■ THE RESOURCE FOR THE INDEPENDENT TRAVELER

"The guides are aimed not only at young budget travelers but at the indepedent traveler; a sort of streetwise cookbook for traveling alone."

—The New York Times

"Unbeatable; good sight-seeing advice; up-to-date info on restaurants, hotels, and inns; a commitment to money-saving travel; and a wry style that brightens nearly every page."

—The Washington Post

"Lighthearted and sophisticated, informative and fun to read. [Let's Go] helps the novice traveler navigate like a knowledgeable old hand."

—Atlanta Journal-Constitution

"A world-wise traveling companion—always ready with friendly advice and helpful hints, all sprinkled with a bit of wit."

—The Philadelphia Inquirer

■ THE BEST TRAVEL BARGAINS IN YOUR PRICE RANGE

"All the dirt, dirt cheap."

—People

"Anything you need to know about budget traveling is detailed in this book."

—The Chicago Sun-Times

"Let's Go follows the creed that you don't have to toss your life's savings to the wind to travel—unless you want to."

—The Salt Lake Tribune

■ REAL ADVICE FOR REAL EXPERIENCES

"The writers seem to have experienced every rooster-packed bus and lunar-surfaced mattress about which they write."

—The New York Times

"A guide should tell you what to expect from a destination. Here Let's Go shines."

—The Chicago Tribune

"[Let's Go's] devoted updaters really walk the walk (and thumb the ride, and trek the trail). Learn how to fish, haggle, find work—anywhere."

—Food & Wine

LET'S GO PUBLICATIONS

TRAVEL GUIDES

Alaska 1st edition **NEW TITLE**
Australia 2004
Austria & Switzerland 2004
Brazil 1st edition **NEW TITLE**
Britain & Ireland 2004
California 2004
Central America 8th edition
Chile 1st edition
China 4th edition
Costa Rica 1st edition
Eastern Europe 2004
Egypt 2nd edition
Europe 2004
France 2004
Germany 2004
Greece 2004
Hawaii 2004
India & Nepal 8th edition
Ireland 2004
Israel 4th edition
Italy 2004
Japan 1st edition **NEW TITLE**
Mexico 20th edition
Middle East 4th edition
New Zealand 6th edition
Pacific Northwest 1st edition **NEW TITLE**
Peru, Ecuador & Bolivia 3rd edition
Puerto Rico 1st edition **NEW TITLE**
South Africa 5th edition
Southeast Asia 8th edition
Southwest USA 3rd edition
Spain & Portugal 2004
Thailand 1st edition
Turkey 5th edition
USA 2004
Western Europe 2004

CITY GUIDES

Amsterdam 3rd edition
Barcelona 3rd edition
Boston 4th edition
London 2004
New York City 2004
Paris 2004
Rome 12th edition
San Francisco 4th edition
Washington, D.C. 13th edition

MAP GUIDES

Amsterdam
Berlin
Boston
Chicago
Dublin
Florence
Hong Kong
London
Los Angeles
Madrid
New Orleans
New York City
Paris
Prague
Rome
San Francisco
Seattle
Sydney
Venice
Washington, D.C.

COMING SOON:

Road Trip USA

ROME

Matthew W. Mahan Editor
Miranda I. Lash Associate Editor

Researcher-Writers
Vedran Lekic
Michael Squire
Elizabeth Thrall

Tzu-Huan Lo Map Editor
Lauren Eve Bonner Managing Editor

St. Martin's Press New York

HELPING LET'S GO If you want to share your discoveries, suggestions, or corrections, please drop us a line. We read every piece of correspondence, whether a postcard, a 10-page email, or a coconut. **Address mail to:**

Let's Go: Rome
67 Mount Auburn Street
Cambridge, MA 02138
USA

Visit Let's Go at **http://www.letsgo.com,** or send email to:

feedback@letsgo.com
Subject: "Let's Go: Rome"

In addition to the invaluable travel advice our readers share with us, many are kind enough to offer their services as researchers or editors. Unfortunately, our charter enables us to employ only currently enrolled Harvard students.

Distributed outside the USA and Canada by Macmillan.

ISBN: 0-312-31996-7

First edition
10 9 8 7 6 5 4 3 2 1

Let's Go: Rome is written by Let's Go Publications, 67 Mount Auburn Street, Cambridge, MA 02138, USA.

ABOUT LET'S GO

GUIDES FOR THE INDEPENDENT TRAVELER

Budget travel is more than a vacation. At *Let's Go*, we see every trip as the chance of a lifetime. If your dream is to grab a knapsack and a machete and forge through the jungles of Brazil, we can take you there. Or, if you'd rather enjoy the Riviera sun at a beachside cafe, we'll set you a table. If you know what you're doing, you can have any experience you want—whether it's camping among lions or sampling Tuscan desserts—without maxing out your credit card. We'll show you just how far your coins can go, and prove that the greatest limitation on your adventure is not your wallet, but your imagination. That said, we understand that you may want the occasional indulgence after a week of hostels and kebab stands, so we've added "Big Splurges" to let you know which establishments are worth those extra euros, as well as price ranges to help you quickly determine whether an accommodation or restaurant will break the bank. While we may have diversified, our emphasis will always be on finding the best values for your budget, giving you all the info you need to spend six days in London or six months in Tasmania.

BEYOND THE TOURIST EXPERIENCE

We write for travelers who know there's more to a vacation than riding double-deckers with tourists. Our researchers give you the heads-up on both world-renowned and lesser-known attractions, on the best local eats and the hottest nightclub beats. In our travels, we talk to everybody; we provide a snapshot of real life in the places you visit with our sidebars on topics like regional cuisine, local festivals, and hot political issues. We've opened our pages to respected writers and scholars to show you their take on a given destination, and turned to lifelong residents to learn the little things that make their city worth calling home. And we've even given you Alternatives to Tourism—ideas for how to give back to local communities through responsible travel and volunteering.

OVER FORTY YEARS OF WISDOM

When we started, way back in 1960, Let's Go consisted of a small group of well-traveled friends who compiled their budget travel tips into a 20-page packet for students on charter flights to Europe. Since then, we've expanded to suit all kinds of travelers, now publishing guides to six continents, including our newest guides: *Let's Go: Japan* and *Let's Go: Brazil*. Our guides are still annually researched and written entirely by students on shoe-string budgets, adventurous travelers who know that train strikes, stolen luggage, food poisoning, and marriage proposals are all part of a day's work. Even as you read this, work on next year's editions is well underway. Whether you're reading one of our new titles, like *Let's Go: Puerto Rico* or *Let's Go Adventure Guide: Alaska*, or our original best-seller, *Let's Go: Europe*, you'll find the same spirit of adventure that has made *Let's Go* the guide of choice for travelers the world over since 1960.

GETTING IN TOUCH

The best discoveries are often those you make yourself; on the road, when you find something worth sharing, please drop us a line. We're Let's Go Publications, 67 Mt. Auburn St., Cambridge, MA 02138, USA (feedback@letsgo.com).

For more info, visit our website: www.letsgo.com.

1 2 3 4 5

PRICE RANGES >> ROME

Our researchers list establishments in order of value from best to worst; our favorites are denoted by the Let's Go thumbs-up (☒). Since the best value is not always the cheapest price, we have incorporated a system of price ranges for quick reference. Our price ranges are based on a rough expectation of what you will spend. For **accommodations,** we base our price range off the cheapest price for which a single traveler can stay for one night. For **restaurants** and other dining establishments, we estimate the average amount that you will spend in that restaurant. The table below tells you what you will *typically* find in Rome at the corresponding price range; keep in mind that a particularly expensive ice cream stand may be marked a ❷, depending on what you will spend.

ACCOMMODATIONS	RANGE	WHAT YOU'RE *LIKELY* TO FIND
❶	€15 and under	Usually hostels or university dorm rooms. Expect bunk beds and a communal bath; you may have to provide or rent towels and sheets.
❷	€16-25	Upper-end hostels or small hotels. You may have a private bathroom, or there may be a sink in your room and communal shower in the hall.
❸	€26-40	A small room with a private bath. Should have decent amenities, such as phone , TV, and AC. Breakfast may be included in the price of the room.
❹	€41-50	Similar to 3, but may have more amenities or be in a more touristed area.
❺	€51 and up	Large hotels or upscale chains. If it's a 5 and it doesn't have the perks you want, you've paid too much.

FOOD	RANGE	WHAT YOU'RE *LIKELY* TO FIND
❶	€5 and under	Mostly street-corner stands, pizza, gelato, or slightly off the beaten path. Hard to find traditional entrees at this price level.
❷	€6-10	Sandwiches, appetizers at a bar, or low-priced entrees. You usually have the option of sitting down, but atmosphere may be lacking.
❸	€11-15	Mid-priced entrees, possibly coming with a soup or salad. Tip'll bump you up a couple dollars, since you'll probably have a waiter or waitress.
❹	€16-20	A somewhat fancy restaurant. You'll have a seperate fork for your salad. Few restaurants in this range have a dress code, but some may look down on t-shirt and jeans.
❺	€21 and up	Food with foreign names and a decent wine list. Slacks and dress shirts will likely be expected.

CONTENTS

discover rome 1

when to go 2
rome by neighborhood 4
to know rome 6
suggested itineraries 9
roman essentials 10

when in rome 15

upon arrival 15
let's get oriented 17
let's get around 17
rome: major streets finder 22
let's get informed 25
let's keep in touch 27
let's speak italian 31

life & times 41

history 41
religion 52
art and architecture 55
music 60

sights 65

rome: major museums and monuments 66
ancient city 69
the roman forum (western section) 72
the roman forum (eastern section) 73
ancient city 78
centro storico 89
piazza di spagna & the corso 105
villa borghese 113
vatican city 115
trastevere 122
termini & san lorenzo 126
southern rome 134
architecture glossary 146

museums 149

principal collections 150
vatican museums 151
other interesting collections 178
revolving exhibitions 181
art glossary 182

food & wine 185

the italian meal 186
restaurant types 186
menu reader 187
restaurants by location 188
dessert 198
caffè 201
wine 202
shopping for food 208

nightlife 211

pubs 211
clubs 218

Bold denotes a map.

entertainment 221

theater & cinema 221
live music & dance 224
spectator sports 228

shopping 231

clothing & shoes 231
non-produce markets 235
miscellaneous 236
music 239
bookstores 240

accommodations 243

accommodations by price 244
accommodations by neighborhood 245
long-term accommodations 256

daytripping 259

central italy 260
lazio 260
lazio (around rome) 261
ostia antica 264
tivoli 268
campania 280
pompeii 293

planning your trip 299

when to go 299
embassies & consulates 300
documents & formalities 300
money 307
getting to rome 311
specific concerns 316
other resources 320

alternatives to tourism 323

volunteering 326
studying abroad 328
working 331

service directory 337

index 344

map appendix

rome: map overview 356
centro storico & trastevere 358
termini & san lorenzo 360
spanish steps & the corso 363
vatican city 364
villa borghese 365
southern rome 366
piazza barberini 367
the appian way 368

HOW TO USE THIS BOOK

PRICE RANGES AND RANKINGS. Our researchers list establishments in order of value from best to worst. Our absolute favorites are denoted by the Let's Go thumbs-up (☒). Since the best value does not always mean the cheapest price, we have incorporated a system of price ranges in the guide. The table below lists how prices fall within each bracket..

SYMBOL:	❶	❷	❸	❹	❺
ACCOMODATIONS	$0-25	$25-35	$35-45	$45-65	$65+
FOOD	$1-10	$10-15	$15-25	$25-35	$35+

PHONE CODES AND TELEPHONE NUMBERS. Area codes for each region appear opposite the name of the region and is denoted by the ☎ icon. Phone numbers in text are also preceded by the ☎ icon.

WHEN TO USE IT

TWO MONTHS BEFORE. Our book is filled with practical information to help you before you go. **Planning Your Trip** (p. 299) has advice about passports, visas, plane tickets, insurance, and more. The **Accommodations** (p. 243) section can help you with booking a room from home.

ONE MONTH BEFORE. Take care of travel insurance, and write down a list of emergency numbers and hotlines to take with you. Make a list of packing essentials (see **Packing,** p. 306) and shop for anything you are missing. Make any reservations if necessary.

2 WEEKS BEFORE. Start thinking about the things you don't want to miss during your stay. **Discover Rome** (see p. 1) lists the city's top sights, with suggested itineraries, themed tours, and Let's Go Picks (the best and quirkiest of Rome). **When in Rome** (p. 15) will be your best friend, dishing the dirt on neighborhoods and offering tips on acting like a true Roman. For navigating, the neighborhood breakdown here is the same as the other chapters: Ancient City, Centro Storico, Piazza di Spagna & the Corso, Villa Borghese, Vatican City and surrounding area. Trastevere, Termini & San Lorenzo, and Southern Rome.

ON THE ROAD. This year, *Let's Go: Rome* features three **walking tours** complete with maps (see p. 12, p. 90, and p. 180). When you reach Rome, you'll spend most of your time in the city flipping through the chapters that follow: **Sights, Museums, Food & Drink, Nightlife, Entertainment, Shopping,** and **Accommodations.** When the city gets to be too much, the **Daytripping** chapter provides a selection of one-day and weekend breaks in the Lazio and Campania regions. The **Service Directory** contains a list of local services. Finally, throughout the book you will find **glossaries** (p. 33, p. 146, p. 182, p. 199, and p. 241) that will help with everything from understanding Renaissance art to ordering the gelato flavor you want. Enjoy.

A NOTE TO OUR READERS The information for this book was gathered by *Let's Go* researchers from May through August of 2003. Each listing is based on one researcher's opinion, formed during his or her visit at a particular time. Those traveling at other times may have different experiences since prices, dates, hours, and conditions are always subject to change. You are urged to check the facts presented in this book beforehand to avoid inconvenience and surprises.

RESEARCHER-WRITERS

Vedran Lekić *Ancient City, Castelli Romani, Centro Storico, Nightlife, Ostia Antica, Tivoli*

The next time you hear of Ved, he'll be on CNN explaining his latest breakthrough in the field of astrophysics or geology, or maybe both. Until then, Ved is enjoying a long stay in Europe; and why not—he speaks plenty of languages. On the job, Ved had an uncanny knack for revising maps and cleaning up choppy writing. Most impressive however, was his ability to get to know Romans—and *Napolitanis*, but that's a different story.

Michael Squire *Lazio, Museums, Southern Rome, Termini & San Lorenzo, Testaccio, Trastevere*

Originally from Cambridge, UK, now hailing from Cambridge, MA, Mike was happy to put off his doctoral studies for a summer in Rome. Despite indecipherable British colloquialisms, his copy was jolly good. In fact, a typical day's work consisted of putting years of *Let's Go* research to shame with his unbounded knowledge of art and the Classics. He also completely overhauled the book's wine coverage and is, for all practical purposes, a seasoned sommelier.

Elizabeth Thrall *Erturia, Food & Wine, Pontine Islands, Spanish Steps & the Corso, the Vatican, Villa Borghese*

Always crafting ready-for-press copy, Lizz was born to edit, but got stuck researching Rome. Don't pity her; Lizz loved this city—so much so that she began referring to herself as an expat and threatened to stay for life. Lizz's most endearing quality was undoubtedly the way she always had "the reader" on her mind—of course, her improvements to the guide will surely pay dividends the next time she attempts to expatriate herself.

Roxana M. Popescu *Editor,* Let's Go: Italy 2004

Emma Firestone *Associate Editor,* Let's Go: Italy 2004

Emily Porter *Associate Editor,* Let's Go: Italy 2004

CONTRIBUTING WRITERS

Andria Derstine was a Researcher-Writer for *Let's Go: Italy 1990* and *1992*, and *Let's Go: Greece 1991*. Her Ph.D. studies in Italian and French art history at New York University have taken her to Rome for the past two and a half years.

Caitlin Hurley, a teacher at Marymount International School in Rome, was a Researcher-Writer for *Let's Go: USA 1994*.

Anna Kim is a Ph.D. candidate in the History of Art and Architecture at Harvard University.

Rabun Taylor is Associate Professor of History of Art and Architecture at Harvard.

Sarah Robinson is a Managing Editor at Let's Go.

ACKNOWLEDGMENTS

Matt thanks: Lizz, Mike, and Ved, thank you for your "smashing" prose and enviable stamina. Miranda and TLo, this book went to press because of you. Scroby, LBon, and boys in Prod, thank you for helping me drag myself across the finish line. Hey city guides, especially pod II, I'll miss wrestling, our raccoon, Parker's mouth, sloshball, collective kvetching about everything, and our CD sharing.

Angela, thank you for your patience, love, and all the food. I wouldn't have the job if it wasn't for you, and I wouldn't have finished it without you. GLo and Peter, thank you for challenging me. Yeah FUP. Kalamchi, Clear, and Salvo, you didn't do a thing for the book, but you're awesome roomies, so thanks for that. Soto, the last-minute spell checking is appreciated. Panamax, thanks for the trip.

Back in CA- Robbie, you're always there for me. DC, Thomas, Vinny, Aid, and the whole Bellarmine crowd: thanks for everything. Mom and Dad, Beth and Megan, thanks for making me who I am; I love you. AMDG. go bells.

Miranda thanks: Matt, thanks for your great attitude and dedication. A huge thanks to our diligent Tzu-Huan and tireless RWs. Scrobins, for smiles and scorpion bowls. Lots of love to my crazy City Guide buds. A big hug to Cristina, who brightened my summer with silliness and charm. I was so happy to have you. Thanks to Becky for making life more fun. A million thanks to my parents for their love and support. To Danny, for your with friendship and affection.

Tzu-Huan thanks: *Mille grazie* to my family for putting up with my hiatus from a career, to my friends, to Matt and Miranda for making this happen, and to Lizz, Mike, and Ved for cleaning up our maps. Editing the Eternal City was more than a satisfactory substitute for the Forbidden City. A.M.D.G. S.P.Q.R.

BYRON

INSIDE

when to go **2**

rome by season **2** holidays and festivals **3**

rome by neighborhood **4**

to know rome **6**

literature **6** film **7**

suggested itineraries **9**

one day **9** three days **9** five days **9** seven days **10**

roman essentials **10**

tried and true **10** a tour less ordinary **10** other random picks **11**

Discover Rome

It seems there is no possible way that Rome can live up to its reputation. In all the books you'll read, in all the pictures you'll see, and in all the pithy sayings you'll hear, Rome will be presented as an idealized city, an eternal metropolis that seamlessly transitions from history to the present in a matter of city blocks. It will be canonized for its invaluable cultural treasures, from ancient temples to Michelangelo's Pietà. In short, the hype will be so extensive that Rome will seem, in a sense, to be unreal.

But Rome *is* exactly what people say it is. The Forum and baths are simply stunning, your first view of the Colosseum will likely stop you in your tracks, and the Sistine Chapel will leave you speechless. These are the sights that attract tourists by the thousands, but that's not why people fall in love with Rome. There is more; there is something about the Roman lifestyle that will draw you in. Maybe it's that you can sit in an espresso bar for as long as your conversation with the owner will keep you there—long after your cappuccino has been drunk—and no one will hint that they want you to leave. Or, maybe it's the way Romans want to share—not sell—their city and its legends. Perhaps it's the way that locals in Trastevere claim, when they try to put into words how they feel about their neighborhood, that they've never seen the other side of the Tiber. Romans have a love for their city that transcends bravado and comparisons: they believe that if this city were to lose its crowded *piazzi* and afternoon shop-closings—in essence, their way of life—in the name of efficiency, functionality, and convenience, they would not be Romans and this city would no longer be their home. Rome's most "eternal" aspect is what Romans can teach you about loving life. So when in Rome, make the city part of you. The Romans do.

Rome by the Numbers

Area: 1494 sq. km. In that space are crammed 981 churches and 280 fountains.

Distance from the Mediterranean: 17 mi.

Official Age of the City: 2755 years. In that time, there have been 168 popes, 73 emperors, and 9.3 million pairs of tight leather pants.

Population: 2.7 million (Metro Rome is home to over 4.5 million). Of those, 94% have their children baptized Catholic; 12% go to mass and confession weekly; and 37% believe they've been afflicted with the "evil eye."

Tourists: 15 million per year. (That's more than five tourists per Roman per year—but who's counting?)

Cars on Rome's Streets: 2 million daily.

Cats on Rome's Streets: do you *really* want to know? Check out p. 143.

Passengers on Rome's Metro: 3 million daily.

Ticket Inspectors: 120.

Gallons of Water Delivered by Ancient Aqueducts: 312,000 hourly.

"Egyptian" Obelisks: 13.

Egyptian Obelisks: 7.

Egyptian Obelisks in Egypt: Fewer than that.

Pyramids in Rome: 1.

Pyramids in Egypt: 4.

WHEN TO GO

Few would dare call a Roman **spring** anything less than heaven. The weather is pleasantly balmy (hovering around 50 to 70°F), but the tourists haven't caught on. By June, both the temperature and the tourist industry have picked up considerably. A Roman **summer** is sweltering (75-95°F) and congested, but you can catch major exhibitions, exciting festivals, and concerts under the stars. When the city gets too thick, cool off in the Mediterranean or in cold volcanic lakes. From late-July through August, the Romans leave town; you may not find as many hole-in-the-wall *trattorie* open, but the crowds will subside a bit. The trend continues into the **fall,** when the temperatures drop (45-60°F) and the prices do, too. **Winter** brings cold (expect temperatures between 40°F and 55°F), rain, and some of the lowest prices of the year, but it also brings the holidays, which are a major to-do in the city of St. Peter.

ROME BY SEASON

SPRING. As soon as the azaleas bloom at the end of March, piles of them are brought to the Spanish Steps to celebrate **La Festa di Primavera,** the coming of spring. The exhibition lasts until the flowers die, usually a week or two. **Good Friday** brings the Pope's **Procession of the Cross** from the Colosseum to the Palatine and a week of services in basilicas across Rome, culminating in the Pope's Easter **Urbi et Orbi** blessing in 50 languages. Don't miss **Rome's birthday:** April 21 sees the Capitoline Hill alive with partyers, Latin poetry, a concert, and fireworks set off from the Circus Maximus. The **Rose Show** arrives in early May at Valle Murcia, on the Aventine above the Circus Maximus, and lasts through June. Also, the **Italian International Tennis Tournament** brings excitement to the Foro Italico in early May.

SUMMER. Festivals and concerts abound, so be sure to check *Roma C'è*. On June 23, the **Church of San Giovanni in Laterano** sponsors a gluttonous banquet of snails and roast pork. **Festa dei Santi Pietro e Paolo,** June 29, is an awe-inspiring religious ceremony for Rome's patron saints, taking place in the Basilica dei Santi Pietro e Paolo. The third Sunday in July brings **Noantri,** a 10-day celebration of the Trastevere neighborhood, complete with midway rides and grand religious processions. Finally, on August 5, the **Festa della Madonna della Neve** is a blizzard of white flower petals representing the legendary out-of-season snow at the **Church of Santa Maria Maggiore.**

FALL. In September, watch out for the **Art Festival** featuring the works of over 100 painters along V. Margutta. Vats of wine make for hazy evenings at the **Sagra Delle Uva** in the Forum's Basilica of Maxentius, and a torch-lit **Medieval Crafts Fair** (late September to early October) on V.dell'orso complements the V.d. Coronari **Antique Fair** (last two weeks of October).

WINTER. Christmas sees P. Navona full of crêche figures for sale and children begging for toys and candy and reciting poems and speeches. On December 8, the Pope and other worshipers leave elaborate floral tributes to the statue of the virgin in P.d. Spagna for the **Festa dell'Immacolata Connezione. Capodanno** (New Year's) merrymaking includes setting off sparklers, throwing old dishes (or clothes, or old bathtubs) from windows, eating *cotecchino* (pig's feet), and washing it all down with *spumante* and an amazing fireworks display. On the first, the faithful light candles and make their way through the catacombs of Santa Priscilla, while the pope gives a solemn High Mass at St. Peter's. On January 17, during the **Festa di Sant'Antonio,** pet cats, dogs, and canaries are blessed after mass on the steps of the Church of Sant'Eusebio all'Esquilino. The **Carnevale** parade (the day before Ash Wednesday) down the Corso is a sight to be seen. Throw on a fancy costume and bring some silly string.

HOLIDAYS & FESTIVALS

Rome doesn't play host to as many balls and concerts as some of its neighbors to the north and sponsors fewer festivals of the Madonna than Sicily or Naples. Nonetheless, Rome enjoys its fair share of general revelry during the course of the year. Religious holidays, a remnant of a more faithful past, still tend to close down the entire city. At other times, locals might be worshiping the sun at the beach, which could very well throw a wrench in your plans to visit sights in the Vatican. It's safe to assume, for instance, that all of Italy will shift its weight to the coasts in August. Expect accommodations and restaurants to be closed, unless you have unimpeachable evidence to the contrary. Museums will generally be open, but some of the smaller ones will have reduced hours.

The following is a list of the most popular Italian and Roman holidays, as well as information about their probable effect on travel plans.

HOLIDAYS AND FESTIVALS	DATE	INFO
New Year's Day	Jan. 1	Europe: closed for business
Epiphany	Jan. 6	was important in Italy; P. Navona is host to crêche makers
Holy Week	Apr. 13-20	penance and ashes, but more important in Italy than in most European countries
Birthday of Rome	Apr. 21	parades and fireworks
Liberation Day	Apr. 25	government shuts down
Labor Day	May 1	some closures
SS. Peter and Paul	June 29	the most important religious holiday; city shuts down
Festa de'Noantri	3rd Sa in July	parade, fireworks, general merrymaking
St. Lawrence Day	Aug. 10	2nd most important religious holiday; city takes the day off
Assumption	Aug. 15	the Virgin is taken to heaven; Romans become pious
Estate Romana	all summer; ends Aug. 22	summer-long music, art, and theater; check *Roma C'e* for listings
St. Francis Day	Oct. 4	patron of the Republic is celebrated
Jazz Festival	Oct. 27-Nov. 4	jazz...oh, yes, jazz
All Saints' Day	Nov. 1	Lives of the saints celebrated with closed shops

HOLIDAYS AND FESTIVALS	DATE	INFO
Christmas Market	Early Dec.	P. Navona is alive with creche makers
Immaculate Conception	Dec. 8	Mary is conceived; most restaurants close
Christmas Vigil	Dec. 24	annual event at the Vatican; address by the pope
Christmas	Dec. 25	*Babbo Natale* (Santa Claus) and big family dinners. Everything closed.

ROME BY NEIGHBORHOOD

No longer defined by the Seven Hills, modern Rome is huge, sprawling over a large area between the hills of the Castelli Romani to the north, the beach at Ostia to the west, and Lake Albano to the south, counting within its boundaries such memorable eyesores as Anagnina, Spinaceto, and Infernetto ("little Hell"). Encircling it is the Grande Raccordo Anulare (GRA), whose name loosely translates to "traffic jams of Biblical proportions." Luckily for you, though, most major sights lie within a comparatively small radius, which can be neatly divided into eight areas.

ANCIENT CITY

Accessible by Metro (Linea B) and buses serving P. Venezia. For ***Sights,*** *see p. 69.*

The Ancient City begins directly south of **Piazza Venezia** (the center of the city and home to the huge Vittorio Emanuele II monument; see p. 89). Directly behind the monument, the **Capitoline Hill,** capped by Michelangelo's P.d. Campidoglio, is accessible by **Via di Teatro di Marcello,** which runs southwest toward the Velabrum and the Tiber. On the other side of the monument, **Via dei For Imperiali** runs all the way to the **Colosseum.** Off V.d. Fori Imperiali are the **Imperial Fora** and the **Roman Forum** itself. Behind the Forum looms the **Palatine Hill** and, beyond that, the **Circus Maximus.**

CENTRO STORICO

Accessible by buses #60 and 117 on the Corso, as well as a number of buses along C. Vittorio Emanuel II. For ***Sights,*** *see p. 89.*

The medieval neighborhood of Rome spreads north and west from **Piazza Venezia,** bordered by Via del Corso on the east and the Tiber to the west. **Corso Vittorio Emanule II** runs northwest from Piazza Venezia toward the Vatican; much of the Centro south of this thoroughfare is taken up by the **Jewish Ghetto.**

PIAZZA DI SPAGNA & THE CORSO

Accessible via Metro Linea A and many buses, including #60 and 492 to P. Barberini and #117 to the P.d. Spagna. For ***Sights,*** *see p. 105.*

East of the Corso, stretching from Piazza Venezia up toward Villa Borghese, is the area around the **Spanish Steps.** The famous steps themselves, which climb from **Piazza di Spagna** up to **Piazza Trinità dei Monti,** are four blocks from the Corso along Rome's most exclusive shopping area, **Via Condotti.** On the western side of the Corso lie the famous Mausoleum of Augustus and the Ara Pacis. South of the Spanish Steps is the über-crowded **Trevi Fountain.** East of the fountain is the **Quirinale,** headquarters of Italian government. **Via del Tritone** runs east from the Corso to **Piazza Barberini,** and continues on toward Termini as **Via Barberini.**

VILLA BORGHESE

M: A-Flaminio or M: A-Spagna. Bus #490 runs through the park. For ***Sights,*** *see p. 113.*

Northeast of Piazza del Popolo and the Spanish Steps is the **Villa Borghese,** a vast park that is home to the **zoo** and several museums. Since it is a park, there are kilometers of verdant paths. The neighborhood of the Villa Borghese stretches around Piazza del Popolo east to cover the environs north of Termini and **Via XX Settembre.**

BORGO, PRATI & VATICAN CITY

Accessible via Metro (Linea A) and many buses, including #64, 492, and 490, which serves northern Prati. For ***Sights,*** *see p. 115.*

Across the Tiber, northwest from the Centro Storico is the **Vatican City.** Crossing the Ponte Vittorio Emanuele II from C. Vittorio Emanuele II takes you directly to **Via della Conciliazione,** the avenue that leads west to P.S. Pietro and **Saint Peter's Basilica.** The **Vatican Museums** are just next door. At the eastern end of V.d. Conciliazione, **Castel Sant'Angelo,** the Pope's historic residence, overlooks the Tiber. Between Castel Sant'Angelo and the Vatican is the quiet **Borgo** neighborhood. To the north is less quiet **Prati,** home to scattered hotels, restaurants, and pubs. **Via Cola di Rienzo** runs through Prati from **Piazza del Risorgimento,** next to the Vatican, across Ponte Regina Margherita to **Piazza del Popolo.**

TRASTEVERE

Tram #13 runs the length of Viale di Trastevere from Largo Argentina in the Centro Storico south past Stazione Trastevere. Among others, buses #23 and 170 provide service to southern Trastevere and bus #870 serves the Gianicolo. For ***Sights,*** *see p. 122.*

Trastevere, easily Rome's most picturesque neighborhood, and certainly its most entertaining to navigate, is south of the Vatican and west, across the Tiber from the Centro Storico. **Viale Trastevere** runs across Ponte Garibaldi all the way to Largo Argentina and C. Vittorio Emanuele II and is the main drag of the neighborhood. Most of Trastevere's points of interest lie near this street, and not far from the river. Between Trastevere and the Vatican is the exclusive and park-like **Janiculum Hill**, or the Gianicolo.

TERMINI & SAN LORENZO

Termini is the transfer point between the 2 Metro lines and is served by countless buses. San Lorenzo is served by bus #492, Esquilino is accessible by buses #70 and 714, and bus #60 runs out of the city along V. XX Settembre (V. Nomentana). For ***Sights,*** *see p. 126.*

Located east of the center of town, this is the area most people see first when arriving in Rome. Get used to it, because it's also where most budget travelers stay. The neighborhood immediately northeast of **Stazione Termini** is jam-packed with hotels, hostels, restaurants, and Internet cafes. East of the station is the **Città Universitaria,** home to Rome's La Sapienza University. South of that is **San Lorenzo,** the student neighborhood, which is home to many cheap and delicious restaurants, as well a healthy dose of left-wing student spirit. South of Termini, along V. Giovanni Giolitti and V. Merulana, is the **Esquilino** neighborhood. San Lorenzo is connected to Esquilino by **Via Tiburtina. Via XX Settembre (Via Nomentana)** cuts through the quieter area northwest of the station. In front of the station, **Via Nazionale** runs from **Piazza della Repubblica** west toward the older center of town. **Via Cavour** runs southeast from the station to the Colosseum.

SOUTHERN ROME

Testaccio, the Aventine, and EUR are served by Metro Linea B and buses #23 and 673. Metro Linea A and buses #673 and 714 run to the Caelian and southeast Rome. For ***Sights,*** *see p. 134.*

Across the river from Trastevere and south of the Jewish Ghetto and the Ancient City are the posh **Aventine Hill** and the working-class **Testaccio** district. The former home to Rome's slaughterhouses is named after a hill of ancient amphora shards and has many of Rome's most popular nightclubs (not to mention its only pyramid). Farther south are **Ostiense** and **EUR,** Mussolini's prototype neighborhood of wide boulevards, nationalistic slogans, and museums. East of the Tiber are the **Caelian Hill,** southeast of the Colosseum and home to the San Giovanni neighborhood, and farther south, the **Appian Way.**

Foro Boario

View from Aventine Hill

Church of Sant'Agnese in Agone

TO KNOW ROME

Though Rome would blow away even the basest philistine, it is impossible to truly appreciate what is arguably the most important city in the history of western civilization without some exposure to its literature and art. Before you even step into the cabin of that 747, *Let's Go* recommends, for your viewing pleasure, the following brief foray into art on the peninsula.

LITERATURE

Anyone who has experienced the distinct pleasure of memorizing Latin verb conjugations will recall some of the heavy hitters of Republican and Imperial literature, from Cicero's masterful "O tempora, o mores!" to Tacitus's self-righteous glorification of the barbarian raiders to the north in the *Histories*. Rome, however, is more than broken kouroi in the sand of the Forum; it's a medieval quarter, a plethora of Renaissance churches, and yes, even the EUR. The following list of works is required reading.

ANCIENT ROME

Catullus's poetry sets a high standard for would-be parodists, while providing a great source of Latin obscenities for future generations of Latin students.

Julius Caesar, *Let's Go*'s honorary researcher-writer, not only penned *De Bello Gallico* about his first military campaigns in France, but conquered his own hometown (literally and literarily) with his first-hand account of the shredding of the Republic in *De Bello Civili*.

Virgil's *Aeneid* links the founding of Rome to the fall of Troy via the wandering of Aeneis.

Ovid, though originally employed by Augustus, was later banished to the Black Sea for his sanction of the escapades of Augustus's promiscuous daughter and grand-daughter, both named Julia. In the meantime, he managed to write the *Amores*, the *Metamorphoses*, and the *Ars Amatoria* (a tongue-in-cheek guide to love and lust). A man for all seasons.

Marcus Aurelius, the philosopher-king managed to rule a Mediterranean empire and pen the *Meditations*.

EARLY CHRISTIAN

St. Clement, 4th Bishop of Rome, liked to write letters. Someone slapped a title on them *(Epistles of St. Clement of Rome)* and published them. Now, wasn't that easy?

St. Jerome's *Vulgate Bible* is essential reading for those planning to visit religious sites in Rome.

Saint Augustine's tales of naughtiness and conversion in *The Confessions* inspired centuries worth of purgations and asceticism.

HEAVEN, HELL, MISCHIEVOUS MONKS, AND A RENAISSANCE

Dante Alighieri, father of the modern Italian language (the *volgare)* and the modern conception of heaven and hell. Michelangelo studied him extensively, and used his *La Divina Commedia* as inspiration for *The Last Judgment* in the Sistine Chapel.

Petrarch's sonnets, most of them in Latin, set the tone for modern Italian poetry.

Giovani Boccaccio's tale of naughty nuns and jousting nobles, *The Decameron*, ostensibly chronicles the adventures of 10 Florentines fleeing their plague-ridden city; in reality, it is more of a literary landscape of Italy's regional foibles and peculiarities.

Benvenuto Cellini, chronicled his life (unsurprisingly, a series of episodes demonstrating indefatigable bravery and determination) in a couple of action-packed autobiographical works.

Giordano Bruno's radical astrological and neo-Platonic observations earned him an execution in the Campo dei Fiori.

ROMANTICISM

Metastasio and **Carlo Goldoni** transformed the stage through melodramas, and, more significantly, Goldoni's *Commedia dell'Arte,* which replaced stock figures with unpredictable characters in works like *Il Ventaglio.*

John Keats and **Percy B. Shelley** resided in a posh convalescent home with a breathtaking view of the Spanish Steps. Shelley wrote that Rome was the "paradise of exiles" while Keats wasted away quietly from tuberculosis.

TWENTIETH CENTURY

Gabriele d'Annunzio, arguably Modernism's most flamboyant character, wrote *Il Piacere* about his cavalier heroics and sexual escapades in Rome.

Alberto Moravia's *Time of Indifference* attacks fascism in a straightforward style, and was promptly censored. He retreated into surrealism afterwards, to avoid being understood by the government. *La Romana* and *The Conformist* are equally famous.

Natalia Ginzburg, the author of several psychological novels centered on the relationship and self, writes in and about Rome in *Famiglia* and *Borghesia.*

Dario Fo proves that being banned by the Catholic Church is and always will be a boost to sales. His *The Accidental Death of an Anarchist* and *We Won't Pay! We Won't Pay!* won him the Nobel Prize for Literature in 1997.

FILM

Just about anything by Fellini is bound to be quintessential Rome, but despite the more ambitious of his post facto claims about having invented Rome for the world to see, cinema didn't begin with Federico. The **Cines studios** created what came to be known as the "super-spectacle": extravagant, larger-than-life productions that replayed historical events with a lot of cosmetics and more than a healthy dose of melodrama. Of this genre, **Enrico Guzzani's** *Quo Vadis* was perhaps the most successful outside of Italy.

Mussolini's propaganda machine began (and ended) at the mammoth **Cinecitta studios,** with the famous director and closet Marxist Luigi Chairini. Chiarini's films are largely indistinguishable from similar, Soviet-style propaganda, but his students **Roberto Rossellini** and **Michelangelo Antonioni** rose to directorial fame

Living in Rome

after the war. Antonioni, to an even greater extent than his colleague Fellini, refused to conform to such "artificial constraints" as plot, form, conflict, resolution, and a cause-and-effect relationship between events. *L'Avventura* (1960) contains some expected bashing of the upper classes. *L'Eclisse* (1962) follows the typical neo-Marxist pattern of condemning materialism. *Blow-Up* (1967), his only script in English, is the story of a photographer in London who inadvertently captures a murder on film.

Italy's non-conventional films continued with Pasolini and Bertolucci, although the latter was far less controversial. Still, the Italian film industry boycotted Bertolucci for the internationalism of his style. He fled abroad to direct such Hollywood epics as *The Last Emperor* and *The Sheltering Sky*.

Palazzo de Quirnale

More recently, *Commedia della Cinema* has replaced Marxism as the preferred form of expression, with directors such as **Nano Moretti** (*Caro Diario;* 1994) and Lina Wermuller (*Ciao, Professore!;* 1993) providing an alternative to the canned Hollywood romantic comedy. The member of the group with the most international currency is **Roberto Benigni,** star of *Ciao, Professore!* The victorious stomp of his film *La Vita e Bella (Life is Beautiful)* through the 1999 Academy Awards is not likely to be forgotten in the film community anytime soon.

So experience Rome, but learn from the mistakes of those who came before you—Gregory Peck (don't fall in love with a stranger), Spartacus (crucifixion isn't fun), Matt Damon (despite the face, Jude Law is not divine), etc.

Vittorio Emanuele II

Gladiator, though slightly inaccurate (Rome's hills aren't that big and Marcus Aurelius was no altruistic Republican), offers invaluable lessons in self-defense. Too bad more Romans don't look like Russel Crowe.

The Talented Mr. Ripley will teach you all about how to dispose of bodies in the Eternal City. Once you get past the inordinate amount of time the film spends in those boring *northern* Italian towns, it's a pretty good psychological thriller.

Roma, Citta Aperta (Rome, Open City) is the Rossellini classic about Rome during WWII, covertly filmed while the city was still occupied by the Nazis.

La Dolce Vita (The Sweet Life), by Fellini, is just plain good. That's all there is to it. Actually, what makes it really good is the sea monster at the end.

Roma, another Fellini flick, this plotless portrait of Rome combines autobiography with both insane and insanely beautiful visual images.

Spartacus is Kubrick and it's flawed, but it's got a young Kirk Douglas. 'Nuff said.

Roman Holiday features Audrey Hepburn and Gregory Peck, and is so sweet you may need to visit a dentist after watching. Watch out for that pesky Bocca della Verità!

Mamma Roma is Pasolini's tale of the allegorical downfall of a passionate and maternal whore who repeatedly tries to prevent her son from joining a band of criminals.

The Conformist, by Bertolucci, makes a study of the effect of fascism on a weak-willed man.

SUGGESTED ITINERARIES

Don't despair if literature and film aren't your thing. No film or novel—nay, nothing—can prepare you for Rome. There is no time to waste, so get out there and allow our suggested itineraries to help you experience the best of La Città Eterna.

ONE DAY

Any attempt to cram the best of the Eternal City into a day will require the nerves of an emperor (think Augustus, not Nero) and Ben-Hur's chariot. In the morning, take our half-day **walking tour** through the medieval Centro Storico (p. 12), but begin at the Spanish Steps so you end at Piazza Navona. Have lunch at one of the restaurants along nearby V.d. Governo Vecchio, hop a bus to P. Venezia, and take our other half-day **walking tour** (p. 90) of the best of the rest of Rome, ending at St. Peter's Basilica in Vatican City. Finish up with dinner at a *pizzeria* in Trastevere (p. 195), then head back across the Tiber for some nighttime fun (p. 211).

THREE DAYS

DAY ONE: GETTING ORIENTED. Begin with our **Best of Rome** walking tour (p. 12). Take your time touring the sights, stopping off in the **Roman Forum** (see p. 69) and the **Bocca della Verità** (p. 87). When you're through, walk down the Tiber to Trastevere, and head for an outdoor *pizzeria* (p. 195). Finish up by heading back up to the Borgo to catch some jazz at **Alexanderplatz Jazz Club** (p. 227).

DAY TWO: VATICAN CITY. Wake up early, go to the **Vatican Museums,** get in line, and race through the galleries to get to the Sistine Chapel before the crowds (p. 150). After you've caught your breath and had your fill of Michelangelo, spend a few hours in the rest of the museum. Be sure to spend some time at **St. Peter's** (p. 115), and make the climb to the top of the dome. Before heading off to dinner, explore Hadrian's mausoleum, better known as **Castel Sant'Angelo** (p. 120).

DAY THREE: BORGHESE AND THE SPANISH STEPS. Your first stop is the **Galleria Borghese** for the most concentrated two hours of art you've ever experienced in your life (p. 165). Relax afterward by wandering through the gardens of the Villa Borghese until you find yourself at the top of the **Spanish Steps** (p. 105). Catch lunch and do some **shopping** (p. 231) there, then take in the big sights in the area—don't miss the **Trevi Fountain** (p. 107). Grab dinner near P. del Popolo (p. 194).

FIVE DAYS

Add the following to the previous three-day tour.

DAY FOUR: SOUTHERN ROME. Spend some time examining the Colosseum up close, then head toward the grand **Church of San Giovanni in Laterano** (p. 136), stopping by the odd little **Church of San Clemente** (p. 134) along the way. From San Giovanni, take bus #218 south to explore the **catacombs** and other sights along the **Appian Way** (p. 139).

DAY FIVE: TIVOLI. Horace and Catullus fled here in search of solitude, although the water park holds almost equal sway with the tourists who make the hour and a half trek from Termini. Take in **Hadrian's Villa** (p. 268) and the **Villa d'Este** (p. 269), but head back to Rome for the night. Accommodations are expensive, but the sunlit terraces can't be beat.

SEVEN DAYS

So you wanted a tropical vacation, but got the hustle and bustle of Rome instead? Not to worry. After five days in Rome, take a two-day sojourn in the **Pontine Islands** (p. 274), just three hours from Rome by public transit. The islands offer pristine shoreline, fantastic seafood, and a little relaxation. You deserve it; this vacation has been hard work.

ROMAN ESSENTIALS...

Our **Tried and True** list is for the first-timer or the Roman holiday-goer who wants a traditional week in the Eternal City. Either way, you can't come to Rome and miss these sights. For **A Life Less Ordinary,** bring your best walking shoes and a healthy appetite. These places don't adorn too many postcards, but they guarantee great memories and sore feet.

TRIED AND TRUE

1. Sistine Chapel. Look up, look down, it doesn't matter. Every square inch is covered in the stuff that postcards (and mousepads, T-shirts, and coffee mugs) are made of. Don't forget the fine (and moderately famous) frescoes along the side walls.

2. The Pantheon. The huge dome of this pagan temple-cum-Christian church still puzzles architects who can't figure out how it was created using 2nd-century building techniques.

3. The Colosseum. No trip to Rome is complete without a brief wander through the rotting hulk of this former stadium, which was pillaged by popes during expansive medieval building projects. Don't get cornered by a gladiator–he'll want €5 for posing in your pictures.

4. Campo dei Fiori. Sight of numerous executions sponsored by those pacifists at the Holy See. Dotted with worthwhile churches, and home to some of Rome's best restaurants.

5. The Spanish Steps. Stop at the ATM and grab your Gucci. It doesn't come cheap, but as one of the world's principle venues for the young and beautiful, it merits an afternoon.

6. Castel Sant'Angelo. The popes fled to this fortress when they needed either solace or a safe haven during invasions. Don't miss the extravagant papal apartments.

7. Palatine Hill. So sayeth the imperial real estate agents: Location, location, location. The hill is home to some of Rome's best ruins and offers a spectacular view of the city.

8. Museo Nazionale Etrusco di Villa Giulia. You could go to Ertruria to see the ruins of this ancient civilization... or you can come here and see all the artifacts plundered from it.

9. Trevi Fountain. This new (1762) addition to the typical tourist route will tempt you to re-enact a classic Fellini moment–but it's going to cost you.

10. Galleria Borghese. Caravaggios, a wooded park, and a nude of Napoleon's sister. What more can you ask of Rome?

A TOUR LESS ORDINARY

1. Domus Aurea. A colossal house, built by Nero to embody his self-proclaimed status as a god, it originally contained a waterfall with fake stalactites and whole lotta gold leaf. Tacitus called it a gross abuse of imperial authority. You be the judge.

2. Jewish Ghetto. Dying for some fried artichokes? They're the local specialty in this ethnic neighborhood. Don't overlook the Sinagoga Askenazita.

3. Cimitero Acattolico per Gli Stranieri. An English roll call of poets who chose to die in Rome, including Percy Shelley and John Keats.

4. EUR. Mussolini's monument to...Mussolini...and the grandeur of Rome, past, present and future. Note the almost Soviet architecture, then head for the amusement park and the artificial lake.

5. Roseto Comunale. Rome's original rose garden was destroyed during WWII, but it was rebuilt on this site in Aventine. With over 800 varieties of rose bushes spread over a gorgeous 10 sq. km, you don't want to skip this sight.

6. San Sebastiano Catacomb. If bones and early Christian iconography don't tempt you, go for the respite from the heat that 10km's worth of underground tunnels can provide. The very best of the Appian Way catacombs.

7. Via Condotti. Account balance, account shmalance. What trip to Rome is complete without a pair of shoes from Ferragamo and a nice little handbag from Louis Vuitton? What? You can't afford it? Be thankful the Romans didn't have a fashion god or you could be in trouble.

8. Da Benito e Gilberto. Perhaps the best little ristorante in the whole Borgo Pio. Splurge for the works: *antipasti, primi, secondi,* wine, dessert, and *espresso.*

...AND OTHER RANDOM PICKS

WHERE TO GO FIRST, LAST, AND WHENEVER CONFUSED. Pierluigi and Fulvia, proprietors of **Enjoy Rome** (p. 25), dish out all the dirt on Rome, tell you what to do with it, and make all the necessary arrangements. Small miracles performed on request.

BEST CHURCH/LIQUOR STORE. **Basilica San Paulo Fuori la Mura** (p. 144), where monks sell homemade benedictine to thirsty believers and passersby.

BEST CHURCH IN WHICH TO SEE SAINTS' HEADS. With both St. Peter's and St. Paul's in one locale, **San Giovanni** (p. 136) is the place to be.

BEST BATHROOM. **Jonathan's Angels** (p. 213).

HANDS-DOWN BEST ITALIAN BEER. **Peroni.** Peroni, Peroni, Peroni.... Was there ever really a doubt?

BEST PICKPOCKETS. The **tiny 10-year-olds** who somehow make it onto the #64 bus (p. 19). We're not kidding.

BEST CLICHÉ ABOUT ROME. **"When in Rome..."** Say it whenever you can; people love it. For our version, see p. 15.

BEST VIEW OF THE CITY. The **cupola atop St. Peter's Basilica** (p. 119) handily beats the keyhole of Piazza del Cavallieri (p. 138). Bring a camera.

BEST PLACES TO BE SEEN. Put on your Gucci, Prada, and Dolce and Gabbana and head over to the **Spanish Steps** (p. 105). By the way, don't even think of going without your cell phone. The **Trevi Fountain** (p. 107) is another hot spot and **Campo dei Fiori** (p. 99) can't be beat on a warm summer night.

BEST DOME. As soon as you get to Rome, drop your bags and go straight to the **Pantheon** (p. 93). Sit there for the duration of your trip. Don't forget to breathe.

BEST FAT OLD ITALIAN POPULAR MUSICIAN. **Vasco Rossi.** This guy is everywhere. Everyone loves him. Do not try to resist, you will be assimilated. First runner-up: Pino Daniele. Older and fatter, yes, but lacks a certain Rossian element of style. For more on the glorious world of Italian pop music, see p. 61.

BEST OF ROME: THE COLOSSEUM TO THE VATICAN

TIME: 3-4hr. walk; longer if you visit the museums along the way.

DISTANCE: about 8km.

SEASON: A sunny day is preferable; bring lots of water.

A highlights tour of ancient Rome

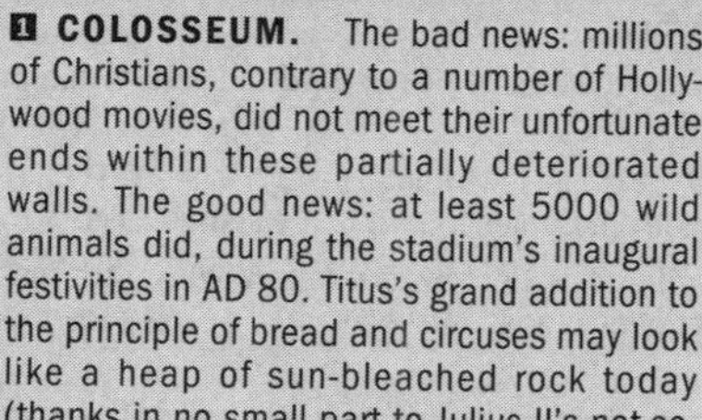

1 COLOSSEUM. The bad news: millions of Christians, contrary to a number of Hollywood movies, did not meet their unfortunate ends within these partially deteriorated walls. The good news: at least 5000 wild animals did, during the stadium's inaugural festivities in AD 80. Titus's grand addition to the principle of bread and circuses may look like a heap of sun-bleached rock today (thanks in no small part to Julius II's not-so-clandestine pillaging during the Renaissance), but in its youth, it was an engineering marvel, containing, among other things, a system of awnings that protected the bloodthirsty populace from the inconveniences of sun and rain. Allow an extra 20min. if you plan to make the climb to the upper tiers of the structure, or stride confidently across the new wooden walkway—just don't look down (p. 76).

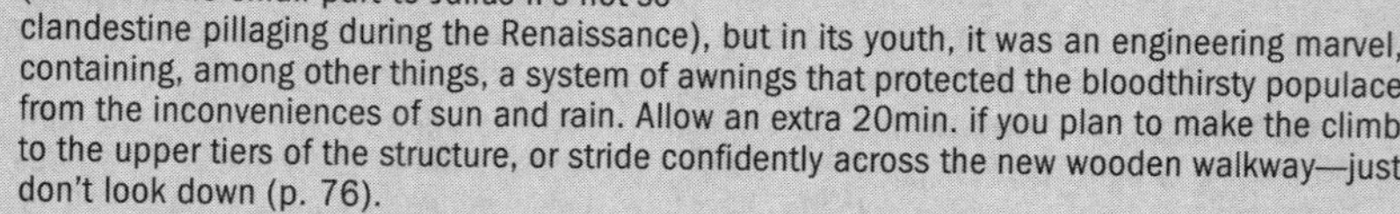

2 SANTA MARIA IN ARACOELI. The archetypal Roman Church. In the first century AD, the Romans worshipped the spirit of money in the guise of Jupiter Moneta. Later, piety replaced productivity, and the mint originally located here became a meeting place for the Franciscans, who were generally uninterested in making money. In the meantime, the Sibyl once quartered within the walls of the old temple informed Augustus that although he did enjoy divine status, one greater than even he would come to rule Rome. In response, the emperor erected the Ara Coeli, or the altar to heaven (p. 85).

3 IL GESU. Historically, the Jesuits were an order known throughout Europe for their commitment to evangelism and their love of extravagant luxury items. The Gesu is the living incarnation of both strains, built in 1584 but left undecorated for more than 100 years (the prescient founders of the Order apparently realized that only Baroque could provide the gilded opulence that such a project required). The Chapel of St. Ignatius and its crowning piece of artistic achievement, the altar topped with an enormous globe of lapis lazuli, are rendered almost unholy by their grandeur, but the real triumph of the church is Baciccia's Triumph of the Holy Name of Jesus, in which sinners, cast from the communion of souls, appear to be hurtling from heaven towards the observers on the ground (p. 91).

4 TEATRO DI MARCELLO. Arranging a walk past the Marcello on a summer evening is a rewarding enterprise: some of Rome's best classical musicians often use the crumbling structure as a venue for concerts in nice weather. Without venturing too far into the stark, dusty collection of ruins, one can visit the oldest building in Rome permanently designated as a theater (p. 88).

5 ISOLA TIBERINA. A stroll around this island, enclosed by the Romans with travertine marble so that it would resemble a ship, is a good way to cross the Tiber on the way to Trastevere. The first structure on the island was a temple to Aesculapius, son of Apollo and god of medicine. During the plague of 293 BC, a statue of him was brought from Greece to the island, which has been dedicated to healing ever since. The Fatebenefratelli (literally "do good brothers") Hospital and San Bartolomeo, Holy Roman Emperor Otto III's church of choice, are both located on the grounds (p. 123).

6 CASTEL SANT'ANGELO. The popes often used this former site of Hadrian's mausoleum as an escape from the pressures, problems, and riots that often plagued St. Peter's. The wealth of the Vatican was often stored here when the Holy Roman Emperors decided that a little trip to the south was the perfect way to fill their coffers. The lower building served as quarters for some of Rome's more rowdy residents, including the boastful autobiographer and sometime artist Benvenuto Cellini, heretical monk Giordano Bruno, and

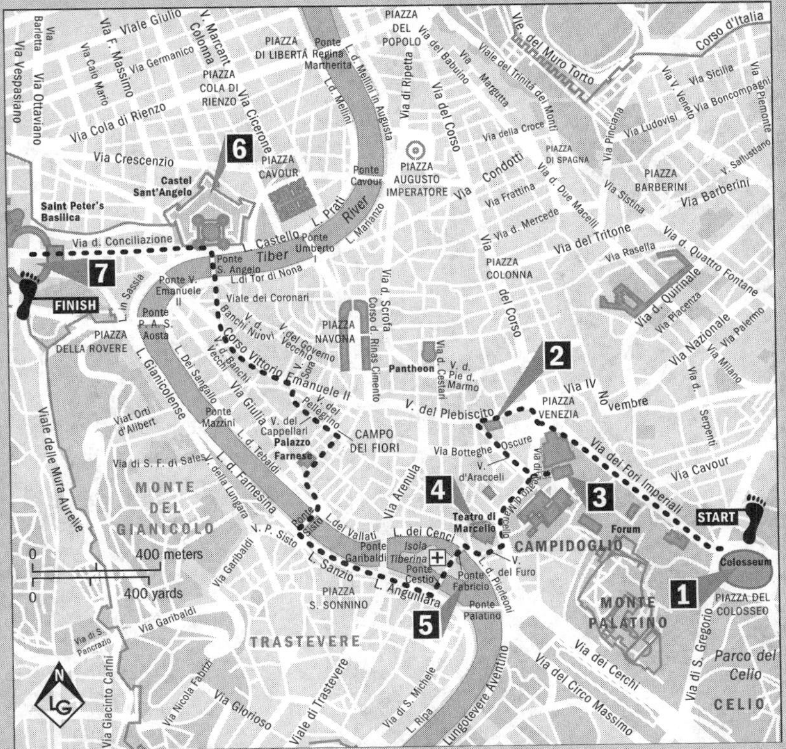

Beatrice Cenci, accused of incest and patricide and memorialized by Shelley's *The Cenci*. The papal apartments are worth a look, especially the Camera d'Amore e Psiche (p. 120).

7 PIAZZA SAN PIETRO. Far too often, tourists eager to rub flesh with millions of other pensive pilgrims in the Sistine Chapel rush past Bernini's masterpiece without a second look. The artist is undoubtedly taking the proverbial route of disgruntled dead people and turning over in his grave; his work was meant to awe the Protestant heretics who came to Rome in order to talk politics with the pope. A set of four colonnades crowned by 140 distinct saints was part of the visual effect planned by Bernini, in addition to the sensation of leaving the narrow streets of the medieval quarter for the comparative openness of the square. Mussolini ruined the characteristic Baroque metaphor (darkness into light) by constructing the Via di Conciliazione, but the square, and the obelisk placed in the middle by Sixtus V, are nonetheless impressive to even the biggest heretic in the crowd (p. 115).

STAR
OLITA
OLIO DI

INSIDE

upon arrival **15**

airports **15** trains **16** early and late flights **17**

let's get oriented **17**

via, piazza, little hell **17** maps **17**

let's get around **17**

buses **18** metro **20** taxis and radio taxis **20** cars **21** bikes and mopeds **25**

let's get informed **25**

tourist offices **25** embassies and consulates **26** print media **26**
broadcast media **27** tipping and bargaining **27**

let's keep in touch **27**

by telephone **27** by mail **29** by email **30** by fax **31**
getting money from home **31**

let's speak italian **31**

When in Rome

In his *History of Rome*, Livy wrote that "the layout of Rome is more like a squatter's settlement than a properly planned city." Two thousand years of city planning later, Rome still seems like an unnavigable sea of one-way streets, dead ends, clandestine *piazze*, and incurable traffic. The following pages will help you get your footing the minute your plane touches down in the Eternal City. Chances are you're still going to get lost—even Roman residents lose their way in Rome's sprawling streets. And when in Rome....

UPON ARRIVAL

Most international flights touch down at Leonardo da Vinci International Airport (☎06 659 51), referred to as **Fiumicino** for the coastal village in which it is located. Up-to-the-minute information on both of Rome's airports is online at www.adr.it.

AIRPORTS

FIUMICINO

Look for touch-screens that display maps and transportation information in English and Italian.

APT (Rome Tourist Authority) (☎06 659 560 74), directly in front of the customs exit of Terminal C. Hotel reservations and brochures. English spoken. Open daily 8:15am-7pm.

Banca di Roma, a small branch sits immediately to the right of customs; go right from customs to the end of the hallway to find the large office. Decent exchange rates. Open M-F 8:25am-1:25pm and 2:40-3:40pm, Sa 8:25-11:55am. **ATM** at both locations accepts AmEx, Cirrus, MC, and V. Its **currency exchange** office is to the right of customs. Open daily 6am-midnight. After midnight and before 6am, use the automatic currency exchange machines which accept 13 foreign currencies.

Luggage Storage, on the right at the end of the hall as you exit customs. Open 6:30am-11:30pm. €2 per bag (under 55kg) for 7hr., or €3.50 for 24hr.

Post Office, next to luggage storage and the large Banca di Roma office. Services include fax and telegrams. Open M-F 8:30-2pm, Sa 8:30am-1pm.

Rent-A-Car/Autonoleggi, two conveyer belts away from the train depot.

CIAMPINO

Most charter and a few domestic flights arrive at Ciampino airport (☎06 794 941). To get to Rome from Ciampino, take the CO.TRA.L bus (every 30min., 6:10am-11pm, €1) to Anagnina station on Metro Linea A (see p. 20). To get to Ciampino, reverse these directions. Another option is taking a train from Termini to Ciampino station and a bus to the airport; check with FS (☎06 488 17 26; www.fs-on-line.com) for details. After 11pm, take a cab to and from Ciampino. Although Ciampino is inside the Rome city limits, there is a supplemental charge of €5.50.

TO & FROM FIUMICINO AIRPORT BY TRAIN

Upon seeing the dozens of people crowded outside customs waiting for loved ones, you may feel compelled to pretend to be related to one of these people and convince them to take you to their Italian home, where you'll enjoy home-cooked meals and a warm bed. Resist this urge. Instead, follow the signs to your left for **Stazione FS/Railway Station.** Go up 2 floors to the pedestrian bridge to the airport train station. From here you can take one of the two trains to the center of Rome.

TERMINI STATION

The Termini line runs nonstop to Rome's main train, Termini (30min.; 2 per hr. 8 and 38min. past the hour 7:37am-10:37pm, extra trains 6:38am and 11:38pm; €8.23, €20 on board). Buy a ticket *"Per Termini"* at the FS ticket counter, the *tabacchi* on the right, or from one of the machines in the station. A train leaves Termini for Fiumicino from track #25 or #26. Follow signs for *"Fiumicino Terminal."* (40 min.; 2 per hr. 22 and 52min past the hour; €8.80). Buy tickets at the Alitalia office (from 9am-7:30pm) at track #25 at the window marked *"Biglietti Per Fiumicino"* or from other designated areas in the station. Validate your ticket before boarding.

TIBURTINA STATION

The Tiburtina/Orte/Fara Sabina train stops at many of the minor train stations (but NOT Termini) on the outskirts of the city center, all of which are, in turn, connected to the city center by bus or Metro. Service is erratic on Sundays and in August, and trains may arrive at Tiburtina after the Metro closes (40min.; every 15min. Su every 30min. 6:27am-9:27pm; extra trains 5:37am, 9:57, 10:27, 10:57, 11:27pm; €4.70). Buy tickets *"Per Tiburtina"* on the right, or from the machines in the station, or on the train after hours. Note that the final destination of this train may be indicated on the signs by *"Orte," "Tiburtina,"* or *"Fara Sabina."* Validate and retain your ticket for the entire trip.

The most convenient way to reach the city center when using this line is to get off at the Tiburtina station, which is connected to the Metro stop "Tiburtina" (Linea B). When you get off the train (track #1), go down the stairs, following the signs for the *Metropolitana.* Buy a ticket (€1), validate it, and take Metro Linea B (dir: "Laurentina"). If you arrive after the metro closes, take the 40N night bus to Termini. A train leaves Tiburtina for Fiumicino from track #4 or #5 (40min., every 15 to 60min. 5:04am-10:33pm, €4.13). Buy tickets at the ticket booths.

EARLY AND LATE FLIGHTS

If your flight arrives at Fiumicino after 10pm or leaves before 8am, you may have transportation difficulties. The most reliable, if expensive, option is to take a **cab,** which costs €35-45. (Request one at the kiosk in the airport or call ☎06 3570, 06 4994, or 06 6645.) In the wee hours, the cheapest option is to take the blue **CO.TRA.L bus** to Tiburtina, which stops at Termini. (1:15, 2:15, 3:30, 5am; €5, pay on board). The bus stop is on your right as you exit through the main doors of Terminal C. To get to Fiumicino from Rome late at night or early in the morning, take bus #40N from Termini to Tiburtina (every 20-30min.), then catch the blue CO.TRA.L bus to Fiumicino from the plaza outside (12:30, 1:15, 2:30, 3:45am; €3.62).

LET'S GET ORIENTED

Most sights and establishments listed in *Let's Go: Rome 2004* are grouped by location and then ranked by interest and quality. Each neighborhood corresponds to a map at the back of this book (on which sights and establishments are plotted). Street names change frequently in Rome; in directions to establishments, this is denoted by placing another street name in parentheses after the initial name. For instance, Via del Quirinale turning into Via XX Settembre would be denoted as "V.d. Quirinale (V. XX Settembre)." **Abbreviations** used include: V. for Via, P. for Piazza, and C. for Corso. First names (as in C.V. Emanuele II) and San/Santa are abbreviated in addresses.

VIA, PIAZZA, LITTLE HELL

No longer defined by the Seven Hills, modern Rome is huge, sprawling over a large area between the hills of the Castelli Romani to the north, the beach at Ostia to the west, and Lake Albano to the south, counting within its boundaries such memorable eyesores as Anagnina, Spinaceto, and Infernetto ("little Hell"). Encircling it is the Grande Raccordo Anulare (GRA), whose name loosely translates as "traffic jams of Biblical proportions." Luckily for you, though, most major sights lie within a comparatively small radius, which can be neatly divided into eight areas. (See **Discover**, p. 3, for a complete list of Roman neighborhoods and their boundaries.)

MAPS

It's impossible to navigate the streets of Rome without a map, and using the free and omnipresent **McDonald's** map will probably get you lost (though you're likely to find at least one of the 35 McDonald's locations in the Eternal City). Instead, pick up the concise and detailed **Charta Roma** map (at EPT or PIT kiosks) or the one published by Enjoy Rome. *Let's Go* publishes a **map guide** to Rome, a pocket-sized map of transportation, sights, etc., with 32 pages of advice on where to sleep, eat, and dance in Rome. The compact Bus/Tram/Metro map available at Termini (free) is relatively useless, so buy a **Roma Metro-Bus** map at a newsstand (€4.13). **Rome A to Z** (sold with **Lazio A to Z**) includes a guide of 20 bike routes (available at newsstands; €6.20). **Tuttocittà,** distributed yearly with Roman phone books, is the best atlas, but isn't sold in stores; ask Roman friends or store owners if you can look at it.

LET'S GET AROUND

Bus and subway tickets (€1) are the same and can be bought at *tabacchi*, newsstands, and vending machines (in stations, on occasional street corners, and at major bus stops). Look for the ATAC label. Each ticket is valid for either one ride on

in recent news

a better life?

Though Italy decriminalized prostitution in 1958, trafficking female immigrants is both illegal and widespread. Italy has roughly 19,000 to 25,000 foreign prostitutes, at least one-tenth of whom have been trafficked. Since 1995, the majority have been Nigerians and Albanians, most 14-18 years old, and most in Rome (according to the London Institute of Race Relations).

Prostitution is hardly safe, but it is very dangerous for immigrants. While many Italians in the sex industry operate out of massage parlors or apartments, foreigners generally work on the street. Worse still, trafficked women are controlled by a ring or a single individual who pays their passage. Enslaved by violence and verbal abuse, they are isolated from family out of fear and shame.

In 1998, legislation allowed foreign prostitutes to apply for an extendable 6-month visa, but only 675 visas were issued from 1998 to 2001. In 1999, immigration officials carried out several mass deportations of Nigerian prostitutes without providing prior notice to Nigeria or assistance for these women. Of those deported, 50% contracted AIDS while in Italy.

the Metro or for unlimited bus travel within 75 minutes of validation. A BIG **daily ticket** costs €4 and allows for unlimited bus or train travel everywhere in the *Comune di Roma*, including Ostia but not Fiumicino; a CIS **weekly ticket** costs €16. Another option is the new 3-day "tourist ticket," which costs €11. Ask for the pass anywhere tickets are sold. Student passes are cheaper, but are only for students studying at Italian universities.

BUSES

Though the network of routes may seem daunting at first, Rome's bus system is very efficient and inexpensive. Buses also cover far more area than the rather scanty metro system. The **ATAC** (*Aziende Tramvie Autobus Communali;* ☎800 431 784, 8am-6pm) intracity bus company has a myriad of **information booths,** including one in Termini. Ask at a tourist office (see color map section) for a useful Bus/Tram/Metro map of central Rome. Each bus stop *(fermata)* is marked by yellow signs listing routes that stop there and key streets and stops on those routes. The name of the stop at which you are standing is boxed; the bus will take you to any of the places listed below the boxed stop. **To go to a stop listed above the box,** cross the street to catch the same bus in the opposite direction.

Temporary bus signs are simple yellow poles with the route marked in cursive; you'll need to check a map to know all the stops. Some buses run only on weekdays *(feriali)* or weekends *(festivi)*, while others have different routes depending on the day of the week. Hours vary by route, but most buses begin around 6am and stop around midnight. Board buses from the front or back doors, not from the middle, then stamp your ticket in the orange machine at the back; exit only through the middle, helpfully marked *uscita.* The ticket is then good for any number of transfers over the next 75min. Stamp the other end of the ticket after your first transfer. If you exceed 75min., **you must stamp a new ticket.** It is wise to carry a ballpoint pen with you because validation machines are often broken. If you encounter a defective machine, mark on your own ticket to indicate that it has been used. There is a **fine of €51 plus ticket price** for not carrying a validated ticket or bus pass, and inspections are becoming more common. Playing the dumb tourist won't help. Buy several tickets and keep them on you: at night and on weekends they can be hard to find.

Night routes are indicated on signs by black shields, owls, and the letter N following the route number. Signal a night bus to stop by standing right under its sign and flailing wildly. They run infrequently, and you may have to transfer several times to get where you want to go. **ATAC** offers *Giro Turistico*, a no-frills, 3-hour circuit of the city. (Bus #110; leaves Termini every 30min, 10am-6pm; €7.75, €12.91 for day use.) They provide a map and some explanation in Italian and quasi-English, whirling you around the city for a comprehensive peek at the city's primary monuments.

A word on **bus etiquette:** If you are young, you really should give your seat to elderly people. Inexplicably, Romans on the bus like to prepare for their grand descent several stops in advance by crowding around the exit doors. If you are standing in their way near the exit, you will be asked repeatedly, *"Scende (la prossima)?"* which means, "Are you getting off at the next stop?" Answer appropriately.

POPULAR ATAC BUS ROUTES

Rome is always revamping its transportation system. Be sure to check a map for the most up-to-date route information.

DAY BUSES

40: Express bus. Termini, V. Nazionale, P. Venezia, Largo Argentina, C.V. Emanuele II, P. Pia.

46: Vatican, C. V. Emanuele II, Largo Argentina, P. Venezia.

60: V. Nomentana, V. XX Settembre. P.d. Repubblica, V. Nazionale, P. Venezia, V. Aventino.

64: Termini, V. Nazionale, P. Venezia, Largo Argentina, C. V. Emanuele II, Vatican (Called by some the wallet-eater, as always, watch out for pickpockets.)

81: P. Malatesta, San Giovanni, Colosseo, Bocca della Verità, P. Venezia, Largo Argentina, P. Cavour, V. Cola di Rienzo, Vatican.

116: V. Veneto, P. Barberini, P.d. Spagna, C. Rinascimento, Campo de' Fiori, P. Farnese, Terminal Gianicolo, V. Giulia, Campo de' Fiori, Pantheon, P. Colonna, P. Barberini, V. Veneto.

117: S. Giovanni, Colosseo, Largo Tritone, P.d. Spagna, P. del Popolo, V.d. Corso, P. Venezia, Colosseo. Weekdays only, from 7:30am-9pm.

119: P.d. Popolo, V.d. Corso, Largo Goldoni, P. Venezia, V.d. Tritone, P. Barberini, P.d. Spagna, V.d. Babuino, P.d. Popolo. Weekdays only, from 9am-8pm.

170: Termini, V. Nazionale, P. Venezia, Bocca della Verità, Testaccio, Stazione Trastevere, V. Marconi, P. Agricoltura.

175: Termini, P. Barberini, V.d. Corso, P. Venezia, Colosseo, Aventino, Stazione Ostienze.

492: Tiburtina, Termini, P. Barberini, P. Venezia, C. Rinascimento, P. Cavour, P. Risorgimento.

TRAMS

3: Stazione Trastevere, Ponte Sublicio, Piramide, V. Aventino, Circo Massimo, Colosseo, S.Giovanni di Laterano, P. Porta Maggiore, San Lorenzo, Nomentana, Trieste, Villa Borghese.

8: Largo Argentina, Ponte Garibaldi, P. Mastai, Stazione Trastevere, Casaletto.

19: P. Risorgimento (Vatican), V. Flaminia, Villa Giulia, San Lorenzo, suburbs.

NIGHT (NOTTURNO) BUSES

You must signal a night bus to stop for you. Buses are supposed to come at 30min.-1hr. intervals, but can be unreliable; try to avoid waiting alone.

29N: Ostienze, Lungotevere de' Cenci, V. Crescenzio (Vatican), V. Belle Arti, V. Regina Marherita, S. Lorenzo, Colosseo. Runs every 30 min.

40N: Approximately the same route as **Metro B**. Runs every 30min.

45N: Western suburbs, Largo d. Porta Cavalleggeri (Vatican), C.V. Emanuele II, Largo Argentina, P. Venezia, V. Tritone, P. Barberini, P. Repubblica, Termini. Runs every 30 minutes.

55N: Approximately the same route as **Metro A**, Runs every 30min.

from the road

Beep Beep

I'd heard the clichés. I'd seen the movies and heard the horror stories; I even learned how to drive stick. But nothing could have prepared me for driving in Italy. A car is a rare treat for a LG researcher-writer, so when faced with the option of speeding up my daytrip reviews in Southern Lazio, I didn't hesitate.

I first sensed that the feat was doomed when the car rental place refused to lend me a map. The saying that 'all roads lead to Rome' overlooks the fact that, inversely, all roads lead out of Rome–and with few signs. After circling for hours in search of the GRA (the beltway encircling Rome), I eventually found an on-ramp. To say that the best strategy was just to close my eyes, pray, and step on it would be a slight overstatement, but I did come to appreciate why so many Roman cars have a plastic Virgin Mary dangling from the rearview mirror.

The GRA itself was no better. I got used to seeing the shoulder used as a fourth lane; but the cars that darted around me as if I were a stationary vehicle remained far more harrowing. Few exits were marked, and I found myself too focused on my own life to find my exit.

Next time, I decided, I'm sticking with the bus.

Michael Squire was a Researcher-Writer for Let's Go:Rome 2004.

60N: Northeastern suburbs, P. Porta Pia, P. Fiume, V. Veneto, P. Barberini, P.S. Silvestro, P. Venezia. Runs every 20min.

78N: P. Clodio, P. Flaminio, P. Cavour, P.S. Andrea d. Valle, Largo Argentina, P. Venezia, V. Nazionale, Termini. Runs every 30min.

BUSES TO RURAL LAZIO

CO.TRA.L buses between Rome and the province of Lazio leave from outside the city center; take the subway to an outlying area and catch a bus from there: M: A-Anagnina for Frascati and the Colli Albani; M: B-Rebibbia for Tivoli and Subiaco; M: A-Lepanto for Cerveteri, Tarquinia, Bracciano, Lago Vico, and Civitavecchia. *Let's Go* lists information in the Daytrips chapter (see p. 259). For more information, contact CO.TRA.L. (☎800 150 008) or a tourist agency (see p. 25).

METRO

Every time they tried to dig more tracks for their subway system, the Romans discovered more ancient ruins. As a result, Rome's subway system is subpar for a city of its size. Many of Rome's sights are a trek from the nearest stop, but for covering large distances quickly, the subway beats the bus—it's comparatively fast and reliable. The two lines (A and B) of the *Metropolitana* intersect at Termini and can be reached by several entrances, including the stairway between the station and P. del Cinquecento. Entrances to Metro stations elsewhere are marked by poles with a white "M" on a red square. **The subway runs daily from 5:30am to 11:30pm.**

You don't have to validate your ticket to pass through the turnstiles on the subway; however, ATAC's ticket inspectors prowl trains and stations, and checks are increasingly-common.

TAXIS AND RADIO TAXIS

Taxis in Rome are convenient but expensive (though less so than in other major cities). You can flag them down in the street, but they are easily found at stands near Termini and in major *piazze*. Ride only in yellow or white taxis, and make sure your taxi has a meter (if not, settle on a price before you get in the car). The meter starts at €2.33. Surcharges are levied at night (€2.58), on Sunday (€1.03), and when heading to or from Fiumicino (€7.23) and Ciampino (€5.16), with a charge per suitcase of €1.04. Standard tip is 10%. Expect to pay about €7.75 for a ride from Termini to the Vatican.

Taxis between the city center and Fiumicino cost around €37. **Radio taxis** will pick you up at a given location within a few minutes of your call. Beware: radio taxis start the meter the moment your call is answered! See the **Service Directory,** p. 342, for a listing of taxi and radio taxis.

CARS

Driving in Rome is a bad idea. Roman drivers are aggressive, and those who drive mopeds appear not to care whether they live or die. Parking is expensive and very difficult to find, and if you don't keep your eyes peeled, you may drive into a car-free zone (certain streets are reserved for public transportation and the police) and incur a fine. Car theft and robberies on cars are rampant, even during the day in busy areas. As if that weren't enough, gas (**benzina** in Italian) is exorbitantly priced (approximately €1.05 per liter). Most gas stations accept credit cards.

Rome is linked to the north and south of Italy by a great north-south highway called the **A1,** which feeds into the **Grande Raccordo Anulare (GRA),** the beltway that encircles Rome. Tolls on these roads are high; a trip to Florence can cost around €11. Besides the highway, there are several good *strade statale* that lead into Rome. From the north, enter on V. Flaminia, V. Salaria, or V. Nomentana. Avoid V. Cassia, V. Tiburtina, and V.d. Mare at all costs; the ancient two-chariot lanes can't cope with modern-day traffic.

When leaving the city, don't try to follow the green *Autostrada per Firenze* signs—get on the GRA instead and follow it around; it's longer but faster. To get to the Adriatic coast, take highway A24. To reach beaches and port towns, try V. Pontina, which sticks close to the sea and connects you to most coastal spots.

INTERNATIONAL DRIVING PERMITS (IDP)

If you plan to drive a car while in Italy, you should obtain an **International Driving Permit (IDP).** Although most car rental agencies don't require the permit, it is required for legal reasons if you drive for more than a month. Your IDP, valid for one year, must be issued in your own country before you depart and must be accompanied by a valid driver's license. You must be 18 years old to receive the IDP. Applications usually need to include one or two photos, a current local license, an additional form of identification, and a fee. Those driving in Italy for more than one year must obtain an Italian license (€36.20).

Australia: Contact local **Royal Automobile Club (RAC)** or **National Royal Motorist Association (NRMA)** in NSW or ACT (☎ 08 942 144 44; www.rac.com.au/travel). AUS$20 plus mailing fee.

Canada: Contact any **Canadian Automobile Association (CAA)** branch office or write to CAA, 1145 Hunt Club Rd., #200, K1V 0Y3 (☎613-247-0117; www.caa.ca/e/travel/id/idp.shtml) Permits CDN$13.

Ireland: Contact the nearest **Automobile Association (AA)** office or write to the UK address below. Permits €5.08. The Irish Automobile Association, 23 Suffolk St., Rockhill, Blackrock, Co. Dublin (☎01 677 94 81), honors most foreign automobile memberships (24hr. breakdown and road service ☎ 800 667 788.)

New Zealand: Contact your local **Automobile Association (AA)** or their main office at Auckland Central, 99 Albert St. (☎09 377 46 60; www.nzaa.co.nz). Permits NZ$12.

South Africa: Contact the Automobile Association of South Africa at P.O. Box 596, 2000 Johannesburg (☎11 799 14 00; www.aasa.co.za). Permits ZAR28.50.

UK: Contact your local AAA or the **AAA Headquarters** (☎0870 600 0371; www.theaa.com), or write: The Automobile Association, International Documents, Fanum House, Basing View, Basing stroke, Hampshire RG21 4EA. To find the nearest location that issues the IDP, see www.theaa.com/getaway/idp/index.html. Permits UK£4.

Rome: Major Streets Finder

see key p. 24

A
B
C
Circ. Trionfale
Via Trionfale
V. d. Giuliana
Vle. Angelico
Viale delle Milizie
Via Lepanto
Via Cesare
Ponte G. Matteotti
L. Michelangelo
Ponte Pietro Nenni
L. Arnaldo da Brescia
Via Flaminia
Viale G. Washington
LGO. TRIONFALE
Via Barletta
Viale Giulio
Via M. A. Colonna
PIAZZA DEL POPOLO
PIAZZALE DEGLI EROI
V. Andrea Doria
Via Leone IV
Via Ottaviano
Via Vespasiano
Via Caio Mario
Via F. Massimo
Via Germanico
PIAZZA DI LIBERTÀ
Ponte Regina Martherita
Via del Babuino
Via Margutta
Vle. Trinità
PIAZZA COLA DI RIENZO
L. d. Mellini
L. in Augusta
Via di Ripetta
Via del Corso
Via Candia
Via Cola di Rienzo
Via Cicerone
Via Crescenzio
PIAZZA CAVOUR
Ponte Cavour
PIAZZA AUGUSTO IMPERATORE
Via della
Via Condotti
Via Frattina
Castel Sant'Angelo
CITTÀ DEL VATICANO
L. Prati
River
L. Castello
Ponte Umberto I
L. Marzio
Saint Peter's Basilica
Via d. Conciliazione
Ponte S. Angelo
Tiber
Via d. Scrofa
PIAZZA COLONNA
Viale Vaticano
Ponte V. Emanuele II
L. di Tor di Nona
V. Zanardelli
L. in Sassia
V. d. B. di S. Spirito
Via dei Coronari
Ponte P.A.S. Aosta
PIAZZA NAVONA
Corso d. Rinascimento
Via Giustiniani
Pantheon
V. d. Seminario
PZA. DELLA ROTONDA
Via Staz. di S. Pietro
V. delle Fornaci
PIAZZA DELLA ROVERE
L. Gianicolense
Corso Vittorio Emanuele II
V. S. Maria d'Anima
V. Monterone
Torre Argentina
V. d. Cestari
V. d. Gesù
V. d. Plebiscito
V. Gregorio VII
Viale delle Mura Aurelie
L. dei Sangallo
Via Giulia
V. d. Monserrato
Viat Orti d'Alibert
Ponte Mazzini
Palazzo Farnese
Via d. Cava Aurelia
Passeggiata di Gianicolo
Via di S. F. di Sales
L. d. Tebaldi
V. d. Giubbonari
Via Botteghe Oscure
MONTE DEL GIANICOLO
V. della Lungara
L. della Farnesina
V. d. Pettinari
Via Arenula
Teatro Marcello
Via del Teatro di Marcello
Ponte Sisto
L. dei Vallati
L. dei Cenci
0
500 yards
0
500 meters
V. P. Sisto
Via Garibaldi
L. Sanzio
Ponte Garibaldi
Isola Tiberina
L. di Pierleoni
L. Anguillara
Ponte Cestio
PIAZZA S. SONNINO
Via Aurelia Antica
Ponte Palatino
Via Garibaldi
Via Luciano Manara
V. d. Genovesi
TRASTEVERE
Villa Doria Pamphili
Via di S. Pancrazio
Via Anicia
Via di S. Michele
Aventino
Via Nicola Fabrizi
Viale Glorioso
V. G. Induno
L. Ripa
Via Giacinto Carini
Via Dandolo
Viale di Trastevere
Porto di Pipa Grande
Ponte Sublico
Lungotevere
V. d. Porta Lavernale
V. Ugo Bassi
Via Marmorata
Via Vittelia
Via Fonteiana
Viale di Villa Pamphili
Via dei Quattro Venti
Via Alessandro Poeria
Via Portuense
L. Portuense
Lungotevere Testaccio
Via Giovanni Branca
Via Donna Olimpia
Via di Donna Olimpia
V. Nicola Zabaglia
Via Galvani
V. Federico Ozanam
Parco Testaccio

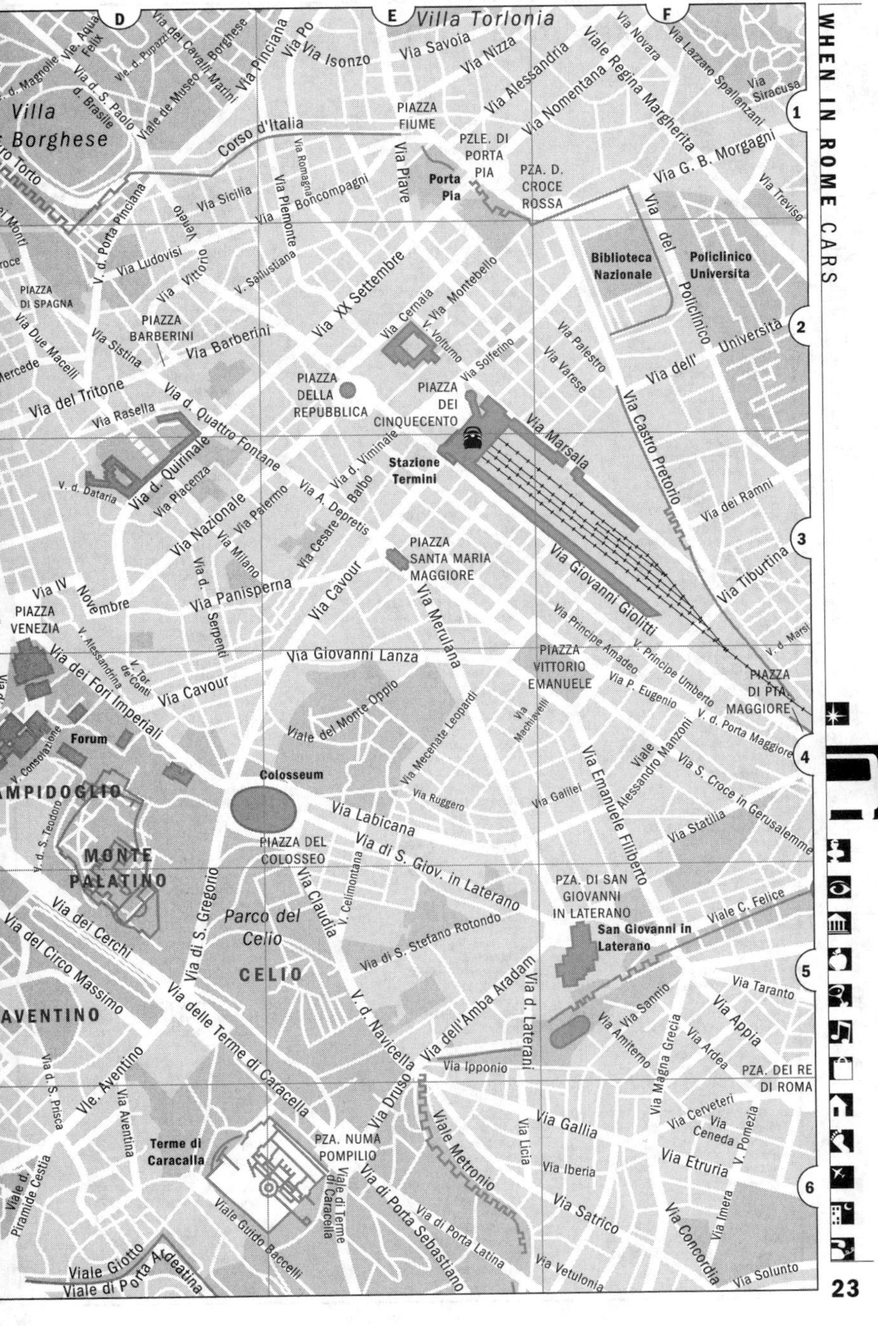
Villa Torlonia
Villa Borghese
PIAZZA FIUME
PZLE. DI PORTA PIA
Porta Pia
PZA. D. CROCE ROSSA
Biblioteca Nazionale
Policlinico Universita
PIAZZA DI SPAGNA
PIAZZA BARBERINI
PIAZZA DELLA REPUBBLICA
PIAZZA DEI CINQUECENTO
Stazione Termini
PIAZZA SANTA MARIA MAGGIORE
PIAZZA VENEZIA
PIAZZA VITTORIO EMANUELE
PIAZZA DI PTA. MAGGIORE
Forum
Colosseum
CAMPIDOGLIO
MONTE PALATINO
PIAZZA DEL COLOSSEO
Parco del Celio
CELIO
PZA. DI SAN GIOVANNI IN LATERANO
San Giovanni in Laterano
AVENTINO
PZA. DEI RE DI ROMA
Terme di Caracalla
PZA. NUMA POMPILIO
Via Savoia
Via Isonzo
Via Po
Via Pinciana
Via Nizza
Via Alessandria
Viale Regina Margherita
Via Nomentana
Via Novara
Via Lazzaro Spallanzani
Via Siracusa
Corso d'Italia
Via Piave
Via G. B. Morgagni
Via Treviso
Via Sicilia
Via Boncompagni
Via Piemonte
Via Ludovisi
Via Vittorio Veneto
V. Sallustiana
Via XX Settembre
Via Cernaia
Via Montebello
Via del Policlinico
Via Sistina
Via Barberini
Via Due Macelli
Via del Tritone
Via Rasella
Via d. Quattro Fontane
Via Palestro
Via Varese
Via dell' Università
Via Castro Pretorio
Via Marsala
Via d. Quirinale
Via Nazionale
Via Piacenza
Via Palermo
Via A. Depretis
Via d. Viminale
Via Cesare Balbo
Via dei Ramni
Via Milano
Via Panisperna
Via Cavour
Via Merulana
Via Giovanni Giolitti
Via Tiburtina
Via IV Novembre
Via d. Serpenti
Via Giovanni Lanza
Via Principe Amadeo
V. Principe Umberto
Via P. Eugenio
V. d. Porta Maggiore
Via dei Fori Imperiali
Viale del Monte Oppio
Via Mecenate Leopardi
Via Emanuele Filiberto
Viale Alessandro Manzoni
Via S. Croce in Gerusalemme
Via Labicana
Via Ruggero
Via Galilei
Via Statilia
Via di S. Giov. in Laterano
Via Claudia
Via di S. Gregorio
Via Celimontana
Via di S. Stefano Rotondo
Viale C. Felice
Via dei Cerchi
Via del Circo Massimo
Via delle Terme di Caracalla
V. d. Navicella
Via dell' Amba Aradam
Via d. Laterani
Via Sannio
Via Amiterno
Via Magna Grecia
Via Ardea
Via Appia
Via Taranto
Via Ipponio
Via Druso
Viale Metronio
Vle. Aventino
Via Aventina
Via d. S. Prisca
Via Gallia
Via Licia
Via Iberia
Via Cerveteri
Via Ceneda
V. Pomezia
Via Etruria
Via Satrico
Via Concordia
Via Imera
Viale di Terme di Caracalla
Viale Guido Baccelli
Via di Porta Latina
Via di Porta Sebastiano
Via Vetulonia
Via Solunto
Viale Giotto
Viale di Porta Ardeatina
Viale d. Piramide Cestia
D
E
F
1
2
3
4
5
6

Rome: Major Streets Finder see map p. 22

STREETS

IV Novembre (V.) **D3**
A. Depretis (V.) **E3**
Alessandria (V.) **E1, F1**
Alessandrina (V.) **D3, D4**
Alessandro Manzoni (Vle.) **F4**
Alessandro Poeria (V.) **B6**
Amba Aradam (V. dell') **E5**
Amiterno (V.) **F5**
Andrea Doria (V.) **A1**
Angelico (Vle.) **A1**
Anguillara (L.) **C4**
Anicia (V.) **C5**
Appia (V.) **F5**
Aqua Felix (Vle.) **D1**
Ardea (V.) **F5**
Arenula (V.) **C4**
Arnaldo da Brescia (L.) **C1**
Augusta (L. in) **C1, C2**
Aurelia Antica (V.) **A4**
Aventino (L.) **C5**
Aventino (Vle.) **D5, D6**
B. di S. Spirito (Via d.) **B3**
Babuino (V. del) **C1**
Barberini (V.) **D2**
Barletta (V.) **A1**
Boncompagni (V.) **E1**
Botteghe Oscure (V.) **C4**
C. Felice (Vle.) **F5**
Caio Mario (V.) **B1**
Candia (V.) **A1, A2**
Castello (L.) **B2**
Castro Pretorio (V.) **F2, F3**
Cava Aurelia (V. della) **A3, A4**
Cavalli Marini (V. dei) **D1**
Cavour (V.) **E3, E4**
Celimontana (V.) **E4, E5**
Cenci (L. dei) **C4**
Ceneda (V.) **F6**
Cerchi (V. dei) **D5**
Cernaia (V.) **E2**
Cerveteri (V.) **F6**
Cesare Balbo (V.) **E3**
Cestari (V. d.) **C3**
Cicerone (V.) **B2**
Circo Massimo (V. del) **C5, D5**
Claudia (V.) **E5**
Cola di Rienzo (V.) **B2**
Conciliazione (V. della) **B2**
Concordia (V.) **F6**
Condotti (V.) **C2**
Consolazione (V.) **D4**
Coronari (V. dei) **B2, B3**
Corso (V. del) **C1, C2, C3**
Crescenzio (V.) **B2**
Croce (V. della) **C2, D2**
Dandolo (V.) **B5**
Dataria (V. della) **D3**
Donna Olimpia (V. d.) **A6**
Druso (V.) **E6**
Due Macelli (V.) **D2**
Emanuele Filiberto (V.) **F4**
Etruria (V.) **F6**
F. Massimo (V.) **B1**
Farnesina (L. della) **B4**
Federico Ozanam (V.) **A6**
Flaminia (V.) **C1**
Fori Imperiali (V. dei) **D4**
Fonteiana (V.) **A5, A6**
Fornaci (V. delle) **A3**
Frattina (V.) **C2, D2**
G. B. Morgagni (V.) **F1**
G. Induno (V.) **C5**
G. Washington (Vle.) **C1**
Galilei (V.) **E4, F4**
Gallia (V.) **F6**
Galvani (V.) **C6**
Garibaldi (V.) **B4, B5**
Genovesi (V. dei) **C5**
Germanico (V.) **B1**
Gesù (V. del) **C3**
Giancinto Carini (V.) **B5, B6**
Gianicolense (L.) **B3**
Gianicolo (Passegiata di) **B2, B3**
Giotto (Vle.) **D6**
Giovanni Branca (V.) **C6**
Giovanni Giolitti (V.) **F3**
Giovanni Lanza (V.) **E4**
Giubbonari (V.) **C4**
Giulio Cesare (Vle.) **B1**
Glorioso (Vle.) **B5**
Gregorio VII (V.) **A3**
Guido Baccelli (Vle.) **D6, E6**
Giuliana (V. della) **A1**
Giustiani (V.) **C3**
Iberia (V.) **F6**
Imera (V.) **F6**
Ipponio (V.) **E5**
Isonzo (V.) **E1**
Italia (Corso d') **D1, E1**
Labicana (V.) **E4**
Laterani (V. dei) **E5**
Lazzaro Pallanzani (V.) **F1**
Leone IV (V.) **A1, A2**
Lepanto (V.) **B1**
Licia (V.) **E6**
Luciano Manara (V.) **B5, C5**
Ludovisi (V.) **D2**
Lungara (V. della) **B4**
M. A. Colonna (V.) **B1**
Machiavelli (V.) **E4, F4**
Magna Grecia (V.) **F5, F6**
Magnolie (Vle. della) **D1**
Margutta (V.) **C1**
Marmorata (V.) **C5, C6**
Marsala (V.) **E2, F3**
Marzio (L.) **C2**
Mecenate Leopardi (V.) **E4**
Mellini (L. di) **C1, C2**
Mercede (V. d.) **C2, D2**
Merculana (V.) **E3, E4**
Metronio (Vle.) **E6**
Michelangelo (L.) **B1, C1**
Milano (V.) **D3**
Milizie (Vle. delle) **A1, B1**
Monserrato (V. di) **B3**
Monte Oppio (Vle. del) **E4**
Montebello (V.) **E2**
Monterone (V.) **C3**
Mura Aurelie (Vle. delle) **A3, A4**
Muro Torto (V. del) **C1, D1**
Museo Borghese (Vle. del) **D1**
Navicella (V. della) **E5**
Nazionale (V.) **D3, E3**
Nicola Fabrizi (V.) **B5**
Nicola Zabaglia (V.) **C6**
Nizza (V.) **E1**
Nomentana (V.) **E1, F1**
Novara (V.) **F1**
Ottaviano (V.) **A1, A2**
Palermo (V.) **D3, E3**
Palestro (V.) **E2, F2**
Panisperna (V.) **D3, E3**
Pettinari (V. dei) **C4**
Piacenza (V.) **D3**
Piave (V.) **E1**
Piemonte (V.) **E1, E2**
Pierleoni (L. di) **C4**
Pinciana (V.) **D1, E1**
Piramide Cestia (Vle. di) **D6**
Plebiscito (V. del) **C3**
Po (V.) **E1**
Policlinico (V. del) **F2**
Pomezia (V.) **F6**
Ponte Sisto (V. di) **B4**
Porta Ardeatina (Vle. di) **D6**
Porta Latina (V. di) **E6**
Porta Lavernale (V. di) **C5, C6**
Porta Pinciana (V. di) **D1, D2**
Porta Maggiore (V. di) **F4**
Porta Sebastiano (V. di) **E6**
Porto di Pipa Grande **C5, C6**
Portuense (L.) **B6**
Portuense (V.) **B6**
Prati (L.) **C2**
Principe Amadeo (V.) **E3, F3, F4**
Principe Umberto (V.) **F4**
Pupazzi (Vle. dei) **D1**
Quattro Fontane (V. delle) **D2, D3, E3**
Quattro Venti (V. dei) **A5, A6**
Quirinale (V. del) **D3**
Raffaello Sanzio (L.) **C4**
Ramni (V. dei) **F3**
Rasella (V.) **D2**
Regina Margherita (Vle.) **F1, F2**
Rinascimento (Corso di) **C3**
Ripa (L.) **C5**
Ripetta (V. di) **C1, C2**
Romagna (V.) **E1**
Ruggero (V.) **E4**
Sallustiana (V.) **D2, E2**
San Francesco di Sales (V. di) **B4**
San Giovanni in Laterano (V. di) **E4, E5**
San Gregorio (V. di) **D4, D5**
San Michele (V. di) **C5**
San Pancrazio (V. di) **A5, B5**
San Paolo di Brasile (V. del) **D1**
San Stefano Rotondo (V.) **E5**
San Teodoro (V. di) **D4**
Sangallo (L. dei) **B3**
Sannio (V.) **F5**
Santa Croce in Gerusalemme (V.) **F4**
Santa Maria d'Anima (V.) **C3**
Santa Prisca (V. di) **D5, D6**
Sassia (L. in) **B3**
Satrico (V.) **E6**
Savoia (V.) **E1**
Scrofa (V. della) **C2, C3**
Seminario (V. del) **C3**
Serpenti (V. dei) **D3**
Sicilia (V.) **D1, E1**
Siracusa (V.) **F1**
Sistina (V.) **D2**
Solferino (V.) **E2, F2**
Solunto (V.) **F6**
Statilia (V.) **F4**
Stazione di San Pietro (V. d.) **A3**
Taranto (V.) **F5**
Tebaldi (L. dei) **B3, B4**
Terme di Caracella (V. delle) **D5, E6**
Terme di Caracella (Vle. di) **E6**
Testaccio (L.) **C6**
Tiburtina (V.) **F3**
Tor de'Conti (V.) **D4**
Tor di Nona (L. di) **B3**
Torre Argentina **C3**
Trastevere (Vle. di) **B5, B6, C5**
Treviso (V.) **F1**
Trinità dei Monti (Vle.) **C1, D1, D2**
Trionfale (Circonvallazione) **A1**
Trionfale (V.) **A1**
Tritone (V. del) **D2**
Ugo Bassi (V.) **B6**
Università (Vle. dell') **F2**
Vallati (L. dei) **C4**
Varese (V.) **F2**
Vaticano (Vle.) **A3**
Vespasiano (V.) **A1, A2**
Vetulonia (V.) **F6**
Villa Pamphili (Vle. di) **A5, A6**
Viminale (V. del) **E3**
Vittorio Emanuelle II (Corso) **B3, C3**
Vittorio Veneto (V.) **D1, D2**
Volturno (V.) **E2**
XX Settembre (V.) **D2, E2, E1**
Zanardelli (V.) **C2, C3**

PLAZAS

Augusto Imperatore (Piazza) **C2**
Barberini (Piazza) **D2**
Cavour (Piazza) **B2**
Cinquecento (Piazza dei) **E2**
Cola di Rienzo (Piazza) **B1**
Colonna (Piazza) **C2**
Croce Rossa (Piazza della) **F1**
Eroi (Piazzale degli) **A1**
Fiume (Piazza) **E1**
Libertà (Piazza di) **B1**
Navona (Piazza) **C3**
Numa Pompilio (Piazza) **E6**
Popolo (Piazza del) **C1**
Porta Maggiore (Piazza di) **F4**
Porta Pia (Piazzale di) **E1**
Re di Roma (Piazza dei) **F5, F6**
Reppublica (Piazza della) **E2**
Rotonda (Piazza della) **C3**
San Giovanni in Laterano (Piazza di) **F5**
Santa Maria Maggiore (Piazza) **E3**
Venezia (Piazza) **D3**

US: Visit any **American Automobile Association (AAA)** office or write to AAA Florida, Travel Related Services, 1000 AAA Drive (mail stop 28), Heathrow, FL 32746 (☎407-444-7000; www.aaa.com/aaa). You don't have to be a member to buy an IDP (US$10). AAA Travel Related Services (☎800-222-4357) provides road maps, travel guides, emergency road services, travel services, and auto insurance.

CAR RENTALS

Economy cars are around €260 per week (€45-90 per day), though you may be able to find deals (without radio or A/C) as low as €150. By reserving in advance, non-residents of Italy are eligible for discounts of up to 60%. Insurance is required, augmenting the rates by as much as €55 a week. Paying by credit card may give you free insurance on rentals; check with your credit card company. All agencies require either a credit card or a cash deposit of at least €155, and most take only plastic. You must be 21 and have a valid driver's license, and preferably an **International Driver's Permit** (see above); the IDP is required for those who drive for more than one month.

You can make arrangements to pick up cars at Termini, the airports, or in the city offices. You may return your car at any rental location in Italy (with an additional charge of roughly €25 north of Rome and a monumental €155 or more to the south). Before making a reservation, ask your airline or travel agent about special deals. For car rental agencies in Rome, see the **Service Directory,** p. 338.

HITCHHIKING

Let's Go does not recommend getting around by thumb as a safe means of transportation, and none of the following is intended to imply otherwise. Never get in the back of a two-door car. Never let go of your bag, and don't put anything in the trunk. If you feel threatened, experienced hitchers recommend you insist on being let out immediately, regardless of where you are. If the driver refuses, many people act as though they're going to open the door or vomit on the upholstery.

BIKES AND MOPEDS

Rome's hilly cobblestone streets, dense traffic, and *pazzo* drivers make the city a challenge for bikes and mopeds. Bikes cost around €3 per hour or €8 per day, and motorini go for €40-50 per day, but the length of a "day" varies according to the shop's closing time. In summer, try the stands on V.d. Corso at P.d. San Lorenzo and V. di Pontifici. (Open daily 10am-7pm.) You need to be 16 years old to rent. Helmets are required by a strictly enforced law, and should be included with your rental. Prices do not include 20% sales tax. For those just interested in an afternoon on a bike, Enjoy Rome (p. 25) offers an informative, albeit harrowing tour of the city's best sights. For bike and moped rental agencies in the city, see the **Service Directory,** p. 338.

LET'S GET INFORMED

TOURIST OFFICES

Enjoy Rome, V. Marghera, 8a (☎06 445 18 43; www.enjoyrome.com). From the middle concourse of Termini (between the trains and the ticket booths), exit right, with the trains behind you. Cross V. Marsala. The office is 3 blocks down V. Marghera. Owners Fulvia and Pierluigi answer questions and offer indispensable tidbits about the city free of charge and in perfect English. Enjoy Rome arranges hotel accommodations (as well as short-term apartments), walking and bicycle tours (see p. 343), and bus service to Pompeii (see p. 292). Additionally, Enjoy Rome offers a full-service travel agency, booking transportation worldwide and lodgings throughout Italy. Open Apr.-Oct. M-F 8:30am-7pm, Sa 8:30am-2pm, Nov.-Mar. M-F 9:30am-6:30pm, Sa 9am-2pm.

PIT (Tourist Information Point) (☎06 489 063 00), at track #4 in Termini. Run by the city, this English-speaking office provides limited information on events, hotels, restaurants, and transportation, as well as countless brochures and a serviceable map of Rome with sights listed on the back. Open daily 8am-9pm. **PIT kiosks** offer the same services at various spots around Rome. Kiosks are located at **Castel Sant'Angelo** (P. Pia; ☎06 688 097 07), **Fori Imperiali** (V.d. Tempio della Pace; ☎06 699 243 07), **P.d. Spagna** (Largo Goldoni; ☎06 681 360 61), **P. Navona** (P. delle Cinque Lune; ☎06 688 092 40), **Trastevere** (P. Sonnino; ☎06 583 334 57), **San Giovanni** (P.S. Giovanni in Laterano; ☎06 772 035 35), **Santa Maria Maggiore** (V.d. Olmata; ☎06 478 802 94), **V.d. Corso** (V. Minghetti; ☎06 678 29 88), **V. Nazionale** (Palazzo delle Espozioni; ☎06 478 245 25), and **Termini** (P. del Cinquecento; ☎06 478 251 94). You can get the same info from the **Call Center Comune di Roma** (☎06 360 043 99), which operates daily 9am-7pm.

APT (Azienda di Promozione Turistica), V. Parigi, 5 (☎06 360 04 399). Similar to PIT. Walk from the station diagonally to the left across P. del Cinquecento (filled with buses) and go straight across P. della Repubblica. Turn right onto V. Parigi, which starts on the other side of the church, at the Grand Hotel. English spoken, but not very well. *Alberghi di Roma* lists all hotels and *pensioni* around Rome registered with the APT. Open daily 9am-7pm.

Centro Turistico Studentesco (CTS), V. Genova, 16 (☎06 462 04 31; general info ☎06 441 111; fax 06 467 92 07; www.cts.it). Open M-F 9:30am-1pm and 2:30-6:30pm. Branch offices: V.d. Ausoni, 5 (☎06 445 01 41); V. Appia Nuova, 434 (☎06 785 79 06); C. Vittorio Emanuele II, 297 (☎06 687 26 72); Terminal Ostiense (☎06 574 79 50); P. Irnerio 43 (☎06 662 85 97).

EMBASSIES AND CONSULATES

*For foreign consular services in Rome, check the **Service Directory** (p. 338). For Italian embassies abroad, see **Planning Your Trip** (p. 300).*

PRINT MEDIA

BROCHURES AND PAMPHLETS

The PIT offices and Enjoy Rome have free brochures and maps of downtown Rome. Enjoy Rome's booklet is packed with information geared toward the English-speaking budget traveler.

MAGAZINES

Roma C'è (€1.00) is the comprehensive, tried-and-true guide to everything from restaurants to church services to discos. It is written in easily decipherable Italian with a small English language section at the end. **Time Out: Rome** (€1.03), a flashy up-and-comer in the market of entertainment and culture mags, has plenty of useful information (entirely in Italian), including special info for women and gays. Both magazines are available on Thursdays. Also on Thursdays, **La Repubblica** publishes **Trovaroma** (€0.77), which lists events and recreational possibilities. **Wanted in Rome** (€0.75), which is published in English on a biweekly basis, offers an extensive listing of upcoming cultural events and classified ads that may prove quite useful for long stays in Rome.

LOCAL NEWSPAPERS

Be advised, the newspapers listed are in Italian. English speakers can still find London's *Evening Standard* and *The New York Times* sold at most *edicole*, albeit at exorbitant prices.

Il Manifesto, good for the latest info on mass culture, celebrity news (www.ilmanifesto.it).

Il Messaggero, one of Rome's most widely circulated newspapers; daily local, national and international news as well as sports, finance and culture (http://ilmessaggero.caltanet.it)

Il Sole 24 Ore, financial and local news in the past 24 hours. (www.ilsole24ore.com)

La Gazzetta dello Sport, the most comprehensive and up-to-date bulletin on sports, specializing in soccer, cycling and motorcar racing. Special section on U.S. sports. (www.gazzetta.it)

La Repubblica, daily national newspaper, with editions for most major Italian cities. Local, national and international news as well as sports, finance, and culture. (www.repubblica.it)

BROADCAST MEDIA

TELEVISION

Rai 1, Rai 2, and **Rai 3** are the three public television channels under the control of the Italian government. Each offers a somewhat interchangeable selection of soaps, educational programs, American sitcoms (dubbed in Italian), variety shows and news. The government also controls three privately owned commercial channels. The only independent and private TV channel, known as the "seventh channel" is **Teleroma 56.** Access to other stations, such as the BBC, often requires cable installation.

RADIO

FM RADIO	STATION	FORMAT
87.9	PUNX	Punk rock, alternative
89.7	Radio 1	Educational, news, geographic info
90.5	M20	Dance, trance, and house
91.7	Radio 2	Talk on politics, music, sports
92.7	TRS	Easy listening, love song requests
93.7	Radio 3	Music, art, and cinema
97.7	Città Futura	Latest international hits
99.3	GR Parlamento	Politics, news from the Senate
101.3	Centro Suono	Urban Contemporary
102.5	RTL	Rome's Top 40
103.3	Isoradio	News, traffic, music for the traveler

TIPPING AND BARGAINING

At many Italian restaurants, a service charge *(servizio)* or cover *(coperto)* is included in the bill. Tips are neither required nor expected, but it is polite to leave a little something (5-10%) in addition. Taxi drivers will expect about a 10% tip.

Bargaining is common in Italy, but use discretion. It is appropriate at outdoor markets, with street vendors, and over taxi fares calculated without a meter (always settle your price *before* taking the cab). Haggling over prices elsewhere is usually inappropriate. Hotel haggling is more successful in uncrowded, smaller *pensioni*. This book usually notes the hotels that are open to bargaining. Never offer what you aren't willing to pay as you're expected to buy once the merchant accepts your price.

LET'S KEEP IN TOUCH

BY TELEPHONE

CALLING ROME FROM ABROAD

Phone numbers in Rome are usually seven or eight digits, although the number of digits in the rest of Italy can range from five to eight. It is necessary to dial the city code (06) for all numbers, even if you are calling from within Rome. Calls to Italy must begin with your country's **international access code** (011 in the US), then Italy's country code (39), and the **city code** without the initial zero (06 becomes 6). **Toll-Free numbers** *(numero verde)* begin with 800 or 167.

CALLING ABROAD FROM ROME

PLACING INTERNATIONAL CALLS. To call home from Rome, dial:

1. The **international dialing prefix.** To dial out of out of Rome to **Australia,** dial 0011; **Canada** or the **US,** 011; the **Republic of Ireland, New Zealand,** or the **UK,** 00; **South Africa,** 09.
2. The **country code** of the country you want to call. To call **Italy,** dial 39; **Australia,** 61; **Canada** or the **US,** 1; the **Republic of Ireland,** 353; **New Zealand,** 64; **South Africa,** 27; the **UK,** 44.
3. The **city/area code.** *Let's Go* lists the city/area codes for cities and towns in Italy opposite the city or town name, next to a ☎. If the first digit is a zero (e.g., 020 for London), omit the zero when calling from abroad (e.g., dial 20 from Canada to reach Rome).
4. The **local number.**

Miraculously, rates have dropped lately for international calls from Italy. At their most expensive, rates to the US are €1.05 for the first minute and €0.80 for each additional minute. Rates are highest on weekdays from 8am to 8pm. Lowest rates are from 11pm to 8am, on holidays, and between 2:30pm on Saturday and 8am on Mondays.

The easiest way to call home is with a pay phone and pre-paid phone card (see **Pay Phones,** below), but a call of any length may require several cards. The English-speaking operator in Italy can put through **collect calls** (☎170), though it's cheaper to find a pay phone and deposit just enough money to be able to say "Call me" and give your number (though some pay phones can't receive calls, and there's no way to tell from just looking at the phone). Some companies have created callback phone services: you call a specified number, let it ring once, and hang up. The company's computer calls back and gives you a dial tone. You can then make as many calls as you want, at rates 20-60% lower than many phone cards. This option is most economical for loquacious travelers, as there may be a monthly minimum of US$10-25. For info, call **Telegroup** in the US (☎800 338 0225).

Depending on your calling plan, a **calling card** may be your best bet; your long distance provider has an international access number (billed as a toll-free or local call) you can dial from Italy to make collect or calling card calls: **AT&T** (☎800 172 444), **MCI** (☎800 905 825), **Sprint** (☎800 172 405), **Bell Canada Direct** (☎800 172 213), **British Telecom Direct** (☎800 172 440), **Telecom Éireann Ireland Direct** (☎800 172 0353), **Telstra Australia Direct** (☎800 172 610), **Telecom New Zealand** (☎800 172 641), and **Telkom South Africa** (☎800 172 294).

Italy is one hour ahead of **Greenwich Mean Time (GMT).** Daylight-saving time starts on the last Sunday in March, when clocks are moved ahead one hour. Clocks are put back an hour on the last Sunday in September.

4AM	7AM	NOON	1PM	8PM	10PM
Vancouver Seattle San Francisco Los Angeles	Toronto Ottawa New York Boston	London (GMT)	Italy Paris Munich Madrid	China Hong Kong Manila Singapore	Sydney Canberra Melbourne

PAY PHONES

Silver and red pay phones are all over the city, although ubiquitous cell phones *(telefonini)* are gradually driving them out. Some still take change, but it is far more convenient to use pre-paid phone cards *(schede telefoniche)*. They come in denominations of €2.50, €5.50, and €7.75, and are available at bars, *tabacchi*, and vending machines. As the most expensive of these cards will only pay for a 3min.

call to the US during peak hours, some *tabacchi* now carry cards in denominations up to €25.50. Once you have purchased the card, break off the perforated corner and insert it into the machine with the magnetic strip facing up. The amount left on the card will be displayed on the screen. Dial away. An initial €0.05 will be taken when your call goes through. It costs €0.10 to connect to mobile phones, which all have the area codes 335, 337, 338, 339, 347, 348, etc. A clicking noise warns you that you're about to run out of money; you can insert another card (or some coinage). Once you have hung up, wait around and savor *la dolce vita* until the phone spits your card back.

TELEFONINI

Because using your local cell service provider back home will most likely necessitate going into extreme debt, renting or buying a cell phone in Rome might be your best bet if you plan to stay for awhile. **Telecom Italia Mobile (TIM)** will allow you to buy a cell phone at one of their ubiquitous (read: there's one on every block) locations for about €50-100, including a €25 prepaid card (a small chip that fits into your phone). The card comes assigned with a number that will expire in 13 months if you do not recharge the card. Recharging the card with TIM is relatively simple: **Ricaricards** are available at tabacchi, at TIM stores, and other places that sell phones. Scratch away the silver and dial the toll free access number (☎4916) from any phone. Follow the prompts to enter your security code, and your phone will be automatically recharged. It is also possible to recharge via the internet at (www.tim.it) using a credit card, although instructions are in Italian only.

The advantage of an Italian cell phone is that **you will not pay a per minute charge for incoming calls.** However, keep in mind that calling to the US will cost you as much as US$0.90/min.. To keep an American number, call your service provider and ask if they have an agreement with TIM or another Italian mobile company (the most popular ones are Blu and Omnitel). You will need to purchase a world phone (approximately US$150-200), and rates will run up to US$0.70/min.

BY MAIL

Although the Italian postal system has drawn snickers from the rest of Western Europe, things are better, partly thanks to new EU standards. Airmail from Italy takes anywhere from one to three weeks to arrive in the US, while surface mail takes a month or longer. Letters and small parcels rarely get lost if they are *raccomandata* (registered), *espresso* (express), or *via aerea* (air mail). Stamps are available at face value in *tabacchi* (they're everywhere; look for the big, white T), but mail letters from a post office to be sure they are stamped correctly.

Rome's **main post office** is at P.S. Silvestro, 19, south of P.d. Spagna (take bus #61, 80, 160, or 850), but will be closed (with only partial access) for renovations during the coming year. While construction continues, visit the branches at P.d. Caprettari 69, V. Terme d. Diovleziano 30, or V. d. Scroffa 61/63 (open M-F 8:30am-6:30pm, Sa 8:30am-1pm), which offer full postal services.

RECEIVING MAIL IN ROME

Those sending you mail in Rome from North America should plan on it taking up to two weeks. Mail can usually be sent to your hotel, though you should let the proprietor know something is coming. The **American Express** office (see **Service Directory,** p. 339) will hold mail for up to 30 days for AmEx card members or travelers' check holders. Have the sender write "client mail" on the envelope, as well as your name, with surname capitalized and underlined. Letters addressed to the main downtown post office should be labeled **Fermo Posta** (held mail) and look like this: SMEDLEY,

the local story

La Economia Nera

Whether you're intrigued by overweight gladiators prowling the Colosseum or accosted by the countless street salesmen peddling "Prada" purses, you cannot avoid Italy's vast unofficial economy. Similarly, many of the desperate—and hopeful—who come to Italy in search of a better life are swept up by the economia nera. Lacking alternatives, many are compelled to take on dangerous and exploitative jobs. The following is an interview with Daniel, 27, who works at a Roman internet shop.

Q: When and why did you come to Italy?

A: Five months ago I came from Romania because life there is very hard. I studied psychology for 4 years at University, but did not have money to pay for all the exams. I worked as a teacher with little children, for €50 a month.

Q: And what do you do in Italy?

A: Here I work 16 hours a day, every day, in an internet shop, and get paid €300 a month. I don't have papers, so my boss has helped me by giving me a job. But, that is not real help. I live in the back of the shop, he took my passport, and I can't

(continued on next page)

Angela; *Fermo Posta;* Piazza San Silvestro, 19; 00187 Roma. You must claim your mail in person at the post office with your passport. The fee is €1.50 per piece.

SENDING MAIL FROM ROME

EXPRESS MAIL, OVERNIGHT MAIL, AND PARCELS

Priority mail through the Italian Postal Service is called *Posta Prioriaria.* It's faster and more reliable than regular mail. Packages of up to 2kg are accepted starting at €0.62. (Info ☎800 222 666.) *Posta Celere* guarantees 24hr. delivery to most locations within Italy for packages up to 30kg. Rates start at €6.20. (Info ☎800 009 966.) Parcels, and unsealed packages under 1kg (500g for Australia) may be mailed from the San Silvestro post office. Sealed packages of up to 20kg and 200cm total outside dimensions (length plus width and height) may be shipped, provided they are wrapped in brown paper, available at any *tabacchi.*

COURIERS

The quickest, most reliable service is available through private couriers. Service and rates are the same between companies. It costs €31.50 to send documents abroad (up to 500g) with guaranteed 48hr. delivery. Mailboxes, Etc. (see p. 31) will accept courier packages. See the **Service Directory** (p. 341) for a list of courier services available in Rome.

PAPAL MAIL

The Vatican administers its own postal service, which is faster and more reliable than Italy's yet costs the same. Visit the locations in P.S. Pietro: one on the left, near the tourist office and another on the right, near the center of the colonnade. There is a branch office on the 2nd floor of the Vatican Museum (open during museum hours, but with no *Fermo Posta*). Packages up to 2kg and 90 cubic cm are accepted. (☎06 698 834 06. Open M-F 8:30am-7pm, Sa 8:30am-6pm.)

BY EMAIL

Internet points, Internet cafes, and even Internet laundromats (p. 340), are breeding like rats. *Let's Go* lists a few with good rates or other attractions. Contact your Internet service provider for information before arriving in Rome.

To set up a new account, check the Yellow Pages under "Internet." Be sure to turn off your modem's "Detect Dial Tone" setting in order to be able to connect.

BY FAX

Most listed Internet cafes and photocopy shops provide fax services (see p. 340). Public fax service is available at the main post office in P.S. Silvestro (9am-6pm) at booths #73-76. (Faxes can be received 24hr. a day; they can only be picked up during business hours; see p. 29.)

GETTING MONEY FROM HOME

WIRING MONEY. It is possible to arrange a **bank money transfer,** which means asking a bank back home to wire money to a bank in Rome. This is the cheapest way to transfer cash, but it's also the slowest, usually taking several days or more. Note that some banks may only release your funds in local currency, potentially sticking you with a poor exchange rate; inquire about this in advance. Money transfer services like **Western Union** are faster and more convenient than bank transfers—but also much pricier. Western Union has many locations worldwide. To find one, visit www.westernunion.com, or call in the US ☎800-325-6000, in Canada ☎800-235-0000, in the UK ☎0800 83 38 33, in Australia ☎800 501 500, in New Zealand ☎800 27 0000, in South Africa ☎0860 100031 , or in Rome ☎800 220 055. Money transfer services are also available at **American Express** (☎06 67641) and **Thomas Cook** offices (☎482 80 82).

US STATE DEPARTMENT (US CITIZENS ONLY)

In dire emergencies only, the US State Department will forward money within hours to the nearest consular office, which will then disburse it according to instructions for a US$15 fee. Contact the Overseas Citizens Service division of the US State Department (☎202-647-5225; nights, Su, and holidays ☎202-647-4000).

LET'S SPEAK ITALIAN

VOWELS

There are seven vowel sounds in standard Italian. **A, I,** and **U** are always pronounced the same way; **E** and **O** have are either tense or lax, depending on where the vowel appears in

the local story

save any money. He gives me some money, but takes much more. And, I have no choice except to sleep in the street. If he hired someone legal, he would be paying more than €300 for the pension and health care. I can't have a pension, and I can't get sick.

Q: Do you know other people in your situation?

A: Many people have come to Italy recently and some have made good money. The minimum salary here is €700-800, and Italians earn ever more. You can work for €35 per day in construction, but there are few jobs. When you walk down V. Nazionale, you can see beautiful girls from Eastern Europe sleeping in the street–in the winter, they go to shelters where they can get clothes and food, but still you need money for everything. And, life is such that it goes and never comes back. All this time is wasted, sleeping in the street, or working for nothing.

Q: Do you have some goal in mind now, since you came to Italy in search of a better life?

A: In my country I had a car, and a job. I worked much more than I do here. But, I worked for myself. Here, I can do nothing but wait, and wait. Maybe something will come my way.

Vedran Lekic was a Researcher-Writer for Let's Go: Rome 2004.

the word, whether it's stressed or not, and regional accent. It's difficult for non-native speakers to predict the quality of vowels. We illustrate the *approximate* pronunciation of the vowels below; don't worry too much about **E** and **O.**

a	*a* as in f*a*ther *(casa)*	**o** (tense)	*o* as in b*o*ne *(sono)*
e (tense) **e** (lax)	*ay* as in b*ay* *(sete)* *eh* as in s*e*t *(bella)*	**o** (lax)	between *o* of bone and *au* of c*au*ght *(zona)*
i	*ee* as in ch*ee*se *(vino)*	**u**	*oo* as in dr*oo*p *(gusto)*

CONSONANTS

Consonants shouldn't be too bad, just remember **H** is always silent and **R** is trilled.

C and G: before **a, o,** or **u, c** and **g** are hard, as in *cat* and *goose* or as in the Italian word *colore* (*koh*-LOHR-eh), "color," or *gatto* (GAHT-toh), "cat." They soften into "ch" and "j" sounds, respectively, when followed by i or e, as in the English *cheese* and *jeep* or the Italian *ciao* (CHOW), "good-bye," and *gelato* (jeh-LAH-toh), "ice cream."

CH and GH: **h** returns **c** and **g** to their "hard" sounds in front of **i** or **e** (see above); making words like *chiave* (key-AH-vay), "keys," and *tartarughe* (tahr-tah-RU-geh), "tortoises."

GN and GLI: pronounce **gn** like the **ni** in *o***ni***on,* thus *bagno (*"bath") is "BAHN-yo." **Gli** is like the **lli** in *million*, so *sbagliato* ("wrong") is said "zbal-YAH-toh."

S and Z: An **s** between two vowels or followed by the letters **b, d, g, l, m, n r,** and **v** is pronounced as a **z;** thus *casa* ("house") sounds like "KAH-zah" and *smarrito* ("lost") like "zmahr-REE-toh." A double **s** or an **s** followed by any other letter has the same sound as English initial **s**, so *sacco* ("bag") is SAHK-koh. **Z** has a **ts** or **dz** sound; thus *stazione* ("station") is "staht-see-YOH-nay," while *zoo* ("zoo") is pronounced "dzoh" and *mezzo* ("half") is "MEH-dzoh."

SC and SCH: When followed by **a, o,** or **u, sc** is pronounced as **sk,** so *scusi* ("excuse me") yields "SKOO-zee." When followed by an **e** or **i,** the combination is pronounced "**sh**" as in *sciopero* (SHOH-pair-oh), "strike." **H** returns **c** to its hard sound **(sk)** in front of **i** or **e,** as in *pesche* (PEH-skeh), "peaches," not to be confused with *pesce* (PEH-sheh), "fish."

Double consonants: The difference between double and single consonants in Italian is likely to cause problems for English speakers. When you see double consonants, think about pronouncing it twice or holding it for a long time. English phrases like "bad dog" approximate the sound of double consonants. Failing to make the distinction can lead to confusion; for example, *pe***nn***e all'arrabbiata* is "short pasta in a spicy red sauce," whereas *pe***n***e all'arrabbiata* means "penis in a spicy red sauce." How long you hold the consonant is a matter of taste.

STRESS & PLURALITY

In many Italian words, stress falls on the next-to-last syllable. When stress falls on the last syllable, an accent indicates where stress should fall: *cit***tà** (cheet-TAH) or *per***ché** (pair-KAY). Stress can fall on the third-to-last syllable as well. It's not easy to predict stress, so you'll have to pick this up by listening to Italian speech.

Italian words form their plurals by changing the last vowel. Words that end in an **a** in the singular (usually feminine), end with an **e** in the plural; thus *mela* (MAY-lah), "apple," becomes *mele* (MAY-lay). Words that end with **o** or **e** in the singular take an **i** in the plural: *conto* (COHN-toh), "bill," is *conti* (COHN-tee) and *cane* (KAH-neh), "dog," becomes *cani* (KAH-nee). There are several exceptions to these rules; for example, *braccio* becomes *braccia* in the plural. Words with final accent, like *città* and *caffè*, and foreign words like *bar* and *sport* do not change in the plural.

PHRASEBOOK

DAYS OF THE WEEK

ENGLISH	ITALIAN	PRONUNCIATION
Monday	*lunedì*	loo-nay-DEE
Tuesday	*martedì*	mahr-tay-DEE
Wednesday	*mercoledì*	mair-coh-leh-DEE
Thursday	*giovedì*	joh-veh-DEE
Friday	*venerdì*	veh-nair-DEE
Saturday	*sabato*	SAH-bah-toh
Sunday	*domenica*	doh-MEH-nee-kah

MONTHS

ENGLISH	ITALIAN	PRONUNCIATION
January	gennaio	jehn-NAH-yoh
February	febbraio	Fehb-BRAH-yoh
March	marzo	MAHRT-soh
April	aprile	ah-PREE-lay
May	maggio	MAHJ-joh
June	giugno	JOON-yoh
July	luglio	LOOL-yoh
August	agosto	ah-GOH-stoh
September	settembre	seht-TEHM-bray
October	ottobre	oht-TOH-bray
November	novembre	noh-VEHM-bray
December	dicembre	dee-CHEM-bray

TIME

ENGLISH	ITALIAN	PRONUNCIATION
At what time...?	*A che ora...?*	ah kay OHR-ah
What time is it?	*Che ore sono?*	kay OHR-ay SOH-noh
It's 3:30.	*Sono le tre e mezzo.*	SOH-noh lay tray ay MEHD-zoh
It's noon.	*È mezzogiorno.*	eh MEHD-zoh-JOHR-noh
midnight	mezzanotte	MEHD-zah-NOT-eh
now	*adesso/ora*	ah-DEHS-so/OH-rah
tomorrow	*domani*	doh-MAH-nee
today	*oggi*	OHJ-jee
yesterday	*ieri*	YAIR-ee
right away	*subito*	SU-bee-toh
soon	*fra poco*	frah POH-koh
already	*già*	jah
after(wards)	*dopo*	DOH-poh
before	*prima*	PREE-mah
early/earlier	*presto/più presto*	PREHS-toh/pyoo PREHS-toh
late/later	*tardi/più tardi*	TAHR-dee/pyoo TAHRdee
early (before scheduled arrival time)	*in anticipo*	een ahn-TEE-chee-poh
late (after scheduled arrival time)	*in ritardo*	een ree-TAHR-doh
daily	*quotidiano*	kwoh-tee-dee-AH-no
weekly	*settimanale*	seht-tee-mah-NAH-leh
monthly	*mensile*	mehn-SEE-leh

TIME

ENGLISH	ITALIAN	PRONUNCIATION
vacation	*le ferie*	lay FEH-ree-eh
weekdays	*i giorni feriali*	ee JOHR-nee feh-ree-AH-lee
Sundays and holidays	*i giorni festivi*	ee JOHR-nee fehs-TEE-vee
day off (at store, restaurant, etc.)	*riposo*	ree-POH-zo
a strike	*uno sciopero*	SHOH-peh-roh
a protest	*una manifestazione*	mah-nee-fehs-taht-see-OH-neh

PHRASES

ENGLISH	ITALIAN	PRONUNCIATION
Hi!/So long! (informal)	*Ciao!*	chaow
Good day/Hello.	*Buongiorno.*	bwohn JOHR-noh
Good evening.	*Buona sera.*	BWOH-nah SEH-rah
My name is...	*Mi chiamo...*	mee Key-YAH-moh
What is your name...?	*Come ti chiami? (informal)/Come si chiama Lei? (formal)*	KOH-may tee key-YAH-mee/KOH-may see key-YAH-mah lay
I'm/We're from . . .	*Vengo/Veniamo dal/dalla. . .*	VAIN-goh/VAIN-ee-Am-oh doll
How are you?	*Come sta/state?*	KOH-may STAH/STAH-tay
Good night.	*Buona notte.*	BWOH-nah NOHT-tay
Goodbye.	*Arrivederci/ArrivederLa.*	ah-ree-veh-DAIR-chee/ ah-ree-veh-DAIR-lah
Please.	*per favore/per cortesia/ per piacere*	pair fah-VOH-ray/ pair kohr-teh-ZEE-ah/ pair pyah-CHEH-reh
Thank you.	*Grazie.*	GRAHT-see-yeh
You're welcome. May I help you? Go right ahead.	*Prego.*	PRAY-goh
Pardon me.	*Scusi.*	SKOO-zee
I'm sorry.	*Mi dispiace.*	mee dees-PYAH-cheh
Yes/No/Maybe.	*Sì/No/Forse.*	see/no/FOHR-say
I don't know.	*Non lo so.*	nohn loh soh
Let's Go! (our favorite)	*Andiamo*	ahnd-ee-AH-moh
Could you repeat that?	*Potrebbe ripetere?*	poh-TREHB-beh ree-PEH-teh-reh
What does this mean?	*Che vuol dire questo?*	kay vwohl DEE-reh KWEH-stoh
Okay/I understand.	*Ho capito.*	Oh kah-PEE-toh
I don't understand.	*Non capisco.*	nohn kah-PEES-koh
I don't speak Italian.	*Non parlo italiano.*	nohn PAR-loh ee-tahl-YAH-noh
I'm an artist	*Sono artista*	SOH-noh ahrt-EE-stah
Is there someone who speaks English?	*C'è qualcuno che parla inglese?*	cheh kwahl-KO-noh kay PAR-lah een-GLAY-zay
Could you help me?	*Potrebbe aiutarmi?*	poh-TREHB-beh ah-yoo-TAHR-mee
How do you say...?	*Come si dice...?*	KOH-may see DEE-chay
What do you call this in Italian?	*Come si chiama questo in italiano?*	KOH-may see key-YAH-mah KWEH-stoh een ee-tahl-YAH-no
Do you have...?	*hai/avete*	Ai/ ah-veh-teh
this/that	*questo/quello*	KWEH-sto/KWEHL-loh
who	*chi*	kee
where	*dove*	DOH-vay
which	*quale*	KWAH-lay
when	*quando*	KWAN-doh

PHRASES

ENGLISH	ITALIAN	PRONUNCIATION
what	*che/cosa/che cosa*	kay/KOH-za/kay KOH-za
why/because	*perchè*	pair-KEH
more/less	*più/meno*	pyoo/MEH-noh

DIRECTIONS AND TRANSPORTATION

ENGLISH	ITALIAN	PRONUNCIATION
Where is...?	*Dov'è...?*	doh-VEH
How do you get to...?	*Come si arriva a...*	KOH-meh see ahr-REE-vah
Do you stop at...?	*Ferma a...?*	FAIR-mah ah
the beach	*la spiaggia*	lah spee-AH-jah
the building	*il palazzo/l'edificio*	eel pah-LAHT-so/leh-dee-FEE-choh
the bus stop	*la fermata d'autobus*	lah fair-MAH-tah DAOW-toh-boos
the center of town	*il centro*	eel CHEN-troh
the church	*la chiesa*	lah kee-AY-zah
the consulate	*il consolato*	eel kohn-so-LAH-toh
the grocery store	*l'alimentari*	lah-lee-men-TAH-ree
the hospital	*l'ospedale*	los-peh-DAH-lay
the market	*il mercato*	eel mair-KAH-toh
the office	*l'ufficio*	loo-FEE-choh
the post office	*l'ufficio postale*	loo-FEE-choh poh-STAH-lay
the station	*la stazione*	lah staht-see-YOH-nay
near/far	*vicino/lontano*	vee-CHEE-noh/lohn-TAH-noh
Turn left/right	*Gira a sinistra/destra*	JEE-rah ah see-NEE-strah/DEH-strah
straight ahead	*sempre diritto*	SEHM-pray DREET-toh
north/south	*nord/sud*	NORd/ SOOd
east/west	*est/ovest*	EHst/OH-vehst
here	*qui/qua*	kwee/kwah
there	*lì/là*	lee/lah
the street address	*l'indirizzo*	leen-dee-REET-soh
the telephone	*il telefono*	eel teh-LAY-foh-noh
street	*strada, via, viale, vico, vicolo, corso*	STRAH-dah, VEE-ah, vee-AH-lay, VEE-koh, VEE-koh-loh, KOHR-soh
Take the bus from... to...	*Prenda l'autobus da... a...*	PREN-dah LAOW-toh-boos dah... ah...
What time does ... leave?	*A che ora parte...?*	ah kay OHR-ah PAHR-tay
the (city) bus	*l'autobus*	LAOW-toh-boos
the (intercity) bus	*il pullman*	eel POOL-mahn
the ferry	*il traghetto*	eel tra-GHEHT-toh
the plane	*l'aereo*	lah-EHR-reh-oh
the train	*il treno*	eel TRAY-no
the car	*la macchina*	lah MAHK-kee-nah
the bicycle	*la bicicletta*	lah bee-chee-CLEH-tah
I would like a ticket for...	*Vorrei un biglietto per...*	vohr-RAY oon beel-YET-toh pair
How much does it cost?	*Quanto costa?*	KWAN-toh CO-stah
How much does... cost?	*Quanto costa...?*	KWAN-toh CO-stah
I would like...	*Vorrei...*	voh-RAY

DIRECTIONS AND TRANSPORTATION

ENGLISH	ITALIAN	PRONUNCIATION
a ticket	*un biglietto*	oon beel-YEHT-toh
a pass (bus, etc.)	*una tessera*	OO-nah TEHS-seh-rah
one way	*solo andata*	SO-lo ahn-DAH-tah
round-trip	*andata e ritorno*	ahn-DAH-tah ey ree-TOHR-noh
reduced price	*ridotto*	ree-DOHT-toh
student discount	*sconto studentesco*	SKOHN-toh stoo-dehn-TEHS-koh
What time does the train for... leave?	*A che ora parte il treno per...?*	ah kay OH-rah PAHR-tay eel TRAY-noh pair
What platform for...?	*Che binario per...?*	kay bee-NAH-ree-oh pair
Where does the bus leave from...?	*Da dove parte l'autobus per...?*	dah DOH-vay PAHR-tay LAU-toh-boos pair
Is the train late?	*È in ritardo il treno?*	eh een ree-TAHR-doh eel TRAY-no
When will the strike be over?	*Quando finisce il sciopero?*	KWAN-doh fee-NEE-shay eel SHOH-peh-roh
the arrival	*l'arrivo*	la-REE-voh
the departure	*la partenza*	la par-TENT-sah
the track	*il binario*	eel bee-NAH-ree-oh
the terminus (of a bus)	*il capolinea*	eel kah-poh-LEE-neh-ah
the flight	*il volo*	eel VOH-loh
the reservation	*la prenotazione*	la pray-no-taht-see-YOH-neh
the itinerary	*l'itinerario*	
the entrance/the exit	*l'ingresso/l'uscita*	leen-GREH-so/loo-SHEE-tah

LANDMARKS

ENGLISH	ITALIAN	PRONUNCIATION
the nation/state	*la nazione/ lo stato*	lah nah-ZEEON-nay/ loh STA-toh
the city	*la città*	lah chee-TAH
the country/small town	*un paese*	oon Pie-eh-zay
the hill	*la collina/un colle*	lah coh-LEE-nah/ oon COH-lay
the mountain/chain of mountains	*la montagna/ una catena di montagne*	lah mon-TAHN-yah/ oona KA-TEH-nah dee mon-TAHN-eh
the volcano	*il vulcano*	eel vool-CAH-no
the sea	*il mare*	eel MAH-ray
the lake	*il lago*	eel LAH-goh
the river	*il fiume*	eel fee-OO-may
the bridge	*il ponte*	eel POHN-tay
the ruins	*le rovine*	leh ro-VEE-nay
the excavations	*gli scavi*	glee SKA-vee

HOTEL RESERVATIONS

ENGLISH	ITALIAN	PRONUNCIATION
Hello? (used when answering the phone)	*Pronto!*	PROHN-toh
Do you speak English?	*Parla inglese?*	PAHR-lah een-GLAY-zay
Could I reserve a single/double room for the second of August?	*Potrei prenotare una camera singola/doppia per il due agosto?*	POH-tray pray-noh-TAH-ray OO-nah CAH-meh-rah SEEN-goh-lah/DOH-pee-yah pair eel DOO-ay ah-GOH-stoh?
with bath/shower	*con bagno/doccia*	kohn BAHN-yo/DOH-cha

HOTEL RESERVATIONS

ENGLISH	ITALIAN	PRONUNCIATION
with bathroom	*con un gabinetto/un bagno/una toletta*	eel gah-bee-NEHT-toh/eel BAHN-yoh/ lah toh-LEHT-toh
open/closed	*aperto/chiuso*	ah-PAIR-toh/KYOO-zoh
a towel	*un asciugamano*	oon ah-shoo-gah-MAH-noh
sheets	*le lenzuola*	lay lehn-SUO-lah
a blanket	*una coperta*	OO-nah koh-PAIR-tah
heating	*il riscaldamento*	eel ree-skahl-dah-MEHN-toh
How much is the room?	*Quanto costa la camera?*	KWAHN-toh KOHS-ta lah KAM-eh-rah
I will arrive at 2:30pm.	*Arriverò alle quattordici e mezzo.*	ah-ree-vair-OH ah-lay kwah-TOHR-dee-chee eh MED-zoh
Certainly!	*Certo!*	CHAIR-toh
I'm sorry but...	*Mi dispiace, ma...*	mee dis-pee-YAH-chay, mah...
We're closed during August.	*Chiudiamo ad agosto.*	kyu-dee-AH-moh ahd ah-GOH-stoh
No, we're full.	*No, siamo al completo.*	no, see-YAH-moh ahl cohm-PLAY-toh
We don't take telephone reservations.	*Non si fanno le prenotazioni per telefono.*	nohn see FAHN-noh lay pray-noh-tat-see-YOH-nee pair tay-LAY-foh-noh
You'll have to send a deposit/ check.	*Bisogna mandare un acconto/un anticipo/un assegno.*	bee-ZOHN-yah mahn-DAH-reh oon ahk-KOHN-toh/oon ahn-TEE-chee-poh/oon ahs-SAY-nyoh
You must arrive before 2pm.	*Deve arrivare primo delle quattordici.*	DAY-vay ah-ree-VAH-ray PREE-moh day-lay kwah-TOHR-dee-chee
Okay, I'll take it.	*Va bene. La prendo.*	vah BEHN-eh. lah PREHN-doh

RESTAURANTS

ENGLISH	ITALIAN	PRONUNCIATION
the breakfast	*la (prima) colazione*	lah (PREE-mah) coh-laht-see-YO-nay
the lunch	*il pranzo*	eel PRAHND-zoh
the dinner	*la cena*	lah CHEH-nah
the appetizer	*l'antipasto*	lahn-tee-PAH-stoh
the first course	*il primo (piatto)*	eel PREE-moh pee-YAH-toh
the second course	*il secondo (piatto)*	eel seh-COHN-doh pee-YAH-toh
the side dish	*il contorno*	eel cohn-TOHR-noh
the dessert	*il dolce*	eel DOHL-chay
the fork	*la forchetta*	lah fohr-KEH-tah
the knife	*il coltello*	eel cohl-TEHL-loh
the spoon	*il cucchiaio*	eel koo-kee-EYE-yoh
the bottle	*la bottiglia*	lah boh-TEEL-yah
the glass	*il bicchiere*	eel bee-kee-YAIR-eh
the napkin	*il tovagliolo*	eel toh-vahl-YOH-loh
the plate	*il piatto*	eel pee-YAH-toh
the waiter/waitress	*il/la cameriere/a*	eel/lah kah-meh-ree-AIR-ray/rah
the bill	*il conto*	eel COHN-toh
the cover charge	*il coperto*	eel koh-PAIR-toh
the service charge/tip	*il servizio*	eel sair-VEET-see-oh
included	*compreso/a*	KOHM-pray-zoh/ah

MEDICAL

ENGLISH	ITALIAN	PRONUNCIATION
I have...	*Ho...*	OH
allergies	*delle allergie*	lay ahl-lair-JEE-eh
a blister	*una bolla*	lah BOH-lah
a cold	*un raffreddore*	oon rahf-freh-DOH-reh
a cough	*una tosse*	OO-nah TOHS-seh
the flu	*l'influenza*	lenn-floo-ENT-sah
a fever	*una febbre*	OO-nah FEHB-breh
a headache	*un mal di testa*	oon mahl dee TEHS-tah
a lump (on the head)	*un bernoccolo*	eel bear-NOH-koh-loh
a rash	*un'esantema /un sfogo/ un'eruzi-one*	leh-zahn-TAY-mah/ eel SFOH-goh/ leh-root-see-OHN-eh
a stomach ache	*un mal di stomaco*	oon mahl dee STOH-mah-koh
a swelling/growth	*un gonfiore*	eel gohn-fee-OR-ay
a venereal disease	*una malattia venerea*	lah mah-lah-TEE-ah veh-NAIR -ee-ah
a vaginal infection	*un'infezione vaginale*	leen-feht-see-OH-nay vah-jee-NAH-lay
My foot hurts.	*Mi fa male il piede.*	mee fah MAH-le eel PYEHD-deh
I'm on the pill.	*Prendo la pillola.*	PREHN-doh lah PEE-loh-lah
I haven't had my period for (2) months.	*Non ho le mestruazioni da (due) mesi.*	nohn oh lay meh-stroo-aht-see-OH-nee dah (DOO-ay) may-zee
I'm (3 months) pregnant.	*Sono incinta (da tre mesi).*	SOH-noh een-CHEEN-tah (dah tray MAY-zee)
blood	*il sangue*	eel SAHN-gweh
the skin	*la pelle*	lah PEHL-lay
a doctor	*il medico*	eel MEH-dee-coh
a nurse	*l'infrmiere/a*	LEEN-fair-mee-air-eh/ah
a gynecologist	*un ginecologo*	jee-neh-KOH-loh-goh

EMERGENCIES

ENGLISH	ITALIAN	PRONUNCIATION
I lost my passport.	*Ho perso il passaporto.*	oh PAIR-soh eel pahs-sah-POHR-toh
I've been robbed.	*Sono stato derubato.*	SOH-noh STAH-toh deh-roo-BAH-toh
The ATM has eaten my credit card.	*Il Bancomat ha trattenuto la mia carta.*	eel BAHN-koh-maht ah trah-tehn-OO-toh lah MEE-ah CAHR-tah
Wait!	*Aspetta!*	ahs-PEHT-tah
Stop!	*Ferma!*	FAIR-mah
Help!	*Aiuto!*	ah-YOO-toh
Leave me alone!	*Lasciami in pace!*	LAH-shah-mee een PAH-cheh
Don't touch me!	*Non mi toccare!*	NOHN mee tohk-KAH-reh
I'm calling the police!	*Telefono alla polizia!*	tehl-LAY-foh-noh ah-lah poh-leet-SEE-ah
Go away!	Vai via!	VY VEE-ah
Go away, cretin!	*Vattene, cretino!*	VAH-teh-neh creh-TEE-noh

LOVE

ENGLISH	ITALIAN	PRONUNCIATION
May I buy you a drink?	*Posso offrirle qualcosa da bere?*	POHS-soh ohf-FREER-lay kwahl-COH-zah dah BAY-ray
I'm drunk.	*Sono ubriaco.*	SOH-noh oo-BRYAH-coh
Are you drunk?	*È lei ubriaco?*	ay LAY-ee oo-BRYAH-coh
I only have safe sex.	Pratico solo sesso sicuro.	PRAH-tee-coh sohl-oh SEHS-so see-COO-roh
You're cute.	*Lei è bello.*	LAY-ee ay BEHL-loh
I'm an anarchist.	*Sono un'anarchica.*	Soh-noh uhn ann-AHR-key-cuh
I am the Pope.	*Sono il Papa*	Soh-noh ell Pah-pah
Your friend is cute.	*Il suo amico è bello.*	eel SOO-oh ah-MEE-cah ay BEHL-loh
I have a boyfriend/ girlfriend.	*Ho un ragazzo/una ragazza*	oh oon rah-GAHT-soh/ oo-nah rah-GAHT-sah
Are you single?	*Sei celibe?*	SEY CEH-lee-beh
I'm married.	*Sono sposato/a*	soh-noh spo-ZA-to/ta
I love you, I swear.	*Ti amo, te lo giuro.*	tee AH-moh, tee loh JOO-roh
I'll never forget you.	*Non ti dimenticherò mai.*	nohn tee dee-men-tee-ker-OH mahy
heterosexual/straight	*etero/sessuale*	EH-teh-roh (ses-SOOAH-leh)
bisexual	*bisessuale*	bee-sehs-SOOAH-leh
gay	*gay*	GAH-ee
lesbian	*lesbica*	LEH-sbee-cah
single	*celibe*	CHEH-lee-beh
transvestite	*travestito/a*	trah-veh-STEE-toh/tah

history **41**

the republic **42** roman empire **44**

rise of christianity **45** middle ages **45**

renaissance & baroque **47** 19th century **48**

20th century **49** today **51**

religion **52**

roman gods **52** mithraism **53** catholicism **53**

art and architecture **55**

classical **55** byzantine **56**

romanesque **57** renaissance **57** baroque **58**

neoclassical **59** fascist **59** post-fascist **60**

music **60**

opera **60** instrumental **61** 20th century **61** pop, rock & rap **61**

Life & Times

HISTORY

VARIOUS BEGINNINGS

Once upon a pagan time, **Aeneas** (a fine fellow remembered as either the progeny of the goddess of love or a distant relative of that famous boatbuilder, Noah), perturbed by the recent wave of certain undesirable elements (i.e. Greeks) into his native Troy, grabbed his aging father, hopped in the Volvo, and commuted to the sunny suburbs of the land of the Latins. Pleased with the climate, friendly peoples, and generous income tax policies, he stuck around and married their princess, Lavinia. He then crowned himself king, and creatively christened the kingdom Lavinium. At this point, Virgil's *Aeneid* leaves off, but that's scarcely all there is to say on the matter.

Shortly after all this happened, according to the ancient Roman historian Livy, a Vestal "Virgin" named Rhea Silvia went bad and gave birth to a bouncing pair of baby boys fathered by Mars, the god of war. Well, as the title implies, this lifestyle choice wasn't really an option for someone in her profession, and her twins were set adrift in the Tiber. Luckily, the boys were found by a motherly she-wolf who had just lost her cubs, and thought the tiny refugees a suitable substitute, until a shepherd came along and "rescued" the twins, who were called **Romulus** and **Remus.** Despite a somewhat troubled childhood, the twins managed to found a city on the Palatine Hill, which they called **Rome,** on April

21, 753 BC, after much debate. Remus's brief insistence on naming the new town after himself ended in the metropolis's first murder. We won't give away which twin won the day, but we'll give you a hint—you're not currently enjoying the witty, irreverent prose of *Let's Go: Reme...*

Pretty as this tale of gods and wolf-boys is, its veracity is somewhat suspect. Pottery dating from as far back as 1200 BC has been found, suggesting older origins. Remains of villages in the area date from about 800 BC; the people who first ruled Rome were the **Sabines.** Three Sabine kings ruled Rome: Numa Pompilius, who took charge in 715 BC, Tullus Hostilius, and Ancus Martius.

The Sabines were soon supplanted by the **Etruscans,** a tribe from the North. (See **Cerveteri,** p. 277, and **Tarquinia,** p. 278, for more information on Etruscan villages.) Responsible for the adaptation of the Latin language and the Latinization of the Greek gods, Etruscan kings inaugurated their control of Rome in 616 BC. Some remains of their civilization can still be seen: notably, the Etruscans built the Cloaca Maxima, the pride and joy of the Roman sewer system. Their rule came to an end in 509 BC when the son of **Tarquinius Superbus** raped the chaste Roman matron **Lucretia.** She committed suicide, and her outraged family led the Roman populace to overthrow the Tarquin dynasty. The next day, the first Roman republic was founded.

Free from Etruscan rule, the Romans turned to affairs of state. Originally, the government was an oligarchy in which land-owning patricians (and after 450 BC, wealthy plebeians) gathered in the Senate to make laws, hear trials, and declare war. A complex bureaucracy made up of *praetores* (judicial officers), *quaestores* (tax collectors), *aediles* (magistrates), and *tribunes* oversaw the city's burgeoning infrastructure. Rome's reach soon extended beyond the Tiber valley as the city conquered neighbors with astounding efficiency. In 395 BC, the Etruscans were put down for good when the Romans captured Veia, their capital. Southern Italy was made safe for Romans in 275 BC, when **Pyrrhus,** the Greek ruler of Tarentum, was defeated at the Battle of Beneventum.

THE REPUBLIC GROWS...

After the conquest of Italy, the republic waged a series of **Punic Wars** (264-146 BC) against Carthage (modern-day Tunisia) for control of key Mediterranean trade routes and territory in Spain and Sicily. During the second of these wars, the Carthaginian **Hannibal** famously marched his army—elephants and all—up through Spain and across the Alps. He swooped down the peninsula, surprising a series of Roman generals, and made it all the way to the walls of Rome, but failed to breach them. His campaign devolved into a cat-and-mouse game with **Fabius Maximus,** who eluded the overeager Hannibal for several years until the starving Carthaginians refused to play anymore and took their tired elephants home. Carthage was decisively defeated at Zama, in Africa, in 202 BC by another great Roman general, **Scipio Africanus.** Pressing the advantage, **Cato the Censor** encouraged Romans to raze the powerless Carthage in the Third Punic War of 146 BC. Rumor has it that Roman soldiers sowed Carthaginian fields with salt to keep the city from causing trouble again.

Traditionally, Roman society was austere and pious, but drunk with a mix of bloodlust and riches, it became a veritable swamp of greed and corruption. Yeoman farmers were pushed off their land by avaricious landowners and driven into slavery or starvation. Less than grateful, the yeomen protested; by 131 BC, popular demands for land redistribution led to riots against the corrupt patricians, culminating in the **Social War** (91-87 BC). Tribes throughout the peninsula fought successfully for the extension of Roman citizenship.

Fed up, **Sulla,** the general who led Roman troops during the conflict, marched on Rome (traditionally a demilitarized zone), seizing control of the city in a military coup. Over 1600 nobles and senators were executed without trial. Sulla's strong-arm tactics set a dangerous precedent for the Republic as generals began to amass private armies funded by huge personal fortunes. In 73 BC, **Spartacus,** rebellious gladia-

An insider's guide to traditional cuisine

The poet Juvenal once said disparagingly of the Roman populace that all it needed was *panem et circenses* (bread and circuses) to remain free of rebellious thought. Luckily for even a temporary resident of the Eternal City oday, Romans no longer live by bread (or ciruses) alone, and Roman bread, in fact, is generlly nowhere near as praise-worthy as its Gallic ounterpart to the north. The two notable excepions to this are *pizza bianca* and *pizza rossa*, oth light, crispy, olive-oil-drizzled flat breads, he latter of which is slathered with a mouth-tanalizing tomato-herb mixture.

Roman cuisine has not yet enjoyed the same ort of notoriety that surrounds that of Tuscany, vith its game dishes, wonderful *pecorino di ienza*, and hearty soups. The invention of pizza tself is a Neapolitan, not Roman, accomplishnent. But Roman cuisine remains a distinct (if enerally underappreciated) entity, with a hisory of its own. Traditionally, much of Roman uisine was based on the *quinto quarto*, the fifth fourth"— that is to say, what was left of a ow, sheep or pig after it was butchered: the nnards and organ meats. Happily, although you an still find dishes based on these in some Roman restaurants, such as *coda alla vaccinara* oxtail stew) and *rigatoni con pajata* (pasta vith the intestines of a milk-fed calf), Roman cuiine today is predominantly created out of the reshest ingredients of the markets in the city, nd enjoying it does not necessitate familiarity vith a butcher's anatomical chart.

At the open markets, be prepared to find a colrful abundance of fresh produce, including reens the likes of which you've never seen efore. Romans love cooked, wilted greens such s *spinaci* and *broccoletti* (spinach and broccoli abe) dressed in garlic and olive oil and spritzed vith a douse of lemon juice, but one of the more nusual is *agretti*, which looks like grass, and vhen boiled for five minutes takes on the consisency of green spaghetti. Another, which, like *gretti*, is in season in winter, is *puntarelle*, stiff reen shoots which are cut and then plunged into old water, causing them to curl up in a spiral hape. Served cold with an anchovy and oil dressing the dish makes a wonderful companion to grilled fish. *Rughetta* is a wild version of *rucola* (arugula) which is grown only around Rome. It is a small, pleasantly bitter-tasting treat as a base for the sweetest tomatoes you'll ever taste (*pomodorini*) and a hunk of *mozzarella di bufala* (buffalo-milk mozzarella). *Fiori di zucca*, zucchini flowers which have been stuffed with mozzarella and perhaps an anchovy, and *carciofi alla giudea* are both deep-fried Roman delicacies; the latter is a whole artichoke plunged in oil, providing crispy, chip-like leaves as an antipasto. *Carciofi alla romana* are equally delectable artichokes, braised with garlic and *mentuccia* (Roman mint). If you're in the mood for a walk through Rome's largest park, the Villa Doria-Pamphilj, you can still find Roman matrons gathering *mentuccia* and pine nuts from the park's plentiful pine trees.

Each region in Italy has its preferred pastas, but in Rome the main idea is to keep things simple. *Spaghetti all'amatriciana* and *alla carbonara* are both flavored with *guanciale* (pork jowl); the former has tomatoes and a dash of *peperoncini* (chili pepper), the latter beaten egg and cheese. But the most simple Roman pasta is *cacio e pepe*, in which the spaghetti is mixed with ground black pepper and grated *pecorino romano* cheese; purists add no oil whatsoever, using just a bit of the pasta's cooking liquid for moisture. Another excellent way to start off a meal is *pasta e ceci*, a thick soup made of pasta and chick-peas, a Roman staple. Other simple pasta dishes include those with sauces of *porcini* mushrooms over *pappardelle*, a wide pasta, or fresh pasta in a *tartufo* (truffle) sauce, whose smoky, earthy flavor will leave you wanting more. For a tasty delicacy, try spaghetti topped with grated *bottarga*, an orange-hued fish roe that comes in solid form and lends a salty fish taste to a simple pasta dish. *Gnocchi*, small potato dumplings which originated in the south of Italy, are traditionally served in Rome on Thursday; for a new twist, however, you might want to try Rome's own version, *gnocchi alla romana*, which aren't made with potato at all, but with semolina, and are flat and circular.

Andria Derstine was a Researcher-Writer for Let's Go: Italy 1990 *and* 1992 *and* Let's Go: Greece 1991. *After living in Rome for three years, she recently returned to the U.S. to complete her Ph.D. at the Institute of Fine Arts at New York University.*

torial slave, led a 70,000-man army of slaves and farmers in a two-year rampage down the peninsula. When the dust cleared, 6000 slaves had been crucified, and **Pompey the Great,** an associate of Sulla, took de facto control of Rome.

Disallowed by the Senate from ruling alone, Pompey ran the city with **Julius Caesar** and **Crassus,** forming the **First Triumvirate.** The threesome went sour, and Caesar, the charismatic conqueror of the Gauls, emerged victorious, having Pompey assassinated in 48 BC. Caesar's reign was brief but memorable: a small senatorial faction, fearful of his power, assassinated him on the Ides of March in 44 BC. In the ensuing power vacuum, a **Second Triumvirate** was formed. This time the ruling all-stars were made up of Caesar's grand-nephew and adopted son, Octavian and Marc Antony (soon to be tangled up with that royal hussy Cleopatra and sent off to Africa) respectively, and Lepidus, a no-account rascal. Octavian soon declared war on Marc Antony and Cleopatra, and spanked them soundly—so soundly, in fact, that they killed themselves in 30 BC.

...AND BECOMES AN EMPIRE

Under his new name **Augustus,** Octavian consolidated power and began assembling an imperial government in 27 BC. His reign (27 BC-AD 14) is considered the golden age of Rome, a flourishing of culture that ushered in the 200 years of the **Pax Romana.** Augustus's power was not only political: he declared himself a god, paving the way for all sorts of mischief among future emperors. Nonetheless, Rome benefited from a huge building boom including a new forum and the first Pantheon. However, the peace was not extended to those who wouldn't sensibly shut up and consent to be ruled. As a result, the emperor's generals busied themselves hacking up Germans.

SONS & LOVERS: JULIO-CLAUDIANS

The descendants of Augustus proved unequal to the task of world government. Drunk with megalomania, they slipped into fevers of debauchery and insanity. **Tiberius** (AD 14-37), who allegedly conducted sexual experiments on goldfish, ushered in an era of decadence. Deranged **Caligula** (who once made his horse *consul*), drooling **Claudius** (AD 41-54), and sadistically wacky **Nero** drained the treasury to support their lifestyles. Much of Rome was burned in the great fire of 64. Nero may or may not have been responsible for the blaze, but took advantage of the situation, building himself a new house, the **Domus Aurea** (p. 81). Nero found a fine set of scapegoats for the fire in the early Christians. Common Romans were entertained and appeased watching Christians dressed in the hides of animals torn to shreds by savage beasts. The Christians who died came to be known as "martyrs," from the Greek "witnesses."

FLAVIANS & ANTONINES

Tired of his quirks, the Senate "persuaded" Nero to commit suicide in AD 68. **Vespatian** (69-79) cleaned up Nero's mess, tearing down the Domus Aurea and erecting the Colosseum. His sons **Titus** (79-81) and **Domitian** (81-96) continued in Vespatian's footsteps. The **Antonine** emperors, starting with **Nerva** (96-98), marked the apex of the Empire. Spanish emperor **Trajan** (98-117) expanded the Empire to its greatest size, conquering Dacia (modern Romania) and the Danube region with feats of engineering and tactical brilliance. Trajan died while conquering Persia, and the general **Hadrian** (118-138) managed to *carpe diem* his way right into the throne. Hadrian preferred philosophy to war and decided to focus his energies on redecorating Rome with his own architectural designs, including another **Pantheon** (p. 93) and his colossal mausoleum, now **Castel Sant'Angelo** (p. 120).

Unfortunately, it was all downhill after Hadrian. The city clung to its status as *Caput Mundi* (head of the world) until the death of the philosopher-emperor **Marcus Aurelius** in 180, but by then, the Empire had grown too large to defend. Emperors, forced to relegate power and money to generals in the field, lay vulnerable to military coups. The tumultuous 3rd century saw no fewer than 30 emperors—only one of them lucky enough to die of natural causes. Despite some enlightened administrations, the brutality and depravity of despots like the unfortunately named **Commodus, Caracalla** (see **Baths of Caracalla,** p. 85), and the confused Elagabalus (who believed he was the sun), did much to undermine the stability of the Empire. **Aurelian** (270-275), who thought that the surest way to solve the city's military and economic crises was to build a wall around it, didn't help the situation much either.

RISE OF CHRISTIANITY & FALL OF ROME

Diocletian (284-305) secured control of the fragmented Empire in 284, established order, and subdivided the Empire into four spiffy and manageable parts. He also intensified the persecution of Christians. Nonetheless, by the end of Diocletian's reign, approximately 30,000 Christians lived in Rome.

After Diocletian, the fortunes of Christianity took a turn for the better. Gallerius, ruling the western part of the Empire, granted freedom of worship to Christians in 311. In 312, while battling it out with Maxentius for the imperial throne, **Constantine** (312-337) saw a huge cross in the sky along with the phrase, *In hoc signo vinces* (By this sign you shall conquer). Sure enough, victory followed, and the next year Constantine's **Edict of Milan** made Christianity the official religion of the Empire. Despite the attempts of **Julian the Apostate** (361-363) to revive old Roman rituals, Christianity became the dominant religion. In 391, **Theodosius** (379-395) issued an edict against paganism.

Constantine hastened the end of Rome's supremacy by moving the capital east to Byzantium (which he humbly renamed **Constantinople**) in 330. Right on cue, armies of northern barbarians knocked politely on Rome's crumbling fortifications, asking if they could please be let in to steal anything not nailed down. First came the **Huns,** who showed up in 375. In 410, **Alaric,** king of the Visigoths, sacked the city. Another sacker-extraordinaire, **Attila the Hun,** arrived on tour in 452, but fast-talking Pope Leo I convinced him to pillage elsewhere. Unfortunately, three years later, Genseric the Vandal wasn't so easily dissuaded. In 476, the Western Roman Empire was finally done in when **Odoacer the Goth** ousted Romulus Augustulus. The Roman Empire was through. Gothic rule wasn't such a bad thing: under Odoacer and his son Theodoric, Roman life proceeded peacefully, perhaps due to the novelty of outside rule.

MIDDLE AGES

The Byzantine emperor **Justinian** brutally conquered much of the western division between 535 and 554, and imposed the *corpus juris,* or codified law of the Empire, which served as Europe's legal model for 500 years. By the 6th century, the Eternal City, once home to nearly a million people, supported only several thousand. When King Totila of the Goths pillaged the aqueducts in 546, the city's fate was sealed. The hills of Rome, once *the* place for Roman domiciles, gave way to the suddenly more appealing neighborhoods on the Tiber. In these days some of the most famous neighborhoods of Rome—Trastevere, Campo dei Fiori, and the area around Piazza Navona—were settled. Starvation and plague ran rampant in ramshackle alleyways near the river, while periodic invasions by barbarians lowered property values.

Rome owed its salvation from the turbulence of the Dark Ages in large part to wealthy popes who attracted cash-laden pilgrims and invoked the wrath of God to intimidate would-be invaders. Pope **Gregory the Great** (590-604) devised efficient strategies for distributing food and spreading the word of God across Europe. His actions laid the framework for the secular power subsequent popes would wield.

MEDIEVAL CHAOS, PART I

Faced again with the threat of invasion from the German Lombards in 752, Pope Stephen II was forced to ask for help from the Frankish warlord Pepin the Short. Pepin's forces prevailed and he gave the city to the "Republic of the Holy Church

Pope Joan

Canonical history holds that Nicholas Breakspear, Pope Adrian IV, was the only English Pope. Popular tradition, however, has it that John VIII (853-855), elected for his saintliness and Greek learning, was not only of English descent but also, to add insult to injury, was a woman. "Joan" was found out when she gave birth during a procession; the enraged citizens of Rome promptly stoned her and the baby to death. The truth of the story of Pope Joan is unclear: historical records are hazy, and the tale has been used polemically to support anti-Catholic, feminist, anti-feminist, and Catholic-reformist agendas. Joan's story gave birth to a tradition in which the elected heir of St. Peter's apostolic seat was required to sit in a special chair with a carved slot for the purpose of having his testicles touched by a young cardinal to verify his gender. In popular culture, Pope Joan inspired the Popess card in the Tarot deck. Bernini may have memorialized her end in some half-hidden sculpting on the famous *baldacchino* in St. Peter's cathedral (see p. 115).

of God" instead of the Byzantine emperor. Pepin's **Gift of Quiersy-Sur-Oise** effectively set up the papal states. Pepin pushed the fledgling republic along for a bit until God took over. **Pope Leo III** slipped a crown on the head of Pepin's son **Charlemagne** on Christmas Day, 800, declaring him "Emperor of the Romans." The relationship between the popes and the Holy Roman Emperors was difficult to maintain. Charlemagne's death in 814 set off another 200 years of anarchy as his descendants killed each other for the dubious privilege of ruling Europe.

In 846, Muslim **Saracens** rowed up the Tiber and plundered several basilicas. Many felt this was God's retribution for clerical misbehavior; indeed, all manner of licentiousness was going on. The most bizarre tale from these years is the posthumous trial of **Pope Formosus.** Formosus's successor **Pope Stephen VI** dug up Formosus and dressed him in ecclesiastical robes to attend a "cadaver synod." After a poor defense, the corpse was convicted on all counts, including coveting the papacy, and, confusingly, perjury. Its three blessing fingers were severed (one can never be too careful), and the corpse formerly known as Formosus was chucked into the Tiber. Pope Stephen himself was later murdered, the next pope was overthrown, and the pope after that was murdered as well.

With the papacy in arrears, power was seized in 880 by a woman named **Theodora,** who set up a secular dominion over Rome. Starting with Anastasius III in 911, the family managed to choose eleven popes, many of them lovers and children of Theodora's daughter. Unfortunately, they never lasted very long. A slightly better fate awaited Marozia's son **Alberic the Younger,** who came to power in 932. Alberic attempted to wrest control of Rome away from the Church, but had no idea how mammoth this task was; the Vatican wouldn't officially excise itself from Roman politics for nearly a millennium.

In 954, Alberic appointed his degenerate teenage son **John XII** as pope. Getting his priorities straight, John installed a harem at the Vatican shortly after his father's death. Before he suffered a stroke while in bed with a married woman in 964, John crowned German monarch **Otto I** Holy Roman Emperor for protection against the Northern Italian **Berengar.** Otto returned the favor by conquering Rome. For the next century, the Emperor picked the pope.

In 1075, Pope **Hildebrand** demanded an end to the Holy Roman Emperor's interference with the Church, forcing Emperor Henry VI, whom he had excommunicated, to beg in the snow for forgiveness. It turned out to be a trick; the next time the emperor was excommunicated he laid siege to Rome, and Hildebrand's followers jumped ship. In 1084, Norman conqueror **Robert Guiscard** remembered—ahead of schedule—that Rome was due for its tercentennial sacking and made convincing work of it.

MEDIEVAL CHAOS, PART II

Romans received a measure of self-rule in the 1122 **Concordat of Worms,** which transferred the balance of power from the Emperor to the Church. Tipsy on its gains, the Church soon predictably arrived in an advanced state of corruption. A secular senate was formed in 1143, but a few hangings later, in 1155, power over the city returned to the pope, Adrian IV, the only English pope.

Unhappy with the popes, Romans kicked them out of the city in 1181. In 1188, during the papacy of **Clement III** (a Roman by birth), the rebels and the Church struck a bargain. The papacy's (super) powers were accepted, and members of the senate swore their loyalty to the pope. In exchange, the Church agreed to recognize the city of Rome as a *comune*, with the power to declare war or peace. This agreement paved the way for the unprecedented power of **Pope Innocent III.** Innocent excommunicated England's King John, declared the Magna Carta (which transferred more power to Europe's aristocracy) null and void, and fought heresy with a vengeance. Innocent declared the Pope to be Vicar of Christ on Earth, "set midway between God and Man," in charge of "the whole world." Innocent's power over the city itself, however, was weak: the citizens maintained earlier reforms, leading to a period of widespread prosperity, if not peace.

Boniface VIII, elected in 1294, antagonized nearly every ruler in Europe with a string of excommunications and the papal edict **Unam Sanctam,** which decreed that it was necessary for salvation that every living thing be subject to the Pope. Fed up, the French assaulted Boniface in his home and accused him of such crimes as sodomy and keeping a pet demon. Poor Boniface died of shock. His successor, the Frenchman Clement V, moved the papacy to Avignon, France, beginning the **Babylonian Captivity** in 1309. For most of the 14th century, popes would conduct their business from Avignon under the watchful eyes of the French kings. Freed from the Church, the city struggled to find peace, but feuding between the Orsini and Colonna families and the outbreak of the **Black Death** in 1348 kept Rome exciting.

At the behest of St. Catherine of Siena, **Pope Gregory XI** agreed to return the papacy to Rome in 1377, restoring the city's greatest source of income. The **Great Western Schism** (1378-1417), the period during which there were two (and occasionally three) popes, however, jeopardized the power of the papacy, and war was widespread. The **Council of Pisa** (1409-1417) resolved the situation to Rome's satisfaction.

RENAISSANCE AND BAROQUE

UP COME THE PROTESTANTS

Taking charge in 1417, **Pope Martin V** initiated a period of Renaissance urbanity and absolute rule in Rome that lasted until 1870. No-nonsense Martin widened and paved roads, and buildings in new Renaissance styles went up. **Julius II** (1503-13) began an ambitious building program, setting out plans for Rome in general and for St. Peter's dome in particular (p. 93). He hired Bramante, who demolished medieval Rome with such enthusiasm and intent that Raphael nicknamed him *il Ruinante*.

When Protestant upstart **Martin Luther** returned to Rome in 1510, he was sorely disappointed by the city's aesthetic indulgence and spiritual dissolution. He was revolted by the sight of Raphael's ornate *Stanze* in the Vatican, in which Christian and pagan symbols mingled—in the buff, no less. While the pope went "triumphing about with fair-decked stallions, the priests gabbled Mass," Luther went about writing the *95 Theses* that kicked off the **Protestant Reformation.**

A Field Guide to Heresy

In the early days of Christianity, there were plenty of heretics. A brief guide to major credences:

Arianism: Following Arius (250-336), they argued that Christ was not eternal, having been created by God the Father. While Arianism was supported by Emperors Constantius II and Valens, the First Council of Nicaea in 325 denounced it.

Docetism: The Docetists (2nd century) argued that Christ's divine nature was incompatible with human suffering and that Christ was not human.

Donatism: The Donatists, a North African sect, split from the church in 312 and survived until the 7th century, when Islam arrived. They believed that the Church should not be tainted with politics and valued personal holiness.

Eunomianism: The Eunomians believed that the only proper name for God the Father, an incomprehensible concept, was "Ungenerated;" everything else, including Christ, had been generated.

Gnosticism: Gnosticism denotes a wide variety of beliefs. In most Gnostic cosmogonies, a creator god was the supreme being; from the creator came a demiurge, a flawed figure who created a flawed world.

(continued on next page)

After excommunicating Luther, **Pope Leo X** (1513-1521) asserted his interest in the humanities, drawing up plans for a new St. Peter's dome and commissioning artists Michelangelo and Raphael. To support their caviar taste, Renaissance popes taxed Romans and their country cousins. Lazio and Umbria soon filed for bankruptcy, and much of the distressed agricultural population up and left. The popes curried favor with and extracted money from whichever foreign nations suited them best at the time. Fragmented alliances left Rome vulnerable to invasion, and soon proved fatal.

SACK OF ROME

The **Sack of Rome,** an intense eight-day pillage by German warriors, Spanish marauders, and 15,000 angry Lutherans, came in May 1527. The city fell to bloodthirsty imperialist troops, who stormed through the Borgo, destroying everyone and everything in sight. Little respect was shown for religious artifacts. One priest was murdered because he refused to kneel and give the Holy Communion to a donkey. The pope, Clement VII, escaped by holing himself up for six months in Castel Sant'Angelo, besieged by the troops of the French King Charles V.

Pope Paul III, disappointed by the sack, set up the **Inquisition** in 1542. It took hold remarkably well, and the burning of books, infidels, and freethinkers carried on until 1610 when all of Rome was clearly in line. Powerful families and the papacy were still hopelessly corrupt, but they didn't seem to be hurting anyone. Having created such havoc, the popes lost much of their political credibility and relevance in the play among European powers during the Thirty Years' War. Most of the 17th and 18th centuries were relatively quiet for Rome.

NINETEENTH CENTURY

Pius VI amiably mishandled conflicts between the church and the Revolutionary French government, and induced anti-clerical sentiment to explode in Paris. Effigies of Pius were set on fire and a severed head landed in the lap of the Papal Nuncio as he was traveling in his coach. Romans, in turn, attacked a French delegation on the Corso in 1793. Homes of French sympathizers were vandalized and the French Academy was set on fire with shouts of "Long live the Catholic religion."

Napoleon Bonaparte arrived on the scene in 1796 to deal with the problem and to refill French coffers with the treasures of Italy. Napoleon refused to depose the pope for strategic reasons, but he brought the Church to its knees, extorting millions in tribute and carrying off precious works of art. Romans watched 500 wagons leave the city loaded with booty; some of the most important pieces of Italian and Roman art are still found in Parisian museums. In 1798, French **General Berthier** stormed the Vatican, kidnapped the pope, and established yet another **Roman Republic.** When Napoleon's empire crumbled, however, the 1815 Congress of Vienna returned the papacy to temporal power in Rome.

In 1849, with the liberal **Risorgimento** raging, Rome voted to abolish the papal state and establish, you guessed it, another **Roman Republic. Pope Pius IX** appealed to Catholic heads of state with success; Rome was once again besieged by a Bonaparte, Napoleon III. The resistance was led by **Giuseppe Mazzini** and **Giuseppe Garibaldi.** The former preached with revolutionary fervor, and the latter led Rome against the French, who still triumphed and reinstated Pope Pius IX.

Nonetheless, regional Italian rulers united the country (except Rome and Venice), declared Rome the capital, and crowned the first Italian king, **Vittorio Emanuele II.** In 1870, when the French left for war with Prussia, there was no one to stop the Italian forces from crashing through the Vatican. The pope, who had just declared the doctrine of Papal Infallibility, "imprisoned" himself, refused to give up, and urged all Italians to support him; he died alone in 1878.

TWENTIETH CENTURY

Rome's recent history may sound vaguely familiar. In a century marked by violent political unrest, public debate between the classes, and a resurgence in new forms of art and culture, citizens are taking part in Caesar's grand Roman tradition. Political fights have moved from the *rostra* to the capitol, although the arguments remained just as heated. Even the *fascisti* of the 1920s took their name from the symbol of authority in ancient Rome, the *fasces*, a bundle of sticks tightly wound around an axe-blade. Today, the Italians (divided principally into northern and southern alliances) heatedly debate the ramifications of sharing resources as a unified state.

IL DUCE

The life of **Benito Mussolini** was a tribute to the bigness of which the littlest man is capable. After stints as a schoolteacher, a journalist,

The world was thus an evil place; salvation could be attained through knowledge, called *gnosis*, ofthe divine spark of god.

Marcionism: Marcion (84-160) denounced the Jewish scriptures as being written in honor of the evil demiurge (see Gnosticism, above) in favor of the Gospel of Luke and the Pauline Epistles. The movement lasted until the 5th century.

Monarchianism: Monarchianism, beginning in the 2nd century, denied the trinity in favor of one godhead. This marked the beginning of tensions between the Eastern and Western churches.

Monophysitism: The Monophysites of the 5th century believed that Christ was wholly divine despite his embrace of human form and mortal nature.

Nestorianism: Nestor (c.381-c.451) argued that Christ was of two persons—one human and one divine. As Mary had given birth only to the human Christ, she could not be called the Mother of God. Nestorianism survives today in Iran, Iraq, and Syria.

Pelagianism: Pelagius, living in the 4th century, rejected the notion of Original Sin and claimed that human free will enables one to earn God's grace. Though Pelagius was excommunicated and his teachings denounced, by the 16th century Roman Catholics held a semi-Pelagianism position on grace, teaching that free will is an important element in overcoming original sin.

and, even a pacifist, Mussolini (or *Il Duce*, "the Leader") started his political career with the militant left, but soon added a dash of Nationalism to his Marx. At the tender age of 25, Mussolini called for the appointment of a "ruthless and energetic" dictator to clean up Italy. Three months later, he conceded that he might be the man needed for the job.

In 1919, Mussolini assembled paramilitary combat groups (*i fasci di combattimenti*), known as the **Blackshirts,** who waged a fierce campaign for power. They broke labor strikes for corrupt industrialists, raided newspapers soft on Bolshevism, and established mini-dictatorships in small cities on the pattern of the Communist rise to power. Mussolini had grown so powerful in Italy that the 1922 **March on Rome** was just for show, as were the reports that 3000 Fascist martyrs had died. When Vittorio Emanuele III named him Prime Minister, Mussolini forged a totalitarian state, suppressing opposition parties, regulating the press, and demolishing labor unions. His few pieces of constructive legislation include revamping the train system to increase efficiency and the **Lateran Pact of 1929,** regulating Vatican-Italian relations.

In 1929, Mussolini moved his office to **Palazzo Venezia,** where he delivered his imperial orations. He fancied himself an emperor in the grandest tradition, and was determined to mark his territory by a series of unfinished, gargantuan architectural schemes. Under his aegis, the government spent more than 33 billion lire on public works; he plowed down medieval, Renaissance, and Baroque works, as well as over three-quarters of the ruins he claimed to be preserving, to create a wide processional street, **Via dei Fori Imperiali.** To symbolize his achievement, Mussolini envisioned a huge forum that would make St. Peter's and the Colosseum look like Legoland. For the centerpiece of his Foro Mussoliano, he commissioned a 263 ft. statue of himself as Hercules. One hundred tons of metal later, with only an enormous foot and head to show for it, the project lost its balance and collapsed.

Impressed by German efficiency, Mussolini entered World War II with Hitler in 1939. Used to relying on propaganda rather than strength, Mussolini squandered his army in France, Russia, and Greece until a coup and the Allied forces deposed *Il Duce*, who was rather ingloriously hanged. Rome's sizable resistance movement made up for Italy's dreadful military performance, protecting Jews and anti-Fascists from the occupying Germans. Serious damage to the city was averted; Hitler had the sense to declare Rome an "open city" as liberating Allies approached in June 1944.

The dreary **EUR** area (p. 145) is a reminder of Mussolini's unsettling vision and his ultimate failure. His legacy lives on in his granddaughter, **Alessandra Mussolini,** who is trying to revive Italian Fascism. Elected to Parliament, she made an unsuccessful bid for mayor of Naples in 1993.

THE ITALIAN NATION

The end of World War II led to sweeping changes in Italian government. The **Italian Constitution** of 1948 established a **Republic** with a president, a parliament with a 315-member Senate and 630-member Chamber of Deputies, and an independent judiciary. Within this framework, the **Christian Democratic Party,** bolstered by American aid (and rumored Mafia collusion), bested the Socialists. Domination by a single party did not stabilize the country; political turmoil has reigned, along with over 50 different governments since World War II.

Postwar instability and industrialization led to violence in the 1970s. The **autunno caldo** (hot autumn) of 1969, a season of strikes, demonstrations, and riots, opened a decade of unrest. The most disturbing event was the 1978 murder of ex-Prime Minister Aldo Moro, who is remembered by a plaque in the Jewish Ghetto where his body was dumped by the leftist Brigade Rosse.

Because the nation is still young, city and regional bonds often prove stronger than nationalist sentiment. The most pronounced split exists between the north's wealthy industrial areas and the south's agrarian territories.

TODAY

The daily minutiae of Italian politics read like a soap opera that, when taken *cum grano salis*, seems more amusing than disturbing. In 1992, **Oscar Luigi Scalfaro** was elected president on a platform of governmental reform, including streamlining of the cabinet. Since then, politics have been characterized by the slow process of electoral law reform, resulting in **"Tangentopoli"** ("Kickback City"); over 2600 politicians have been implicated in corruption scandals. Reaction to the crackdown on corruption and the Mafia in politics has included such acts of violence as the 1993 bombings of the Uffizi, Florence's premier art museum, as well as several sites in Rome, including the Church of San Giorgio in Velabro (p. 87), the "suicides" of 10 indicted officials over the past four years, and open Mafia retaliation against judges.

Current and former Prime Minister **Silvio Berlusconi** (who moonlights as a billionaire publishing and television tycoon, in addition to being a part-owner of AC Milan) presided over a "Freedom Alliance" of three right-wing parties: his conservative **Forza Italia,** the reactionary **Lega Nord,** and the formerly neo-fascist **Alleanza Nazionale.** When the Lega Nord pulled out in 1994, Berlusconi lost his majority and was forced to resign as Prime Minister.

The elections of 1996 brought the center left-coalition, the **Olive Tree** (L'Ulivo), to power, and **Romano Prodi** was elected Prime Minister. Prodi's major designs were balancing the budget and the stabilization of Italian politics. He now serves as president of the European Union Commission. Despite his removed position in Brussels, Prodi's voice still carries weight: he's in the unique position of having left the presidency without first horribly disgracing himself.

In 1998, **Massimo D'Alema** came to power also representing a variation of the center-left. His policy is largely similar to Prodi's. In June 1999, a government bureaucrat was found assassinated in the streets of Rome. The same night, a 19-page manifesto was found in trash cans across the city. It was feared that this might mark a resurgence of the anarchic Italy of the 1970s, and *carabinieri* in the city were on full alert. Though the incident seems to have been an isolated one, D'Alema saw his support crumble at the end of the year as he failed to push through welfare reforms and alienated unions in trying to do so.

D'Alema struggled to please both the ex-communist wing of the party and his moderate base, a problem that eventually forced him to resign in May of 2000. He was replaced by his former Treasury Minister, **Giuliano Amato.** Known as "Dr. Subtle" for his ability to perceive the fine points of argument and his deft trimming of government spending, Amato (alongside Ciampi and D'Alema) is largely credited with the institution of the successful 1999 budgetary reforms, though his anti-graffiti campaign failed entirely. Master writers have been catching "why me?" all over *bella Italia* since Amato's first day in office. Perhaps the nickname derives from Amato's ability to avoid scandal; he was one of few to emerge unscathed from corruption crack-downs in the early 90s, one of which led to late Socialist Party leader Bettino Craxi's exile in Tunisia. As the top untainted Socialist, he led a shaky 12-party coalition for just one year. In Italy's 2001 general election, Berlusconi (a.k.a. moneybags) led a center-right coalition that took back Parliament, propelling him back into the corner office. To expect stability would be to ignore Italian history.

Despite the Left's ardent effort to unseat him, Berlusconi has proven quite adept at hardball. Just when it looked certain that he would have to sell part of his media empire because of conflict of interest charges, Parliament approved (with plenty of prodding no doubt) a bill that allowed him to keep his 90% of the country's television broadcasts so long as he agreed not to manage them; his children now run them. Then again, in the summer of 2003, Parliament spared him from legal proceedings over allegations of corruption by granting the country's top government officials immunity from prosecution while in office. Only days prior to the legislation, Berlusconi made headlines by attending his trial and asserting that "one citizen is equal to another [in the eyes of the law] but perhaps this one is slightly more equal than the rest..." Lest you think that it doesn't quite live up to detractors' allegations of totalitarianism, it should be noted that the Berlusconi government hasn't been shy in its use of force, either. During the 2001 G8 meeting in Genoa, the *carabinieri* (who were later exonerated by Parliament, surprise, surprise) severely beat protestors, killing one man and seriously injuring dozens in a midnight raid on their headquarters. Given his penchant for legal nuance and large-event management, many Europeans are apprehensive as Berlusconi begins a year-long term as President of the EU (it is a rotating office).

Currently, the city of Rome is run by center-leftist Mayor **Walter Veltroni.** Veltroni, who has been out of the media spotlight thus far—though that is to be expected when the opposition owns the media—was elected mayor during the 2001 general elections. His victory was crucial in proving that the center-left was still a force in Italian politics. Rome is not only a large city, but it is one of the few places in Italy to buck the country's recent trend towards conservatism. Should the "War on Terror," corruption charges, and Labor's dissatisfaction make Berlusconi vulnerable, look for Veltroni and Rome to lead the Left's resurgence.

RELIGION

Religion has been a major force in the shaping of Roman history, politically as much as socially. From the Pantheon to St. Peter's, the majority of sights in Rome are or were connected with religion. This section aims to be a history of belief: for information on religion and politics, see **History** above.

GODS OF THE ROMANS

Early Roman religion is difficult to piece together, mostly because the ancient Romans themselves were involved in forgetting it by the first century BC. All that can be certain is that the Romans had the typical Indo-European *paterfamilias* structure of a male head of household who bore sacral life-and-death power over the rest of the family. **Lares** were attached to a particular household, worshiped by the family and its slaves. **Penates** were also household gods, but they were associated more with the storage cupboards of the household and the care of the hearth. Along with war rituals, the hearth was an area of strong religious importance, and the cult of **Vesta** (with her league of Vestal Virgins; see **House of the Vestal Virgins,** p. 74) was one of the most fundamental elements of early Roman religious practice.

Like the vast majority of inhabitants of the ancient world, the Romans practiced animal sacrifice, believing it important to achieve a state of *pax deorum* (peace of the gods) instead of *ira deorum* (the wrath of heaven.) War rites of the Romans were even known to include human sacrifice in cases of dire crisis, though this was outlawed by the more refined citizenry of later centuries. Romans were introduced to the entire package of Greek gods and goddesses by the Etruscans. The awed Romans soon adopted most of the Greek religious cast, simply transposing Hellenic names into Latinate versions for use at home. As the god of war, **Mars** was declared patron of belligerent Rome.

Roman polytheism was of a tolerant sort; religion was seen as a local practice, and foreign gods were frequently "interpreted" as versions of the Greco-Roman gods under other names. The Romans didn't impose their religion on anyone, and even the notorious "cult of the emperor"—which began with Julius Caesar and Augustus, who were deified posthumously—actually began by popular demand in one of the eastern provinces, where local inhabitants had a custom of deifying their rulers. Many of the more educated Romans were non-religious, having absorbed the Stoic, Epicurean, and Platonic elements of Greek philosophy.

MITHRAISM

Mithraism, a religion with strong similarities to Christianity that flourished in the first few centuries AD, was the first successful monotheistic religion in the Empire. Imported from Persia, it centered around the god **Mithras,** who created the world by killing a sacred bull. Mithraism remains shrouded in mystery, mainly because it was a secretive cult based on the celebration of **mysteries** known only to initiates. The vast majority of our knowledge about the religion comes from archaeological remains. Their place of worship, the **mithraeum,** was usually built underground, and several Christian churches, notably the **Basilicas of San Clemente** (p. 134) and **Santa Prisca,** were constructed on top of them. Although only eight mithrae have been excavated in Rome, there may have been over 700 at the height of the movement. Several mithrae have also been excavated in Ostia Antica (**Daytrips,** p. 263).

The mithraeum was usually an artificial cave with stone benches facing a depiction of Mithras killing the sacred bull. Several other minor figures were present in the scene, including a scorpion, a dog, a snake, the sun, the moon, and a male figure named Cautopates holding a torch. The best-preserved artifact of the scene is the bull sculpture in the Room of the Animals at the Vatican Museums.

Mithras, the central figure in the religion, originated as a minor Zoroastrian and Hindu deity. An Apollo-like figure, he was the god of the sky, the sun's light, contracts, and mediation. The cult's Roman popularity began around AD 100. Historians speculate that Mithraism was a social religion for bourgeois Roman military veterans. With nothing but artificial ties to its Zoroastrian roots, it was a sort of Roman New Age religion.

CHRISTIANITY & CATHOLICISM

> Suppressed for the moment, the deadly superstition broke out again, not only in Judea, the land which originated this evil, but also in the city of Rome, where all sorts of horrendous and shameful practices from every part of the world converge and are fervently cultivated.
>
> —Tacitus, *Annals* 15:44

Since Peter and Paul arrived shortly after Christ's death, Christianity has been big in Rome. Christ said to give unto Caesar what is Caesar's and unto God what is God's; in reality,

A field guide to Roman deities

Touring the Forum without the faintest idea of Jupiter's identity is the fastest way to turn an otherwise pleasant afternoon into a walk through hell. Each god or goddess below is paired with what he or she primarily represented to the Romans.

Jupiter: King of the Gods; lawmaker; propensity for approaching women in the form of various wild animals.

Juno: Queen of heaven; goddess of women and marriage; Jupiter's...sister.

Mars: god of war and the spirit of battle.

Vulcan: God of fire; divine smith; ugly.

Ceres: Goddess of Earth and fertility.

Venus: Goddess of love and lust; patron of prostitutes; noted philanderer.

Vesta: Goddess of the family and city hearth; virgins.

Minerva: Goddess of war, handicraft, and wisdom; born fully grown from Jupiter's ponderous head.

Neptune: God of the sea and water; Jupiter's brother.

Apollo: God of the sun, music and song; Diana's twin.

Diana: Goddess of the moon, wild animals, hunting, vegetation, chastity, and childbirth.

Mercury: God of animals, wealth, commerce, shrewdness, persuasion, and travelers (don't forget to sacrifice to this guy).

in recent news

Cast into darkness

In July 2002, Pope John Paul II returned from World Youth Day in Toronto to some trouble brewing back home (or, more accurately, in the Danube). An Argentine bishop famous for thumbing his mitre at the Vatican had, it seemed, taken nine women by boat to the middle of the river and ordained them in defiance of papal law. The Church responded by calling the ceremony a "cultish spectacle." Several prominent theologians, however, used the occasion to remind the College of Cardinals that the exclusive ordination of men had no scriptural basis, merely a traditional one.

Some speculated that the Church would ignore the ceremony in an attempt to illegitimize the proceedings. But on Aug. 6, seven of the women were excommunicated for the sin of celebrating mass with their families and friends. They had failed to meet their deadline for repentance and a return to orthodoxy on July 22, and thus, according to the Vatican's statement, had committed an "affront to the dignity of all women." The seven, two of them theologians and one of them a teacher from Munich, announced that they would continue to fight the Vatican and its chief ideologue, Cardinal Joseph Ratzinger, who handed down the excommunications.

separating politics and religion hasn't been quite so simple. As early as AD 35, the Senate declared Christianity to be "strange and unlawful." Nonetheless, in 42, **Saint Peter,** the first Bishop of Rome, set up shop in the city. **Saint Paul,** the codifier of Christian thought, dropped by often, until he was beheaded in 62, near EUR. Peter met his end in upside-down crucifixion near the site of the Vatican in 67. The duo are recognized as Rome's patron saints.

Persecution of Christians began in earnest after the Great Fire of Rome in 64, and it continued sporadically for the next 240 years. From 200 to 500, Christians used the **catacombs** outside of the center of Rome as cemeteries by Christians (p. 139). Although the Christians did not live there, as commonly assumed, much has been learned about the early church from the decorations inside.

Christian persecution in Rome ended just before Christianity was made the state religion in 315. The church struggled to find its feet. The **Nicene Creed** of 325 was the first cohesive statement of belief by the Pistic (Orthodox) church, nailing down the basics of Christianity. Soon, with the banning of paganism, Christianity found itself with a monopoly on the soul trade. A flurry of theological literature ensued: a Latin translation by **St. Jerome** standardized the Bible, while Rome's own **St. Augustine** wrote the *City of God* and *Confessions*, the framework of most Christian theology.

During this period, most of the major basilicas of Rome were begun, though in forms vastly different from their current states. The **crucifix,** today the ubiquitous symbol of Christianity, only became widely used around 550. In 490, the Council of Chalcedon declared that Jesus was of both human and divine nature, answering a question that had spawned innumerable heretic sects. In 787, the Second Council of Nicaea declared that the Holy Spirit proceeds from the Father and the Son. The first major break in the church began to form, and in 1054, the Eastern and Western halves of the church separated in an event known as the **Great Schism.** Rome and Constantinople were too far apart for effective government, and Roman religious rule grated on the Byzantines. In addition, there was theological dissent: the Eastern church believed in the special religious significance of icons, while the Western church did not.

The (Western) Church's history during the Middle Ages was tumultuous. Papal succession was political, and greed and corruption were rampant. Pope Urban II kicked off the **First Crusade** in 1047 in order to unify the Church and squelch partisanship. While this crusade, like those that followed, failed to retake the Holy Land and created all manner of havoc in the Middle East, it succeeded in bringing a rebirth to a religion in danger of becoming stagnant. For similar reasons, Pope Gregory II initiated the first incarnation of the **Inquisition** in 1232.

The 14th century, during which the papacy jumped borders, duplicating and even triplicating itself, was only dress rehearsal for the confusion that would come with the **Protestant Reformation** of the 1500s. In 1517, Martin Luther's accusatory *95 Theses* significantly threatened Rome's religious power. Ignatius of Loyola founded the Jesuits in 1534 to combat the Protestant menace; from 1534-1563, the Council of Trent met to plan the **Counter Reformation** and further define what had become known as Roman Catholicism.

Since World War II, the Church has spread its message globally with renewed strength and vigor, particularly in Eastern Europe and the developing world. Meanwhile, back in Rome, the Church has lost much of its following: less than 10% of Romans attend mass regularly. The Church's responses to public affairs during this century have been contradictory. While Pope Pius XII insisted that the Church would stay out of politics, a 1950s papal decree forbade Catholics from associating with the Communist party. Ironically, in many other Western European countries, the Church was directly affiliated with Socialist parties. The **Second Vatican Council** (1962) was an attempt to improve relations with other religions and to make the Church more accessible to the layperson. The most visible results of the Council, which concluded under Paul VI in 1965, included the replacement of Latin with the vernacular in the mass, the increased role of local clergy and bishops in administration, and the re-evaluation of the place of scripture with regard to belief.

Since 1981, Pope John Paul II's international approach to papacy—including his overt use of the media and constant traveling—has reflected the Church's intention to establish a more direct relationship with believers without the interference of politics. The fact that the current pope is Polish (Italian newspapers don't call him Giovanni Paolo II but Wojtyla, his last name) has removed the Pope from Italian politics, and the papacy has concerned itself primarily with global issues.

ART AND ARCHITECTURE

Before Rome was Rome, Etruscans lived, worked, and made art that influenced the Roman conquerors who would later take over their territory. They are most famous for their subtle, reddish pottery, which took heavy inspiration both from the Greeks and from Oriental, Phoenician, and Hittite sources. Their earliest pottery (9th century BC) took the form of funerary urns, mostly decorated with stippled or incised patterns. In the 7th century, the **bucchero** style—shiny black or grey funeral pottery that looks like metal—came into style, a must-have for every Etruscan lady. Just as typical, however, are the earthy **terra-cotta** bas reliefs that the Etruscans introduced and the Romans went on to claim. Nationalistic Roman orator Cato even had the nerve to announce, several hundred years later: "I hear too many people praising the knick-knacks of Corinth and Athens, and laughing at the terra-cotta antefixes of our Roman gods."

CLASSICAL ROME

The emerging Roman styles in art fall mainly into two large categories—art in service of the state and private household art, which originates in the votive statues of household gods (the *lares* and *penates*) created by ancient Roman tribes. Household art was a democratic form, splashed across the interiors of houses, courtyards, and shops. Most private Roman art took the form of **frescoes,** Greek-influenced paintings that were daubed onto wet plaster so that both plaster and paint would dry together, forming a lasting and time-resistant patina. Da Vinci's *The Last Supper* is probably the most famous fresco. Proud household owners often embellished their abodes with sneaky **trompe l'oeil** doors or columns to make the place look bigger. **Mosaic** (painting with tiles) was another popular genre from the Hellenistic period onward; a favorite subject was the watchdog, often executed on the vestibule floor, with the helpful inscription *cave canem* ("beware of dog"). Craftsmen-artists fashioned these mosaics by painting scenes into the floor (or occasionally wall) of a building, pressing finely shaded **tesserae** (bits of colored stone and glass) onto the painting's surface, and squeezing a soft bed of mortar in between the cracks to cement everything in place. An even more personalized art form of sorts—graffiti—was also widely practiced by citizens of the ancient Roman Empire. Look out for walls in Pompeii or excavated buried buildings to see the full range of uninhibited ancient self-expression—everything from love declarations to denunciations of Christianity as a cannibal religion, as well as such judiciously weighed sentiments as "Marcus Lucius has a very large ass."

Public art in Rome was commissioned by the Roman government and usually reflected the tastes and victories of whoever was in power at the time. At first the Romans simply exploited Greek design features for their buildings, but soon they developed the revolutionary technology of the **arch** from earlier Etruscan vaults. This, along with the happy invention of **concrete,** revolutionized their conceptions of architecture and made possible such monuments as the **Colosseum** (p. 76), triumphal arches celebrating military victories, aqueducts, amphitheaters, basilicas, and much more. The Romans then finessed the arch, lengthening it into a **barrel vault,** crossing two arches to make a **groin vault,** or rotating it in a tight circle to build **domes.** Monumental public buildings either reminded the spectator of a particular emperor's exploits in battle (like the artistically sublimated propaganda of Trajan's Column) or functioned as frenzied arenas of mass entertainment intended to pacify an unruly populace. Some of the most famous building occurred around AD 80, when the normally affable ex-plebe emperor Vespatian built the blood-soaked arches and columns of the Colosseum, and when Titus had his triumphal **Arch of Titus** constructed to provide a suitable backdrop for him to parade his booty and slaves.

Religion, Marx noticed, has a way of keeping the people busy and out of trouble. The Roman government scooped him on this, making sure to spend money on the construction of religious temples and on festivals and rites to calm and patriotically inspire the populace by offering it a spectacle of spiritual unity and power. Temples were usually constructed along the Greek model, with a triangular portico supported by the classical row of columns and decorated with strips of friezes on strategic flat surfaces. In capitals (the decorative upper portion of a column), Romans used the Greek orders of Doric, Ionic, and Corinthian, making the latter more elaborate than ever by supplementing its crown of acanthus leaves with all kinds of ornate curlicues. Later on, the Romans would begin to transfer column style and the full panoply of Greek architecture to almost any building.

The earliest and most sacred man-made monument in Rome was the Temple to Vesta, although its white simplicity was soon overshadowed by more pragmatic temples, such as those devoted to the deified Augustus and Julius Caesar. Rome's most important architect was **Vitruvius,** who originated the idea that harmonious buildings would base their measurements and proportions on the human body—a.k.a. the "measure of man." Later on, Romans became more interested in theaters and basilicas for distraction and contemplation. At this point, basilicas were still used as courthouses and shopping arcades, although the cool and climate-adapted design of a long rectangle with arch-and-column supports would be recycled by later Christian and Byzantine emperors as the first floorplan for early churches.

BYZANTINE DECADENCE

When Constantine transferred the capital of the Roman Empire in AD 330 from Rome to **Constantinople** (then known as Byzantium, and now reincarnated as modern-day Istanbul), artistic influences in Rome took a decidedly Asiatic twist. Born from the aesthetic traditions of the Christian catacombs and the Greek and Oriental styles, Byzantine art favored immobile, mystical, slender-fingered figures against flat gold or midnight blue backgrounds, shadowy domes, and an atmosphere of enigmatic and flooding holiness. Spread the world over by the Emperor Justinian and his powerful wife Theodora, the Byzantine style reveled in gorgeously ornate mosaics, some of which can still be seen in the churches of Santa Cecilia in Trastevere, Santa Prassede, and Santa Maria in Domenica, although the best examples of this style in Italy are all in Ravenna. Despite the fact that the religious Byzantine emperors erected countless costly palaces, only their religious buildings have survived subsequent sackings, medieval recycling, and modernization. These buildings were built on the model of Roman **basilicas** (law courts); instead of having a cathedral shape, they are rectangular and domed, with stony cold sarcophagi and the dim gold glare of far-off mosaics and anemic saints.

Piazza Farnese

A TOUCH OF ROMANESQUE

Given the chaos of the 3rd and 4th centuries, emperors' minds tended to turn to making war, not art. The gaze of the Christian art that eventually emerged in the Middle Ages was fixed firmly on heaven. From roughly AD 500 to 1200, Romanesque-style churches dominated Europe. In Rome, these fashions slowly and incrementally overtook the older Byzantine style, retaining the basilica floorplan but updating it with rows of pillared round arches, low ceilings, oriel windows, peeling wooden statues of saints, and an elaborate and arcane bestiary of men and beasts cavorting in the caps of pillars and the reliefs above doorways. Wall frescoes and mosaics from this period abound in Rome, in **San Paolo fuori le Mura** (which also hoards mosaics imported *in toto* from Byzantium), **Santa Maria Maggiore,** and **Santa Prassede.**

Horse Carriage

RENAISSANCE IN ROME

The succession of wealthy Renaissance popes eager to leave their mark on the city in the form of new buildings, paintings, and sculpture gave a sagging Rome its most striking stylistic

Piazza Navona

tummy-tuck since its ancient days. This age heralded the split between science and faith, and the Church condemned both Galileo and Giordano Bruno for their astronomical assertions that the earth was not the center of the universe. Painters, sculptors, and architects relied heavily on subjective experience while at the same time employing the technical discoveries of the Age of Science, such as the newly reinvented trick of creating **perspective.** Although Rome was certainly not the center of the Italian Renaissance, it did manage to lure many of the most famous Florentine artists to come refurbish the imperial city's image, including Michelangelo, Brunelleschi, and Raphael. It is also home to one of the period's trendiest churches, the Mannerist Jesuit headquarters, **Il Gesù** (p. 91).

The supreme artist with the supremely tortured soul, **Michelangelo Buonarroti** (1475-1564), grew up among the stonemasons of Tuscany; as the man later said: "with my wet-nurse's milk, I sucked in the hammer and chisels I use for my statues." During this period, Michelangelo honed his knowledge of the human body after he swapped his crucifix for the privilege of dissecting corpses in the Cloisters of Santo Spirito. At the age of 21, he headed to the already ancient capital city to seek his fortune. Originally commissioned by the pope for some minor works, Michelangelo was deluged with requests for work once he became well-known in Rome. It is for one of these commissions that he created the profoundly sorrowful and career-making **Pietà** in St. Peter's (p. 117).

In 1502, Pope Julius II sent for Michelangelo, now almost 30 and at the height of his career, to return once more to Rome to build the pope's **tomb** (in San Pietro in Vincoli). The relationship that was to last 10 years between the overbearing, irascible, and demanding Julius II and the introverted and temperamental Michelangelo was hardly a meeting of like minds. The colossal tomb was left unfinished when Julius got carried away instead with plans for St. Peter's. Irritated, Michelangelo abandoned Rome in 1504, but Julius managed to sweet-talk the moody artist into returning to Rome to paint the **Sistine Chapel** ceiling. Mikey spent the next four years slaving over—or rather under—the problem-ridden project, beginning by learning how to paint frescoes. In the following years, he threw away his original pictorial design, redesigned his plans, fired his assistants, and ended up doing the whole job himself. The ceiling was finished in 1512, four months before Julius's death, and Michelangelo escaped to Florence. Thirty years later, Michelangelo returned to Rome, greeted by the new Pope Paul II, who called the aged Michelangelo back to the Sistine Chapel for arguably his most important work, **The Last Judgment** (p. 161). Michelangelo would continue his architectural designs, but he would never paint again. Before his death at the age of 89, he expressed his wish to be buried in Florence. To circumvent the Romans, who would certainly want to claim Michelangelo's body, his casket was smuggled to Florence and interred.

Michelangelo's Florentine contemporary **Raphael** (Raffaello Sanzio) also made the obligatory pilgrimage to Rome for prestige and generous papal commissions. Julius had him fresco his private rooms, now world-famous as the **Raphael Stanze.** Raphael profited from his stay in the Vatican to covertly learn some of Michelangelo's techniques for creating realistic and dynamic art, much to Michelangelo's annoyance.

BERNINI + BORROMINI = BAROQUE

The Baroque in Rome can be summed up in the work of two heavily lionized artists: **Gian Lorenzo Bernini** and **Francesco Castelli Borromini.** The personality differences between effervescent, cavalier boy-genius Bernini and dark, temperamental Borromini are abundantly clear in their works. Known as the "greatest European" in his day, the architect, sculptor, painter, and dandy Bernini more than set the standard for the Baroque during his prolific career. Bernini's father, a Florentine sculptor, brought his son to Rome to start work; he was immediately signed on for training and didn't stop working until the age of 80. He died having worked for every pope that was in power during his lifetime.

Along with his charged **St. Teresa in Ecstasy** (in Santa Maria della Vittoria), Bernini's Hellenistic **David** (in the Galleria Borghese, p. 165) stands in great contrast to Michelangelo's classical version. Although sculpture was only one facet of Bernini's career, he made great contributions to Rome in the architecture department. The oval of the *piazza* of St. Peter's was the culmination of a life's work; he personally supervised the construction of each and every one of the 284 Doric columns of travertine marble. Bernini's churches and monuments (including the grand **baldacchino** at St. Peter's and his own favorite, the church of **Sant'Andrea al Quirinale**) exemplify the exuberantly showy, theatrical, illusory style that came to define the Baroque.

The non-conformist Swiss **Borromini** spent much of his career fitfully working against the gaudy showiness of the Baroque. Borromini was commissioned to design some of the details on Bernini's *baldacchino*, but it became increasingly apparent that Bernini and Borromini's styles were wholly incompatible. In works like the church of **San Carlo alle Quattro Fontane,** Borromini created an entirely new architectural vocabulary that fused sculpture and architecture. Eventually the complexity of Borromini's work caught up with him; he became obsessed with his calculations and machinations and withdrew completely from society. A few days after burning a final series of architectural plans, he impaled himself on a sword.

NEOCLASSICAL RE-REVIVAL

In the late 1700s, southern Italy would provide the long-awaited reaction to the Baroque in the form of **Neoclassicism.** Morbidly infected by the excitement surrounding the excavations in Pompeii, Herculaneum, and Paestum, Neoclassical artists reasserted the values of Greco-Roman art that the Renaissance already had taken a shot at imitating. The greatest artists of this period weren't Roman but they soon immigrated to Rome. Foremost among the Neoclassicists was **Jacques-Louis David** (1748-1825), who studied in Rome at the French Academy. In sculpture, the coldly pure lines of **Antonio Canova** also found fans, leading the Borghese to install some of his marble statues in their gardens.

Pope Benedict XIV preferred restoring Rome for tourists over conducting church business; street signs and historical markers appeared for the first time. He commissioned paintings for St. Peter's and mosaics for Santa Maria Maggiore, redesigned by prominent architect **Fernando Fuga.** Baroque artists managed to resist the tide of Neoclassicism, as **Nicola Salvi's** Baroque Trevi Fountain (p. 107)—completed in 1762—testifies. The tumultuous Risorgimento put a damper on construction in the mid-1800s; once the country was unified, large-scale building began, to accommodate the new government. The undeveloped area east, southeast, and northeast of Termini was soon crowded with apartment buildings. A number of buildings were lost in expansion, including Henry James's favorite, the **Villa Ludovisi.**

FASCIST ART

Mussolini was the biggest proponent of public works since the cadre of popes who built St. Peter's and the rest of the Vatican complex. Most of the monuments he erected, like his philosophy, are pompous, rigid, geometrical, and based on an artistic model that subjugates the individual to the public masses. Much of the Fascist legacy in Roman architecture can be found in the **EUR** neighborhood on the outskirts of Rome (p. 145), including one building (the Palace of Labor) that architect **Marcello Piancentini** described proudly as a "square Colosseum." The **Foro Italico,** meant to be the monumental symbolic center for a heroic nation, is also a prime example of the Fascist notion of artistic expression—not too different from their notion of political expression. Note the excessive use of "DUCE A NOI" in the tilework, as well as the nude figures wrestling, swimming, laboring, and piloting biplanes.

POST-FASCIST ART

Things got a little more complicated and a lot less megalomaniacal after Mussolini was out of the picture. Although Italy and Rome are perhaps best known in modern times for their celluloid art (see p. 7 for more on **Italian cinema**), Italian visual artists had some degree of fame. Several turned to more traditional forms for less than traditional purposes: neo-*neo*-Classicist Felice Casarotti kicked it with the old *old* school, while **Giorgio di Chirico** painted surrealist landscapes that combined ancient Roman architecture with signs of Italian modernity like trains and cars—Vespa meets Vespatian, so to speak. Textures and artistic materials also became more important, with Lucio Fontana exploring the aesthetics of the disgusting in sculpture and painting, and multimedia sculptor **Alberto Burri** melding masterpieces out of scraps of plastic, fabric, and cellophane. No tour of Roman museums is complete without ogling **Amedeo Modigliani's** paintings of voluptuously sexy nude women—they're always lurking around the corner in Roman museums.

MUSIC

The Italians have long been slaves to a pretty tune. Italians, with help from the French, invented the system for musical notation still in use today. Before Julie Andrews came along as a singing nun in curtain couture, there was Guido D'Arezzo, who invented *solfege*, the "do, re, mi" syllable system of expressing the musical scale. A 16th-century Venetian printed the first musical scores with moveable type. Cremona offered violins by Stradivarius and Guarneri; the piano (actually *pianoforte*, which means "soft-loud") is an Italian invention. For Italians, vocal music has always occupied the position of highest glory. **Madrigals,** free-flowing secular songs for three to six voices, grew in popularity. One of the greatest contributors to Italian madrigals and sacred music was **Giovanni Pierluigi da Palestrina.** Born and bred in Lazio, he served as a choirboy at the Church of Santa Maria Maggiore and went on to direct choirs at Santa Maria Maggiore, and San Giovanni in Laterno.

OPERA

Born in 16th-century Florence, nurtured in Venice, and revered in Milan, the opera is the greatest musical innovation in Italian history. Invented by the **Camerata,** an artsy clique of Florentine poets, noblemen, authors, and musicians, opera began as an attempt to recreate the dramas of ancient Greece by setting lengthy poems to music. As opera spread from Florence to Venice, Milan, and Rome, the styles and forms of the genre grew increasingly distinct. Contemporaneous with the birth of opera was the emergence of the **oratorio.** Introduced by the Roman priest **St. Philip Neri,** the oratorio set biblical text to dramatic choral and instrumental accompaniment.

In opera, Baroque ostentation yielded to classical demands of moderation. To today's opera buffs, the words "Italian opera" generally connote Rossini, Bellini, Donzietti, Verdi, and Puccini—all composers of the 19th and early 20th centuries. **Giuseppe Verdi** had become a national icon by mid-life, writing such masterpieces as the tragic, triumphal *Aïda*, and *La Traviata*. Another great composer of the period, **Gioacchino Rossini,** boasted that he could produce music faster than copyists could reproduce it, but he proved such an infamous procrastinator that his agents resorted to locking him in a room with a single plate of spaghetti until he finished composing. Apparently that was some pretty amazing spaghetti, as his *Barber of Seville* remains a favorite of modern audiences. Finally, **Giacomo Puccini**, composer of *Madama Butterfly*, deserves a nod for his kick-ass female characters (despite their various predispositions toward ending in tuberculosis or violent suicide).

INSTRUMENTAL MUSIC

Instrumental music began to establish itself as a legitimate enterprise in 17th-century Rome. During the Baroque period, **Corelli** developed the *concerto* form, distinguished by its contrasting moods and tempos, which added drama to technical expertise. **Antoni Vivaldi** wrote over 400 *concerti* while teaching at an orphanage in Venice. His *Four Seasons* remains one of the best-known Baroque orchestral works. In the mid-17th century, operatic overtures began to be performed separately, resulting in the creation of a new genre. The *sinfonia* (symphony) was modeled after the melody of operatic overtures, but simply detached from its setting. At the same time, composer **Domenico Scarlatti** wrote over 500 harpsichord sonatas.

Italy's choke-hold on the music world continued into the 19th century. Relying on pyrotechnic virtuosity and a personal style of mystery and scandal, violinist **Nicolo Paganini** brought Europe to its knees. One of the first musicians to make publicized concert tours, he inspired **Franz List** to become a virtuoso pianist; the pair became the 19th-century equivalent of rock stars, complete with their very own groupies.

TWENTIETH CENTURY

Italian classical music continued to grow into the 20th century. **Otto Respighi,** composer of the popular *Pines of Rome* and *Foundations of Rome*, experimented with orchestral textures. Known for his work with meta-languages, **Luciano Berio** defied traditional instrumentation with his *Sequenza V* for solo trombone and mime, and other works for solo wind instruments and voice. Among performers, **Luciano Pavarotti** retains followers, despite the loss of his voice; his 1990 concert with the two "other" tenors, Placido Domingo and Jose Carreras, drew a full-capacity crowd to the Baths of Caracalla. A 1997 repeat filled the stadium at Modena, and the 1998 reunion during the World Cup in Paris reportedly drew one million people.

POP, ROCK & RAP

Once upon a time, Italian pop had its own unique and indigenous character, which blended Italian folk songs and Mediterranean rhythms with pop beats. Pino Daniele, Lucio Battisti, **Vasco Rossi,** and others used to perform folk-inspired ballads for captive audiences composed largely of university students. Since the 1980s, however, traditional Italian pop has been assimilated into the global hegemony of the American/British pop scene. Some of these earlier stars have faded from the pop sky, while others, like Rossi, have adapted to suit the trends, and remain very popular. There are still a good number of native pop talents, among them Renato Zero, Gianna Nannini, **Laura Pausini,** and 883. The aging Renato keeps churning out hits, and the Romans love him for it: In the summer of '99 he was able to fill the Foro Italico for six nights in a row. Nini's "Lupi Solitari" was the anthem of all angsty 15-year-olds, while 883's ballad "Come Mai" has been suggested as the new Italian national anthem. Since Laura Pausini conquered the Italian pop scene, she has begun to try to swim in more international waters, albeit with somewhat uneven success.

Italian rock acts are generally better than their pop counterparts. **Zucchero,** who has played stadiums with the likes of Pavarotti and Sting, is the tried and true warhorse of Italian rock, with a solid international fan base as well. The aforementioned Vasco Rossi has turned from folk to rock; his "Rewind" was an anthemic hit in 1999. **Liftba,** with their U2-esque stylings and a lead-singer with highly impressive cheekbones, is perennially popular, though some fans complain that they have sold out, leaving their socially conscious roots in the wake of popular success.

Though many would be hard-pressed to believe it, Italian rap exists, and it's not bad. Well, it's not that bad. Well, it's not *terrible...* The ultra-left wing and super-silly **99 Posse's** reggae and rap hybrid stylings were featured in the controversial film *Sud,* while curly-haired **Jovanotti** has turned from TV-variety show pop star to rapper. **Articolo 31,** though its more pop/rock than rap, also puts in a good showing—it takes its name from the Italian law banning pot smoking, in case you were wondering. Rome's contributions to Italian rap include **Er Piotta,** whose "SuperCafone '99" ignited dance floors and *coatti* everywhere, the pseudo-gangster rapper **Flamino Maphia,** and **Colle de Fomento,** whose "Il Cielo su Roma" explains all you'll ever need to know about why living in Rome is so damn cool.

INSIDE

ancient city **69**
centro storico **89**
walking tour of centro storico **90**
piazza di spagna & the corso **105**
villa borghese **113**
vatican city **115**
trastevere **122**
termini & san lorenzo **126**
southern rome **134**
architecture glossary **146**

Sights

Rome wasn't built in a day, and you won't see any substantial portion of it in 24 hours, (although you can try, using one of our walking tours). Ancient temples and forums, medieval churches, Renaissance basilicas, Baroque fountains, 19th-century museums, and Fascist architecture all cluster together in a city bursting with masterpieces from every era of Western civilization. Rome is possibly the greatest exposition of human endeavor on the planet. Enjoy.

No matter which sights you choose to see, there are a few general pieces of advice that pertain to many of them. First and foremost, most sights are best visited in the morning—the earlier, the better. Not only do you avoid the crowds, but in the summer you miss the crushing heat that descends upon the city. During the afternoons, you can visit some of Rome's countless galleries and museums, or do as the Romans, and take a siesta. Remember that most churches are only open from 8:30am to 12:30pm and from 4 to 7pm, so plan accordingly. If you are planning to visit one of the city's countless churches or Vatican City, remember to dress appropriately or you will be asked to leave. For women, this means no shorts or miniskirts (above the knee), sleeveless shirts, or sundresses. For men, no shorts or hats. Jeans and t-shirts are permitted. A final note about site-seeing in Rome: hours of operation are always subject to change—nation-wide strikes, a proprietor's whim, and everything in between can and will thwart your plans, so be ready to throw your hands up, let out a yell of frustration, and go buy some gelato.

Rome: Major Museums and Monuments
see key on p. 68
A
B
C
PIAZZA GIUSEPPE MAZZINI
Viale Giuseppe Mazzini
PIAZZALE CLODIO
Via della Giuliana
Circ. Codia
Via Trionfale
Circ. Trionfale
Viale Medaglie d'Oro
Viale Angelico
Via G. Ferrari
Via L. Settembrini
Lepanto
Via Cesare
L. delle Armi
L. delle Navi
Ponte G. Matteotti
L. Arnaldo da Brescia
Ponte Pietro Nenni
L. Michelangelo
Via Flaminia
Via di S. Eugenia
Viale delle Milizie
Via Barletta
Viale Giulio
Via Marcant. Colonna
LGO. TRIONFALE
PIAZZALE DEGLI EROI
Via Andrea Doria
Via Leone IV
Via Vespasiano
Via OttaViano
Via F. Massimo
Via Caio Mario
Via Germanico
PIAZZA COLA DI RIENZO
PIAZZA DI LIBERTÀ
Ponte Regina Martherita
L. d. Mellini
L.d. Mellini in Augusta
PIAZZA DEL POPOLO
Via del Babuino
Via di Ripetta
Via del Corso
Via Candia
Via Cipro
Via Cola di Rienzo
Via Cicerone
Via Crescenzio
PIAZZA CAVOUR
Ponte Cavour
PIAZZA AUGUSTO IMPERATORE
Via Angelo Emo
Viale Vaticano
CITTÀ DEL VATICANO
Castel Sant'Angelo
Vatican Wall
Saint Peter's Basilica
Via d. Conciliazione
L. Castello
L. Prati
Ponte S. Angelo
Tiber River
Ponte Umberto
L. Marianzo
L. di Tor di Nona
Ponte V. Emanuele II
Viale dei Coronari
Via d. Scrofa
Corso d. Rinascimento
Viale Vaticano
Via Aurelia
Via S.Maria Mediatrice
Via Staz. di S. Pietro
L. in Sassia
Ponte P. A. S. Aosta
PIAZZA DELLA ROVERE
L. Gianicolense
corso Vittorio Emanuele II
PIAZZA NAVONA
V. d. Seminario
Pantheon
L. Dei Sangallo
Via Giulia
V. d. Cestari
Viat Orti d'Alibert
Ponte Mazzini
Via Gregorio VII
Via d. Cava Aurelia
Viale delle Mura Aurelie
Palazzo Farnese
L. d. Tebaldi
V. Botteghe
Via di S. F. di Sales
L. d. Farnesina
V. della Lungara
MONTE DEL GIANICOLO
Ponte Sisto
L. dei Vallati
Via Arenula
Teatro Marcello
V. P. Sisto
L. Sanzio
L. dei Cenci
Ponte Garibaldi
Isola Tiberina
Ponte Cestio
Via Garibaldi
L. Anguillara
PIAZZA S. SONNINO
Pte. Palatino
0 500 yards
0 500 meters
Via Aurelia Antica
Villa Doria Pamphili
Via di S. Pancrazio
TRASTEVERE
Via Nicola Fabrizi
Via Glorioso
Via Dandolo
Viale di Trastevere
Via di S. Michele
L. Ripa
Ponte Sublicio
Lungotevere
Porto di Pipa Grande
Via Marmorata
Via Giacinto Carini
Via dei Quattro Venti
Via Alessandro Poerio
Via Cavalcanti
Via Portuense
L. Portuense
Lungotevere Testaccio
Via Giovanni Branca
Via Nicola Zabaglia
Via Galvani
Parco Testaccio
Ponte Testaccio
TESTACCIO
Stazione Magliana
Via d. Tre Fontane
TO CENTRAL ROME (5km)
Via C. Colombo
Palazzo della Civiltà del Lavoro
PIAZZALE D. NAZIONI
TO 60 & 61 (500m)
PIAZZA G. MARCONI
Palazzo dei Congressi
Viale Pasteur
Viale Europa
Viale Asia
Viale Civiltà Romana
V. Lincoln
Viale America
PIAZZA G. AGNELLI
Viale dell'Arte
Via Cristoforo Colombo
Via C. Colombo
Palazzo dello Sport
EUR

D
E
F
TO 47 (1.7km)
TO 54 (500m)
1
2
3
4
5
6
Villa Borghese
Vle. d. Belle Arti
Viale del Giardino Zoologico
Vle. G. Washington
Viale dei Cavalli Marini
Viale Aqua Felix
Pupazzi
Via d. Magnolie
Viale de Museo Borghese
Via d. S. Paolo d. Brasile
Via Pietro Raimondi
Via Pinciana
Vle. d. Muro Torto
Corso d'Italia
Via Salaria
Via Po
Via Adda
Villa Torlonia
Viale Regina Margherita
Via Arno
Via Isonzo
Via Savoia
Via Nizza
Via Alessandria
Via Dalmazia
Via Novaro
Via Nomentana
Via Lazzaro Spallanzani
Via Alessandro Torlonia
Via Giovanni
Via Siracusa
Via Bari
PIAZZA FIUME
PIAZZA PORTA PIA
Porta Pia
PIAZZA CROCE ROSSA
Via Piave
Via Romagna
Via Boncompagni
Via Piemonte
Via Sicilia
Via V. Veneto
Via Ludovisi
V. Sallustiano
Via XX Settembre
Via Montebello
Via Cernaia
Biblioteca Nazionale
Policlinico Universita
Via Treviso
Via Pavia
Viale Regina Elena
Via del Policlinico
Via dell' Università
Città Universita
Vle. d. Trinità dei Monti
Margutta
V. d. Croce
PIAZZA DI SPAGNA
Condotti
Via Frattina
Via d. Due Macelli
Via Sistina
PIAZZA BARBERINI
Via Barberini
Via d. Mercede
Via del Tritone
Via Rasella
Via d. Quattro Fontane
PIAZZA COLONNA
Via del Corso
Via d. Quirinale
Via Piacenza
Via Nazionale
Via Milano
Via Palermo
Via A. de Pretis
Via Cesare Balbo
Via d. Viminale
PIAZZA DELLA REPUBBLICA
PIAZZA DEL CINQUECENTO
Via Solferino
Via Palestro
Via Varese
Via Castro Pretorio
Stazione Termini
Via Marsala
Via dei Ramni
Via Tiburtina
Via dei Sardi
Via dei Marsi
PIAZZA SANTA MARIA MAGGIORE
Via Giovanni Giolitti
Via Cavour
Via Merulana
Via Principe Amadeo
Via Principe Umberto
Via IV Novembre
Plebiscito
PIAZZA VENEZIA
Oscure
Via d. Serpenti
Via Giovanni Lanza
PIAZZA VITTORIO EMANUELE
Via P. Eugenio
Via dei Fori Imperiali
Via del Teatro di Marcello
Forum
Viale del Monte Oppio
Via Mecenate Leopardi
Via Machiavelli
Via Emanuele Filiberto
Viale Manzoni
Via D. Pta. Maggiore
PIAZZA DI PTA. MAGGIORE
CAMPIDOGLIO
ESQUILINO
Via Ruggero
Via Galilei
Via S. Croce in Gerusalemme
Via Labicana
Colosseum
PIAZZA DEL COLOSSEO
Via Statilia
Villa Wolkonsky
Pierleoni
MONTE PALATINO
Via di S. Gregorio
Via Claudia
Via di S. Giov. in Laterano
Via Celimontana
P. DI SAN GIOVANNI IN LATERANO
Viale C. Felice
Aventino
Via dei Cerchi
Parco del Celio
Via di S. Stefano Rotondo
San Giovanni in Laterano
Via del Circo Massimo
CELIO
Via d. Laterani
Via Taranto
Via Sannio
Via Amiterno
Via Appia
Via Aosta
Via delle Terme di Caracalla
Porta di Metronia
Via dell'Amba Aradam
Via Magna Grecia
Via Ardea
AVENTINO
Via d. S. Prisca
Viale Aventino
Via Ipponio
P. DEI RE DI ROMA
Via Druso
Via Gallia
Via Cerveteri
Via Ceneda
Nuova
Terme di Caracalla
PZA. NUMA POMPILIO
Viale Metronio
Via Iberia
Via Etruria
Viale d. Piramide Cestia
Viale G. Baccelli
Viale di Terme di Caracella
Via di Porta Sebastiano
Via di Porta Latina
Via Satrico
Via Concordia
Via Acqui
PZA. OSTIENSE
Viale Giotto
Viale di Porta Ardeatina
Via Vetulonia
Via Solunto
Via Ostiense
TO 66 (1.8km)
Vle Marco Polo
TO EUR (SEE INSET, 5km)
TO 52 (50m)
Via Acacia
Via Siria
24 29 44 25 33 39 42 48 63 26 38 68 30 20 49 18 22 31 35 37 67 65 43 36 23 69 40 41 19 55 32 45 28 51 62 53 34 27 50 46 21

Rome: Major Museums and Monuments

see map on p. 66

MUSEUMS	
dell'Alto Medioevo, **57**	**inset**
d'Arte Moderna, **24**	**D1**
d'Arte e Tradizioni Populari, **56**	**inset**
Galleria Borghese, **44**	**E1**
Campidoglio (Capitoline), **23**	**D4**
Canonica, **32**	**D1**
di Civiltà Romana, **59**	**inset**
Galleria Colonna, **30**	**D3**
Galleria Corsini, **4**	**B4**
Doria Pamphilj, **20**	**C3**
Keats-Shelley Memorial House, **25**	**D2**
Mario Praz, **7**	**C3**
Nazionale d'Arte Moderna, **33**	**D3**
Nazionale d'Arte Orientale, **65**	**E4**
Nazionale Etrusco di Villa Giulia, **14**	**C1**
Nazionale Romano Palazzo Altemps, **64**	**C3**
Nazionale Romano Palazzo Massimo, **63**	**E3**
Nazionale Romano Terme di Diocleziano, **48**	**E2**
Palazzo Barberini, **42**	**D3**
Palazzo Venezia, **22**	**D4**
Preistorico ed Etnografico, **58**	**inset**
Galleria Spada, **8**	**C4**
Degli Stumenti Musicali, **55**	**F4**
Vatican Museums, **1**	**B2**
Villa Farnesina, **5**	**B4**

PLACES OF WORSHIP	
Abbazia delle Tre Fontane, **60**	**inset**
Il Gesù, **18**	**C4**
Pantheon, **12**	**C3**
S. Apostoli, **68**	**D3**
S. Cecilia in Trastevere, **13**	**C5**
S. Clemente, **51**	**E5**
S. Croce in Gerusalemme, **62**	**F5**
S. Giovanni in Laterano, **53**	**E5**
S. Marco (Piazza di Venezia), **22**	**D4**
S. Maria in Aracoeli, **67**	**D4**
S. Maria in Cosmedin, **19**	**C4**
S. Maria Maggiore, **49**	**E3**
S. Maria in Palmis, **52**	**E6**
S. Maria del Popolo, **10**	**C2**
S. Maria in Trastevere, **6**	**C5**
S. Paolo Furori le Mura, **66**	**D6**
S. Pietro (St. Peter's Basilica), **70**	**B3**
S. Pietro in Vincoli, **43**	**D4**
S. Stefano Rotondo, **50**	**E5**
S. Trinità dei Monti, **25**	**D2**
Sinagoga Ashkenazita, **15**	**C4**

ROMAN MONUMENTS	
Ara Pacis, **11**	**C2**
Arch of Constantine, **28**	**D4**
Basilica of Maxentius and Constantine, **40**	**D4**
Baths of Caracalla, **46**	**D6**
Baths of Diocletian, **48**	**E2**
Bocca della Verità, **19**	**C4**
Campidoglio (Capitoline), **23**	**D4**
Castel S. Angelo, **3**	**B3**
Catacombs:	
S. Agnese, **54**	**F1**
S. Callisto, **52**	**E6**
S. Domitilla, **52**	**E6**
S. Priscilla, **47**	**E1**
S. Sebastiano, **52**	**E6**
Circus Maximus, **34**	**D5**
Colosseo (Colosseum), **45**	**E4**
Domus Aurea, **69**	**E4**
Forum of Augustus, **37**	**D4**
Forum of Trajan and Trajan's Column, **31**	**D4**
The Forum, **36**	**D4**
Mausolueum of Augustus, **11**	**C2**
Palatine Hill, **32**	**D4**
President's House, **38**	**D3**
Pyramid (of Gaius Cestius), **21**	**D6**
Teatro Marcello, **16**	**C4**
Temple of Venus and Rome/S. Francesco Romana, **41**	**D4**
Trajan's Market, **35**	**D4**
Velabrum, **55**	**D4**
Via Appia Antica, **52**	**E6**

PARKS AND FOUNTAINS	
Cimitero Acattolico per gli Stranieri, **17**	**C6**
Fontana dei Quattro Fiumi (Fountain of the Four Rivers), **9**	**C3**
Fontana di Trevi, **26**	**D3**
Fontana del Tritone, **39**	**D2**
Giardino Zoologio, **29**	**D1**
Il Grotto delle Tre Fontane, **61**	**inset**
Orto Botanico, **2**	**B4**
Roseto Comunale, **27**	**D5**

PIAZZE	
Campo dei Fiori, **8**	**C4**
Piazza di Spagna, **25**	**D2**
Piazza Augusto Imperatore, **11**	**C2**
Piazza Barberini, **39**	**D2**
Piazza del Cinquecento, **48**	**E2**
Piazza del Colosseo, **45**	**E4**
Piazza Navona, **9**	**C3**
Piazza del Popolo, **10**	**C1**
Piazza della Rotonda, **12**	**C3**
Piazza Venezia, **22**	**D4**

ANCIENT CITY

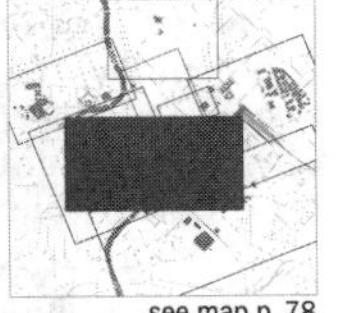
see map p. 78

In the midst of the countless, scattered stones, walls, and columns of the **Roman Forum** and the **Palatine** stands a small, truncated column. This spot was the **Umbilicus Urbis,** the "navel of the city," marking the geographical center of the ancient city. More than any other monument in Rome, it symbolizes the city's past status as the *ombelico del mondo*— the center of the West's political, economic, social, and religious life. Despite the ravages of time, the glory of Rome's history is still palpable. In a relatively small area, one can see the venues of Roman government, religion, entertainment, privilege, and even sanitation. Over the millennia, much of Rome's ancient heritage has been built upon, built over, reused, and modified; as a result, the ancient city presents visitors with an organic whole, where residences rest on ancient theaters, churches on ancient temples, and excavations proceed everywhere. Exploring the ancient city is time-consuming and involves a great deal of walking; **give yourself a full day to visit the Forum, Palatine, and Colosseum thoroughly.**

ROMAN FORUM

Main entrance: V.d. Fori Imperiali, at Largo C. Ricci, between P. Venezia and the Colosseum. Other entrances are opposite the Colosseum at the start of V. Sacra and at the Clivus Capitolinus, near P. del Campidoglio. M: B-Colosseo, or bus to P. Venezia. Open in summer M-Su 9am-7:15pm; in winter M-Su 9am-4pm; occasionally closes early. Free. Guided tour with archaeologist available at noon in English only, €3.50; audioguide tour for Forum in English, French, German, Italian, Japanese, or Spanish €4; both available at "biglietteria palatino" located at the end of V. Nova past the Arch of Titus. Access to the Forum is unpredictable–many areas are fenced off for excavation or restoration at irregular intervals.

The Forum— once a marshland prone to flooding and eschewed by Rome's Iron Age (1000-900 BC) inhabitants— spreads from the Colosseum west toward the Capitoline Hill. Today, many of the Forum's structures are reduced to piles of jagged rocks, and the locations of many sites are uncertain.

In the 7th and 8th centuries BC, Etruscans and Greeks used Tiber Island as a crossing point for trade and the Forum as a market. Rome itself was founded as a market town for sober farmers who came to trade and perform religious rites; the Romans were peacefully dominated by the more advanced Etruscans until 510 BC, when the Republic was established. The **Curia,** the meeting place of the Senate; the **Comitium Well,** or assembly place; and the **Rostra,** the speaker's platform, were built here to serve the young government. Across Via Sacra, Rome's oldest street, temples to Saturn, Castor, and Pollux were dedicated in honor of the revolution. The conquest of Greece in the 2nd century BC brought new architectural forms to the city. The lofty **Basilica Aemilia** was used as a center for business and judicial work before Christians transformed it and many of the existing structures in the Forum into churches.

The Forum was never reserved for any single activity. Senators debated the fates of far-flung nations over the din of haggling traders. The **Vestal Virgins** kept the city's eternal flame burning in their house on a street full of prostitutes. Elsewhere, priests offered sacrifices in the temples, generals led triumphal processions up to the Capitoline, and pickpockets relieved tourists of their possessions. Some things never change.

The Forum witnessed political turbulence in the Republic in the first century BC. **Cicero's** orations against the antics of corrupt young aristocrats echoed off the temple walls and **Julius Caesar's** dead body was cremated, amid rioting crowds, in the small temple that bears his name. Augustus, Caesar's great-nephew and adopted son, exploited the Forum to support his new government, closing off the old town square with a temple to the newly deified Caesar and building a triumphal arch honoring himself. His successors followed suit, clotting the old markets with successively grander tokens of their majesty (often looted from the monuments of their predecessors). The construction of the imperial palace on the Palatine in the first century AD and of new *fora* on higher ground to the north cleared out the old neighborhoods around the square, so that, by the 2nd century, the Forum, though packed with gleaming white monuments, had become a deserted ceremonial space. A century later, emperor Constantine's Christian city government closed the pagan temples. By the 5th century the looting of the Forum by barbarians attested to Rome's dramatic decline.

In the Middle Ages many buildings were converted to churches and alms houses; the Forum gradually became Campo Vaccino, a cow pasture, with only the tallest columns peeking through the tall grass. The last bits of the Forum's accessible marble were quarried by Renaissance popes for their own monumental constructions. Excavations since 1803 have uncovered a vast array of remnants, but also rendered the site extremely confusing—the ruins of structures built over and on top of each other for more than a thousand years are now exposed to a single view.

CIVIC CENTER

The Forum's main entrance ramp leads directly to V. Sacra. To your immediate left is the Temple of Antoninus and Faustina. To the right, the Capitoline Hill and the Arch of Septimius Severus stand in the distance. V. Sacra cuts through the old market square and civic center; the Basilica Aemilia is to your immediate right, and the brick Curia building is just beyond.

BASILICA AEMILIA

Completed in 179 BC, the Basilica Aemilia was the judicial center of ancient Rome. It also housed the guild of the *argentarii* (money-changers), who operated the city's first *cambiomat* and provided Roman *denarii* for traders and tourists (doubtless at the same great rates found today at Termini). The basilica was damaged several times by fire and rebuilt; in the pavement you can see bronze marks from the melted coins lost in these blazes. In AD 410, the basilica received its death blows from Alaric and his raiding Goths, and the broken bases of columns are all that remain of the interior. The foundations of the row of *tabernae* (shops) that once faced the Forum are still visible along the path. In the back right corner of the basilica are reliefs of the *Rape of the Sabine Women* and the *Death of Tarpeia.*

CURIA

Mussolini's restorations revealed an inlaid marble pavement and long steps where Roman senators placed their own chairs for meetings; even prior to this work, the Curia (to the left of the Basilica Aemilia as you face it) enjoyed the distinction of being one of the oldest and most significant buildings in the Forum. Tullus Hostilius, the third king of Rome, started putting marble in place for the first Curia, but the current building dates to Diocletian's reign (AD 283). In 630 it was converted to a church. The stone base shows where Augustus's legendary golden statue of Victory rested until the end of the 4th century, when Christian senators irked by paganism had the statue destroyed. The Curia also houses the **Plutei of Trajan,** two sculpted parapets that decorated the Rostrum, depicting the burning of the tax registers and the distribution of food to poor children. To the left of the Curia is the **Church of Santi Luca e Martina,** once the **Secretarium Senatus.** Farther up the hill, below the **Church of San Giuseppe dei Falegnami,** is the 2nd century BC **Mamertine Prison** (p. 85), where St. Peter is said to have been imprisoned and miraculously summoned water to appear in order to baptize his cellmates.

COMITIUM

The broad space in front of the Curia was the Comitium, where male citizens came to vote and representatives of the people gathered for public discussion. This space was also home to the famed **Twelve Tables,** bronze tablets upon which the first codified laws of the Republic were inscribed. To the left of the Arch of Septimius Severus is the large brick **Rostrum,** or speaker's platform, erected by Julius Caesar in 44 BC (just before his death). The term *rostra* refers to the metal ramrods on the bows of warships. *Rostra* from warships captured at Antium in 342 BC decorated the platform. The literal *rostrum* is gone, but regularly spaced holes in its platform remain. Senators and consuls orated to the Roman plebes from here, and any citizen could mount to voice his opinion (theoretically, at least). After his assassination, Cicero's head and hands were displayed here as a warning to those who practiced unbridled free speech. Augustus's rebellious daughter Julia is said to have voiced her objections to her father's legislation promoting family values by engaging in amorous activities with Augustus's enemies on the spot where the laws had been announced.

ARCH OF SEPTIMIUS SEVERUS

The hefty Arch of Septimius Severus stands between the Comitium and the slopes of the Capitoline Hill. Dedicated in AD 203 to celebrate the emperor's victories in the Middle East, the arch is covered with reliefs that depict the imperial family. After Caracalla, Severus's restless son and successor, grabbed the throne by killing his brother Geta and scraping his name and portrait off of the arch. Directly behind the arch the grey tufa walls of the **Tabularium** line the rear of the Forum. Once a repository for the Senate's archives, this structure now serves as the basement of the Renaissance **Palazzo dei Senatori.**

MARKET SQUARE

The original market square (in front of the Curia) was occupied by a number of shrines and sacred precincts. Immediately down the stairs from the Curia lies the **Lapis Niger** (Black Stone), surrounded by a circle of bricks. Republican Romans believed this is where the legendary founder of the city, Romulus, was murdered. Modern scholars now think the Lapis Niger was actually an early shrine to Vulcan. The shrine was considered passé even during the Republic, when its statuary and columns were covered by gray pavement. Below the Lapis Niger rest the underground ruins of a 6th-century BC altar, along with a pyramidal pillar where the oldest known Latin inscription in Rome warns the public against defiling the shrine. In front of the Rostrum, half-way between the Curia and the **Basilica Julia,** the **Three Sacred Trees** of Rome—olive, fig, and grape—have been replanted by the Italian state (never mind that grapes grow on vines).

The "newest" part of the Forum is the **Column of Phocas,** erected in 608 to celebrate the visiting Byzantine emperor, Phocas—a sacrilege that would have probably made early Republican Romans roll over in their graves. The marketplace may also have been home to three important markers: the Umbilicus Urbis, the Golden Milestone, and the Vulcanal. The exact locations of these, which not only marked the center of the city, but also that of the entire Roman world, is a matter of speculation.

LOWER FORUM

To the south of the Arch of Septimius Severus lie the Basilica Julia and the three extant temples of the lower Forum: the Temple of Saturn, the Temple of Castor and Pollux, and the Temple of the Deified Julius. The remnants of these ancient monuments are across the Market Square from the Curia and the Basilica Aemilia.

TEMPLE OF SATURN

Eight columns mark the Temple of Saturn, one of the first buildings constructed in Rome. The Romans believed that Saturn had taught them the art of agriculture, and filled his statue inside the temple with fresh olive oil. The temple was the site of Saturnalia, the Roman winter bash that signified the end of the year. During this raucous party, class and social distinctions were blurred as masters served slaves.

Behind the temple are (left to right): twelve columns of the **Portico of the Dei Consentes** dedicated to the twelve most important Roman gods; the three Corinthian columns of the **Temple of Vespatian,** completed by his son Domitian; and the foundations of the **Temple of Concord,** which was built to celebrate the peace between patricians and plebeians in 367 BC.

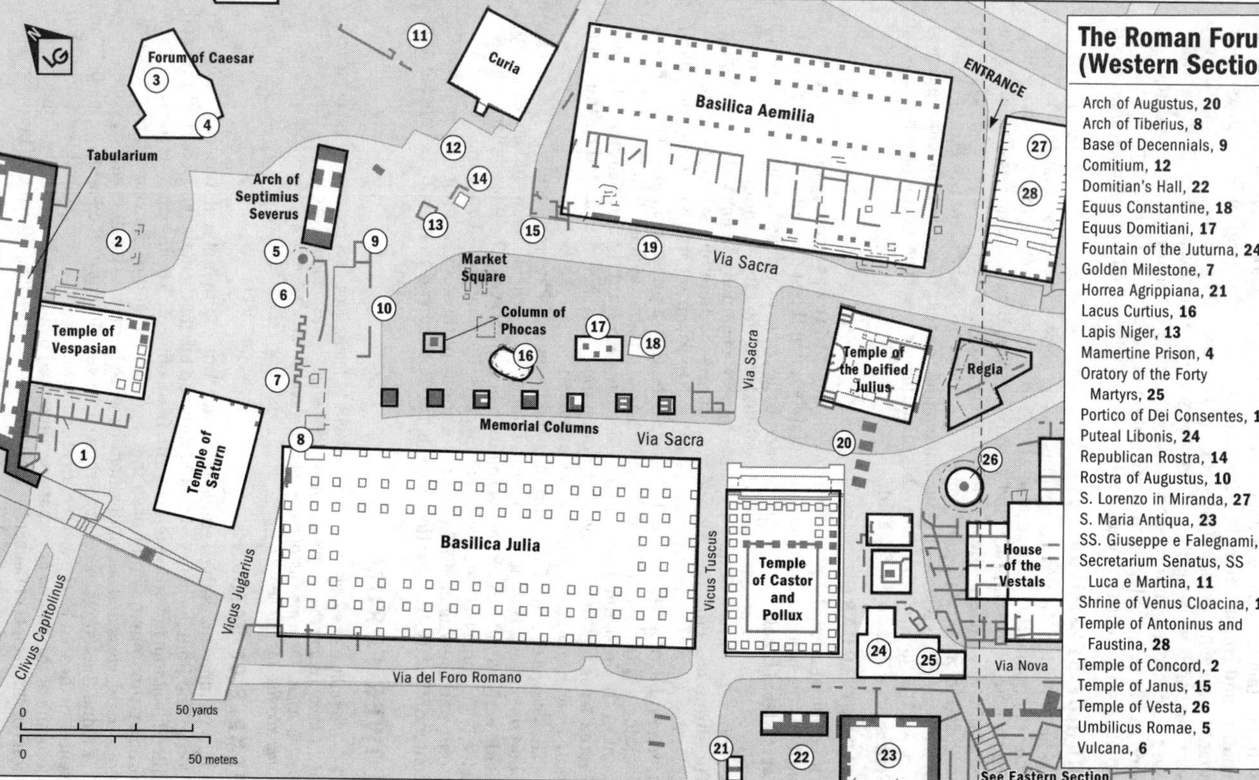
The Roman Forum (Western Section)
Arch of Augustus, 20
Arch of Tiberius, 8
Base of Decennials, 9
Comitium, 12
Domitian's Hall, 22
Equus Constantine, 18
Equus Domitiani, 17
Fountain of the Juturna, 24
Golden Milestone, 7
Horrea Agrippiana, 21
Lacus Curtius, 16
Lapis Niger, 13
Mamertine Prison, 4
Oratory of the Forty Martyrs, 25
Portico of Dei Consentes, 1
Puteal Libonis, 24
Republican Rostra, 14
Rostra of Augustus, 10
S. Lorenzo in Miranda, 27
S. Maria Antiqua, 23
SS. Giuseppe e Falegnami, 3
Secretarium Senatus, SS Luca e Martina, 11
Shrine of Venus Cloacina, 19
Temple of Antoninus and Faustina, 28
Temple of Concord, 2
Temple of Janus, 15
Temple of Vesta, 26
Umbilicus Romae, 5
Vulcana, 6
Forum of Caesar
Tabularium
Curia
Basilica Aemilia
ENTRANCE
Arch of Septimius Severus
Market Square
Via Sacra
Temple of Vespasian
Column of Phocas
Temple of the Deified Julius
Regia
Temple of Saturn
Memorial Columns
Basilica Julia
Vicus Tuscus
Temple of Castor and Pollux
House of the Vestals
Vicus Jugarius
Clivus Capitolinus
Via del Foro Romano
Via Nova
50 yards
50 meters
See Eastern Section

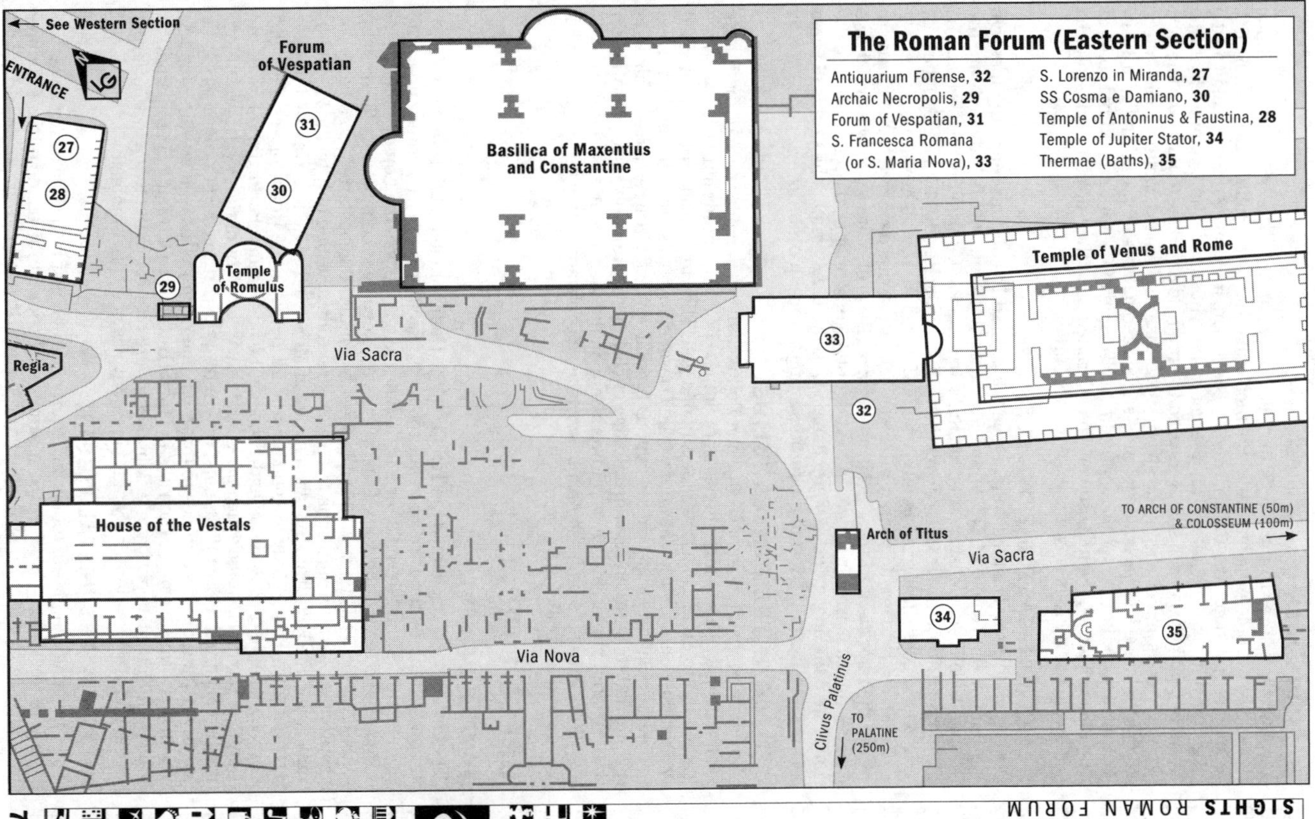
The Roman Forum (Eastern Section)
Antiquarium Forense, 32
Archaic Necropolis, 29
Forum of Vespatian, 31
S. Francesca Romana (or S. Maria Nova), 33
S. Lorenzo in Miranda, 27
SS Cosma e Damiano, 30
Temple of Antoninus & Faustina, 28
Temple of Jupiter Stator, 34
Thermae (Baths), 35
See Western Section
ENTRANCE
Forum of Vespatian
Basilica of Maxentius and Constantine
Temple of Romulus
Temple of Venus and Rome
Regia
Via Sacra
House of the Vestals
Arch of Titus
Via Nova
Clivus Palatinus
TO PALATINE (250m)
TO ARCH OF CONSTANTINE (50m) & COLOSSEUM (100m)

BASILICA JULIA

Around the corner to the left of the Temple of Saturn, rows of deserted column bases are the sole remains of the Basilica Julia. Begun by Julius Caesar in 54 BC, completed by Augustus, and restored by Diocletian, it followed the same plan as the Basilica Aemilia (see above) on a larger scale. The central hall, flanked by three rows of columns on each side, was used by tribunals of judges to lay down the law. Look for grids and circles in the steps where anxious Romans, waiting to go before the judge, played an ancient version of snakes and ladders. If you've had your fill of culture, the end of the basilica opposite the Temple of Castor and Pollux is part of the **Cloaca Maxima,** the huge sewer which drained from the Forum directly into the Tiber. Do not try to avail yourself of this resource.

TEMPLE OF CASTOR & POLLUX

At the end of the Basilica Julia, three white marble columns mark the massive podium of the **Temple of Castor and Pollux,** dedicated in 484 BC to celebrate the Roman rebellion against their tyrannical Etruscan king, Tarquinius Superbus. The Romans attributed their victory over the Latins at Lake Regillus in 499 BC to the help of the twin gods Castor and Pollux, who outflanked the mortal Etruscans.

Legend says that immediately after the battle the twins appeared in the Forum to water their horses at the nearby **Lacus Juturnae** (Basin of Juturna). Now marked by a reconstructed marble *aedicula* to the left of the gods' temple, the site was once the location of the ancient city's water company. Behind the temple, the **Church of Santa Maria Antiqua** is the oldest in the forum, dating to the 6th century.

TEMPLE OF THE DEIFIED JULIUS

Across from the Temple of Castor and Pollux is the rectangular base of the **Temple of the Deified Julius,** which Augustus built in 29 BC to honor his murdered adoptive father and to proclaim himself the son of a god. The circular altar of rocks housed within the temple marks the spot where Caesar's body was cremated in 44 BC, and where Marcus Aurelius gave his famous funeral speech. Little remains of this temple beyond the altar and its surrounding enclave which are now covered with a tin roof. Wistful monarchists leave flowers here on the Ides of March. In his own modest glory, Augustus built the **Arch of Augustus,** a triple arch (only the bases are visible now) that straddled V. Sacra.

UPPER FORUM

TEMPLE OF VESTA

The circular building behind the Temple of the Deified Julius is the Temple of Vesta, originally built by the Etruscans but rebuilt by Septimius Severus at the end of the 2nd century AD. Designed after a Latin hut, the temple was the home of the Vestal Virgins, who tended the sacred fire of the city, keeping it continuously lit for more than 1000 years (when it went out in the 4th century, things started to go badly for the Romans). Within one of the temple's secret rooms, visited only by the Vestal Virgins, stood the **Palladium,** the small statue of Minerva that Aeneas was said to have brought from Troy to Italy. Behind the temple, between the House of Vestal Virgins and the Temple of Antoninus and Faustina, lies the triangular **Regia,** office of the Pontifex Maximus, Rome's high priest and titular ancestor of the Pope. Long before the first Pontifex (Numa Pompilius) took it over, as early as the 6th century BC, the Regia was the site of sacrifices to the gods of agriculture (as well as Mars, Jupiter, Juno, and Janus). One of the rites performed was the October harvest ritual, in which the tail and genitalia of a slain horse were brought to the Regia in an offering to the god of vegetation. Sadly, this ceremony has been discontinued.

HOUSE OF THE VESTAL VIRGINS

The sprawling complex of rooms and courtyards behind the Temple of Vesta was the House of Vestal Virgins. Here, in spacious seclusion in the shade of the Palatine, lived the six virgins who officiated over Vesta's rites, chosen for their purity and physical perfection and ordained at the age of seven. As long as they kept their vows of chastity, the Vestal Virgins were among the most respected citizens of ancient Rome; they were the only women allowed to walk unaccompanied in the Forum and could protect or pardon anyone. This easy life had its price; if a virgin strayed from celibacy, she was buried alive with a loaf of bread and a candle on the assumption that the sustenance that it provided would give her time to contemplate her sins during her prolonged death. Only a handful of women met this fate.

Off-and-on restoration often means that visitors can only peer through the iron gates surrounding the House of the Vestal Virgins. Still, there is a view (head up to the Palatine to get a really good view) of the central courtyard where statues of the priestesses who served between AD 291 and 364 reside, including one whose name was scraped away (8th on the left as you enter the courtyard). The erased priestess is thought to have been Claudia, the Vestal Virgin who, at the end of the 4th century, converted to that new-fangled religion from the south, Christianity.

TEMPLE OF ANTONINUS & FAUSTINA

Back on V. Sacra is the Temple of Antoninus and Faustina (opposite the Temple of Vesta, to the immediate right as you face the entrance ramp), whose strong foundation, columns, and rigid lattice ceiling have preserved it unusually well over the ages. In the 7th and 8th centuries, the **Church of San Lorenzo in Miranda** was built in the interior of the abandoned temple. The temple's columns and frieze were incorporated into the Christian structure. This is not to say that the Christian rulers didn't try to destroy the pagan temple: the deep grooves at the top of the columns show where cables were tied in attempts to demolish this steadfast symbol of pagan worship. The original building was constructed by Emperor Antoninus and dedicated to his wife Faustina (his name was added after his death in AD 161.). In the shadow of the temple (to the right as you face it) is an archaic **necropolis,** with Iron Age graves dating to between the 10th and 8th centuries BC, which lend credence to Rome's legendary founding date of 753 BC. The bodies from the ancient graveyard were found in hollow tree trunks. The remains are visible in the Antiquarium (see **Velia,** below).

TEMPLE OF ROMULUS

Closed to the public.

Farther up V. Sacra stands the round Temple of Romulus, which retains its original bronze doors, with a working lock, from the 4th century AD. The name of the structure, however, is misleading for two reasons. First, the "Romulus" in question here was probably the son of the 4th-century emperor, Maxentius, not the legendary founder of Rome. Second, the temple probably wasn't a temple at all but an office of the urban magistrate during the Empire. The temple now houses the **Church of Santi Cosma e Damiano** (p. 83). Across V. Sacra from the structure, remains of fortifications from between 730 and 540 BC have been discovered. Behind the temple, recently excavated ruins of Vespatian's **Forum Pacis** (Forum of Peace) are visible along V.d. Fori Imperiali, beginning just past the main entrance.

VELIA

Take V. Sacra out of the Forum proper, toward the Arch of Titus.

BASILICA OF MAXENTIUS AND CONSTANTINE

The Antiquarium Forense is to the right of the front entrance to the Church of Santa Francesca Romana. Open daily 9am-6:30pm, but subject to unannounced closures. Free.

The gargantuan Basilica of Maxentius and Constantine is on the left as you walk down V. Sacra. The three gaping arches that remain are only the side chapels for an enormous central hall, whose coffered ceiling covered the entire gravel court and three chapels on the other side. Emperor Maxentius began construction of the basilica in 306, but was overthrown by Constantine at the Battle of Milvian Bridge in 312 before its completion. Constantine oversaw completion of the basilica, but refrained from converting it into a church despite his conversion to Christianity, out of reverence for the pagan traditions of the Forum. He built the basilica of **San Giovanni in Laterano** instead, based on a similar architectural plan (see p. 136). Constantine's new religious piety failed to impact the size of his inflated ego. The middle apse of the basilica once contained a gigantic statue of him; the body was bronze, and the head, legs, and arms were marble. The remains that were found (on exhibit at the **Museo Capitolino;** see p. 168) include a 6½ ft. long foot. The enormous statue met a less exalted end in the 7th century, when all the bronze in the basilica was melted down to cover the first basilica of St. Peter's.

The Baroque facade of the **Church of Santa Francesca Romana** is built over Hadrian's Temple to Venus and Rome *(Amor* and *Roma)*. It hides the entrance to the **Antiquarium Forense,** a small museum that houses artifacts from the Forum. Among the items on display are skeletons from the *necropolis*.

ARCH OF TITUS

On the summit of the Velian hill, where V. Sacra intersects with the road down from the Palatine, is the Arch of Titus, built in AD 81 by Domitian to celebrate his brother Titus's destruction of Jerusalem 10 years earlier. Though the paranoid Frangipane family turned it into a fortified tower in the Middle Ages, Pope Pius VII ordered it restored to its original state in 1821. On the interior of the arch is a famous frieze depicting Titus's victory and the treasure he took from the Great Temple, which appears to have been spent by Titus on the construction of the Colosseum.

THE COLOSSEUM

M: B-Colosseo. Open daily May-Oct. 9am-6:30pm; Nov.-Apr. 9am-4pm. €8 for a combined ticket to the Colosseum and the Palatine Hill, EU citizens 18-24 €4, EU citizens under 18 and over 65 free. To avoid long lines at the Colosseum, buy tickets at entrance to the Palatine Hill in the Roman Forum. 7-day Archaeologia Card good for entrance to the four Musei Nazionali Romani, the Colosseum, the Palatine Hill, the Terme di Diocleziano, and the Crypti Balbi. €20, EU citizens 18-24 €10, EU citizens under 18 and over 65 free. Tours with archaeologist €3.50; audioguide in English, French, German, Italian, Japanese, or Spanish €4.

The Colosseum is the enduring symbol of the Eternal City—a hollowed-out ghost of travertine marble that dwarfs every other antiquity in Rome by reputation, if not by sheer size alone. Recently completed renovations have cleaned the exterior and reconstructed several missing sections (in brick instead of marble, unfortunately) to give a better sense of what the ancient amphitheater looked like, although the interior is still barren. Use your imagination (or scenes from *Gladiator*), or pick up an audioguide (*telefonini* on steroids) to make the visit more interesting. The city of Rome does its part to make the Colosseum come alive by hiring poor souls to dress up as gladiators and centurions outside, as well as the occasional historically inaccurate but provocatively dressed gladiatoress. They're amusing enough to look at, but what they want is to have their picture taken with you for a cool €5. Enter on the lowest level of seating (the arena floor is off-limits) and take stairs to the upper level.

The term "Colosseum" is actually a nickname for the *Amphitheatrum Flavium*, which Vespatian began building in AD 72 to block out the private lake that Nero had installed. The nickname derives from the colossal bronze statue of Nero as sun-god that used to grace the area next to the amphitheater (see the **Domus Aurea,** p. 81). The Colosseum was completed in 80 by Titus, with spoils from the emperors' campaigns in Judaea. Titus allegedly threw a monster bash for its inauguration: a 100-day fête that saw 5000 wild beasts perish in the bloody arena (from the Latin for sand, *harena*, which was put on the floor to absorb blood). Though the maximum capacity is still debatable, it is thought that the Colosseum was capable of hosting crowds of at least 50,000. Because the Colosseum events took place for the "public good," tickets to see the slaughter were always free.

Chances are that the house was packed for Trajan's celebration of his Dacian victories, when 10,000 gladiators and 11,000 beasts duked it out for a month. Over the centuries, it wasn't only gladiator fights that filled the arena: in the mornings, as a warm-up for the evening's battles, exotic animal hunts were a huge draw. It's also said that the elliptical interior was flooded for sea battles, although some archaeologists and native Romans insist that it would have been impossible, citing the Circus Maximus as the more probable locale. Gladiatorial games were suspended in 438 by a Christian-dominated empry and Senate, and animal hunts soon bit the dust as well. The Colosseum was used briefly as a fortress in the Middle Ages and as a quarry in the Renaissance, when popes, beginning with Urban VIII, pillaged marble for use in their own grandiose enterprises, including St. Peter's Basilica (see p. 115) and Palazzo Barberini (see p. 109). The former pagan symbol became the site of Christian liturgical rites in the 17th and 18th centuries, and a chapel and rows of crosses were eventually built on the north end of the hollowed-out amphitheater. The crosses were removed in the 19th century when excavations began on the Colosseum, leaving the structure, with the exception of the ongoing exterior renovations, as it is today.

The outside of the arena, with the layers of Doric, Ionic, and Corinthian columns, was considered the ideal orchestration of the classical architectural orders, from the most staid to the most ornamental. On the outer side opposite the entrance, look for five marble posts on the edge of the pavement. These posts are remnants of anchors for a giant *velarium*, the retractable shade that once covered the amphitheater. During each game, 1000 naval troops operated the *velarium*. Inside, the tremendous wooden floor is gone, revealing brick cells, corridors, ramps, and elevators that were used to transport wild animals from their cages up to the arena level.

Note the large cross across from the side entrance. It symbolizes the Colosseum's escape from total destruction at the hands of pillagers by a lucky mistake. The Pope, in order to commemorate the martyrdom of the thousands of Christians supposedly killed in the amphitheater, declared the monument a sacred place and forbade any more demolition. Since that time, it has been discovered that no Christians had been killed in the Colosseum. These days, in fact, the Pope holds occasional masses there. Additionally, in the summer of 2000, the Colosseum was used as a stage for several Italian TV variety show extravaganzas as well as Greek drama and classical music performances. Organizers bragged that it was the first time in 15 centuries that it had been used as an entertainment venue, though the maximum audience of 700 for these events paled by comparison to the arena's former glory.

ARCH OF CONSTANTINE

Between the Colosseum and the Palatine Hill, marking the tail end of the V. Sacra, is the Arch of Constantine, one of the latest and best-preserved imperial monuments in the area. The Senate dedicated the arch in AD 315 to commemorate Constantine's victory over his rival Maxentius at the Battle of the Milvian Bridge in 312 (see **History**, p. 45). The arch's friezes show how heartfelt that dedication actually was: one side's images depict life in Constantine's camps and images of war; on the other side, the images depict life after Constantine's victory and the virtues of peace and humanity. There are a few rough 4th-century friezes that demonstrate just how much Roman sculptural art declined from the onset of the millennium, but otherwise the triple arch is cobbled together almost entirely from sculptural fragments pilfered from earlier Roman monuments. The four sad-looking men near the top, for example, are Dacian prisoners taken from one of Trajan's memorials; the medallions once belonged to a monument for Hadrian and include depictions of his lover, Antinous; the rest of the scatterings celebrate the military prowess of Marcus Aurelius.

PALATINE HILL

The Palatine rises to the south of the Forum. Open daily 9am-7:15pm; in winter daily 9am-4pm; sometimes closes M-F 3pm, Su and holidays noon. Last entrance 45min. before closing. Combined ticket to the Palatine Hill and the Colosseum €8; EU citizens between 18 and 24 €4;

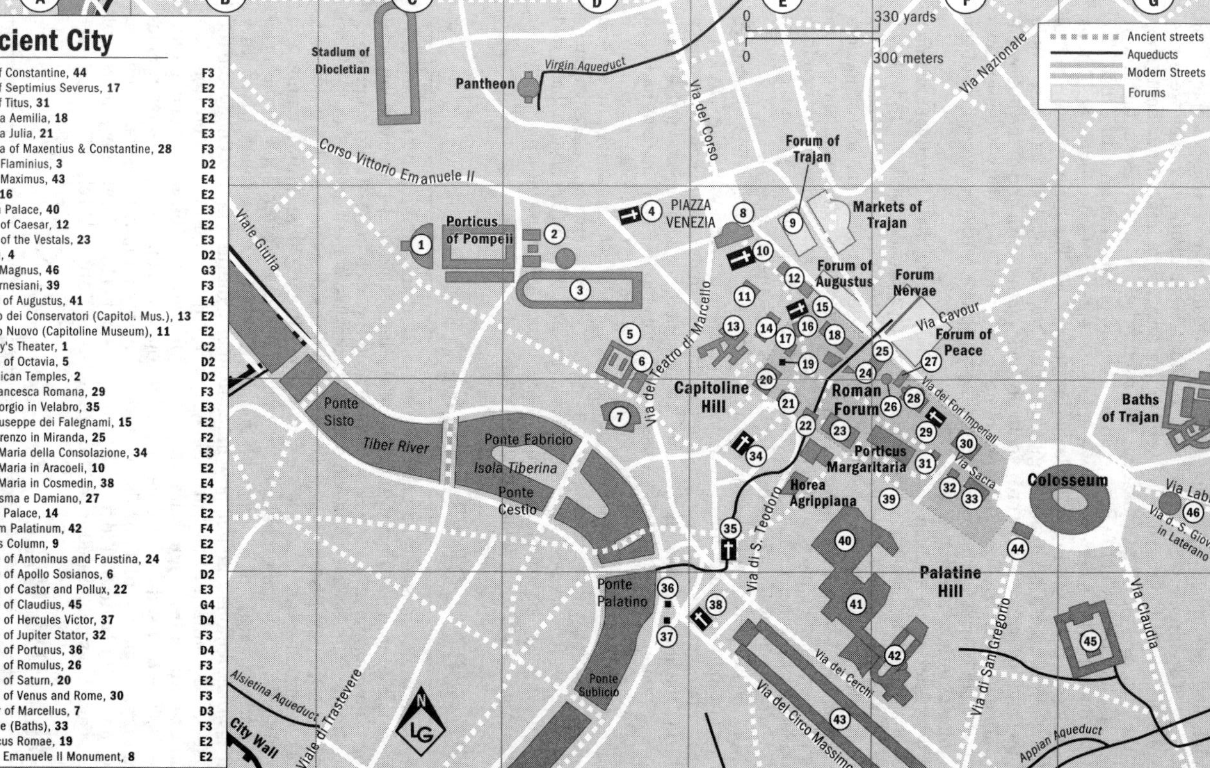
Ancient City
Arch of Constantine, 44 F3
Arch of Septimius Severus, 17 E2
Arch of Titus, 31 F3
Basilica Aemilia, 18 E2
Basilica Julia, 21 E3
Basilica of Maxentius & Constantine, 28 F3
Circus Flaminius, 3 D2
Circus Maximus, 43 E4
Curia, 16 E2
Flavian Palace, 40 E3
Forum of Caesar, 12 E2
House of the Vestals, 23 E3
Il Gesu, 4 D2
Ludus Magnus, 46 G3
Orti Farnesiani, 39 F3
Palace of Augustus, 41 E4
Palazzo dei Conservatori (Capitol. Mus.), 13 E2
Palazzo Nuovo (Capitoline Museum), 11 E2
Pompey's Theater, 1 C2
Portico of Octavia, 5 D2
Republican Temples, 2 D2
San Francesca Romana, 29 F3
San Giorgio in Velabro, 35 E3
San Giuseppe dei Falegnami, 15 E2
San Lorenzo in Miranda, 25 F2
Santa Maria della Consolazione, 34 E3
Santa Maria in Aracoeli, 10 E2
Santa Maria in Cosmedin, 38 E4
SS. Cosma e Damiano, 27 F2
Senate Palace, 14 E2
Stadium Palatinum, 42 F4
Trajan's Column, 9 E2
Temple of Antoninus and Faustina, 24 E2
Temple of Apollo Sosianos, 6 D2
Temple of Castor and Pollux, 22 E3
Temple of Claudius, 45 G4
Temple of Hercules Victor, 37 D4
Temple of Jupiter Stator, 32 F3
Temple of Portunus, 36 D4
Temple of Romulus, 26 F3
Temple of Saturn, 20 E2
Temple of Venus and Rome, 30 F3
Theater of Marcellus, 7 D3
Thermae (Baths), 33 F3
Umbilicus Romae, 19 E2
Vittorio Emanuele II Monument, 8 E2
Ancient streets
Aqueducts
Modern Streets
Forums
0 330 yards
0 300 meters
Stadium of Diocletian
Pantheon
Virgin Aqueduct
Via del Corso
Corso Vittorio Emanuele II
Via Nazionale
Forum of Trajan
Markets of Trajan
PIAZZA VENEZIA
Porticus of Pompeii
Viale Giulia
Forum of Augustus
Forum Nervae
Via Cavour
Forum of Peace
Via del Teatro di Marcello
Capitoline Hill
Roman Forum
Via dei Fori Imperiali
Baths of Trajan
Ponte Sisto
Tiber River
Ponte Fabricio
Isola Tiberina
Ponte Cestio
Porticus Margaritaria
Via Sacra
Colosseum
Via Labicana
Via d. S. Giovanni in Laterano
Horea Agrippiana
Via di S. Teodoro
Palatine Hill
Ponte Palatino
Via Claudia
Via di San Gregorio
Via dei Cerchi
Via del Circo Massimo
Ponte Sublicio
Alsietina Aqueduct
Viale di Trastevere
City Wall
Appian Aqueduct

EU citizens under 18 and over 65 free. Guided tour at noon, in English only, €3.50; €2.50 with Archeologia Card. May be purchased at the "biglietteria palatino," located at the end of V. Nova past the Arch of Titus, or 100 yards down V.d. S. Gregorio from the Colosseum. Visit the Palatine after the Forum; you will better appreciate the views of the Forum having seen it up close. Sections of the "Orti Farnesini," the hills best for viewing, as well as the Houses of Augustus and Livia are closed for renovations through the summer of 2004.

The Palatine offers— for the rather steep admission price— not only vast temples and imperial palaces, but also some of the best views of ancient Rome imaginable. Striking views aside, the hill, a square plateau rising between the Tiber and the Forum, contains some of the oldest and "newest" Roman ruins. As early as the 1500s, Palatine became the site of research concerned with Rome's imperial past; excavations continue to this day.

Arch of Constantine

The first and final chapters of the ancient Empire unfolded atop the Palatine's heights. The she-wolf that suckled Romulus and Remus had her den here, and it was here that Romulus built the first walls and houses of the city, a legend corroborated by the discovery of 9th-century BC huts on the southeastern side of the hill. During the Republic, the Palatine was the city's most fashionable residential quarter, where aristocrats and statesmen, including Cicero and Marc Anthony, built their homes. In 36 BC, with the construction of his relatively modest house, Octavian Augustus transformed the hill into the official residence of emperors. Later emperors, starting with Nero, built progressively more luxurious palaces illustrative of their absolute power. By the middle of the first century AD, Palatine was transformed into a gargantuan palace complex; indeed, the hill's Latin name, Palatium, became synonymous with the palace that dominated it. After the fall of Rome, the hill suffered the same fate as the Forum, although Byzantine ambassadors and even popes sometimes set up house in the crumbling palace.

Palatine Hill

ORTI FARNESIANI

Take your first right as you start up the hill from the Arch of Titus.

The Orti Farnesiani opened in 1625 as the first botanical gardens in the world. They were built on the foundations of Augustus's imperial palace. For incredible Forum views, follow the signs for the *"Affacciata sul Foro."* At the end opposite from the Forum, terraces look down on several structures that are currently being excavated (and will likely be off-limits through 2004). On the far right are the foundations of the Temple of

A Roman Forum

Cybele, constructed in 204 BC on the orders of a prophecy from a Sibylline book. Immediately to its left are the remains of a 9th-century BC village, the **Casa di Romulo** (House of Romulus). The Iron Age inhabitants (who may well have included the legendary twin) built their oval huts out of wood; all that remains are the holes they sunk into the tufa bedrock for their roofposts.

Left of the temple is the **House of Livia.** Livia was Augustus's wife, the first Roman empress, and according to Robert Graves's *I, Claudius,* an "abominable grandmother." She had the house, with its vestibule, courtyard, and three vaulted living rooms, connected to the **House of Augustus** next door. Along the pathways between the House of Livia and the House of Augustus, excavation and restoration continue on rooms once lined with marble and gold.

IMPERIAL COMPLEX

Descending the stairs from the terrace to the Domitian's (AD 81-96) imperial complex, you cross the long, spooky **Cryptoporticus,** a tunnel that connected Tiberius's palace with the buildings nearby. Used by slaves and imperial couriers as a secret passage, it was built by Nero in one of his more paranoid moments. The mosaic tiles lining the tunnel remain in excellent condition, one of the few surviving remnants of Nero's famed "Golden House." Domitian, equally paranoid about the threat of assassination, incorporated the secret passageway into his own palace as a potential escape route. Unfortunately, the tunnel was unable to prevent his eventual assasination at the hands of his wife and bodyguard.

DOMUS FLAVIA

The sprawling Domus Flavia is the former site of a gigantic octagonal fountain that occupied almost the entire courtyard. The building was divided into three halls, and was used by the emperor for a variety of social, political, and religious functions. It was also the site of a huge throne room where Domitian could preside over public audiences. He clearly had a thing for fountains, because the ruins of a smaller, elliptical one remain intact next to the sunken **Triclinium,** where imperial banquets were held between a set of twin oval fishponds. On the other side of the Triclinium, a walkway offers sweeping views of the grassy **Circus Maximus** (see p. 82) and, farther to the left, the **Baths of Caracalla** (see p. 85).

DOMUS AUGUSTANA

Next door, stands Domus Augustana, which served as the first emperor's court, and was constructed on Palatine's most sacred site, where, according to legend, Romulus founded the city. The exterior walls that remain are so high that archaeologists are still unsure how they were roofed over. The structure, based on a Hellenistic palace, was built on the side of the hill, with three floors descending below the level of the main hall, including a sunken courtyard with a fishpond. The emperor's quarters were in the maze of staircases and corridors behind the courtyard leading toward the side of the hill. Farther down the hill were the **Paedagogium,** the servants' quarters, and the **Domus Praeconum,** which served as the palace's physical plant.

HIPPODROME

Perhaps the most visible ruins on the Palatine are in the east wing of the palace, where the Stadium Palatinum, or **Hippodrome,** stands. Set below the level of the Domus Augustana, this curious stadium has at its southern end a sunken oval space, once surrounded by a colonnade, now decorated by the Archaeological Superintendency with fragments of porticoes, statues, and fountains. Although it is fairly certain that this was not a racetrack for hippopotamus, its exact nature remains uncertain. There are two prominent theories: first, that it was a private arena, where the imperial family would get their kicks watching the lesser classes fight for their lives; and second, that it was a private garden. It likely served a dual purpose. From the northern end of the stadium, a winding path leads around to the **Domus Severiana,** a later addition to the imperial complex that featured a central heating system.

PALATINE ANTIQUARIUM

Between the Domus Augustana and the Domus Flavia. 30 people admitted every 20min. 9:10am-6:20pm. Free with entrance to Palatine. Visiting time limited to 20 min. per floor.

Built on the ruins of Domitian's imperial palace, the museum chronologically traces Palatine's development over the last 50,000 years. Since the museum was built around the palace's foundation brick remnants of Domus Flavia and other imperial structures protrude between ground floor exhibits. Ground floor rooms showcase recently discovered evidence of human presence during the Middle Paleolithic Era (100,000 - 35,000 BC) as well as remains of the Romans' earliest dwellings. Rooms on the upper floor trace Palatine's imperial past, and feature many frescoes and sculptures- both Roman originals and Roman copies of Greek masterpieces.

DOMUS AUREA

On the Oppian Hill, below Trajan's baths. From the Colosseum, walk through the gates up V.d. Domus Aurea and make 1st left. Reservations ☎06 399 677 00. Open M and W-Su 9am-7:45pm. Groups of 30 admitted every 20min. €5, EU citizens 18-24 €2.50, EU citizens under 18 and over 65 free. Visits supervised by guards who give rather spartan tours in Italian. A better bet is the audioguide (€2). Italian and English tour with archaeologist €3.50. Reservations recommended for all visits: additional €1.50.

The recently reopened Domus Aurea was only a small part of Emperor Nero's residence, which once took up one-third of Rome. "Golden House" is something of a misnomer, as this edifice was a series of banquet halls and galleries; Nero's private rooms were likely on the Palatine.

Having determined, like so many before him, that he was a god, Nero had the architects Severus and Celer design a palace to suit divinity. "Using art and squandering the wealth of the Emperor," writes Tacitus, they created "eccentricities which went against the laws of nature." Between the Oppian and Palatine palaces was an enclosed lake, where the Colosseum now stands, and the Caelian Hill became private gardens. The Forum was reduced to a vestibule of the palace; Nero crowned it with a colossal statue of himself as the sun. Standing 35m tall, it was the largest bronze statue ever made and was justly called the Colossus.

The party didn't last long, however. Nero was forced to commit suicide only five years after building his gargantuan pleasure garden, and his memory was condemned by the Senate. Following suit, the Flavian emperors who succeeded Nero replaced all traces of the palace with monuments built for the public good. The Flavian Baths were built on top of the Caelian Hill, the lake was drained, and the Colosseum was erected. Trajan filled the Domus Aurea with dirt (so that it would make a stronger foundation) and built his baths on top of it in AD 115, and Hadrian covered the western end with his **Temple of Venus and Rome** in 135. The Domus Aurea itself was rediscovered in the 14th century.

Even though most of Domus Aurea is now cold, damp, and dark, try to visualize what it would have looked like in Nero's day, when the whole building was illuminated by sunlight streaming in through skylights and aligned corridors (after all, Nero did fancy himself the sun god). Fortunately, Trajan did not completely fill in the Domus Aurea, and many artists, including Raphael, lowered themselves down into the building with ropes in order to study the best-preserved frescoes, which were on the ceilings. Artists were not the only ones who managed to lower themselves into the magnificent house; signatures of other adventurers can be seen on many of the ceilings. Early archaeologists removed many of the treasures Nero had accumulated during his year of "study" in Greece. Among others, the Laocoön sculpture group and *The Dying Gaul* (now in the **Capitoline Museums,** see p. 168) once graced the Domus Aurea.

The tour begins in a corridor of Trajan's baths, but quickly progresses into the palace itself, meandering through several small rooms before reaching the **Corridor of the Eagles,** notable for the detailed artwork that once covered the ceiling. Fragments of friezes of eagles and vegetation can be made out, as well as a central scene thought to be Ariadne after she was abandoned by Theseus.

The tour passes through the **Nymphaeum of Ulysses and Polyphemus,** which was supposed to resemble a natural grotto: fake stalactites and an artificial waterfall were installed. A statue of the Muse Terpsichore was found here, and there is still a pentagonal mosaic of Ulysses and Polyphemus on the ceiling. The next notable sight is the **Golden Vault,** once a sumptuous banquet hall covered in gold leaf. Traces of the precious metal are still visible, but this is also where you can see just how high dirt was piled in the Domus Aurea before its excavation, as there is a huge heap of it in an adjoining room.

Shortly after the Golden Vault is the **Room of Achilles at Scyros.** On the ceiling is an image of cross-dressing Achilles (his father, who had received a prophecy that he would die in the Trojan War, ordered him into drag to avoid it). Farther down the corridor is the most hyped room in the Domus Aurea, the **Octagonal Room.** Some ancient historians contended that Nero's palace was so extravagant that he had a rotating banquet hall that turned throughout the day, and this might have been it. Unfortunately, there is no evidence of the equipment needed to achieve this effect, so a few modern scholars have posited that it was all an optical illusion: the room is, in fact, designed so that sunlight circles its walls throughout the day (sunlight still streams into the room, making it by far the brightest), and this may have made the room appear to spin (especially at the end of a drunken banquet). Just off the Octagonal Room is the last stop on the tour, the **Room of Hector and Andromache,** notable for its elaborate friezes and vault.

CIRCUS MAXIMUS

Walk down V.d. San Gregorio from the Colosseum. Open 24hr.

Cradled in the valley between the Palatine and Aventine hills, the Circus Maximus is today only a grassy shadow of its former glory. This rather plain hollow of a park was the sight of all the uproar depicted by Charlton Heston in *Ben Hur*. After its construction around 600 BC, more than 300,000 Romans often gathered here to watch the careening of chariots around the quarter-mile track. Obelisks in the arena's center served as distance markers, and the turning points of the track were perilously sharp to ensure enough thrills 'n' spills to keep the crowds happy. The excitement of the chariot races was interspersed with a variety of other competitions ranging from bareback horse-racing to more esoteric events like tent-pegging. Emperor Augustus watched from special terraces built onto the Palatine palaces. Crowds still fill the Circus Maximus today for triumphant celebrations, on the rare occasion that A.S. Roma wins a game.

FORI IMPERIALI

The sprawling Fori Imperiali lie on either side of V.d. Fori Imperiali, stretching from the **Basilica of Maxentius and Constantine** to P. Venezia. **"Excavations will proceed indefinitely"** means that the area is closed off, but you can still get free views peering over the railing from V.d. Fori Imperiali or V. Alessandrina. The large conglomeration of temples, basilicas, and public squares was constructed by emperors from the first century BC to the 2nd century AD in response to increasing congestion in the old Forum. Excavation in the area began in the early 1930s.

VISITOR CENTER

Across the Basilica of Maxentius and Constantine on V.d. Fori Imperiali. ☎06 679 77 86. Open daily 9:30am-6:30pm. Free.

The newly opened visitor center offers visitors shade and a history lesson. There is an exposition center with busts of Augustus, Vespatian, Domitian, Nerva, and Trajan, as well as a computer station where you can learn about the emperors' endeavors. Audio guides for the Imperial Fora are available in Italian and English (€3.10). Guided tours are offered Saturday and Sunday at 4pm in Italian (€6) or other languages (€7). Call for reservations.

FORUM OF CAESAR

On the left-hand side of V.d. Fori Imperiali, just past the Forum as you walk toward P. Venezia.

Julius Caesar was the first Roman leader to expand the city center outside the Forum proper, constructing the Forum of Caesar in 46 BC. Caesar's motivations were political: the new forum and temple he built in honor of Venus, his supposed ancestress, seriously undercut the prestige of the Senate and its older precinct around the Curia. The remains of the **Temple of Venus Genetrix** are marked by three columns. Additions from the reign of Trajan include the brick **Basilica Argentaria,** an ancient bank, and the heated public bathroom—the semi-circular room with holes along the walls. Nearby, a replica of a bronze statue of Caesar from his forum has been placed on the sidewalk of V.d. Fori Imperiali for foreign tourists to have their pictures taken with and Italian teenagers to deface.

FORUM OF AUGUSTUS

The first ruins on the right as you walk up V.d. Fori Imperiali toward P. Venezia (although they are better seen from V. Alessandrina, if it is open)

Completed in 2 BC, the Forum of Augustus was dedicated to *Mars Ultor* (Mars the Avenger). It commemorates Augustus's victory over his adoptive father Julius Caesar's murderers, Brutus and Cassius, at the Battle of Philippi in 42 BC. Three columns remain of the **Temple of Mars Ultor,** which centered upon a statue of Mars (oddly enough, it bore a striking resemblance to a certain avenging Emperor) and lined with statues of Roman history's most important figures. A copy of the Mars statue can be seen at the Capitoline Museums (see p. 168).

The hefty wall behind the temple, built to protect the precious new monument from the seamy Subura slums that spread up the hill behind it, doesn't run exactly straight. As the legend goes, when the land was being prepared for construction, even Augustus couldn't convince one stubborn homeowner to give up his domicile, so the great wall was built at an angle around it.

The aptly named **Forum Transitorium** (also called the **Forum of Nerva**) was a narrow, rectangular space connecting Augustus's forum with the old Roman Forum and the forum of Vespatian (near present-day V. Cavour). Most of it now lies under the street, but new excavations have begun to uncover more. Although Domitian began it, Emperor Nerva inaugurated the Forum in 97, displaying the wit that Roman emperors were known for: he dedicated the temple to Minerva, the deity whose name was closest to his own.

CHURCH OF SANTI COSMA E DAMIANO

Near the entrance to the Roman Forum at the intersection of V. Fori Imperiali and V. Cavour. Open daily 9:30am-12:30pm and 3-6:30pm.

The only remnant of **Vespatian's Forum** was built in 527 out of a library in Vespatian's complex. The interior displays a set of 6th-century mosaics including a multi-color Christ with his robes blowing in the wind. A recently installed viewing window allows for a look into the adjacent Temple of Romulus the Divine. In the north-west corner of the church courtyard is a large Neapolitan nativity scene, featuring more than 130 human figures.

MARKETS OF TRAJAN

Enter at V. IV Novembre, 94, up the steps in V. Magnanapoli, to the right of the 2 churches behind Trajan's column. ☎06 679 00 48. Open Tu-Su 9am-7pm. Last entrance 1 hr before closing. €6.20, EU citizens under 18 and over 65 free, EU citizens 18-24, teachers, and with ISIC €3.10.

Across V.d. Fori Imperiali from the Vittorio Emanuele II monument stand the brick **Markets of Trajan.** The three-floor, semicircular complex, built during the early 2nd century BC, is perhaps the first example of a Roman shopping mall. It was designed to buttress sections of the Quirinal Hill which was excavated to make room for the **Forum of Trajan.** The market had space for 150 shops, selling everything from imported fabrics to Eastern spices. Recent scholarship has confirmed that the long and somewhat bizarre Roman fascination with pubs began here, with the taverns that lined the street outside the market. As you enter the markets, you will find yourself flanked by three levels of vaulted chambers within the Great Hall, which was most likely designed for official functions. Between this hall and the rest of the markets runs via Biberatica, named for the beverages sold in shops on either side of it. The Torre delle Milizie, dating from the 12th century, rises from atop the central semicircular complex. This tower was originally part of a palace, which was later fortified, most notably by Pope Boniface VIII.

FORUM OF TRAJAN

Marked by an imposing column, the Forum of Trajan, the largest, newest, and most impressive of the imperial *fora*, is hard to miss. Built between 107 and 113, the forum was a celebration of Trajan's campaigns in modern-day Romania. The complex included a colossal equestrian statue of Trajan and a triumphal arch. In the back of the forum, the enormous **Basilica Ulpia** once stood in judicial might. The largest basilica ever built in Rome (17m x 60m), the Ulpia is today just two rows of truncated columns and fragments of the friezes.

TRAJAN'S COLUMN

At one end of the decimated forum stands the almost perfectly preserved spiral of Trajan's Column, one of the greatest surviving specimens of Roman relief sculpture ever found. At 40m, it is exactly the same height as the hill leveled in order to build Trajan's Forum. The continuous frieze that wraps around the column narrates the Emperor's campaigns. From the bottom, you can survey Roman legionnaires preparing supplies, building a stockaded camp, and loading boats to cross the Danube. Twenty-five hundred figures in all have been making their way up the column since 113. The statue of their Emperor that crowned the structure in ancient days was destroyed in the Middle Ages and replaced by the figure of St. Peter in 1588. The column survived the 6th and 7th centuries only because Pope Gregory I was so moved by some of the reliefs that he prayed for Trajan's acceptance into heaven. The Pope then claimed that God had come to him in a vision, ensuring Trajan's safe passage but refusing to admit any other pagans. The small holes in the column are actually windows that illuminate an internal staircase. In the column's base is a door that leads to the tomb of Trajan and his wife, where Trajan's ashes rested in a golden urn only to be stolen in the Middle Ages.

CAPITOLINE HILL

PIAZZA DEL CAMPIDOGLIO

Go up La Cordonata, the 2nd staircase down V.d. Teatro di Marcello, which is on the right as you face the front of the enormous monument of Vittorio Emanuele II.

The Capitoline was the smallest of ancient Rome's seven hills, but also one of the most important and sacred. The highlight of the modern hill is the spectacular P. del Campidoglio, designed by Michelangelo in 1536 in honor of the visit of Emperor Charles V and in celebration of the hill's ancient glory. In ancient times, the hill was the site of a gilded temple to Jupiter (dedicated in 509 BC); also on the hill were the state mint, senatorial archives, and the Department of Throwing People off the Capitoline Hill. The northern peak of the hill was home to Juno's sacred geese, which saved the city from ambush by the Gauls in 390 BC by honking so loudly that they woke the populace. In keeping with the hill's ancient significance, Michelangelo set up the statues of the twin warriors **Castor and Pollux** that flank the wide and gently sloping staircase, as well as the two reclining river gods and the statue of the goddess Roma. To the right and left of P. del Campidoglio stand **Palazzo dei Conservatori** and **Palazzo Nuovo,** home to the **Capitoline Museums** (p. 168). At the far end, opposite the stairs, is the turreted **Palazzo dei Senatori** (Rome's city hall).

In the center of the *piazza* stands the famous equestrian statue of **Marcus Aurelius,** brought here from the Lateran Palace. The gilded bronze was one of a handful of ancient bronzes to escape medieval meltdown, and then only because it was thought to be a portrait of Constantine, the first Christian emperor. Unfortunately, both man and steed succumbed to the assault of modern pollution and were removed for restoration in 1981, leaving behind only their pedestal. The emperor now resides in climate-controlled comfort in the courtyard of the Palazzo Nuovo, and the statue you see now is a weatherproof copy. Across the way, in the courtyard of the Palazzo dei Conservatori, lie the gargantuan foot, head, arm, and kneecap of the statue of Constantine that once graced the Basilica of Maxentius.

On the open side of the *piazza*, rejoin *La Cordonata* to make the descent to P. Venezia. The staircase was designed so that Charles V, apparently penitent over his sack of the city a decade before, could ride his horse up the hill to meet Paul III during his triumphal visit. On the right-hand side of La Cordonata stands a dark statue of a hooded man, **Cola di Rienzo,** the leader of a popular revolt in 1347 that attempted to reestablish a Roman Republic. The statue marks the spot where the disgruntled populace tore him limb from limb shortly after electing him first consul.

MAMERTINE PRISON

Walk downhill from Piazza del Campidoglio, past the left side of the Palazzo dei Senatori, toward the Forum. Open daily 9am-12:30pm and 2:30-6:30pm. Donation requested.

The gloomy, slightly claustrophobic Mamertine Prison, consecrated as the **Church of San Pietro in Carcere,** once held St. Peter, who supposedly caused water to flood into his cell and used it to baptize his captors. Although a stairway now leads down to the dank lower chamber, a small hole used to be the only access to the dungeon. The Romans used the lightless lower chamber as a holding cell for prisoners awaiting execution. Inmates were tortured and occasionally strangled to death in the dark by order of the government. Among the more unfortunate residents were Jugurtha, King of Numidia; Vercingetorix, chieftain of the Gauls; and the accomplices of the dictator Catiline.

SANTA MARIA IN ARACOELI

Climb 124 pilgrims' steps up from the left side of La Cordonata. Open daily 9:30am-12:30pm and 2:30-5:30pm.

The 7th-century Church of Santa Maria in Aracoeli lies on the site of the Temple to Juno Moneta. "Aracoeli" comes from a medieval legend, in which the Emperor Augustus has a vision of the Virgin Mary, causing him to raise an altar to Heaven *(Ara Coeli)* on the spot she indicated; this explains the rather unusual fresco of Augustus and the Tiburtine Sibyl in the company of saints and angels. The stunning **Bufalini Chapel** (on the right as you face the altar) is home to **Pinturicchio's** Renaissance frescoes of St. Bernardino of Siena. The third chapel on the left houses a beautiful fresco of St. Antonio of Padova, the only one left of a late 15th-century series by Benozzo Gozzoli.

BATHS OF CARACALLA

From the eastern end of Circus Maximus, walk up V.d. Terme di Caracalla. Open Tu-Su 9am-6:30pm, M 9am-1pm; in winter 9am-2:30pm. €5, EU citizens 18-24 €2.50, EU citizens under 18 or over 65 free. Tours with guide €3.50 on Sundays at 10:30am, in Italian only; audioguide €4.

The Baths of Caracalla were constructed in AD 212 and fully operational until the 6th century, when the invading Goths severed the supply of water from the aqueducts. The largest baths at the time they were built, they are also the best preserved, erected under the watchful guidance of Caracalla, the same emperor who killed his brother Geta, stole the throne from his father Severus, and then scratched his brother's image off the arch of Janus and the arch of Septimus Severus.

NERO SUM

Nero, son of Claudius's fourth wife, began a sadistic reign of terror, torture, and debauchery at the tender age of 16, after his mother fed her ex-husband poisonous mushrooms. Nero started out mildly, guided by his overbearing but well-meaning mother; he was too timid even to sign the standard death warrants. Soon, though, he proved to be one of the most ill-adjusted teens in history. He transmogrified into a megalomaniacal monster and ordered the cruel murders of his mother, Agrippina, and his 19-year-old wife, who was found tied up in a hot bath with her veins slashed. He made his best friend and advisor, famed philosopher and tragedian Seneca, cut his own wrists. Nero was haunted by paranoid visions—he often woke up screaming from nightmares of his mother—so he initiated a one-man witch-hunt, condemning senators, army officers, aristocrats, and others to be beheaded as traitors. Many blame Nero for the fire of 64 BC—guilty or not, he certainly took advantage of its destruction, commandeering acres of burnt-out land to construct the Domus Aurea. Ultimately, Nero pushed the patience and the coffers of his empire too far; the Senate sentenced him to death by flogging. Nero, in disguise, escaped on horseback to have a servant slit his throat, as he didn't have the guts to do so himself. The notoriously bad musician and actor did, however, have enough panache to utter in his last moments, "What an artist dies with me."

Thought Caracalla was not perhaps best known for his sunny disposition, construction of this monumental complex nonetheless proved beneficial to the entire Roman population. The monstrous baths were capable of handling approximately 2000 Romans at any given time; men bathed in the mornings, women in the afternoons, and slaves in the evenings. The colorful mosaic floors are remarkably well preserved, especially in the *apodyteria* (dressing rooms), and extremely intricate in design. The original tiling alone warrants a trip to the gigantic *thermae*, but it is the size of the proto-health club that continues to amaze the plebes. The complex had a central hall opening onto a round, warm swimming pool on one side and a cold pool on the other. Romans would follow a particular regimen for cleaning, beginning with the warm bath, followed by a procession from hot *(caldarium)* to colder rooms (the lukewarm *tepidarium* and the cold *frigidarium*), finishing with a dip in the *natatio*, which was a cold, open-air pool. Remains of a rectangular brick wall mark the boundary of the ancient gym where Romans played sports, sipped juices, and had their body hair plucked by special servants. Rome's opera company used to stage Verdi's *Aïda* here, complete with horses and elephants, until it was discovered that, due to either the weight of the animals or the sopranos' voices, the performances caused structural damage.

VELABRUM

The best way to access its sights is to walk down V. Teatro di Marcello, to the right of the Vittorio Emanuele II monument, from P. Venezia.

The Velabrum is a low plain west of the Forum and south of the Jewish Ghetto in the shadow of the Capitoline and Palatine hills. This Tiber floodplain was a sacred area for the ancient Romans, and for that reason there are a number of ancient ruins there. It was believed that the mighty Hercules kept his cattle here and that it is where Aeneas first set foot on what was to become Rome. It was also here that baby Romulus and Remus were found by the she-wolf that nursed them in their infancy according to Roman legend. During the days of the Republic, the area's proximity to a port on the Tiber made it an ideal spot for the city's cattle and vegetable markets. Civic-minded merchants spotted the riverbanks with temples, arches, and a grandiose theater, all dedicated to the gods of trade and commerce. Even after the empire's fall, the area remained a busy market center.

BOCCA DELLA VERITÀ

Two blocks south of the Theater of Marcellus along V. Luigi Petroselli. Portico and church open daily 9am-7pm. Byzantine mass Su 10:30am.

The **Church of Santa Maria in Cosmedin,** originally constructed in the 6th century to serve the local Greek colony, is not the reason that most tourists make the trek from the Theater of Marcellus. In the eternal quest to get up close and personal with the parts of the Roman landscape that have been featured in Hollywood movies, most people visit for the famous **Bocca della Verità** in the portico. Originally a drain cover carved as a river god's face, the circular relief was credited with supernatural powers in the Middle Ages, when it was claimed that the hoary face liked to chomp off the fingers of anyone who dared the gods by speaking an untruth while his hand was in its mouth. To keep the superstition alive, the caretaker-priest used to stick a scorpion in the back of the mouth to sting the fingers of suspected fibbers. The Bocca made a cameo in *Roman Holiday;* during the filming, Gregory Peck stuck his hand in the mouth and jokingly hid his hand in his sleeve when he yanked it out, causing Audrey Hepburn to yelp in shock. The scene wasn't scripted, but it worked so well that it was kept in the movie. For more medieval fun, test the honesty of your friends at home with clay replicas of the Bocca that sell for €2.50-5.50 in the gift shop.

FORO BOARIO

Call ☎06 39 967 700 to obtain information about visiting the round temple on the 1st and 3rd Su of each month.

P. della Bocca della Verità is also the site of the ancient Foro Boario (cattle market). Its two ancient **temples** are among the best-preserved in Rome. The rectangular **Temple of Portunus,** once known as the Temple of Fortuna Virilis, reveals both Greek and Etruscan influence. The present construction dates from the late 2nd century BC, although there was likely a temple on the site for years. The **circular temple** next door, thought to be the Temple of Hercules Victor, was believed to be dedicated to Vesta because of its similarities to the Temple of Vesta in the Forum (see p. 74).

CHURCH OF SAN GIORGIO IN VELABRO

One block from Foro Boario on V.d. Velabro in the direction of the Capitoline Hill. Open daily 10am-12:30pm and 4-6:30pm.

Behind the hulking **Arch of Janus** (built in the 4th century AD as a covered market for cattle traders) once stood the little Church of San Giorgio in Velabro. A marvelous edifice, it boasted a 9th-century porch and pillars, a simple early Romanesque interior, and a brick and stone arch *campanile* (bell tower). The oldest written records suggest that the main portion of the church's modern day structure was constructed in the late 7th century under the auspices of Pope Leo II (682-3). The bell tower was first added in the 12th century and then rebuilt in 1837 after the original was struck by lighting. A terrorist car bombing in 1993 reduced the church's famed portico to a single arch and part of a stone beam. Both the church and the arch have been summarily rebuilt. To the left of the church, the **Arch of the Argentarii** was erected in the 3rd century AD by the *argentarii* (money changers) and cattle merchants who used the *piazza* as a market in honor of Emperor Septimus Severus.

CHURCH OF CONSOLATION

From P. Bocca della Verità, take V.G. Decollato 2 blocks uphill to the P. della Consolazione. Open daily 6am-noon and 3:30-6pm, closes at 6pm in winter.

Here in P. della Consolazione, prisoners in ancient times were given a prayer, a pat on the back, and a "good luck out there," before they were put to death. The church itself was once home to an order of monks (equipped humanely with smelling salts and liquor flasks) who were dedicated to giving succor to the condemned and accompanying them on their last mortal journey.

Arch of Janus

Bocca della Verità

Theater of Marcellus

THEATER OF MARCELLUS

The Teatro di Marcello is the round building reminiscent of the Colosseum two blocks down from the Piazza Venezia on the right side of V. Teatro di Marcello. You cannot enter the theater, but excellent views are available from the outside. The theater was begun by Caesar and finished by Augustus in 13 BC. It bears the name of Augustus's nephew, a potential successor of whom he was particularly fond, and whose early and sudden death remains a mystery. He may have been poisoned by Augustus's wife, Livia, who intended her own son from a previous marriage, Tiberius, to be the next emperor.

The arches and pilasters on the exterior of the theater served as a model for the Colosseum. It represents the classic arrangement of architectural orders, which grow more complex from the ground up: stocky Doric pilasters support the bottom floor, Ionic capitals hold up the middle, and elaborate Corinthian columns once crowned the top tier. Vitruvius and other ancient architects considered this arrangement the most perfect possible exterior decoration, inspiring Michelangelo, Bramante, and other Renaissance architects to copy the pattern. The exterior is all that remains, as a succession of medieval families used its seats and stage as the foundation for fortified castles. The park around the theater is open for classical concerts on summer nights. See **Entertainment,** p. 221, for more information.

SAN NICOLA IN CARCERE

Adjacent to Teatro di Marcello at V.d. Teatro di Marcello and V.d. Foro Olitorio. ☎06 686 99 72. Open M-F 7am-noon and 4-7pm, Su 9:30am-1pm and 4-7pm. Closed Aug.

The 12th-century church rests on the foundations of three Republican temples, which were built and dedicated to the gods Juno, Janus, and Spes (Hope) during the hairy times of the First Punic War. The ancient buildings were converted into a prison during the Middle Ages—hence the name *carcere*, meaning "prison." The only captives in the deserted interior today are well-labeled paintings and restored engravings, including part of the church's original dedication from May 12, 1128. On the right side of the church lies the best-preserved temple, its Ionic columns scattered in the grass and embedded in the church's wall. The left wall preserves the Doric columns of another temple. The third temple is buried beneath the church and its remains can be accessed through a staircase near the narthex. Ask about accessing the buried temple in the office to your left as you enter the church.

PORTICO D'OTTAVIA

At the bend of V.d. Portico d'Ottavia in the Jewish Ghetto, a shattered pediment and five marble columns in the shadow of the Theater of Marcellus are all that remain of the once magnificent Portico d'Ottavia, one of Augustus's grandest contributions to Rome's architecture. Built by Quintus Metellus in 149 BC, it was revamped and imperially restyled by Augustus, who dedicated it to his sister Octavia in 23 BC. The portico was a rectangular enclosure sheltering temples to Jupiter and Juno, some libraries, and public rooms adjunct to the Theater of Marcellus. The Romans stuck many of their imported Greek masterpieces here, including the famous Medici *Venus*, now in Florence's Uffizi. She was rediscovered under the crumbling detritus and refuse that had accumulated on the site thanks to the ravages of a nearby fish market. In fact, a church was built into its wall in AD 755 (see p. 104).

TEMPLE OF APOLLO SOSIANUS

Through the fence to the right of the portico are the polished white columns of the Temple of Apollo Sosianus. The temple is best viewed from V.d. Teatro di Marcello, directly to the right of the Theater of Marcellus, since the area around it has been closed in recent years. While the temple dates as far back as 433 BC, it was rebuilt by Gaius Sosius who attached his own name to it. The three Corinthian columns support a well-preserved frieze of bulls' skulls and floral garlands. The temple's ornate original 5th-century Greek pediment is visible in the **Museo Centrale Termoelettrica Montemartini** (see p. 177).

CENTRO STORICO

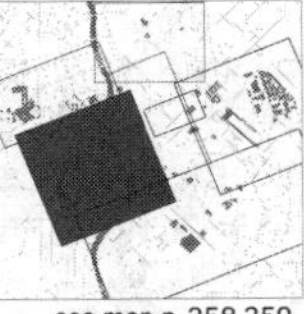
see map p. 358-359

This sprawling maze of ancient streets and alleys—the historic center of Rome—brims with dim Baroque churches, cramped picture galleries, ancient ruins, and vast *piazze*. V.d. Corso, runs from P. Venezia nearly a mile north to P. del Popolo, forming a rough eastern boundary for the area; the Tiber is its boundary to the West.

PIAZZA VENEZIA & VIA DEL CORSO

VITTORIO EMANUELE II MONUMENT

Stairs open daily 9am-5pm.

Also known as the *Vittoriano* or "Mussolini's typewriter," this confection of gleaming white marble looms over P. Venezia like a glacier. It is a memorial to King Vittorio Emanuele II (under whom Italy was first united) begun in 1885, the day after his death. At the top of the staircase on the exterior is the *Altare della Patria* (Altar of the Fatherland), which has an eternal flame guarded night and day by two members of the armed forces. Behind it is the **Tomb of the Unknown Soldier,** and above is an impressive equestrian bronze of the man of honor. Brave the many stairs for an excellent view of the city, and a close look at all sorts of 19th-century allegorical reliefs. Around the left side toward the forum are the **Sacrario delle Bandiere, Museo del Risorgimento** (p. 179), and the **Complesso del Vittoriano.**

PALAZZO DI VENEZIA

This building, on the left as you stand with your back to the *Vittoriano*, is the oldest extant example (begun in 1455) of a Renaissance Roman *palazzo*. Its formidable tower and fortress-like facade keep one foot in the Middle Ages. The *palazzo* housed the embassy of the Venetian Republic from 1564 to 1797 and later the French and Austrian embassies. Mussolini made the building his personal residence and seat of the Fascist Grand Council, and delivered some of his most famous speeches

TIME: 3 hr. walk.

DISTANCE: about 3km.

SEASON: Year-round, but spring is best.

A complete tour of the medieval Centro Storico neighborhood.

1 PIAZZA NAVONA. The site of Domitian's stadium, the *piazza* was a special pet project of a number of 17th-century popes. The result was a Baroque masterpiece that today houses Bernini's Fontana dei Quatto Fiumi (p. 97) and pushy vendors alike. The Church of Sant'Agnese in Agone (p. 97) is also worth a look, if for nothing else than the saint's head, which is on prominent display.

2 PANTHEON. A 2000 year old temple currently masquerading under the name Church of Santa Maria ad Martyres. When the ancient Romans dedicated it to all of the pagan gods, they topped the round temple with the largest masonry dome ever constructed. Enter and marvel at the magnificent structure (p. 93).

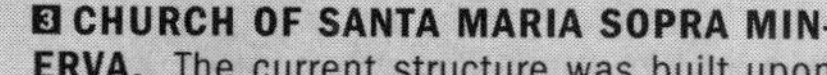

3 CHURCH OF SANTA MARIA SOPRA MINERVA. The current structure was built upon (sopra) the old Roman temple to Minerva, and is one of the few examples of Gothic architecture in Rome. Under the main altar is the tomb Catherine de Siena, who convinced the Pope to remove the papacy from wicked, wild France a back to sober, discreet Italy. Other highlights include the final resting place of the artist F Angelico, and Michelangelo's *Risen Christ* (p. 95).

4 GALLERIA DORIA PAMPHILJ. Taking V.d. Seminario to the east and a right onto Sant'Ignazio will lead you directly to the place where the term "nepotism" was first coined. Histo in the making. The Doria Pamphilj's family's relations with Innocent X are largely responsible f the contents of their palace, which can only be described as opulent. Velasquez's painting Innocent X is one of the finest papal portraits in Rome (p. 177).

5 TREVI FOUNTAIN. All roads lead to this tourist monstrosity. Just face the facts: you'll end u here at some point, bathed in the flashbulbs of thousands of Kodak disposable cameras, ar tossing a coin over your shoulder. If you can, take a moment to enjoy the Neptune fountain, bu into the side of a *palazzo*. A trip to nearby **San Crispino** (p. 199) is reward enough for being normal tourist for a night.

6 PIAZZA BARBERINI. Bernini's Fontana del Tritone is the centerpiece of this square, built f Urban VIII (of the same clan of Barberini bees that decorate the bronze canopy in the Vatican). short walk up V. Veneto to the Capuchin Crypt in the Chiesa Santa Maria della Concezione is spooky (and cool) way to spend a hot afternoon (p. 109).

7 SPANISH STEPS. Home of all that's Italian chic, the Spanish Steps are host to a number overpriced and famous cafes, a couple of decent churches (for the materialistic sinners in Arma that congregate in the nearby *piazze*), and everything that you need to know about internation fashion (p. 105).

from its balcony. It is now home to the **Museo Nazionale del Palazzo di Venezia,** which has temporary exhibits and a small permanent collection (see p. 182). Walk inside (around the corner, on V.d. Plebiscito) to look at the garden.

The Museo shares this former embassy building with the **Basilica of San Marco.** (Open daily 9am-1pm and 4:30-6:45pm.) The church is dedicated to the patron saint of Venice, and served as the *palazzo*'s chapel. It's foundation can be traced to AD 336, when the church was founded by Pope Mark. Every few centuries parts of the church were restored, making it a kaleidoscope of different artistic styles. Inside the church, Melazzo da Forli's *San Marco Evangelista* hangs in the chapel, right of the high altar. The 9th-century mosaic in the apse depicts Christ and Pope Gregory IV holding a model of the recently restored church.

BASILICA DEI SANTI APOSTOLI

With your back to the Vittorio Emanuele II Monument, turn right on V.C. Battisti. P.S. Apostoli is two blocks down on the left. Open daily 7am-noon and 4-7pm.

Tucked in the corner of the *piazza,* this church was built in the 15th century for Pope Martin V. It has an arcaded portico with sculptures above and below. If you're brave enough to get past the lions guarding the entrance, you'll marvel at the imperial eagle, a scary 2nd-century Roman relief, and the largest altarpiece in Rome.

IL GESÙ

With your back to the Vittorio Emanuele II Monument, turn left on V.C. Battisti, which becomes V.d. Plebiscito and intersects P.d. Gesu; the church is on the left at this intersection. Open daily 6am-12:30pm and 4-7:15pm. Apartments open M-Sa 4-6pm and Su 10am-noon.

The impressive and sumptuous Il Gesù is the principal Jesuit church in Rome, and one of the richest in the city. Its construction was decreed in 1540 by St. Ignatius Loyola, founder of the Jesuit order. The Jesuits, known for their superior education, organization, and dedication, advanced Catholicism through missionary efforts, founding colleges, and building political ties. Jacopo Barozzi began constructing Il Gesú church 1568; it was completed in 1577 by Giacomo della Porta, who drew from some of Michelangelo's designs for St. Peter's, including the paired pilasters.

Architecturally, Il Gesù became the standard for Counter Reformation churches. It was designed with a wide single nave in a Latin rather than a Greek cross, so that people attending the church would focus their attention on the altar.

The interior is lavishly ornate; the Jesuits' motto is *"Ad maiorem dei gloriam"* ("to the glory of God") and impressive churches were believed to glorify God and inspire faith and respect. On the ceiling of the nave, Il Baciccia's celebrated fresco, *Triumph of the Name of Jesus,* uses spectacular perspective, painted panels, and stucco figures to draw the painting into the same space as the viewers. Baciccia also decorated the brilliant dome. The large monogram "IHS" in the apse is the Jesuits' insignia and represents the first three letters of Jesus' name in Greek.

Look left of the dome for the enormous **Cappella di Sant'Ignazio di Loyola,** dedicated to the founder of the order lying under the altar of bronze, marble, and lapis lazuli. Across the apse is another altar, this one displaying the hand of St. Francis Xavier, Ignatius's friend who led missions to India and Japan. Next to the church, St. Ignatius's **apartments** contain artifacts and paintings.

PIAZZE DEL COLLEGIO ROMANO & SANT'IGNAZIO

V. Lata, two blocks up V.d. Corso from P. Venezia on the left, leads into P. del Collegio Romano. P. di Sant'Ignazio is one block off V.d. Corso on V.d. Caravita (four blocks up from P. Venezia, on the left).

PALAZZO DORIA PAMPHILJ

P. del Collegio Romano's stalwart *palazzo* harbors the extensive art collection of the **Galleria Doria Pamphilj** (see p. 177). Dating from the early 15th century, the *palazzo* has been inhabited by the Doria-Pamphilj family for four centuries. Although their part of the building is off-limits, you can look at one of the *palazzo*'s lavish apartments in the gallery.

CHURCH OF SAN MARCELLO AL CORSO

Across from Palazzo Doria Pamphilj, one block up V.d. Corso, in P. San Marcello. Open M-Sa 7:15am-12:30pm and 4:30-7pm, Su 8:30am-noon and 4-7pm; Sept.-June closed Su.

The church has received worldwide attention because of its Holy "Miraculous Crucifix," which survived unscathed from a fire in 1519 that destroyed the rest of the ancient basilica. The crucifix has attained special spiritual significance, even drawing recent blessings from The Vatican. On the west wall is a stark and moving fresco of the *Crucifixion* by Giovanni Battista Ricci da Novara. The fourth chapel on the right has three excellent busts by Algardi.

CHURCH OF SANT'IGNAZIO DI LOYOLA

In P. Sant'Ignazio. Take V. Caravita from V.d. Corso. Open daily 7:30am-12:30pm and 4-7:15pm.

This Jesuit church is modeled after the Gesu, and on roughly the same scale. The ceiling is decorated with Andrea Pozzo's *trompe l'oeil* fresco, *The Triumph of St. Ignatius*. Pozzo designed the ceiling so its figures appear to exist in the same space as the church's architecture, and used foreshortening to make it appear as though several more stories continued above before breaking into Heaven. The fresco shows St. Ignatius being received into heaven, while figures from all the continents embrace Christianity, an allegory of the Jesuits' missionary efforts. Be sure to see Legros's reliefs at the altar to St. Louis Gonzaga, a Roman noble who gave up his wealth to join the Jesuits (the chapel to your right at the crossing). Pozzo painted the false dome after a group of neighboring nuns stopped the construction of the real one, fearing that it would cut off the light to their garden.

PIAZZA COLONNA

COLUMN OF MARCUS AURELIUS

A few blocks further up the Corso is P. Colonna, named for the massive column that dominates it. The monument was erected after Marcus Aurelius's death in AD 180. Modeled on that of his great-grandfather Trajan, the column depicts the Stoic philosopher-emperor's wars against German and Sarmatian barbarians. Trajan's wars had extended the empire so far that Aurelius was forced to spend much of his reign fighting off invasions. Compared to Trajan's, the column's reliefs are rough and unrefined. Unless you're 90 ft. tall or can fly, the best way to look at the column reliefs is to go see the plaster casts of them at the **Museo della Civiltà Romana,** in EUR (p. 176). The statue on top of the column is not Marcus Aurelius, but rather St. Paul, and it was placed there by Pope Sixtus V in the 16th century.

PALAZZI

On the western side of the *piazza*, away from the Corso, **Palazzo Wedekind** (home to the newspaper *Il Tempo*) was built in 1838 with Roman columns from the Etruscan city of Veio. Check out the magnificent clock supported by four strange human figures. **Palazzo Chigi,** built in the 16th and 17th centuries and now the official residence of the Prime Minister, forms the north side of the *piazza*. Guards with really big guns prevent public entrance, but you can look through into the courtyard. Colonna's northwest corner flows into P. di Montecitorio, dominated by Bernini's **Palazzo Montecitorio,** seat of the Chamber of Deputies. The 6th-century BC obelisk in front of the *palazzo* was brought from Egypt to serve as a sundial in Augustus's *Ara Pacis* complex (see p. 83). Running off P. Colonna to the south, V. Bergamaschi leads to **Piazza di Pietra,** where the colonnaded portico of the **Temple of Hadrian** (dedicated to the emperor in AD 145 by his son, Antonius Pius) forms the facade of the **Palazzo della Borsa,** which houses the chamber of commerce.

PIAZZA DELLA ROTONDA

In the middle of P. della Rotunda, among the hordes of tourists and McDonald's patrons gawking at the Pantheon, Giacomo della Porta's late-Renaissance fountain supports an **Egyptian obelisk.** The phallic monolith was added in the 18th century, when obelisks—popular among ancient Romans—had come back into fashion.

PANTHEON

In P. della Rotonda. Open M-Sa 8:30am-7:30pm, Su 9am-6pm; holidays 9am-1pm. Free.

Originally dedicated to all the gods (the name is derived from the Greek *pan*—"all"—and *theos*—"god"), the Pantheon has stood for nearly 2000 years, with its granite columns, pediment, and soaring domed interior remarkably the same as the day it was erected, save superficial decorative alterations. The Pantheon emerged unscathed from centuries of Christian neglect toward other pagan monuments in Rome because it was given by Byzantine Emperor Phocas to Pope Boniface IV in and it was consecrated as the **Church of Santa Maria ad Martyres** in 609, its official name to this day. The Pantheon contains several important tombs: Raphael's final resting place, the third chapel on the right, is decorated by the artist's beautiful *Madonna del Sasso* (commissioned by Lorenzetto). Three members of the Italian royal family are also buried here: King Vittorio Emanuele II (second chapel on the right) and King Umberto I and his wife Margherita (second on the left). The real attraction, however, is the building itself, which Hadrian had building constructed between AD 118 and 125 (on the site of a 27 BC temple that had served the same purpose). He may have also contributed to its design as well, since he is credited with the revolutionary design of the Temple of Venus and Rome in the Forum (see p. 76), the sprawling Villa Adriana at Tivoli, and his own mausoleum (see **Castel Sant'Angelo**, p. 120).

The Pantheon weathered the Middle Ages, though it sometimes filled in as a fortress and even a fish market (the spotty low holes on the interior walls are marks from the wooden stands vendors built right into the structure). The building has served as the inspiration for countless Renaissance and Neoclassical edifices, including the Jefferson Memorial in Washington, D.C. Michelangelo, who used the Pantheon as a model for St. Peter's Basilica, is said to have designed his own dome 1m shorter in diameter, out of respect for the ancient temple. The 17th century wasn't quite so deferential. Barberini Pope Urban VIII melted down the bronze door (which has since been replaced), the bronze eagle that adorned the tympanum, and other elements to make cannons for Castel Sant'Angelo (as well as the *Baldacchino* of St. Peter's). In horror the Romans remonstrated: "What the barbarians didn't do, the Barberini did."

EXTERIOR

The traditional triangular pediment, inscribed dedication, and Corinthian columns of the exterior deceive the first-time visitor into expecting an equally traditional interior. In fact, the only purpose of the large rectangular brick element that rises behind the pediment is to hide the dome from the view of those approaching, although this effect worked better in the days of the Roman Empire, when the level of the surrounding *piazza* was some 7m lower and the temple had to be approached via a staircase. The inscription across the frieze on the facade is deceptive too. It reads in Latin: "Marcus Agrippa, son of Lucius, made this in his third consulship." This refers to the earlier temple, which Hadrian tore down after a fire in AD 117. He presumably had the old inscription copied here to avoid accusations of excessive pride.

DOME

All modesty was left at the door. The breathtaking dome, which is the largest ever made out of masonry, used to be decorated with bronze rosettes. It was constructed entirely out of poured concrete in a series of rings decreasing in thickness

A lesson in architectural forensics

The Pantheon is one of Rome's most famous ancient buildings, and certainly its best-preserved one. Yet in many ways it remains a mystery. Even the historian Dio Cassius, writing in Rome in the early third century, about 240 years after the Pantheon was initially conceived, was uncertain about its origins, purpose, and symbolism. His conjectures are the only ones that survive from antiquity; naturally they have hardened into dogma over the years. Dio thought this great domed building was built by Agrippa, the famous general under Augustus. So did modern interpreters until the late nineteenth century, when excavations of the porch and floor and careful investigation of the building's brick stamps proved definitively that the building had existed in three phases, and that the version Dio knew—and that we know today—was built entirely under the emperor Hadrian around AD 120, nearly a century and a half after Agrippa's original. (Mischievously, Hadrian reproduced Agrippa's dedicatory inscription on his own creation, fooling even the scrupulous Dio.)

Lacking a written history, the Pantheon is its own best document. Its fabric reveals all kinds of information to the careful observer. Focusing on the building's exterior, we begin with a well-documented event in early modern history: the reconstruction of the left side of the porch. If you look closely, you will notice four anomalies on this side: the monolithic column shafts have been shattered and mended; two are of pink granite, whereas their companions on the other side, and on the facade, are gray granite; the capitals on this side are in much better condition than the others; and large parts of the outer marble facing of the intermediate structure between the porch and the rotunda are missing. From this, you could conclude that the original columns and superstructure on this side collapsed, and that the column shafts and capitals were not reused; that the collapse pulled off some of the marble facing of the intermediate block; and that the restorers salvaged two pink granite columns from somewhere else, and carved new capitals on this side. But why are the column shafts so damaged? This is the usual state of fallen Roman shafts when they are excavated. In fact, if you detour to the *piazza* just to the west of the Pantheon, you will see a couple of pink-granite columns of exactly the same proportions, and roughly the same state of repair, standing on the far side of the square; they were re-erected in the 1930s. Many identical columns once adorned a bath building in this area. Granite was long unavailable in Italy until recently, except to the extent that it could be extracted from existing Roman ruins. The restorers, aware of the existence of these "spare parts" for the Pantheon in the vicinity, successfully recovered some fallen granite shafts from the buried baths. Thanks to various documents, including inscriptions on the Pantheon itself, we know that the restoration was begun under Urban VIII. In 1625-26 he reerected the left front corner column (apparently the original) with a new capital, and famously purloined the bronze trusses from the porch roof to be melted down for cannon. The restoration was completed under Pope Alexander VII in 1666. Could we have known this without textual evidence? Partly. Carved into the top of the corner replacement capital is a bee, the symbol of Urban's clan, the Barberini. On the other two capitals, and the underside of the cornice above, are the arms of Alexander VII Chigi: six mountains and a star.

From most perspectives the porch looks suitably monumental for the astounding rotunda that lies behind it—yet it is smaller than Hadrian intended. There is no written evidence of this change of architectural plan; the clues exist in the building itself. If you look at the intermediate block as it rises above the roof of the porch, you'll see a second, higher triangular pediment embedded in it. This was the roofline as originally intended. Roman column shafts were often manufactured in standard sizes; on the top end of the spectrum were 40-foot, 50-foot, and 54-foot shafts. Those on the Pantheon today are 40 Roman feet high; but the roof as originally planned would have accommodated 50-footers, or even the hulking 54-footers that adorned the Basilica of Constantine in the Forum. The original plan was compromised—most likely because bad planning and a cramped work space precluded the erection of the larger shafts in their necessary sequence.

As you walk around the Pantheon, see if you can find other clues to this disruption, or to other events in the building's history. You may be surprised at how much the building alone can reveal.

Rabun Taylor is an Associate Professor of History of Art and Architecture at Harvard.

and weight, without supporting vaults, arches, or ribs. With a radius and a height of 21.3m, it is a perfect half-sphere—if a sphere were placed inside the building, it would touch both the top and bottom of the room. The 9m *oculus* provides the only source of light, which was originally used to mark time on a sundial. During rainstorms, a column of water comes down through the *oculus* in a perfect circle.

PIAZZA DELLA MINERVA

One block down V.d. Minerva from P. della Rotunda, behind the Pantheon.

ELEFANTINO

An oddly poignant monument marks the center of this tiny *piazza:* a statue of a baby elephant known as the Elefantino, or **Pulcin della Minerva.** Crafted by Bernini, it supports a 6th-century BC Egyptian obelisk. The monument was set up in 1667, in honor of Pope Alexander VI. The gist of the inscription is that it takes a strong mind (the elephant is symbolic of Alexander's mind) to support wisdom (the obelisk).

CHURCH OF SANTA MARIA SOPRA MINERVA

Open M-Sa 7am-7pm, Su 7am-1pm and 3:30-7pm.

The gleaming Church of Santa Maria Sopra Minerva was built on top of a temple incorrectly attributed to Minerva, Goddess of Wisdom. Begun by the Dominicans in 1280, this is the only Gothic church in all of Rome, despite its simple exterior, which was redone in the 19th century. To the right of the entrance, six plaques mark the high-water levels of Tiber floods over the centuries. The Gothic interior is spangled with colored shadows from the beautiful stained glass windows. The highlight of the church is Fra Filippo Lippi's magnificent fresco cycle showing the life of St. Thomas Aquinas, in the **Carafa Chapel.** To the left of the high altar is Michelangelo's 1520 sculpture, *Christ the Redeemer*. The chapels on the right house a number of treasures as well, including a panel of the *Annunciation* by Antoniazzo Romano, a pupil of Pinturicchio. Many altars in Rome house a holy relic, and Santa Maria Sopra Minerva has a great one—the body of St. Catherine of Siena, the famous 14th-century ascetic and church reformer. To the left of the altar, another medieval great, the painter-saint **Fra Angelico**, lies under a tomb surrounded by a bronze-leafed fence.

PIAZZA SAN LUIGI DEI FRANCESI

CHURCH OF SAN LUIGI DEI FRANCESI

One block down V.d. Salvatore from C. Rinascimento as it passes P. Navona. Open F-W 7:30am-12:30pm and 3:30-7pm, Th 7:30am-12:30pm.

The simple and sooty Church of San Luigi dei Francesi serves as the French National Church in Rome (Bastille Day is celebrated in the *piazza*) and is home to three of **Caravaggio's** most famous ecclesiastical masterpieces. Between 1597 and 1602, the flamboyant artist decorated the last chapel on the north side, dedicated to the evangelist St. Matthew. *The Calling of St. Matthew*, to the left of the chapel's altar, is the most famous piece, but *St. Matthew and the Angel*, in the center, and the *Crucifixion of St. Matthew*, to the right, are also breathtaking. You must pay €0.10 to shed light on the works, or it'll be impossible to see anything. All of the paintings are characterized by Caravaggio's dramatic use of light to highlight the theological and emotional point of the paintings and to accentuate his careful compositions. He grants careful attention to natural and even grimy details, so much so that the picture of *St. Matthew and the Angel* was toned down because the patrons of the chapel found the first one inappropriate.

CHURCH OF SANT'IVO

One block down V. Dogana Vecchia from S. Luigi dei Francesi; turn right as you exit the church. Entrance to cloister around the corner at C. del Rinascimento, 40. Open M-F 10am-4pm, Sa 10am-1pm, Su 9am-noon.

Pantheon

Church of Santa Maria in Cosmedin

Circus Maximus

Borromini's stunning Baroque masterpiece, the Church of Sant'Ivo flaunts its famous corkscrew cupola over the Palazzo della Sapienza, the original home of the University of Rome. The entrance to the **cloister** provides the best view of the recently restored Borromini facade and cupola, originally designed in 1660. The interior of the church is breathtaking—completely white and designed in the complex geometric pattern of a star. The view of the facade from the courtyard is remarkable in the light of the late afternoon sun.

PIAZZA SANT'AGOSTINO

CHURCH OF SANT'AGOSTINO

Go up V.d. Scrofa; turn left as you exit the church of S. Luigi dei Francesi. Make a left on V.d. Coppelle. P.S. Agostino is immediately on your left. Open daily 7:45am-noon and 4:30-7:30pm.

The simple Renaissance facade of the **Church of Sant'Agostino** is a sharp contrast with its ornate interior; its 15th-century design was augmented by layers of Baroque and Rococo stucco and frippery. Keep an eye out for Raphael's shiny *Prophet Isaiah,* on the third pillar on the left aisle. For €0.10, turn on the lights in the chapel on the left to see the detail of Caravaggio's shadowy *Madonna of the Pilgrims,* which is considered to be one of his most beautiful paintings.

PIAZZA NAVONA AND ENVIRONS

Navona is the archetypical Roman *piazza.* Built over ancient ruins, made lavish by Baroque popes, and always the scene of lively street life, almost every visitor to Rome passes through here. The street vendors have shifted from tomatoes and sausages to caricatures and fake soccer jerseys, but the *piazza* is still lively from the morning until well after midnight. Pickpockets ply their trade in the shadow of Navona's three fountains, while customers of the expensive *enoteche* and restaurants nearby do their best to look like jaded sophisticates, even while shooing away rose-selling *vu cumpràs.*

The *piazza's* oblong shape is due to its past as a stadium. You can still see some of the stadium's foundations in P. Tor Sanguigna, outside the northern end of Piazza Navona. Contrary to popular belief, Domitian never used this 30,000-person venue to shred Christians; it was a racetrack. From its opening day, the stadium witnessed daily contests of strength and agility: wrestling matches, javelin and discus tosses, foot and chariot races, and even mock naval battles, for which the stadium was flooded and filled with fleets of ships skippered by convicts.

As the Empire fell, real-life battles with marauding Goths replaced staged contests, the stadium fell into disuse, and Romans used its crumbling outer walls as foundations for new houses. Crowds returned to the *piazza* when the space hosted the city's general market from 1477 to 1869. Festivals and jousts were commonplace, as was the contest of the *Cuccagna*, during which contestants shimmied up a greased pole to win fabulous prizes. These days, the market, selling beautifully crafted porcelain *presepi* (nativity scenes), marzipan fruit, and *Befane* (the Epiphany witch) of every size, comes to the *piazza* only from Christmas until Epiphany (Jan. 6). Legitimate portrait artists (and less legitimate caricaturists) roost here year-round, as do multilingual fortune tellers.

Navona owes much of its existence to a case of pure one-upsmanship. Innocent X, the Pamphilj pope who came to the papal throne in 1644, was eager to distract the Roman people from the achievements of his predecessor, the ubiquitous Barberini Urban VIII. Innocent cleared out the old stadium (where his family had a palace for centuries) and set about constructing a new *piazza* and palace to rival those of the Barberini family across town (see **Piazza Barberini,** p. 109).

FOUNTAIN OF THE FOUR RIVERS

The towering, rippling bodies in Bernini's famous Fountain of the Four Rivers *(Fontana dei Quattro Fiumi)* command the center of the *piazza* with the grandeur that Innocent intended. In an effort to sabotage his nemesis, the Pope managed to divert the flow of a repaired channel, which had been supplying the Fontana del Tritone in *Piazza* Barberini. Having stolen old Urban's thunder, Innocent commissioned Bernini to make something impressive out of it. Each of the river gods represents one of the four continents of the globe (as they were thought of then): the Ganges for Asia, the Danube for Europe, the Nile for Africa (veiled, since the source of the river was unknown), and the Rio de la Plata for the Americas. Beneath the figure of the Plata is a strange looking armadillo, representing American wildlife, and a bag of coins suggesting the wealth of New Spain.

According to legend, Bernini designed the Nile and Plata statues to shield their eyes from his arch-rival Borromini's Church of San Agnese in Agone. The rivalry continued when Borromini perched his statue of St. Agnes on top of the church to look out beyond the *piazza*, not deigning to drop her gaze onto Bernini's work.

OTHER FOUNTAINS

At the southern end of the *piazza*, the **Fontana del Moro** attracts pigeons and small children alike. Originally designed by Giacomo della Porta in the 16th century—Bernini renovated it in 1653 and added Il Moro. The central figure, supposedly modeled on a king of the Congo who died in Rome while on a mission to the Pope, perches precariously on a mollusk while struggling with a fish. The tritons around the edge of the fountain were moved to the Giardino del Lago in the Villa Borghese in 1874 and replaced by copies. Balancing the whole scene is the **Fontana del Nettuno,** flowing in the north end of the *piazza*. It too was designed by della Porta and spruced up by Bernini. It was without a central figure until 1878, when Antonio della Bitta added the Neptune.

CHURCH OF SANT'AGNESE IN AGONE

Western side of P. Navona, opposite Fontana d. Quattro Fiumi. Open daily 9am-noon and 4-7pm.

According to legend, in ancient times St. Agnes rebuffed the advances of the lascivious son of a magistrate and was stripped naked in Domitian's stadium as punishment. Miraculously, her hair instantly grew to cover her shameful nudity.

Piazza Colonna

Camp dei Fiori

Piazza dell'Orologio

Unhappy with this miracle, her persecutors tried to burn her at the stake. When the flames didn't singe her, efficient Diocletian decided to cut her head off. It worked. The church marks the spot where she was nearly exposed and houses her severed skull (referred to as the *Sacra Testa*, or Holy Head) in its sacristy. The chapels above the altars are decorated with reliefs and statues instead of paintings, largely by Bernini's pupil Ferrata. Borromini designed the dome and facade with twin bell towers.

SANTA MARIA DELLA PACE

CHURCH OF SANTA MARIA DELLA PACE

Take V.d. Tor Millina from the western side of P. Navona. Turn right on V.d. Pace. Open daily 7:45am-noon and 4:30-7:30pm. Temporarily closed for restoration since the summer of 2003.

Enter the church through **Bramante's cloisters.** Originally built in 1482, the church's facade got a facelift from the imaginative Baroque architect da Cortona in 1656, giving it a charming semicircular porch and making it so popular among Rome's upper crust that the *piazza* became jammed with the carriages of devout patricians. It was only in the 19th century that the *piazza* was expanded, a development so popular that a Latin inscription was put up declaring that no stone in the *piazza* could ever be moved. The **Chigi chapel** (first on the right) is decorated with *The Sybils* by **Raphael.**

CHURCH OF SANTA MARIA DELL'ANIMA

V.d. Pace, 20. Across from S. Maria della Pace. Open daily 8am-1pm and 2-7:30pm. Ring the bell.

The unassuming German National Church in Rome hides a fragrant courtyard and a spookily deserted, dark interior. Keep an eye out for the bizarre skull-cherub reliefs everywhere and the smooth imitation of Michelangelo's *Pietà*, along with Peruzzi's beautiful tomb of the Dutch Pope Adrian VI.

VIA DEL GOVERNO VECCHIO

V.d. Governo Vecchio runs west from the southern end of P. Navona, and is best known for its art and antique galleries and restaurants. The street, which heads west to the Vatican, used to be a papal thoroughfare, lined with the townhouses of prosperous bankers and merchants.

PIAZZA PASQUINO

Here, at the beginning of the road, a misshapen figure is all that remains of poor Pasquino, an ancient Roman bust that has been used as a a *statua parlante* or "talking statue" ever since Cardinal Caraffa put him here in 1501. Bringing together Rome's classical past, popular life, and repressive governments, irate citizens are free to cover Pasquino with their complaints about government, the church, or anything else. Though in earlier times people wrote directly onto the statue, nowadays signs and posters are taped to it.

PIAZZA DELL'OROLOGIO

Farther down the street, Borromini's Baroque clock tower stands guard—when it's not shrouded in scaffolding. Don't miss the beautiful Virgin supported by cherubs carved into the rear corner of the oratory below the clock tower. Beyond P. dell'Orologio, V.d. Governo Vecchio becomes V.d. Banchi Nuovi, and ends in P. Banco di Santo Spirito. In the 15th century, the *via* and *piazza* made up a banking district that attracted moguls from all over Italy. Not only did they change and hoard money here, but they also acted as bookies, taking bets on anything from sporting events to papal behavior. (The "pope eating a baby" 300-to-1 longshot was never cashed in.) The **Palazzo di Banco di Santo Spirito** was founded by Pope Paul V to provide credit to poor Romans. The dank little **Arco dei Banchi,** on the left down V.d. S. Spirito toward the Tiber, houses a Virgin and lamp to which Catholic passersby say a quick Hail Mary. Just inside the entrance and to the left, the arch shows the height of the 1277 flood.

CHIESA NUOVA

Bus #64 or 40. Seven blocks down C.V. Emanuele II from P. Sant'Andrea della Valle. Open daily 8am-noon and 4:30-7pm.

Originally founded in the 12th century as Santa Maria in Vallicella, Chiesa Nuova became the home base for Philip Neri's congregation of Counter-Reformation Oratorians. He rebuilt the church in 1575, calling it the "new church." The compassionate Neri was one of the great church reformers in the Counter Reformation and organized pious associations that cut across social lines to unite people. He often tested the piety of his aristocratic followers by making them do ridiculous things to test their faith, such as wearing foxtails through the streets or working as manual laborers on his church. During construction, the future St. Philip had a vision of the Virgin rescuing parishioners by supporting a collapsing section of the old church; inspection of the beams proved that they were indeed about to fall. **Pietro da Cortona** represented this mini-miracle in a 1644 ceiling painting. He also painted the decorations of the dome and the apse over the altar. The altar is decorated with three excellent early paintings by **Peter Paul Rubens.** The chapel on the left holds the remains of St. Philip Neri and is decorated with a mosaic version of Guido Reni's painting of the saint. Head through the door to the left of the altar to enter the sacristy. It was designed by Borromini and decorated with an excellent statue of St. Phillip Neri by Algardi. Ask if the **rooms of the saint** are open—they contain more paintings by Reni, Cortona, and Guercino. Next door is the 17th-century **Palazzo dei Filippini,** designed by Borromini, featuring his trademark complex concave and convex surfaces.

CAMPO DEI FIORI

Two blocks south of C.V. Emanuele II (on P. della Cancelleria or V.d. Paradiso) stands Rome's most frenetic *piazza*, **Campo dei Fiori,** a bustling marketplace during the day and a meatmarket of drunken young foreigners when the sun goes down (see p. 212). Until papal rule ended in 1869, the area was the site of countless executions. In the middle of the Campo, a statue commemorates the death of its most

Mausoleum of Augustus

Villa Medici

Piazza Farnese

famous victim: **Giordano Bruno** (1548-1600), who rises above the hubbub with his arms folded over a book. Scientifically and philosophically out of sync with his time, Bruno sizzled at the stake in 1600 for taking Copernicus one step too far: he argued that the universe had no center at all. Now the only carcasses that litter the *piazza* are those of the fish in the colorful **market.** Open M-Sa 6am-2pm.

NEAR CAMPO DEI FIORI

PALAZZO DELLA CANCELLERIA

Just down P. Cancelleria from the Campo, the entrance to the palazzo is on the left. Open daily 7am-noon and 5-8:30pm; winter 7am-noon and 4:30-8pm. No admission beyond courtyard.

A stone coat of arms marks this early Renaissance *palazzo.* Designed in 1485, it impressed an array of popes and cardinals, who in turn affixed their sacred insignias to it. The building's designer remains unknown, but its size and style have led some to suspect Bramante. While Bramante may not have had anything to do with the building itself, his fingerprints are all over the **courtyard,** which is ringed by three stories of *loggie* supported by Doric columns and resembles his restoration of the adjoining **Basilica of San Lorenzo in Damaso.** Today, the Cancelleria is the seat of the three Tribunals of the Vatican and is considered part of Vatican City.

THEATER OF POMPEY

Walk out of Campo dei Fiori on Passetto del Biscione; go right at V.d. Grotta Pinta.

The V. Grotta Pinta is a canyon of curved *palazzi* built over the remains of the semi-circular Theater of Pompey. Pompey the Great, one of the power-hungry generals of the first century BC, competed with his rival Julius Caesar in both war and peace. Aggravated by Caesar's popular victories in Gaul, the arrogant Pompey built a grandiose theater, the first of its kind in the city. Unfortunately, the prudish Senate had outlawed permanent theaters because it feared they would corrupt public morals. To outwit the censors, Pompey built a small shrine at the top of the stands and called the whole complex a temple. Though Caesar bested Pompey politically, the old general still got the last laugh: it was in Pompey's portico, built to surround his sumptuous theater, that Caesar was assassinated on the Ides of March, 44 BC. A note to archaeology nuts: on the back side of the theater on V.d. Biscione, two restaurants, **Ristorante San Pancrazio** and **Ristorante da Costanza,** have basement dining rooms built out of the theater's substructure.

PALAZZO MASSIMO "ALLE COLONNE"

The Church of San Pantaleo is open for mass M-Sa 7:30am and 7:15pm; Su 7:30, 11:30am, and 7:15pm.

Just across C. Vittorio Emanuele II from P. della Cancelleria in P.S. Pantaleo, this *palazzo* was built by Baldassare Peruzzi from 1532-1533 and is home to a family that traces its origins all the way back to the Roman general Fabius Maximus (hence "Massimo") Cunctator, who kept Hannibal from capturing Rome in the late 3rd century BC. The *palazzo* has a curved exterior because it rests on the foundations of Domitian's ancient Odeon theater. Behind the *palazzo,* a solitary column remains from the ancient edifice. The back wall of the palace preserves a cycle of 16th-century monochrome paintings; most houses in Rome once boasted such intricate decoration, but few have resisted the assaults of wind and rain as well as this one. Also in P.S. Pantaleo, is the 1216 **Church of San Pantaleo.** Giuseppe Valadier added the strange facade in 1806.

PALAZZO DELLA FARNESINA AI BAULLARI

Just across C. Vittorio Emanuele II from Palazzo Massimo, this little *palazzo,* also known as the **Piccola Farnesina,** holds its own against the Campo's other stunning *palazzi.* Built in 1523 by Antonio da Sangallo the Younger for Thomas Le Roy, an English diplomat, the *palazzo* got its name from a case of mistaken identity. Le Roy's brilliant career in Rome was rewarded when he was made a nobleman and given special permission to add the lily of France to his coat of arms. The lilies were mistaken for the flowers that represent the Farnese family. The 19th-century interior houses the **Museo Barracco's** Greek, Roman, Egyptian, and Assyrian art.

PIAZZA FARNESE

PALAZZO FARNESE

The palazzo *is 1 block southwest of Campo dei Fiori down V.d. Baullari. The* palazzo *is closed to the general public: in order to see the interior, permission from the French embassy is required. Contact the French embassy 1 month prior to your visit.*

This stately and recently renovated *palazzo* was begun in 1514, and is today considered the greatest of Rome's Renaissance *palazzi.* The **Farnese,** a noble family from the backwoods of Lazio, parlayed Pope Alexander VI's affair with Giulia Farnese into popehood for her brother Alessandro. He became **Pope Paul III,** set up the Council of Trent, reinstated the Inquisition, and commissioned the best architects of his day—da Sangallo, Michelangelo, and della Porta—to design his abode. He also continued the trend of papal hijinks, having four illegitimate children and granting legitimacy to three.

Although the facade and entrance passage are remarkable, the most impressive part of the building is **Michelangelo's** cornice. Note the band of *fleurs de lis* encircling the building. Since 1635, the French Embassy has rented the *palazzo* for 1 lira per year in exchange for the Hôtel Galiffet in Paris, home of the Italian Embassy. The Farnese family had two huge tubs (the present-day fountains) dug up from the Baths of Caracalla (see p. 85) to serve as "royal boxes" from which members of the patrician family could view the parties and shows they hosted in the square during the 16th and early 17th centuries. The interior is decorated with Annibale Caracci's ceiling relief, showing the loves of the gods, decorated with *tromp l'oeil* architecture. On the northwest side of the *piazza* stands the **Church of Santa Brigida,** whose portal upstages its *palazzo.* The Swedish St. Bridget lived here until her death in 1373.

Church of l'Immacolata Concezione

Piazza Mattei

Piazza del Poppol

PALAZZO SPADA

To the east of Palazzo Farnese, off P. Capo di Ferro, the Baroque **Palazzo Spada,** built in 1544 for Cardinal Girolamo Capodiferro, houses the picture collection of the **Galleria Spada** (see p. 175) and also all sorts of *carabinieri* and dignitaries visiting the Council of Ministers elsewhere in the building. The *palazzo* is a treasure in itself, recently restored to its original creamy whiteness. Outside, eight ancient Roman kings, generals, and emperors stand proudly under Latin inscriptions describing their achievements. Inside, 18 even less modest Roman gods stand, buck naked, around the court—even the prudish Vesta. Cardinal Bernardino Spada, who acquired the palace in the 17th century, commissioned the elaborate decorations to compensate for the relatively puny size of his palace, but to make the palace seem bigger he went beyond naked gods and had Borromini design an illusionistic colonnade beyond the library on the right side of the courtyard. The colonnade seems to stretch back through a spacious garden, framing a life-size Classical statue. In reality, Borromini manipulated perspective by shrinking the columns and pavement dramatically. The colonnade is only a few meters long, the statue stands a meter tall, and the garden is no more than a narrow alley.

VIA GIULIA

As part of his campaign in the early 1500s to clean up Rome after the Babylonian Captivity (when the popes moved to Avignon and the city fell into serious disrepair; see p. 47), Pope Julius II commissioned Bramante to construct a straight road leading to the Vatican. V. Giulia (ah, modesty) runs parallel to the Tiber northwest from Ponte Sisto to P. d'Oro. Don't be confused by the fact that the odd building numbers begin near Ponte Sisto, while the evens begin at P. d'Oro. This relatively wide road was a contrast to the narrow and winding medieval streets of the day. Throughout the 16th century, the charming road was a fashionable neighborhood, and later architects built its expensive residences in accordance with Bramante's restrained, Classical vision. In the 17th century, Innocent X built a prison here to slum down the area and make his own P. Navona more important. It didn't work: the tiny neighborhood still attracted popes, nobility, and artists, including Raphael, who lived at #85, while P. Navona attracted second-rate caricaturists and pickpockets. V. Giulia remains one of Rome's most exclusive streets, with well-maintained *palazzi*, antique stores, and art galleries.

MICHELANGELO'S FOOTBRIDGE

Perhaps the most striking of the area's sights is the ivy-draped bridge that spans V. Giulia from the back of the **Palazzo Farnese** (p. 101) to the Tiber embankment. Michelangelo designed the bridge, which was originally intended to be the first leg of a much longer bridge that would cross the Tiber. Alessandro Farnese wanted to connect his *palazzo* with the Villa Farnesina on the other side with a private walkway, but funds dried up before its completion (see **Museums,** p. 149). Off the southeast corner of the *palazzo* lurks the **Fontana del Mascherone.**

CHURCH OF SAN GIOVANNI DEI FIORENTINI

In P. Dell'Oro, at the northern end of V. Giulia. Open M-Sa 7am-noon and 4:30-7:30pm, Su and holidays 7:30am-1pm and 4:30-8pm.

Seated at the center of Rome's Renaissance Florentine community, this church was built by Pope Leo X, a Medici from Florence, in hopes of illustrating the glories of his hometown. All the famous artists competed for the privilege of building it; Jacopo Sansovino didn't live long enough to finish, so the work was farmed out to da Sangallo and della Porta, and finally wrapped up by Carlo Maderno in 1614. Ask the sacristan to show you the *crypta Falconieri*, an impressive family tomb designed by Borromini and located behind the altar. Borromini is also buried in the church—look for his gravestone on the pill ars on the left. Salvator Rosa painted the dramatic altarpiece on the right transept altar. Notice the church's two busts: Bernini's on the right and a work by his lesser-known father, Pietro, on the left.

LARGO ARGENTINA

Toward the beginning of C. Vittorio Emanuele II lies Largo di Torre Argentina, a busy cross-street that sees too much of Rome's bus and taxi traffic. The largo is named for the square *Torre Argentina* that dominates its southeastern corner.

AREA SACRA DI LARGO ARGENTINA

This sunken area in the center of the largo is a complex of four Republican temples unearthed in 1926 during Mussolini's project of demolishing the medieval city. Their excavation is as much testament to *il Duce's* disregard for Rome's medieval heritage as it is a tribute to his reverence for its antiquities. Archaeologists don't know to whom the temples were dedicated, but it is believed that they were connected with the larger complex built around the **Theater of Pompey** (see p. 100). The site is now a **cat shelter,** and dozens of cats patrol its grounds, providing the photos of cats sitting on broken columns that calendar makers love so much. The shelter (☎687 21 33; www.romancats.com) appreciates donations to help feed the cats.

CHURCH OF SANT'ANDREA DELLA VALLE

One block west of Largo Argentina, in the direction of the Vatican and the Tiber River, on C. Vittorio Emanuele II. Open M-Sa 7:30am-noon and 4:30-7:30pm.

Begun in 1591 by Grimaldi and completed by Baroque bigwig Carlo Maderno, this church sports a 1665 facade by Rainaldi, who challenged the contemporary style by displaying rows of columns and pediments in place of swirls and curls. The conventional interior, where Puccini's opera *Tosca* begins, is modeled on **Il Gesù** (p. 91) and dominated by an array of excellent Baroque paintings. Lanfranco frescoed the dome with its depiction of layers of angels, while Domenichino painted the pendentives and the scenes of the life of the saint in the curved area above the altar, with their beautiful landscapes. The most striking paintings are Mattia Preti's scenes of the martyrdom of St. Andrew behind the altar.

JEWISH GHETTO

South of Largo Argentina. Bordered by V. Arenula (tram #8) and by V.d. Teatro di Marcello (bus #44, 63, or 170). The Service International de Documentation Judeo-Chrétienne, V. Plebiscito, 112, an information center for Jewish-Christian relations, has half-day walking tours of the Ghetto during the school year. ☎06 679 53 07. €2.58 donation.

Although Dickens declared the area "a miserable place, densely populated, and reeking with bad odours," today's Jewish Ghetto is one of Rome's most charming and eclectic neighborhoods, with family businesses dating back centuries and restaurants serving up some of the best food in the city (see **Food** p. 191).

The Jewish community in Rome is the oldest in Europe, and began in the late Roman Republic when migrants arrived to be near the political and economic hub of the Mediterranean. After 1,500 years of relatively peaceful cohabitation, Pope Paul IV (1476-1559) decided that the Jewish population of Rome should be confined to its own neighborhood, and erected the walled ghetto in a neighborhood prone to flooding. He restricted its inhabitants to careers in money-lending and used-clothes peddling, and required them to swear oaths of submission to the pope in annual ceremonies by the **Arch of Titus** (p. 76), a monument celebrating the Roman conquest of Jerusalem. The ghetto was torn down after Italy's unification, and more than 2,000 of Rome's Jews were deported to concentration camps during the Nazi occupation.

CHURCH OF SANTA MARIA IN CAMPITELLI

Off of V.d. Teatro di Marcello in P. di Campitelli. Open M-Sa 7am-noon and 4-7pm. Mass Su and holidays 7:30, 10am, noon, 6:30pm.

The Counter-Reformation plan to beautify Rome led to the construction of a new church, Santa Maria, in the swanky and very central *Piazza* di Campitelli. Designed by Carlo Rainaldi and constructed in 1662, the church was intended to give thanks to Mary for delivering the city from the plague in 1656. It houses the statuette believed to have miraculously ended the plague.

PALAZZO CENCI

Technically outside the Ghetto, Palazzo Cenci is at the end of V. Catalana, which runs parallel to V.d. Portico d'Ottavia. This *palazzo* was home to Beatrice Cenci, made famous by Dickens's and Shelley's accounts of her execution after she, along with her brother and stepmother, murdered her cruel and incestuous father at the end of the 16th century.

SANT'ANGELO IN PESCHERIA

Toward the eastern end of V.d. Portico d'Ottavia. Prayer meetings W 5:30pm and Sa 5pm.

This church was built right into the Portico d'Ottavia (see p. 89) in 755 and was named after the fish market that once stood here. You can still see an official plaque requiring that the head and body up to the first fin of any fish longer than the length of the plaque be given to the Conservators of Rome. It was here that the Jews of the Ghetto were forced to attend mass every Sunday from 1584 until the 19th century—they quietly resisted the forced evangelism by stuffing their ears with wax.

SINAGOGA ASKENAZITA

At the corner of Lungotevere dei Cenci and V. Catalana, opposite the Theater of Marcellus. ☎06 68 40 06 61. Temple open for services only.

The heavily guarded synagogue symbolizes the unity of the Jewish people in Rome and proclaims its unique heritage in a city of Catholic iconography. Built between 1874 and 1904, it incorporates Persian and Babylonian devices, attempting to create a different architectural style from Christian churches. A gray metal dome tops the temple, and inside, the front is graced with seven massive gold menorahs below the rainbow-colored dome. Orthodox services, to which anyone is welcome, are segregated by gender and conducted entirely in Hebrew. Rome remains keenly aware of the Holocaust, and the tarnished reputation it earned during World War II, and generally does an excellent job protecting the religious freedom of its citizens. The temple itself is heavily guarded after a 1982 terrorist attack by the Palestinian Liberation Organization (PLO). To protect civilian worshipers from further attacks, the doors are bolted from the inside during services. The synagogue houses the **Jewish Community Museum** (see p. 179), a visit to which gets you a brief tour of the temple itself.

PIAZZA MATTEI

The center of the Ghetto, accessible by walking down toward the river on V. Paganica from V.d. Botteghe Oscure (which runs between V. Arenula and P. Venezia).

TREVI FOUNTAIN

The 16th-century *Fontana delle Tartarughe*, in which four little boys are portrayed standing on the backs of small dolphins while pushing tortoises into the water, is the center of this hidden *piazza*. Designed by Florentine Giacomo della Porta, the fountain wasn't graced with turtles until Bernini restored it in 1658. According to local legend, Duke Mattei, a notorious gambler, lost everything in one night, and his father-in-law-to-be was so disgusted that he rescinded his approval of the marriage. The Duke, in a bid to wrest his name from the mud of scandal, had the fountain built in one night to prove that a Mattei could accomplish anything, even when completely destitute. Apparently it worked; he got the girl, although she blocked up her window so she would never have to see the fountain that got her married.

PIAZZA DI SPAGNA & THE CORSO

M: A-Spagna. Touring the area should take about half a day.

see map p. 363

If you need directions to the Piazza di Spagna, you're lost. The most self-consciously glamorous spot in Rome, the azalea-decked Spanish Steps rise from a crowded *piazza* to a rosy church flanked by palm trees—it's no wonder postcard photographers abound. For years this area was the artistic and literary center of Rome, but today the only artists you'll see will offer to paint your portrait for a few Euros. There's still plenty to do in and around the *piazza*: relive the past with a *cappuccino* at **Antico Caffè Greco** (p. 202), indulge in some high-end retail therapy, or simply sit on the steps with a gelato and enjoy your Roman Holiday—just like Audrey Hepburn.

The Spanish Steps and P. d. Spagna were once literally Spanish. The area around the Spanish ambassador's residence, located in the western end of the hourglass-shaped *piazza* since 1622, once held the privilege of extra-territoriality. Wandering foreigners who fell asleep there were liable to wake up the next morning as grunts in the Spanish army. Nowadays, they're more likely to wake up with no wallet.

SPANISH STEPS

Designed by an Italian, paid for by the French, named for the Spaniards, occupied by the British, and currently under the sway of American ambassador-at-large Ronald McDonald, the Spanish Steps *(Scalinata di Spagna)* could be an alternate location for the United Nations. The 137 steps were constructed from 1723 to 1725 to link the *piazza* to important locales above it, including the **Pincio** and the **Villa Mèdici.** The beginning of May heralds the world-famous flower show, when the steps are covered with azaleas and photographers, and each July an evening fashion show is held on the steps. When the area first opened to the public, Romans hoping to earn extra *scudi* as artists' models flocked to the steps dressed as the Madonna and Julius Caesar. Posers of a different sort abound today, and dressing like a virgin does not seem to be the main objective. At night, hordes of virile adolescent males, along with tipsy foreigners imitating their Italian counterparts, descend on the *piazza* in search of women.

FONTANA DELLA BARACCIA

Barges are hardly inspirational objects, however, when one such vessel was washed into the *piazza* after the Tiber flooded on Christmas Day, 1598, Gian Lorenzo Bernini's less famous father Pietro was so moved that he decided to immortalize it in stone. The fountain was built below ground level to compensate for meager water pressure in the area.

OTHER SIGHTS

At the southern end of the *piazza* rises the **Column of the Immaculata,** an 1857 celebration of Pope Pius IX's declaration of the Immaculate Conception. On December 8, the Pope kneels at the base, while Roman firemen climb their ladders to place a wreath atop the column. Just behind the column stands the **Collegio di Propaganda Fide,** or, as the Latin inscription above the entrance reads, the *Collegivm Vrbanvm de Propaganda Fide* (City School of Good Propaganda). Though it sounds like a leftover from the fascist era, the college was actually founded to train missionaries in the 16th century. The undulating facade along V.d. Propaganda was designed by Borromini. Just across from **Sant'Andrea delle Fratte**, at V. Mercede, 12, a plaque commemorates the building, now full of offices, where Bernini died.

NEAR THE STEPS

CHURCH OF SANT'ANDREA DELLE FRATTE

V.S. Andrea, 1. Facing the Spanish Steps, walk to the right on V. d. due Macelli, then follow the right fork along V. d. Propaganda until it intersects V. Mercede. Open daily 6:30am-12:30pm and 4-7pm. This is a fully operational church; be respectful of the devout. Masses at 7am, 7:30am, 8am-noon hourly, 6pm, and 7pm.

Capped by a Borromini bell tower, Sant'Andrea dominates the Via Capo le Case—just as its architects intended. Borromini died before the church was completed, allowing other masters to have a hand in its design. Bernini was involved; check out one of his later works, the two seraphim near the altar, which originally decorated the Ponte Sant'Angelo. Their companions can still be seen along the bridge in front of Castel Sant'Angelo (see p. 120). Also make sure to stop at the second chapel on the left, dedicated to the miraculous appearance of the Madonna to Jewish banker Alphonse Ratisbonne on January 20, 1842. Alphonse immediately converted to Christianity, became a man of the cloth, and later worked as a missionary in Palestine. Hundreds of lace hearts now hang on the altar and its surrounding columns to commemorate the event.

CHURCH OF SANTA TRINITA DEI MONTI

Top of the Steps. Open daily 8am-1pm. ***Tours*** *Tuesday and Friday at 11am, in Italian and French only. €3. Call ☎06 679 41 79 in advance for reservations.*

After indulging in the 5th sin (gluttony) at your choice of establishments on V. Condotti, ascend the stairs of heaven to the Church of Santa Trinita dei Monti. (Confessionals on the right.) The Neoclassical church was designed by Carlo Maderno and provides a worthy incentive to climb the steps, not to mention a sweeping view of the city. Known as the Church of the Kings of France, Santa Trinita was built in 1502 under the auspices of French King Charles VIII. Shortly thereafter the church was unceremoniously pillaged during the infamous 1527 sack of the city by Spanish King Charles V. Work was completed on the new building in 1570, and it was consecrated in 1595. This time, the church lasted over 200 years until it was sacked anew in 1798 by armies of Revolutionary France. The church was restored after the fall of Napoleon; today, the only original part is the transept, above the largest altar.

The third chapel on the right and the second chapel on the left contain works by Michelangelo's star pupil, Daniele da Volterra. The last figure on the right of his *Assumption* depicts his cantankerous teacher, but is currently undergoing restoration. Poussin rated Volterra's other painting, *Deposition from the Cross*, as one of the three greatest paintings ever. Having been restored twice and traveled to the Medici Villa and back, the painting is a bit worse for the wear. The fourth chapel on the left in the north transept was frescoed in the 16th century by the Zuccari brothers. The obelisk in the center of the church's *piazza* was brought to Rome in the 2nd century; its hieroglyphics were plagiarized from the obelisk in P. del Popolo.

Also worth a visit is the cloister attached to the church. Now a private school, the cloister features frescoed portraits of the kings of France, a garden with striking views of Rome, an *astrolabe*, and various *trompe l'oeil* effects designed by a monk turned mathematician. (You must take the tour to see all but the frescoes.)

VILLA MEDICI

Villa Medici, Via Trinita dei Monti, 1. ☎06 676 13 20; www.villamedici.it.

On the left as you face Santa Trinita, the Villa Medici houses the **Academia di Francia.** Founded in 1666 to give young French artists an opportunity to live in Rome (Berlioz and Debussy were among the beneficiaries), the Academy continues to house creative Francophiles and arranges excellent exhibits, primarily of French art. Behind the severe facade lies a beautiful garden featuring sculpted hedges, modern art, and at least one obelisk—as well as sweeping views of the city. Due to ongoing restorations, there are no regularly scheduled exhibitions and no regular hours. Call or check the Internet for current exhibitions (mostre) and opening times. Groups may arrange garden visits by calling in advance.

PIAZZA DI TREVI

M: A-Barberini or A-Spagna. Or, take a bus to P.S. Silvestro or Largo del Tritone.

TREVI FOUNTAIN

Nicolo Salvi's extravagant and well-touristed Fontana di Trevi emerges from the back wall of **Palazzo Poli.** The fountain was completed in 1762 by Giuseppe Pannini, who may have altered the original design. The fountain may

Minimi

Santa Trinita dei Monti is celebrating its 500th anniversary, an occasion to remember the original inhabitants of the church, the Minimi di Francesco di Paola (Minimi for short). The word "Minimal" refers to the fact that this order was probably the first organized group of vegans in history. Unlike their latter-day counterparts in The States' more decadent universities, these monks were not radicals for animal rights, but rather chose the simple, meatless life in imitation of Christ and the early apostles. This naturally brought them into conflict with the papacy; one of the favorite pranks of the otherwise somber Vatican was to send succulent, decidedly non-vegan fare to the good brothers. Tours of the famous, newly-restored dining hall (*refettorio*) where the monks categorically rejected such dubious peace offerings are available, but the real highlight of the church is a solar clock built to keep time using a single beam of sunlight and various astronomical charts. The monks were known not only for their scientific achievement, but also for their art. Their *anamorfosi* paintings, which can be viewed on the tour, are particularly impressive. These works are mathematically calculated to display different images from different viewpoints (precursor to the modern hologram).

Muro Torto

Triton Fountain

Pietà

also have been based on designs by Bernini who elaborated upon a simpler one by Leon Battista Alberti; the idea for combining the fountain and *palazzo* was based on a project by da Cortona. Regardless of its dubious architectural heritage, Fontana di Trevi has become a Roman staple, thanks to countless filmmakers (and the pack-instinct of most tourists).

RELIEFS AND SCULPTURES

Not surprisingly, the figure in the middle of the fountain is Neptune, the god of the sea. Neptune's chariot is drawn by two winged horses, guided by two Tritons (representing calm and stormy seas, respectively). Allegories of abundance and health can be found in the two niches on either side of the burly mermen, while the Four Seasons calmly survey the madness from on high, just under the Corsini family arms. In good old Roman style, the fountain's source is an aqueduct—specifically the **Acqua Vergine** aqueduct, which also supplies the spouts in P. Navona and P. d. Spagna. The relief at the top of the fountain on the left shows the fountain's namesake, Trivia, the maiden who allegedly pointed out the spring for the aqueduct to thirsty Roman soldiers. The opposite relief shows Augustus's right-hand man, Agrippa, giving the go-ahead for the aqueduct in 19 BC.

The fountain cleverly incorporates the facade of the *palazzo* into its design, effectively becoming a part of the *piazza's* architecture. Not everyone in the neighborhood was happy about this project, however; it's said that the proprietor of 85 Via del Stamperia complained so loudly and for so long that a wave was built in front of his store—business has been bad ever since. Just above the wave, notice that the window in the upper right is not a window at all, but a painting of one. A young Corsini took his own life one day by taking a dive out of the original window, and his family bricked it up.

TOSSING A COIN

Legend has it that the traveler who throws a coin into the fountain will have a speedy return to Rome. Proper form is to put one's back to the fountain and toss over the left shoulder with the right hand. As the donation increase, so do the rewards—the traveler who tosses two coins will fall in love in Rome, and after three coins the wedding bells begin to toll. Years of romantic hopes have done their damage: the coinage eats away at the travertine and stains the pool. Since the restoration, travelers have been advised not to follow the custom, but this hasn't put an end to the tradition.

TAKING A DIP

In Fellini's *La Dolce Vita*, the uninhibited Anita Ekberg takes a midnight wade in the fountain. Squads of roving policemen and policewomen armed with whistles and attitude keep others from re-enacting the famous scene. Though we won't say how we came to know this, illicit bathing will cost you upwards of €500 and a stern talking-to in Italian. Impossibly buxom "model" Anna Nicole Smith tried to do her own Ekberg impression in 1997 and had to cough up the dough. Save yourself the trouble and *spend that money* on gelato from nearby **San Crispino** (p. 199) instead.

CHURCH OF SANTI VINCENZO AND ANASTASIO

Opposite the Trevi Fountain. ☎ 06 678 30 98. Open daily 7:30am-12:30pm and 4-7pm.

The Baroque Church of Santi Vincenzo and Anastasio, rebuilt in 1630, was the parish "Church of the Popes" for many years. A church in some form has stood at this location since the 10th century. In its current incarnation, the church boasts a facade by Martino Longhi the Younger (completed from 1646-50) and a ceiling fresco by Francesco Manno. Coincidentally, S.S. Vincenao and Anastasio houses a crypt that preserves the **hearts and lungs of popes** from 1590 to 1903 in marble urns, which, unfortunately for you anatomy fans, is closed to the public.

PIAZZA BARBERINI

see map p. 367

Rising from the hum of a busy traffic circle at the end of V.d. Tritone Bernini's Triton Fountain (**Fontana del Tritone)** seems overwhelmed by the cars and motos speeding around P. Barberini. Banks, hotels, a cinema, and a large 24hr. Internet cafe give the *piazza* a distinctly modern feel. On the corner of V.V. Veneto, Bernini's **Fontana delle Api** (Bee Fountain), buzzes with the same motif that graces the Barberini coat of arms.

CHURCH OF L'IMMACOLATA CONCEZIONE

V.V. Veneto, 27a. Walk up V.V. Veneto away from P. Barberini. Open F-W 9am-noon and 3-6pm. Donation strongly suggested.

This severe 1626 Counter-Reformation church holds the tomb of Cardinal Antonio Barberini, the church founder. Perhaps the only modest

in recent news

Fishing in the Trevi

Roberto Cercelletta was no stranger to the Roman *carabinieri* (national police), who affectionately called him by his nickname, D'Artagnan, and looked the other way as he looted about €1000 per day from the Trevi Fountain. Six mornings a week, clad in galoshes and armed with a large magnet on a pole, he carried away the coins tossed into the fountain by tourists and destined for a number of Roman charities. On the seventh day, he rested, watching from afar the civic officials who came to collect the money, which, somehow, was always less than they expected.

For 34 years, it wasn't clear that Cercelletta was actually breaking any laws. The coins didn't belong to anyone, not even the city of Rome. An ordinance passed in 1999 to protect city monuments, however, hefted a fine upon anyone who waded in the fountain. Cercelletta was charged several times, but police found no indication, despite his staggering daily take, that he was able to pay. He owned a moped and a cell phone, but little else. In August 2002, after the Italian media made his crime public, he was arrested after one of his early morning wades and charged.

The Bone Collectors

The bones of 4000 Capuchin friars (for whom cappuccino is named) decorate the four rooms of the Church of L'Immacolata Concezione's Capuchin Crypt, one of the most bizarre and elaborately macabre settings in Rome. A French monk inaugurated the crypt in 1528, but never saw his brilliant concept brought to its completion because the crypt was not finished for another 350 years. Angels deck the halls, with hip bones serving as wings. The bodies of more recently dead friars stand, robed and hooded, beneath bone arches. Even the hanging lights are made of bones. Dirt was shipped in especially from Jerusalem to line the floors. The last chapel displays two severed arms with mummy-like skin hanging on the back wall. Also featured in this chapel is a child's skeleton plastered to the ceiling, holding a scale and a reaper, and accompanied by the uplifting inscription: "What you are now we used to be, what we are now you will be."

member of the family, his tomb's inscription reads "Here lies dust, ashes, nothing." Walk downstairs for the main attraction: the bones of 4000 dead friars in the **Capuchin Crypt** (see **The Bone Collectors,** p. 110). Five rooms of methodically arranged bones show off the creative, if morbid, sides of the 18th-century Capuchin friars. The church upstairs also offers less melancholic altarpieces by Baroque painter Guido Reni as well as works by Domenichino Caravaggio, Pietro da Cortona, and Lanfranco.

PALAZZO BARBERINI

Walk on the southern side of P. Barberini, up V.d. Quattro Fontane to the Palazzo.

Carlo Maderno began this *palazzo* in 1624 on commission from Pope Urban VIII, and then took on Bernini and Borromini to form a Baroque architecture tag-team. Maderno and Bernini designed the perspective effect that makes the third floor windows look the same size as those on the first floor, while Borromini designed a spiral staircase to the right behind the main facade. Inside, da Cortona decorated the main hall's ceiling with an exaltation of the various virtues of the Barberini, so they could be reminded of just how cool they really were. The *palazzo* houses the **Galleria Nazionale d'Arte Antica** (p. 174).

VIA VITTORIO VENETO

The Veneto curves north toward the Villa Borghese.

This street, which once symbolized the glamor of Rome in the 50s and 60s, now houses slightly less chic airline offices, embassies, and lux hotels. At the turn of the 19th century, pushy real estate developers demolished many of the villas and gardens, including the wooded preserve of the **Villa Ludovisi.** The speculator who bought the Ludovisi built a colossal palace in its place, but soon even he couldn't afford those crazy 19th century Italian taxes, and the government repossessed the palace. The US embassy now inhabits the immense *palazzo* (currently called the Villa Margherita), which it received in return for tons of surplus WWII goods in 1945. The rise of the movie industry and tourism in the 1950s marked V.V. Veneto's heyday. The grand cafes and hotels attracted bigwigs like Roberto Rossellini and Ingrid Bergman, eager paparazzi, and wide-eyed Americans. V.V. Veneto's prominence has faded, though pricey cafes and restaurants still offer tourists an American Breakfast or a *Menú Turistica.*

PIAZZA DEL POPOLO

M: A-Flaminio. Exit the station and pass under the city walls to the northern entrance to the piazza. A visit to the sights below should take about an hour.

The southern end of the square marks the start of three major streets: V.d. Corso, which runs to P. Venezia (you can see the gleaming *Vittoriano* at the end); V.d. Ripetta on the right, built by Pope Leo X for service to the Vatican; and V.d. Babuino on the left. Outside the Porta del Popolo is an entrance to the **Villa Borghese** (see p. 113).

At Napoleon's request, architect Giuseppe Valadier provided the ornamentation for the once-scruffy *piazza* in 1814, adding the travertine fountains on the western and eastern sides. To the west, a beefy Neptune splashes in his element with two Tritons. The eastern figures represent Rome flanked by the Aniene and the Tiber. Also present is the she-wolf suckling Romulus and Remus. Walls extending from both sides of the fountains form two semi-circles that enclose the square. Each end of the walls displays one of the four seasons. Once upon a time in a grislier era, P. del Popolo was a favorite venue for popes to perform public executions. Today the "people's square" has become a lively place, though executions are infrequent at best, and the Pope just isn't as lively as he used to be. Masked revelers once filled the square for the torch-lit festivities of the Roman carnival, and the *piazza* remains a favorite arena for communal antics. After a soccer victory or government coup, the *piazza* resounds with music and celebration.

CHURCH OF SANTA MARIA DEL POPOLO

On the north side of P. del Popolo. ☎06 361 08 36. Open M-Sa 7am-noon and 4-7pm, Su and holidays 8am-1:30pm and 4:30-7:30pm.

Don't let the unassuming facade of the church deceive you into passing it by—within its walls are many Renaissance and Baroque masterpieces. The gilded relief above the altar depicts the exorcism that led to the church's foundation. Pope Pascal II chopped down a walnut tree marking the legendary spot of Nero's grave, clearing ground for the church and allowing the terrified neighbors to live free of his ghost. The apse behind the altar was designed by **Bramante**—look for his signature shell pattern on the walls. In the vault of the apse, Pinturicchio painted a cycle of the *Coronation of the Virgin*. It is illuminated by 16th-century stained glass windows (the first in Rome) by Frenchman Guillaume de Marcillat.

DELLA ROVERE CHAPEL

Immediately to the right after the main entrance, this chapel harbors an *Adoration* by Pinturicchio. The fresco and its lunettes depict the life of St. Jerome. More frescoes by Pinturicchio's pupils are in the third chapel on the right; note its interesting *trompe l'oeil* benches.

CERASI CHAPEL

The Cerasi Chapel, to the left of the main altar, houses two spectacular **Caravaggios;** located on the right is the *Conversion of St. Paul*. Unlike previous painters, Caravaggio used contrasts of light and shadow instead of images of angels or God to show the apostle's conversion to Christianity as an internal spiritual experience. On the left is the somewhat less famous *Crucifixion of St Peter*, while over the altar, Carracci's *Assumption of the Virgin* demonstrates the artist's mastery of color.

CHIGI CHAPEL

Open daily 7am-noon and 4-7pm.

The Chigi Chapel, second on the left, was designed by **Raphael** for the wealthy Sienese banker Agostino Chigi, reputedly the world's richest man (see **The Era Before Dishwashers,** p. 174). Raphael proved especially ingenious in his designs for the mosaic of the dome. Instead of representing the angels as flat figures, he used perspective and foreshortening to make them seem to stand on top of the chapel, peering down from their gilded empyrean. A century later, Bernini completed the chapel for Cardinal Fabio Chigi, the future Pope Alexander VII. Bernini added two medallions of faces to the pyramids and the marble figure of Death in the floor. Bernini also designed the statues of Habakkuk and Daniel (with the lion at his feet).

OTHER SIGHTS

OBELISK OF PHARAOH RAMSES II

Restored in 1984, the obelisk commands the center of the *piazza*. Some 3200 years old, it was already an antique when Augustus brought it back as a souvenir from Egypt in the first century BC. Flanked on four sides by floppy-eared lions spouting water, its foundation provides a sensational rendition of the city.

CHURCHES OF SANTA MARIA DI MONTESANTO AND SANTA MARIA DEI MIRACOLI

At the southern end of P. del Popolo. S. Maria di Montesanto open M-Sa 4-7pm, Su 11am-1pm. S. Maria dei Miracoli open M-Sa 6am-1pm and 5-7:30pm, Su and holidays 8am-1pm and 5-7:30pm.

If you look closely, you'll see that the Baroque "twins" aren't quite identical. S. Maria di Montesanto, on the left, with a facade by Bernini, is the older sibling (1662). Santa Maria dei Miracoli was completed by Fontana in 1681. Carlo Rainaldi planned the site to integrate the three streets, the churches, and the *piazza* into a whole.

Although the twins are chock full of 17th-century Italian art, S. Maria di Montesanto has a few contemporary pieces as well. In *Supper at Emmaus* (1981), by Tommasi Ferroni, one of the dinner guests is wearing sneakers and jeans. Creative black tie, anyone?

PIAZZA AUGUSTO IMPERATORE

M: A-Flaminio. Walk down V.d. Ripetta from the south side of P. del Popolo. After years of restoration, the mausoleum has re-opened. Open Sa-Su 10am-1pm. €2.10. Free for those under 18 and over 65. *Ara Pacis is closed for renovation until Feb. 8, 2004.*

The mausoleum, the Ara Pacis, and an obelisk that now stands in P. Montecitorio were once part of an intricate plan to use sculpture, architecture, and even the movements of the sun to legitimize and exalt the Emperor Augustus. His mausoleum and the Ara Pacis were designed to showcase the probity of his rule and its connection to Roman traditions. On the day and hour of the anniversary of Augustus's birth, the shadow of the obelisk would point directly at the center of the Ara Pacis. In the 2000 years that have passed since the construction of the complex, however, only the mausoleum has remained in its original position.

MAUSOLEUM OF AUGUSTUS

The circular brick mound of the Mausoleum of Augustus once housed the funerary urns of the Imperial family. The oversized tomb (about 87 meters in diameter) may have been inspired by Alexander the Great's mausoleum, which Augustus visited while in Egypt. Cyprus trees once, and again today, line the tomb's circumference; a colossal statue of the emperor may have stood at its peak. Two obelisks, now relocated to other *piazze*, once guarded the entrance. Later centuries saw the mausoleum converted to a Colonna family fortress, a wooden amphitheater where Goethe watched some bear-baiting in 1787, and even a concert hall, until Mussolini restored it in 1936 and surrounded it with Fascist buildings, trying as always to associate himself with his hero, Augustus.

ARA PACIS

To the right of the mausoleum (coming from P. del Popolo). Heavy construction currently blocks the altar from street side view.

The Ara Pacis stands as a monument to both the grandiosity of Augustan propaganda and the ingenuity of modern-day archaeology. The marble altar, completed in 9 BC, was designed to celebrate Augustus's success in achieving peace after years of civil unrest and war in Gaul and Spain. The reliefs on its front and back include depictions of allegorical figures from Rome's most sacred myths: a Roman Lupercalia, Aeneas (founder of Rome and Augustus's legendary ancestor) sacrificing a white sow, Tellus the earth goddess, and the goddess Roma. The side panels show the procession in which the altar was consecrated, with realistic portraits of Augustus and his family and various statesmen and priests, all striding off to sacrifice cattle on the new altar to peace.

The altar, which stood alongside the ancient **Via Lata** (now the Corso), was discovered in fragments over the course of several centuries and only pieced together within the last century by Mussolini's archaeologists. The excavation was almost permanently halted, as it was discovered that the altar, buried some 10m underground, was supporting one of Rome's larger *palazzi.* To make matters worse, the water table of the city, having risen with the ground level over the past two millennia, had submerged the monument in over 3m of water. Archaeologists and engineers devised a complicated system of underground supports for the palace and, after freezing the water with carbon dioxide charges, painstakingly removed the precious fragments. Mussolini provided the colossal, aquarium-like display case.

VILLA BORGHESE

see map p. 365

M: A-Spagna and follow the signs. Alternatively, from the Flaminio (A) stop, take V. Washington under the archway into the Pincio. From P. del Popolo, climb the stairs to the right of Santa Maria del Popolo, cross the street, and climb the small path. BioParco, V.d. Giardino Zoologico, 20. ☎06 321 65 64. Open M-F 9:30am-6pm, Sa-Su 9:30am-7pm. €8.50, ages 3-12 €6.50, under 3 free. Santa Priscilla catacombs, V. Salaria, 430, along with the gardens of Villa Ada, are best reached by bus #310 from Termini, or the #630 from Venezia, or in P. Barberini. Get off at P. Vescovio and walk down V.d. Tor Fiorenza to P. di Priscilla to the entrance to the park and the catacombs. ☎06 862 062 72. Open Tu-Su 8:30am-noon and 2:30-5pm. €5.

The park of the **Villa Borghese** covers almost 7 sq. km north of the Spanish Steps and V.V. Veneto. Its shaded paths, overgrown gardens, scenic terraces, and countless fountains and statues are a refreshing break from the fumes and chaos of the city, as well as a great place to spend time when everything else is closed for the afternoon. Many workers eat lunch or enjoy siestas on park benches, ignoring both tourists who tool around in silly bicycle-car contraptions and couples making out on park benches.

In celebration of becoming a cardinal, Scipione Borghese hired architect Flaminio Ponzio and landscaper Domenico Savino da Montepulciano to build a little palace in the hills. They did him proud: the Borghese became the vastest and most variegated garden estate in the city and one of the first to follow the Baroque craze of edging ornamental gardens with contrived "wilderness." Completed by Dutch architect Jan van Santen in 1613, the building remained in the hands of the Borghese family until 1902, when it and all the works of art inside were purchased by the Italian state and subsequently handed over to the city of Rome.

Abutting the gardens of the Villa Borghese to the southwest is the **Pincio,** first known as the *Collis Hortulorum* (Hill of Gardens) for the monumental gardens the Roman Republican aristocracy built there. The hill is graced with the **Moses Fountain,** which depicts the spiritual leader as a wee babe in a basket. During the Middle Ages,

the local story

Secret gardens

Beth Blosser is a guide at the Villa Borghese's Giardina Segreta, where she supervises programs for children and gives tours of the garden installed by Cardinal Scipione Borghese.

Q: Was the entire park always part of the villa?

A: There were actually three enclosures in the villa, called *recinti*. The first was in front of the villa, basically an Italian landscape garden with a grid of paths. Where they intersected, there would be something interesting, like a fountain. The first enclosure had very high hedges. It was a typical garden in Rome, a dense forest. Although it was private, it was open several times a year and was created to entertain large groups. So, in other words, it was a public area of the private gardens.

From the first building near the back on, though, it became a completely private park, called the *parque dei dine*. It was stocked with deer, and you couldn't get to it except by going through the house. It was really only intended for the Borghese pope and the cardinal.

Q: What's the best time of the year to see the gardens?

A: The second of the secret gardens is really beautiful at the end of Feb. or the beginning of Mar., when the bulbs are in

(continued on next page)

the area served as a *necropolis* for bodies denied a Christian burial. Claudius's third wife, Messalina, created quite a stir in the nearby **Villa of L. Licinius Lucullus** by murdering the owner. When she later ran off with her lover, her infuriated husband sent his troops to track down and kill her. The Pincio family took possession of the storied villa in the 4th century. Since then, fleets of Vespas, skippered by surly teenagers, have replaced the Victorian carriages, but the view is still one of the best in Rome.

The elegant terrace of restaurants and cafes in **Casina Valadier,** rising above P. del Popolo, would offer an even better view if it were open. The Casina is being renovated for an as-yet-undetermined period of time and the restaurants have moved elsewhere or closed down. This locale has fed an unusual clientele of politicians and celebrities, from Gandhi to Chiang Kai-shek. The north and east boundaries of the Pincio are formed by the **Muro Torto,** or "crooked wall," so named for its irregular lines and centuries-old dilapidation. Parts of the wall have seemed ready to collapse since Aurelian built it in the 3rd century. When the Goths failed to break through this pile of rocks in the 6th century, the Romans decided St. Peter must be protecting it and refused to strengthen or fortify it, giving St. Peter a chance to do his job.

Northwest of the Pincio is the rose-planted **Villa Giulia,** home of the resplendent Museo Nazionale Etrusco (see p. 170). Villa Giulia also hosts outdoor classical concerts during the month of July (see p. 224). The park's other major museums are the **Galleria Borghese** (see p. 165), which houses one of Rome's finest sculpture Renaissance paintings collections, and the **Galleria Nazionale d'Arte Moderna** (see p. 170).

The villa's art is not limited to its museums; in the English-style **Giardino del Lago** (Garden of the Lake), Jacopo della Porta's *Tritons* look suspiciously like those in Piazza Navona. These are the real thing, moved here in 1984—the ones in Piazza Navona are copies. In the lake itself is the **Temple of Aesculapius.** Get a picturesque close-up from a rowboat (€3 for 20min.). Finally, there's an imitation medieval fortress, now the **Museo Canonica** (see p. 179). The **BioParco** is no world-class zoo, but it has plenty of animals, most of whom are sluggish in the Roman heat. North of Villa Borghese are the **Santa Priscilla catacombs** and the gardens of **Villa Ada.**

Although it might seem a little ridiculous, a tandem bicycle or bicycle-car hybrid is probably your best bet for getting around the park, which boasts a circumference of 6km. Several stands around the park, including one near P. le

Brasile, rent a variety of these vehicles. Expect to pay about €10/hr. for a 3-person hybrid, or about €7/hr. for a regular bicycle.

VATICAN CITY

M: A-Ottaviano, bus #64 (beware of pickpockets), #492 from Termini or Largo Argentina, #62 from P. Barberini, or #23 from Testaccio. ☎06 69 82.

see map p. 364

Perched on the western bank of the Tiber and occupying 108½ independent acres within Rome, Vatican City is the last foothold of the Catholic Church, once the mightiest power in Europe. Since the Lateran Treaty of 1929 (see **History,** p. 50), the Pope has reigned with full sovereignty over this tiny theocracy but must remain neutral in Roman and Italian politics. As the spiritual leader of millions of Catholics around the world, however, the Pope's influence extends far beyond the walls of his tiny domain. The nation preserves its independence by minting the Vatican Euro (something of a collector's item), running a separate postal system and radio station, and having its own governor (appointed by the Pope). The Vatican is protected by the Swiss Guards, the world's most photographed military men. The guards wear flamboyant uniforms designed, *not* by Michelangelo, as tour guides insist, but by some nameless seamstress in 1914, perhaps inspired by a fresco in the Raphael Rooms of the Vatican Museum (p. 155). Although priests, nuns, and other official visitors are allowed in all areas, tourists are only admitted to the Basilica and the stellar **Vatican Museums** (see p. 150). Visitors reserving in advance may also tour the Vatican gardens (see p. 120).

What's it like to live in the Vatican? It's no party. More than 95% male, the population must conform to a set of rules even the draconian hostel owner would never dare to enforce. The curfew is 10pm, when the last city gates lock up for the night, and no commercial entertainment is permitted. The 900 inhabitants are nonetheless very well connected: the Vatican's phone per capita ratio is the highest in the world.

ST. PETER'S BASILICA

*Multilingual confession available; languages– about 20–are printed outside the confessionals by the main altar. **The Pilgrim Tourist Information Center** is located*

the local story

flower. It's called the aviary garden, because the Cardinal used to have a collection of rare birds. The garden next to the aviary was used for the Cardinal's other collection, rare bulbs. When the garden is really extraordinary is in Apr. or May, when the two or three varieties of irises and 15 or 16 types of antique roses are blooming. When they redesigned the gardens, they were sure to only plant the things that would have been here in the early 17th century, when the gardens were built.

Q: How did they redesign the gardens?

A: We don't have graphic documentation of how the gardens were originally, so they designed based on what we know about gardens from that period in general. One thing we did have was a list of the plants, because of the Borgheses' careful accounting. We also know about the uses of the flowers. The roses in particular were used widely, on tables, in drinking water, and even on the ground to perfume the path for people running foot races.

Q: What's an interesting thing about the Villa Borghese that average tourists might not know about?

A: Behind the museum, there's a garden, built in the 1920s. It has a little Venus fountain, and in the back, there's a piece of stone. It's the tomb of the Borghese dog.

on the left between the rounded colonnade and the basilica, and offers a multilingual staff, Vatican post, free brochures, and currency exchange. Next to the Information Center is a ***first-aid*** *station and free bathrooms. Open daily Apr.-Sept. 7am-7pm; Oct.-Mar. 7am-6pm. Mass M-Sa 8:30, 10, 11am, noon, 5pm; Su and holidays 9, 10:30, 11:30am, 12:10, 1, 4, 5:30pm; Vespers at 5pm. Plan on spending at least 2hr. in St. Peter's.*

Of all the Church's treasures, St. Peter's Basilica may be its most prized. To provide a fitting introduction to the heart of the Vatican City, the Church hired Baroque sculptor Gian Lorenzo Bernini to design the Piazza San Pietro. It seems that Bernini wanted the marble *piazza* to greet pilgrims as a surprise after their wanderings through the medieval Borgo district. Mussolini, as it happens, had other ideas for the *piazza*. In the 1930s, he built V.d. Conciliazione, a column-lined avenue that approached the basilica from the east. The road provided Benito with a prime parade route, and offered a grand, if austere, entrance to the elliptical Piazza San Pietro. Yet even without the element of surprise, Bernini's masterful *piazza*— with its 96 statues, two fountains, and one Alexandrian obelisk—is truly overwhelming.

Although the Piazza San Pietro shows traces of Bernini's genius, the basilica itself has an even more impressive artistic pedigree. Designed in turn by Bramante, Raphael, and Michelangelo, St. Peter's marks the resting spot of the bones of St. Peter, the church's founder. (For more on church history, see p. 53.) A Christian structure of some kind has stood on this spot since Emperor Constantine made Christianity the state religion in the middle of the 4th century. In 1506, with Constantine's original brick basilica aging, Pope Julius II called upon **Donato Bramante** to carry out his monumental vision of a new church for what he saw as a new world. Bramante designed the basilica with a centralized Greek-cross plan—a decision which proved contentious for the next 100 years. Bramante's work was so expensive that he continually asked the cardinals for money. To pay the bills, the cardinals sold indulgences, which eventually contributed to the Protestant Reformation, and a boatload of religious dissidents who settled America.

Bramante died before completing his project, and **Raphael** was tapped to continue his work. Raphael, like Bramante, died before getting the job done. Construction all but halted until 1539, when Paul III appointed **Antonio da Sangallo the Younger** to continue the project. Sangallo spent seven years working on a 25 ft. model of his design, which cost as much as a small church to build. Both Raphael and Sangallo envisioned St. Peter's as a Latin cross, with one hall of the church longer than the others. In 1546, Paul III handed 72-year-old **Michelangelo** the job of completing the basilica, with three times the budget. Even though he and Bramante reportedly hated each other, Michelangelo reverted to the Greek-cross plan because of his love of symmetry. Unfortunately, Michelangelo, too, was finished before his project. **Carlo Maderno** put the final touches on the basilica, lengthening St. Peter's nave and adding three chapels. The basilica's famous double-shelled dome was designed by Michelangelo, and its central apex lies directly over St. Peter's bones. **Giacomo della Porta** altered the ribs and lantern after Michelangelo's death. To get a sense of scale, you might look at the golden ball just below the cross on the top of the dome—16 people can comfortably fit inside.

AROUND THE BASILICA

After walking through Bernini's colonnade, you'll be in the rectangular part of the *piazza* just before the basilica. In the warmer months, a stage and a mind-boggling number of chairs are set up in this area for the Pope's weekly audiences (W 10:30am). To the left, before the basilica, are the bathrooms, information center, and first aid station. Just before the steps on the left of the basilica is a courtyard vigilantly protected by Swiss Guards. If you want to see the Tomb of St. Peter and the Pre-Constantine Necropolis (p. 119) ask the Swiss Guards to let you go to the Ufficio di Scavi, through this courtyard. To the right of the basilica, just at the end of the colonnade, is the entrance to the Prefettura della Casa Pontifica, where you may get tickets to a papal audience. This entrance is not marked; you must inquire with the Swiss Guards at the top of the stairs to gain admission to this office as well.

PORTICO AND ENTRANCE

Before entering St. Peter's, glance up at the central balcony. Flanked by pink marble, this is where the new pope is announced and subsequently gives his first blessing. Inside the portico, five doors with scriptural themes mark the entrance into the basilica proper. Unless the Pope is celebrating in the basilica, the central bronze door—taken from the old St. Peter's—is closed. The small door to the right is the *Porta Sancta* (Holy Door) and can only be opened by the Pope. Every quarter century, and on special anniversary years, the Pope knocks on its bricked-up center with a silver hammer to initiate Jubilee years of holy celebration.

PIETÀ

Chances are you'll be blinded by flashbulbs immediately as you enter the basilica. No, it's not the Italian paparazzi, but something more sublime: Michelangelo's *Pietà*. The marble *Pietà* (1497-1500) lies in the first chapel in the right aisle behind a wall of glass. Created when Michelangelo was 25, the piece established him as the preeminent contemporary sculptor in Rome. Michelangelo crowned his achievement by signing his name on the band directly across the Madonna's robe, making the *Pietà* the only sculpture he ever deemed worthy of his signature.

The sculpture was originally created for the chapel of the French Kings (Santa Petronilla) in the original St. Peter's, where it would have been viewed from the right. The current frontal display is thus incorrect (Christ, not the Virgin should face the viewer), and it is best to view the *Pietà* from the right. From this angle, the Virgin's piteous gesture is emphasized (she extends her hand toward the viewer) and Christ's elongated limbs and torso are appropriately foreshortened.

The Pietà made Michelangelo and the image of the Madonna cradling the dead Christ extremely famous. The theme originated in 14th-century Germany and was popularized in France; Michelangelo was simply the first to portray the unwieldy pose with such elegance. The finish on this statue, most visible on Christ's body, is extraordinary—Michelangelo never again finished a sculpture to this level of refinement. His Madonna is unusually youthful—too young to be the mother of a 32-year-old man. For this, Michelangelo was accused of heresy; he claimed that Mary's virginity preserved her youth. This interpretation of the Madonna could also be based on Michelangelo's readings of Dante and Petrarch, who thought of the Madonna as both the mother and daughter of God.

In 1962, the *Pietà* was sent to the World's Fair in New York, but it no longer travels. In 1972, a axe-wielding maniac attacked the famous sculpture, smashing the nose and breaking the hand off the Madonna. Since then, the *Pietà* has been restored by meticulous sculptors who examined the 1934 copy which stands in the Treasury of St. Peter's (see p. 120). Farther down the right aisle is the **Chapel of the Sacrament.** This chapel is reserved solely for prayer, and no photographs are allowed. You can catch a glimpse of the sanctuary through the windows on both sides of the entrance—Bernini's bronze ciborium, a model of Bramante's *Tempietto* at Rome's other St. Peter's (San Pietro in Montrorio, p. 125), and Bernini's bronze angels definitely merit a look.

ST. PETER

Moving from the Chapel of the Sacrament into the central nave of the basilica, you'll see a **bronze of St. Peter** presiding over the crossing from a marble throne on the right-hand pier. His feet have been worn smooth by visitors who stop to kiss or rub them. While this statue was once thought to date from the Middle Ages, research in the 1990s suggests that it may be the work of **Arnolfo di Cambio,** c.1300. St. Peter is decked out in full religious regalia on holidays. Joining him in the four corners of the crossing are statues of St. Helena, St. Veronica, St. Andrew, and St. Longinus holding sacred relics. Next to St. Andrew (on the left-hand pier closest to the entrance of the basilica) is the staircase leading down to the **Vatican Grottoes.**

ST. PETER'S DOME

High above the *baldacchino* (p. 118) and the altar rises Michelangelo's dome, which is built with a double shell, but designed as a circular dome, like the Pantheon (see p. 93). Out of reverence for that ancient architectural wonder, Michelangelo is said to have made this cupola a meter shorter in diameter than the Pantheon's, but its measurements are still eye-popping. The dome's highest point towers 120m above the floor and its diameter measures 42.3m across. When Michelangelo died in 1564, only the drum of the dome had been completed. Work remained at a standstill until 1588, when 800 laborers were hired to complete it. Toiling round the clock, they finished the dome on May 21, 1590.

Around the bottom of the drum is inscribed the biblical passage that gives the basilica its name: "You are Peter, and upon this rock I will build my church; I will give you the keys to heaven." As the scriptural justification for the opulence that is St. Peter's, references to these lines appear throughout the rest of the Vatican, especially in the Sistine Chapel. The remainder of the dome is decorated with images of Mary, Christ, and the Evangelists, as well as choirs of angels. At the very top God presides on high.

BALDACCHINO

In the center of the crossing, the *baldacchino*, another work by Bernini, rises on spiraling dark columns over the marble altar, reserved for the Pope's use. The Baroque structure, cast in bronze pillaged from the Pantheon, was unveiled on June 28, 1633 by Pope Urban VIII, a member of the wealthy Barberini family. Bees, the symbol of the Barberini family, buzz here and there (as well as on buildings and statues all over Rome), while vines climb up toward Michelangelo's cavernous cupola. The striking helical twist of the columns was inspired by columns from the Basilica of Constantine, upon which Jesus was said to lean while preaching to his disciples at the Temple of Solomon. One of these columns used to reside next to the *Pietà;* it can now be seen in the Treasury of St. Peter's (p. 119). In front of the *baldacchino*, 70 gilded oil lamps burn, illuminating Maderno's sunken *Confession*. Two semi-circular marble staircases lead to St. Peter's tomb, directly beneath the papal altar. These staircases are closed to the public, but a better view of the tomb is possible from the grottoes.

TRIBUNE

Bernini's masterful bronze tribune (completed in 1666) encloses a 4th-century throne taken from the palace of Maxentius, the emperor defeated by Constantine at the Milvian Bridge. The throne was so venerated in the Middle Ages that it was called Peter's chair, referring to the office of the pope and not to the actual historical figure. Carbon dating in the 20th century established the throne's actual age. Above the throne is a stained glass window illuminating the symbol of a dove, and located to the throne's right and left, tombs of Pope Urban VIII and Pope Paul III face each other.

To the left of the Cathedral Petri, in the left aisle and behind the statue of St. Veronica in the crossing, is Bernini's last work in St. Peter's, the Baroque **monument to Alexander VII.** A melodramatic example of a rather melodramatic style, a bronze skeleton symbolizing death emerges from a doorway with an empty hourglass in his bony fingers, telling the Pope that his time is up. Apparently unconcerned, Alexander prays calmly above miles of fluid drapery, surrounded by the four Christian Virtues. The hourglass soon ran out for Bernini as well, who died two years after he finished this statue.

Nearby, in the **Cappella della Colonna** (diagonally across from Alexander VII, moving toward the Tribune), is the monument to St. Leo the Great, surrounded by the tombs of not-quite-as-great St. Leo II and St. Leo III. The chapel holds Algardi's famous relief of St. Leo the Great, as pope, meeting Attila the Hun. Walking down the left aisle to the doors of the basilica, you'll find the **Cappella Clementina,** where a monument to Pius VII was sculpted by Thorvaldsen in 1823.

TREASURY OF SAINT PETER'S

To the left of the large Confession Chapel in the left hand aisle of the basilica, a door leads into the Treasury. Open daily Apr.-Sept. 9am-6:15pm, Oct.-Mar. 9am-5:15pm. Last admission 5:30pm. Closed when the Pope is celebrating in the basilica and on Christmas and Easter. €5, children 12 and under €3. Photographs not allowed. Wheelchair accessible. Plan to spend 30min.

The Treasury of St. Peter's holds some of the gifts donated to his tomb in past centuries. The marble plaque to the right on the entrance hall lists all the Popes in order, starting with Peter in AD 64. Among the highlights of the nine-room museum are: a massive column from the Basilica of Constantine; the "dalmatic of Charlemagne," an intricately designed robe that the illiterate Holy Roman Emperor donned for sacred ceremonies; the copy of the *Pietà* made in 1934; a clay statue of one of Bernini's angels (also seen on the Ponte S. Angelo); the magnificent bronze tomb of Sixtus IV; and the stone sarcophagus of Junnius Bassius (4th century), which is decorated with 10 biblical episodes from Creation to the capture of St. Peter. Lest you think Christianity was a bed of gilded diamond-encrusted roses, note the forboding device labeled *"strumento usato per torturare i cristiani"* (instrument used for the torture of Christians).

VATICAN GROTTOES

Near the statue of St. Andrew, which is the statue on the left, closest to the doors of the basilica, steps lead down to the Grottoes. Open daily 7am-6pm; Oct.-Mar. 7am-5pm. Wheelchair accessible by entering through the exit, near the entrance to the cupola. Photographs allowed. Plan to spend about 15min.

The Vatican Grottoes are the final resting place of many Catholic VIPs, including popes, emperors, and Queen Christina of Sweden. The passages are lined with tombs both ancient and modern, but bright lights, a fresh coat of paint and reassuring guards make this grotto anything but creepy.

CUPOLA

Ticket office is located at the exit of the grottoes; from inside the basilica, exit the building, and reenter the door to the far right as you face the basilica. On foot €4, by elevator €5. Rooftop terrace is wheelchair accessible, but cupola is not. Lines can be long, especially in the afternoon; you may want to consider visiting the cupola before the basilica, depending on the length of the line. Open daily Apr.-Sept. 8am-5:45pm; Oct.-Mar. 7am-4:45pm. Closed when the Pope's inside.

For unforgettable views of the interior of St. Peter's and the skyline of Rome, take the elevator or climb the steps to the base of the dome and the rooftop terrace. To get an even better perspective on the city, tackle the 330 stairs that lead to an observatory atop the dome. No elevator can save you from this climb, which will leave even the fittest *Let's Go* reader light-headed. But it's well worth it. Standing 370 ft. above the ground, you'll be able to spot most of Rome's major sights, the seven hills, and the Tiber's course. It's also a great opportunity to check out the Pope's backyard, complete with hedges in the shape of the papal seal, a fleet of shiny automobiles, and 10 satellite dishes. On the way down, drop a postcard in the Vatican mailbox on the terrace—everyone sends a postcard from the Vatican, but how many send one from the very top?

TOMB OF ST. PETER AND PRE-CONSTANTINIAN NECROPOLIS

On the left side of the Piazza San Pietro is the entrance to the necropolis, beyond the information office. ☎06 698 853 18; scavi@fsp.va. Open M-F 9am-5pm. You must reserve a spot in advance in order to see the necropolis. To request a tour, write to The Delegate of the Fabbrica di San Pietro, Excavations Office, 00120 Vatican City. Give a range of times and languages. Phone calls only accepted for reconfirmations. Book as far ahead as possible. €9.

Legend holds that after converting to Christianity, Constantine built the first basilica directly over the tomb of St. Peter, who had been crucified for preaching the Gospel. In order to build on that exact spot, the emperor had to level a hill and destroy the first-century necropolis that stood there before. There was no

St. Peter's Basilica

Castel Sant'Angelo

Galleria Borghese

proof for this story, however, until 1939, when workers came across ancient ruins beneath the basilica. Unsure of finding anything, the Church secretly set about looking for St. Peter's tomb. Twenty-one years later, the saint's tomb was identified under a small *aedicula* (temple), directly beneath the altars of both the Constantinian and modern basilicas. The saint's bones, however, were not found in the crude grave. A hollow wall nearby held what the church later claimed to be the holy remains— although archaeologists disagreed. It is quite possible that the bones were displaced from the tomb during the Saracen's sack of Rome in AD 849.

Multilingual tour guides will take you around the streets of the necropolis, which holds several well-preserved mausolea (pagan and Christian), funerary inscriptions, mosaics, and sarcophagi.

THE VATICAN GARDENS

For a guided tour of the gardens, make a reservation in advance. To request a tour, call ☎ 06 698 844 66 or 06 698 844 55. Tours: every day except W in summer, and Sa-Su in winter. €9.

Apart from those who are fortunate enough to have an office here (the municipal officers who run The Vatican), relatively few people venture into the gardens. All the better to see you with, fair greenery. Book early to guarantee a desirable viewing hour, especially during the summer.

CASTEL SANT'ANGELO

Down V.d. Conciliazione from St. Peter's. To enter the castle, walk along the river with St. Peter's behind you, and the towering castle to your left. Signs will point you to the entrance. Alternately, cross the Tiber on Bernini's Ponte S. Angelo, which leads directly to the entrance of the Castel. ☎ 06 687 50 36 or 06 697 91 11. Open Tu-Su 9am-7pm. €5, EU citizens under 18 and over 65 free. EU students 18-25 €2.50. Tours of the dungeon detailing art history Su 12:30pm in Italian, 2:30pm in English; call for information and reservations ☎ 06 681 91 11. Bookstore offers information and reservations; audio guide in English, French, German, Italian, and Spanish €4. No photos in rooms with frescos.

St. Peter's may have popes and the Colosseum gore galore, but only Castel Sant'Angelo boasts a 3-for-1 special, all under one roof. Rising from the banks of the Tiber, the massive Castel Sant'Angelo began as a mausoleum and was subsequently recycled as a fortress, prison, and palace— and it's easy to see why. The round building lies on prime Roman real-estate (within shouting distance of St. Peter's and a bridge away from the Pantheon). It remained an important political landmark until it was turned into a museum in the 1930s. The metamorphosis of this ancient structure provides a quick-and-dirty general history of Rome after Augustus, as well as the once-in-a-lifetime chance to see a papal bathroom.

Castel Sant'Angelo was originally constructed as a mausoleum by Hadrian (AD 117-138), an emperor who dabbled in architecture. Hadrian's mausoleum didn't last long as such, and was incorporated into the walls of Rome by Aurelian in 271. After the castel was sacked by Alaric in 410 and the besieging Goths in 537, Pope Gregory the Great saw a vision of Archangel Michael atop the fortress, which he interpreted as a sign of the end of the plague. As luck would have it, the plague did end shortly thereafter, and the fortress was renamed Castel Sant'Angelo. (Michael, although an angel, is sometimes called "St. Michael.")

The castle was frequented thereafter by various Popes; during the sack of Rome in 1527, Pope Clement VII ran for his life along the Leonine wall between the Vatican and the fortress, while the imperial invaders took potshots at his streaming white papal robes. Pope Paul III had a more sedentary term in the castle, building a sumptuous suite of apartments atop the ancient foundations. Pesky heretics and troublemakers, including the revolutionary astronomer Giordano Bruno and thieving artist Benvenuto Cellini (who was once stored for a day in one of the larger vertical ventilation ducts), were relegated to the depths of the former mausoleum. If you'd like more information, the **audio guide** is probably your best bet, as there is relatively little written information within many of the rooms.

RAMPARTS & MAIN CASTLE ROOMS

Directly opposite the ticket booth, iron stairs lead down to a spiral ramp that at first glance, looks like part of Hadrian's private parking garage. Although the ramp used to be a straight shot to the big guy's tomb, it now serves as a remarkably well-preserved reminder of Imperial Rome. Note the low lighting, damp air, and the occasional floor mosaic. At the top of the ramp, you can turn right and climb to the fortress ramparts and four circular bastions, named for the four evangelists. From the ramparts you can see the massive cement remains of Hadrian's mausoleum and bits of the travertine and marble that once encased it completely.

Back toward the ramp's exit, a bridge leads into the mausoleum. Inside, a wooden ramp (built by Alexander VII) rises steeply over the emperor's tomb while creepy incendiary urns, typical of those that held the ashes of many a Roman emperor, sit in niches in the walls. Try not to sneeze—all of Hadrian's descendants, ending with Caracalla, were cremated in the mausoleum.

The ramp leads outside into **The Court of the Angel,** where you'll find the Archangel Michael, sculpted by Raphael "not the really famous Raphael" di Montelupo in 1544. To the right of the statue is Michelangelo's **Facade of The Medici Chapel,** built for Pope Leo X, a Medici himself, in 1514. The facade captures the Renaissance admiration of balanced classical form.

This courtyard leads into the **Sala di Apollo,** which contains *grotteschi* frescoes painted in imitation of ancient Roman designs. Two rooms adjoining the Sala di Apollo display 15th- and 16th-century paintings. From the adjacent **Courtyard of Alexander VI,** stop to study the enormous crossbows and cannonballs that once served as the castle's defense. Another stairway, on your right as you enter the courtyard, climbs to the **bathroom of Pope Clement VII** nearby. Formerly heated by hot furnace air pumped behind the walls, it is still heavily frescoed with flighty grotesques painted for Clement's personal contemplation.

The stairway to the left of Clement's toilette leads to a gallery that circles the citadel, decorated at intervals with *grotteschi*, stuccos, and *loggie* built by Popes Julius II and Paul III. The bar offers shady tables in vine-covered niches overlooking St. Peter's, and provides a delightful spot for a pick-me-up.

Basilica of Santa Cecilia

PAPAL APARTMENTS

The extravagant Papal Apartments include the lush **Sala Paolina,** financed by Pope Paul III, where a fresco of Hadrian stares at a fresco of—who else?—Archangel Michael. Scenes from the life of Alexander the Great and St. Paul are also represented in fresco. Before the Pope was Paul III, he was Alexander Farnese, hence the choice of subject matter. Paul saw the Christian tradition as a continuation of the Greco-Roman one, and he venerated heroes from both eras. Don't miss the out-of-place black-coated man peeking out from a faux doorway on the right as you enter the room—it's speculated to be a caricature of Raphael di Montelupo, the sculptor of the first Michael statue. Also check out the papal bedroom nearby, where a sumptuous double bed raises the eyebrows of pious tourists.

Casa di Dante

OTHER ROOMS

The rest of the castle is less exciting; high points include the **Camera del Perseo, Camera di Amore e Psyche** (frescoed and filled with furniture), the **Pompeian Corridor** (with 16th-century graffiti), and the **Hall of the Library** (awash with scenes of cavorting sea gods and lined with stucco reliefs). Political prisoners of the popes were kept in the stone cells along the rim of the fortifications as late as the 19th century.

Keep climbing through temporary exhibition rooms, which usually show the work of recent Italian painters or photographers, to reach a broad, circular terrace with excellent views of the city. A large map outlines the principal sites, and the view of St. Peter's is well worth the 66 stairs. Above you on the terrace stands Peter Verschaffelt's bronze statue of Michael, completed in 1752.

Church of Santa Susanna

TRASTEVERE

Trastevere—a name that refers either to its *trans Tevere* (across the Tiber) location or its settlement during the reign of Tiberius—has a distinct Roman vibrance all its own. The *Trasteverini* claim to be descendants of the purest Roman stock—*Romani dei Roma* (Romans from Rome). Some residents even claim never to have crossed the river.

The legendary founder of Ostia, King Ancus Martius, first founded Trastevere not as a residential spot but as a commercial and military outpost to protect the valuable salt-beds at the base of the Tiber. The Vatican and Gianicolo hills that flank Trastevere became important outposts for defending the city from Etruscan invasions. During the Empire, sailors in the imperial fleet inhabited the area, building mud and clay huts along the river's banks. The success of a commercial port started by Hadrian lured Syrian and Jewish merchants to the neighborhood, and the maritime business flourished alongside such cottage industries as tanning, carpentry, milling, and prostitution.

By the Middle Ages, Trastevere's commercial activity began to wane and many residents retreated to the other side of the river. In his 1617 guidebook, editor Fynes Moryson warned readers, "because the aire is unwholesome, as the winde that blows here from the South, Trastevere is onely inhabited by Artisans and poore people." The popes took little interest in the neighborhood and rarely extended their wealth to build churches or monuments here. The community remained fiercely self-sufficient and in keeping with its independent spirit, Trastevere supported two revolutions in the 19th century: Mazzini's quest for a Republic in 1849 and Garibaldi's resurgence in 1867.

After World War II, things began to change—drastically. The cause was gentrification, as the quaintly 'backward' ways of Trasteverini slowly became celebrated by wealthy bohemian types and tourist operators. An recent influx of yoga stores, souvenir vendors, and middle-aged tourists has brought the threat of banality to this famously "authentic" Roman neighborhood. Thanks to rent control and centuries of fiery patriotism, however, the area has more or less retained its gusto. To keep the spirit of independence alive, **Noantri** ("We others," in dialect) is celebrated during the last two weeks of July. Though a bit tacky, the festival features grand religious processions, masses dedicated to protecting "the life of Trastevere," some kiddie rides, and a *porchetta* (roast pig) on every corner.

ISOLA TIBERINA

According to legend, Tiber Island shares its birthday with the Roman Republic—after the Roman tyrant Tarquin raped the virtuous Lucretia, her outraged husband killed him and threw his corpse in the river, where muck and silt collected around it, forming a small land mass. These violent origins may have deterred Republican Romans from settling the island; its first living inhabitants were slaves abandoned after they'd become too weak to work. On the island, the pitiful slaves prayed to Asclepius, the Greek god of healing. Rumor has it that when the Romans took his statue from the sanctuary at Kos and dragged it up the Tiber in 293 BC, the god appeared to them as a snake and slithered onto the island. The Romans took it as a sign that Asclepius wanted his temple here and, with their typical architectural aplomb, encased the island in marble, building its walls in the shape of a boat to commemorate the god's arrival. Traces of the original travertine decoration on the southeast side of the island are still visible—look for the serpent carved in relief near the "prow." The Romans built a large Aesclepius temple with porticos where the sick could wait for the god to visit them in their dreams and prescribe a cure. Nearby, archaeologists have found pits full of *ex voto* statuettes of arms, legs, and other body parts offered in thanks.

FATEBENEFRATELLI HOSPITAL

The demise of Aesclepius's worshippers in the fourth century AD was not enough to undo the island's long associations with healing. In 1548, a group of charitable Fatebenefratelli monks erected a hospital on the site which still occupies the northwestern half of the island (modernized in the 1930s). It was here that English King Henry I's courtier, Rahere, reputedly fought off malaria, a fatal disease in those pre-quinine days. He was so thankful that he promised to build a church and hospital in gratitude back in England (apparently he thought that Aesclepius already had Rome covered). True to his word, he built the structures that still stand in London's Smithfield district. Expectant Roman mothers consider the hospital the most fashionable place in the city to give birth. That's not surprising: it looks like a tropical villa on the outside and like a church, replete with open-air *piazze*, on the inside.

BRIDGES

The footbridge leading from the east bank of the river (on the Centro Storico side) is the **Ponte Fabricio** (commonly known as the **Bridge of Four Heads** for its two busts of Janus, the two-headed god of beginnings and endings). It's the oldest in the city, built by Lucius Fabricius in 62 BC. From the *lungotevere*, you can see the inscription Lucius carved into the bridge to record his public service. From the bridge, the beleaguered **Ponte Rotto,** one of Rome's less fortunate ancient constructions, is also visible to the south. Built in the 2nd century BC, the poor bridge underwent medieval repair after medieval repair, each time succumbing to the Tiber's relentless floods. Since its last collapse in 1598, it had been slowly disintegrating until it was accidentally blown up during the construction of the current metal bridge just downstream, the **Ponte Palatino.** Now all that remains is a single marble arch planted squatly, but proudly, midstream. On the other side of the island, the **Ponte Cestio** (originally built by Lucius Cestius in 46 BC and rebuilt in 1892) takes you across to Trastevere. The little bridge offers a stellar view of the Gianicolo and the Church of Santa Maria in Cosmedin. Stairs lead to the bank, where lovers, graffiti artists, and other social derelicts enjoy the many charms of secluded anonymity.

CHURCH OF SAN BARTOLOMEO

In P.S. Bartolomeo dell'isola. Open daily M-Sa 9am-12:30pm and 4-6:30pm.

This 10th-century church has been flooded and rebuilt many times, and is now something of an architectural chimera, with a Baroque facade, a Romanesque bell tower, 16 ancient columns, and avant-garde 20th-century stained glass windows.

CENTRAL TRASTEVERE

From the Ponte Garibaldi, V.d. Trastevere opens onto P.G.G. Belli and then P. Sonnino, Trastevere's transportation hub (centered on the ever-charming golden arches of McDonald's). A right onto V.d. Lungharetta takes you to P. di Santa Maria in Trastevere.

PIAZZA SIDNEY SONNINO

*The **Torre degli Anguillara (Casa di Dante)** is to the left. The **Church of San Crisogno** is opposite Casa di Dante, on P.S. Sonnino. Open daily 7-11:30am and 4-7:30pm. €1.55 donation to enter ruins. To reach the **Church of San Francesco a Ripa** from P.S. Sonnino, go down V.d. Trastevere and turn left on V.d. S. Francesco a Ripa. Open M-Sa 7am-noon and 4-7pm, Su 7am-1pm and 4-7:30pm.*

The 13th-century **Torre degli Anguillara** stands over a *palazzo* of the same name. The various members of the Anguillara family were notoriously active as priests, magistrates, warlords, criminals, and swindlers. The building now stands in honor of Dante Alighieri as the **Casa di Dante.** Across the street is the **Church of San Crisogno,** etched with the name of Cardinal Borghese. Although founded in the 5th century, the church has been rebuilt many times; twenty feet beneath the most recent structure lie the visitable remains of the original. To visit the ruins, walk into the room left of the altar; an attendant will lead you down the wrought-iron staircase. Traces of original wall paintings and some well-preserved sarcophagi and inscriptions are visible. On the left side of the church you can view a memorial and listen to an explanation of the life and times of Beata Anna Maria Taigi, housewife and saint who did good works while tending seven sons and her husband, "a difficult, rough character." Wives may wish to use this moment to chastise their husbands for being lazy pigs. Nearby, one of the first Franciscan churches in Rome, the **Church of San Francesco a Ripa,** showcases Bernini's *Beata Lodovica Albertoni* in a chapel on its left side. She lies in a state of surprising euphoria for a sculpture of a dead corpse, and is flanked by cherubim busts and suspended as if floating in thin air.

BASILICA OF SANTA CECILIA IN TRASTEVERE

From P.S. Sonnino, walk away from the river and go left on V.G.C. Santini, which runs into V.d. Genovesi. From V. Genovesi, go right on V.S. Cecilia. Open daily 7am-1pm, 3:30-7pm. Cloister open Tu and Th 10-11:30am, Su 11:30am-noon. Donation requested. Crypt €2.

During the 3rd century, Cecilia converted to Christianity and also managed to convert her husband Valerian and brother-in-law with her. The boys were later beheaded for their refusal to worship Roman gods. Cecilia inherited a considerable fortune from them both, becoming one of the richest women in Rome and inciting such resentment that the prefect of Rome ordered her death in 230. She was locked in her own steamroom to die, but miraculously survived. Her relations tried to behead her, but despite three tries, the executioners botched the job and she survived for three more days, slowly bleeding to death. Tirelessly optimistic, the hemorrhaging evangelist converted over 400 people before she died. She bequeathed her palace to build this beautiful church. Cecilia is known as the patron saint of music because she was found singing after her three-day stint in the steamroom. On November 22, St. Cecilia's day of martyrdom, churches hold a musical service.

Pope Urban I consecrated the church in her palace in the 5th century, but Pascal I rebuilt it in 821 when, according to one Vatican account, he dreamed that St. Cecilia revealed her true burial grounds in the catacombs of St. Callisto. He had her body exhumed and moved to the new church. Stefano Maderno's **statue of Santa Cecilia** lies under the high altar, showing what she looked like when exhumed from her tomb in 1599 in Maderno's presence—pretty good for a 1200-year-old corpse.

Sadly, Rococo restorers wreaked havoc on the medieval frescoes by **Pietro Cavallini** that once covered the church. However, fragments of his magnificent 1293 *Last Judgment* remain in the gated **cloister** on the right. Beneath the church lie the ruins of Roman buildings and an ancient church. The entrance is on the left as you enter the church, marked *"cripta e scavi."* Cardinal Rampolla, the man responsible for the excavations, is memorialized in the last chapel outside the church.

SANTA MARIA IN TRASTEVERE

From P.S. Sonnino, take V.d. Lungaretta. Open M-Sa 9am-5:30pm, Su 8:30-10:30 am, noon-5:30pm.

The church has the distinction of being the first in Rome dedicated to the Virgin Mary. Though this structure dates from the 12th century, an earlier basilica existed on the site under Calixtus in the 3rd century. The mosaics of the Virgin and the ten saintly women lining the exterior give way to a sea of gold and marble inside. The 12th-century mosaics in the apse and the chancel arch depict Jesus, Mary, and a bevy of saints and popes in rich Byzantine detail.

GIANICOLO

PIAZZA SAN PIETRO IN MONTRORIO

Take V. della Scala from P.S. Encidio to Vico del Cedro. Take V.d. Cedro to the end and climb the stairs to the piazza (you must cross V. Garibaldi half way up). Church and Tempietto open May-Oct. daily 9:30am-12:30pm and 4-6pm, Nov.-Apr. 9:30am-12:30pm and 2-4pm. Mausoleo Ossario Garibaldino open Tu-Sa 9am-1pm. Free.

Built on the spot once believed to be the site of St. Peter's upside-down crucifixion, the biggest draw of the **Church of S. Pietro in Montorio** is a masterly *Flagellazione di Gesu,* painted on slate by Sebastiano del Piombo from designs by Michelangelo. The church also contains the tombs of Irish noblemen, exiles persecuted by English Protestants. Next door in the center of a small courtyard is the stunning **Templete of Bramante** (1499-1502). A combination of Renaissance and Classical architecture, it provided the inspiration for the larger dome of St. Peter's.

Visible from the Church, just up the hill, is **Mausoleo Ossario Garibaldino,** a starkly fascist monument erected in 1941 to enclose the remains of Goffredo Mameli, the composer of the Italian national anthem. If you want to continue the national theme, a decent hike further up the hill (taking V. Garibaldi past the fountain and then veering right onto Passeggiata del Giancolo) will bring you to **P. Giuseppe Garibaldi,** the site of a patriotically over-blown statue-complex crowned by the revolutionary leader himself. (Take V. Garibaldi past the fountain and then veer right onto Passeggiata del Giancolo, continuing up past the kiddie carousel.) The *piazza* marks one of the last places that Garibaldi's ragtag Italian troops tried to hold off Napoleon. Even if you fail to experience a surge of Italian nationalism, you're likely to appreciate the sweeping panoramic view of the city.

BOTANICAL GARDENS

At the end of V. Corsini, off V.d. Scala (V. della Lungara), at Largo Cristina di Svezia, 23A. Grounds open Tu-Sa 9:30am-6:30pm; Oct.-Mar. M-Sa 9:30am-5:30pm. Greenhouses open at gardeners' discretion. Closed Aug. and during bad weather. €2.07; ages 6-11 and over 60 €1.04, under 6 free, handicapped people plus one companion free. Free tour sheets available at entrance.

Filled with well-labeled specimens of trees and flowers, the gardens remain green and luxuriant even when the rest of Rome is dull and brown. The remarkable assemblage of flora stretches from valleys of ferns through groves of bamboo to a hilltop Japanese garden. Of interest are the garden of roses cultivated during the Baroque period in Rome, containing the two founding bushes from which all domesticated Italian roses supposedly have sprung, and the stellar Garden for the Blind, a star-shaped garden of various plants labeled in braille.

TERMINI & SAN LORENZO

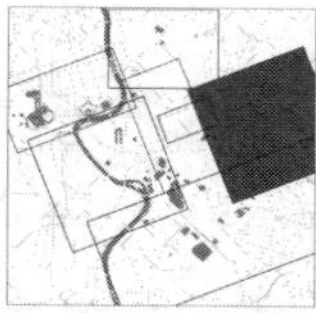

see map p. 360-361

At first, the Termini area might not seem the most promising area for sightseeing, but don't make the mistake of overlooking the district entirely. The further east you head, the more real (and less eternal) the city becomes: the cheap shopping and eating options around the San Lorenzo district testify to the large student population here. Termini not only gives a second chance to those with nostalgia for college life, but also offers a more genuine peek into daily life in modern Rome.

PIAZZA DEL QUIRINALE & VIA XX SETTEMBRE

M: A-Barberini. Walk two blocks south along V. delle Quatro Fontane, turn right on XX Settembre; the piazza is a few blocks straight ahead.

PIAZZA DEL QUIRINALE

This *piazza,* at the southwest end of V.d. Quirinale, occupies the summit of the tallest of Rome's original seven hills. From the belvedere, the view takes in a sea of Roman domes, with St. Peter's in the distance. In the middle of the *piazza,* the heroic statues of **Castor and Pollux** (mythical warrior twins whom the ancient Romans embraced as their protectors) flank yet another of Rome's many obelisks. The fountain over which they preside was once a cattle trough in the Roman Forum.

PALAZZO DEL QUIRINALE

The palazzo is not open to the public.

Since 1947, the President of the Republic has officially resided in this imposing *palazzo,* following in the tradition of the popes and Italian kings before him. The *palazzo* is a Baroque collaboration by Bernini, Carlo Maderno, and Domenico Fontana. Maderno designed the front, while Bernini set himself to the *manica lunga* (long sleeve) on V.d. Quirinale. Look through the portals on the *piazza* for a glimpse of the white-uniformed, silver-helmeted Republican Guards (each of whom must be at least 6ft. tall to get his job) and the *palazzo's* lush gardens. The neighboring white stone **Palazzo della Consulta** houses the constitutional court. Though the President has reserved most of the *palazzo* for himself, the humble public may enter the former papal stables that now house revolving exhibitions (see p. 182).

CHURCH OF SANT'ANDREA AL QUIRINALE

At P. Quirinale, take V. Quirinale. Open Sept.-July M and W-Su 8am-noon and 4-7pm; Aug. M and W-Su 8am-noon.

Another stunning church courtesy of Bernini: in fact, this oval church was reputedly Bernini's favorite, and its small scale gives it an intimacy that is lost in larger basilicas. Sant'Andrea nicely exemplifies Bernini's ability to combine sculpture with architecture to create a dynamic and lively space, and his use of light and different colored stone in a coherent project. Statues of angels and cherubs clamber over the dome of the church and play with architectural garlands, while Sant'Andrea looks upward to the symbol of the Holy Spirit. Look for the statues of men with nets, representing Saint Andrea's fellow fishermen. Left of the altar are the rooms of St. Stanislaus, a Jesuit saint, immortalized in an amazing sculpture.

CHURCH OF SAN CARLINO

Near the corner of V. Quirinale (V. XX Settembre) and V. Quattro Fontane. Open M-F 10am-1pm and 3-5pm, Sa 10am-1pm. If the interior is closed, ring at the convent next door.

This ingenious church by Francesco Borromini, officially **San Carlo alle Quattro Fontane,** provides a sharp contrast to neighboring Sant'Andrea al Quirinale and highlights the architect's unique vision. Borromini avoided the kind of mixed-media and multicolored extravaganzas that Bernini perfected. The interior of the church is undecorated, but is organized in a complex mathematical system incorporating the church's undulating curves and pairs of columns. The dome further illustrates his mathematical approach to architecture, with interlocking geometric forms receding to give an illusion of depth. The church has the distinction of being both Borromini's first and last work: though he designed the simple interior early on in his career, he finished the more ornate facade just before his suicide. Borromini also designed the **cloister** next door, which holds the **crypt** where it is said that he hoped, in vain, to be buried.

VIA XX SETTEMBRE

The beginning of V. XX Settembre showcases one of Pope Sixtus V's more gracious additions to the city. In an effort to ease traffic and better define the city's regions, the 16th-century pontiff straightened many of Rome's major streets and erected obelisks at important junctions. From the crossroads with V. delle Quatro Fontane (yes, from the middle of the road, so be careful), you can survey the obelisks at P. Quirinale, at the top of the Spanish Steps, and at Santa Maria Maggiore. V. Quirinale becomes V. XX Settembre at V. Quattro Fontane, heading east, and after a few blocks opens into the Baroque **Piazza San Bernardo,** site of Fontana's colossal **Fontana dell'Acqua Felice,** built in 1587 where Pope Sixtus V's aqueduct entered the city. Prospero Antichi's beefy and ill-proportioned statue of Moses was inspired by Michelangelo's, but is supposedly glowering at having been carved by such an inept sculptor.

CHURCH OF SANTA MARIA DELLA VITTORIA

On the south side of P.S. Bernardo, away from P. Repubblica. Open daily 7am-noon and 3:30-7pm.

This church has one of Bernini's most stunning ensembles, which is dedicated to Spanish mystic **St. Teresa of Avila.** In the **Cornaro Chapel** (the last one on the left) Bernini shows the saint in ecstasy as an angel pierces her with a golden arrow. The scene was subsequently elaborated to resemble a theater, with members of the Cornaro family looking on.

CHURCH OF SANTA SUSANNA

The Church is located on the north side of P.S. Bernardo. Open daily 9am-noon and 4-7pm.

The Church of Santa Susanna, the American parish in Rome, is run by an exceptionally friendly community of Cistercian nuns. Note the church's distinctive Counter-Reformation facade by Carlo Maderno. Inside, Baldassarre Croce's Mannerist frescoes of the life of the biblical Susanna cover the walls, and Giovanni Antonio Paracea's four large statues of the prophets stand on pillars dating from the 9th century. St. Susanna, niece of Pope Caius, converted to Christianity as a youth and "sacrificed herself to God, making an offering to him of her virginity." When she refused Emperor Diocletian's orders to marry his son and worship an idol of Jupiter, he had her beheaded in his home.

BATHS OF DIOCLETIAN

P. dei Cinquecento, 78. ☎06 488 05 30. Open Tu-Sa 9am-7:45pm. Free.

The tattered brick remains of the Baths of Diocletian tower over news kiosks and vendors camped out around Termini. The baths were a colossal construction project, undertaken by Diocletian's brother Maximianus, employing 40,000 Christian slaves from AD 298-306. The baths, which could serve up to 3,000 people, once contained gymnasiums, art galleries, gardens, libraries, and concert halls. Going to the heated public toilet was a social event in itself, as it could accommodate 20 people at a time. The cold pool (*frigidarium*) alone measured 2500 sq. m, the size of a small lake. The baths were modeled on Trajan's thermal baths, the first to abandon a strict north-south axis to make better use of solar energy; the *calidarium*, or hot bath, faced southwest, thus facing the sun during the warmest parts of the day, and the *frigidarium* faced northeast. The complex fell into ruin in 538 when the aqueducts supplying water for the baths were destroyed, perhaps out of jealousy, by Witigis and his dirty Ostrogoths. Damn barbarians.

ROTONDA AND BATHS EXHIBIT

V. Romita, 8. Baths and rotunda on right after exiting S. Maria degli Angeli, between V. Cernaia and V. Parigi. Open Tu-F 9am-2pm, Sa-Su 9am-1pm. Free.

This section of the baths is a dramatic home to two of the most important **Hellenistic sculptures** in existence. One is a first-century depiction aging boxer, looking up tiredly, complete with cauliflower ear, and signed by Apollonius. The other is a general leaning on a lance, in imitation of Lysippos's famous statue of Alexander the Great; his nudity (not to mention his rippling muscles) exhibits his semi-divine nature. Glass sections of the floor provide a peek at the foundations of the baths.

CHURCH OF SANTA MARIA DEGLI ANGELI

Church open M-Sa 7am-6:30pm, Su 8am-7:30pm.

It was a long time coming, but the Christians avenged their persecution and exploitation under Diocletian with this church. Centuries after Diocletian's death (and his bath's demise), a Sicilian priest had a vision of a swarm of angels rising from the baths; he subsequently pestered Pius IV to build a church on the dilapidated site. So, in 1561 Pope Pius IV ordered Michelangelo, then 86, to convert the ruins into a church. This would be his last architectural work. Imitating the architecture of the baths, Michelangelo used the remains of the *calidarium* as the church facade. This is how it appears today, although much of his interior plan was changed after the Pope and Michelangelo died three years later. Despite the departure from Michelangelo's plan and the many years of design revisions, the interior preserves a sense of the ancient baths. The church was constructed in the ancient *tepidarium* (lukewarm baths); Michelangelo scavenged material from the baths to construct the red porphyry columns that line the church interior. A sundial, located in the floor leading from the east transept to the altar, provided the standard time for Roman clocks for hundreds of years. The sacristy leads to ruins of the *frigidarium* as well as a small exhibit on the construction of the church.

VIA NOMENTANA

Beginning at the *Porta Pia* (designed by Michelangelo), this breezy road is lined with pleasant villas, embassies, and parks. Hop on bus #36 in front of Termini or head to V. Cernaia and catch the #60; both traverse the boulevard.

VILLA TORLONIA

☎06 442 311 85. Open June-Aug. daily 7am-8:30pm, Apr.-May and Sept. 7am-7:30pm, Oct.-Feb. 7:30am-5pm, Mar. 7am-6pm. Museo della Casina delle Civette and Museo del Casino dei Principi ☎06 442 500 72 open Apr.-Sept. 9am-7pm, Oct.-Mar. 9am-5pm. €2.60, €1.60 reduced.

About a kilometer from the Porta Pia is Mussolini's former estate, which he 'leased' from the Torlonia family for the princely annual sum of one lira. The house was long abandoned after WWII, though over the last few years as the park has been in the midst of an extensive redevelopment program. Walk in through the foreboding gates to see over 50 species of birds and 100 types of trees and shrubs. The **Museo della Casina delle Civette** displays numerous framed art deco designs for, and pieces of, stained glass; but the real attraction is the house's various architectural oddities like the 'thinking room' upstairs. The **Museo del Casino dei Principi** houses Mussolini's bed and other such memorabilia, in addition to an important collection of 18th-century neoclassical sculpture by Antonio Canova and Bartolomeo Cavaceppi.

BASILICA & CATACOMBS OF SANT'AGNESE FUORI LE MURA

V. Nomentana, 349. ☎06 862 054 56 or 328 565 24 14 to make tour reservations. Open daily 9am-noon and 4-6pm; closed Su mornings and M afternoons. Catacombs €5.

Under this 7th-century basilica winds a network of Rome's best-preserved and least-crowded **catacombs** (AD 100-500) containing the remains of **Saint Agnes,** a 12-year-old martyred by Diocletian for refusing to marry, and almost 7,000 other graves. Although the catacombs were ransacked (along with the rest of Rome) in the 5th century, you can still get up close and personal with some skeletons. The tour guide explains the early Christian method of marking the tombs of the dead and the use of private family chapels. The church's 7th-century apse shows off the extraordinary Byzantine-style mosaic of the young saint with a pair of popes.

MAUSOLEUM OF CONSTANZA

V. Nomentana, 349. ☎06 862 054 56 or 328 565 24 14 to reach tour guide Danilo. Open daily 9am-noon and 4-6pm; closed Su mornings and M afternoons. €1 donation requested. Make sure to call before visiting; it is a popular spot for weddings and is consequently closed to tourists.

This early round church originally served as the mausoleum of Constantine's eldest daughter, Constantina, and is decorated with stunning 4th-century mosaics, showing animals, and wine making, predating most Christian imagery. Constantina was cured of leprosy while sleeping on St. Agnes's tomb, leading her to convert to Christianity and build her own tomb, which was later transformed into a baptistry, and then a church. Right next to the mausoleum are the ruins of the 4th-century basilica of St. Agnes.

ESQUILINE HILL

The Esquiline and Caelian (see p. 134) hills are the largest of ancient Rome's seven hills, and are today home to some of the city's greatest traffic chaos. In ancient times, Nero built his decadent Domus Aurea (see p. 81) between these hills: the

Baths of Diocletian

Church of San Pietro in Vincoli

Piazza Sonnino

area's densely constructed ancient buildings provided early Christians with a quarry from which to build their basilicas.

BASILICA OF SANTA MARIA MAGGIORE

From Termini, exit south onto V. Giolitti, and walk down V. Cavour. At P. dell' Esquilino, walk around to southeastern side of the basilica to enter. Open daily 7am-7pm. Museum open M-Sa 9am-6:30pm: €4, reduced €2. Loggia ☎06 483 058; open M-Sa 9:30am-1pm; €2.70. Museum entrance through souvenir shop. Dress appropriately (shawls provided for women).

Take a moment and prepare yourself; you are about to enter one of the world's oldest and best preserved basilicas, home to an original cycle of early Christian mosaics that have looked down upon worshippers here continuously for some sixteen centuries. The Basilica of Santa Maria Maggiore, which crowns the summit of the Esquiline hill, combines glittering ancient mosaics with the splendor and bravura of Renaissance and Baroque additions. Fourth among the seven major basilicas traditionally visited on the pilgrimage to Rome, it is also one of the five churches in Rome granted extraterritoriality, making it officially part of Vatican City.

According to legend, the Virgin Mary appeared before Pope Liberius in August 358 and requested that he build a church in her honor. The location of the church was to be the place that would be covered in snow the next morning. On the morrow, the Pope discovered that snow had indeed fallen on the hill's crest. He promptly set out to design and build the church, first named Santa Maria della Neve (St. Mary of the Snow). Romans recreate the miracle with white rose petals every 5th of August.

It appears that the basilica was actually built 80 years later by Pope Sixtus III, who noticed that Roman women were still visiting a temple dedicated to the mother goddess Juno Lucina, built on the hill next to Liberius's smaller church. Sixtus enthusiastically tore both down to build a new basilica, not only substituting a Christian cult for a pagan one, but also celebrating the recent Council of Ephesus, which declared Mary to be imbued with a divinity that raised her above general humankind. Most of the mosaics inside are designed to commemorate her new status.

Maria Maggiore has a deceptive exterior: while the shell Ferdinando Fuga built for it in 1750 is 18th century Baroque, inside is one of the best-preserved Classical basilicas. Ancient columns divide the rectangular church into a central nave with two side aisles surmounted by celestial windows. The triumphal arch over the high altar swims in mosaics honoring the Holy Virgin Mary; the image (on the right) of Mary spinning a basket of purple wool to make a veil dates from the 5th century. Although difficult to see without the aid of binoculars, the mosaics on the left side of the church contain scenes from the lives of Abraham, Jacob and Isaac, and, on the right, of Moses and Joshua. The coffered ceiling above it all is believed to have been gilded with the first gold sent from America by Columbus.

In the subterranean *confessio* before the altar, a marble Pope Pius IX kneels in front of a relic of the baby **Jesus' crib.** Though now sheathed in globs of silver, the crib is revealed each Christmas morning. A dazzling *baldacchino* looms over the altar, which enshrines the famous image of the Madonna. To the right of the altar, a marble slab marks the **tomb of Gian Lorenzo Bernini.** A visit to the *loggia* grants access to the one-time private chambers of Pope Paul V and Bernini's spiral staircase.

CHURCH OF SANTA CROCE IN GERUSALEMME

P.S. Croce in Gerusalemme. M: A-San Giovanni. From P.S. Giovanni north of the Metro stop, go east on V. C. Felice; the church is on the right. From P.V. Emanuele II, take V. Conte Verde (V.S. Croce in Gerusalemme). Open daily 7am-7pm. Museum open Tu-Sa 10am-12:30pm and 3:30-6:30pm. Free.

This unique church is home to a mother lode of major relics, housed in the appropriately named and Fascist-designed "Chapel of the Relics," off of the left aisle, which contains fragments of the "true cross" found by St. Helena. It also houses a chunk of the cross of Dismas (the Good Thief), thorns from Christ's crown, and a nail used in the crucifixion. Perhaps the eeriest of the chapel's relics is the dismembered finger used by doubting Thomas to probe Christ's wounds. The church is believed to have been built around 326, but was rebuilt twice: in 1144, when the *campanile* was added, and in 1744, when the facade got a facelift. At the end of the right aisle in the church's interior, the **Chapel of St. Helena** contains 15th-century mosaics depicting Christ, Peter, Paul, and Helena. The latest addition to the basilica (in 1999) is a museum just before the altar on the right. On display are the brightly-painted 12th-century frescoes that once adorned the nave and which were discovered in 1913, as well as particularly grumpy-looking fourteenth-century statues of St. Peter and St. Paul.

PORTA MAGGIORE

The area around the Porta Maggiore (also called the Porta Prenestina) might be one of the smoggiest, not to mention slowest, of Rome's traffic intersections, but spend a moment appreciating the large inscribed arch erected by Emperor Claudius in AD 52. The well-preserved arch, which supported one of Imperial Rome's major aqueducts, was later built into the Aurelian walls which surround the city. Just outside the wall are the curious remains of the **Tomb of the Baker:** the funerary monument, decorated with sculpted bakery ovens below and a frieze charting the processes of bread-making above, was erected in honor of Marcus Virgilius Eurysaces in 30 BC to celebrate the lowly cause of bakers everywhere. Once you've seen it, leave promptly to avoid succumbing to the monument's own fume-fatigued, and generally dilapidated, fate.

CHURCH OF SANTA PRASSEDE

From the front of Santa Maria Maggiore, walk up V. Merulana, taking the first right onto tiny V. San Giovanni Gualberto. The church is at the dead-end. Open daily 7am-noon and 4-6:30pm. Free.

Built in 822, the Church of Santa Prassede houses a stunning set of Christian **mosaics**. Prassede and Pudenziana, the daughters of the powerful senator Pudens, reputedly buried the corpses of 3,000 persecuted Christians and were converted themselves by St. Peter around AD 50. The Vatican doubted this story enough to remove the girls from the register of saints in 1969. In the apse is the New Jerusalem, a triumphal lamb, and the two sister saints being presented to Christ, with Peter and Paul encouraging them. From the right aisle step into the **Chapel of St. Zeno,** a small glittering room of mosaics, lit by a machine outside the door (€0.50 per 5min). The chapel is populated by various saints, while four angels hold up a Byzantine Christ floating in a sea of gold. Note the Empress Theodora above the doorway leading into the gift shop, who has a square halo, indicating that she was still alive when the mosaics were made (i.e. before her death in the early 9th century). Another reading, understandably less popular with the Vatican, is that this represents a female bishop. The chapel holds part of a column of rare oriental jasper retrieved from Jerusalem in 1228 during the 6th Crusade, reputedly the column to which Christ was strapped and flogged before his crucifixion.

CHURCH OF SANTA PUDENZIANA

From behind Santa Maria Maggiore, walk down V.A. Depretis and turn left onto V. Urbana. Church is on the right. Open M-Sa 8am-noon and 3-6pm; Su 9am-noon and 3-6pm.

Legend has it that this small church was built by Pope Pius I in AD 145 on the property of the late senator Pudens, in gratitude to his daughters. The original windows, though walled up, are still visible, as are remnants of the original buildings behind the altar. The mosaic of Christ teaching the Apostles in the apsidal vault, dating from the late 4th century, is the oldest known mosaic in a Roman place of worship.

PIAZZA VITTORIO EMANUELE II

The piazza *is down V. Carlo Alberto from the front steps of Santa Maria Maggiore.*

This large *piazza* used to be famous for its free-for-all outdoor market with piles of fresh fish, fresh fruit, clothes, shoes, and luggage. The market has since moved to the covered Mercato Esqulino (on the intersection of V.G. Pepe and V. G. Giolitti, on the southeast side of Termini, open M-F mornings). The market may have moved, but the area still brims with a multicultural mix of shops and restaurants. Its small park houses the curious remains of a 4th-century fountain. The **Porta Magica,** a few steps away, reveals an alchemist's ancient instructions for turning lead into gold. Nearby, and with considerably more success, contemporary alchemists are hard at work producing fake Prada bags.

SANTA BIBIANA

Follow V. Giolitti which runs alongside Stazione Termini to the intersection with V. Cairoli, near the end of the station. Church is alongside station wall. Open daily 7:30-11am and 4:30-7:15pm.

Tucked away next to Termini, a water tower and the grime of Esquilino, Santa Bibiana is Bernini's first church and its interior hides several impressive works of art that make it worth a visit. Bernini carved a statue of the saint for the altarpiece, while the great Baroque painter **Pietro da Cortona** painted a series of frescoes of her life and martyrdom for refusing to sacrifice to pagan gods. The sacristan will turn on the lights for you upon request.

THE AUDITORIUM OF MAECENAS

In Largo Leopardi, down V. Merulana from S.M. Maggiore, or V. Leopardi from P.V. Emmanuele II. Open Tu-Sa 9am-7pm, Su 9am-1:30pm. €2.58, children €1.55.

This underground Roman ruin was once romantically thought to have been the site for Horace and Virgil's poetic recitations to their patron, Maecenas, in the first century BC (hence the name). Today, the general consensus is that it formed part of his luxurious summer dining complex. The remains of frescoes, especially those depicting an outside garden viewed through false windows, are still visible behind the stairs.

BASILICA OF SAN LORENZO FUORI LE MURA

Bus #492 from Termini to P. Verano, or tram #3 from Porta Maggiore. Open daily 8am-12:30pm and 3-7pm.

This basilica, dedicated to Rome's *numero tre* saint after Peter and Paul, long remained one of the seven pillar-churches of a pilgrimage to Rome—that is, before a wayward American bomb missed its Stazione Tiburtina target and severely damaged the church and its priceless artwork on July 19th, 1943 (an event commemorated with due bitterness 60 years later, in July 2003). Restoration projects were speedily completed by 1949, and the church (in fact comprised of two basilicas, one from the 6th and one from the 13th century, joined together) still houses a 6th-century mosaic of Christ seated on a globe (mounted on the triumphal arch). The church's 12th-century cloister fared better in the bombing, and leads to the catacombs where San Lorenzo was supposedly buried after being burned alive in 258.

CAMPO VERANO & THE JEWISH CEMETERY

Bus #492 from Termini to P. Verano. To the right of Basilica S. Lorenzo Fuori le Mura, down V. Tiburtina, in San Lorenzo. A bus runs through the cemetery Sa and holidays. Open daily 7:30am-6pm; Oct.-Mar. 7:30am-5pm.

More beautiful than bone-chilling, Campo Verano, Rome's largest public cemetery, features a maze of underground tombs, topped with elaborate marble huts and decked with fresh-cut flowers, statuary, and a fetishistic number of photographs of the dead incorporated into tombstones. On November 1 and 2, All Saints' and All Souls' Days, Romans make pilgrimages to the tombs of their relatives, placing chrysanthemums on the stones. The Jewish Cemetery is next door on the far side of the Campo Verano cemetery.

OPPIAN HILL

Now capped with the large public Parco Oppio, the Oppian Hill once housed part of Nero's Domus Aurea (p. 81) and the Baths of both Titus and Trajan.

CHURCH OF SAN PIETRO IN VINCOLI

M: B-Cavour. Or bus #75 to Largo V. Venosta. From Cavour Metro, walk west down the V. Cavour. Take the steep flight of stairs, opposite Hotel Palatino, on the V. di S. Francesco di Paola to P.S. Pietro in Vincoli. Open daily 7am-12:30pm and 3:30-6pm. Dress appropriately.

The 5th-century *San Pietro in Vincoli* (St. Peter in Chains) is named for the sacred chains in which St. Peter was supposedly bound after having been imprisoned on the Capitoline. The two chains were separated for more than a century, one in Rome and one in Constantinople, but reunited in the 5th century, and if you're into that kind of thing, you can view them below the altar.

Most tourists head right for Michelangelo's looming **Moses,** which is currently undergoing restoration but is still open to the public (be prepared for extensive scaffolding). This Moses was meant to serve as the centerpiece for the unfinished *Tomb of Pope Julius II*, but a series of budget cuts and delays that would have made the current Italian government proud, put a stop to the project. Julius had planned a gargantuan sepulchre for himself, with roughly forty statues, but, alas, he died before the monument was completed. Needless to say, his successors were less interested in immortalizing his death, and Julius ended up in an unmarked grave in the Vatican. Besides, at the time, Michelangelo had other things on his agenda—namely the Sistine Chapel.

No, Moses didn't transform into a goat in a little-known passage at the end Exodus. Those really are horns you're seeing, but they're the product of a medieval mistranslation. According to Exodus, when Moses descended from Sinai with the Ten Commandments, "rays" (similar to "horns" in Hebrew) shone from

Ecstasy of St Teresa

Appian Way

Catacombs

his brow. Those adoring females at his side, Leah and Rachel, are actually in the New Testament and here represent active and contemplative lives, respectively.

SOUTHERN ROME

CAELIAN HILL

Just east of the Colosseum, the Caelian and its neighbor, the Esquiline, are the largest hills in Rome.

see map p. 366

CHURCH OF SAN CLEMENTE

M: B-Colosseo. Turn left out of the station, walk east on V. Fori Imperiali (V. Labicana) away from the Forum, and turn right onto P.S. Clemente. From the Manzoni (A) stop, walk west on V.A. Manzoni (V. Labicana), and turn left onto P.S. Clemente. ☎06 704 510 18. Open M-Sa 9am-12:30pm and 3-6pm, Su and holidays 10am-12:30pm and 3-6pm. Lower basilica and mithraeum €3.

Sewers, Masolino, and St. Clement (the fourth pope) might appear to be an odd combination, but, after all, this is Rome, perhaps the only place in the world where one can visit a 12th-century church built upon a 4th-century sanctuary built on the temple of an ancient religion that was supplanted by Christianity. Rome ain't called the 'Eternal City' for nothing.

The upper church, reached through a 12th-century courtyard to the east, holds medieval mosaics of the Crucifixion, saints, and apostles. A series of frescoes by Masolino (possibly executed with help from his pupil Masaccio), dating from the 1420s, graces the **Chapel of Santa Caterina** at the back of the church. Hooligan pilgrims scrawled their names on the fresco of St. Christopher that decorates the left wall. The 6th-century marble choir enclosure displays a Romanesque paschal candlestick that belonged to the lower church.

However, it's the lower cluster of buildings and foundations that makes San Clemente unique. The early plan of the 4th-century lower church has been obscured by piers and walls built to support the upper church. With a little imagination (or the excellent color-coded *Guide to the Three Levels* series of excavation maps, available at the gift shop for €3.10) one can trace the lines of the original nave, aisles, and apse, which retain rare 11th-century frescoes. On this level are a few curiosities, including the tomb of St. Cyril (responsible for the Cyrillic alphabet) and a series of frescoes depicting scenes from the life of St. Clement. Also on display (on the left wall immediately after the staircase) are a number of ancient Roman inscriptions re-used by early Christians.

Descend a third, 4th-century flight of stairs to view even earlier buildings, including a large late 2nd-century shrine to Mithras with a ritual room, dining room, and Mithraic schoolroom. Mithraism, the last pagan state religion in Rome, was introduced by soldiers returning from Asia Minor in 67 BC, but it disappeared by the end of the 4th century. More passages lead through Roman basements, while below an underground river flows through Republican-era sewers.

CHURCH OF SANTI GIOVANNI E PAOLO

Just southeast of the Colosseum, take V. Claudia and turn right onto V.S. Paolo della Croce. Open M-Sa 8:30am-noon and 3:30-6pm, Su 3:30-6pm. Case Romane entrance is just west of the church, down the Clivo di Scauro. Call for advance booking/guided tours ☎06 704 54 44. Open daily 10am-1pm, 3-6pm. €6, reduced €4. Villa Celimontana open daily dawn-dusk. Free.

The Church of San Giovanni e Paolo lies directly opposite its medieval campanile, curiously adorned with brightly-colored Islamic ceramic plates; the present basilica dates to the 12th century. The real attraction here, though, is the set of rich Roman houses, complete with even richer decoration, which formed the foundations for an earlier church on the site (probably in the 5th century). Only reopened to the public in 2002, and with excellent explanatory panels in both Italian and English, the site contains brilliantly preserved wall paintings from the 2nd and 3rd centuries. A small museum (called the Antiquarium) houses the artifacts found during the excavations. Opposite the Church, the beautifully-kept gardens of the Villa Celimontana reward you for the detour with a secluded spot for a picnic.

CHURCH OF SANTI QUATTRO CORONATI

V.d. S.S. Quattro Coronati, 20. From San Clemente, bear south down the V. dei Querceti and head up the Via dei Santi Quattro; the church is on the right at the top of the steep hill. Basilica open M-Sa 6:15am-8pm, Su 6:45am-12:30pm and 3-7:30pm. Chapel of S. Stefano M-Sa 9:30am-noon, 4:30-6pm; Su 9-10:40am, 4-5:45pm; donation requested. Cloister currently closed.

Named for four sculptors who were martyred by Diocletian for refusing to carve (or worship) statues of the Roman god Aesculapius, this church, though small and inconspicuous, has played a prominent role in Roman ecclesiastical history. Due to its proximity to the Lateran Palace (the early seat of the papacy), the church housed high-ranking Catholic officials for many years.

Located on Caelian Hill, the Church was in a good position to defend the Lateran area, which is why the massive western walls were raised in the 13th century. Consequently, the church became a refuge for Popes under siege, as well as visiting royalty like Charles of Anjou, earning it the moniker, "The Royal Hospice of Rome." The little **chapel** to the right, off the entrance courtyard, next to the *Monache Agostiniare* sign, contains an extraordinary fresco cycle of the life of Constantine painted in 1248. Ring the bell of the convent; the cloistered nuns will send you a key on a lazy susan. Inside the small Church itself, note the 12th-century upper storey: a *matroneum* for female participants.

Just off the aisle, the 13th-century **cloister** ranks as one of the most beautiful in the city. Unlike the artistically striking cloisters at San Paol Fuori le Mura and San Giovanni in Laterano, the cloister here strikes the senses with its elegant simplicity and peacefulness. It is currently undergoing an extensive restoration, but you can peer through the glass to check its progress.

CHURCH OF SANTO STEFANO ROTONDO

V.S. Stefano Rotondo, 7. From P.S. Giovanni, take V.S. Giovanni. The road forks twice; stay to the left. The Church was closed for restoration in July 2003. Call ☎06 421 199 in advance to check progress.

Built in the late 5th century, the Church of Santo Stefano Rotondo is one of the oldest circular churches in existence. Long-needed restoration continues on the church; it certainly takes some imagination to picture the building in its original form. It was once structured in three concentric rings, but centuries of decay and remodeling reduced it to the two inner rings by 1450.

SAN GIOVANNI

CHURCH OF SAN GIOVANNI IN LATERANO (ST. JOHN LATERAN)

M: A-San Giovanni or bus #16 from Termini. Call ☎06 698 863 92 to confirm hours of operation. Basilica open daily 7am-6:45pm. Sacresty open daily 7am-noon, 4-6pm. Cloister open daily 9am-6pm; €2, €1 for students. Museum open daily 9am-6pm; €1, free for students. Dress appropriately. Just west of the church on the southwest end of P. di S. Giovanni in Laterano lies the baptistery. Open daily, 7am-12:30pm, 3:30-7:30pm.

Although the pope doesn't hang his *zucchetto* here, the immense Church of San Giovanni in Laterano is technically part of the Vatican City, and shares its extraterritoriality. A terrorist bomb heavily damaged the basilica in 1993 (a simultaneous blast devastated the Church of San Giorgio in Velabro): the north facade received the most damage but it has since been restored. The church (and the adjoining Lateran palace) were home to the papal court before the Avignon papacy in the 14th century. Some of the grandeur of the old days returns on Corpus Christi, the ninth Sunday after Easter, when a triumphant procession, including the College of Cardinals, the Swiss Guard, and hundreds of Italian Girl Scouts, leads the pontiff back to the Vatican after mass. The doors of the main entrance, facing the P.S. Giovanni, were moved here from the Curia, the Roman senate house in the Forum. Inside, Borromini's remodeling in the 17th century obscures the original plan of the basilica, creating a dramatic series of niches for 12 imposing statues of the Apostles.

The stately Gothic *baldacchino* over the altar houses two golden reliquaries containing **the heads of Saints Peter and Paul,** and an altar from which only the Pope can celebrate mass. A door to the left of the altar leads to the 13th-century **cloister,** home to the church's collection of sacred relics and regalia (along with the small museum of gold and precious vestments). The twisted double columns and inlaid pavement are typical of the Cosmati family, who designed much of the stone inlaid with marble chips that decorates medieval Roman churches.

Originally built by Constantine, the octagonal **baptistery of Saint John** served as the model for its more famous cousin in Florence. According to legend, all Christians were once baptized here. Today, however, services are reserved only for Rome's upper echelon.

SCALA SANTA

M: A-San Giovanni or bus #16 from Termini. Across from the main entrance of the church, on the east side of P. di S. Giovanni in Laterano. ☎06 772 66 41. Open M-Sa 6:15am-noon and 3-6:15pm, Su 6:15am-noon and 3:30-6:45pm.

The Scala Santa holds what are believed to be the 28 marble steps (now covered in walnut wood for protection) that were part of Pontius Pilate's house in Jerusalem which Jesus ascended several times on the day of his crucifixion. Medieval pilgrims apparently knocked several years off their time in Purgatory by similarly making their way up the steps (but on their knees, and reciting proscribed prayers along the way).

The tradition stood unquestioned until an unruly German named Martin Luther, in the middle of his way up, decided that the act was one of futility and false piety. He went on to stir up some minor trouble back home (which, of course, is not referenced in the official rendition of the steps' history, which you can find at the top of the staircase). Today the stairs remain a genuine place of pilgrimage, creaking with the traffic of earnest Catholics struggling up this metaphorical stairway to heaven.

If the mere thought of climbing these steps on your fragile kneecaps fills you with a Luther-like distaste for the Church, use the secular stairs on either side. In the sanctuary you'll find, among other relics, the *Acheropita* image, a depiction of Christ supposedly painted by St. Luke with the assistance of an angel, the image of which was carried in processions to stop the plague.

AVENTINE HILL

M: B-Circo Massimo. From Piazza Venezia, you can take the 81 bus. Walk down V. Circo Massimo to P. Ugo La Malta. On the left is V. d. Valle Murcia, which turns into V.d. Santa Sabina.

Just a short walk south of the ancient Circus Maximus and you could almost forget that you were still in Rome. With steep, narrow, winding streets, framed by high, shady trees, the Aventine Hill is the place to head for a quiet afternoon reading that Dante (or Grisham) you promised yourself you would read. This exclusive area is relatively free from fellow travellers, and consequently from bars, restaurants, and cafes. But what the Aventine lacks in tourist amenities it makes up for in, well, churches. While Santa Sabina is the most famous, the churches of Sant' Alessio e San Bonifacio, San Saba, and Santa Prisca (which was built over a 3rd-century Mithraeum, like San Clemente) can all boast a similar first-millennium ancestry. A full tour will take around an hour and a half; reward your labors by bringing your own picnic and stopping in the Giardino degli Aranci.

ROSETO COMMUNALE

The garden lies along V.d. Valle Murcia, up from P. Ugo la Malfa, across the Circus Maximus from the Palatine Hill. ☎ 06 574 68 10 for information. Open daily May-June, 8am-7:30pm.

If Lewis Carroll ever put his hand to designing a garden, this would be it. With over 800 varieties of rose bushes (but, sadly, no playing cards, swinging paint cans, or Queens of Hearts painting the town red), the Roseto Comunale is the place to stroll, rest, and, yes, smell the roses. A number of benches also make this an ideal place to spend a quiet afternoon reading, sitting in the sun, or watching the tourists pant their way up the Palatine Hill in the distance. Each May, the horticultural world descends upon the Roseto to compete for the **Premio Roma,** the prize given to the best new variety of rose. Twenty-one countries compete for the honor, and you will find the winners displayed in the lower section of the Roseto's 10 sq. km grounds.

The first Roseto in Rome was destroyed during World War II, but intrepid gardeners built this new version on the site of the old Jewish Cemetery, which was relocated to Campo Verano. When asked for the land by the city, the Jewish community leader agreed, but requested that the old site be memorialized. As a result, steles of the Ten Commandments flank the entrances and the upper section is shaped like a menorah.

GIARDINI DEGLI ARANCI

Also known as Parco Savello, in P. Pietro d'Illiria, right next to the Church of Santa Sabina. Open daily dawn to dusk.

Ah, smell the citrus. The ripe fruit scattered all over the ground of this *giardini* is only one of the attractions. Spectacular views of Rome are also yours to enjoy. The park is well kept and quiet, its peace only disturbed by occasional parties of picnicking school children and businessmen on lunch break. Luckily, even they turn off their *telefonini* to enjoy the sights.

Aventine Hill

Porta San Sebastiano

Basilica of Santa Maria Maggiore

CHURCH OF SANTA SABINA

At the southern (uphill) end of Parco Savello, in P. Pietro d'Illiria, next to the Giardino degli Aranci. Entrance to the Church through the vestibule. Suggested donation for the cloister: €1. Open daily 6:30am-12:45pm and 3:30-7pm.

The famous residents of the adjoining monastery (the first monastery of the Dominican order) have included St. Dominic, Pius V, and St. Thomas Aquinas, but the actual church was built much earlier, during the reign of Celestine I in the 5th century. The mosaics are colorful and the wooden doors are a rare find; they depict a variety of different Biblical scenes, including one of the earliest representations of Christ hanging between two thieves (note Christ's cross-less crucifixion). The vestibule also leads to the recently opened monastic cloister, a 13th-century colonnade with a beautifully maintained garden.

PIAZZA DEI CAVALIERI DI MALTA

At the end of V.S. Sabina, past the Church dei Santi Bonifacio e Alessio. Entrance to grounds at P. Cavalierie, 4. ☎06 675 812 34 for information. Open Sa 10 and 11am; closed July and Aug. €5 donation requested.

Although it is rarely open to the public, this postcard-perfect *piazza* is home to the Knights of Malta, a charitable organization officially known as the Order of the Knights of St. John of Jerusalem. The order dates to the 12th century when their military services were offered to assist pilgrimage to the Holy Land. More easily accessible is the **keyhole view** of St. Peter's Basilica. Peek through the keyhole in the large green gate at #3 for a view of the dome of St. Peter's, framed by superbly manicured foliage.

APPIAN WAY

Parco dell'Appia Antica: V. Appia Antica, 42. ☎06 512 63 14. Bus #218 from San Giovanni; get off before Domine Quo Vadis. Bus #118 from Pyramide and Circo Massimo along the V. Appia Antica to V. Appia Pignatelli. Or, forgo the info office and begin on the other end of the Way by taking the slightly faster and simpler route of bus #660 from Metro Colli Albani; get off the bus at V. Appia Antica and V. Cecilia Metella (the last stop). Open daily 9am-5:30pm (hours may vary); free guided tours on Su.

The Appian Way (see map on p. 368) was built by Appius Claudius in 312 BC and has been called the "queen of roads" ever since. It once traversed the entire Italian peninsula, providing a straight path for legions heading to and from conquests to the south. It was the site of the grisly crucifixion of Spartacus's rebellious slave army in 71 BC—bodies reputedly lined the road from Rome to Capua. In 37 BC, the Appian Way saw Virgil's 375km pilgrimage to Brindisi; and it was this road that St. Peter traversed on his first trip to Rome in the company of his disciples in AD 42. Since burial inside the city walls was forbidden during ancient times, fashionable Romans made their final resting place along the Appian Way, while early Christians secretly dug labyrinthine catacombs under the ashes of their persecutors.

Some of Italy's modern expressways follow the ancient path, but a sizeable portion of the road remains in its antique state. The area surrounding the road was turned into a 3500 hectare regional park in 1997. If you make it far enough south, past the tomb of Cecilia Metella, you will get to a stretch of the road paved with enormous original paving stones, lined with fragments of white tomb statues and cornices, and bordered by horse pastures and views of the valley below. It will also take you past a minor Italian military base. Don't miss the ruins of the large Villa dei Quintilli and the Casal Rotondo. The few restaurants and cafes around the path, especially around the Catacombs of S. Callisto, S. Domitilla and S. Sebastiano, are overpriced for the quality of their fare and service. A better option is to bring a picnic and stop in the luscious Campanian valley on either side of the V. della Caffarella. Bikes can be hired at Nolo Bike rental next to the Basilica of S. Sebastian.

Exercise **caution** when walking or biking on V. Appia Antica and Via Ardeatina, particularly from Porta San Sebastiano toward the catacombs. As in antiquity, the Appia Antica remains a very busy thoroughfare, and the modern day drivers zooming down it during rush hour aren't likely to make room for you—shoulders are virtually non-existent. The road is **closed to private traffic** on Sundays and holidays from 9:30am-7pm, making it a safer and more pleasant time to walk or bike along the road. If your feet are tired, try riding the **Archeobus,** which leaves Piazza Venezia every hour and transports passengers between major sights. (☎06 469 546 95; single ticket is valid all day, €7.75.)

CATACOMBS

M: A-San Giovanni. Take bus #218 from P.S. Giovanni to intersection of V. Ardeatina and V.d. Sette Chiese, walk up V.d. Sette Chiese to the intersection with V. Ardeatina. At least 2 catacombs open every day, see individual listings. €5, 15 and under €3. Visitors follow a free guided tour in the language of their choice every 20min.

Due to their belief in the resurrection of their bodies, early Christians chose to bury rather than cremate their dead (which was the contemporary Roman norm). Burial within the city walls was forbidden and therefore, between the 2nd and 5th centuries, they hacked eerie, underground galleries for the dead out of the pliant local *tufa* (a soft volcanic rock). The resulting multi-story cellars for the dead stretch through tunnel after tunnel for up to 25km on as many as five levels. Of the 60 catacombs near Rome, five are open to the public; the most notable are those of San Callisto, Santa Domitilla, and San Sebastiano, which cater to the catacomb fanatic in their close proximity to one another on V. Appia Antica.

In the Jewish tradition, bodies were typically swathed in linen before being placed in simple slots in the tunnels, to be sealed with slabs of marble. The deceased were identified and eulogized on the marble slabs (first in Greek, the language of the New Testament, and later in Latin). The graves were mass-produced and thus affordable; even the *tufa* removed for the sake of burials was used to make bricks. Joining the ranks of impoverished Christian peons were a number of martyrs, whose notoriety transformed the catacombs from mere burial grounds to holy pilgrimage sites.

After a series of vain looting attempts for gold (Christians did not bury their dead with precious objects), the long-lost mazes fell into disuse in the 9th century, to be rediscovered in the 16th century. Excavation didn't begin until the 19th century. Early pilgrims filched bones to sell as relics; consequently, the bones remaining in the parts of the catacombs open to the public have long since been interred in Roman churches. Most of what remains of the burial sites are vacant slots where the bodies were placed and wall paintings spared by the grave robbers. **Tours**

Fontana del Acqua Felice

Pyramid of Gaius Cestius

Testaccio

through the catacombs are not recommended for people who are claustrophobic or have difficulty walking. Although the oil lamps of Roman Christians and the candelabras of Victorian tourists have been replaced by a multiplicity of electric lamps, the tunnels are not recommended to those who travel with their night-light.

SAN SEBASTIANO

V. Appia Antica, 136. From the #218 bus stop near S. Callisto and S. Domitilla, walk down V. Sette Chiese to V. Appia Antica and turn right. Or walk past the Mausoleum of Cecilia Metella and the Circus of Maxentius from the #660 bus stop at V. Metella. ☎06 785 03 50. Open Dec.-Oct. M-Sa 8:30am-noon and 2:30-5:30pm. Adjacent church open daily 8am-6pm.

Arguably the most historically significant of the Appian Way catacombs, San Sebastiano was the most revered of the catacombs during the first millennium. It offered a safe haven to the bodies of Peter and Paul during a particularly severe period of Christian persecution in the 3rd century (or so ancient graffiti on its walls suggests). San Sebastiano's three levels accommodate 160,000 tombs and are dotted with animal mosaics, disintegrating skulls, and fantastic early Christian iconography. In addition to being comprehensible, guides here tend to be remarkably well-informed, expertly leading groups through a sizeable chunk of the 10km of tunnels. Bernini's bust of St. Peter resides in the chapel on the first level. In addition to the Christian tombs, three elaborate pagan tombs were recently unearthed and are in marvelous shape.

Above ground, the **Basilica di San Sebastiano,** originally constructed by Constantine in AD 340, is the current home to an **arrow** that reputedly **wounded Saint Sebastian.** His persecutors clubbed him to death after an unsuccessful onslaught of arrows, which were later plucked from his body by St. Agnes. His miraculous endurance has induced painted depictions of the archery scene. A more significant relic is the hunk of stone supposedly bearing **Christ's footprints.** Controversially, *Domine Quo Vadis* (p. 141) claims to possess a similar relic of Jesus' meeting with St. Peter along the Appian Way. In August 1999, the church was robbed; although the thieves snatched the busts of the apostles, they tossed the footprints on the side of the road as they left the church; criminals with a conscience.

SAN CALLISTO

V. Appia Antica, 110. Take the private road that runs northeast to the catacombs's entrance. ☎06 513 015 80. Open Th-Tu 8:30am-noon and 2:30-5:30pm; closed Feb.

The first public Christian cemetery, the catacombs of San Callisto are Rome's largest, with almost 22km of subterranean paths and 500,000 graves. They are now also the most developed for tourists and can be the most crowded. The four serpentine levels once held 16 popes (nine were buried in what's now called "The Crypt of the Popes" or, more jovially, "The Little Vatican"), seven bishops, and St. Cecilia (the patron saint of music—her remains can now be found in the Church of S. Cecilia in Trastevere, see p. 125). Most spectacular of all are the 3rd century tomb paintings, including a depiction of the Last Supper with seven, rather than twelve, diners.

SANTA DOMITILLA

V.d. Sette Chiese, 280. Facing V. Ardeatina from the exit of San Callisto, cross the street and walk right up V. Sette Chiese; catacombs on the left. ☎06 511 03 42. Open Feb.-Dec. M and W-Su 8:30am-noon and 2:30-5pm; closed Jan.

Santa Domitilla is acclaimed for its paintings (a 3rd century portrait of Christ and the Apostles remains intact) and its collection of inscriptions from tombstones and sarcophagi. The tour includes a visit to an ancient frescoed pagan tomb adjoining the catacombs. This is the least crowded of the catacombs on V. Appia Antica. Take a moment to rest your feet and enjoy the flowers while sitting at the picnic tables in the pleasant garden behind the church.

OTHER SIGHTS

PORTA SAN SEBASTIANO

V.d. Porta S. Sebastiano, 18. Take bus #218 to the intersection of V. Mura Latine and V. Appia Antica. ☎06 704 752 84. Museum open Tu-Sa 9am-7pm, Su 9am-2pm. €2.60; reduced €1.60; EU citizens under 18 and over 65 free. Gate closed for restoration in summer 2003.

Marking the beginning of the Appian Way, this is the largest and most intact of the nine surviving gates (out of the 18 original third-century Aurelian walls). Nicknamed a 'killing gate,' the actual gate was left incredibly weak, but when invaders stormed through they were trapped in an inner court, where archers picked them off like sitting ducks. Inside, the gate has been converted into an excellent **Museo delle Mura,** exploring the 19km wall's two-millennia history with displays in Italian and English.

DOMINE QUO VADIS? (CHURCH OF SANTA MARIA IN PALMIS)

At the intersection of V. Appia Antica and V. Ardeatina. Bus #218 from P.S. Giovanni. Open M-Sa 7am-12:30pm and 3-6:30pm, Su 8:30am-1pm and 3-7pm.

St. Peter is said to have had a vision of Christ at this spot as he was fleeing Rome. Upon being asked *"Domine quo vadis?"* ("Lord, where are you going?"), Christ replied that he was going to Rome to be crucified again because St. Peter had abandoned him. Peter instead returned to Rome and suffered his own martyrdom. In the middle of the aisle lie the alleged **footprints of Christ** in a piece of stone (San Sebastiano also claims a pair, see p. 140); if the gargantuan prints do belong to Christ, he should have played basketball.

MAUSOLEO DELLE FOSSE ARDEATINE

Bus #218 to the intersection of V. Ardeatina and V.d. Sette Chiese. Walk down V. Ardeatina; it's to your right. ☎06 513 67 42. Open M-F 8:15am-5pm, Sa-Su and holidays 8:15am-3:30pm.

One of the only modern monuments on the Appian Way is at the Fosse Ardeatine, site of a WWII atrocity. In these caves, Nazis slaughtered 335 prisoners (including 75 Jews and twelve adults who remain unidentified) as a reprisal for an attack by Roman partisans who killed 32 German military police. To hide the corpses and cover their tracks, the Nazis demolished those sections of the cave with explosives. The bodies were recovered and placed in a mass grave that is

Piazza di Siena

Vittorio Emanuel II

Piazza di Campidoglio

marked by a monument and a sculpture. Families still bring fresh flowers daily to the tomb of their loved ones. A small museum (all labelled in Italian) on site charts the history of Nazi oppression, torture and butchery alongside the Italian resistance.

VILLA MASSENZIO

V. Appia Antica, near the tomb of Cecilia Metella. Open Tu-Su 9am-7pm; in winter Tu-Su 9am-5pm. €2.60; reduced €1.60.

The **Villa of Maxentius** lies half-buried in cricket-filled greenery. Emperor Maxentius built the villa in the first decade of the 4th century, but he never got to enjoy it, having been ejected by the newly Christian Constantine. Over 0.5km in length, the circus was intended for chariot races and other pagan pastimes. The **Tomb of Romulus,** inside a giant brick portico, housed the remains of the emperor's son, named for the city's mythological founder, but is currently closed indefinitely for restoration.

MAUSOLEUM OF CECILIA METELLA

Intersection of V.d. Cecilia Metella and V. Appia Antica. Open Tu-Su 9am-6:30pm. €2.

This towering turret-like structure, seemingly an imitation of Augustus's mausoleum (see p. 112), was built in 30 BC for the patrician Cecilia, wife of a powerful Roman senator. It was preserved by its conversion into a fortress in the fourteenth century, when its famous crenelations were added. Used as a medieval roadblock of sorts, it stopped travelers to "request" a payment for the Caetni family coffers. The medieval complex includes the ruins of a Gothic church (rare in Rome), Chiesa San Nicola a Capo di Bove, which is across the street.

TESTACCIO

PYRAMID OF GAIUS CESTIUS

M: B-Piramide, bus #175 from Termini, or bus #23 from P. Risorgimento. Directly across from Metro station.

Egyptology has almost as proud a tradition in Rome as it does in England; the craze peaked after the defeat of Cleopatra's armies in the first century BC. Gaius, tribune of the plebes under Augustus, used his legions of slaves to complete the 27m high *Piramide di Caio Cestio* in 330 days. Aurelian had the pyramid built into his city walls in the 3rd century for protection from the Goths. Medieval tradition asserts that it stands over Remus's grave. Nowadays, it's a favorite hangout for Rome's feline population.

CIMITERO ACATTOLICO PER GLI STRANIERI

V. Caio Cestio, 6. From the Piramide station, follow V. R. Persichetti onto V. Marmorata, immediately turning left onto V. Caio Cestio. Ring bell for admission. Donation requested. Open Tu-Su 9am-5pm.

The Protestant Cemetery, or, to be blunt, the Non-Catholic Cemetery for Foreigners, is the only non-ancient burial space in Rome for those who don't belong to the Catholic Church. Crowded tombstones fight for attention with stray teams of meowing cats in the shade of lush tamarind trees. In the far left corner of the "Old Cemetery," **John Keats** lies beside his friend, Joseph Severn. At his request, the tombstone itself doesn't mention Keats by name, though the cemetery's directing placards do. It soberly states to contain "all that was mortal of a Young English Poet," and (after a quick disclaimer written by friends) records the words Keats wished to be inscribed on his grave: "Here lies one whose name was writ in water." On the other side of the small "New Cemetery," **Percy Bysshe Shelley** rests in peace beside his friend Trelawny, under a simple plaque hailing him as *Cor Cordium*, "Heart of Hearts." Also buried here are Goethe's son Julius, Italian socialist Antonio Gramsci (no self-respecting Italian cemetery would have him, even dead), and Richard Henry Dana, author of *Two Years Before the Mast*.

PORTA SAN PAOLO

M: B-Piramide: next to the Pyramid of Gaius Cestius. Museum entrance in the back. Open daily 9am-1:45pm. Additional hours Tu, Th 2:30-4:30pm.

Called *Porta Ostiensis* in antiquity, this gate began the famous Via del Mare, which linked Rome to its major port at Ostia. It is one of sixteen gates along the 3rd-century Aurelian Walls. Today, this colossal fragment keeps watch over the gnarls of traffic converging at Piramide. Inside lies **Museo Della Via Ostiense,** an excellent little history museum with impressive models of life on V. Mare.

MONTE TESTACCIO

Follow V. Caio Cestio from V. Marmorata until it ends at V. Nicola Zabaglia. Continue straight onto V. Monte Testaccio. The hill is ahead and to the right.

One of the most famous and historically significant landfills around, Monte Testaccio once served as a transfer area for grain, oil, wine, and marble unloaded from river barges. After goods were stored, ancient Roman merchants tossed leftover terra cotta urns (*testae*, from which Testaccio gets its name) into a vacant lot. The

Matilda Talli has run ***Roman Cat Sanctuaries*** *for twenty years. Matilda, and her feline friends, can be visited daily between 2:30-4:30pm from the gate next to the Pyramid of Gaius Cestius (p. 142). To find out more about the program's work, or to make a donation, ☎574 41 36 or visit www.igattidellapiramide.it.*

Q: Where do the cats you look after come from?

A: All over. We look after the stray cats in the Protestant cemetery, but the majority are abandoned pets. Tourists love to see kittens climbing around the ruins, but the reality here in Rome is that we often find a box with a cat and five kittens at our gate with a note saying "sorry, had to leave my apartment." Sometimes we manage to give the kittens away for adoption; usually, however, they live their lives here.

Q: How many cats do you have?

A: We currently care for over 100 cats, which all have to be fed, medically cared for, neutered and housed.

Q: How do you pay for this?

A: We are largely dependent on the good will of people visiting the cemetery next door, but we also organize a lottery and a garden party in September. In terms of practical work, which is often quite gruelling, we have about a dozen volunteers and we are always looking for more.

Mausoleam of Cecilia Matella

Isola Tiberina

Piazza San Bernardo

pile grew and grew, and today the ancient garbage dump, contrary to all intuition, rises in green splendor over the rest of the city. The park is now closed to the public as a *zona archelogica*, and pilfering pot shards is illegal, but V. Monte Testaccio, which surrounds the base of the hill, is home to many Roman nightclubs.

OSTIENSE

South of Testaccio lies Ostiense, a neighborhood largely born of turn-of-the-century urban migrations. It remains primarily a residential suburb, and certainly feels like it, although the Basilica and the huge wholesale *Mercati Generali* on V. Ostiense (M: B-Garbatella) on weekday mornings merit a side trip for sights and produce.

BASILICA SAN PAOLO FUORI LE MURA

M: B-Basilica San Paolo, or take bus #23 or 769 from Testaccio at the corner of V. Ostiense and P. Ostiense. Open in summer daily 7am-6:30pm; in winter 7am-6pm. Cloister open M-Sa 9am-1pm and 3-6:30pm; in winter 9am-1pm and 3-6pm. Dress appropriately.

Only the Pope can say mass at the massive high altar of this church, which shares extraterritorial status with San Giovanni in Laterano, Santa Maria Maggiore, and St. Peter's (hence the Vatican post-boxes). Until the construction of the new St. Peter's, San Paolo was the largest basilica in Rome. St. Paul, after being beheaded at nearby Tre Fontane, is believed to have been buried under the altar, demarcated by a red light (his body, that is; the head keeps the excellent company of St. Peter's noggin in San Giovanni). The original church was built in AD 324 by Constantine; the current incarnation was constructed after a huge fire in 1823. Yet another tragedy beset the church five years ago, when vandals painted the courtyard's statue of St. Paul fire-engine red.

Warmly lit by high alabaster windows, the mammoth layout of the basilica is in the Latin cross style (the shape of a "T"), with two aisles flanking the nave on each side. The triumphal arch around the altar, which was reassembled after the fire, is set with 5th-century mosaics depicting Christ giving benediction in the company of the apostles. Over 200 mosaic medallion portraits of the popes, from St. Peter to John Paul II, line the basilica's periphery. There is only space for eight more portraits, and legend says that when the wall fills up, the world will end.

Don't miss the **cloister:** its gorgeous mosaic-filled columns (called *'Cosmatesque'*, after its designer) resemble those in the cloister of San Giovanni, although here you can actually walk across the cloister. The gift shop sells monk-made **benedictine liquor** (€4-15), along with other potent potables and sundry delights.

EUR

M: B-EUR-Palasport, M: B-EUR-Fermi or bus #170 from Termini or P. Venezia.

The EUR (AY-oor), south of Ostiense, stands apart from Rome's other neighborhoods because of its completely different aesthetic and its markedly slower pace of life. Instead of ancient *piazze*, Roman ruins, and meandering, narrow streets, EUR is composed of wide, straight boulevards in a strangely perfect street grid, brimming with apartment high-rises that house many of Rome's white-collar doctors and lawyers. Built in a modern Neoclassical style all its own, EUR was to be the site of the 1942 World's Fair that Mussolini intended to showcase Imperial (well, let's be honest, Fascist) achievements. Apparently, the new, modern Rome was to shock and impress the rest of the world with its futuristic ability to build dozens of rectangular buildings that all look the same. World War II meant cancellation of the fair and demands on manpower and material, ensuring that EUR would never complete Mussolini's dream of extending Rome to the sea.

German and Allied occupation during the war left EUR in such bad shape that it was labeled a "modern Pompeii." Although it was rebuilt for the 1960 Rome Olympics, the under-touristed area feels like it is missing something: restaurants and shops. Failing all other alternatives (a few expensive eateries can be found on V. Europa), there is, appropriately enough, a McDonald's at 270 V. America.

Arriving via the EUR-Fermi stop delivers you to the foot of the *laghetto* (little artificial lake). Behind it, you will see the massive dome of the **Palazzo dello Sport,** which is used today as a major sports and concert venue. In front of the lake reside a few of Rome's only skyscrapers. A turn right down V.C. Colombo will take you to **Piazza Marconi,** laden with museums and Mussolini's 1939 obelisk, embodying the Fascist mantra that citizens exist to serve the state. Continuing on V. Cristoforo Colombo, and then turning left down V.d. Civilta del Lavoro will bring you to the **Palazzo della Civilta del Lavoro,** undoubtedly EUR's definitive symbol. A distinctly Modernist marble rectangle, it still manages to evoke Classical architectural allusions, winning it the accolade of "square Colosseum." If modern and postmodern Neoclassical architecture is your thing, be sure also to compare the **Palazzo dei Congresso** (at the other end of V della Civilta del Lavoro) and the **Piazzale degli Archivi** (at the east end of V. Europa).

ABBAZIA DELLE TRE FONTANE

M: B-Laurentina. Exit the metro station and walk straight ahead to V. Laurentina; take a right and proceed about ¾ mi. north on V. Laurentina and turn right onto V.d. Acque Salve. The abbey is at the bottom of the hill. Or take bus #761 north (catch it on the same side of the street as the metro stop) from the Laurentina stop; ask when to get off for the intersection of V. Laurentina and V. Acque Salve. Open daily 8am-1pm and 3-7pm.

St. Paul is said to have been beheaded at the site of this Trappist abbey. According to legend, his head bounced on the ground three times, creating a fountain with each touch. The now defunct fountains are contained within the Chiesa del Martirio di San Paolo, the last of three churches lying along the path through the compound's gate. A millennium later, St. Bernard stayed here during his 12th-century visit to Rome. Pick up some potent eucalyptus liqueur (€5-13) and divine chocolate (€9.80 for a gargantuan 900 gram bar), as well as marmalade, body cream, and shampoo, all made on the premises by Trappist monks.

IL GROTTO DELLE TRE FONTANE

V. Laurentina, 450. ☎06 591 46 30. Diagonally across the street from L'Abbazia delle Tre Fontane. Open sunrise to sunset. Mass held in the grotto M-Sa 10:30am and 5pm (6:30pm in the summer), Su 9, 10:30am, noon, and 5pm (6:30pm in the summer).

On April 12, 1947, Bruno Cornacchiola, an extreme leftist trolleyman, and his three children were taking a hike through a grove at the Tre Fontane. His youngest son lost his ball, and when Bruno went to help, he saw a vision of the Virgin of Revelation. She persuaded him (undoubtedly with visions of hellfire) to dispense with his plan to assassinate the pope. To commemorate the conversion, Catholics flock to the outdoor chapel built on the site and pray to the Virgin to preserve the pope's health. A tunnel to the right of the chapel is lined with personal photographs and hand written messages asking the Virgin for assistance.

LUNEUR PARK

V. Tre Fontane. ☎06 592 59 33. From P. G. Marconi, walk north on V. C. Colombo, turning right onto P. dell'Industria. The piazzale *dead-ends into V.d. Industria; turn left, there are entrances all along V.d. Industria. Take a right onto V. Tre Fontane for the main entrance on the right. Open in summer M-F 4pm-midnight, Sa 10am-1pm and 3pm-2am, Su 10am-1pm and 3pm-midnight; in winter Sa-Su 10am-1pm and 2pm-midnight. Pay by the ride, usually €2-3.*

Tired of museums, ruins, and churches? Itching to see some real life Italian carnies? Head to LunEUR, an old-fashioned amusement park with no high-culture strings attached. While it's no Disney World, the park caters to children and older daredevils alike. Cheap thrills like the "Himalaya Railroad," "Musik Express," and "Gravitron" abound, although a slow moving ferris wheel for less stable digestive systems resides at the back of the park.

LAGHETTO ARTIFICIALE

Just south of M: B EUR-Palasport and EUR-Fermi, at Largo G. Pella.

It's a lake. It's artificial. It's also a perfect rectangle. The shape is jarring for those accustomed to more realistic imitations, but it gets the job done, just as Mussolini presumed it would. Locals kayak up and down and couples stroll along the banks in the well-manicured Parco Centrale. Pedal-powered boats can be rented on the south side of the lake (opposite side from the Metro), and, in a pinch, overpriced restaurants cater to tired wannabe sailors on all four shores.

ARCHITECTURE GLOSSARY

TERM	EXPLANATION
abbazia	also *badia*, an abbey
anfiteatro	amphitheater
arco	arch
apse	a semicircular, domed niche projecting from the altar end of a church
atrium	an open central court, usually to an ancient Roman house
baldacchino	stone or bronze canopy supported by columns over the altar of a church
basilica	a rectangular building with aisle and apse; no transepts. Used by ancient Romans for public administration. Christians later adopted the style for churches
battistero	a baptistry, usually a separate building near the town's *duomo*, where the town's baptisms were performed
campanile	a bell tower, usually freestanding
cappella	chapel
castrum	the ancient Roman military camp layout, which many Italian cities were originally built on: a rectilinear city with straight streets, the chief of which was called the decumanus maximus
cenotaph	An empty tomb, in dedication to someone one buried elsewhere or whose corpse was lost. Cenotaphs to Dante Alighieri are often found in large churches
chancel	the space around the altar reserved for clergy and choir
chiesa	church

cloister/chiostro	a courtyard; generally a quadrangle with covered walkways along its edges, often with a central garden, forming part of a church or monastery
confessio	tomb of a saint or martyr in a church
cupola	a dome
duomo	cathedral; the official seat of a diocesan bishop
facade	the front of a building, or any wall given special architectural treatment
in restuaro	under restoration; a key concept in Rome
loggia	a covered gallery or balcony
mausoleum	a large tomb or building with places to entomb the dead above ground
nave	the central body of a church
necropolis	ancient burial site; definitely spooky
palazzo	an important building of any type, not just a palace. Many were built as town-houses for wealthy families
reliquary	holding place for a saint's relics, which usually consist of bones, but are often much much stranger
scalinata	stairway
thermae/ terme	ancient Roman baths and, consequently, social centers
telamoni	large, often sensual, statues of men used as columns in temples
transept	in a cruciform church, the arm of the church that intersects the nave or central aisle (i.e. the cross-bar of the T)
travertine	a light-colored marble or limestone used in many of the buildings in Rome
villa	a country house, usually a large estate with a formal garden. In Rome, villa refers to the area surrounding the estates that have become public parks.

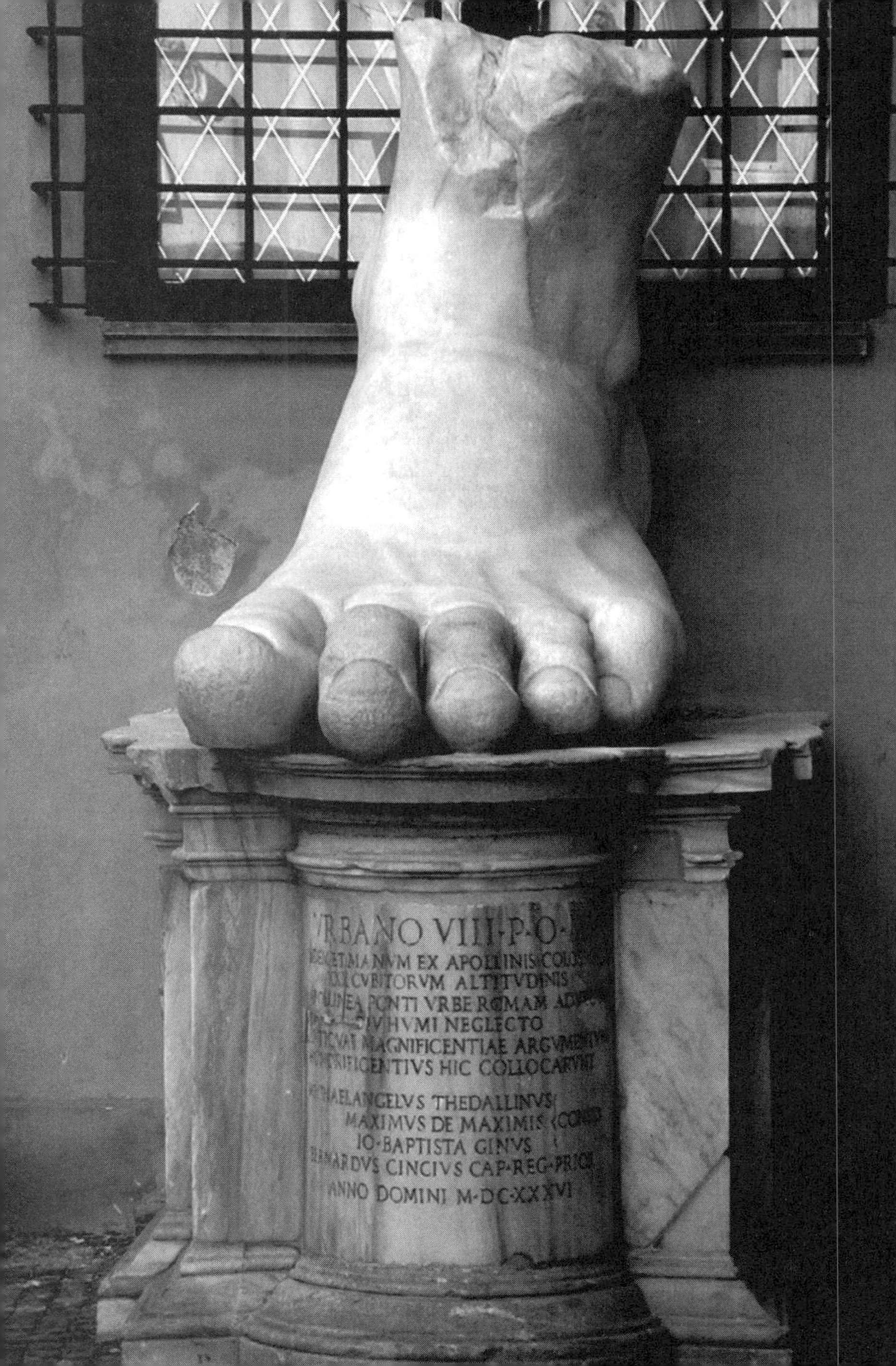
RBANO VIII·P·O·
MANVM EX APOLLINIS
CVBITORVM ALTITVDINIS
PONTI VRBE ROMAM
HVMI NEGLECTO
MAGNIFICENTIAE
ENTIVS HIC
MAXIMVS DE MAXIMIS
IO·BAPTISTA GINVS
CINCIVS CAP·REG·
ANNO DOMINI M·DC·XXXVI

INSIDE

principal collections **150**

the vatican **150** galleria borghese **165** capitoline museums **168**
museo nazionale etrusco di villa giula **170** galleria nazionale d'arte moderna **170**
musei nazionali romani **171** villa farnesina **173** museo nazionale d'arte antica **174**
galleria spada **175** EUR museums **176** recommended collections **177**

other interesting collections **178**

larger collections **178** smaller museums **179**

revolving exhibitions **181**

art glossary **182**

Museums

Some cities have museums; Rome, on the other hand, is one living, breathing, inescapable museum. Skip the bars, the clubs, the tiny *ristoranti* tucked into a side alley, and you still have Rome, bulging at the seams with the contents of your art history book and proof that once, not so long ago, this was the center of the western world.

Although faithful art-lovers from around the world have been making pilgrimages to the works of Michelangelo and Bernini for centuries, they still haven't figured it out. They approach Rome like a checklist of pagan and Christian treasures, to be checked off each day in a flurry of museum-hopping excess. (N.B. Despite the seeming contradiction, the *Let's Go* picks in **Discover** (p. 10) don't include any works of art. Hah, thought you had us, didn't you?) A proper museum experience, rather, ought to begin with an idea of what you would like to see and a *cappuccino*. Go early and take your time, pause at works that interest you; do not feel any obligation to read the info blurbs and listen to the audio clips, especially if the work doesn't grab you; there are plenty that will. Most importantly, stop (sit if you can) when you are moved by something, even if it is not famous or on your list. Leave the museum when you are burnt out, or when they kick you out.

Be prepared, Roman museums may have inconvenient hours and galleries that close inexplicably; some are not handicapped-accessible. Many museums retain the 18th-century presentation of their collections (thirty paintings to a wall is not uncommon), and labels range from highly informative, multi-lingual placards to none at all.

Helpful Hints: For some museums, reservations are a must; for others, they simply alleviate tiresome lines. Rome's museums are generally closed on Sunday afternoons and all day Monday, as well as major holidays. Be sure to call ahead to ask if all the galleries of the museum you wish to see are open, as renovations and labor shortages cause many unannounced closings. For up-to-the-minute information on many of Rome's museums, visit **www.museionline.it.**

EU citizens, people under 18 or over 65, and students should never pay full price for admission. Ask about discounts, and always carry your ISIC card. Students of art and architecture may be eligible for a special pass, or *tessera*, which allows them to visit certain national museums and monuments for free or at a discount. The bureaucratic bonanza for said pass begins at the **Ufficio Centrale Beni Culturali,** Divisione VI, V.S. Michele, 22, 00153 Roma. Applications should include a letter from your school, verifying your course of study, as well as two passport photos. The letters will be processed more quickly if written in Italian.

PRINCIPAL COLLECTIONS

The museums and galleries described below are the largest and most famous in Rome, and constitute the heart of the city's collections. Most of these museums are wheelchair accessible, but call ahead to request assistance.

VATICAN MUSEUMS

Walk north from the right-hand side of P.S. Pietro along the wall of the Vatican City about 10 blocks. From M: Ottaviano, head south on V. Ottaviano until you reach the Vatican City wall, turn right, and follow the wall to the museum's entrance. ☎06 698 849 47 or 06 698 850 61. Information and gift shop on the ground level past the entrance of the building. Very useful guidebook, €7.50. ***Currency exchange*** *and* ***first-aid*** *stations near ticket booths. Valuable newly revised CD-ROM audio guide with information and amusing anecdotes €5.50. Guides are available in major languages, and most of the museums' staff speak English. For information about guided tours, call ☎06 698 838 60. All major galleries open M-F 8:45am-4:45pm, Sa 8:45am-1:45pm. Schedule is liable to change so call in advance. Last entrance 1½hr. before closing. Closed on major religious holidays. €10, with ISIC card €7, children under 1m tall free. Free last Su of the month 8:45am-1:45pm. Most of the museum is* ***wheelchair accessible,*** *though less visited parts, such as the upper level of the Etruscan Museum, are not. Various galleries close without explanation; call ahead. Snack bar between the collection of modern religious art and the Sistine Chapel; full, reasonably priced cafeteria near main entrance. Dress appropriately. Plan to spend at least 4-5hr.*

Going to the Vatican Museums is a bit like psychotherapy: too much at once is a bad, bad thing. Taken in small doses, the Vatican Museums' world-renowned collections of sculpture, paintings, frescoes, and manuscripts can be both delightful and rewarding. With eight minor museums and millions of visitors a year, the Vatican Museums are not particularly hospitable to aimless wanderers. Plan to arrive 45min. prior to the stated opening times to avoid the legendary lines, or enter during lunchtime. Avoid visiting on Saturdays, which are notoriously crowded, and Mondays, as the museum is closed Sundays and thus gets double traffic on Monday.

In an attempt at traffic-control, the Vatican has three color-coded routes that guide you through the collections, organized by the amount of time visitors can spend. However, the routes tend to be hard to follow and crowded, as organized tour-groups are required to follow them. The Vatican Museums are best seen over an extended period of time. If you are strapped for time follow Routes A and B, but if you have Herculean fortitude and stamina Route C will give you a more complete tour of the Vatican's best.

Route A: Quattro Cancelli and the Egyptian Museum (45min.), Belvedere Courtyard (15min.), Chiaramoni Museum (30min.), Pio-Clementine Museum (1hr.), Etruscan Museum (1hr.).

Route B: Gallery of the Candelabra, Gallery of Tapestries, Gallery of Maps (45min. for all three), Raphael Rooms (45min.), Sistine Chapel (45min.), Galleria Urbano VIII, Library of Sixtus V, Galleria Clementina (30min.), Pinoteca (1hr.).

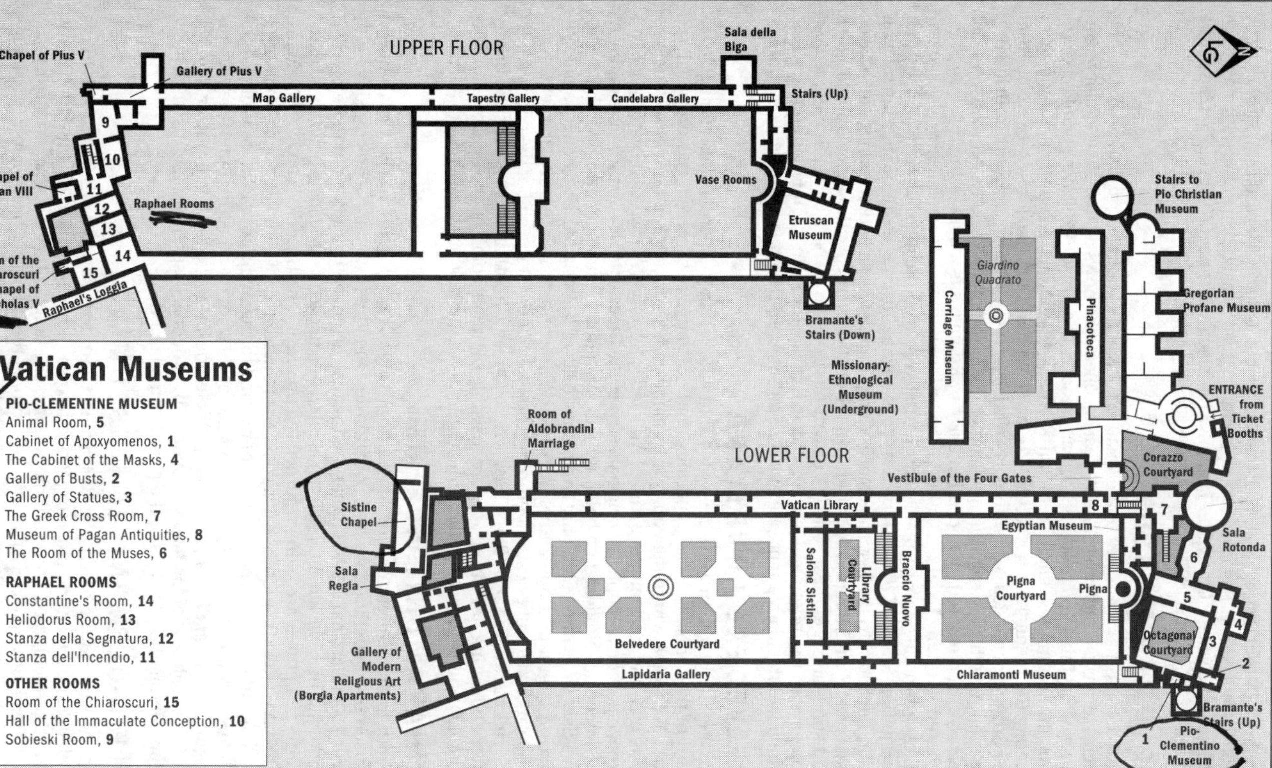
UPPER FLOOR
Chapel of Pius V
Gallery of Pius V
Map Gallery
Tapestry Gallery
Candelabra Gallery
Sala della Biga
Stairs (Up)
Vase Rooms
Etruscan Museum
Bramante's Stairs (Down)
Chapel of Urban VIII
Raphael Rooms
Room of the Chiaroscuri & Chapel of Nicholas V
Raphael's Loggia
9
10
11
12
13
14
15
Stairs to Pio Christian Museum
Gregorian Profane Museum
Pinacoteca
Giardino Quadrato
Carriage Museum
Missionary-Ethnological Museum (Underground)
ENTRANCE from Ticket Booths
Corazzo Courtyard
LOWER FLOOR
Room of Aldobrandini Marriage
Vestibule of the Four Gates
Vatican Library
8
7
Sala Rotonda
Egyptian Museum
Sistine Chapel
Sala Regia
Gallery of Modern Religious Art (Borgia Apartments)
Belvedere Courtyard
Salone Sistina
Library Courtyard
Braccio Nuovo
Pigna Courtyard
Pigna
6
5
4
3
2
1
Octagonal Courtyard
Lapidaria Gallery
Chiaramonti Museum
Bramante's Stairs (Up)
Pio-Clementino Museum
Vatican Museums
PIO-CLEMENTINE MUSEUM
Animal Room, 5
Cabinet of Apoxyomenos, 1
The Cabinet of the Masks, 4
Gallery of Busts, 2
Gallery of Statues, 3
The Greek Cross Room, 7
Museum of Pagan Antiquities, 8
The Room of the Muses, 6
RAPHAEL ROOMS
Constantine's Room, 14
Heliodorus Room, 13
Stanza della Segnatura, 12
Stanza dell'Incendio, 11
OTHER ROOMS
Room of the Chiaroscuri, 15
Hall of the Immaculate Conception, 10
Sobieski Room, 9

Route C: Quattro Cancelli, Gallery of the Candelabra, Gallery of Tapestries, Gallery of Maps (45min. for all four), Raphael Rooms (45min.), Sistine Chapel (45min.), Egyptian Museum (45min.), Belvedere Courtyard (15min.), Chiaramoni Museum (30min.), Pio-Clementine Museum (1hr.), Etruscan Museum (1hr.), Pinoteca (1hr.).

EGYPTIAN MUSEUM

Past the information booth in the Quattro Cancelli, to your left, at the top of the first flight, turn right and enter. The Vatican's collection shows a small, high-quality sampling of Egyptian and pseudo-Egyptian (read: Roman-made) statuary, paintings, coffins, and mummies, snatched from Roman excavations or purchased by popes. Among the highlights: in Room 1, Coptic (Egyptian Christian) funerary steles from the 3rd-6th centuries AD, with early Christian iconography; in Room 2, brilliantly painted polychrome sarcophagi complete with mummies (one has equally colorful hair dye) and painted linen death masks; in Room 5 sits a bust of the Pharaoh Mentuhotep II, dating from c. 2050 BC. The 3rd and 4th rooms are filled with colossal fakes: enormous, mostly black marble first-century Roman emulations of Egyptian antiquities. Many of these statues were excavated from the site of Hadrian's Tivoli villa. Tucked into the last rooms are Mesopotamian seals and ceramics and a large variety of Sumerian and Assyrian bas-reliefs, featuring mythological animal-gods and some of the earliest samples of writing. Don't look too closely, though, should you happen to understand hieroglyphics: this is all Roman-manufactured nonsense, which had the inadvertent side effect of baffling pre-Rosetta stone archaeologists.

BELVEDERE COURTYARD

Exiting the Egyptian Museum, you'll find yourself in the **Cortile della Pigna** (Courtyard of the Pinecone), the uppermost end of Bramante's Belvedere Courtyard. It's not hard to see where the courtyard's name came from; a gigantic bronze pinecone rests on a capital from the baths of Alexander Severus (AD 222-235) flanked by two bronze peacocks (copies of originals now in the **Braccio Nuovo**) on the stone railing of the Michelangelo-designed balcony. The 1st-century pinecone, cast by Publius Cincius Salvius, is one of the only surviving works of the original Vatican Museums collection begun by Pope Julius II in 1506. The center of the courtyard features a modern bronze spherical sculpture by Gio Pomodoro. At the end of the courtyard on the right is the **Tower of the Winds,** where Queen Christina of Sweden lived briefly after abdicating her throne, before insisting on more comfortable apartments. The sundial inside was used in the 16th century to cast doubt on the Julian calendar.

CHIARAMONTI MUSEUM

When facing the giant pinecone, a door to your right leads to the Chiaramonti Museum, a 300m long vaulted corridor designed by Bramante. The corridor holds over 1000 Classical busts, statues, and reliefs, arranged by Canova in the early 19th century. The Chiaramonti Museum is often one of the first to close; head there early, as the sculptures are better appreciated up close. The Braccio Nuovo (New Wing; currently closed), another gallery of Roman marble copies of Classical Greek originals, is undergoing renovations. Connecting to the midpoint of the corridor of the Chiaramonti, this collection of life-size (and larger) statues includes the famous **Augustus of Prima Porta,** a portrait of the emperor at the height of power, and the reclining **Colossus of the Nile,** surrounded by crocodiles, sphinxes, and 16 small boys, representing the 16 cubits of the river's annual flood.

PIO-CLEMENTINE MUSEUM

Up the stairs at the end of the Chiaramonti corridor, a domed vestibule leads to the stellar Pio-Clementine Museum, thought to be the Western world's finest collection of antique sculpture. The vestibule contains the first-century AD **Apoxyomenos** a strikingly realistic depiction of an athlete scraping the oil off his body before a competition. The statue is a Roman copy of 330 BC piece by Lysippos, a renowned Greek sculptor. A door leads from the vestibule into the Octagonal Court.

OCTAGONAL COURT

To the left of the vestibule is the outdoor Octagonal Court, the birthplace of the Vatican Museums. Julius II began the rich tradition of papal art collecting when he filled the courtyard with Classical sculpture from his private collection. The courtyard itself was designed by Bramante, but it was square until 1772 when Pope Clement XIV commissioned the architect Michelangelo Simonetti to redesign it. As part of his tenure as papal architect, Simonetti also designed the Room of the Muses, the Sala Rotondo, the Greek Cross Room and the staircase bearing his name, which connects the Egyptian, Etruscan and Pio-Clementine Museums.

To the left of the entrance stands the sublime **Apollo Belvedere,** another Roman copy of a Greek original. The god's placid features and posture (capturing the moment just after Apollo has shot an arrow) inspired innumerable Renaissance copies in stone and on canvas. During the 18th century, Apollo became the holy grail for aesthetes on their Grand Tours. Turning clockwise, you encounter the tortured **Laocoön** group, a sculpture that was famous even in ancient times for its vivid grotesqueness. Virgil's *Aeneid* tells the story of Laocoön, a Trojan priest who was punished by Athena, protectress of the Greeks, for advising his people against drawing the Trojan Horse into their city. Athena sent two sea serpents to devour Laocoön and his sons; the Trojans misinterpreted the omen, and happily dragged the "gift" into Troy. Make sure to look at the realistic detail on this sculpture; the veins and muscles are clearly visible. Laocoön's raised arm was discovered and reattached in the 20th century, but many art historians now debate the authenticity of this appendage.

Directly across the courtyard stands the **Cabinet of Canova,** which exhibits Antonio Canova's **Perseus with the Head of Medusa,** flanked by the boxers Kreugas and Damoxenos. These Neoclassical marbles depict violent mythological themes: Perseus killed the monstrous Medusa with the help of the gods; while the surly Damoxenos (on the right), not satisfied with a tie, stabbed his opponent in the stomach and gutted him alive (Damoxenos was then disqualified and Kreugas was declared the posthumous winner. After Napoleon plundered much of the Vatican's collection in 1800, these contemporary works were installed as a replacement (see **History,** p. 48). In the Cabinet of Hermes, do not miss the **Venus Felix** and the **Sarcophagus with battle of Amazons,** which captures the moment when Achillies simultaneously murders and falls in love with Penthesilea, one arm breaking her fall in the forefront while the other stabs her in the unseen background.

OTHER ROOMS

Two slobbering Molossian hounds guard the entrance to the **Room of the Animals,** a marble menagerie that reveals much about the prominence of brutality in Roman pastimes. Through the zoo is the **Gallery of Statues**—home to Apollo, Hermes, Ariadne, and others—at the end of which are stony faces in the Room of the Busts (which showcases a thoroughly engaging 1m foot and calf muscle). **The Cabinet of the Masks,** also adjacent to the Room of the Animals, houses the Venus of Cnidos. When staff is short, these rooms are often closed.

The **Room of the Muses** connects to the animal room and centers around the inscrutable **Belvedere Torso.** The torso has long been thought to represent Hercules sitting on the skin of the Nemean lion, but recent scholarship has suggested that it more likely depicts a suicidal Ajax or Dionysus in a thoughtful moment. During the Renaissance, the torso sat in the center of the Octagonal Court (where the fish pond currently serves as a poor substitute) and was drawn by Raphael and Michelangelo. The unusually muscled Christ in the Sistine Chapel's *Last Judgment* (see p. 161) shows that Michelangelo paid close attention. Through the arch, the Pantheon-inspired **Round Room** houses colossal Roman statues including two of Antinous Hadrian's ill-fated boy-toys and one of the Emperor Claudius in a general's uniform (his reputed obesity and propensity to drool tactfully forgotten), and a breathtakingly gaudy gilded Hercules. The statue was found carefully buried near the Theater of Pompey; the inscription on the its "tombstone" explains that the statue was struck by lightning and instantly rendered sacred; a proper burial was thus required. In the middle of the Round Room stands a mammoth fountain measuring 13m in circumference. The **Greek Cross Room,** the last in the museum, contains the enormous **sarcophagi** of St. Helen on the left, and Constance on the right, mother and daughter, respectively, of Constantine. The sarcophagi are made of porphyry, a luxurious and notoriously difficult to carve stone. Constance's was made in Alexandria, which possessed the last shop in the empire capable of working the material. It was dragged to the Vatican in 1790 on a cart pulled by 40 oxen. The relief on Constance's sarcophagus focuses on the wine harvest. Though traditionally associated with that most pagan of pagans, Bacchus, the harvest's theme of rebirth and eternal life became popular with early Christians as well. On either side of the exit, enormous 2nd-century red granite sphinxes might pose riddles before permitting you to leave.

ETRUSCAN MUSEUM

The next flight of the Simonetti Staircase climbs to the **Etruscan Museum,** which is filled with artifacts from the *necropolises* of Tuscany and northern Lazio. This newly renovated museum provides a welcome, peaceful change from the rest of the Vatican, but its galleries are often closed. However, the splendid contents of the **Regolini-Galassi Tomb,** a *tumulus* (burial mound) found intact and treasure-filled outside the necropolis at Cerveteri, are always visible. In Room II, the case on the right holds an extraordinary bronze chariot and bed with which a deceased 7th-century BC couple were supplied for their journey to the other side. Room III contains the rare 5th-century BC bronze **Mars of Todi** and Room IV holds a diverse collection of 4th- to first-century BC sacrophagi, sculptures, and reliefs carved from soft volcanic stone. Room IX has an excellent display of red- and black figure amphora imported from Greece by wealthy Etruscan traders. More far-flung rooms keep smaller bronzes, terra cotta figures, and jewelry. At the end of the Etruscan Rooms, visit the excellent **Rooms of the Greek Originals,** the **Stairway of the Assyrian Reliefs,** and the **Vase Collection.**

OTHER GALLERIES

GALLERY OF THE CANDELABRA

Back on the landing of the Simonetti Staircase is the **Room of the Biga.** "Biga" means chariot in Greek, and the room appropriately holds a first century AD marble chariot outfitted with newly sculpted wheels and horses. The chariot served as an elaborate throne for the bishops of the Church of San Marco. Request a tour for access to the room. Ask at the information desk of the museum, or just peek through the gate. Past the door of the Biga is the Gallery of the Candelabra, named for the marble candlesticks standing under each of six archways. This hall holds more ancient statuary, including a late-Hellenistic depiction of Dionysus as a young boy carried on the shoulders of a satyr. Also note the statue of Artemis with several rows of what appear to be breasts (although the **audio guide** helpfully notes that they might also represent bull's testicles). The image represents fertility and comes from the Cult of Artemis, popular in Asia Minor several centuries before the birth of Christ.

GALLERY OF THE TAPESTRIES

The Gallery of the Tapestries is next as you exit the Gallery of the Candelabra. Not surprisingly, its walls are hung with massive tapestries, executed by Raphael's workshop from original cartoons after the artist's death. (Examples of old-school Raphael tapestries designed for the Sistine Chapel can be seen in the Vatican's Pinacoteca, p. 164.) On the left wall hang 16th-century Flemish depictions of the life of Christ, including three gory panels displaying the slaughter of the innocents. On the right, Roman tapestries illustrate stories of obscure Popes. Pope Pius VI built this corridor and, humble man that he was, had scenes from his life detailed on the ceiling.

GALLERY OF THE MAPS

The Gallery of the Maps is a long, gilded walkway of cartography designed by Egnazio Danti, the Vatican's true Renaissance man: Danti was a Dominican cosmographer, mathematician, architect, and painter. The 40 frescoes depict maps of Italy, the Apennine Mountains, and Avignon in gorgeous greens, blues, and golds. The map of the Adriatic, with winged lions and whiskered fish, is a must see, as is the splendid fresco, stucco, and gold-leaf work on the ceiling.

APARTMENT OF PIUS V

The Apartment of Pius V comes next along the thoroughfare to the Sistine Chapel, holding still more tapestries. At the end of the "apartment" there is a shortcut staircase down to the Sistine Chapel. To the left, the longer journey through the museum continues with the **Sobieski Room,** the **Room of the Immaculate Conception,** and the Raphael rooms.

SOBIESKI ROOM

The Sobieski Room is named for the Polish work that takes up the north wall, "Sobieski Liberates Vienna," in which Sobieski, the king of Poland, defeats the Turks in battle and saves Christendom from takeover by Islamic warriors. What this painting lacks in quality, it more than makes up for in size. The mosaic in the center of the floor is ancient Roman, excavated from the port city of Ostia (see **Daytripping,** p. 263).

ROOM OF THE IMMACULATE CONCEPTION

The Room of the Immaculate Conception holds 52 rare books in dozens of languages, all delivering a single statement: Pius IX's 1854 decree announcing the doctrine of Mary's permanent and unsullied virginity. The main fresco portrays Pope Pius IX proclaiming the controversial dogma, in case anyone missed it the first time.

RAPHAEL ROOMS

While the Sistine Chapel awes viewers with its vast frescoes and heroic scale, the smaller—but no less exquisite—Raphael Rooms provide an up-close-and-personal look at some of the world's best wall paintings. Known primarily by the self-explanatory adjective *terribilita*, it appears that Pope Julius II had a bit of the suburban housewife in him as well. Upon becoming Pope in 1503, Julius announced his need to redecorate: he simply could not live in the downstairs apartments, looking at portraits of his predecessor, the nefarious Span-

Laocoön

Vatican Museums

Museo Nazionale d'Arte Antica

ish Pope Alexander VI of Borgia. So he promptly hired the best painters of his day (including Perugino, Peruzzi, and Il Sodoma) to decorate a cozy little *cubiculum* (bedroom) for himself. Work was progressing nicely until a certain Raphael Sanzio coasted into town and painted a trial piece for Pope Julius, a little work called **The School of Athens.** The pope was so impressed with Raphael that he immediately fired his other painters, had their frescoes destroyed, and handed the entire suite of rooms over to Raphael. The commission marked the beginning of Raphael's brilliant career in Rome.

CONSTANTINE'S ROOM

A detour down an outdoor walkway over the Belvedere Courtyard takes you to Constantine's Room, *completed after Raphael's death*, where the not-so-subtle theme is Christianity's victory over paganism. The tip-off might be the ceiling where a statue of a pagan god lies broken on the ground in front of a gleaming gold crucifix on a pedestal. On the wall to the left of the entrance, Constantine addresses his soldiers and sees the vision of the cross; the opposite wall holds the baptism of Constantine; in the window wall, Constantine donates the city of Rome to Pope Sylvester; on the wall facing the window, Constantine defeats Maxentius at the Battle of the Milvian Bridge. These frescoes were designed to look like tapestries, hence their subdued colors. Despite the tour guides who proclaim otherwise, none of these frescoes were painted by Raphael's hand, although a few of the designs may have been taken from his sketches.

ROOM OF THE CHIAROSCURI AND THE CHAPEL OF NICHOLAS V

The Room of the Chiaroscuri displays coffered wooden ceilings and frescoes of the apostles. The small Chapel of Nicholas V (often closed during the summer) forms the oldest section of the palace. The chapel was decorated by Fra Angelico between 1447-51 with frescoes depicting events from the lives of St. Stephen and St. Lawrence. Exit the Room of the Chiaroscuri and pass through the gift shop (also completed after Raphael's death) into the Heliodorus Room.

HELIODORUS ROOM

The Heliodorus Room was under renovation during summer 2003.

The Heliodorus Room (1511-14) was designed as the secret antechamber of the apartments. The room's obscure subjects were chosen by Julius to illustrate God's miraculous protection of the Church at various times in history. Directly opposite the door is Raphael's depiction of the providential deliverance of St. Peter from the Tullianum Prison on the Capitoline Hill. Raphael's unique composition and his exquisite use of light (daylight, moonlight, angelic light, and real light from the window below) make this fresco one of the Vatican's most moving.

The right wall tells the biblical story of Heliodorus, who had come to loot the Temple of Jerusalem, but was tossed out by a couple of angels. On the entrance wall is the miracle of Bolsena: a priest, who had trouble believing in transubstantiation, came to mass in Bolsena and saw the wine and bread become blood and flesh. Raphael painted Julius himself in the guise of Pope Urban IV, who, after the miraculous appearance of blood on the altar linen at Bolsena, instituted the feast of Corpus Christi. Note the Swiss Guards, dressed just as festively as they are today, kneeling on the right. On the long wall is Pope Leo the Great expelling Attila from Rome.

STANZA DELLA SEGNATURA

The Stanza della Segnatura (1508-12), originally the Pope's library, where official documents were signed, is considered Raphael's Vatican masterpiece. The walls represent four branches of learning—theology, law, philosophy, and poetry. On the wall of the entrance is the splendid **School of Athens,** in which ancient philosophers and scientists (many of whom Raphael painted with the features of his friends and fellow artists) stroll through an airy architectural fantasy. The centerpiece is an argument between Plato, who points to the sky, and Aristotle, who gestures to the assembly as a comment on his rationalist (earthly) philosophy. In the lower right, Euclid, explaining geometry on the ground, has Bramante's face. To the far right of the composition stands Raphael, in three-quarter profile, and his friend and fellow artist, Il Sodoma. In the center we see the isolated and brooding figure of Heraclitus writing. X-rays have proven that the figure was added as an afterthought and it is believed to be a portrait of Michelangelo. Legend has it that Raphael was given a sneak preview of the Sistine Chapel and was so moved that he changed his style of painting entirely. He added the portrait to his work in progress in order to honor his former rival. Another interesting aspect of the fresco is that it was executed with remarkable speed. Raphael supposedly drew up the elaborate cartoons for the frescoes in a matter of days. Furthermore, it appears that Raphael spent as much time working on the face of Heraclitus as on the left half of the fresco.

Opposite the entrance is the **Disputation of the Holy Sacrament,** in which theologians, authors (look for Dante, wearing a crown of laurels, on the right), and church doctors crowd around a monstrance that holds the communion host. Above them is the community of heaven, conversing more peacefully, as they have reached complete understanding of the truths debated below. **Parnassus** is a representation of poets, musicians, and their inspirational muses on the mountain for which the work is named; on the left, note Homer in blue, Dante in profile, and Sappho holding a scroll bearing her name. On the right, the cardinal and the theological virtues of the law, are represented, respectively, by Gregory IX approving the Decretals and Justinian publishing the Pandects.

STANZA DELL'INCENDIO

The final room is the Stanza dell'Incendio (the corner of which you passed through before), containing works largely designed by Raphael but executed by Raphael's pupils, including Giulio Romano. By the time of their painting (1514-17), Pope Leo X Medici had taken up residence in the *stanze*, and portraits of earlier Leos dominate the room, which served as a dining room. The riotous *Fire in the Borgo* depicts the 847 blaze that was miraculously extinguished when Leo IV made the sign of the cross from the *loggia* of St. Peter's. The painting depicts the facade of the old Constantinian basilica that was pulled down to make way for the new St. Peter's. The painting, hinting at the style that Raphael would adopt at the end of his life, is attributed predominantly to the master himself. Other scenes show the coronation of Charlemagne in 800, the victory of Leo IV over the Saracens at Ostia, and the oath of Leo III. The ceiling, painted by Perugino, is all that remains of the earlier work on the apartments; it is said that Raphael left it out of respect for his master. Yet the contrast between the two sets of frescoes shows (perhaps intentionally) that the student quickly surpassed his teacher. From here, exit through the **Chapel of Urban VIII,** decorated by Pietro da Cortona.

BORGIA APARTMENTS & MUSEUM OF MODERN RELIGIOUS ART

The Vatican is known for old, old things, but the museum has made an effort to spice things up with some modern art, albeit of a religious nature. Buttressed with a few big-name works, this collection is not among the Vatican's strongest and can be bypassed (look for signs) en route to the Sistine Chapel. Still, if you're looking for a break from the noisy crowds and your feet aren't hurting yet, it's worth a look.

The **Borgia Apartments,** named after the infamous Alexander VI Borgia, father of the even more infamous Lucrezia and Cesare, comprise six rooms decorated by Pinturicchio from 1492-95. Today, the only visible embellishments are the lunettes and ceiling vaults; the walls have been covered by the Vatican's collection of modern religious art. Matisse's glorious, colored clerical capes (designed for a chapel despite his atheism), and a cast of Rodin's famous *Thinker* are the stars of the apartments. In the **Room of the Sibyls,** legend has it that the ambitious Cesare Borgia had his brother-in-law Alfonso d'Aragone murdered in order to free his sister Lucrezia to marry Alfonso d'Este.

Outside the Borgia Apartments, the **collection of modern religious art** (largely assembled by Pope Paul VI) continues for many more rooms. The collection is not organized according to any apparent theme, but works by Beckmann, Chagall, Dali, Gauguin, Kandinsky, Klee, Modigliani, Morandi, Munch, Picasso, Rivera, and Shahn can be found by the intrepid wanderer.

SISTINE CHAPEL

With its frescoes plastered on everything from mouse pads and calendars to sweatshirts and coffee mugs, it's easy to forget that the Sistine Chapel is just that—a chapel. Technically part of St. Peter's Basilica, the Sistine Chapel was originally a private chapel for the Popes, and it is still the chamber in which the College of Cardinals elects popes; a tradition since the 16th century. While Michelangelo's frescoes receive the most attention, the ones along the side wall were painted first, for Sixtus IV from 1481 to 1483. Michelangelo then painted the ceiling from 1508 to 1512, and Pope Leo X had Raphael's tapestries (now in the Vatican Museum's Pinoteca) hung below the frescoes on the side walls in 1519. Finally, Michelangelo painted his *Last Judgment* between 1535-41, replacing earlier frescoes by Perugino. In 1980-94 the ceiling frescoes and *Last Judgment* were cleaned, amid much heated debate; the side-wall frescoes were restored in 1999. Regardless of your interest in art history, the Sistine Chapel will blow you away.

While in the chapel, **speak quietly** and **refrain from taking flash photos,** even if you see others around you doing it. The light of the flash damages the frescoes, and you can buy much better shots (actually cheaper than using your own film) on postcards in the ubiquitous gift shops.

WALL FRESCOES

Before craning your neck, prepare yourself by taking in the older, all too often ignored frescoes on the side walls. As you face the *Last Judgment*, the wall on your left holds six scenes from the life of Moses, while six scenes from the life of Christ appear on the right wall. The cycle was completed by an all-star team of artists working under Perugino that included Botticelli, Ghirlandaio, Roselli, Pinturicchio, Signorelli, and della Gatta.

LIFE OF MOSES

Starting at the altar, the first fresco in this cycle is Pinturicchio's *Moses and Zepporah*, which shows Moses circumcising his son and returning to Egypt. Botticelli's remarkable *Burning Bush* comes next, in which Moses hears God speaking out of the burning bush, instructing him to free the enslaved Israelites. A busy man, Moses also defends Jethro's daughters from Midianites at the well, and kills an Egyptian who had beaten an Israelite slave. The third fresco, by Biagio di Antonio, depicts the crossing of the Red Sea. The newly freed Israelites (left), have passed safely across the sea, which was conveniently lifted, while the pursuing Egyptian troops drown (at right).

The next fresco, by Cosimo Roselli, shows Moses receiving the Ten Commandments. The Israelites immediately break the new laws by worshipping a golden calf, which incites Moses to smash the tablets in anger. Botticelli's *Punishment of Korah, Dathan, and Abiram* follows, in which the three are punished for trying to stone Moses. Behind Moses, on the far right, the figure in black is Botticelli's self-portrait. The last fresco in this cycle ties up loose ends: Moses hands his staff to his successor Joshua, an angel shows Moses the promised land, and Moses dies.

LIFE OF CHRIST

The first fresco, as you face the altar, was painted by Perugino and Pinturicchio and depicts the baptism of Christ by John the Baptist. In the background, Christ preaches (left) while John steps back in time, predicting Christ's coming (right). In the second fresco (by Botticelli) Christ is tempted by the devil, who suggests that he test God by throwing himself from various high places to see if angels save him.

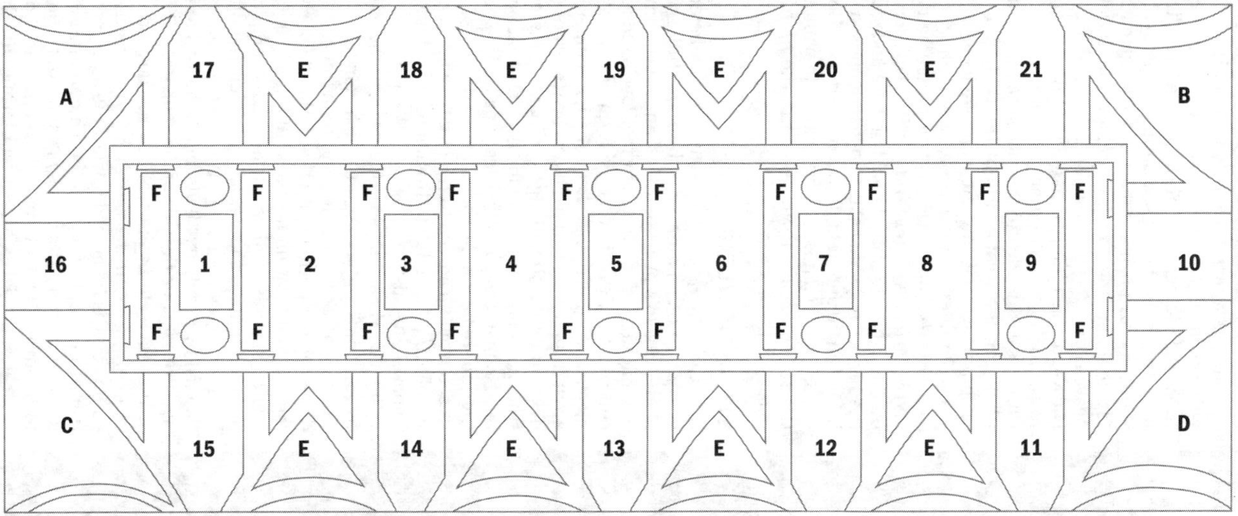
North Wall: Life of Christ
West Wall: Last Judgment (Entrance)
East Wall: Exit
South Wall: Life of Moses
A
B
C
D
E
F
1
2
3
4
5
6
7
8
9
10
11
12
13
14
15
16
17
18
19
20
21

The Sistine Chapel Ceiling

BIBLE STORIES

A The Bronze Serpent
B Judith and Holofernes
C The Punishment of Hamen
D David Slaying Goliath
E Jesus' Forefathers
F The Ignudi

FROM THE CREATION TO THE FLOOD

1 God Separates Light from Darkness
2 Creation of Sun, Moon, and Plant Life
3 God Separates the Water and the Earth and Creates Life in the Sea
4 Creation of Adam
5 Creation of Eve
6 Original Sin and Expulsion from the Garden of Eden
7 Noah's Sacrifice
8 The Flood
9 The Drunkenness of Noah

THE PROPHETS AND SIBYLS

10 Zacharia
11 Joel
12 Erythraean Sibyl
13 Ezekiel
14 Persian Sibyl
15 Jeremiah
16 Jonah
17 Libyan Sibyl
18 Daniel
19 Cumaean Sibyl
20 Isaiah
21 Delphic Sibyl

in the know

Reading list

Being a painter during the Renaissance meant more than having talent with a brush. Intellectual education was taken seriously. Michelangelo was a Dantista, a Dante scholar, and took much of his inspiration from *La Divina Commedia.*

Even the less formidably intellectual artists were forced to acquire a knowledge of Biblical and extra-Biblical sources, because of the number of commissions that came from the papacy and other religious orders. Here are a few appropriate readings to complement your visit to the Vatican:

Budding Michelangelo

St. Augustine, *The City of God*

Dante, *The Divine Comedy*

St. Jerome, the Vulgate Bible

Aspiring Mediocrity

St. Jerome's Vulgate: Genesis, Exodus, Numbers 16 and 22:8, Deuteronomy 33, Matthew, Revelation, Judith 13:8-10, Samuel 17: 41-51

Dante, *Inferno*

In line at the Vatican

St. Jerome's Vulgate: Genesis 1,8; Exodus 2:11-20, 3:1-6, 4:20, 14:23-30, 15:1- 20, 23:12-15, 32:1-19.

Cliff's Notes: Inferno I-X, XXXIII.

Next, Christ calls the first apostles, fishermen named Peter and Andrew, in a fresco by Ghirlandaio. In the fourth fresco, by Cosimo Rosselli, we see Christ giving the Sermon on the Mount. In the right foreground, Christ heals a leper. The next fresco is the most famous in the cycle, showing Christ handing the keys to the kingdom (symbolizing the power to decide who enters heaven) to Peter, the first pope. The final fresco shows the Last Supper, painted by Roselli and Antonio. Judas, the disciple who betrayed Christ, is easy to identify: he's sitting across from Christ on the wrong side of the table and is unsurprisingly the only one without a halo.

The far inferior frescoes on the wall opposite *The Last Judgment* (*Resurrection* on the left and *St. Michael Defending the Body of Moses* on the right) are not original but were added in the 1570s where Michelangelo was supposed to have painted another full wall masterpiece. Botticelli, Ghirlandaio, and Fra Diamante painted the series of popes who stand in the niches between the windows.

SISTINE CEILING

Ironically, the project was given to Michelangelo as a consolation prize by Pope Julius II. Michelangelo's plans to create a massive tomb for Julius II were thwarted by the Pope's sudden edifice fetish, which took the form of improvements to St. Peter's. To keep the hot-tempered artist from fleeing to the hills (as he was wont to do), Julius let Michelangelo repaint the star-studded ceiling of the Sistine Chapel. That bad boy Bramante apparently suggested his rival for the job, believing Michelangelo's distaste for fresco would lead him to reject the assignment, which would then fall to Bramante or his buddy Raphael. Big mistake. Huge.

Sulking, Michelangelo set about learning how to fresco, firing assistants with remarkable rapidity after he learned the technique, and developing a permanent crick in his neck (he did not paint flat on his back, but standing up and craning his head backwards). His complex and ambitious design primarily depicts the Biblical story of Genesis in the central panels, flanked by Prophets, Sibyls and nudes reclining on thrones along the side of the vault.

Michelangelo began work at the far end of the ceiling, painting the Creation narrative backwards as he moved toward the altar (contrary to Church tradition, in which paintings surrounding the altar always came first). Suffering from a lack of funds, Michelangelo took a six-month hiatus after completing half the ceiling in 1510-11. The division between his earlier, crowded panels and the later, more streamlined panels is quite striking. The scale of Michelangelo's figures increased dramatically as he painted—check out the size of Zachariah's feet (above the exit) compared to those of Jonah (above the *Last Judgment*).

While focusing on the central panels, don't overlook the three-dimensional *Apostles and Sibyls* (whose brawny arms are said to be the result of Michelangelo's exclusive use of male models) and the often amusing *ignudi* (nude figures). Some of Michelangelo's best painting, these nudes support green sacks full of acorns (the symbol of the della Rovere family, of which Pope Julius II was a member). Often ignored, the nudes serve an important function by framing the panels (observe how strange the flood panel looks due to the collapse of a small fresco). In the four corner spandrels are depictions of *David and Goliath*, *Judith and Holofernes*, *The Bronze Serpent*, and *The Punishment of Haman*.

THE CREATION OF EARTH

Looking from *The Last Judgment* toward the chapel's rear, the panels show the first five days of Creation, beginning with *Separation of Light from Darkness*. Both the *Creation of the Sun, Moon, and Planets* and *Separation of Land from Water* focus primarily on the figure of God, clad in a pink robe, surrounded by nebulous clouds.

ADAM AND EVE

In the next panel, *Creation of Adam*, Michelangelo revolutionizes conceptions of Man's birth. By depicting both God and man in human form, Michelangelo places mortals on nearly equal footing with God. Chalk one up for large-scale representations of hubris. Much scholarly attention has been devoted to the "tension" in the gap between the two fingers. Michelangelo, true to Genesis, used the same cartoon to create the images of God and Adam to ensure that God creates Adam in his own image. Interestingly, the nebular assortment of angels and pink raiment about God looks exactly like a human brain. In the central panel, God for the first time in art history appears on Earth for *Creation of Eve*. Eve rests next to the stump of a tree, an allusion to the cross. In *Temptation and Expulsion from Paradise*, Adam and Eve reluctantly retire from the garden while the serpent slithers past.

LIFE OF NOAH

The last three panels take up the life of Noah, with God conspicuously absent. These frescoes depict the **Sacrifice of Noah** (where Noah thanks God for saving him and his family from the flood), **The Flood,** and the **Drunkenness of Noah,** in which Noah forgets himself after the flood in a bout of shameful and ungodly revelry, thus proving the sinful nature of all mankind, even God's favorites. Though Michelangelo could have ended with the *Flood*, it was theologically important to include the *Drunkenness of Noah* as a reminder that though sinners were picked off in the flood, God's children still "die" from sin. This underscores mankind's need for a savior, and thus reinforces the role of Christ and the Church. A close look at *The Flood* reveals slight damage to a corner, which occurred as a result of an explosion in the nearby Castel Sant'Angelo in 1508.

THE LAST JUDGMENT

Leaving behind frolicking *ignudi* for the flames of hell, Michelangelo, now around 60, was at the height of his artistic powers when he turned his brush to the story of *The Last Judgment* (1535-41) for Pope Paul III. In the 23 years between the completion of the ceiling frescoes and the start of the *Last Judgment*, the character of Rome changed dramatically, as the Sack of Rome and the Protestant Reformation wreaked havoc on the city and her beliefs. A Dante scholar, Michelangelo gave his interpretation several Infernal references, notably in the depiction of ferryman Charon whacking the damned in the lower right-hand corner of

the fresco. The location of *The Last Judgment* above the altar places the most sacred part of the church in the mouth of hell. Paul III was satisfied with the results of his commission: upon the unveiling of the altarpiece, he fell to his knees on the marble floor, crying, "Lord, charge me not with my sins when Thou shalt come on the day of judgment!"

In order to paint *The Last Judgment* above the altar, three previous frescoes were destroyed and two windows were filled. The resulting fresco shows Christ, whose beefy body is supposedly modeled after the Belvedere Torso (see p. 153), in the center, with Mary averting her eyes from the grotesque spectacle of damnation on the left. St. Peter returns the keys to the kingdom to Christ, who is painted in front of a golden light representing the monstrance of the Holy Spirit. He initiates two vortices; with his "right hand of power" he sends the damned spiraling to hell as he effortlessly lifts the saved with his left hand. Surrounding Christ, the saints are portrayed with the instruments of their martyrdom. Amid the saintly entourage is St. Bartholomew, who was flayed alive, holding his own skin (the face of the skin is a rather morbid self-portrait of the 65-year-old artist).

In the center, below Christ, angels with trumpets hold two books; the very large book of the damned and the very small book of the saved. On the left of the fresco, angels pull the lucky souls into heaven, while on the right, demons drag the damned into an abyss. On the bottom left corner of the work, a grim skeleton looks directly at the rest of the chapel, while on the right resides the famous figure of a damned man who looks into hell. Also in the lower right corner, Minos, Master of the Underworld, sports a coiling tail and ass-ears. His face is a portrait of Biagio da Cesena, who, speaking for Pope Paul III, objected to Michelangelo's use of "shameless nudity in a holy space." The figures' nudity, however, plays a symbolic role in Michelangelo's work. None of the angels have wings or other fine digs as they do on the Sistine Ceiling, and all of the figures were originally painted nude by Michelangelo. This was to show that in the end all illusion would be wiped away and all the worldly goods that we mistakenly valued on earth would be valueless before the judgement of truth by God. After Michelangelo's death, the Counter-Reformation and other periods of prudishness led to several rounds of loin cloth painting over the nude figures. During the painting's restoration the fate of the cover-up was hotly contested by pro-nudity and anti-nudity camps. In the end, only the earliest coverings painted by Michelangelo's pupil, Daniele da Colterra (nick named *il braghettone*, the maker of breeches), were left. Nudists 1, anti-nudists 0.

OTHER MUSEUMS

Plan to spend a total of 20min. in these galleries.

CHAPEL OF ST. PIUS V

From the exit along the left-hand wall of the Chapel, several corridors return to the Galleries of the Library and back to the Belvedere Courtyard. The corridors pass numerous rooms containing artifacts collected during the reigns of various popes. In the second room, the Chapel of St. Pius V, a reliquary case contains fragments of saints retrieved from the treasury of *Sancta Sanctorum*, including the *Reliquary of the Head of St. Praxedes*. The blue and gold starred ceiling above the exit is similar to the ceiling of the Sistine Chapel before Michelangelo's frescoes.

ROOM OF THE ALDOBRANDINI MARRIAGE

A short way up on the left, the Room of the Aldobrandini Marriage hides a series of rare ancient Roman frescoes, including the celebrated wedding scene, set in a flowering park filled with animals.

The contested legacy of the Sistine Chapel

When Michelangelo painted his sibyls, *ignudi*, and scenes from the Old Testament on the ceiling of the Sistine Chapel, it was without any knowledge of the controversy that his pigments would ouch off in art circles nearly 500 years later.

By the 19th century, visitors to the famous hapel were beginning to notice something: the rescoes were almost impossible to see. oethe, who craned his neck upwards like any ourist in 1786, predicted that the paintings vould someday be entirely obscured by the ayers of the centuries. What were these lay-rs? The expected dirt, grime, and soot, carried rom the bodies of tourists milling below by an ir current to collect on the frescoes, but also, urprisingly, a commission of noted art histori-ns created by the Vatican to look in the prob-em discovered that a layer of glue had been pplied at some point in the past.

The glue, an only slightly more refined (and istorically exalted) version of the substance hat children apply to the surface of finger-aintings to give them a professional sheen, vas brushed over the frescoes sometime dur-ng the 18th century. It blackened with age, ecause of its ingredients, adding to the effect roduced by the rainwater seeping in through he roof and the soot from when candles were urned on the premises, not to mention the weat and grime from millions of tourists.

The Vatican's international crack team of art istorians and professional conservationists, owever, found themselves confronting ethical bjections to the restorations when they nnounced the plans to clean the frescoes and emove the glue. Other experts fretted over the act that stabilization and repair often has the nintended effect of changing the work of art. reserving the integrity of a work is the first enet of any respectable restorationist, but mistakes can occur during the process. It was alleged by those who opposed the restorations that Michelangelo had intended the glue to be placed on the ceiling. The Vatican team proved in short order that this was not the case, but was still forced to subject its own methods to the most careful scrutiny.

The actual restoration process was meticulous, grueling work. A mixed solvent with a gelatinous consistency was applied with brushes to very small areas of the frescoes, and left alone for three minutes. The grime dissolved into the solvent, which was removed with sterilized natural sponges soaked with twice-distilled water. If necessary, the process was repeated again 24 hours later. In some cases, small portions of the fresco had flaked away. The restoration team did not repaint these part of the frescoes, but did retouch them with thin parallel strokes of watercolor. These parallel strokes can be easily distinguished from the original painting upon closer examination, but for us on the ground, they are undetectable.

During the process of restoration, the Vatican team recovered details of the original cleaning of the frescoes, which began only a few years after Michelangelo completed the project in 1512. Their methods were not nearly as careful as the ones utilized by the most recent restoration: they scrubbed the Sistine ceiling with wine and sponges made from stale bread. Nonetheless, this history of restoration was what the Vatican team needed to prove that theirs was a valid project, not a result of 20th century mores about the importance of art. When the Sistine Chapel was revealed after the restorations in the original colors that Michelangelo intended, flashbulbs exploded over the restored frescoes ablaze in rich hues and, for the first time in centuries, visible in all of the detail that Michelangelo wanted.

Anna Kim is a Ph.D. candidate in the History of Art and Architecture at Harvard University.

ROOMS OF THE PAPYRUS

The Rooms of the Papyrus contain 29 facsimiles of medieval papyrus sheets with Latin writings dating back to the 16th century. The corridor continues past cases of uninspiring modern religious art (skip the *Mute Swans of Peace*) as well as antique globes, bells, and maps. The papal geocentric "universe" globes, midway down on the left side, are worth a glance.

THE SISTINE HALL

The Sistine Hall, leading off the main corridor to the right, is used for exhibitions from the Vatican Library's superb collection of books and manuscripts. Access to the library is difficult to obtain; you must visit the information desk at the entrance with letters of introduction and possibly proof of enrollment from your university. At the end of the corridor, you'll find the Vestibule of the Four Gates, from which the stairs on the opposite side lead up to the Sistine Chapel. On the left is the **Atrium of the Four Gates** and the **Court of the Pinacoteca,** with an excellent view of St. Peter's.

PINACOTECA

The Pinacoteca, the Vatican's painting collection, spans the 12th to 18th centuries, and now holds more than 460 works, including masterpieces by Giotto, Poussin, Leonardo da Vinci, Titian, Raphael, and Caravaggio.

ROOMS 1-7

These galleries hold mostly Florentine and Sienese Gothic altarpieces and triptychs from the 12th to 14th centuries, painted in brilliant colors with extraordinary detail. Particularly impressive is Giotto's two-sided *Stefaneschi Triptych* in **Room 2.** Originally created for the high altar of Constantine's Basilica and part of the Sacristy of the old St. Peter's, it is named for the cardinal who commissioned it. Cardinal Stefaneschi is shown in the central panel, presenting the throned St. Peter with a model of the triptych itself. Notice that the model depicts the now lost frame around the triptych. In **Room 3,** catch Fra Angelico's *Madonna and Child,* and Fra Filippo Lippi's *Coronation of the Virgin.*

In **Room 4,** Melozzo da Forli's *Sixtus IV and Platina* shows Sixtus inaugurating the Vatican library by nominating Bartolomeo Platina as prefect. **Room 5** contains works by various 15th-century painters, including Ercole de' Roberti's **Miracoli di San Vincenzo Ferrari. Room 6** is primarily filled with polyptychs, although it also includes a stylized depiction of St. Sebastian by the Botticelli school. **Room 7** houses various works from the Umbrian school and includes *St. Jerome Enthroned* by Giovanni Santi (Raphael's less-famous progenitor) and **Madonna with Four Saints** by Perugino.

ROOM 8

In the center of the room are three works by Raphael, from left to right the *Madonna of Foligno*, the sublime *Transfiguration*, and the *The Coronation of the Virgin. The Coronation of the Virgin,* painted when Raphael was still in his teens, established the artist's mastery of the Florentine style. The *Transfiguration,* considered by some to be Raphael's greatest work, is straight out of Matthew 17, when Christ, alight with heavenly glory, spoke with Moses and Elijah in the presence of his disciples. Displayed on the walls are the tapestries designed by Raphael, which once hung on the lower walls of the Sistine Chapel until they were plundered during the sack of Rome (only to be returned later). The tapestries were recently restored; *La Pesca Miracolosa* is among the best.

ROOMS 9-10

These rooms house Giovanni Bellini's *Il Seppellimento di Cristo* and an unfinished Leonardo da Vinci panel of St. Jerome. Da Vinci's painting was almost certainly separated into five pieces at some point in time; the divisions in the panels are still obvious. Room 10 holds Titian's *Madonna of San Nicoletta dei Frari* (look for Titian's name on the wall depicted the painting).

ROOMS 12-15

Room 12 is your introduction to the devilishly cruel world of Baroque devotional art. Don't miss Caravaggio's sensual *Deposition from the Cross* and Nicholas Poussin's grisly *Martyrdom of St. Erasmus*, who had his intestines rolled out on a winch. The tamer *Last Communion of St. Jerome* by Domenichino can also be seen here. The last three rooms tend toward the obscure and can be skipped.

MINOR MUSEUMS

All four minor museums were closed for renovations in 2003.

The Gregorian Profane Museum, on the left as one heads toward the museum entrance, offers a respite from the bustle and bombast of the other museums. Look for the statues of Marsyas, the satyr who dared to play Athena's pipes (and was skinned alive for doing so), and the fragmentary *Chiaramonti Niobid.* Niobe, a mother of 14 children, had taunted Leto for having given birth to only two. Unfortunately for Niobe, the two were Apollo and Diana, and the irritated gods avenged their insulted mother by shooting down all 14 of Niobe's kiddies. The gallery also contains reliefs from imperial monuments, many depicting buildings of ancient Rome. Next door, the **Pio-Christian Museum** holds artifacts of a fascinating historical synthesis—the marriage of the Greco-Roman sculptural tradition to the newer iconography of the Christian Church. The sarcophagi and statuary here date from the earliest centuries AD, when the Roman Empire and its artistic vocabulary were still alive and well. Many a small statue of the Good Shepherd stands among the many intricately carved sarcophagi. Nearby, the **Ethnological-Missionary Museum** displays non-Christian religious articles alongside missionary-inspired works from Third-World cultures. The **Carriage Museum** contains comparatively recent papal goodies, including armor, guard uniforms, and carriages.

GALLERIA BORGHESE

Piazzale Scipione Borghese, 5. M: A-Spagna; take the exit labeled "Villa Borghese," walk to your right to P. Porta Pinciana; then take V.d. Museo Borghese to the museum. Alternatively, take bus #910 from Termini to Via Pinciana or follow Villa Borghese exit signs, and head left up the road to reach V. del Museo Borghese. Brown signs in the park point the way. ☎ 06 841 65 42. Open daily 9am-7pm. Entrance on the hr., visits limited to 2hr. Tickets include ground floor galleries and Pinacoteca. Tickets (including reservation, tour, and bag charge) €8; EU citizens 18-25 €5.25; EU citizens under 18 and over 65 and students €2. Audio guide €5. Limited capacity, so reservations are a must. Reservations ☎ 06 328 10, open M-F 9am-6pm, Sa 9am-1pm; www.ticketeria.it. The basement of the palace contains inexpensive snack bar, restrooms, cloakroom (bags must be checked before entering the museum), and the bookshop, which sells guidebook €13.

Housed in the former residence of the opulent Cardinal Scipione Borghese (Pope Paul V's nephew), Galleria Borghese attests to the buying power of those close to the Pope. The works include Classical sculptures, important Renaissance and Mannerist paintings, and more Bernini than you thought possible. Unfortunately, Napoleon's sticky fingers were here too—instead of plundering the Borghese by force, he bought a large part of its Classical sculpture from his brother-in-law Camillo Borghese in 1807. For more Villa Borghese's history and sights, see p. 113.

After purchasing a ticket in the basement of the villa, either go back outside and head up the grand staircase to join the rest of the group in the sculpture-filled **main galleries** or start in the Pinacoteca and enjoy the paintings in relative peace.

GROUND FLOOR

On your way into the sculpture galleries, don't rush past the ancient statuary, including some colossal feet and several figures of Hercules, recognizable by his lion skin cloak and signature club. Next is the grand entrance hall, which features a gorgeous ceiling fresco the *Apotheosis of Romulus* by Mariano Rossi and 4th-century gladiator mosaics. Also worthy of note is a fragment thought to be a discarded version of the head of Christ from Michelangelo's last work, the *Rondanini Pietá*. To prepare yourself for the Bernini still to come, take a look at his unfinished, naked *Truth* and the first century AD *Fighting Satyr*, which he restored with his father Pietro.

ROOM 1

The highlight of this room is undoubtedly 19th-century Neoclassicist Antonio Canova's nude statue of Pauline Bonaparte Borghese as *Venus*. Supposedly, Pauline's husband thought the figure so luscious that he forbade anybody else to see it. Asked by a 19th-century tabloid writer if she felt uncomfortable posing disrobed, Pauline coolly replied, "No, the room was quite warm." The marble figure holds an apple, a reference to the beauty contest that launched the Trojan War, depicted in the ceiling fresco by Domenico de Angelis (1790). According to mythology, Eris, the goddess of discord, disrupted an Olympian wedding by throwing a golden apple inscribed "For the Fairest" amid the gods. Hera, Athena, and Aphrodite immediately claimed the title. Zeus wisely brought in a second opinion, that of Paris, the most beautiful mortal man. Each goddess tried to entice Paris to choose her: Hera offered unlimited power, Athena unsurpassed knowledge and wisdom, and Aphrodite the love of the most beautiful mortal woman. Being the shallow man that he was, Paris chose the last, and made off with a certain Helen. The four smaller *frescoes* flanking the beauty contest, which tell the story of Troy's destruction and the subsequent flight of Aeneas, remind us how well that worked out.

ROOM 2

Nicknamed the "Room of the Sun," this is the Borghese's Hero room. Bernini's **David** crouches tensely, his slingshot ready, while Perseus and Hercules duke it out with various wild beasts on nearby sarcophagi. David's grimacing face is supposedly Bernini's own—check out Bernini's self-portrait on the second floor and decide for yourself. As will become evident, Cardinal Borghese was a big fan of this emerging star, commissioning several of Bernini's greatest sculptures, most of which remain in the Galleria Borghese. The Borgheses seemed to have a thing for the baby Hercules; you'll find several maudlin renditions of him in this room too.

ROOM 3

At 24, Bernini sculpted **Apollo and Daphne,** considered by many to be the finest work of his early career. Two figures, the hunter-god and a wood nymph, are portrayed in an extraordinarily dynamic pose. Apollo, enamored of the lovely sprite, is depicted mid-chase, his limbs and draped garment flying. Meanwhile, the maiden morphes into a laurel tree, her curls sprouting foliage, her toes twisting into gnarled roots. According to Ovid (and the **Pietro Angeletti** painting on the ceiling), the chaste nymph was unable to outrun her insistent suitor, and so called on her father, the river god, for aid. He transformed her into a tree to protect her virginity. As Apollo clasped Daphne in his arms, he could still feel her heart beating beneath the spreading bark. Bernini originally advised Cardinal Borghese to position the sculpture in the far right hand corner as you enter, so that the figure of Daphne was only gradually revealed to the viewer.

ROOM 4

Follow the religiously-themed chapel-hallway to **Room 4,** where pagan myth once more takes over in the form Bernini's **Rape of Proserpina** (1622-5). According to myth, Pluto carried off the young daughter of Ceres (variously Gaia or Demeter), the goddess of harvest, as she picked flowers in a field. This little abduction didn't go over well with Ceres, who withheld the earth's harvest in a brilliant act of collective bargaining, or Zeus, who demanded that Pluto return the girl to her frantic mother. Unfortunately, a hungry Proserpina had already eaten six pomegranate seeds, the *specialità della casa* of Hades, and was thus eternally bound to her new husband.

The Olympic divorce court eventually decided on joint custody; Prosperina would spend six months a year with her mother on earth (summer), and the rest in Hades as queen of the underworld (winter). The seventeen 17th-century porphyry and alabaster busts of Roman emperors give the room its name and, along with elaborate mosaics, line the walls.

ROOMS 5-7

In summer 2003, Rooms 6 and 7 were closed indefinitely for renovations.

In **Room 5,** a first-century Roman sculpture with a modern head depicts the enigmatic Hermaphrodite. Perhaps the original Lady (of sorts) in Red, Hermaphrodite can also be found in the ceiling panels, sporting a red gown in each scene. In **Room 6** (named the Gladiator Room after the former tenant, *Borghese Gladiator,* was sold to Napoleon), a weary-looking Aeneas, followed by his son Ascanius, carries his elderly father away from the burning city of Troy. This piece, *Aeneas and Anchises*, was one of Bernini's first commissions, which he executed at just 21 with help from his sculptor father. While Bernini's characteristic sense of movement is somewhat limited in this early sculpture, he seems to have hit a groove early on with the all-important consideration of hairstyles. **Room 7** showcases a Roman portrait of the goddess Isis in black marble, six sphinxes, and a marble border featuring pyramids, owls, cranes, and hieroglyphics.

ROOM 8

Called the Room of Silenus, after yet another work *(Silenus and Bacchus)* taken to France, **Room 8** centers around a pirouetting 2nd-century Roman satyr. Don't let him distract you from the room's real attractions—no fewer than six **Caravaggios** grace the walls. Two early paintings (*Boy with Fruit* and *Self-Portrait as Bacchus*, c. 1590) exhibit Caravaggio's exploration with color and light, more fully realized in his famous *St. Jerome* (1605). *David with the Head of Goliath* (1609-10) is considered to be one of Caravaggio's finest works. His concern for the beheaded Goliath is deeply personal: after killing Ranuccio Tommassoni in a 1605 duel, Carravaggio is said to have sent the painting to the Pope with a plea against capital punishment. Carravaggio's *Madonna of the Palafrenieri* was booted from its original home in St. Peter's, due to a lack of "decorum."

PINACOTECA

The Pinacoteca at the Galleria Borghese is accessible from the gardens in back of the gallery by a winding staircase. Go outside by the door you came in and walk around the building to find the door on the opposite face of the building.

ROOM 9

Room 9, given the moniker The Dido Room for its ceiling frescoes, features primarily Florentine painters of the 16th century, and few genuinely famous works. Raphael's *Deposition* (1507) was painted in part to ease the pain of Atalanta Baglioni, who lost her son in a war over Perugia. If Christ looks familiar, it's because he was modeled after Michelangelo's *Pietá*, which Rapahel greatly admired. Other religious works, like *Crucifixion with St. Jerome and St. Christopher*, attributed to Pinturicchio, and Fra Bartolomeo's *Adoration of the Christ Child*, share the walls with Raffaellino del Colle's *Madonna and Child with the Infant St. John the Baptist.* In the summer of 2002, experts announced that this work was actually a touch-up on an early painting by Raphael. Images of the underpainting, discovered through multispectral technology, are displayed alongside the complete work. In Raphael's original, Mary embraces her son more tightly, thought by some to be an auger of Christ's execution. Speculation continues, but there's one thing that everyone can agree on: there's a reason history remembers Raphael, and not Raffaellino del Colle.

ROOMS 10-13

Room 10 showcases Italian Mannerism and the dangers of excessive lust—the cupid in Cranach's lovely *Venus* eats honeycomb (a symbol of pleasure) while simultaneously getting stung by nasty-looking bees. Inexplicably, Venus remains unscathed. The room also houses a Correggio, briefly owned by Queen Christina of Sweden, which shows Zeus appearing to a reclining Danae as a thunder cloud raining bright golden sparks toward her pelvis. Zeus's infidelity (he was married to Hera) gave rise to an important demigod: Danae gave premature birth to Bacchus, the god of wine, and several months later the vengeful Hera struck the unlucky mistress down with lightning. **Rooms 11** through **13** hold a variety of smaller, more minor works. **Room 11** features works from the Ferrarese School; **Room 12** the Sienese, Lombard, and Venetian schools, including a copy of Leonardo's *Leda and the Swan;* and **Room 13** lesser-known Florentine painters.

ROOMS 14-16

Room 14 is called the Gallery of Lanfranco; if you wonder why, look up. The large hall to the left (facing the stairway) provides beautiful views of the curlicue French gardens below. The macho-macho men holding up the ceiling are done in *trompe l'oeil*, which is an extremely detailed style of painting that aims to give a life-like effect to the work. Notable as well are the three small self-portraits by Bernini. The red walls of **Room 15** are home to Bassano's sweet *Sheep and Lamb*, juxtaposed (a dark joke by the curators?) with a his rendition of the *Last Supper*—note the less-than-subtle lamb's head on a plate. Directly across in **Room 16** is Zucchi's fabulous *Allegory of the Discovery of the New World*, which depicts an amusing take on the founding of America.

FINAL ROOMS

The doorway next to Cleopatra leads to **Room 17** and its excellent 17th-century Dutch and Italian interior paintings, notably Frans Francken's whimsical *Antique Dealer's Gallery* and two views of Rome by Canaletto. You will find an uncharacteristically pudgy Christ in Rubens's *The Deposition* in **Room 18.** Titian's best work in Rome, *Sacred and Profane Love*, resides in **Room 20** with three of his later works.

CAPITOLINE MUSEUMS

On top of the Capitoline Hill behind the Vittorio Emanuele II monument. ☎ 06 399 678 00. Open Tu-Su 9am-8pm. €7.80, with ISIC €5.80, EU citizens under 18 and over 65 free. Guidebook €7.75, audio guide €4, Guided tours in Italian Sa 5pm, Su at noon and 5pm. Reservations necessary for groups on Sa and Su, additional €25. Plan to spend 2-3hr.

The Capitoline Museums, founded in 1471 by Pope Sixtus IV, comprise the world's oldest public museum, one of Rome's most important repositories of Greek and Roman sculpture. The beautiful *piazza* and the facades of both *palazzi* were designed by Michelangelo. The museums' impressive collection is arranged for architectural symmetry and overall ornamental effect rather than historical, archaeological, or artistic integrity. So bring your sketchbook and revel in the incongruity.

The Palazzo Nuovo (to the left as you enter) contains hundreds of unlabeled statues from the 4th century BC through the 3rd century AD, while the Palazzo dei Conservatori (on the right), houses some famous Hellenistic Roman bronzes and Renaissance art.

PALAZZO NUOVO

In the underground passageway from Palazzo Conservatori to Palazzo Nuovo, follow the signs for a quick detour to the Tabularium. The balcony underneath the ancient arches provides perhaps the best possible view of The Roman Forum—without the crowds or heat. Inside the Palazzo Nuovo's courtyard, the original 2nd-century gilded bronze statue of philosopher-king **Marcus Aurelius** sits astride his bronze horse, commemorating the empire's victories over Germanic tribes. (A copy is in the middle of the P. Campidoglio, where Michelangelo intended the original to stand.) The statue is the only equestrian bronze to survive from ancient Rome; most bronzes were melted down during the Middle Ages. Lucky Marcus survived by mistake, as he was thought to be Constantine, the first Christian emperor.

On the second floor, notice the delicate *Capitoline Venus* in a polygonal room on the right as you walk down the central corridor. One of the more celebrated sculptures in the museum's expansive collection, it is understood as an allegory of Roman notions of feminine beauty. The Hall of Emperors, to the left at the end of the hallway, showcases 67 busts, including a delicate bust of a Roman woman, **Dama Flavia,** c. AD 98-117, with curls that would put Little Orphan Annie to shame. The next room, aptly named the Hall of Philosophers, holds 79 busts and 23 reliefs of figures including Homer, Pythagoras, Socrates, Euripides, and Cicero. Unfortunately, it is difficult to associate names with faces, as the sculptures are woefully unlabeled. Oh, if these busts could talk. At the center of the Hall of Gladiators stands the **Statue of the Dying Galatian,** believed to be originally accompanied by two other Galatian figures now displayed in the Museo Nazionale Romano Palazzo Altemps. The *Faun Statue* **(Room VII)** stands out from the rest of the exhibit for its color, if nothing else. It was constructed out of a special red marble called *rosso antico* and was discovered in Hadrian's villa in Tivoli.

Museo Nazionale d'Arte Antica

Arte Antica

PALAZZO DEI CONSERVATORI

In Palazzo dei Conservatori's courtyard reside sundry limbs long separated from their owner, the 12m 4th-century **Colossus of Constantine;** don't miss your chance to get a picture of yourself beside his big toe. This colossus stood in the basilica in the Forum, a dedication to Constantine's victory over Maxentius. On a landing before the first floor, four reliefs from a monument to Marcus Aurelius show scenes (right to left) of the emperor offering a sacrifice, driving a triumphal chariot, bestowing clemency on captives (with the same gesture as in his equestrian statue), and receiving the ominous "orb of power."

At the 2nd landing, a door depicting episodes from the life of Romulus leads to the **Sala dei Conservatori.** Giuseppe Cesari frescoed the giant main room with episodes from the reigns of the early kings that were linked to the mythological origins of Rome—a little

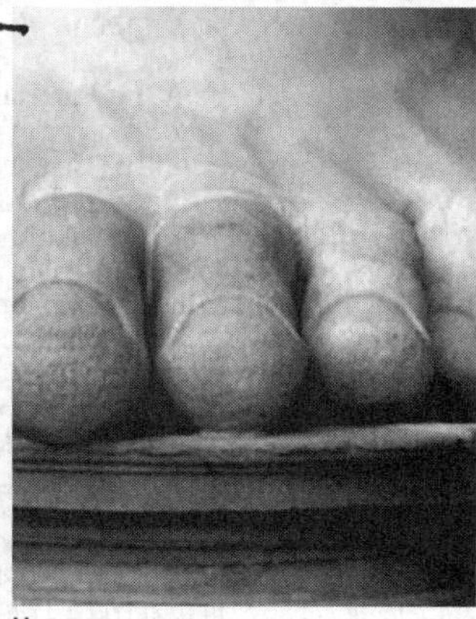

Museums

love, a little religion, and a whole lot of carnage. The **Spinario,** a Hellenistic bronze of a boy quietly picking a splinter out of his foot, is two rooms down **(Room III),** while the famous **Capitoline She-Wolf,** a 6th- or 5th-century BC Etruscan bronze, stands in the center of the next room **(Room IV).** The *She-Wolf* is thought to be the work of the renowned Vulca of Veii, although Antonio Pollaiuolo added Romulus and Remus to the sculpture in the 16th century. On the walls are the *Fasti*, the archival records of the ancient Pontifex Maximus, excavated from the Regia in the forum. The third floor contains a large collection of oil paintings in the Pinacotea Capitoline. Among the masterpieces not purloined by the popes in **Room III** are Bellini's *Portrait of a Young Man* and Titian's *Baptism of Christ.* Speed through the **Cini Gallery** to see **Caravaggio's** rendition of *St. John the Baptist*, in which a ram appears instead of the traditional lamb, indicating that the boy portrayed might be Isaac and not John. A few doors down, in the Sala di Santa Petronilla, named for the 12m *Il Guercino* altarpiece of the burial of said saint, is quite possibly the biggest frame in Rome. Also worthy of a look is **Peter Paul Ruben's** masterpiece *Romulus and Remus*, as well as a self-portrait by Velazquez.

MUSEO NAZIONALE ETRUSCO DI VILLA GIULIA

In Villa Borghese at P. Villa Giulia, 9. M: A-Flaminio or bus #19 from Piazza Risorgimento or #52 from P.S. Silvestro. From Galleria Borghese, follow V. Dell'Uccelliera to the Zoo, and then take V.d. Giardino to V.d. Belli Arte. The museum is on your left, after the Galleria Arte Moderna. ☎06 320 19 51. €4, EU citizens under 18 and over 65 free. Audio guide €4, guidebook €15, available at the bookstore outside the museum entrance. Open Tu-Su 8:30am-7:30pm. Plan to spend 1½-2hr.

The national Etruscan museum is housed in the Villa Giulia, built in 1552 by Pope Julius III, who was criticized by contemporaries for leading a frivolous life while the Council of Trent erupted around him. Designed by Vignola, with some input from Michelangelo, the villa's decorative sculpture was partially scraped away by more conservative popes. Luckily, Vignola's nymphaeum, a sunken goldfish pond with prolific ferns and mermaid columns, was preserved.

Though every town in the region seems to host an Etruscan museum, Rome's collection is by far the strongest. The 35 rooms of this museum are well labeled in English and Italian, with instructive maps and historical and archaeological details. Don't miss the ceramic uteruses used as fertility charms **(Room 5),** or the statues from the portico of the Temple of Apollo in **Room 7,** who brazenly stick their tongues out at passing visitors. **Room 9** holds a graceful 6th-century BC terra cotta sarcophagus of a husband with his arm around his wife, which is the best-known piece of Etruscan art. The entire work was hand-modelled by the same artist who created the Louvre's famous *Sarcofago degli Sposi.*

Room 20 houses a collection of Etruscan and Roman jewelry that showcases pearls imported from the Far East, emeralds from Egypt and the Urals, and sapphires from Sri Lanka. Look for the tiny **Room 22**, which holds a couple of gold sheets with inscriptions in Etruscan and Phoenician; these are the oldest historical sources from pre-Roman Italy. In **Rooms 30** and **31,** archaeologists have reconstructed fragments of the facade of an Etruscan temple, complete with terra cotta gargoyles, chips of original paint, and a fresco of the Greek warrior Tydaeus biting into the brain of a still-living adversary while Athena, who was about to give him the gift of immortal life, turns away in disgust. Before you leave, make sure to see an unusually large skeleton (6 ft. long) lying in a tree trunk in **Room 32.**

GALLERIA NAZIONALE D'ARTE MODERNA

In Villa Borghese, V. delle Belle Arti, 131. M: A-Flaminio. Enter park, walk up V. George Washington. ☎06 322 98 315. Open Tu-Su 8:30am-7:30pm. €9, art and architecture students €6. Wheelchair accessible. ***Cafe delle Arte*** *M 7:45am-6pm, Tu-Sa 7:45am-8pm. Extended hours Apr.-Sept. 7:45am-midnight. Plan to spend 1-1½hr.*

They say that books should not be judged by their covers, and the Galleria Nazionale D'Arte Moderna proves that art museums should not be either. Despite its overwhelming Neoclassical facade, designed by **Cesare Bazzani** in 1911 and enlarged in 1933, the museum holds a large collection of mostly Italian 19th- and 20th-century art in a conspicuously modern interior. The central salon features well-chosen temporary exhibitions by contemporary Italian artists in a range of media and deserves careful scrutiny. The 19th-century galleries (to your left as you enter) are mainly arranged by artist and do not present any notable works, with the exception of Canova's depiction of Hercules holding Lica upside-down by his ankle.

You may ask yourself if that is really a urinal suspended from the ceiling. Yes, it is. Welcome to the world of early 20th-century art (towards the back of the museum). The urinal belongs to **Marcel Duchamp**, (1887-1968) who not only led, but quickly eclipsed the movement away from strict artistic conventions. Indeed, by age 20 he had experimented with Post-impressionism, Fauvism, and Cubism. At 25, he presented his unprecedented *Nude*, which was rejected by his contemporaries in Paris but enthusiastically embraced in New York. Shortly thereafter Duchamp stopped painting. Aside from Duchamp's work, the gallery also includes Klimt's *Three Ages of Man*, a Cubist piece by Georges Braque, and Modigliani's *Portrait of a Lady with a Collar.*

A sculpture-filled hallway, featuring a **Henry Moore** centerpiece flanked on either side by **Alberto Viani's** depictions of a voluptuous white *Nude*, leads to galleries of art from 1950 to the present. Inside the gallery, works by Giacometti stand in a room adjacent to one of Arnaldo Pomodoro's broken spheres, *Sfera n. 2.* Nearby is an undulating bronze wall by Gio Pomodoro. A smattering of internationals (Pollocks, a Calder, and a Kandinsky) also hang in these galleries, but are outdone in sheer outlandishness by the Italian works, such as **Lucio Fontana's** slashed canvases and **Alberto Burri's** charred cellophane creations. Upstairs is a case featuring drawings by Moore, Morandi, and Twombly and a photograph of Castel Sant'Angelo wrapped by **Christo.**

MUSEI NAZIONALI ROMANI

A **seven-day ticket book** is good for the Palazzo Massimo, the Palazzo Altempts, the Crypti Balbi, and the Terme di Diocletian for €9; admission to the Colosseum, the Palatine Hill, and the Terme Caracalla bumps the price up to €20 (ask for the **Archaeologia Card** package). These special ticket offers are available at the ticket office.

MUSEO NAZIONALE ROMANO PALAZZO MASSIMO

Largo di Villa Peretti, 1. In the left-hand corner of P. dei Cinquecento as you stand with your back to Termini. ☎06 481 55 76; group reservations ☎06 399 677 00. Open Tu-Su 9am-7:45pm; last entrance 7pm. €6, EU citizens ages 18-24 €3, EU citizens under 18 and over 65 free. Audio guide in Italian and English €2.50. Guided tours of museum in Italian €3.50. For information call ☎06 481 55 76. No photographs, video cameras, or cell phones allowed. Wheelchair accessible.

The often overlooked Palazzo Massimo contains many magnificent Greek and Roman marble statues of Apollo, Dionysus, and Aphrodite, among other ancient heroes. The spacious, well-lit *palazzo* is designed around an apricot-colored inner courtyard boasting a goldfish pond. The basement floor holds an impressive catalogue of Roman coins, starting in the 4th century BC and ending with Vittorio Emanuele II. Vault doors worthy of Lloyd's of London guard the approximately 3,600 different coins on display. On the ground floor, Roman sculpture and portraiture from 11 BC to AD 1 is on display, as well as Greek sculptures and later Roman copies. A Greek sculpture of the *Maiden of Anzio*, taken from Nero's beach bungalow in Anzio, can be found on the first floor. Particularly amusing are the series of gymnast sculptures in the gallery on the right, where the *Discobulo* (not the original) looks primed for the next Olympics. Look for door knockers in the form of various violent beasts. Also keep an eye out for an impressive sarcophagus dating from the 3rd century AD, that depicts a battle with the Germans. The Roman commander who used to be in the sarcophagus is portrayed advancing in the center of the front panel.

The superb mosaics and wall paintings of the top floor are only accessible with a guide, and you must arrive at the time stated on your ticket. The 45min. tour first takes you to Livia's summer dining room, painted to resemble a Mediterranean garden, which was restored in the 1990s. In order to be relocated to the museum, these frescoes had to be adhered to a surface with a natural glue, allowing for them to stay in one piece as the wall behind them was cut. The rest of the tour leads you down a decorated cryptoporticus to some erotic bedrooms of Villa Farnesina, as well as through rooms showcasing mosaics from Imperial Rome.

MUSEO NAZIONALE ROMANO TERME DI DIOCLEZIANO

Museum: P. dei Cinquecento, 78. Opposite Termini. Reservations ☎ 06 399 677 00. Open Tu-Su 9am-7pm. €5, EU citizens 18-24 €2.50, EU citizens under 18 and over 65 free. Audioguide €4; guided tour with archaeologist Su at noon and 5:30pm, €3.50.

Stretching over 15 hectares of prime Roman real-estate between the present-day *piazza* dei Cinquecento and the via XX Settembre, the Baths of Diocletian, completed in AD 306, were once the largest baths in the Western Hemisphere. Now, the baths' vaulted halls provide a striking display space for various temporary exhibitions. If you happen to visit when this Aula Grande is closed, be sure to look in through the large glass doors. The permanent exhibitions are housed in the recently renovated buildings associated with the convent of the **Madonna degli Angeli,** which was commissioned by Pius IV, in 1561. Most of the museum is dedicated to epigraphy, which is the study of inscriptions set apart by their durability and sacred or public use, and is unique in that the inscriptions are presented in a historical context, demonstrating their usefulness in understanding ancient history. Epigraphs housed in the museum speak of the masses of slaves laboring under the Roman patricians, the rise of the classes of freemen, as the eventual rise of Christianity (note how fishes, doves, and dates of death, start appearing on tombstones during the 3rd century). The rest of the exhibits are concerned with pre-history. Be sure to stroll past the one hundred ancient columns that make up the arcade of the *Chiostro Michelangiolesco*, a peaceful cloister littered with fragments of ancient sculpture, including a central fountain teeming with goldfish.

AULA OTTAGONA

Aula Ottagonale: V. Romita, 8. Walk toward P. Repubblica, pass S. Maria degli Angeli on your right; the Aula is on the next block to your right. ☎ 06 399 677 00. Open Tu-Sa 9am-2pm, Su 9am-1pm. Free.

This elegant octagonal room holds a number of important Classical sculptures, mostly 2nd-century AD Roman copies of much older Hellenistic originals, recovered from three imperial baths— those of Caracalla, Constantine, and Diocletian. Two magnificent bronzes stand in the center of the room: the 2nd century BC Principe Ellenistico and the seated boxer (Pugilatore), created a century later.

MUSEO NAZIONALE ROMANO PALAZZO ALTEMPS

P. Sant'Apollinare, 44. Just north of P. Navona. Museum ☎ 06 783 35 66, ticket office ☎ 06 683 35 66. Open Tu-Su 9am-7pm. €5, EU citizens 18-24 €2.50, EU citizens under 18 and over 65 free. ***Audio guide*** *€4.* ***Guidebook*** *in gift shop €8.20. Plan to spend 1-2hrs.*

A few steps from the chaotic tourist frenzy that is the Piazza Navona lies the 15th-century Palazzo Altemps, which now houses a collection of ancient Roman sculptures. Arranged around a courtyard, the galleries display Classical works with a modern twist (most have been restored and modified over the centuries). The way the sculptures were restored and altered reveals a great deal about Romans' preferences—and obsessions—during the 15th-19th centuries.

On the ground floor, note the Hermae—statues that portray realistic torsos, but turn into columns below the waist. The genitals of these statues were left visible, legend has it, so that travelers could rub them for good luck. Also on the ground floor is a more modest *Parthenon Athena*, a first-century BC copy of a 5th-century original by Phidias that stood 12m-high and sported a body covered with gold leaf, a head of ivory, and eyes of precious stones. Upstairs you can find the *Ludovisi Throne*, featuring a relief of Aphrodite being born from the waves. Sculpted in the 5th century BC for the Temple of Epizephiris, the throne was meant to receive the cult statue of goddess Aphrodite during the annual re-enactments of the goddess's birth. Outside the Palazzo's chapel stands a statue of the *Suicidal Gaul*, who killed himself and his wife in order not to fall into the hand of the advancing Greeks. This statue is a copy of the original bronze that stood on the acropolis of Pergamum to commemorate the Greeks' victory over the barbarians in 238-234 BC. Nearby lies a sarcophagus with a striking depiction of a battle scene commemorating 3rd-century AD Roman victories over the Ostrogoths. The sarcophagus has not been restored and is one of Altemps' most famous pieces.

VILLA FARNESINA

V. della Lungara, 230, just across from Palazzo Corsini. Bus #23; get off between Ponte Mazinni and Ponte Sisto. ☎06 680 272 68; www.villafarnesina.it Open M-Sa 9am-1pm. Extended hours Dec., March 15 to June 30, and Sept. 15 to Oct. 31 M and Sa 9am-4pm. €4.50, EU citizens ages 14-18 €3.50, EU citizens under 14 and over 65 free. Plan to spend 1hr.

Thought to be the wealthiest man in Europe in his day, Agostino "il Magnifico" Chigi entertained the stars of the Renaissance papal court in his sumptuously decorated villa and its extensive palm gardens. The interior decoration boasts frescoes by Raphael, Peruzzi, Il Sodoma, and Giulio Romano. After the banker's death in 1520, however, the villa fell into disrepair and was bought by the Farnese family.

FIRST FLOOR

To the right upon entering the villa lies the fantastical Sala of Galatea. The villa's architect, Baldassare Peruzzi, bears most of the responsibility for the frescoes. The ceiling frescoes are symbols of astrological signs, which, taken with the two central panels of Perseus decapitating Medusa and Callisto (in a chariot drawn by oxen), add up to a symbolic plan of the stars in the night sky at 9:30pm, November 29, 1466—the moment of Chigi's birth. But the masterpiece of the room, on the long wall opposite the windows, is Raphael's vibrant fresco, *The Triumph of Galatea*, in which Galatea surfs on a conch-shell chariot drawn by two dolphins. Galatea was the lover of Polyphemus, the Cyclops whom Odysseus kills in the *Odyssey*. Prior to his Homeric debut, Polyphemus had his mistress stolen by Venus, who took pity on the nymph's love for another man (one with two eyes).

One room over is the lovely **Loggia di Psiche,** which was an entrance hall before the Farnese family glassed it in to protect the frescoes. The 1520 ceiling fresco recreates the adventures of *Psyche on Earth*, including her love affair with Cupid and the ensuing jealousy of Venus. It's speculated that this love affair is supposed to mirror that of Chigi and his wife, Francesa Ordeaschi, who can be seen to the far left of the second ceiling fresco, offering a bowl to Mercury. **Raphael** was commissioned to paint these and even drew up designs for them, but rumor has it that he was too obsessed with his new mistress, la Fornarina, to do any work. The frescoes are attributed to Penni, Giovanni da Udine, and Giulio Romano.

SECOND FLOOR

Upstairs you'll find two rooms decorated with impressive frescoes that celebrate Chigi's wedding to a young Venetian noblewoman whom he had abducted and kept cloistered in a convent for several years. The first, the **Sala delle Pers-**

The era before dishwashers

The Villa Farnesina used to be one of *the* spots where that legendary Roman excess took place. Artists, ambassadors, courtesans, cardinals, and even Pope Leo X were known to enjoy Agostino Chigi's extravagantly lavish parties.

Stories of his largesse are legendary. He once invited the Pope and the entire College of Cardinals to dinner in a gold-brocaded dining hall so imposing that the Pope reproached him for not treating him with greater familiarity. Chigi, an honorable man, ordered the hangings removed and revealed to his astonished guests that they'd actually only been eating in his stables.

At another infamous banquet in his *loggia* overlooking the Tiber, Chigi had his guests pay their tab by tossing his gold and silver dishes into the river after every course. Slyly, the shrewd businessman had already hidden nets under the water to recover his original treasures.

pettive, is embellished on two ends by Baldassare Peruzzi with views of 16th-century Trastevere (right) and the Borgo (left), framed between *trompe l'oeil* columns. The geometry's not all there, but it's worth a look. Vulcan sits above the fireplace, and 11 Olympian gods relax atop vine-covered arches. The adjacent **Stanza delle Nozze** (Marriage Room), which recently underwent extensive restoration, is the real reason for coming. The Stanza delle Nozze was frescoed by Il Sodoma, who had been busy painting the papal apartments in the Vatican until Raphael showed up and stole the commission. Il Sodoma rebounded well, making this masterful fresco (1509) of Alexander the Great's marriage to the beautiful Roxanne. The side walls show the family of Darius the Persian surrendering to Alexander and a rather awful depiction of Bellerophon the Pegasus-tamer that was painted by another (unknown) hand.

MUSEO NAZIONALE D'ARTE ANTICA

This collection of 12th- through 18th-century art is split between Palazzo Barberini and Galleria Corsini. The former displays more masterpieces, but the latter collection is certainly worth a visit.

PALAZZO BARBERINI

V. delle Quattro Fontane, 13. M: A-Barberini. Bus #492 or 62. ☎06 420 036 69. Open Tu-Su 9am-7:30pm. €6, EU citizens 18-24 €3, EU citizens under 18 and over 65 and EU university students €1. Plan to spend 1-1½hr.

The Barberini contains paintings from the medieval through Baroque periods and an impressive central stairway full of Barberini bees, designed by Bernini. The Barberini family lived here from 1625, when Pope Urban VIII built it to commemorate his accession, through 1960, despite the sale of the *palazzo* to the state in 1949. Twice an hour, guards open the upper floor and allow you to wander through the Rococo apartments once belonging to Cornelia Costanza Barberini. The museum's collection goes back to the 12th century, and has more than 1,400 paintings, and more than 2,000 decorative art objects. Among these are a number of masterpieces by del Sarto, Il Sodoma, Bernini, Holbein, Lippi, Raphael, Caravaggio, and Poussin. Of particular note on the first floor is Raphael's recently restored *La Fornarina*, a portrait of a baker's daughter who also happened to be his mistress, Piero di Cosimo's beautifully restrained *Mary Magdalene*, and a vibrant *Annunciation and Two Donors* by Fillipo Lippi. Upstairs in the first hallway is Guido Reni's *Portrait of a Lady*, depicting the legendary Beatrice Cenci. After a *cause celebre* involving incest, patricide, and execution, Beatrice was also immortalized by Shelley, Dickens, and Hawthorne.

GALLERIA CORSINI

V. della Lungara, 10. Opposite Villa Farnesina in Trastevere. Take the #23 bus and get off between Ponte Mazinni and Ponte Sisto. ☎ 06 688 023 23. Open Tu-Su 8:30am-7:30pm. €4, EU students €2, Italian art students and EU citizens over 65 free. Guidebooks in Italian €10.50. Wheelchair accessible. Plan to spend 1hr.

Follow signs to the second floor of the Palazzo Corsini, where the gallery showcases a crowded collection of 18th-century furniture, ancient and modern sculpture, and paintings from the 14th-18th centuries. Among these are works by the Dutch masters Rubens and Van Dyck, and Italian virtuosi Fra Angelico, Titian, and Caravaggio. In **Room 2,** note in particular Fra Angelico's triptych of the *Last Judgment*, the *Ascension of Christ*, and *Pentecost* to the left of the door, Titian's *Portrait of Philip II of Spain* and Rubens's *St. Sebastian*. Nicolas Poussin's *Triumph of Ovid* in **Room 6** is remarkable. Try not to miss the bedroom where Queen Christina of Sweden died—it's marked by a plaque of her dying words in Italian and Swedish ("I was born free, I lived free, and I will die free"), as well as a rather unflattering portrait of her painted as the goddess Diana.

GALLERIA SPADA

P. Capo di Ferro, 13, in the elaborate Palazzo Spada. From Campo dei Fiori, take any of the small streets leading to P. Farnese. With your back to Campo dei Fiori, take a left onto Capo di Ferro. Bus #64. ☎ 06 68 74 896. Open Tu-Su 8:30am-7:30pm. Last tickets sold 30min. before closing. €5, EU students €2.50, EU citizens under 18 and over 65 free. Reservations €1 extra. Guidebooks €10.50. Guided tour Su 10:45am from museum bookshop. Pamphlet guides in English available for each room of the exhibit. Plan to spend 1hr.

Yet another cardinal with money to burn and friends to impress, Bernardino Spada filled his grand *palazzo* with gorgeous visual goodies. Various well-connected descendants added to the stash, which was acquired by the state in 1926. Time and luck have left the palatial apartments nearly intact, and a visit to the gallery offers a glimpse of the luxurious Baroque court life. The gallery occupies only four rooms of the Palazzo Spada; the rest is the State Council, so mind your behavior. Before entering the gallery, ask at the ticket counter to see *Perspective* by **Borromini.** Using a clever combination of light and angles, Borromini's optical illusion makes a 12m hallway look like a fabulous colonnade.

ROOMS 1-2

In **Room 1,** Spada hung numerous family portraits, including three portraits of himself, by Il Guercino, Guido Reni, and Cerini. In **Room 2,** look for the **Tintoretto** work *Portrait of Archbishop of Luca Stella*, Reni's portrait of St. Jerome, and Prospero Fontana's *Astrologer*, complete with astrological globe. There are also several impressive portraits by **Titian,** including *Portrait of a Musician*. This painting employs mostly dark colors and is noteworthy for the complete absence of red, the color for which Titian is renowned. **Lavinia Fontana,** one of the few female painters whose work survived from the 16th century, painted the rather masculine-looking

Cleopatra. Above the windows is a frieze by del Vaga, originally meant to serve as a model for a tapestry that was to be hung below Michelangelo's far less cherubic *The Last Judgment*; alas, the tapestry was never made.

ROOMS 3-9

Room 3 houses 17th-century portraits and grandiose mythological scenes along its capacious walls. The award for best melodrama goes to *Death of Dido*, by **Il Guercino,** which shows the scorned Carthaginian queen throwing herself onto both her sword and her funeral pyre simultaneously. In the distance, Aeneas's ships set sail for Italy, while an unconcerned Cupid loads another arrow. In Trevisani's *Banquet of Mark Antony and Cleopatra*, a midget holds a dalmatian in check, while a monkey on a leash skulks in the foreground of *The Rape of Helen* by Campana. Hanging nearby is Pietro Testa's gruesome, yet fascinating, *An Allegory of the Massacre of the Innocents*. Two large globes by the Dutch cartographer Wilhelm Blaeu occupy the middle of the room, a terrestrial globe from 1622 and a celestial globe from 1616. The fresco on the ceiling, painted by Ricciolini in 1698, portrays allegorical figures representative of the "four parts of the world," the "four elements," and the four seasons.

EUR MUSEUMS

M: B-EUR-Palasport or B-EUR-Fermi. Walk north up V. Cristoforo Colombo, or take bus #714 from Termini.

Make your final destination P. Giuglielmo Marconi; the museums are splayed about Mussolini's obelisk. One morning is enough to see all the museums.

MUSEO DELLA CIVILTÀ ROMANA

P.G. Agnelli, 10. Down V. Civiltà Romana. ☎06 592 60 41. Open Tu-Sa 9am-6:45pm, Su and holidays 9am-1:30pm. €6.20, EU citizens 18-25 €3.10, under 18 and over 65 free.

If ever there was an intimidating museum facade, this is it. This museum was constructed during the Fascist period, and charged with the small task of explaining the history of Imperial Rome. It accomplishes this through an absurd number of scale models, which are really worth a look. Elsewhere, a life-size model of a Roman library and a cast of Trajan's Column are laid out.

MUSEO DELL'ALTO MEDIOEVO

V. Lincoln, 3. ☎06 542 281 99. Open Tu-Su 9am-8pm. €2, under 18 and over 65 free. Wheelchair accessible.

Come see how the Longobords overran the remains of the Roman Empire in the smallest of the EUR museums, dedicated to Late Antiquity and the early Middle Ages. Among the collection of weapons, jewelry and household items are stone fragments with intricate arabesque designs and finely woven tunics. Unfortunately, "look but don't learn" is the idea here; the museum's Italian placards are only slightly informative and there aren't any in English.

MUSEO NAZIONALE DELLE ARTI E TRADIZIONI POPOLARI

P. G. Marconi, 8. ☎06 591 07 09; www.ips.it/musis/museo_arti. Open Tu-Su 9am-8pm. Closed New Year's, May Day, and Christmas. Call for tours in Italian or Braille. €4, reduced price €2, EU citizens 18-25 €2, under 18 and over 65 free.

This museum is a veritable treasure trove of recent Italian culture. Roman marionettes sway beside wine presses, Carnevale costumes dance next to toy sailboats, and Queen Margherita's sumptuous gondola is beached on the 2nd floor. Exhibits are very well labelled, though background information is rarely translated into English. Frequent temporary exhibitions on the first floor.

MUSEO PREISTORICO ED ETNOGRAFICO LUIGI PIGORINI

P. G. Marconi, 14. ☎06 54 95 21. Reservations ☎06 841 23 12; guided tours in Italian, ☎06 440 33 86. Open daily 9am-8pm. €4, EU citizens ages 18-25 €2, under 18 and over 65 free.

The collection is strong in ethnographic artifacts from Italy and contains the skull of the famous Neanderthal Guattari Man, discovered near Circeo. The museum holds more than 61 skulls (all in a row) and countless skeletons, in addition to an exhibition that traces the evolution of man from apes to Marilyn Monroe.

RECOMMENDED COLLECTIONS

MUSEO CENTRALE MONTEMARTINI

V. Ostiense, 106. M: B-Piramide. From P. Ostiense, head right of the train station to V. Ostiense. Then, walk or take bus #702 or 23 three stops. ☎06 574 80 30. Open Tu-Su 9:30am-7pm. €4.13, EU citizens ages 18-24 €2.58, EU citizens under 18 and over 65 free. Joint Capitoline Museum ticket €8.26.

Electric generators and Classical sculptures aren't typical bedfellows, but Athena never looked so good. **Montemartini,** the first Roman power plant, was converted to hold overflow sculpture from the Capitoline Museums in the 1990s, and today houses over 400 statues. Highlights include the *Hercules' Presentation at Mount Olympus* group (a huge, well-preserved floor-mosaic of a hunting scene, best viewed from the staircase to the right), a first-century BC funeral bed made out of bones, and the 1.5m head of the goddess Fortuna.

GALLERIA COLONNA

V. della Pilotta, 17. Just north of P. Venezia in the Centro Storico. ☎06 667 843 30. Open Sa 9am-1pm. €7, students €5.50, children under 10, adults over 65, military and disabled persons are free. Guide included in ticket at 11am in Italian and 11:45am in English. Closed Aug. Tours of Princess Isabella's apartments available by appointment; groups of 10 required; €13.75 per person. Free tours in English 11:45am.

For a mere €7, you can spend a morning sitting on a plush velvet couch contemplating priceless works of art under a frescoed ceiling. This 18th-century *palazzo* holds the Colonna family's collection, which includes Tintoretto's *Narcissus* and Bronzino's *Venus, Cupid, and Satyr*. The ebony desk in the next room is adorned with an ivory relief of Michelangelo's *The Last Judgment*. The grand salon is second in length only to the Hall of Mirrors at Versailles.

GALLERIA DORIA PAMPHILJ

P. del Collegio Romano, 2. From P. Venezia, walk up V. del Corso and take your 2nd left. ☎06 679 73 23. Open F-W 10am-5pm, last tickets 4:15pm. Closed New Year's Day, Easter, May Day, Aug. 15, and Christmas. €7.30, students and seniors €5.70. Audio guide included. Useful catalogue with €5.16 deposit. Private apartments (10:30am-12:30pm) €3.10.

The Doria Pamphilj family, whose relations with Pope Innocent X coined the term nepotism, still owns this stunning private collection, on display in their palatial home. It is arranged in stackable 18th-century fashion and includes Titian's *Salome*, Raphael's *Double Portrait*, but only one Bernini, as the sculptor was out of favor with Innocent. Make sure to look closely at Caravaggio's *Rest During the Flight in Egypt*—the sheet music in the painting can be played—and Velasquez's portrait of *Innocent X*, by far the jewel of the collection and the best papal portrait in Rome.

MUSEO NAZIONALE D'ARTE ORIENTALE

V. Merulana, 248. In Palazzo Brancaccio on the Esquiline Hill. ☎06 487 44 15. Open M, W, F 9am-2pm; Tu and Th 9am-7pm; Su 9am-1pm. Closed 1st and 3rd M each month. €4.13, Italian citizens under 18 and over 65 free.

Italy's most treasured collection of Oriental art, this museum sports an array of artifacts dating from prehistory up to the 19th century, divided into six main sections: evolution of art in the Near East, Islamic art, Nepalese and Tibetan art, Buddhist art from India, and Southeast Asian art. Highlights include Stone Age fertility dolls and psychedelic paintings of the Buddha.

OTHER INTERESTING COLLECTIONS

LARGER COLLECTIONS

MUSEO CRIMINOLOGICO

V. del Gonfalone, 27. Near Ponte Mazzini. ☎06 683 002 34. Open Tu-W 9am-1pm and 2:30-6:30pm, Th 2:30-6:30pm, F-Sa 9am-1pm. May be closed Aug. €2, under 18 and over 65 €1.

After overdosing on "artwork" and "culture," get your aesthetic stomach pumped at this museum dedicated to crime and punishment (the only museum in Rome run by the Dipartimento dell'Amministrazione Penitenziaria). Torture devices comprise the majority of the first floor, as well as some olde English etchings of rather frightening scenes, among them *A Smith Has His Brains Beaten Out With a Hammer.* On the 2nd floor, learn all about the phrenology of criminals and the secret language of tattoos. The 3rd floor contains terrorist, spy, and druggie paraphernalia, as well as a room filled with stolen goods. The Roman police cannot determine who owns them. Children will learn a great deal.

MUSEO DELLE CERE

P. Santi Apostoli, 67. Two blocks to your left at the end of V.d. Corso facing the Vittorio Emanuele II monument. ☎06 679 64 82. Open daily 9am-8pm. €5. Call to arrange group discounts.

Billing itself as an "emulation" of London's Madame Tussaud's—it's more like a photocopy of a photocopy—this **wax museum** presents major historical and bizarre scenes. Lowlights include the *Last Meeting of the Fascist Grand Council in Piazza Venezia*, featuring a very sickly-looking Mussolini, heroes of the Risorgimento, Italian pop stars of the 1960's, and soccer stars.

MUSEO MARIO PRAZ

V. Zanardelli, 1, top fl. At the east end of Ponte Umberto, right next to Museo Napoleonico. ☎06 686 10 89. Must visit museum with small tour groups (35-45min.) that leave on the hour in the morning and on the half-hour in the afternoon. Open M 2:30-6:30pm, Tu-Su 9am-1pm and 2:30-6:30pm. Free.

This eccentric, smallish museum is housed in seven ornate rooms, the last home of Mario Praz (1896-1982), an equally eccentric and smallish professor of English literature and 18th- and 19th-century art collector. Neighbors believed that Praz had supernatural powers: when they saw him they spat or flipped coins.

KEATS-SHELLEY MEMORIAL HOUSE

P. di Spagna, 26. M: A-Spagna. Right of the Steps as you face them. ☎06 678 42 35. Open May-Sept. M-F 9am-1pm and 3-6pm, Sa 11am-2pm and 3-6pm. €2.60.

The house where Keats lived until his death in 1821 houses both interesting artifacts and morbid curiosities. On the morbid side are plaster casts of Keats's face before and after he succumbed to tuberculosis, a lock of his hair, and his deathbed correspondence with his sister. More scholarly exhibits include his impressive library. Both Keats and Shelley are buried in the **Protestant Cemetery** (p. 143) at Piramide.

JEWISH COMMUNITY MUSEUM

Lungotevere Cenci, 15. Take bus #23, which runs along the Tiber. ☎06 684 00 61. To see the synagogue interior, you must take a tour, which usually leave on the hour in Italian and on the half hour in English. Call ahead. Open May-Aug. Su-F 9am-7:30pm; Sept.-Apr. M-Th 9am-4:30pm, F 9am-1:30pm, Su 9am-12pm. No cameras. €6, reduced price €3. Services Th 8:30pm, F 8pm, Sa 8:30pm.

Sinagoga Askenazita's museum houses a small collection of objects that were hidden during the nine-month Nazi occupation of Rome: magnificently decorated torahs, altar cloths, and various ceremonial objects, as well the original plan of the ghetto (see **Jewish Ghetto,** p. 104). The synagogue itself is lavishly decorated in bright and beautiful Art Deco designs. Like all Jewish temples in Italy, this is an Orthodox synagogue, meaning services are segregated by gender.

MUSEO CANONICA

V. Pietro Canonica, 2. ☎06 884 22 79. In Villa Borghese. Open Tu-Sa 9am-7pm, Su 9am-1:30pm. €2.58, students €1.55, under 18 and over 65 free.

The home and studio of Pietro Canonica, who created the reliefs and statues that decorate many Italian squares. The museum houses a collection of his sculptures.

IL VITTORIANO

*P. Venezia in the V. Emanuele II monument. Open daily 9:30am-7:30pm (last entrance 6:30pm). Free. **Sacrario delle Bandiere:** ☎06 647 355 002. Open Tu-Su 9am-1pm. Free.*

If you can't bear the thought of climbing all the steps of the V. Emanuele in the raging heat, it's cooler to do it inside the monument while taking in a plethora of history at the **Museo di Risorgimento** (which documents Italy's revolution in 1870), the **Hall of Flags,** and the **Tomb of the Unknown Soldiers.** The **Sacrario delle Bandiere** is in the basement of the Vittorio Emanuele II monument and salutes 20th-century Italian war efforts, displaying battle-weary flags and hulking World War I submarines. Enter on the left side of the monument as you face it.

SMALLER MUSEUMS

ARTS AND LETTERS

***Museo Comunale Birreria Peroni:** V. Cagliari, 29. ☎06 884 49 30. Open Apr.-Sept. M-Sa 10am-8pm. €3. **Museo della Casina delle Civette:** in the Villa Torlonia, bus #36 from Termini. ☎06 442 500 72. Open Apr.-Sept. Tu-Su 9am-6pm; Oct.-Mar. Tu-Su 9am-5pm. €2.80, students €1.55, EU citizens under 18 and over 65 free. **Goethe Museum:** V. del Corso, 18, ☎06 326 504 12. Open M, W-Su 10am-6pm. €3, students €2. Booking required for the **Museo Internazionale del Cinema e dello Spettacolo:** V. Bettoni, 1. 90min. Tours offered Tu, Th, Sa. ☎06 370 0 266. **Museo e Biblioteca Teatrale del Burcardo:** V. del Sudario, 44. ☎06 681 94 71. Open M-F 9am-1:30pm. Free.*

If you come to the **Museo Comunale Birreria Peroni,** just off V. Nomentana, looking for beer, you'll be disappointed, but if you seek contemporary Italian painting and sculpture in an ex-brewery, look no further. The **Museo della Casina delle Civette** is full of art nouveau stained glass. The **Goethe Museum,** near P. del Popolo, is in the writer's former house, and celebrates his life through books and paintings. The **Museo Internazionale del Cinema e dello Spettacolo** lies across the river from Testaccio. The **Museo e Biblioteca Teatrale del Burcardo** contains costumes, scripts, and other artifacts of the stage.

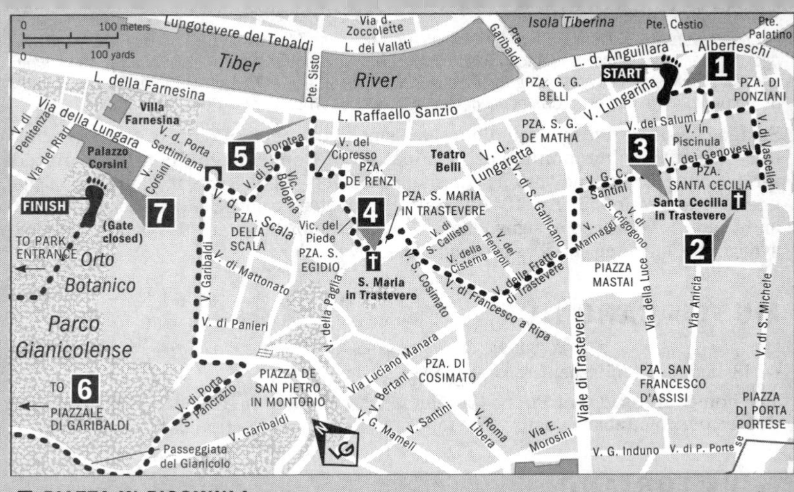

1 PIAZZA IN PISCINULA. The Ripa Grande, Rome's original port, spawned thousands of tiny *piazze* and avenues around the main square. Each is worth a look, but V.d. Lungaretta, P.d. Gencola, V. in Piscinula, and V. Lungarina are notable for their comparative lack of loud tourists and fine *trattorie*.

TIME: 2.5hr. walking

DISTANCE: 2-4mi., depending on the number of detours taken

SEASON: A spring or summer day is best; plan to finish the walk in the late afternoon, remembering that the route through the Orto Botanico is closed Tu-Sa after 6:30pm.

2 SANTA CECILIA IN TRASTEVERE. Saint Cecilia was a Roman aristocrat who, after escaping a botched murder attempt in her own bath, was beheaded by Diocletian for her refusal to renounce Christianity. Despite several severe hacks by her executioner, she managed to stay alive for several days and convert thousands.

3 CHIOSTRO SAN GIOVANNI DEI GENOVESI. Ring the bell at no. 12 to be admitted to the 15th-century cloister by a friendly custodian (3-6pm in summer; 2-4pm in winter). A bit of Florence in Rome, the architectural harmony of the building is attributed to Bacio Pontelli. The *chiostro* is rarely visited by even the most knowledgeable tourists.

4 SANTA MARIA IN TRASTEVERE. Legend has it that on the day that Christ was born, the *piazza* overflowed with oil, signifying the coming of Christ's sanctifying grace. During the day, a stop at nearby Pizzeria San Callisto (p. 195) is recommended. Follow Vic. del Piede to Piazza de Renzi, then V. del Cipresso, turning right onto Vic. del Cinque.

5 PIAZZA TRILUSSA. The **Ponte Sisto** links this square with the more ancient part of Rome across the Tiber, but it is by no means lacking in historical pedigree. The beloved dialect poet Trilussa is immortalized here by a statue.

6 PALAZZO CORSINI AND ORTO BOTANICO. Stopping by the Galleria Nazionale d'Arte Antica might well add an additional 3-4hr. to your tour of Trastevere, but at least take a moment to climb the 17th century stone staircase. If you want to sit and pause before the grande finale, skip the stairs in favor of the Orto Botanico, Baroque fountains, and gardens.

7 GIANICOLO. At the end of the day, the hike to the top of the Janiculum provides the sort of views that drive writers about Rome crazy with cliches. To escape the rambling triteness that so often plagues the first-time visitor, go for the noontime cannon blast instead.

DEFENDING ROME AGAINST BARBARIAN HORDES

Museo delle Mura Porta San Sebastiano: *V. di Porta San Sebastiano, 18. Take bus #760 from the Circus Maximus or 218 from San Giovanni, or walk from the baths of Caracalla. ☎06 704 752 84. Open M-Sa 9am-7pm, Su 9am-2pm. €2.58, students €1.55, EU citizens under 18 and over 65 free.* ***Museo Storico dell'Arma dei Carabinieri:*** *P. del Risorgimento. ☎06 689 66 91. Open Tu-Su 8:30am-12:30pm. Free.*

The ancient defense of Rome is chronicled in the **Museo delle Mura Porta San Sebastiano.** The **Museo Storico dell'Arma dei Carabinieri,** near the Vatican, is dedicated to the glorious history and heroism of the machine-gun-toting Italian military police (the *carabinieri*). Please, don't laugh at the tiny toy Fiats.

MUSEO NAPOLEONICO

V. Zanardelli, 1, 1st fl. At the east end of Ponte Umberto. ☎06 688 062 86. Open Tu-Sa 9am-7pm, Su 9am-1:30pm. €2.58, students €1.55.

The Primoli family, to whom this *palazzo* belonged, married into the Bonapartes in the 19th century and decided this was as good a reason as any to amass a collection of portraits and letters of sundry members of Napoleon's family. Live out your dream of seeing lithographs of every one of Napoleon's nieces.

OH, THOSE MAD SCIENTISTS

Museo della Matematica: *P. Aldo Moro, 5. Take bus #492. Reservations necessary, call ☎06 583 310 2.2. Open M-F 9am-6pm. Admission and multi-lingual guided tour free.* ***Museo Storico Nazionale dell'Arte Sanitaria:*** *Lungotevere Sassia, 3. ☎06 683 51. Open M, W, F 10am-noon. €1.55.*

Rome plays host to a few intriguing museums focusing on mathematic and scientific collections. The **Museo della Matematica** is located in the math department of La Sapienza. All manner of medical instruments from the 16th century to the present are contained in the **Museo Storico Nazionale dell'Arte Sanitaria,** across Ponte Vittorio Emanuele II on the Vatican bank.

PASTA, PRESEPIO, AND PURGATORY

Museo Nazionale delle Paste Alimentari: *P. Scanderbeg, 117. Follow signs from P. di Trevi. ☎06 699 11 19. Open daily 9:30am-5:30pm. €9, under 20 €6. Audio guide included.* ***Museo Tipologio Nazionale del Presepio:*** *V. Tor dei Conti, 31a, near the intersection of V. dei Fori Imperiali and V. Cavour. Call ☎06 679 61 46 to arrange a visit.* ***Piccolo Museo delle Anime del Purgatorio:*** *Lungotevere Prati, 12. ☎06 688 065 17. Open daily 7-11am and 4:30-7:30pm. Free.*

The **Museo Nazionale delle Paste Alimentari's** ultimate purpose is ending world hunger with pasta. In the meantime, the museum will be happy to tell you everything you've ever wanted to know about Italy's favorite *primi*. Crêche scenes, 3000 of 'em, are the focus at the **Museo Tipologio Nazionale del Presepio.** The **Piccolo Museo delle Anime del Purgatorio,** near Ponte Cavour inside the Chiesa del Sacro Cuore del Suffragio, displays communications (burn marks left by hands and fingers on books, clothing, etc.) from souls trapped in Purgatory.

REVOLVING EXHIBITIONS

While a number of museums listed above occasionally host temporary shows, the galleries below exclusively host temporary exhibitions. Major exhibitions are usually listed in the English section of *Roma C'è* or in *L'Evento.* Information can also often be found at www.beniculturali.it; www.commune.roma and www.romeguide.it. The Commune di Roma constantly organizes themed exhibitions which are shared between dozens of museums at one time (☎06 492 71 41; www.festivalroma.org.) The Commune di Roma also offers a special English-speaking information line (☎06 06 06. Open M-Sa 4pm-7pm).

MUSEO NAZIONALE DEL PALAZZO VENEZIA

V. del Plebiscito, 118. On the left-hand side of P. Venezia as you stand with your back to the Vittorio Emanuele II monument. ☎ 06 679 88 65. Open Tu-Su 9am-7pm. Permanent collection €4, EU citizens under 18 and over 65 free. Admission varies for the exhibits. Guided tours available.

The museum (an impressive 1455 *palazzo* that once belonged to the embassy of the Venetian Republic) hosts Rome's most prominent exhibitions. These are held in three large rooms, including the **Sala del Mappamondo,** the office where Mussolini used to deviously leave his light on all night, earning the title "Sleepless One." To find out what's showing (usually on a Roman theme) watch the ads the museum routinely projects onto the facade of the building opposite. Don't miss the inner garden, a remarkable oasis of peace next to one of Rome's busiest intersections.

SALA DEL BRAMANTE

P. del Popolo. M: A-Flaminio. Entrance on right side of the church; in the small courtyard to the rear of Church of Santa Maria del Popolo. ☎ 06 326 005 69. Open daily 10am-6:30pm. €2.58.

A small gallery that unveils temporary exhibitions, including a wildly popular Goya show. Past favorites include Mark Chagall, ceramics through the ages, and Dalí.

MUSEO DEL CORSO

V. del Corso, 320. ☎ 06 678 62 09. www.museodelcorso.it. Open Tu-Su, 10am-8pm. €5, €4 reduced.

An imposing palazzo that has become Rome's center for revolving modern art exhibitions. Dali, Picasso and 19th-century Spanish paintings were favorites in the past.

PALAZZO RUSPOLI

V.d. Corso, 418. ☎ 06 687 47 04. Open Su-Th 9:30am-8:30pm, Sa 9:30am-10:30pm. M-F €8, reduced €7; Sa-Su €9, reduced €8; EU citizens under 18 and over 65 free. Audio guide included with ticket.

This palace on the Corso between P. Colonna and V. Condotti hosts major exhibitions, such as an excellent show of Velazquez in 2003.

MUSEO CENTRALE DEL VITTORIANO

V.S. Pietro in Carcere, off V.d. Fiori Imperiali at the left-hand rear corner of the V. Emanuele monument. ☎ 06 678 06 64. Open M-Th 9:30am-7:30pm, F-Sa 9:30am-11:30pm, Su 9:30am-8:30pm. €8.50, students €6.

This museum hosts some of Europe's principal touring exhibits. An exhibition on Italian artists in St Petersburg, a popular Cezanne show and a huge showcase of Impressionist paintings were recent attractions.

SCUDERIE PAPALI AL QUIRINALE

V. XXIV Maggio. Across the street from Palazzo del Quirinale. ☎ 06 399 675 00; www.scuderie-quirinale.it. Open Su-Th 10am-8pm. €9, reduced €6.

The Scuderie Papali is housed in the former papal stables on the Quirinal Hill and was restored as modern exhibition space in 2000. Rome's newest display venue made its debut with the highly renowned *La Maesta di Roma* last year.

ART GLOSSARY

TERM	EXPLANATION
assumption/ *assunta*	image of a blessed person (usually the Virgin Mary or a saint) rising into heaven
baroque	predominant style during the 17th and first half of the 18th century; typically florid and dramatic, designed to appeal to the emotions and used to describe the painting of Caravaggio, Rubens, Giordano, and Tiepolo, the sculpture of Bernini, and the architecture of Borromini.

bozzetto	rough, preliminary version of a composition, either the outline of a picture or a sketch for a sculpture (usually in clay)
cartoon	full-sized drawing used to transfer a preparatory design to the final work, especially to a wall for a fresco
cassone	large, lavishly decorated chests made in Italy from the 14th century to the end of the 16th century, often painted, a famous example being Botticelli's *Primavera*
cenacolo	"Last Supper"; A depiction of Christ at dinner on the evening before his crucifixion, often found in the refectory of an abbey or convent
chiaroscuro	the balance between light and dark in a painting, and the painter's ability to show the contrast between them
classicism	the adoption of architectural motifs and sculptural style from ancient Greece and ancient Rome, often seen in works of the High Renaissance (think Michelangelo's David). All the rage in Rome during the early 16th century, when streamlined columns, marble, and rounded domes and arches came back into fashion
cosmati work	mosaic on marble, found in early Christian churches around Rome
deposition/ *deposizione*	scene of the disciples lowering the dead Christ from the cross
diptych	a painting in two parts or panels
forum	in an ancient Roman town, a square containing municipal buildings and/or market space. Smaller towns usually have only one central forum, while large cities, such as Rome, can have several
fresco	a painting made on wet plaster. When it dries, the painting becomes part of the wall
frieze	a band of decoration in any medium. Architecturally, can also refer to the middle part of an entablature (everything above the columns of a building) between the architrave and the cornice
futurism	an Italian movement in painting, scuplture, and literature from 1909-1920, seen as an offspring of Impressionism and a forerunner to Expressionism. Its followers (incl. Boccioni and Balla) extolled movement, speed, technology, and violence.
grotesque	painted, carved, or stucco decorations of fantastic, distorted human or animal figures, named for the grotto work found in Nero's buried Golden House
High Renaissance	The culmination of the Italian Renaissance circa 1500, known for its brilliant use of color, detailed realism, mastery in conveying movement, the human body, and large-scale, multi-figured compositions in perfect perspective. In Rome, this movement flowered under Pope Julius II, who commissioned works by Michelangelo and Raphael and sponsored Bramante's designs for Saint Peter's basilica.
Intarsia	inlay work, usually of marble, metal, or wood
lunette	a semi-circular frame in the ceiling or vault of a building that holds a painting or sculpture
maestà	an image of the Virgin enthroned as queen of heaven, usually holding the infant Jesus on her lap, most typical of the early Renaissance 1300-1450
mannerism	style during the early 16th to late 17th century. An offspring of the High Renaissance with even further exaggerations of the human body, movement, and color for the sake of expression and immediacy, characteristic of Pontormo and Tintoretto
Pietà	a scene of the Virgin mourning the dead Christ
polyptych	altarpiece with more than three panels
presepio	nativity scene
putto	(pl. *putti*) the little nude babies that flit around Renaissance art occasionally, and Baroque art incessantly
sinopia drawing	a red pigment sketch made on a wall as a preliminary study for a fresco.
stigmata	miraculous body pains or bleeding that resemble the wounds of the crucified Christ; many works depict this miracle
travertine	a light colored marble or limestone used in many of the buildings in Rome
triptych	a painting in three panels or parts
trompe l'oeil	literally, "to fool the eye," a painting or other piece or art whose purpose is to trick the viewer, as in a flat ceiling painted to appear domed

Caffé Greco

INSIDE

the italian meal **186**
restaurant types **186**
menu reader **187**
restaurants by location **188**
dessert **198**
caffè **201**
wine **202**
shopping for food **208**

Food & Wine

In ancient Rome, the patricians' dinners were lavish, festive affairs that lasted hours on end. Roman writers like Petronius and Juvenal reported the erotica, exotica, and excess characteristic of the Imperial dinner table—peacocks, flamingos, and herons were served with their full plumage meticulously replaced after cooking. Acrobats and fire-eaters distracted guests between courses of dormice and camels' feet. Food orgies went on *ad nauseam*, literally—after gorging themselves, guests would retreat to a special room called the *vomitorium*, throw it all up, and return to the party to eat still more.

These days, however, Roman food rituals are considerably tamer. Breakfast, if you're lucky enough to get it, is usually just a gulp of cappuccino and a pastry—often a poor imitation of a croissant called a *cornetto*. Lunch is traditionally the day's main meal, though some Romans now eat lunch on the go during the week, *all'americana*. Keep in mind that restaurants tend to close between 3pm and 7:30pm.

Traditional Roman cuisine is not generally ranked as the best in Italy, but we promise you won't starve. As a cosmopolitan city, Rome has excellent restaurants specializing in the various other Italian regional cuisines, as well as food from around the world. New trends include postmodern decor, weekend brunch, and Chinese food. A note on Chinese eateries: a few are good; most are dirt cheap; several are health hazards. Look for establishments whose menus include Chinese translations.

THE ITALIAN MEAL

The traditional Italian meal, believe it or not, is a product of medieval poverty. Meat was scarce, and when it was available, it was savored. Pasta (as cheap and filling then as it is today) was tossed in the same sauce as the meat, so it would carry the flavor. The family filled up on the **primi** (first course) before enjoying meats.

In Rome, a full meal begins with **antipasti,** or appetizers. It is acceptable to order *antipasti* alone for lunch, but it is considered gauche at dinner. Next, the *primi* arrives: usually some sort of pasta, risotto, or soup. Especially on Thursdays, many restaurants serve up homemade *gnocchi*, dense dumplings of potato or semolina flour, frequently in a gorgonzola or four-cheese sauce. While *lasagna al forno* (baked lasagna) may be tempting, know that it is often prepared well in advance and will probably not be particularly fresh.

The **secondi** (second course) usually consists of meat or fish. Innards and other random parts of the cow or pig distinguish traditional Roman cuisine. Seafood is common although often expensive. Calamari is excellent here, especially when grilled. Items with asterisks on the menu are *surgelato* (frozen). Don't necessarily rule them out; frozen seafood might in fact taste better than the stuff that's been sitting out in the market all day. Keep in mind that for *secondi*, what you order is what you get— no vegetables on the side. If you want something to go with your meat or fish, you can sample the numerous **contorni** (side dishes), which are usually vegetable specialties. Even the most devoted carnivores will enjoy dishes like *fagiolini* (tender string beans) or *pomodori* (fresh tomatoes and fresh basil in olive oil). A perennial option, Roman mixed salads *(insalata mista)* are usually full of veggies.

Dolce (desserts) are typically accompanied by the essential espresso. Freshly made *tiramisù* (sponge cake soaked in espresso and rum) is a classic Italian dessert. *Profiteroles*, delicate rolled pastries with chocolate and cream filling, are also exquisite. *Panna cotta* is a cream custard, covered in chocolate sauce or *frutti di bosco* (berries). And if *gelato* isn't rich enough for you, try *tartufo*, truffly ice cream that comes in *bianco* (vanilla) and *nero* (chocolate) versions.

For a **digestivo** (after-dinner drink), try *grappa* (doubly distilled yellowish liqueur made from old grape pressings) or *sambuca con le mosche* (anise liquor "with flies"—that is, with coffee beans floating on top). If *grappa* and *sambuca* make your eyes water, you might prefer *limoncello*, a sweet lemon-flavored liqueur.

The billing at Roman restaurants can be a bit confusing. Usually, bottled water is automatically served and charged to your bill: ask for *frizzante* (fizzy) or *naturale/non gasata* (still). Many restaurants add a cover or bread charge of €1-2 per person. *Servizio*, if not included in food prices, may be added to the bill at 10-15%. Tipping in Rome is a little ambiguous. In general, it is not common practice, although in more touristy locales waiters may expect it. To reward unusually good service give 5% in cash, so that the owner doesn't pocket the tip before the waiter even sees it.

RESTAURANT TYPES

Ristorantes are the most elegant eateries, with dolled-up waiters, linen tablecloths, and expensive (though not necessarily better) cuisine. A **trattoria** has a more casual atmosphere and lower prices. An **osteria** or **hostaria** is more casual still; some serve traditional home-style Italian cooking, while others have a more creative flair. Another cheap option is the **tavola calda** or **rosticceria,** where you buy platefuls of pastas, cooked vegetables, and well-seasoned meats to eat on the spot or wrap up for a picnic elsewhere.

There are two kinds of **pizzerias.** At a *pizzeria forno a legno*, you sit down to your own plate-sized pizza. A Roman-style crust is light, crispy, and blackened a little around the edges, unlike the famous Neapolitan pizzas, which are thicker. In a *pizzeria rustica* or *a taglio*, order a slice or particular weight of any of the pizzas displayed at the counter. But be warned: all types of establishments, especially in a touristed city like Rome, might choose to call themselves "ristoranti."

MENU READER

ANTIPASTI	
antipasto rusto	assortment of cold appetizers
bruschetta	crisp baked slices of bread with tomatoes or other toppings
prosciutto e melone	cured ham and honeydew melon
PRIMI	
pasta aglio e olio	in garlic and olive oil
pasta al pomodoro	in tomato sauce
pasta alla puttanesca	in a tomato sauce with olives and capers
pasta all'amatriciana	in a tangy tomato sauce with onions and bacon
pasta all'arabbiata	in a spicy tomato sauce
pasta alla bolognese	in a red meat sauce
pasta alla boscaiola	in a cream sauce with peas and bacon
pasta cacio e pepe	with pepper and pecorino cheese
pasta ai funghi porcini	with a sauce of large wood mushrooms
pasta alla carbonara	in a creamy sauce with egg, cured bacon, and cheese
pasta alle cozze	in a tomato sauce with mussels
pasta alla pizzaiola	tomato based sauce with olive oil and red peppers
pasta alla pescatore	with several kinds of clams and mussels, and sometimes squid
pasta al tartufo	with a truffle sauce
pasta alle vongole	in a clam sauce; *bianco* for white, *rosso* for red
gnocchi	dumpling-like pasta made from potatoes
polenta	deep fried cornmeal
risotto	rice dish (comes with nearly as many sauces as pasta)
PIZZA	
ai carciofi	with artichokes
ai fiori di zucca	with zucchini blossoms
ai funghi	with mushrooms
alla capriciosa	with ham, egg, artichoke, and olives
con alici	with anchovies
con bresaola	with cured beef
con melanzana	with eggplant
con prosciutto	with ham
con prosciutto crudo	with cured ham (also called simply *crudo*)
con rucola (rughetta)	with arugula (rocket for the Brits)
margherita	plain ol' tomato, mozzarella, and basil
napoletana	with anchovies, tomato, and cheese
peperoncini	chilies
polpette	meatballs
quattro formaggi	with four cheeses
quattro stagioni	four seasons; a different topping for each quarter of the pizza, usually mushrooms, *crudo*, artichoke, and tomato
SECONDI	
animelle alla griglia	grilled sweetbreads
calamari alla grigliata	grilled squid
carciofi alla giudia	fried artichokes
coda alla vaccinara	stewed oxtail with herbs and tomatoes
filetto di baccalà	fried cod
fiori di zucca	zucchini flowers; filled with cheese, battered, and lightly fried
involtini al sugo	veal cutlets filled with ham, celery, and cheese, topped with tomato sauce
melanzane parmigiana	eggplant parmesan
osso buco	braised veal shank
pasta e ceci	pasta with chick peas
saltimbocca	slices of veal and ham cooked together and topped with cheese
scamorza grigliata	a type of grilled cheese

SECONDI	
suppli	fried rice ball filled with tomato, meat, and cheese
trippa	tripe; chopped, sautéed cow intestines, usually in a tomato sauce
CONTORNI	
broccoletti	broccoli florets
cicoria	chicory
fagioli	beans (usually white)
fagiolini	green beans
funghi	mushrooms
insalata caprese	tomatoes with mozzarella cheese and basil, drizzled with olive oil
insalata mista	mixed green salad
melanzana	eggplant
piselli	peas
spinaci	spinach
COOKING BASICS	
aceto	*vinegar*
burro	*butter*
al pezzo (l'etto)	*by weight (per 100g)*
bollito	*boiled*
crudo	*raw*
filetto	*fillet*
fritto	*fried*
formaggio	*cheese*
misto	*mixed/assorted*
riso	*rice*
sale	*salt*
trancia	*slice*
uovo	*egg*
zucchero	*sugar*

RESTAURANTS BY LOCATION

ANCIENT CITY

see map p. 78

The area around the Forum and the Colosseum is home to some of Italy's most egregious tourist-traps, replete with €13 *menù turistici*. The snack carts lining the streets will serve you no better; expect to pay €2 for water and €3.50 for a quasi-sandwich. If you forgot to pack a lunch and the stroll down V.d. Fori Imperiali seems impossible in the heat, there are a few places that offer meals at fair prices.

I Buoni Amici, V. Aleardo Aleardi, 4 (☎06 704 919 93). From the Colosseum, take V. Labicana to V. Merulana. Turn right, then left onto V.A. Aleardi. A long walk, but the cheap and excellent food is well worth the hike. Choices include the *linguine all'astice* (linguini with lobster sauce, €6.50), *risotto con i funghi* (€5.50), and *penne alla vodka* (€5.50). Cover €1. Open M-Sa noon-3pm and 7-11:30pm. AmEx/D/MC/V. ❶

Taverna dei Quaranta, V. Claudia, 24 (☎06 700 05 50), off P. del Colosseo. Shaded by the trees of the Celian Park, outdoor dining at this corner *taverna* is a must. The menu changes weekly, and in summer often features the sinfully good *oliva ascolane* (fried olives stuffed with meat, €3.90) and *ravioli all'Amalfitana* (€7.75). House wine €5.20 per L. Cover €1. Reservations suggested, especially for a table outside. Open daily 12:30-3:30pm and 7:30pm-midnight. AmEx/D/MC/V. ❷

Hostaria da Nerone, V.d. Terme di Tito, 96 (☎06 481 79 52). M: B-Colosseo. Take the stairs to the right (with your back to the Colosseum) and walk up to V.N. Salvi. Turn right, and then left onto V.d. Terme di Tito. Outdoor dining near the Colosseum with views of the Baths of Titus. Traditional specialties like *tegamino di cervello burro e funghi* (brains with butter and mushrooms, €8) are worth joining the tourist scene. Pasta €6-6.50. Cover €1.29. 10% service. Open M-Sa noon-3pm and 7-11pm. Closed Aug. AmEx/MC/V. ❷

Luzzi, V.S. Giovanni in Laterano, 88 (☎06 709 63 32). M: B-Colosseo. Walk away from the Colosseum for two blocks along V.S. Giovanni in Laterano. This *trattoria* manages to combine affordability with plentiful outdoor seating near the Colosseum. Generous servings and unbeatable prices. *Primi* €3-6; *secondi* €4-8. Open Th-Tu noon-3pm and 7pm-midnight. AmEx/MC/V. ❶

RESTAURANTS & PIZZERIE BY PRICE

UNDER €10 ❶

I Buoni Amici (188)	AC
Luzzi (189)	AC
Pizzeria Baffetto (190)	PN
Trattoria da Sergio (190)	CF
La Pollarola (191)	CF
L'Oasi della Pizza (191)	CF
L'Insalata Ricca (191)	CF
Il Portico (191)	JG
Franco e Cristina Pizzeria (192)	JG
Pizza e Festa (192)	JG
Pizza Re (193)	PS
Cacio e Pepe (194)	BPV
"Lo Spuntino" da Guido e Patrizia (195)	BPV
Pizzeria San Callisto (195)	TV
Augusto (196)	TV
Dar Poeta (196)	TV
Cave Canem (196)	TV
Pizzeria La Maschere (198)	SL
Il Capellaio Matto (198)	SL
Volpetti Piu (198)	TA

€10-20 ❷

Taverna dei Quaranta (188)	AC
Hostaria da Nerone (189)	AC
Pizzeria Corallo (190)	PN
Trattoria Gino e Pietro (190)	PN
Zampano' (190)	CF
Trattoria Da Luigi (191)	CF
Ristorante Arnaldo ai Satiri (191)	CF
La Taverna del Ghetto "Kosher" (192)	JG
Vini e Buffet (192)	PS
Arancio d'Oro (192)	PS

€10-20 ❷ CONTINUED

Al Piccolo Arancio (193)	PS
Centro Macrobiotico I. N. Club (194)	PS
Franchi (194)	BPV
San Marco (195)	BPV
Trattoria "da Dante" (195)	BPV
Ristorante a Casa di Alfredo (196)	BPV
Ouzeri (196)	BPV
Tulipano Nero (196)	BPV
Osteria dei Belli (196)	BPV
Ristorante al Fontanone (196)	BPV
Africa (197)	NT
Al 39 (197)	NT
Hostaria da Bruno (197)	NT
Il Pulcino Ballerino (197)	SL
Arancia Blu (197)	SL
La Pantera Rosa (198)	SL
La Cestia (198)	TA
Trattoria da Bucatino (198)	TA
Luna Piena (198)	TA

€20-30 ❸

Trattoria dal Cav. Gino (190)	PN
Taverna Lucifero (190)	CF
Trattoria da Giggetto (191)	JG
Il Giardino Romano (191)	JG
Il Margutta (193)	PS
Taverna Angelica (195)	BPV
Il Tunnel (197)	SL

€30-45 ❹

UKIYO Japanese Restaurant (193)	PS
Velando (195)	BPV

€45 AND OVER ❺

Presidente (193)	PS
La Pergola at the Cavalieri HIlton (194)	BPV
Da Benito e Gilberto (195)	BPV

AC Ancient City BPV Borgo, Prati & Vatican City CF Campo dei Fiori ESQ Esquilno JG Jewish Ghetto PS Piazza di Spagna PV Piazza Navona SL San Lorenzo NT North Termini TV Trastevere TA Testaccio & Aventino

CENTRO STORICO

see map p. 358-359

PIAZZA NAVONA

There are plenty of delicious, inexpensive *trattorie* and *pizzerie* near P. Navona, but it often takes a short stroll to reach them. A walk down V.d. Governo Vecchio reveals some of the best restaurants in the city, often charging less than their more convenient neighbors in the *piazza*. If you're really lucky, you'll happen upon one of the smaller *enoteche* and *trattorie*, some of which advertise themselves with no more than a beaded curtain guarding an open doorway—Romans who know will tell you that these places offer a constantly changing menu at unbeatable prices. No matter where you eat, you can expect to be subjected to numerous performances by street performers.

Pizzeria Baffetto, V.d. Governo Vecchio, 114 (☎06 686 16 17). At the intersection of V.d. Governo Vecchio and V. Sora. Once a meeting place for 60s radicals, Baffetto now overflows with hungry Romans. It's gotten famous—be prepared to wait a long time for a table outdoors (as well as for your delicious pizza once you're seated). Pizza €4.50-7.50. Open daily 8-10am and 6:30pm-1am. Cash only. ❶

Pizzeria Corallo, V.d. Corallo, 10-11 (☎06 683 077 03). Off V.d. Governo Vecchio near P. del Fico. This *pizzeria* is a great place to grab a cheap, late dinner before losing your life's savings at the chi-chi bars nearby. Pizzas €4-9. Excellent *primi* pastas €5-9. Reservations accepted. Open daily 6:30pm-1am; in winter closed M. MC/V. ❷

Trattoria dal Cav. Gino, V. Rosini, 4 ☎06 678 34 34). Off V.d. Campo Marzio across from P. del Parlamente. The very affable Gino greets you at the door at this *trattoria*, and points at a sign above the door, announcing that *tonnarelli alla ciociala* (€7) is the house specialty. Another sign proclaims Gino's philosophy: *In Vino Veritas*. Agreed. *Primi* €6-7; *secondi* under €20. Reservations accepted. Open M-Sa 1-3:30pm and 8-10:30pm. Cash only. ❸

Trattoria Gino e Pietro, V.d. Governo Vecchio, 106 (☎06 686 15 76), at the intersection of V. Savelli. Basic Roman food without any frills, like *gnocchi verdi al gorgonzola* (with potatoes, spinach, and gorgonzola cheese, €7.50) and *saltimbocca alla romana* (with *prosciutto* and sage, €8.90). Reservations accepted. Open F-W noon-3pm and 6:30-11pm. Closed first 20 days of Aug. AmEx/MC/V. ❷

CAMPO DEI FIORI

If you're not in a rush, take the time to navigate the labyrinth of crooked streets and alleyways that surround Campo dei Fiori. While you might get yourself horribly lost, you will certainly find several exceptional *ristoranti* that can provide sustenance until the search party arrives. If your friends can't find you after dinner, just go pubbing in the Campo and make some new ones (see p. 212).

Trattoria da Sergio, V.d. Grotte, 27 (☎06 686 42 93). Take V.d. Giubbonari and turn your 1st right. Just far enough away from the Campo to keep away the tourists, Sergio offers a simple ambience (the waiters don't bother with menus) and hearty portions. Try the *spaghetti Matriciana* (with bacon and spicy tomato sauce, €6). Fresh fish Tu and F. Reservations suggested. Open M-Sa 12-3pm and 6:30-11:30pm. MC/V. ❶

Zampano', P. della Cancelleria, 83 (☎06 689 70 80), between C.V. Emanuele II and the Campo. This swank *hostaria* is running out of space in its front window to plaster all the awards they've won over the years. Recently renovated, Zampano' offers creative pizzas (€7-9), more than 200 wines, and a changing menu. *Primi* €7-8; *secondi* €12-13. Top it all off with a savory dessert (€4.50-€6). Open daily noon-2:30pm and 7:30-11pm. AmEx/MC/V. ❷

Taverna Lucifero, V.d. Cappellari, 28 (☎06 688 05 536), off Campo dei Fiori. Pleasant owner knows and greets his guests at the door. While the menu changes daily, the delicious meat or cheese fondues never fail to delight. The Taverna also offers homemade pastas, tender fillets, 400 varieties of red wine, and 45 kinds of grappa. Expect to order a full, Roman dinner (€25 without drinks). The white truffles are worth the price (€1-7 per g depending on season). Two seatings: 8:30pm and 10:30pm. Call for reservation (two weeks in advance for Sa). Open Sept.-June daily 8pm-2am. Cash only. ❸

Trattoria Da Luigi, P.S. Cesarini, 24 (☎06 686 59 46), near Chiesa Nuova, four blocks down C.V. Emanuele II from Campo dei Fiori. Enjoy inventive cuisine such as the delicate *carpaccio di salmone fresco con rughetta* (€8), as well as simple dishes like *vitello con funghi* (€9.50). Open Tu-Su noon-3pm and 7pm-midnight. AmEx/MC/V. ❷

La Pollarola, P. Pollarola, 24-25 (☎06 688 016 54), Take V.d. Biscione on the right as you approach Campo dei Fiori. As the Romans motto goes, *"si mangia bene e si spende giusto"* ("one eats well and pays a fair price"). Typical but superlative dishes like *spaghetti alla carbonara* (€7). *Secondi* €8-15. Tip included in prices. Open M-Sa noon-3:30pm and 6pm-midnight. AmEx/MC/V. ❶

L'Oasi della Pizza, Via della Corda, 3-5. (☎06 687 28 76; www.info.pizzeriaoasi.tiscalinet.it). Within shouting distance of Campo dei Fiori, this pizzeria offers delicious, classic pizzas at reasonable prices. It also serves up delightful fish dishes. The *capricciosa* (tomato, mozzarella, ham, eggs, and mushrooms €9) is great. You'll get your vegetables with the leafy margherita (€7). Basket of bread €2. Open Th-Tu noon-3pm and 7-11:30pm. ❶

L'Insalata Ricca, Largo di Chiavari, 85-6 (☎06 688 036 56), off C.V. Emanuele II near P.S. Andrea della Valle. What kind of salad would you like? They have *all* of them (€5.20-8.30). If you don't like this location, there are 11 others around town, including the following: P. Pasquino, 72; V.d. Gazometro, 62-66; P. Albania, 3-5; V. Polesine, 16-18; P. Risorgimento, 5; and V.F. Grinaldi, 52-54. Reservations suggested for dinner. Open daily 12:30-3:30pm and 6:45-11:45pm. US$ accepted. AmEx/D/MC/V. ❶

Ristorante Arnaldo ai Satiri, V.d. Grotta Pinta, 8 (☎06 686 19 15). Take Largo dei Chiavari off C. Vittorio Emanuele II and turn right on V.d. Grotta Pinta. Unusual dishes include spicy *Fusili con melanzane* (with eggplant; €8) and the house specialty, *rigatoni alla crema di cavoli* (with cream of cabbage; €8). Glowing with red light bulbs and candles, the interior resembles a cross between a bordello and a darkroom. Outdoor dining in summer. Open W-M 12:30-3pm and 7:30pm-1am. AmEx/MC/V. ❷

JEWISH GHETTO

On the other side of V. Arenula from Campo dei Fiori, the former Jewish Ghetto has patiently endured centuries of modernization, anti-Semitism, and tourism. Quiet, cozy *trattorie* line the streets of this neighborhood, each serving traditional Roman-Jewish dishes, like *carciofi alla giudia* (fried artichokes) and *fiori di zucca* (zucchini blossoms filled with cheese and anchovies, battered, and lightly fried).

Trattoria da Giggetto, V.d. Portico d'Ottavia, 21-22 (☎06 686 11 05). Rightfully famous but increasingly pricey, Giggetto serves up some of the finest Roman cooking known to humankind in outdoor tables overlooking the ruins of the Teatro Marcello. Their *carciofi alla giudia* (€4.50) are legendary, but be daring and go for the *fritto di cervello d'abbacchino* (fried brains with mushrooms and zucchini, €12). Cover €1.50. Reservations needed for dinner. Open Tu-Su 12:15-3pm and 7:30-11pm. AmEx/MC/V. ❸

Il Giardino Romano, V.d. Portico d'Ottavia, 18 (☎ 06 688 09 661; www.ilgiardinoromano.it). The shaded garden in the back is the perfect place to enjoy a relaxing lunch or dinner. If you don't feel like barbecued meats or fresh fish, Il Giardino Romano also offers a selection of pizzas (€5-9). *Primi*, €4-8; *Secondi* €10-15. Reservations recommended for dinner (esp. in the garden). 10% ISIC discount. Open Tu-Su noon-3:30pm and 6:30pm-midnight. AmEx/MC/V. ❸

Il Portico, V.d. Portico D'Ottavia, 1b (☎06 687 47 22). Il Portico is a low-key, family restaurant in the middle of the Jewish Ghetto. Tourists go for the tasty pizzas (*proscuitto* €5.20, *funghi* €5.20), while locals gravitate toward the wide variety of salads (€5.70-7.80). Open daily noon-3:30pm and 6:30pm-midnight. MC/V. ❶

Master Your Pasta

In Rome, pasta has been a way of life as much as a way of eating for over eight centuries. Once a humble peasant food, the all-in-one nutritional feast is now taken very seriously in here. Woe betide any prospective son- or daughter-in-law not cooking the pasta *al dente* (firm to the bite). If you ever hope to impress mama, you'd better get a handle on the various types of pasta:

anelletti: Nothing special; think Spaghetti-O's.

cannelloni: Lasagne sheets bent into giants tubes filled with baked meat or spinach and ricotta. They might look similar, but **paccheri** are shorter and rarely baked.

conchiglie: Shell shapes; a favorite accompaniment to tuna sauces.

farfalle: Bow ties, for those who dress-up for dinner.

fettucini: Like linguine, but wider; served with creamy sauces. Variations in width produce **tagliattele**, **taglionini**, and **tagliarini**.

fusilli: Corkscrew shapes; often served cold with olive oil. The hollow version is **torchietti**, and spiralled strips are called **fusilli bucatini**.

continued on next page

Franco e Cristina Pizzeria, V. Portico d'Ottavia, 5 (☎06 687 92 62), serves delicious classic Roman-style pizza by the slice. A great place to grab a bite to eat if you are on a busy schedule, especially since the ingredients are fresh and the toppings overflowing. Try the *caprese* or *rughetta e salmone*. Open M-Sa 8am-9pm. ❶

KOSHER OPTIONS

Numerous options for traditional Italian-Jewish cuisine line V.d. Portico d'Ottavia. Most restaurants and delis have large signs out front that advertise themselves as "kosher." If you are in the mood for a quick pizza (€2.60) or sandwich (€2.60-3), try **Pizza e Festa,** V.d. Portico d'Ottavia, 1/B. (☎06 689 32 35. Open Su-Th 9:30am-3:30pm and 6:30-10:30pm, F 9:30am-3:30pm.) **La Taverna del Ghetto "Kosher,"** V.d. Portico d'Ottavia, 8, offers excellent homemade pastas and other sit-down meals for those who wish to rest their weary feet. (☎06 688 097 71. Open Sa-Th noon-3pm and 6:30-11pm, F noon-3pm).

PIAZZA DI SPAGNA

see map p. 363

Though the Spanish Steps area may seem very different from the less affluent environs of Termini, there is one similarity—lots and lots of bad, bad food. The frustrating part of it all is that while a crappy restaurant at Termini might set you back €10, the same awful food here will cost twice as much. The best food in the area tends to be toward the Ara Pacis, across the V.d. Corso, and away from the hordes of tourists.

Vini e Buffet, P. Torretta, 60. (☎06 687 14 45). From V.d. Corso, turn onto P.S. Lorenzo in Lucina. Take a left on V. Campo Marzio, and quick right onto V. Toretta. Vini e Buffet is a favorite spot for chic Romans with a penchant for regional wines. Also available are patés, *crostini,* and *scarmorze* (a tangy variety of cheese) for €6.50-8.50. Don't leave without getting one of their signature yogurt, almond, and cassis combination bowls (€4). Reservations are recommended but not necessary. M-Sa 12:30-3pm and 7:30-11pm. Cash only. ❷

Arancio d'Oro, V.d. Arancio, 50-52 (☎06 686 50 26). Take V.d. Condotti from P. di Spagna; take the 1st right after V.d. Corso, then the 1st left. Escape the overly touristy *piazza* with the locals. They'll order the fried artichokes (€4.50), and the less inhibited might go for the *taglioni* with cuttlefish ink (€7.50). No meal is complete without *panna cotta* (cream custard with fresh fruit). Dinner reservations suggested. Open M-Sa 12:30-3pm and 7:30-11:30pm. AmEx/D/MC/V. ❷

PizzaRè, V. di Ripetta, 14 (☎06 32 11 468). Take V. di Ripetta for one block away from P. del Popolo. For those looking for a cheap vacation to the south, PizzaRé serves up Neapolitan-style pizza as well as regional wines and desserts. The "PizzaRé," with buffala mozzarella and cherry tomatoes, is a favorite. It may be a chain (with a second location on V. Oslavia, 39a, near P. Mazzini), but this isn't Domino's. Open daily 12:45-3:30pm and 7:30pm-12:30am (stays open until 1am F and Sa). AmEx/MC/V. ❶

Il Brillo Parlante, V. Fontanella, 12 (☎06 324 33 34 or 06 323 50 17; www.ilbrilloparlante.com). Take V. del Corso away from P. del Popolo and turn left onto V. Fontanella. The wood-burning pizza oven, fresh ingredients, and excellent wine attract many lunching Italians. Sophisticated food and shady outdoor tables available. Thin-crusted pizza €7-10. Restaurant open Tu-Su 12:30-5:30pm and 7:30pm-1am; *enoteca* (wine bar) open Tu-Su 11am-2am. MC/V. ❶

Al Piccolo Arancio, V. Scanderbeg, 112 (☎06 678 61 39). Facing the Trevi Fountain, go right on V.d. Lavatore; V. Scanderbeg is on the right. This friendly *trattoria* is a stone's throw from the Trevi Fountain, but its side street location insulates diners from street vendors. *Ravioli all'arancia* (with ricotta and oranges; €6.90) is a specialty, and the *abbacchio al forno* (roasted lamb; €9.80) is popular. Bread €1.05. Open Tu-Su noon-3pm and 7pm-midnight. Closed two weeks in mid-Aug. AmEx/D/MC/V. ❷

Al Presidente, V. Arcione, 95 (☎06 679 73 42). Facing the Trevi Fountain, walk right on V. Lavatore and bear left onto Arcione. Fish from the ocean, not from a farm. You can taste the difference in dishes like the toad thighs in seaweed. Homemade pasta with truffles is not to be missed. Primi €12, secondi €17. Open Tu-Su 7:30-midnight, Sa-Su noon-3pm.❸

UKIYO Japanese Restaurant, V.d. Propaganda, 22 (☎06 678 60 93; www.ukiyo-restaurant.it). Sushi Chef Yoichi Takumi brings Japanese cuisine along with attentive service to Italy for the delight of both tourists and locals. The fish is fresh and prepared to the exacting standards of a Japanese sushi kitchen. Their specialty is a subtle mackerel, ginger and sesame roll (€5). Full meal of assorted sushi (€28.50) and tasting menu available (€42). Open Th-Tu noon-2:45pm, 7-10:45pm. Wheelchair accessible. AmEx/MC/V. ❹

Il Margutta, V. Margutta, 118 (☎06 326 505 77; www.ilmargutta.it), off V.d. Babuino, near P. del Popolo. This upscale scene is all vegetarian, all the time. The food is green, and the atmosphere and service are excellent. A mushroom and soy burger is €8; lunch, buffet style €15; all-you-can-eat brunch €25.

gnocchi: Dumplings, often filled with potatoes.

lasagne: Thin sheets served densely packed with cheese, tomato sauce, and sometimes meat.

linguine: Very thin strips of pasta.

orrecchiette: Little ears of pasta, larger variety called **cencioni**.

penne: Small tubes (**pennete** is even smaller, but not as small as **rigatoni**) often served with thin sauce.

ravioli: Small or large pockets of pasta stuffed with meat, cheese, or veggies.

rigatoni: Tubes; sized just between **pennete** and **macaroni**.

spaghetti: Ever reliable. If hollow, call it **bucatini**.

tortellini: Baby ravioli, often filled with meat.

vermicelli: Long and thinner than **spaghetti**.

ziti: Curved tubes; longer and thicker than macaroni.

Confused? Just order the risotto.

the BIG $plurge

Divine dining under the stars

La Pergola at the Cavalieri Hilton, V.A. Cadlolo, 101 (☎06 350 921 52; www.cavalieri-hilton.it). Located atop the luxurious 5 star Hilton hotel. If those rarely broken €50 bills are burning in your pocket, consider taking a plunge worth every penny. Dine in style at the famous La Pergola, ranked for the past 6 consecutive years as the best restaurant in Rome and one of the top ten in Italy. Overlooking the city, the hotel beholds a panoramic view almost worth the expense in itself. German-born Chef Heinz Beck (who visits each table) offers his take on traditional Mediterranean cuisine, sprinkled with influences from the south of France and Asia. Some divine concoctions include *gnocchi* with caviar, ricotta *souffle* with litchi "soup," and squid tempura with pineapple ravioli. For dessert (if the bank's not broken), indulge in the balsamico ice cream and black truffle served beside *foie gras*. The wine cellar's collection of 48,000 bottles, assembled by sommelier Monte Mario, has won several awards in a country that doesn't joke about its alcohol. Jacket required. Complete meal €130 without wine. Open Tu-Sa for one seating per evening. **Reservations strongly recommended.**

Full bar to help meat lovers drown their sorrows. Reservations suggested at night. Open daily 12:30-3:30pm and 7:30-11:30pm. AmEx/MC/V. ❸

Centro Macrobiotico Italiano-Naturist Club, V.d. Vite, 14, 4th fl. (☎06 679 25 09), just off V.d. Corso. Probably the only restaurant in Rome where you're offered ground sesame seeds with your salad, the Centro Macrobiotico has provided Romans with a healthy alternative to pasta and pastries for the last 30 years. The Club also houses a small health food store. *Primi* €8-9; *secondi* €9-11:50, organic wine €12-16. Predictably, no smoking allowed. Open M-Sa 12:30-3pm and 7:30-11pm. MC/V. ❷

BORGO & PRATI (NEAR VATICAN CITY)

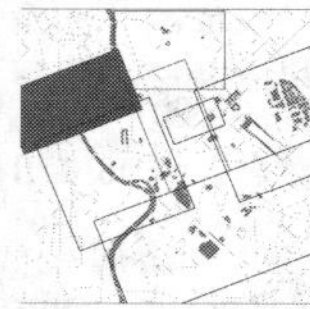
see map p. 364

The streets near the Vatican are paved with bars and *pizzerie* that serve mediocre sandwiches at hiked-up prices. For far better and much cheaper food, head to the residential district a few blocks north and east of the Vatican Museums, home to specialty shops with fresh bread and pastries and small family-run *osterie*. They might run you a few more euros than the average Roman fare, but chances are, you'll be dining next to a couple of nuns and an Italian movie star or two. Who can put a price on the world's freshest veal, anyway?

Franchi, V. Cola di Rienzo, 204 (☎06 687 46 51; www.franchi.it). Benedetto Franchi ("Frankie") has been serving the citizens of Prati superb *tavola calda,* prepared sandwiches, and other luxurious picnic supplies for nearly 50 years, and not an unsatisfied customer yet. Delicacies include various croquettes (€1.10), marinated munchies such as anchovies, peppers, olives, and salmon, and pastas (€5.50 per generous portion). More expensive than buying bread and cheese for a midday snack, but certainly cheaper and better than most Vatican area snack bars. Open M-Sa 8:15am-9pm. AmEx/MC/V. ❷

Cacio e Pepe, V. Giuseppe Avezzana, 11 (☎06 321 72 68). From P. Mazzini take V. Settembrini to P. dei Martiri di Belfiore, then left on V. Avezzana. Great pasta for cheap; no wonder Cacio e Pepe has been a neighborhood favorite since 1964. All the homemade pasta is delicious, but yes, the *Cacio e Pepe* is their specialty. Lunch under €10, a full dinner around €15. House wine and beer only. M-F 8-11:30pm, Sa 12:30-3pm. Reservations accepted. Cash only. ❶

"Lo Spuntino" da Guido e Patrizia, Borgo Pio, 13 (☎06 687 54 91). Near Castle Sant'Angelo. This place has real character; don't be fooled by the checkered tablecloths and bow tie adorned waiters at other establishments nearby. The atmosphere is casual, with plastic plates and forks–but the food is homey and popular with lunching locals. Guido himself holds court behind a counter filled with all the makings of a beautiful *tavola calda* (snack bar). Prices vary, but a full meal (*primi, secondi,* and wine) will run you less than €8. Usually open M-Sa 8am-8pm. Cash only. ❶

Da Benito e Gilberto, V.d. Falco, 19 (☎06 686 77 69 or 338 152 78 92) off Borgo Pio, marked only as "Hostaria." Frequented by Italian celebrities and less glitzy locals alike, this small *ristorante* offers fresh seafood in excess. There is no menu (you're eating what was freshest at the market), but your waitress will do her best to bridge the language gap by bringing you everything. The best things in life, however, are not free; *antipasto, primi, secondi,* desert, caffe, and a bottle of wine will put you back about €65. Dress well, but no tuxes required. Reservations required. Tu-Sa 7:30pm-whenever they want to close. AmEx/MC/V. ❺

San Marco, Via Tacito, 27-29 (☎06 323 55 96), off P. Cavour. San Marco has been dousing hungry Romans with mozzarella for the past 50 years. Perfect Roman crust and fresh toppings (€6-10). The conventional pizzas are delicious, but try their special pies for something a little more unique–like smoked swordfish and greens (€9.80). Homemade *tiramisu* (€4.10) is as close to heaven as most of us will get. Open Su-F noon-4pm and 6:30pm-12:30am. Sa 6:30pm-12:30am. ❷

Taverna Angelica, P. Amerigo Capponi, 6 (☎06 687 45 14), just south of V. d.Crescenzio. Classy copper and wicker interior off the main thoroughfare with fresh and creative dishes to match. Reasonable prices (*primi* €10, *secondi* €15) although some portions are stylishly small. Meats are excellent, but fish is the specialty here. Amazingly, a good bottle of wine goes for €15. Open daily 7:30pm-around midnight. Reservations accepted. AmEx/MC/V. ❸

Velando, Borgo Vittorio, 26 (☎06 688 099 55), at Via Plauto. This small and elegant spot serves Umbrian cuisine with a twist. The service is excellent, as dishes like strawberry risotto or chestnut pasta with cuttlefish and greymullet roe rush to your table. With *primi* as little as €12 and *secondi* (with *contorni*) €15, you can afford to be adventurous. Strong wine list, with a few bottles by the glass for €4. For dessert, baked peaches in chocolate sauce are balanced and not too sweet. Open M-Sa 12:30-3pm and 7:30pm-midnight. AmEx/MC/V. ❹

Trattoria "da Dante," V. Monte Santo, 36a. (☎06 375 155 37) near P. Mazzini. As many variations in the menu as there are regions of the underworld. If hearing English at the table next to you is making you think of hell's fires, da Dante's local feel will renew your faith. Moreover, prices here (primi €6, secondi €8-10, good house wine €6) are quite reasonable. Veal is the house specialty. M-Sa 12:30-3pm and 7:30pm-1am. AmEx/MC/V. ❷

TRASTEVERE

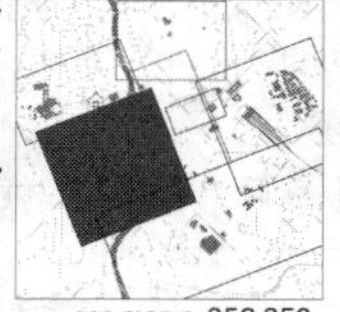
see map p.358-359

You can't say you've been to Rome without having savored a pizza and swilled some tasty Perroni in one of the rowdy outdoor *pizzerie* in Trastevere. Trastevere is home to raucous pubs, hopping pizza joints, and a loud bohemian population. By day, the cobblestone streets rumble with the sounds of children and Vespas, but when night falls, hippy expats add their voices to the madding throng in P. di Santa Maria di Trastevere. You may have trouble finding a table outside in the summer months without a reservation. On the plus side, almost any restaurant you stumble upon will be worth your while, provided you stay clear of glossy, lit-up menus sporting color pictures of every dish offered.

Pizzeria San Callisto, P.S. Calisto, 9a (☎06 581 82 56). Off P.S. Maria in Trastevere. Simply the best damn pizza in Rome: shame about the service and the long, long, long waits for a table. Gorgeous thin crust pizzas so large they hang off the plates (€4.20-7.80). The *bruschetta* (€2.10) alone is worth a postcard home. Open Tu-Su 7pm-midnight. MC/V. ❶

Augusto, P. de' Renzi, 15 (☎06 580 37 98). North of P.S. Maria in Trastevere. Enjoy the daily pasta specials at lunch (around €5), and the *pollo arrosto con patate* (€5.50). The homemade desserts are wonderful. Dinner is chaotic, lunch features laid-back discussions between waiters and clientele. No reservations. Open M-F 12:30-3pm and 8-11pm, Sa 12:30-3pm. Closed Aug. ❶

Dar Poeta, Vicolo del Bologna 45-46 (☎06 588 05 16; www.darpoeta.it). From P. S. Egidio, head down V. delle Scala and turn right. Hardly a tourist in sight. Eighteen types of bruschetta (all €2) and unusual pizzas amid the old favorites (€4-8.50). Save room for the desserts, homemade daily by owner Marco's mamma (€3.50). No smoking inside; the heat-sensitive should be wary of sitting near the fiery wood oven. Open 7:30pm-1am. AmEx/MC/V. ❶.

Cave Canem, P. S. Calisto, 11 (☎06 589 82 17). Just south of P. S. Maria in Trastevere. More bruschetta toppings than you could shake a toasted piece of bread at (€1.60-3.10; try 'em all for €7.30). Pizzas (€4.50-8) almost rival Pizzeria S. Calisto's, but here service does come with a smile. Homemade pasta (ravioli with butter and sage, €5.50). Open daily 7:30pm-midnight. AmEx/MC/V. ❶

Ristorante a Casa di Alfredo, V. Roma Libera, 5-7 (☎06 588 29 68). Off P. Cosimato. Whether you opt for the "sea" menu or "land" menu, you are destined to find something to your liking. Try the *gnocchi con gamberi* (€8) or the specialty *tonarelli all' Alfredo* (€8) to start and the grilled *calamari* (€10.50) or the filetto a pepe verde (€13) as a main dish. Open daily noon-3pm and 7:30-11:30pm. AmEx/MC/V. ❷

Ouzeri, V.d. Salumi, 2 (☎06 581 82 56). Either go left off V.d. Trastevere or take V. Vascellari from Lungotevere Ripa and then go right onto V.d. Salumi. Ouzeri may advertise itself as a "Taberna Greca," but the waiters will tell you it is actually a Greek Cultural Association complete with Greek live music and dancing lessons (Oct.-Apr., W and Sa). Meals are large and worth every cent. To get inside, ring the doorbell. €1.50 membership required. Reservations suggested. Open M-Sa 8:30pm-2am. Cash only. ❷

Il Tulipano Nero, V. Roma Libera, 15 (☎06 581 83 09). Take V.d. Trastevere; turn right on V. E. Morosini. Some of the more innovative pizzas (€4-7) in Rome. Almost removed from the nighttime chaos of P.S. Maria in Trastevere, this pizzeria is smack in the middle of the nighttime chaos of P. Cosimato. Iron palates can attempt the *pennette all'elettroshock* (€7.50). Portion size ranges from large to gigantic. Open Tu-Su 6pm-2am. AmEx/MC/V. ❷

Osteria dei Belli, P. Sant'Apollonia, 11 (☎06 580 37 82). Off V.d. Lungaretta near P.S. Maria in Trastevere. A bustling *trattoria* specializing in Sardinian cooking, especially seafood. Nice outdoor seating area, if rather full of tourists taking photographs. Ravioli *sardi* (in tomato cream sauce) €8. Excellent grilled *calamari* €12. Reservations suggested. Open Tu-Su 11:30am-2:30pm and 7:30-11:30pm. AmEx/MC/V. ❷

Ristorante al Fontanone, P. Trilussa, 46 (☎06 581 73 12). Directly opposite Ponte Sisto. Serves traditional Roman cuisine, including *rigatoni cacio de pepe*, with peccorino cheese and pepper (€6). When you realize you're paying partly for the location, remember the queues at San Callisto and console yourself with the renowned *carciofi alla Romano* (€4). Open M, Th-Su noon-2pm and 7-11pm, W 7-11pm. Closed mid-Aug. to mid-Sept. MC/V. ❷

TERMINI & SAN LORENZO

see map p. 360-361

NORTH OF TERMINI

You're near the train station, hungry, and in a hurry. This is no reason to subject yourself to the nightmare of shady tourist establishments offering a €8 "quick lunch" (and pre-cooked tourist menus). Heading northwest away from V. Marsala onto V. Vulturno is a reasonable bet for a traditional and inexpensive lunch. Otherwise, the following provide good service and food for a largely local clientele.

Africa, V. Gaeta, 26-28 (☎06 494 10 77), near P. Independenza. Decked out in yellow and black, Africa continues its 20-year tradition of serving excellent Eritrean/Ethiopian food. The meat-filled *sambusas* (€2.50) are a flavorful starter; both the *zighini beghi* (roasted lamb in a spicy sauce; €8) and the *misto vegetariano* (mixed veggie dishes; €6) make fantastic entrees, while the thick yogurt (€1.55) goes well with spicy dishes. If you're in the mood to get messy, try your hands at their spongy Ethiopian flat bread, known as *injera*. Cover €1. Open M-Sa 8am-midnight. MC/V. ❷

Al 39, V. Palaestro 39a-41a (☎06 444 12 13). Between the intersection of V. S Martino d. Battaglia and V. Gaeta. The locals' lunch joint. Ingredients are fresh, the waiters friendly, and the food is a good value (*bruschetta al pomodoro*, €1.30). Carnivores should try the specialty, *bisteca Al 39*, (€10). Vegetarians won't go hungry with the superb *rigatoni vignaroli* (€5). The pizza oven is not wood fired, but the pizzas (€4-7) are served bubbling. Open M-Sa noon-3:30pm, 7-midnight. AmEx/MC/V. ❷

Hostaria da Bruno, V. Varese, 29 (☎06 490 403). From V. Marsala, next to the train station, walk three blocks down V. Milazzo and turn right onto V. Varese. A neighborhood favorite with daily specials. Start with the *tortellini con panna e funghi* (with cream and mushrooms; €6.50) or the tasty homemade *gnocchi* (€6) and continue with the delicious *osso buco* (€8). Bruno, the owner, makes *crépes*, and he's very good at what he does: note the picture of him shaking hands with the Pope upon presentation of one of his little masterpieces. Open M-F noon-3:15pm and 7-10:15pm. Closed Aug. AmEx/MC/V. ❷

SAN LORENZO

San Lorenzo is Rome's university district so if under 30 you'll be treated like any other of the region's local *regazzi* and *regazze*. A discriminating student palate, combined with student financial resources, have ensured that just about every restaurant here is good and cheap. Even Saint Lawrence himself emerged as a foodie upon martyrdom: on being grilled alive, he reputedly instructed his tormenters: "turn me over, I'm done." The San Lorenzo area also has the distinct advantage of being closed to traffic between June and October (W-Su nights). Come late July, when exams are over, the district sinks into a summer slumber, waking up again in time for the new semester in late September. Although the district feels lively and safe, it is best to avoid north and east of P. Tiburtina if you're alone at night. There is also not much else to see or do in this area besides eat. From Termini, walk south on V. Pretoriano to P. Tiburtino, or take bus #492 to P. Verano (at the other end of V. Tiburtina from P. Tiburtino).

Il Pulcino Ballerino, V.d. Equi, 66-68 (☎06 494 12 55). Take a right off V. Tiburtina. An artsy atmosphere with cuisine to match. The cook stirs up dishes like *conchiglione al "Moby Dick"* (shells with tuna, cream, and greens) and *risotto* (various types; €5.16-6.20). Excellent vegetarian dishes like *scamorza* and potato casserole (€6.20). You can also skip the chef altogether and prepare your own meal on a warm stone at the table. Cover €1. Open M-Sa 1-3:30pm and 8pm-midnight. Closed 2nd and 3rd weeks of Aug. AmEx/MC/V. ❷

Il Tunnel, V. Arrezo, 11 (☎06 442 368 08). From M:B-Bologna, walk down Vle. della Provincie, take the fourth right onto V. Padova, and the second left onto V. Arezzo. It's a bit of a trek, but this is a family-run Roman *hostaria* just as it should be, and the locals' choice. Golden crispy pizzas are served for lunch and dinner (from €4); pizzas in the centro storico will seem miniscule in comparison. All pastas dishes (€4-10) are made fresh and the *bisteca alla Fiorentina* is unrivalled in Rome (priced by weight, around €15 per person). The Italian wine list is small but well chosen, and advice is freely given (bottles start at €6). Open Tu-Su noon-3pm, 7pm-midnight. Closed August. MC/V. ❸

Arancia Blu, V.d. Latini, 65 (☎06 445 41 05), off V. Tiburtina. This elegant and popular little vegetarian restaurant serves up an inventive and excellent take on food. Enjoy elaborate dishes like *tonnarelli con pecorino romano e tartufo* (pasta with sheep cheese and truffles; €6.20) or fried ravioli stuffed with eggplant and smoked *caciocavallo* with pesto sauce (€8.50). Extensive wine list. Open daily 8:30pm-midnight. MC/V. ❷

Pizzeria La Maschere, V. degli Umbri 16 (☎06 446 29 90). Heading east from Ple. Tiburtino on V. Tiburtina, V. degli Umbri is the third street on the right. Have a gargantuan pizza here (€5.50-12) and you'll be upset that you settled for anything smaller anywhere else. Drinks are an excellent value too (40oz. beer, €2.55), as are the *bruschette* (with tomatoes, €1.30). The frozen desserts are not such a bargain. Open daily, 4:30pm-2am. No credit cards. ❶

Il Capellaio Matto, V.d. Marsi, 25. From V. Tiburtina, take the 4th right off V.d. Equi. Vegetarians, rejoice! This offbeat place (named for the Mad Hatter) offers pasta and rice dishes like *riso al pepe verde* (with green peppercorn, €5.50), imaginative salads like *insalata di rughetta, pere, e parmigiano* (arugula, pears, and parmesan, €4.20), and a variety of crepes (€4-6). Plenty of meat dishes, too. Cover €1. Open W-M 8pm-midnight. ❶

La Pantera Rosa, P. Verano, 84-85 (☎06 445 63 91). At the eastern end of V. Tiburtina. The house specialty is the innovative creamed salmon pizza (€6). There's also a variety of excellent *primi* such as *bucatini all'Amatriciana* (thick spaghetti with spicy tomato sauce, €6). Open M-Tu and Th-Su noon-3pm and 6:30pm-12:30am. MC/V. ❷

TESTACCIO & AVENTINO

Once home to a giant slaughterhouse *(il Mattatoio)*, Testaccio now contains some excellent restaurants, many of which serve traditional Roman fare. It is also the center of Roman nightlife. True to their roots, Testaccio eateries offer food made of just about every animal part imaginable. The gastronomically adventurous can sample local delicacies such as *pagliate* (calf intestines with milk), *animelle alla griglia* (grilled sweetbreads), and *fegato* (liver).

La Cestia, Viale di Piramide Cestia, 69. M: B-Piramide. Walk across P. di Porta San Paolo to V. di Piramide Cestia; restaurant is on the right. La Cestia's offerings, particularly their fish, are so beloved that employees of the Food and Agriculture Organization make the trek from their headquarters near the Circus Maximus to grab lunch. The fish you just ate for dinner was likely on display as you walked in the door, eyes and all. The pizza and pasta are excellent for light meals. Open Tu-Su 12:30-3pm and 7:30-11pm. D/MC/V. ❷

Trattoria da Bucatino, V. Luca della Robbia, 84-86 (☎06 574 68 86). Take V. Luigi Vanvitelli off V. Marmorata, then the first left. A friendly neighborhood *trattoria* bringing you the animal entrails you know and love, and plenty of gut-less dishes as well. Delicious mounds of *tripe alla romana* (€7) stay true to the traditions of Testaccio. More conventional (but equally good) dishes include *cosse alla marinara* (€5). Pizza €5-7. Cover €1.50. Open Tu-Su 12:30-3:30pm and 6:30-11:30pm. Closed Aug. D/MC/V. ❷

Volpetti Piu, V. Alessandro Volta (☎06 574 43 06). Take a left onto V.A. Volta off of V. Marmorata. Join the locals at this authentic *gastronomica* for a quick lunch at one of their self-service tables. Fresh salads, pizza, and daily specials from €4. Open M-Sa 10am-10pm. ❶

Luna Piena, Via Luca della Robbia, 15-17 (☎06 575 02 79). From V. Marmorata take a left onto V.A. Volta, and then your first right. Serving innovative cuisine along with traditional Roman dishes, this *ristorante* is one of Testaccio's best. Experiment with *primi* (€4-6) such as *risotto* with pumpkin and peas or, if you're feeling brave, *secondi* like beef tail or tripe (€6.70-8.78). For a lighter meal, opt for a hearty salad (€5-6.50). Open Th-M 12:30-3pm and 7:30-11:30pm, F-Sa 12:30-3pm and 7:30pm-midnight. D/MC/V. ❷

DESSERT

Though loosely translated as "ice cream," *gelato* is in a league of its own. Unfortunately, shops catering to naive tourists may sell you commercially made, pitiful imitations of true *gelato:* to avoid this sad fate, try our recommended *gelaterie*, or at least look for shops advertising *gelato artigianale* or *propria produzione*, which means they make it themselves. If the *gelato* flavors are grayish and barely distinguishable, instead of an artificially colored rainbow, it's a good sign that you're getting the good stuff. Saying *"con panna"* when you order will usually add a mound of fresh whipped cream to your serving for free. Most *gelaterie* require you to pay before you eat, so first head for the *cassa* (cash register) and then present your receipt to the scooper when you order. Now for some flavorful gelato vocabulary:

ITALIAN WORD	DESCRIPTION	ITALIAN WORD	DESCRIPTION
amaretto	almond	**amareno**	sour cherry
ananas	pineapple	**arancia**	orange
baci	chocolate and hazelnut	**cannella**	cinnamon
cassata	nuts and candied fruits	**cocco**	coconut
cocomero	watermelon	**fragola**	strawberry
frutti di bosco	mixed berries	**lampone**	raspberry
latte/panna/crema	cream	**limone**	lemon
liquirizia	black licorice	**mela**	apple
menta	mint, often chips	**meringa**	meringue
miele	honey	**mirtillo**	blueberry
nocciola	hazelnut	**pesca**	peach
pistacchio	pistachio	**pompelmo**	grapefruit
nutella	hazelnut chocolate	**riso**	rice pudding
stracciatella	chocolate chip	**tiramisù**	rum, coffee, and cream

Another option is a slushy flavored ice treat called **granita.** Three common flavors are *limone* (lemon), *amareno* (sour cherry), and *caffè* (slushy frozen espresso). Alternately, try visiting a **grattachecce** stand. At these little booths (usually around parks and busier streets), muscled vendors will scrape shavings off a block of ice for you on the spot with a metal shovel, then spike your drink with any of the flavored syrups they have on hand. The Roman specialty in *grattachecce* is a combo flavor called **lemoncocco,** a yummy mix of lemon and coconut flavors with bits of fresh coconut fruit mixed in.

San Crispino, V.d. Panetteria, 42 (☎06 679 39 24). Very near the Trevi Fountain. Facing the fountain, turn right onto V. Lavatore and take your 2nd left; it is inset on the right. Crispino is almost universally acknowledged as the best *gelato* in Rome. Every flavor made from scratch. Don't miss the honey-infused "gelato di San Crispino"; they recommend pairing it with "Islay single malt scotch," which is sublime in its own right. Cups €1.70-6.30. Also at V. Acaia, 56 (☎06 704 504 12), south of the center in Appio. Both locations open M, W-Th, Su noon-12:30am, F-Sa noon-1:30am.

The Old Bridge, Vle. dei Bastioni di Michelangelo (☎06 397 230 26), off P. del Risorgimento, perpendicular to Vatican museum walls. Have someone hold your place in the Vatican line and come to this outpost. Huge cups and cones (€1.50-3) filled with your choice of 20 homemade *gelato* flavors, some of the best in the city. Open M-Sa 9am-2am, Su 3pm-2am.

Da Quinto, V.d. Tor Millina, 15 (☎06 686 56 57). West of P. Navona. Eccentric interior decoration, huge lines, and icy, lighter gelato. The fruit flavors are especially good, as are the house specialty banana splits (€4.13). Enormous *macedonia* of fruit with yogurt, *gelato,* or whipped cream topping (€6.50). Fresh fruit smoothies sweetened to order. Open daily 11am-2am; winter occasionally closed W.

Giolitti, V.d. Uffici del Vicario, 40 (☎06 699 12 43; www.giolitti.it). From the Pantheon, follow V.d. Pantheon to its end and then take V.d. Maddelena to its end; V.d. Uffici del Vicario is on the right. Makes wonderful *gelato* in dozens of flavors, as well as ices laden with fresh fruit, both to take-out or eat-in. Choose your flavors before you step up to the bar. Festive and crowded at night. Cones €1.55-2.60. Open daily 9am-1am. AmEx/D/MC/V.

Tre Scalini, P. Navona, 30 (☎06 688 019 96). This chic, old-fashioned spot is famous for its *tartufo,* a hunk of truffled chocolate ice cream rolled in chocolate shavings (€3.20 at the bar, €6.50 sitting). A touristed location with very high prices. Bar open Th-Tu 9am-1:30am; pricey restaurant open Th-Tu 12:30-3:30pm and 7:30-9pm.

the local story

Oil and Bacchanalia

Fabio Parpelli, 27, is the owner and sommelier at Apicius, an oleoteca and wine shop.

Q: How did you get interested in olive oil and wine?

A: I always had good oil at home. My mother taught me a lot. For wine, it started when I was young (about 15). I preferred wine to beer, which I guess is uncommon for young people. I went to stores to buy wines, and tasted the difference. Then I started to study it. I went to the AIS, the only Italian sommelier school in the world that's accredited.

Q: What are some of the challenges of opening a new store in Italy?

A: Well, I think you need to start with an idea of what you want. I wanted to showcase oil, because people usually don't care about it. Until 2 or 3 years ago, people bought bad stuff. I saw that other wine shops sold oil, but they didn't showcase it like they did with their wines. My mother was like a "sommelier" for oil, and so I learned from her. I am very particular about it. When I go into a restaurant, I have to know what I'm using.

Q: What makes a good oil?

A: A good olive oil comes from a small farm that presses olives from their own region, like they did a long time ago.

Palazzo del Freddo Giovanni Fassi, V. Principe Eugenio, 65-67 (☎06 446 47 40), off P.V. Emanuele II, southeast of Termini. Also at V. Vespasiano, 57, near the Vatican. This century-old *gelato* factory is famous throughout Rome. Try *riso*, try *coco*, try them all. Its most famous flavor is *la caterinetta,* a delicate honey and vanilla concoction. Cones, cups, and shakes €1.30-2.60. *Frulatti* (fruit glazed with sugar) and ice cream sandwiches €1.80. Open Tu-F noon-12:30am, Sa noon-1:30am, Su 10am-12:30am.

Yogufruit, P. G. Tavani Arquati, 118 (☎06 589 76 12), off V.d. Lungaretta near P.S. Sonnino. No tradition here; it's filled with the young and the fruitful. Tart frozen yogurt blended with just about anything: fruit, M&Ms, even cornflakes. Cups or cones €1.50-€2.50. Open M-Su noon-2am.

PASTRY

Italian pastries are generally from the southern part of Italy, so don't be put off by the signs advertising traditional Neapolitan *sfogiatelle. Pasticcerie* (pastry shops) are scattered around Centro Storico and distinguish themselves from the typical bar with a glorious selection of sweets to wash down with your *caffè*. Pastry is usually sold by weight.

Pasticceria Ebraica Boccione, Portico d'Ottavia, 1 (☎06 687 86 37). A tiny, take-out only pastry bakery deep in the Jewish Ghetto. Little fanfare, just long queues of locals who line up for what they all acknowledge to be the best pastry in Rome. *Torta Ricotta Vicciole* and *Torta Ricotta Cioccolate* are the most famous of their creations, all sold at excellent prices (€10.33 per kg). Open Su-Th 8am-8pm, F 8am-5:30pm. Closed Jewish holidays.

Il Fornaio, V.d. Baullari, 5-7 (☎06 688 039 47). Across from P.S. Pantaleo, south of P. Navona. Run by the Italian mothers you never had. Wonderful, fresh-baked cakes, pies, and cookies. *Torta di mele* (€2 per big slice), delicious *biscotti* (€1 per *etto*). *Ricotta torte* (about €2 per slice) may require that you go to confession afterwards. Open daily 7am-8pm.

Dagnino, V.V.E. Orlando, 75 (☎06 481 86 60; www.pasticceriadagnino.com). Off P. Repubblica, in the Galleria Esedra. This *pasticceria* extraordinaire serves fabulous Sicilian pastries, *gelato* (€1.60-2.10 at the bar), marzipan wonders, almond drinks, and exquisite, never-soggy ricotta *cannoli siciliani* (€1.65 at the bar, €3.10 at the table). Don't miss the splendid, sticky *cassatina* (€2.07-€4.15), a heavy mix of candied orange and lemon peel, green icing, almond paste, and sweet, moist ricotta. Understandably busy at lunchtime, given that *primi* are €5.20 sitting down. Open daily 7am-10pm. MC/V.

CAFFÈ

Italian coffee is the world's best, and coffee itself is the perfect solution to early hostel lockouts, hangovers, and hordes of belligerent tourists. It's also incredibly cheap and readily available. What to order? **Caffè** or **espresso** is a small cup of very strong coffee. A **cappuccino** is espresso with steamed milk and foam, often with a sprinkle of *cacao* on top. Italians only drink it for breakfast, but you can get it anytime you like, if you don't mind the bartender's snickering. A **caffè latte** is a shot of espresso with an entire glass of hot milk. If you want skim milk, request a **latte scremato. Caffè macchiato** is espresso with a spot of milk. **Latte macchiato** is a steamed milk with a spot of espresso. **Caffè ristretto** (or **alto**) is espresso with less water than usual. A **caffè lungo** has more water than normal, for non-Italian nervous systems. **Caffè corretto** is a black espresso "corrected" with a spot of liqueur. **Caffè americano** may be either filtered coffee or a *caffè lungo*. **Decaffeinato** coffee is available and may be made into any of the above delicacies. Better than decaf, though, is **caffè orzo,** a coffee-like drink made from barley—it tastes better than decaf and contains no trace caffeine.

Note that in most cafes and bars, you pay one price to stand at the bar, and a higher price (as much as double) to sit down. There is usually a menu on the wall of the bar listing the prices *al bar* or *al banco* (standing up) and *a tavola* (at a table). The streets around Campo dei Fiori and Trastevere hide some of the best *caffès*. The bars around the Spanish Steps cater to rich tourists and are often packed and over-priced. Also avoid the numerous bars near the Vatican; the prices are some of the highest in Rome, and the quality tends to be poor. Wander a few blocks north to V. Cola di Rienzo to find more authentic *caffès*.

Bar Giulia (a.k.a. Cafe Peru), V. Giulia, 84 (☎06 686 13 10), near P.V. Emmanuele II. No other bar is crazy enough to open near this tiny, 50-year-old institution located in a building that Raphael once called home. The owner, Alfredo, serves what may be the cheapest (and most delicious) coffee in Rome (at bar €0.57, sitting €0.72) and will add your favorite liqueur at no extra charge. You may have to crowd surf over the hordes of locals to get your cup of fresh-squeezed orange juice. Open M-Sa 4am-9:30pm.

Tazza d'Oro, V.d. Orfani, 84-86 (☎06 679 27 68). Standing with your back to the Pantheon's portico, you'll see the yellow-lettered sign on your right. No seating, but some of the best coffee in Rome (their own "regina" blend of arabica coffees from around the world) at great prices (*caffè* €0.65; cappuccino €0.80). Jamaican Blue Mountain available (€1.50). Superlative *granita di caffè* with fresh whipped cream (€1.30). Open M-Sa 7am-8pm.

Bar San Calisto, P.S. Calisto, 4 (☎06 583 58 69). Join Trasteverean youth and Roman elders as they engage in conversation over excellent, inexpensive cappuccino (€0.80 sitting or standing), iced tea (€1), or *Peroni* (€1.55). Small selection of excellent homemade *gelato* (€1-2). Low prices keep the hordes coming to this popular spot. Open M-Sa 6am-2am. Closed Su and 1wk. in Aug.

Caffè della Pace, V.d. Pace, 3-7 (☎06 686 12 16), off P. Navona. Dark wood interior, marble tables outside. Great people-watching, although you'll see nearly as many Americans sedately writing postcards as Italians wildly gesticulating on their cell phones. Stylish and soothing location raises the prices. *Espresso* €2, cakes €4, *apertivi* €5-8. Cheaper at the bar. Prices go up (about €2.50) after dark. Open Tu-Su 9am-2am.

Il Caffè Sant'Eustachio, P.S. Eustachio, 82 (☎06 688 020 48). Take a right on Via Palombella behind the Pantheon, towards the right as you face it. Rome's "coffee empire," this cafe was once a favorite haunt of Stendhal. Though the coffee is excellent, the modern-day struggling artist may not be able to afford the habit. Try a *granita di caffè* with all the works (at bar €3.85, sitting €5.70), or their very own *gran caffè speciale* (€2.10/3.60). If you don't like your espresso heavily sugared, specify "*caffè amaro*." Open Su-F 8:30am-1am, Sa 8:30am-2am.

Babington's Tea Rooms, P. di Spagna, 23 (☎06 678 60 27). God save the queen! Sit at your wicker covered table and order a complete high tea any time of day (€21). Some of the world's finest, from the sublime rose-infused Chinese black tea (€8 a pot) to the YinZhen

in the know

Swilling like a pro

The language and rituals of wine experts may be intimidating, but some understanding may be useful for even us simpletons. Sit back, pull out your best corkscrew, and drink in this list of vocabulary, overgeneralizations, and tips.

Start with the **label.** Most will yield information about the region and the type of grape in addition to the producer and the alcoholic content. For the best wines (CRU quality), the vineyard will also be named.

Body, called *struttura* in Italy, refers to the physical quality of the wine in the mouth. A full-bodied wine has more complex and longer-lasting flavor. Usually, this distinction refers to reds, which require aging and breathing time far more often than whites. **Aging** is dependent upon a number of factors, including the year and region in which the wine was produced. The old adage is red with meat and white with fish, but there are exceptions.

Legs refer to the pattern of the wine on the glass when it is swilled; **nose** to the smell upon opening the bottle. In a well-choreographed ritual, the waiter brings the bottle to the table and shows you the label. Nod if you've gotten what you ordered. He or she will pour a small amount in your glass. Swill it and inhale deeply; if it reeks of vinegar, something's gone horribly wrong.

"silver needle," a tea in the Chinese imperial-style, in which leaves are hand-picked twice a year at dawn (€30). Open W-M 9am-8:15pm.

Antico Caffè Greco, V. Condotti, 86 (☎06 679 17 00), off P. di Spagna. One of the oldest and most famous cafes in the world, this posh house, founded in 1760, has entertained the likes of European kings, Goethe, Wagner, Baudelaire, Byron, Shelley, John F. Kennedy, among others who could afford to spend too much on their caffeine habits. *Cappuccino* (at bar €1.25, sitting €5.20). Hot chocolate with cream (€2.40/€6.20). Sherry (€2.40/€6.20). Rumor has it that walking straight to the back library room and ordering in your best Italian will earn you a discount. Open M-Sa 8am-8:30pm.

WINE

It used to be the case that in Italy food came first, wine second. Indeed, until just a few years ago, imbibing wine was much like buying bread: you bought what was made locally, considered it essential to a meal, and did not think to make distinctions much beyond what some of the older *trattorie* still yank down from the rafters to offer with your pasta today (house white and red, without any other nuances). In many Italian *pizzerie*, you may even still receive a strange look for ordering wine rather than the usual staple, namely beer; and in many Roman *trattorie*, the best, cheapest and sometimes only option continues to be the *vino della casa*.

Appreciation for Italian wine is, in fact, a fairly recent phenomenon, boosted by the international wine festival, **Vinitaly,** held annually in Verona each April. French and American connoisseurs have now begun to realize what the Italians long knew: Italian climates, topography, and soil variation make for a variety of wines that goes unparalleled throughout the world. Natural land and climate diversity has provided for a number of different native grapes, which are grown alongside "international" varieties like Chardonnay, Merlot, and Cabernet Sauvignon. Once nicknamed Oinotria ('Wine-land') by the Greeks, Italy has begun, once again, to win international renown for its wine. Indeed, today Italy annually produces more wine than anywhere else in the world.

Organization of national industries has never been Italy's strong point, but a makeshift system (vino di tavola, IGT, DOC, DOCG, in order of increasing quality) at least guarantees that the wine in question is produced in the region on the label, and in line with the production methods specified by the government. The best Italian wines, however, operate outside the system. One of the key factors in Italian wine production at the moment is the issue of *barrique:* storing wines in large, wooden barrels imbues them with a rich, wooden and vanilla-tainted taste that a number of producers have recently eschewed in favor of the 'real flavor' of the wine.

Italian wines are usually named for their region, although sometimes *also* for their grapes. The good news is that a superb, write-home-to-your-mama bottle of wine will rarely cost more than €50; the bad news is that ordering one of them will involve learning the names of more regions and subregions than you ever thought existed. The *Let's Go* guide (all tasted in the line of duty, you understand) is a starting point; for a more comprehensive explanation, always buy your wine from an *enoteca* that has at least one sommelier on staff.

Wine

WINE TASTING

Most of the bottles listed by region and name below were selected by and purchased from **Apicius** (p. 207), ever wary of the most renowned, and consequently expensive without cause, labels. Any of the *enoteche* we list will be able to help you choose something similar if they do not carry the specific bottle. Wines are listed by name and vineyard.

Cheese

PIEMONTE

The Piemonte (literally 'at the foot of the mountains') region is just south of the Alps and its superb wines approach those of France in terms of their fruity and autumnal maturity. Its two most famous reds are the *nebbiolo* grape-based **Barolo** (a rich and full-bodied wine comparable in complexity to Bordeaux) and **Barbaresco.** The Piemonte had a great year in 1996, but anything from 1997-2000 will also do well. In 2002, hail storms damaged the crop, bumping up consumer prices. The Piemonte also produces the more fruity **Barbera d'Asti** and **B. d'Alba.** The most famous firm, with a price label to match, remains **Gaja.**

Sassisto, produced by Bera in Langhe, is one of the best value wines on offer at only €14; the combination of 80% barbera and 20% nebbiolo grapes give the wine a body to die for. Also keep a sharp eye out for the barbera bargain **L'Armangia** (€12.70), made on a small family farm which experiments with alternatives to barrique. **Fornaci,** produced by Gavi (€21.60) is a wonderful white whose 14.5% volume means that, unlike most other Italian whites, it can improve with age. Dessert wines are also big here: the **Barolo**

Est!Est!Est!

Chianato from Chiarlo (€18) is best accompanied by chocolate, and any excuse can justify the various **Moscato d'Asti** options, lower in alcohol, high in sugar but still with a wonderful fruity bouquet.

From the Peimonte region, *Let's Go* recommends **Barolo** (MicheleChiarlo, €31; Cerequio, €55), **Barbaresco** (MicheleChiarlo, €28), **Barbera** (Cascina Castel't, €8.80; Vendemmia Tardiva, €23.25), **Gavi** (Chiarlo, €10.85), and **Muscato** (Chiarlo, €8.20).

TUSCANY

The most famous and productive wine region in Italy, with over 30 DOC regulated regions and six DOCG regions. **Chianti** is the name of the game here (think velvet, smooth elegance and Silence of the Lambs), and **Chianti Classico** the most renowned of all Italian wines. Chianti is made from a combination of four grape varieties, dominated by the Sangiovese grape; Chianti Classico gets its name from one of the specific six Chianti areas in Tuscany, and a cockerel motif on the bottle guarantees its quality. Although they might look pretty, bottles covered in a straw flask will very rarely have a taste to match. The full-bodied **Brunello di Montalcino** and lighter **Rosso di Montalcino** are made from close relatives of Chanti Sangiovese grapes. If you've ordered *vino della casa* at a better *trattoria*, chances are that you were served a **Montepulciano d'Abruzzo** (not to be confused with the finer **Vino Nobile di Montepulciano**). Carmignano wine, distilled from a mixture of aged Sangiovese, Canailol Nero, Cabernet Franc, and Cabernet Sauvignon grapes, is a close cousin to the wines from Vernaccia di San Gimignano. A new generation of Tuscan wine, often using international grape types called "Super Tuscans," is red, bold and can be expensive. The region had a fantastic year in 1997, but 1999 will do almost as well.

In terms of best values, you can't beat **Pazzesco** (meaning 'madness'), **Castello del Trebbio** (€6.50) or **Tenute di Petrolo**, Petrolo, a fabulous merlot (price not yet determined). For an amazing Tuscan white, try the coastal **Verdicchio dei Castelli di Jesi**, Tenute di Tavignano (€7), which is dry, pale and perfect as an aperitif.

Other *Let's Go* recommendations include **Brunello di Montalcino** ('97 Fanti, €40), **Rosso di Montalcino** (Fanti, €14), **Vino Nobile di Montepulciano** ('97 Tenuta Vadipiatta, €18), **Chianti Classico** (Villa Cafaggio €14; '98 Riserva Villa Cafaggio €25), **Chianti** (Villa Artimino, €6), and **Supertuscan** (Torrione, €29).

SICILY

Wine quality in the region around Mt. Etna is currently in the midst of its own explosion, but prices have been (thankfully) slow to follow. A perfect climate and 3000 year tradition are central to the wine-making approach, even as international grapes and growing methods begin to encroach from the north. In keeping with the Sicilian love for all things sweet, the **red marsala** and the amazing white **Muscato Passito di Pantelleria** are famous exports.

International grapes by Planeta include **Chardonnay** (€18.80), **Merlot** (€19.60), and Sicily's famous red wine, **Lamoremio** (€25).

If you're looking for Sicilian grapes, check out **Cometa** (Fiano, €22), **Fontanelle Curto** (Nero D'Avola, €15.50), **Fratello Sole** (Nero D'Avola, €7.40), **Sorella Luna** (Insolita e Grecanico, €7.40), **Madre Terra** (Nerello Mascalese €14), **Pietramarina** (€17.20), **Rovitello** (Nerello Mascalese e Nerello Cappuccio, €23), **Moscato Passito di Pantelleria** (Martingana by Salvatore Murana, €54), **Khamma** (S. Murana, €42), and **Mueggen** (Murana, €25).

CAMPANIA

A southern region famous for white wines like **Greco di Tufo, Falanghina** and **Fiano di Avellino,** which all should be drunk as young as possible. Campania also produces great full bodied red wines like **Taurasi** and **Aglianico.** The Camarato by top producer Villa Matilde is perhaps the best deal at €9.50.

Falanghina (Feudi di San Gregorio, €9), **Fiano di Avellino** (Feudi di San Gregorio, €11.70), **Greco di Tufo** (Feudi di San Gregorio, €11.70), **Selve di Luoti** (Feudi di San Gregorio, € 23.40), **Falangina** (Colle si San Domenico, €6.70), **Greco di Tufo** (Colle si

San Domenico, €8.25), and **Fiano di Avellino** (Colle si San Domenico, €8.25) number among Campania's best values.

LAZIO

Rome's surrounding area around has been manufacturing wine since before Horace (he was particularly partial to wines from Falernum in Compania). The region is best known for its whites from Castelli Romani and Frascati. The notorious white **Est! Est!! Est!!!** comes from Montefiascone. Lazian wine may be the most underrated of all Italian regions, which makes for some killer bargains. L'Olivella, *the* producer for the region, makes **Racemo** (Frascati Superiore, €7.50), **Concento** (Cesanese and Sangiovese, €6.50), **Tre Grome** (Frascati Superiore, €14.85). Another great label, Mottura, makes **Latour a Civitella** (Grechetto, €12) and **Magone** (Pinot Nero 85%-15% Montepulciano, €15).

Cafe Greco

VENETO

This northeastern region is home to the full-bodied wines. **Amarone** grapes are left in the sun to breathe for two months or more, increasing the sugar concentration to make the wine more alcoholic. Another famous Venetian wine is **Recioto della Valpolicella. Prosecco,** which some insultingly call "Italian champagne," is a dry sparkling white.

For more full-bodied wonders, try **Amarone** (Monte Sant'Urbano from Speri '97, €44) **Recioto della Valpolicella Classico** (Vigneto I Comunai by Speri, €35.50) **La Poja** (Allegrini, €44), **Prosecco** (Bellenda, €8.90) and **Pinot Nero (Noir)** (Campo alle More by Gini, €16).

Filetti di Baccala

FRIULI VENEZIA GIULIA & TRENTINO ALTO ADIGE

White wines are Trentino's and Alto Adige's claim to fame. Although they overlap physically, Trentino and Alto Adige are entirely distinct in terms of the wines produced. Very near Germany and Austria, inhabitants speak German and many wine makers from the region have Italian names but produce wines often thought of as German. Note the German labels and Gothic-style writing.

Try Alto Adige's Cantina Produttori Valle Isarco's **Sylvaner Dominus** (€10), **Kerner** (€7), **Muller Thurgau** (€8.10), and **Gewurztraminer** (€10.85). Franz Hass, the region's other big producer, offers wine fans **Gewurztraminer** (€13) and **Pinot Nero (Noir)** (€20).

Tazza d'Oro

From Trentino, top choices include **Teroldego Rotaliano Granato** (Foradori, €35), **Terodego Rotaliano** (Foradori, €15), **San Leonardo** (Tenuta San Leonardo, €45), **Traminer Aromatico** (Castel Sallegg, €10.60), **Pinot Bianco** (Castel Sallegg, €8.30), and **Pinot Grigio** (Castel Sallegg, €8.30).

WINE BARS & ENOTECHE (WINE SHOPS)

Enoteche (or *bottiglierie*), traditional wine and olive oil shops, have become an economical and more common lunchtime alternative to pricey *trattorie.* The evolution of wine shops into makeshift restaurants began when shop proprietors had the common decency to feed the men who delivered barrels of the local harvest. Eventually word got out, and the wine shops had to install card tables, put up signs *"vino e cucina,"* and turn family members into waiters. In the 60s and 70s, students, hippies, and political activists gathered in such places to discuss Marx and Marcuse. (Note to aspiring radicals: Marcuse's prose still merits a stiff drink and a sense of humor.) *Enoteche* bars are now to be found on almost every street corner in almost every neighborhood and can be distinguished from restaurants primarily by their knowledgeable sommeliers and locally produced gastronomic delicacies (like cured meats, Italian cheeses and *crostini*). *Enoteche* often converge into wine bars, which offer more upscale, elegant foods and settings. Here you'll often find smoked fish, imported cheese, delicate desserts in multicolored exotic syrups, in addition to the typical pizza and salad dishes. Anyone looking for tasty, inexpensive food in an informal, personable setting will enjoy the cuisine and company in these neighborhood establishments. A huge selection of wines is available by the glass (from €1), and the best food option in nearly all cases is the plate of mixed *antipasti* (around €6). Most are open only on weekdays during lunchtime (approximately noon-3pm); the trendiest open again during the evening.

Bar Da Benito, V.d. Falegnami, 14 (☎06 686 15 08), off P.Cairoli in the Jewish Ghetto. For 40 years and counting, a bar counter lined with bottles and hordes of hungry workmen. Glasses of wine from €1; bottles from €5.50. Two hot pastas prepared daily (€4.50), along with fresh *secondi* like prosciutto with vegetables (€5). Spacious and fan-cooled seating area, next to take-out bar. Always packed, noisy, and incredibly hectic, but exceedingly friendly. Lunch noon-4pm. Open M-Sa 6:30am-7pm. Closed Aug.

Cul de Sac, P. Pasquino, 73 (☎06 688 010 94). Off P. Navona. One of Rome's first wine bars, Cul de Sac has kept the customers coming with an extensive wine list (from €2 a glass), outdoor tables, and dishes perfect for complementing wine. House specialty paté (such as pheasant and mushroom; €5.40) is exquisite, as are the scrumptious *escargot à la bourguigonne* (€5.10). Open M 7pm-12:30am, Tu-Sa noon-4pm and 6pm-12:30am. MC/V.

Trimani Wine Bar, V. Cernaia, 37b (☎06 446 96 30), near Termini, perpendicular to V. Volturno (V. Marsala). Their shop is around the corner at V. Goito, 20. Probably the city's most influential wine bar, at least to those in the know; it is indisputably Rome's oldest. Simple, wonderful salads (like the avocado and feta; €6.90), filling quiches (try the spiny lobster and leek quiche; €5.50), smoked fish (€13.50), impressive cheese and salami plates (€6.20-9.90), and unpretentious desserts. Despite all that, the wines are the real feature here, with almost 30 served from just €2.30 a glass. Reservations recommended for dinner. Happy hour 11:30am-12:30pm and 4-7pm. Open M-Sa 11:30am-12:30pm. AmEx/MC/V.

Enoteca Cavour 313, V. Cavour, 313 (☎06 678 54 96). Just north of the V. dei Fori Imperiali, on the left hand side of V. Cavour. The manager confesses to changing the menu whenever he or his staff "have a new idea." Regulars go straight for the couscous plate of the day and taste the offerings by the glass (€2.80-5), which change bi-weekly. Wonderful meats and cheeses, numerous salads (€5-7), and rich desserts (€3-5). The friendly staff will help you select from the wine list, organized by region (€11-260; many good bottles under €15; don't bother with the few non-Italian offerings). Open M-Sa 10am-2:30pm and 7:30pm-1am, Su 7:30pm-1am (kitchen closes 12:30am). Closed Aug.

'Gusto, P. Augusto Imperatore, 9 (☎ 06 322 62 73; www.gusto.it). On the north side of the *piazza*, just north of Ponte Cavour. Patrons have given up debating whether this culinary extravaganza is really a pizzeria, a posh *ristorante*, or a glorified *enoteca*. Pizzas start at €5, but don't come expecting just your average salami *piccanti*. With dishes like shallot quiche with a 'gelato' of balsamic vinegar (€9.50) and over 15 wines to choose from (from €3.30 per glass), who cares? Open daily 12:30pm-2am; kitchen open 12:30-3pm and 7:30pm-1am. AmEx/MC/V.

Il Simposio di Piero Costantini, Pzza. Cavour, 16 (☎06 321 15 02). Essentially a restaurant bar. 20 wines by the glass, all €4-5 and native products. Open M-Sa 6:30pm-midnight. Closed Aug. Closed Sa in late July. AmEx/MC/V.

Il Piccolo, V.d. Governo Vecchio, 75 (☎06 688 017 46), off the southwest corner of P. Navona. Simple but refined food served by struggling writers and musicians. Jazz floating out to street-side tables in the evening makes this a bohemian haven. Large selection of wines by the glass changes monthly (from €1.05). Salads and pasta for lunch €5.50-7 and assorted *antipasti* at night €5. Open daily noon–2:30am. AmEx/D/MC/V.

Enotecantica, V.d. Croce, 76b (☎06 679 08 96; www.enotecantica.com), off P. di Spagna. Relax at the elegant, J-shaped bar after a draining day at Cartier. Sip wine (€3-7 per glass) and console yourself with the delusion that money can't buy happiness or have a laugh at the picture of Jack Nicholson with the owner. Mixed plate of antipasti €7, larger plate €10. Salads €4.50-8.50. Pizza from €5.50. Open daily noon-1am. AmEx/D/MC/V.

Enoteca Buccone, V. Ripetta, 19 (☎06 361 21 54). Two blocks south of P. del Popolo on the left. Choose from hundreds of wines by the bottle, dozens by the glass, and head into the back room for elegant light fare. Delicate quiches €3, tiny *tartini* €1, and cold pasta salads €5. *Secondi* €6.50-10.50. Wines by the glass (€1.80-6.20) are all high-quality representatives of their variety and more than fairly priced. Try the opulent and concentrated Amarone (€6.50). Lunch served noon-3:30pm; dinner F-Sa evenings. Open M-Th 9am-8:30pm, F-Sa 9am-midnight, No Sa dinner in July. AmEx/D/MC/V.

Curia di Bacco, V.d. Biscione, 79 (☎06 689 38 93; www.lacuriadibacco.it), off Campo dei Fiori. A mead hall reminiscent of Beowulf, complete with candle-lit long wooden tables along a brick-lined cave interior. Choose from over 200 bottles (€10-100). Also offers an extensive imported beer list (€3-5), and a large menu of Italian midnight munchies (€3-10). If that's not enough, rumor has it that Julius Caesar was slain on the site. Open daily 5pm-2am; in winter, 6pm-2am. AmEx/MC/V.

La Vineria (a.k.a. Enoteca Reggio), Campo dei Fiori, 15 (☎06 688 032 68). Founded in 1800, the owners claim it was the first to sell wine by the glass and it remains one of the most popular and lively choices. Occupying a large swath of outdoor seating in the Campo, it's full of expats during the day; at night, throngs of young Italians and tourists fight to be served surprisingly cheap wines (glasses starting €2.30, €1.30 at bar) and harder drinks (gin and tonic €4.65, at bar €3.10). Open M-Sa 9am-2am. AmEx/D/MC/V.

WINE SHOPS

Enoteca, shops that sell only wine or are physically separate from their associated wine bar or restaurant, are the cheapest places to buy a bottle and the best for advice.

Apicius, V. Giula, 86 (☎06 682 179 52; www.enotecapicius.it). Approximately 100 wines from small producers throughout Italy are hand selected by Fabio, the English-speaking sommelier-cum-owner. He's happy to give you wine lessons, complete with tastings (call for information). Or just ask for advice while investing in a bottle (€6-200 a bottle). Many of the wines on the *Let's Go* wine tasting list (p. 203) are available here. Also a certified *oleoteca,* with many fine olive oils. 20 or more oils from small farms, hand-bottled *pates* and preserves, and other Italian specialities all organically produced. Open M 3-9pm, Tu-Sa 10am-1:30pm and 3-9pm; in winter Tu-Sa 10am-1:30pm and 3-9pm. Open daily in Dec. Closed 3 wks. in Aug. MC/V.

Il Simposio di Piero Costantini, P. Cavour, 16 (☎06 321 15 02; www.pierocostantini.it). The 1st floor showcases a multitude of spirits and wine paraphernalia, but head downstairs for a daunting collection of wines from around the globe. A gated cave holds an extraordinary collection of rare wines; ask the sommelier for admittance. Prices per bottle are competitive, ranging from €2 (get drunk) to €6-€50 (for enjoyment) to €1500+ (trust fund). Open M 4:30-8pm, Tu-Sa 9am-1pm and 4:30-8pm. AmEx/MC/V.

Trimani, V. Goito, 20 (☎06 446 96 61 or 800 014 625; info@trimani.com). Near Termini. Founded in 1821, Trimani remains Rome's most famous wine shop. Vast selection of wines, which range from very affordable to way-beyond-your-credit-card-limit. Expert staff will be happy to advise you in selecting a bottle to fit your palate and wallet. A number of Italian liquors also available. Open M-Sa 8:30am-1:30pm and 3:30-8pm. AmEx/D/MC/V.

SHOPPING FOR FOOD

Once the ATM starts shooting blanks you know it's time to shop for—and make—your own meals. For those with rarefied tastes, **alimentari** carry a selection of Italian specialty foods and liquors far superior to those found at your typical supermarket. They generally carry basic groceries, dry goods, and deli items, and are superb for "food souvenirs." For specialty cheeses, fresh bread, and meats, head to a **panificio** (bakery) or a **salumeria** (delicatessen). A little **pane** (bread) and an **etto** (100g) of meat or cheese will make a cheap but satisfying sandwich. Be aware that these smaller establishments usually close between 1-4pm, though it is becoming more common to stay open "non-stop." For produce, open-air markets are best for freshness and price. Seek out small **frutta e verdure** shops and stands. Besides markets, **supermarkets** are usually the cheapest way to purchase mainstream foods. They are also quieter, air-conditioned, and open longer; however, the produce is much less fresh and you have to walk quite a distance from any tourist locale. See the **Service Directory** (p. 342), for listings of major supermarkets in Rome.

ALIMENTARI AND OTHER DELIGHTS

Franchi, V. Cola di Rienzo, 204 (☎06 874 651; www.franchi.it), off V. Cola di Rienzo at V.d. Terenzio. Hanging ham hocks, huge wheels of cheese and a terrific selection of wine and olives are among the more mundane buys to be had at Franchi. Check out the lobster tails (€93/kg) and *foie gras* (€78/kg) artfully displayed. Open M-Sa 8:15am-9pm. AmEx/MC/V.

Antica Caciara Trasteverina, V. S. Francesco a Ripa, 140a/b (☎06 581 28 15). Off Viale di Trastevere. The usual buys, plus amazing salami and sausages. It's a mortal sin to leave Rome without trying at least one of their cheeses. This family-owned store has drawn acclaim for its incredible regional selection: Ricotta Romana, Castel Magno, Burrata Pugliese, Pecorino Pienza, and much more. Open M-Sa 7:30am-2pm and 3:30-8pm. AmEx/MC/V.

Castroni, V. Germanico, 64 and 70 (☎06 397 232 79; www.castronigroup.it). Near the Vatican, this gastronomical mecca covers two locations. One is a massive specialty shop where every olive oil and pasta imaginable is sold fresh. Ground coffee goes for €8-11 per kg alongside a large assortment of pastries (€1-2). Next door, satisfy your cravings for, well, everything at the international store. Cafe outside serves coffee, cocktails, and diverse panini. Open M-Sa 7:15am-8pm, international store 9am-1:30pm and 3:30-8pm. AmEx/MC/V.

Fratelli Fabbi, V.d. Croce, 27-28 (☎06 679 06 12; www.fabbi.it). A Gucci bag may be the ultimate Spanish Steps shopping souvenir, but perhaps one could learn to be happy with a 1kg bag of meter-long spaghetti (€5.90) instead. This packed delicatessen offers a plethora of Italian culinary goodies, including buffalo mozzarella (€13.90/kg) and baked rice-stuffed tomato (€11/kg). Open M-Sa 8am-8pm, closed a few days in Aug. AmEx/D/MC/V.

Albero del Pane, V.S. Maria del Pianto, 19-20 (☎06 686 50 16) in the Jewish Ghetto. This is where Rome's health-conscious citizens come for natural foods and cosmetics. This unique *alimentari* also caters to vegetarians with bread made without yeast or milk, and a similarly prepared rice pudding and raisin tart. Dairy section ranges from live culture yogurt (€2.55/500g) to soy skim milk. Open M-Sa 9am-7:30pm; in mid-June and July closes at 1:30pm on Sa; in Aug. 9am-1:30pm and 5-8pm. AmEx/MC/V.

Cooperative Latte Cisternino, V.d. Gallo, 20 (☎06 687 28 75), off Campo dei Fiori. Fresh *latte* (milk; 1L from €1.14) and *formaggio* (cheese) galore. Excellent selection, especially of young milky cheeses. Small selection of fine olive oils, wines, and fruit preserves. Open M-F 8am-2pm and 5-8pm, Sa 8am-1:30pm. Closed some evenings in Aug.

Drogheria Innocenzi, P. San Cosimato, 66 (☎06 581 27 25). Dry-goods store with a huge selection of foreign imports and Italian specialties. Stocks teas from around the world–Christopher Columbus could have saved everyone a lot of trouble if he had just shopped here. Open daily 7am-2pm and 4:30-8pm; closed Th in winter and Sa in July and Aug.

OUTDOOR PRODUCE MARKETS

Ah, one of the joys of continental living: outdoor market vendors keep their own hours based on how quickly their product sells. They close when they run out and stay open late when they are overstocked. You can find dealers in fruit, cheeses, meats, loaves, and fishes. Fish stands close first (before noon), so arrive before 9am to ensure that your *gamberi* are still crawling. Produce stands close last. When no hours are specified, Monday through Saturday 7am-1pm is a safe estimate, but remember that these hours are merely a guideline. Generally, vendors will do business before they have officially opened and after they have officially closed. **Beware of pickpockets.** Also note that most vendors will pick out your selection for you and will not be pleased if you handle the merchandise.

Mercato Rionfale, V. Cola di Rienzo at V. Properzio. Good selection and reasonable prices for produce, fish, meat, and dairy. Open M-Sa 7am-7pm; July and Aug. 6am-4pm.

Mercato Trionfale, M: A-Ottaviano at V.S. Maura and V. Andrea Doria. Vast assortment of fruit, vegetables, dairy, and meat products, as well as some baked goods.

Mercato Testaccio, P. Testaccio. M: B-Piramide. Your one-stop shopping option. Come here for clothing, shoes, and books. Excellent options and prices on fish as well.

Mercato di Piazza Mazzini, north of P. Cavour. M: A-Lepanto, then take V. Lepanto (which becomes V. G. Ferrari) until V. Speri. A vast array of fruits, veggies, fish, meat, dairy, and non-food items, such as clothing and cosmetics.

Mercato di Piazza San Cosimato, in Trastevere. A lively produce market with meat and cheese in abundance. Walk up V. Trastevere away from river, turn right on V. Fratte di Trastevere, and turn left on V.S. Cosimato.

Mercato di Campo dei Fiori, at P. d. Cancelleria and V. d. Pellegrino. Fruits, veggies, cheese, fish, and a pittance of flowers. Come for the produce, stay for the nightlife.

Mercato di Piazza Vittorio Emanuele II, slightly south and west of Termini. The usual produce and mayhem, this time with clothes.

Mercato Rionfale di Monti, V. Baccina at V. d. Garofone. Produce, fish, dairy, and meat products. A few other stands nearby, on V. d. Serpentei and in P. Madonna d. Monti.

Mercato di Via Milazzo, north of Termini, between V. Varese and V. Palestro. M: B-Termini or Castro Pretorio. A smaller selection of the usual items.

Mercato di Via del Lavatore, near the Trevi Fountain. Only produce, but located on a prime tourist route.

INSIDE

pubs **211**

centro storico **212** borgo, prati & vatican **214** trastevere **214**
termini & san lorenzo **215** testaccio & ostiense **217**

clubs **218**

centro storico **218** termini **218** testaccio **219**

Nightlife

When you're frustrated about the random afternoon closing times of restaurants, museums, and just about everything else in the so-called Eternal City remember that everyone is sleeping now, so they don't have to after dark. This chapter lists the best places in Rome to meet, drink, and grind. Keep in mind that the hours we list are controlled by the government, and are only guidelines. Few clubs will ask you to stop ordering after they are officially "closed."

PUBS

Exactly why the Irish pub has become the *de facto* model for Roman nightlife is unclear, but it has. Rome has more pubs than Dublin, and more on the way. Not all of Rome's pubs are Irish: some claim to be English, Scottish, American, or Brazilian, and many are distinctly Roman concoctions. Nationality is in the eye of the drinker.

Many Roman pubs feature live music, dancing, and entertainment. The tradition of staying *all'aperto* is alive and well in Rome's pubs—most have outdoor seating in the hot summer months. A more traditional drinking experience lives on in the slightly more upscale **wine bars** (see p. 206), where you can drink without the darkness, smoke, and pick-up scene of the bars.

Listed below are some of our favorites for your pub-crawling pleasure. Of course, *Let's Go* researchers are not allowed to drink while on duty because ramble they be too drinking gin much merry if happiness...

Artu Cafe

Johnny's Angels

The Drunken Ship

CENTRO STORICO

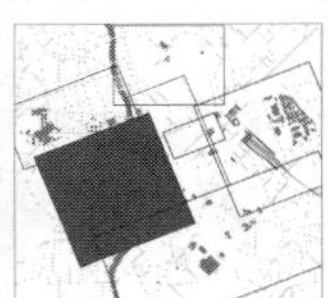

see map p. 358-359

The area is well-served at night by Bus #45N on C. Vittorio Emanuele II.

CAMPO DEI FIORI

The statue of Giordano Bruno looks down on the insanity taking place nightly in the Campo with an expression of dismay. This may have to do with the screaming twenty-somethings, or perhaps his facial expression is due to the imminent prospect of being burned at the stake. Do your best to ignore him, have a drink at one of the hordes of pubs and bars, and go find another lonely backpacker. You diligently threw your coins in the Trevi Fountain; here's your chance to capitalize in this frat-like neighborhood.

The Drunken Ship, Campo dei Fiori, 20-21 (☎06 683 005 35; www.drunkenship.com). Given up trying to break the language barrier? Rest assured, there's someone here who speaks your language. A Heineken will set you back €5, €2.50 for students (who also qualify for €1 shots throughout the week). Nightly themes 8-10pm. A takeout window completes the American aesthetic. Su Ladies' night; M free shots for girls who flash the bartender; Tu €1 shots; W power hour (all the Heineken you can drink between 9-10pm €5); Th 2 pints of Heineken, get one free. Happy Hour daily 5-8pm. W 9-10pm power hour (all you can drink, €6). Open daily 11am-2am. AmEx/MC/V.

Sloppy Sam's, Campo dei Fiori, 9-10 (☎06 688 026 37). Three words: drink, drink, drink. Then make bestest friends with the table next to you. Feel like you were just here? No, that was The Drunken Ship. Sam's is slightly more upscale, but themed nights persist: ranging from "manic" Mondays (beers €2 from 9pm until the keg kicks) to 'thirsty' Thursdays (ladies' night, beer and long drinks €2.50). Beer €3.50; shots €2.50. Happy Hour daily 4-8pm. Open M-F 4pm-2am, Sa-Su 11am-2am. AmEx/MC/V.

Taverna del Campo, Campo dei Fiori, 16 (☎06 687 44 02). When munchies strike, head here for the famous shell-peanuts and other great snacks to soak up the alcoholic over-indulgence: *Panini* €4-6; *bruschetta* €3; salads €5-9. Wine by the glass €2.60-10; beer €3-4; cocktails €8. 3Less touristy than the rest of the Campo, but of course, everything's relative. Open Tu-Su 8:30am-2am; in Aug. food service until 10:30pm. AmEx/MC/V.

Crisca Nimagiu, P. della Cancelleria, 87 (☎06 683 088 88). A pub, wine bar, gelateria, restaurant, and live music venue all rolled into one. Silver bar stools and chairs give the joint a 50s atmosphere. Copious outdoor seating. Bottled beer €3-4.50, cocktails €5.50, wine by the glass €2-5. Live music Th. Open M-F 7:30am-2am, Sa-Su 10:30am-2am.

PIAZZA NAVONA

Enter the three-ring circus and attempt to fend off henna tattoo artists and the rose vendors, who become more aggressive as the night (and their bouquets) fade. V.d. Governo Vecchio is home to some fantastic cocktail bars filled with young and trendy locals as much as in-the-know tourists. So forget the college mayhem in Campo dei Fiori and settle in for a more grown-up evening.

Jonathan's Angels, V.d. Fossa, 14-16 (☎06 689 34 26). West of P. Navona. Take V. Pasquino (V. Governo Vecchio) from the southwest end of P. Navona, a right on V. Parione, a left on V.d. Fossa and head for the lights. Not since Pope Julius II has there been a case of Roman megalomania as severe as that of Jonathan, whose face serves as the theme for the decor in this parallel-universe of a bar. Even Michelangelo's accomplishments pale before the loo, the **finest bathroom** in Rome, nay, Italy. Jonathan himself holds court in the right bar, while his son and successor, Jonathan II, spins underground techno on the left. Medium beer on tap €5; delicious cocktails/long drinks €8. Mercifully free of pub-crawlers. Open M-F 5pm-2am, Sa and Su 3pm-2am.

Abbey Theatre, V.d. Governo Vecchio, 51-53 (☎06 686 13 41). One of the only establishments in Rome where you can drop in for a mid-morning Guinness (€5). Stay for lunch (a lot of vaguely Irish dishes, such as beef in Guinness, €6.50), watch MTV, and admire the rather touching painting of a drugged-out-looking Yeats. Before you know it, it'll be time for Happy Hour (M-F 3:30-8pm). Should you have the staying power, dinner's also available. 40min. Internet access and one drink €5. Open daily 11am-3am. AmEx/MC/V.

ELSEWHERE IN CENTRO STORICO

Trinity College, V.d. Collegio Romano, 6 (☎06 678 64 72; www.trinity-rome.com). Off V.d. Corso near P. Venezia. Yet another Irish pub, yet more pub-crawlers. Offers degrees in such diverse curricula as Guinness, Harp, and Heineken. Tuition at €5 per beer. Pub food served for lunch and dinner (double burger, €10). Happy Hour noon-8pm. Classes held every day 11am-3am. AmEx/MC/V.

Night and Day, V.d. Oca, 50 (☎06 320 23 00). Off V. di Ripetta near P. del Popolo. Don't even think of coming until the rest of the bars close. At 2am, Italians who don't let dawn stop their fun stream in. Buy a membership card (€5) for discounts on drinks. Beer €3-5, Guinness €4.50. Happy hour until midnight. Open Tu-Su 7pm-6am. Closed part of Aug.

Bartaruga, P. Mattei, 7/8 (☎06 689 22 99), in the Jewish Ghetto. Named after the tortoise-shaped fountain in the *piazza,* Bartaruga provides a refreshing smidgen of northern Italian campery. The setting is surreal: a myriad of Murano glass, light blue and pink sofas, and tassled drapery. On weekends it overflows with Italian men in tight clothes. Wide variety of cocktails available; beer €5. Open M-Sa 3pm-2am, Su 3-10pm. Closed part of Aug.

Rock Castle Café, V.B. Cenci, 8 (☎06 688 079 99). In the old days, people would wish that there were a disco-pub with a frat-house atmosphere in the Jewish Ghetto. And they would wish that they could find Red Dog somewhere in the Eternal City. With the advent of the Rock Castle Café there's nothing left to wish for. Resist the urge to drink Budweiser; the Guiness (€4.50) is much better for you. Popular in winter with study abroad students (who receive a 10% discount). DJs and specials every night; Tu cocktails €4 and W 9-10pm all you can drink Beck's €5. Live music Sept.-June M night. Open daily 9pm-3am.

Victoria House, V. di Gesù e Maria, 18 (☎06 320 16 98). Near P. del Popolo; look for the large Union Jack. If this place were any more British, you'd be in London. Pretty much everything inside was shipped from Sheffield. Shepherd and steak pies and fish & chips (€8) served with several kinds of beer. Smashing. Happy Hour daily 6-9pm. Pints €4.50. Open Tu-Th 5pm-12:30am, F-Sa 5pm-1:30am, Su 5pm-12:30am.

The Nag's Head, V. IV Novembre, 138b (☎06 679 46 20). Off P. Venezia. Pier, the bartender, who is straight out of *Cocktail* (and advertises himself as a master of *"flair estremo"*), makes this place worth a visit. After the bottle-twirling and other excesses, you almost don't mind the €0.50 he tacks on to your bill as a "tip." Dance floor inside; live music twice a week. Beer €3-5; cocktails €8. Cover (imposed by slick bouncers with gratuitous ear pieces) €5; F and Sa men €7.75; *gratis* Su. Open daily in summer 8pm-2am; winter noon-2am. MC/V.

BORGO, PRATI & VATICAN CITY

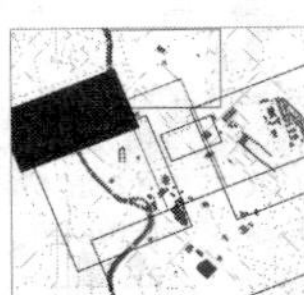
see map p. 364

The area around the Vatican is largely residential and full of clergy, making for quiet nights. After-hours bars still abound, however. Well, at least there isn't a lack of confessionals for your post-hangover crises of conscience.

Nuvolari, V. degli Ombrellari, 10 (☎06 688 030 18). Off Borgo Vittorio. This cocktail bar also functions as an *enoteca* with wine by the glass (€3.50), a diverse wine list that changes weekly, and the usual salads (choose from 30, €6 each). Meat and cheese platters €7.50. Homemade deserts €3.50. In winter, free buffet until 8:30pm. Kitchen closes M-Th 12:30am, F-Sa 1:30am. Open M-Sa 8pm-2am.

The Proud Lion Pub, Borgo Pio, 36 (☎06 683 28 41). The outside of the pub says "Rome, Borgo Pio," but the beer and scotch says "I don't forget my Highland roots." Affiliated with the Italian Dart Club; call and ask about upcoming tournaments. 11 beers on tap, over 30 different bottled varieties available. Beer and cocktails €4; single malts €4.50-5. W and Sa Happy Hour all night. Open M-Sa 8:30pm-2am.

Su & Giú, Via Tacito, 42 (☎06 320 03 29). Three blocks north of P. Cavour. If you're tired of ordinary bars passing themselves off as *enotecas*, you might find Su & Giú a pleasant change. This stylish and tranquil family-run *enoteca* has a comprehensive offering of wines by the bottle (€10 and up) and by the glass (€3 and up). Also serves light meals (primi €5-8). Open daily noon-3pm and 9pm-2am.

Morrison's, V. E.Q. Visconti, 88 (☎06 322 22 65). Two blocks north of P. Cavour. Harp, Kilkenny, and Guinness on tap, and an excellent selection of Irish and Scotch whiskey and bourbon. Wall slogans celebrate being one pint from the floor. For those in the literary know, the James Joyce (blue curacao and Harp) is a must. Pint of Guinness €5; cocktails €6.50. Open daily 6:30pm-2am. AmEx/MC/V.

TRASTEVERE

see map p. 358-359

Follow the crowds wandering the narrow streets: you're bound to find something. Still, since wandering time is just wasted drinking time, make a beeline for one of the following:

Artu Cafe, Largo Fumasoni Biondi, 5 (☎06 588 03 98). In P. San Egidio, directly behind Santa Maria in Trastevere. A small, dark wood bar bathed in colored light, Artu offers a random melange of people on their way to dinner or fresh from partying in Trastevere. Good selection of drinks (beer €4.50; wine €3-5.50 per glass; specialty cocktails €6.20-7.20). Free *apertivi* buffet 6:45-9pm. Open Tu-Su 6pm-2am. MC/V.

Enoteca Trastevere, V.d. Lungaretta, 86 (☎06 588 56 59). Off P.S. Maria in Trastevere. The name says it all. A fine wine bar offering dozens of wines by the glass (€2.60-9.50). Large list of beers (€4.50), cocktails and fine spirits (€6-7.70). Open daily 5pm-2am. Closed 1wk. in mid-Aug.

Ombre Rosse Caffè, P. S. Egidio, 12 (☎06 588 41 55; www.ombrerosse.com). A mellow place to sit outside and people watch. Wine by the glass €4-5.50, cocktails €6, pint of beer €4.50-5.50. Huge selection of grappas and spirits (from €4.50). Live jazz/blues Oct.-Mar., Su 7pm, Th 10pm. Open daily 7:30am-2am. Closed second week of August. AmEx/MC/V.

Antilia, V. della Scala, 1 (☎6 583 357 88). Just north of P. S. Egidio. Drinks flow freely for a young crowd of tourists and students from nearby John Cabot University swilling an extensive range of bottled beers (€3-5). Cocktails €6, wine by the glass €3-10. The house snack is *piadine* (pita bread sandwiches €5-8). Live music every night, Oct.-Mar. 10:30pm. Open daily 6pm-2am. Closed mid-August. MC/V.

La Scala, P. della Scala, 60 (☎06 5803763). On the left on V.d. Scala behind Santa Maria in Trastevere. The food in the restaurant is good (appetizers from €2.50), but the locals come there for the bar, which they sometimes turn into a *discoteca*. Live music (i.e. an electric keyboardist and singer) Tu 9:30pm; live DJ spins a large variety of music W-Su. Burgundy lounges and bar stools are put to shame by the best seat in the house—the infamous *mezza maquina* (half car) booth. Serves dinner until 1am. Cocktails at the bar from €6.20 (€0.50 extra for table-seating). Open Tu-Su noon-2am, M 6:30pm-2am. AmEx/DC/MC/V.

TERMINI & SAN LORENZO

Termini might have been the convenient *zona* to find a place to sleep, but it's not the best area to take in a lively night-cap. If you're in the mood for several night-caps, however, the following pubs make for a reasonably short stumble home.

see map p. 360-361

Friend's, V. Piave, 71 (☎06 420 142 85). From Piazza Independenza take V. Goito, then cross V. XX Settembre onto Via Piave. Plenty of outdoor seating and intriguing stainless steel interior. Chill music and all manner of cocktails (€5.50 bar/€6.50 table) including tropical and frozen varieties. Beer €4-4.50. Premium spirits €7.50-8.50. Breakfast until 12:30pm, lunch until 3:30pm, tea snacks until 7pm, light food for drinking until midnight. Free plate with drink during Happy Hour 7-9:30pm. Open M-Sa 7:30am-2am, Su 6pm-2am. Another location in Piazza Trilussa, 34 (☎06 581 61 11) with full dinner and free Internet access. AmEx/V/MC.

Julius Caesar, V. Castelfidardo, 49 (☎347 590 15 05; www.juliuscaesarpub.com). Just north of Termini near P. dell'Indipendenza, on the corner of V. Solferino. Come here for live music, cheap drinks, and good times with fellow travelers. Upstairs features beer on tap (€4.50-5.50), cheeky Roman busts, and even cheekier Roman babes, while the downstairs is filled with blaring live music most nights (10:30-11:30pm). Happy Hour half-price until 6:30pm; in summer, pints of Heineken €3. Cocktails €7; wine €3.50 per glass. Residents at local hostels receive a 20% discount. Open daily 4:30pm-3am.

Druid's Rock, P. dell'Esquilino, 1A (☎06 474 13 26; www.druidspubrome.com). Opposite the back end of S. Maria Maggiore, on the northeast corner of P. dell'Esquilino. A pool table and ample televisions for viewing sports events draw Italians and tourists alike. F-Sa live music from 10pm. Happy Hour 10am-9pm. Beer €5 per pint, €7.50 per liter. Cocktails €6. Open daily 10am-2am. MC/V.

SAN LORENZO

The vibrant university district, San Lorenzo, is home to one of the most energetic (and least expensive) pub and bar scenes in Rome: one night here and you'll wish you discovered it sooner. Tourists rarely venture into San Lorenzo, making it all the more tempting as a slice of genuine Roman youth nightlife. San Lorenzo is a 10min. walk from Termini and from P. Repubblica, through which night buses run every 30min. for your ride home.

Il Simposio, V.d. Latini, 11 (☎0328 907 785 51). Off V. Tiburtina. Ah, the sweet smell of turpentine. The symposium's walls are cluttered with the Jackson Pollock-esque works of local artists, and chances are good that on any given night a splattered painter will be

Bar de Benito

Abbey Theater

Johnny's Angels

hard at work beautifying a discarded refrigerator. With cocktails from €3.50 and a glass of *fragolino* for €2.75, even starving artists can afford the place. Membership card required, €3 per month, €6 per year. Open daily 9pm-2am. Closed July-Aug.

Pub Hallo'Ween, P. Tiburtino, 31 (☎06 444 07 05), at the corner of V. di Porta Labicana and Ple. Tiburtina. Abandon all hope of not having fun, all ye who enter here. The plastic skulls and fake spiders and spiderwebs confirm your suspicions: this is indeed a gateway to the darkest pits of Hell. Draft beer €3.70-4.20, bottles €3.70. Cocktails €4.20-5.20. Enjoy sandwiches (€2.70-5.20) such as the Freddy (salami and mozzarella €3.70) or the Candyman (nutella €2.60). Open daily 8:30pm-2:30am. Closed Aug.

Lancelot, V.d. Volsci, 77a (☎06 445 46 75). Near the intersection of V. Volsci and V. dei Etruschi. An intimate, albeit smoky, underground labyrinth with painted castle walls and red leather benches. Huge selection of board games: test your language skills with Italian Trivial Pursuits, or let the artist in you shine in a round of Pictionary. Filled with thirsty scholars swilling €3 bottles of beer and eating €2 panini. Salads €3-5. Cocktails €4. During the winter there can be a wait to get in. Open daily 8:30pm-2am.

Legend Pub, V.d. Latini, 25 (☎06 446 38 81). Off V.d. Volsci. Gleefully rowdy crowds of soccer fans gather here to enjoy cheap beer (€4), appetizers (€2), pizza (€5.50) and the house specialty, fat and juicy steaks with fries (€10). The occasional bucket of water is thrown by neighbors unhappy with the loud masses gathered under their windows in the ample outdoor seating area. Open Tu-Su 4pm-3:30am. Closed Aug. AmEx/MC/V.

Ferrazza, V. dei Volsci 59 (☎06 490 506; enotecaferrazza@libero.it). At the intersection of V. dei Volsci and V. dei Latini. So you fancy yourself as a native San-Lorenzian, huh? Just like the dilettante residents, this ultra-popular bar is smart, elegant and trendy, while still retaining reasonable prices. Wine by the glass, €2.50-5. Beer, €4. Cocktails, €3.90-5. Open M-Sa 9am-3:30pm and 5pm-2am.

360°, V.d. Equi, 57. (☎06 590 22 37). Off V.d. Sabelli. Live music, every night, is this place's big draw. Shows start after 11pm. In the morning, music and painting lessons are given and in the afternoon a music school hosts jam sessions. Weekends offer the most mainstream music sessions, although the school's experimental performances during the week attract decent crowds of music lovers. Beer €3, cocktails €4.50. Happy hour 9-11pm. Open 9pm-5am. Closed late July-Aug.

Rivegauche2, V.d. Sabelli, 43 (☎06 445 67 22). One of the best Irish pubs in Rome, Rivegauche2 maintains a degree of chumminess despite being arena-like in comparison to other tiny San Lorenzo bars. The Guinness-themed interior gives way to a wonderful selection of Irish beers (properly poured; €4.65) and a long list of spirits from the UK, including some of the best single-malt scotches (€4-€20). Happy hour until 9pm (€1 off). Open M-Sa 7pm-2am, Su 6pm-2am. MC/V.

Drome, V.d. Latini, 49-51 (☎06 446 14 92). Just off V. dei Sabelli. A small cocktail bar/lounge with orange chairs straight off the set of The Jetsons and live jazz during non-summer months. An assortment of Middle Eastern foods nicely compliment all sorts of Italian liquors. Internet €3.20 per hr. Open M-Sa 8pm-3am. Closed July-Aug.

Pigmalione, V. di Porta Labicana, 29 (☎06 445 77 40). Off V.d. Sabelli. Mellow rock and blues play under the watchful gaze of a massive Aztec calendar painted on the wall. An eclectic mix of Indian, Egyptian, and astrological decor. More conducive to long, intimate conversations than its Irish counterparts, in addition to being better lit and less smoky. Beer and cocktails €4. Shots €1.70. Salads and panini €3.50-4. Open daily 7pm-2am. Closed Aug.

Dalhu' Pub, V.d. Equi, 38-40 (☎06 445 73 69). Off V. Rutoli. Quiet, small Irish pub attracts a somewhat older crowd. Beers from €3.50; cocktails from €5. Open 8:30pm-2am. Closed late July-Aug.

TESTACCIO & OSTIENSE

Testaccio and Ostiense are nightlife-central. Bus #20N heads up V. Ostiense, stopping by the Pyramid of Gaius Cestius every 30min. Alternatively take the Metro B Line to Piramide.

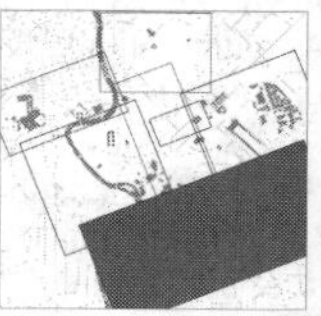

see map p. 366

Shanti, Via dei Conciatori, 11. (☎06 330 465 662). From M: Piramide, head down V. Ostiense; take second street on the right. Yes, that really is incense beckoning you into this chilled, two-floored North African haven. And yes, these surely are some of the best cocktails (€6-7) to be had in Rome. Great Hookahs (€2.60 per person). Belly dancing, 11pm-1am, W, Th, F, Sep-Mar. Open daily 9pm-1am. Closed on Su in July, all of Aug.

Ketumbar, V. Galvani, 24 (☎06 573 053 38). Do you miss SoHo? Are you willing to pay €10 for a cocktail and €5 for a Coke in the original glass bot-

the BIG $plurge

Bar del Fico, P. del Fico, 26-28 (☎06 686 52 05). Off V.d. Governo Vecchio. A place to see and be seen with Romans, Fico is almost always mobbed with locals at night. Lounge under the heated, ivy-covered awning or have your drink inside in one of the three oh-so-chic sitting rooms. Wide range of drinks, but pricey: 0.5L beer €6.20. Open daily 8am-2am.

Bar della Pace, V.d. Pace, 4-5-7 (☎06 686 12 16). Off V.d. Governo Vecchio. Its proper name is Antico Caffe della Pace, but you won't hear it called that very often. One of *the* places to be for celebrity-watching in the Eternal City by night, this locale is upscale and knows it. Sit outside or in one of the two gorgeous rooms, which are tastefully appointed with wood furniture and cushy armchairs. The waitresses seem to have been picked out of a beauty contest, and you know why. Prices are out of sight, but that's why you're here. Open daily 9am-2am.

tle? Here's a taste of New York decadence in the middle of Italy. It even doubles as an a pricey Japanese restaurant. Wear black and look pretentious; everyone else will. Open M-Sa 8pm-3am. Closed Aug. AmEx/MC/V.

Mount Gay Music Bar, V. Galvani, 54 (☎06 574 60 13). Grab a pillow on the floor and sip your cocktail (€8) alongside Rome's young and beautiful. Two cave-like rooms are filled with attractive Italians and the sounds of two turntables above. A cool catacomb-styled room for dancing, in winter and spring, lies below. Open Tu-Su 11pm-dawn. MC/V.

Four XXXX Pub, V. Galvani, 29 (☎06 575 72 96; www.fourxxxxpub.it). From Piramide, turn left at the pyramid on to V. Marmorata, then left on V. Galvani. This themed Australian-cum-South-American bar serves up its namesake beer, a light Australian lager (€5) and many others. Live jazzzz, bluessss, and soullll on the lower level in winter F-Sa 9:30pm. Local and Latin American food. Burgers €5, Tex-Mex pizza €8. consumed in crowded tiki huts on the first floor. Open M-F 12:30-3:30pm; daily 7:30pm-2am. AmEx/D/MC/V.

CLUBS

CENTRO STORICO

see map p. 358-359

Groove, V. Savelli, 10 (☎06 687 24 27). Head down V.d. Governo Vecchio from P. Pasquino and take the 2nd left. Look for the black door. Lose it to acid jazz, funk, soul, and disco. F and Sa 1-drink minimum (€5.16). Open W-Su 10pm-2am. Closed most of Aug.

TERMINI & SAN LORENZO

see map p. 360-361

NORTH OF TERMINI(SALARIO)

Alien, V. Velletri, 13-19 (☎06 841 22 12; www.aliendisco.it). One of the biggest discos in Rome attracts a well-dressed crowd and plays the house you know and love. As of this writing, the comfy chill-out room had not yet reached 1987. Cover varies (about €15, including a drink). Occasional theme nights. Open Tu-Su 11pm-5:30am. In summer, moves to Fregene.

Piper, V. Tagliamento, 9 (☎06 841 44 59; www.piperclub.it). From V. XX Settembre, take V. Piave (V. Salaria). Take a right on V. Po (V. Tagliamento). Alternatively, take bus #319 from Termini to Tagliamento. A popular club that occasionally hosts gay nights. 70s, rock, disco, as well as the standard house and underground. Very gay friendly all the time. Teenaged crowd on some afternoons. Cover €10-18 (includes a drink). Open F-Sa 11pm-4:30am; in summer Sa and Su 11pm-4:30am.

Black Out, V. Saturnia, 18 (☎06 704 967 91; www.blackoutclub.com). From the Colosseum, take V. Claudia (V.d. Navicella/V. Gallia) southeast; turn right on V. Saturnia. Punk and Britpop. Occasional bands. Cover €8 (includes 1 drink). Open Th-Su 11pm-4am. Closed mid-Jun to Aug.

SAN LORENZO

Il Giardini di Adone, V.d. Reti, 38a (☎06 445 43 82). Off V.d. Sabelli. Though it fancies itself a "spaghetti pub," the happy students who frequent this little place would remind you that tables are properly used for dancing, not for eating linguini. Cover €6 (includes a drink). Open Tu-Su 8pm-3am.Closed late July-Aug.

TESTACCIO

Welcome to the Carnival. A weekend night of drinking at Trastevere bars is logically followed with a trip across the river to the V. Monte di Testaccio area, the club kid's playground. Clubs here cater to goths, gays, plain' ol party-goers, and lots of scantily clad girls. Most *locali* in Testaccio are open-air or subterranean tunnels built into the side of an ancient Roman trash dump (note the pottery shards lining some interiors) and so can withstand the heat that closes down other nightspots. In June clubs sprout up in parking lots as part of **Testaccio Village,** an outdoor music and dancing extravaganza. The clubs on V. di Monte Testaccio have only meat-packers and car repair shops as neighbors, so let's get loud. We won't be waking anyone up.

see map p. 366

Charro Cafe, V. di Monte Testaccio, 73 (☎06 578 30 64). So you wanted Tijuana, but ended up in Rome. Weep no more, *mis amigos.* Make a run for Charro, home of the €2.60 tequila bum bum. Italians guzzling beer (€5) and strong Mexican-themed drinks (€6) dance themselves silly to pop and house. In summer no cover; in winter, entrance €5, with drink €11. Restaurant open M-Sa 8:30pm-midnight; club midnight-3am. Closed in Aug.

Coming Out Pub, V.S. Giovanni in Laterano, 8 (☎06 700 98 71). Right behind the Colosseum, next to the gladiator school. Great BGLTQ hang-out. In winter, pub hosts live music Th, games Tu, and karaoke W. Enjoy a bite to eat (€5-7) before having a satisfying cocktails (€5.50). Open daily 5pm-5am. Cash only.

Aquarela, V. di Monte Testaccio, 64 (☎06 575 90 58). You want pottery shards? You got pottery shards. A fine example of urban renewal, Roman-style. Built out of trash, then used for years as a vegetable market, the club has two underground tunnels that remain cool even when the party's hot. Entrance (€10) includes a drink. Open Tu-Su 8:30pm-4am.

Radio Londra Caffè, V. di Monte Testaccio, 65b (☎06 575 00 44). Italian bands covering rock classics badly. Packed with an energetic, good-looking, young crowd. Jam sessions M. Pint of beer €4-5. Pizza, *panini,* and hamburgers (€4.20-5.20). 1 yr. membership €8 (includes one free drink) required. Open M-Sa 9pm-3am.

Chic and Kitsch, V.S. Saba 11a (☎06 578 20 22). Uniting the elegant with the eclectic; music (often House or a variant) is selected by resident DJ Giuliano Marchili. Cover: men €13, women €10 (includes a drink). Open W-Su 11:30pm-4am. Closed Aug.

Classico Village, V. Libetta, 3 (☎06 375 185 51). M: B-Garbatella. Exit onto V. Argonauti and take a left on V. Libetta. One of the best-known *centri sociali* in Rome—your one-stop shop for all things countercultural. Hosts live music, films, art exhibits, poetry readings, African cuisine tastings, and more. Open daily, hours and cover vary (€8-10).

Jungle, V. di Monte Testaccio, 95. Small, smoky disco bar full of Italian Goths (on Sa) clad in black leather dancing to the Cure and Italian pop. Extravagant, if somewhat disorienting light effects. Cover €5-8. Free before 11pm. Beer €5. Cocktails €7.75. Open F-Sa 11pm-5am.

L'Alibi, V. di Monte Testaccio, 40/44 (☎06 574 34 48 or 338 450 04 92). Traditionally a gay club, L'Alibi now draws a mixed crowd. Its two floors host drag queen shows and hip DJ's alike. The roof garden, decorated with leopard prints, plays chill music and serves cocktails (€8). Cover F & Sa only €13-15. Open W-Su midnight-5am.

Coyote, V. di Monte Testaccio, 48b (www.coyotebar.it). The newly-opened club sports a Tex-Mex look and caters to the homesick American tourist. Hosts Italian DJ's. Its spacious terrace is a welcome escape from the revelry inside. No cover. Open daily 9pm-4am.

INSIDE

theater & cinema **221**
live music & dance **224**
classical music & opera **224** summer events **225**
jazz **226** rock & pop **227** dance **228**
spectator sports **228**

Entertainment

Roman entertainment just isn't what it used to be. Back in the day, you could swing by the Colosseum to watch a man viciously clawed to death by a bear. Now, Romans seeking diversion are far more likely to go to the opera, a soccer game, or the latest Hollywood flick. Is this progress? Perhaps. But this is no reason for you, bloodthirsty traveler, to content your restless heart with eating *gelato* next to a monument or people-watching in a *piazza*. Rome is full of more entertaining entertainment options.

Roma C'è, Time Out, and **TrovaRoma** contain lists of events and venues (see p. 26), and *Roma C'è* includes a section in English detailing goings-on of special interest to English speakers. Check out the *Roma C'è* web site at www.romace.it. Tourist offices (p. 25) also have lots of information on cultural activities—ask for *Un'Ospite a Roma*. Of course, the city's walls are plastered with advertisements for upcoming concerts, plays, operas, parties, and circuses.

THEATER & CINEMA

Contrary to popular belief, Roman theater predates the moment that Nathan Lane first donned a toga in *A Funny Thing Happened on the Way to the Forum.* Current shows are mostly toga-less, thankfully, and Rome is host to a number of quality productions.

Stardust

Roman Forum

Festa de l'Unite

Shows range from mainstream musicals to black box experimental theater and are mostly in Italian. In summer, most theaters close, but the city-wide **Estate Romana** festival features numerous performances in open-air theaters. Ancient Greek and Roman plays are performed in Italian at the ancient theater in Ostia. The city's two major festivals add to the repertoire considerably with international productions: **Festival Roma-Europa** in summer and early fall; and **Festival d'Autunno** in fall. Check newspapers for listings. For information on plays and musicals in English, check tourist offices or the English section of *Roma C'è.* The following are other web sites to consult:

www.musicali.it, The best place to check up on upcoming music concerts throughout Italy and recent headlines on your favorite Italian singers. Listings vary from boy bands like Luna Pop to classic crooners like Paolo Conte.

www.romaturismo.it, Your one-stop English link to Roman events, exhibitions and music venues. Check out "Happenings in Rome" for city festivals. Most listings include comprehensive information on dates, locations, phone numbers, and descriptions of the kinds of dance, film and food offered. Roma turismo also goes the extra mile to list photography exhibits, literature readings and fitness activities. (Site also in Italian).

www.comune.roma.it, English version provides general information on how to contact centers such as the Cinema office of Rome or The House of Literature, as well as other useful tourist tips. Calendar of Events in Italian.

THEATER

Teatro Argentina, Largo di Torre Argentina, 52 (☎06 688 04 601 or 06 687 54 45). Bus #64 from Termini or Tram #8. Considered to be the most important theater in Rome and home to the Teatro di Roma company, Argentina hosts plays (in Italian), concerts, and ballets. Built in the 18th century, today Teatro Argentina is also the head of many drama/music festivals taking place throughout the year. Call for specific information. Box office open M-F 10am-2pm and 3-7pm, Sa 10am-2pm. Tickets €10-26 (students €10-21). AmEx/D/MC/V.

Teatro Colosseo, V. Capo d'Africa, 5 (☎06 700 49 32). M: B-Colosseo. Walk away from the station with the Colosseum to your right for 1 block. Turn right and walk 2 blocks through P. Colosseo, then turn left onto V. Capo d'Africa. Offers a selection of alternative plays (Italian or translated into Italian) but also has an English theater night, featuring new works from American and British playwrights. Box office open Tu-Sa 6-9:30pm. Tickets €10-20, students €7.75. Closed in summer.

Teatro Ghione, V.d. Fornaci, 37 (☎/fax 06 637 22 94; www.ghione.it). South of P. S. Pietro. Ghione has been putting on 10 plays a year (between Sept.-May), in addition to an extensive annual musical program, for twenty years. For further information, see p. 224.

Teatro Nazionale, V.d. Viminale, 51 (☎06 478 251 40). M: A-Repubblica. From P. della Repubblica, walk 1 block toward Termini and right on V.d. Viminale. Bus #64 also services the theater. Mostly original Italian plays; some translations of international works. Box office open daily 9am-5pm. Tickets €16.75-25.80. AmEx/D/MC/V. Closed in summer.

Teatro Sistina, V. Sistina, 129 (☎06 420 07 11; www.ilsistina.com). M: A-Barberini. Turn right on V. Sistina from P. Barberini. One of the biggest mainstream theaters. Recent productions: *Can-Can, Rugantino, L'Anatra all'Arancia,* exclusive engagement of *Sister Act* (in English), and The Who's *Tommy* (in Italian). Box office open daily 10am-1pm and 3:30-7pm. Tickets starting around €17. AmEx/D/MC/V.

Teatro Valle, V.d. Teatro Valle, 23a (☎06 688 037 94; www.teatrovalle.it), near C.V. Emanuele II, southeast of P. Navona. An excellent variety of shows. Box office open Tu-Sa 10am-7pm, Su 10am-1pm. Tickets €16-29, under 26 and over 65 €11-20. Closed June-Aug.

Teatro dell'Arte Studio, V. Urbana, 107 (☎06 488 56 08 for tickets), hosts the Ford Entertainment English Theatre of Rome, F nights until June. Full length play at 8pm followed by 10min. sketches at 10pm. Also sponsors the **Summer English Theatre Festival.** Contact Ford Entertainment for additional information (☎06 444 13 75; www.porticus.com/offnight).

CINEMA

Italy, much to the horror of foreign cinema-goers, insists on dubbing all the film and video it imports. Unless you know Italian well and get a kick out of hearing a very squeaky-sounding Woody Allen speak it, this idiosyncrasy poses a definite obstacle to your Roman cinematic enjoyment. Undubbed English-language films are hard to find, especially recent releases. However, an increasing number of cinemas in central tourist locations are beginning to realize that travellers like to see films too. These theaters are slowly beginning to offer one Hollywood film in English. A few valorous Cineclubs show foreign films, old classics, and an assortment of favorites in the original language. Check newspapers or *Roma C'è* for listings. A v.o. or l.o. in any listing means *versione originale* or *lingua originale* (i.e. not dubbed, usually with Italian subtitles). All first-run theaters offer lower priced tickets for the first two screenings of the day from Monday to Friday (around 4:30 and 6:30pm), as well as all day Wednesday.

Though popular Italian film of late has tended toward the banal, it's definitely worth checking out, particularly Nanni Moretti's thoughtful and humorous work. The antics of Roberto Benigni are amusing even without understanding dialogue.

Il Pasquino, P. Sant'Egidio, 10 (☎06 580 36 22), off P.S. Maria in Trastevere. Take tram #8 from Largo Argentina to the first stop across the river. Go right on V. della Lungaretta to P.S. Maria in Trastevere. Rome's biggest English-language movie theater with 3 different screens showing English films. Program changes daily, so call for the schedule or stop by and pick one up. Tickets €6.20, matinee €7.23. Look for the Roma International Film Festival during the summer in *Roma C'è* or *Roma Estate*.

Warner Village Moderno, P. della Repubblica 43/45 (☎06 477 791 91; www.warnervillage.it). Well-touristed location. For those who want to watch their movies while munching on "pic 'n mix". One recent (by Italian standards) Hollywood blockbuster (in English) each week. Tickets €7.30, matinee and under 12 €5.50.

Nuovo Sacher, Largo Ascianghi, 1 (☎06 581 81 16). Take V. Induno from V.d. Trastevere. This is the famed Italian director Nanni Moretti's theater and shows a host of Indy films. M and Tu films in the original language. Tickets €7, matinee and W € 4.50.

the local story

La Giovane

Giulia Rapponi, 23, tour guide at Santa Trinita dei Monti and film student, provides a first-hand glimpse of what it's like to be young and Roman.

Q: What's it like for young people your age when they leave their universities? Do they live with their parents?

A: Yes. They don't want to spend money on the rent. The state helps people who have to leave home to attend school pay for board, but many of my friends still live with their parents.

Q: When do most people finally leave home?

A: Late, when they find a job. My uncle left when he was 33, but this was old even by European standards.

Q: How does this affect romantic relationships?

A: It's different. The Italian family always gets in the middle. The mother always wants to meet your boyfriend or girlfriend.

Q: Do Romans diet?

A: Yes, but men more than women. They do their eyebrows, and they go to tanning salons and hair removal places. The men wear tight shirts that show you the muscle and tight pants that show you the...well, you know. They

(continued on next page)

Giulio Cesare, V.G. Cesare, 259 (☎06 397 207 95). M: A-Ottaviano. M films in the original language. Tickets €7.25; matinee and W €4.25.

Greenwich, V.G. Bodoni, 59 (☎06 574 58 25). In Testaccio. Bus lines #75, 673, and 719. Films in the original language with Italian subtitles. Tickets €7, matinee and W €4.50.

Alcazar, V. Cardinal Merry del Val, 14 (☎06 588 00 99), in Trastevere. Take tram #8 from Largo Argentina to the second stop across the river. M films in the original language. Tickets €7, matinee and W €4.50.

LIVE MUSIC & DANCE

CLASSICAL MUSIC & OPERA

The stage of the Baths of Caracalla (see p. 85) used to host summertime opera performances, but this lively tradition was halted once it was discovered that performers' voices, or "screeching," as the brochure kindly puts it, were literally bringing the ancient house down. The live elephants that were brought on stage for productions of *Aïda* also did little to fortify the structure. There are still smaller classical music concerts that sporadically pop up in the crazy emperor's baths.

There are many opportunities to see strong musical performances in Rome. *Telecom Italia* hosts a classical music series at the **Teatro dell'Opera** (see p. 225). At 9am on concert days, unsold tickets are given out for free at the box office. Be prepared to get in line early; tickets go on a first-come, first-serve basis. Local churches often host free or inexpensive concerts—check newspapers, tourist offices, and church bulletin boards for details. Finally, and perhaps most interestingly, the *carabinieri* frequently give rousing concerts of various Italian composers in P. di San Ignazio and other outdoor forums free of charge. Other venues occasionally offer special discounts, so keep your eyes peeled.

PRINCIPAL VENUES

Accademia Nazionale di Santa Cecilia, V. Vittoria, 6 (☎06 361 10 64 or toll-free 800 90 70 80; www.santacecilia.it). Off V. del Corso. This conservatory, named for the martyred patron saint of music, was founded by Palestrina in the 16th century and is home to Rome's official symphony orchestra. Orchestra and chamber concerts are held at the **Parco della Musicain,** V. Pietro di Coubertin, 30, near P. del Popolo. Regular season runs Oct.-June, covering the classics, occasional special presentations, such as piano-playing jazz god Keith Jarrett and Jimi Hendrix played by a string quartet. From late-June to late-July, the company moves outdoors to the *nymphaeum* in Villa Giulia.

Teatro Ghione, V.d. Fornaci, 37 (☎06 637 22 94; www.ghione.it), near the Vatican. This red velvet theater hosts Euromusica's classical concerts and other big-name musical guests. Season Oct.-Apr. Box office open daily 10am-1pm and 4-8pm. English-speaking staff. Tickets €9-21. Call for info on morning concerts, with discounts. MC/V.

Teatro Olimpico, P. Gentile da Fabriano, 17 (☎ 06 360 051 84; www.teatroolimpico.it). The *piazza* is intersected by Lungo Tevere Flaminio along the river, north of the Vatican. Bus #910 or Metro A: Flaminio and bus #225. This newer auditorium with good acoustics is home to many different classical music, theater, and dance events. Season runs Oct.-May. Box office open M-F 10am-1pm and 2-5:30pm. Ticket prices vary. MC/V.

Teatro dell'Opera di Roma, V. Firenze, 72 (☎06 481 602 87 or 06 481 7517; www.opera.roma.it). Take V. Viminale from P.d. Cinquecento, in front of Termini, to P.B. Gigli. The theater also runs seasonal concerts at Stadio di Olimpico and the Baths of Caracalla (primarily in the summer). Look out for occasional performances during the year at the Teatro Valle, the Teatro Manzoni, and the Loggia della Villa Medici. Box office open Tu-Sa 9am-5pm, Su 9am-1:30pm, plus days of performances from 9am-5pm and 1hr. before the starting time until 15min. after. Tickets €8-21. Substantial student discounts available. AmEx/MC/V.

Parco della Musica, V. Pietro di Coubertin (☎06 808 20 58; tickets, toll-free 800 90 70 80; www.musicaperroma.it), off V. Flaminia. Tram #2. Rome's long-awaited auditorium is finally open. A variety of musical concerts are held in the new arena, including performances by the Accademia Nazionale di Santa Cecilia. The music conservatory jointly operates the new auditorium. Box office open M-F 11am-6pm. Tickets €15-40. AmEx/MC/V.

SUMMER EVENTS

The classical scene in Rome goes wild in the summer. The smaller festivals that run from mid-May to August are part of the larger **Roma Estate festival**, a city-wide cultural binge that encompasses a wide variety of artistic genres (www.romaestate.com). Highlights include the

the local story

spend a fortune on their clothing. €250 for shoes.

Q: How do they get the money?

A: They spend all the money they have. They can afford it because they live with their parents, where you have your mother to cook and clean for you. Why would you cook and clean if you can stay at home and relax and do things for your pleasure?

Q: Do you think this is right?

A: No, but that's the way it is.

Q: How do young people meet?

A: First in school, and then in university. Not so much in the clubs, because you go there to be with friends you already have, not to meet new people. Men mostly go to find women.

Q: Do you have any advice for college students looking to move to Rome and meet people?

A: There are the social centers. They used to be mainly communist, but now they are just filled with normal people, with concerts featuring artists from all around the country. They're very cheap. It used to be better, but now there is a lot of fighting outside, and people who stay there and smoke and drink too much. People who go to them should be careful. You have to be on your guard.

Festa de l'Unite

Baths of Caracalla

Stardust

Summer at the Fora, at the Markets of Trajan, Via IV Novembre, 94 (☎ 06 692 050 630), which includes theatrical and musical events from July 4 until September 28, as well as evening tours of the archeological site. Performances at 9pm, €12. Guided tours €6.50. Also visit the **Castel Sant'Angelo** from July 4 to August 10th for a evening of jesters, acrobats, musicians and wine-tasting. Performances daily, 9pm-12:30 am. (Info and bookings ☎ 06 399 676 00). Quite close to Rome is the **Spoleto Festival (Festival Dei Due Mondi)** in Umbria, held during the last week of June and first week of July. This world-renowned music and art festival celebrated its 45th anniversary in the summer of 2002. Visit the festival's Rome office at V.C. Beccaria, 18, open M-F 10am-5pm. (☎ 06 808 83 52; www.hellotickets.it.) Also popular is the **New Opera Festival di Roma** held at the Cortile della Basilica di S. Clemente in San Giovanni (☎ 06 561 15 19; www.newoperafestivaldiroma.com). The box office is open 10am-1pm and 3-7pm on the day of events and tickets range from €15-22. It all starts with the Festa Europea della Musica, a weekend of non-stop music at the end of June—most concerts are free and in fabulous locations. Imagine Michelangelo's Campidoglio in orange and purple strobe lights. For tickets to other summer events, try the **Associazione Il Tempietto,** V. in Selci, 47 (☎ 06 871 315 90; www.tempietto.it), which organizes frequent concerts in churches and at the **Notti Romane al Teatro di Marcello** in summer. Shows start at 8:30pm. Tickets €15, though some concerts held in church venues are free.

JAZZ

Rome is no New Orleans. Even so, jazz swings on within the confines of the eternally hip city. Listings are in *Roma C'è* and *Time Out;* the latter does a slightly better job with jazz, though *Roma C'è* tends to translate most of their jazz listings into English. During the summer, Alexanderplatz (see below) organizes the popular **Jazz & Image** festival in the **Villa Celimontana,** the ruin-filled park that stretches from the Colosseum to the Baths of Caracalla. For tickets, call **Orbis Agency,** P. d. Esquilino, 37 (☎ 06 482 74 03). From mid-June to mid-Aug., films about jazz are shown on an outdoor screen at 9pm. Entrance to the festival is usually €8, though the price may be hiked up significantly (to the tune of €21) for bigger names. In past years, the festival has hosted the Manhattan Transfer, Branford Marsalis, Herbie Hancock, Ray Brown, and Cedar Walton. The world-renowned **Umbria Jazz Festival** in

July takes place in Perugia, only a few hours away by train. Past performers include Joao Gilberto, B. B. King, Joe Henderson, and Sonny Rollins (☎075 573 33 63). Another alternative is the **Dolce Vita Jazz Festival** (☎800 90 70 80 for info; www.dvjazzfestival.com) at **La Palma Club,** which runs from the beginning of June to the beginning of August. Shows usually start at 10pm. Tickets €8-40; 10 concerts of your choice €100; festival card €200. AmEx/MC/V.

PRINCIPAL VENUES

The streets of Trastevere are the best romping grounds for those in search of a good jazz joint. Wander the winding streets, listening for sax riffs and vocalists doing a damn good job with mostly English lyrics, or try some of our favorites:

Alexanderplatz Jazz Club, V. Ostia, 9 (☎06 397 421 71). M: A-Ottaviano. Head left on V.G. Cesare, take 2nd right onto V. Leone IV and 1st left onto V. Ostia. Night buses to P. Venezia and Termini leave from P. Clodio. Known as one of Europe's best jazz clubs, the smoky atmosphere conveys the mythical feeling of a 40s jazz joint, while sparkling walls and a funky bar suggest a modern side. Read messages left on the walls by the greats who played here, from old pros like Art Farmer and Cedar Walton to young stars like Steve Coleman and Josh Redman. Cocktails €6.20. Required *tessera* (€6.20), good for 2 mos. Shows start 10pm. Open Sept.-June daily 9pm-2am. Moves outside in the summer to Villa Celimontana.

Big Mama, Vicolo S. Francesco a Ripa, 18 (☎06 581 25 51; www.bigmama.it). From V. di Trastevere with your back to the river, make a left on to Via S. Francesco a Ripa and then a right onto the Vicolo. Blues, blues, and more blues. A *tessera* (€12) is valid for a year and allows you into the club's many free concerts. Occasional €5.16 cover for big-name groups. Open Oct.-June daily 9pm-1:30am; sometimes closed Su and M.

Stardust, V. dei Renzi, 4 (☎06 583 208 75). Take a right off V. Lungaretta onto V.d. Moro just before P.S. Maria in Trastevere; V. dei Renzi is the 2nd street on the left. Low-key cocktail bar; great to chill and listen to live jazz (most nights, but call to confirm). When's the next time you'll to get to do it while eating crepes? Cocktails €5.50-6.50; beer €4-4.50. Su brunch noon-5pm. Open daily 5pm-2am. Cash only.

Fonclea, V. Crescenzio, 82a (☎06 689 63 02; www.fonclea.it), near P. Risorgimento. Metro A: Ottaviano or bus #492 to V. Crescenzio. Pub and restaurant with live music. In the summer, moves outside for music and movies; €6 cover for movies. Shows start at 9:30pm. Open daily 8pm-2am. MC/V.

ROCK & POP

Big-name shows (which usually play at the **Palazzo dello Sport** in EUR or at the **Foro Italico** north of Flaminio) will invariably have massive poster campaigns. If you still feel inadequately in touch with the local music scene, ticket agencies and tourist offices have information on upcoming shows. In summer, the city's pop and rock scene explodes with concerts and festivals that run late into the night. **Ticket agencies** (see p. 343) can arrange reservations and provide more information about major rock concerts. Tickets and info for many concerts are also available at the RicordiMedia (see p. 239) shops scattered throughout the city. The more popular festivals and performances include:

Cornetto Free Music Festival Roma Live (enter to win free tickets at www.cornettoalgida.it), at a number of different locations around the city, including Stadio Olimpico and Valle Giulia. Concerts by the likes of Pink Floyd, the Cure, the Backstreet Boys, Ziggy Marley, Lou Reed, and Joan Baez, among others.

Gay Village nel Testaccio Village, V. di Monte Testaccio, 16 (☎ 340 060 54 03; www.gayvillage.it). Live, mostly local music of all kinds mid-June to mid-Aug. plus other events. Tickets Su-Th €5/day, F-Sa €10/day; 7 days in a row €20. Tickets available at www.tkts.it.

Roma Incontra il Mondo, Laghetto di Villa Ada, V.d. Ponte Salario (☎06 418 03 69 or 06 582 015 64; www.villaada.it), north of Villa Borghese. A festival of world music and *"musica etnica,"* livens up the lake in Villa Ada. Performers have included the late Nusrat Fateh Ali Khan, Ruben Gonzales, and Blonde Redhead. Festival runs late June to early Aug. Concerts start at 10pm. Tickets sold at the door; €8. Cash only.

Fiesta, Ippodrome delle Capannelle, V. Appia Nuova, 1245 (☎06 712 998 55; www.fiesta.it), M: A-Colli Albani or bus #664. An extremely popular festival running all summer, featuring all things Latin American. Performers have included Cesaria Evora, Jose Feliciano, and Burning Spear. Don't know how to salsa? Don't worry, you too will be assimilated. Concerts start at 8:30pm. Attendance can swell to over 30,000 on weekends. Tickets €8. Advance tickets can be ordered (☎199 109 910) with a credit card, or can be bought in person at Orbis, Messagerie Musicali, and many other locations.

DANCE

The **Rome Opera Ballet,** affiliated with the **Teatro dell'Opera,** shares its ticket office, information line, and, sometimes, its stage. Both companies stage joint performances in the summer at P. di Siena in Villa Borghese. During the rest of the year, the company performs at the ex-Aquarium, in P. Fanti, south of Termini. (☎06 481 70 03, tickets 06 481 60 255.) A smaller venue is **Argilia Teatri,** at V.d. Argilia, 18 (☎06 638 10 58) south of the Vatican City. In summer, there is also a festival of dance, art, and culture called **RomaEuropa,** with venues throughout the city (information ☎06 474 23 19). You can also pick up a program at the **Museo Nazionale degli Strumenti Musicali,** P.S. Croce in Gerusalemme 9a, near P. Vittorio Emanuele. The museum hosts the **Invito Alla Danza** festival in July. (☎06 442 021 71; tickets ☎06 442 02 440; www.invitoalladanza.it; tickets €10-18.) The Teatro Greco Dance Company sometimes sponsors performances in P. Vittorio Emanuele II (which also hosts a massive outdoor film festival in summer). Previously listed theaters may also host dance performances; check local listings.

SPECTATOR SPORTS

While other spectator sports may exist in Rome (and the key word is "may"), the only one that matters is **calcio**—soccer. Rome has two teams in Italy's A League: **A.S. Roma** and **S.S. Lazio.** Traditionally, Lazio's fans come from the suburbs and countryside around Rome, while Roma fans are from the city itself, especially the Centro Storico, Trastevere, Testaccio, and the Jewish Ghetto. Lazio, which is literally owned by the man from Del Monte, has lately spent close to a hundred million euros on a revolving cast of expensive players. Roma relies on superstar Italian playmaker Francesco Totti, protagonist of the 2000 European national championship, and legendary Argentine striker Gabriel Batistuta.

Games at the **Stadio Olimpico,** in the Foro Italico (Metro A: Ottaviano and bus #32), are the closest modern-day equivalent to the spectacles that once delighted thousands in the Colosseum. *Tifosi*, as hardcore fans are called, show up hours before each game to drink, sing team songs, and taunt rivals. Unfortunately, the festivities sometimes turn ugly, with fans displaying offensive banners and shouting obscenities at the visiting team. For the most part, though, the celebrations are cheerful and melodious: fans wave flags to strains of the "Macarena," while Queen's "We Are the Champions" blends imperceptibly into the background of tens of thousands of fans reciting fight songs to the tune of the "Battle Hymn of the Republic." League matches are held almost every Sunday and sometimes Saturdays September to June, with European cup matches often played mid-week. The can't-miss appointments of the season are the two Roma-Lazio matches, which often prove decisive in the race for the championship. While each team has close to 50,000 season ticket holders, they also sell single-game tickets, which typically start at €15.50. Tickets can be bought at the stadium box office before games (although the tickets often run out), and also at the team's stores: **A.S. Roma Store,** P. Colonna, 360 (☎06 678 65 14; www.asromastore.it. Open daily 10am-8pm, tickets sold 10am-6:30pm. AmEx/MC/V), or V. Appia Nuova, 130 (☎06 775 906 56), or V. Cola di Rienzo 136/A (☎06 321 27 41); and **Lazio Point**, V. Farini, 34/36, near Termini. (☎06 482 66 88; www.laziopoint.superstore.it. Open M-F 9am-7pm, Sa 9am-1pm. AmEx/D/MC/V.)

Italy is also one of the hosts to the **6 Nations Cup,** Europe's premier Rugby Union tournament. Italy joined the 133-year-old competition in 2000, and the Italian Rugby Federation has decided to keep the games in Rome, although much of the fan base resides in northern Italy. Visitors will find that despite rising interest, good seats are readily available. The events take place in mid-February and early March at the Flaminio Stadium (Metro A: Flaminio. Then take the #2 tram to the V. Tiziano stop. The stadium is located near the intersection of V. Tiziano and V.M. Pilsudski). For more information visit www.6-nations-rugby.com.

The ultra-trendy **Concorso Ippico Internazionale** (International Horse Show), is held at P. di Siena in the Villa Borghese in May. Tickets (€44-180) are available at the Ufficio Biglietteria MAS S.r.l. at V. Gregorio VII, 267 (☎06 638 38 18; Open M-F 10am-1pm and 2pm-6pm.) For more information, check *Roma C'è* or contact the **Federazione Italiana Sport Equestrio,** V. Tiziano, 74 (☎06 368 584 94; www.piazzadisiena.com.)

The beginning of May also witnesses the **Italian Open Tennis Championship,** a warm-up event for the French Open that draws many of the world's top players. For more information, call the Italian Tennis Federation. (☎06 368 51 or 06 368 584 06; www.federtennis.it.)

In mid-July, Rome is home to the **Golden Gala,** one of the seven most important international athletics competitions in the world. The event, which takes place at the Stadio Olimpico, was instituted immediately after disastrous the 1980 Moscow Olympics, which was boycotted by Western countries. An important milestone for the competition came in 1983 when a world record was broken there for the first time. (Ticket Office ☎06 32 810; visit www.goldengala.it. Open M-F 9am-6pm, Sa 9am-1pm).

Tickets for many sporting events can be bought at the **Orbis Agency,** P. dell'Esquilino, 37 (☎06 482 74 03).

GE

INSIDE

clothing & shoes **231**

boutiques **232** cheap and chic **233**

department stores **234** shoes **234**

non-produce markets **235**

miscellaneous **236**

jewelry **236** perfumerias **237** stationery **237**

toys **238** home furnishing **238** luggage **239**

music **239**

bookstores **240**

Shopping

CLOTHING & SHOES

Everything you need to know about Italian fashion is summed up in one simple phrase: *la bella figura.* This term describes a beautiful, well-dressed, put-together woman, and it is taken very, very seriously in Rome. Begin with a pair of big, dark sunglasses with a (preferably gold) logo prominently displayed. If you're under forty, consider tinted sunglasses—blue or purple will do, although many Romans are inclined to clear these days. Whatever you do, don't remove them indoors. Then you'll need a bag; **Prada** and **Gucci** will immediately increase your social status by a factor of ten, while **Louis Vuitton** and **Fendi** are also acceptable. Logos, of course, should continue to be prominent, and it's also wise to tuck in a pack of cigarettes and an especially expensive telefonino with a signature ring. As for shoes, the rules are simple: wear heels. High heels. Very high heels. All the time. Ignore cobblestones, steep stairs, and the high cost of cabs—the Romans all do. With your key accessories in place, wear black. All black, all the time. For men, the best thing to do is to buy one glorious Italian suit—**Armani** or **Dolce & Gabanna**—and then spend the rest of your life praying you don't spill.

Some advice before setting out with credit card in hand: sales in Italy happen twice a year, in mid-January and mid-July. Don't be surprised if you can't try on everything in all stores. Finally, be clear about exchanges and returns *before* giving a store your money; Italy is not exactly known for its customer service. These listings are a teaser; for the latest shopping information, pick up a free copy of *Where Rome* at any tourist information booth.

CLOTHING SIZE CONVERSIONS

WOMEN'S CLOTHING							
US SIZE	**4**	**6**	**8**	**10**	**12**	**14**	**16**
EUROPE SIZE	32	34	36	38	40	42	44
WOMEN'S SHOES							
US SIZE	**5**	**6**	**7**	**8**	**9**	**10**	**11**
EUROPE SIZE	36	37	38	39	40	41	42
MEN'S SUITS/JACKETS							
US SIZE	**32**	**34**	**36**	**38**	**40**	**42**	**44**
EUROPE SIZE	42	44	46	48	50	52	54
MEN'S SHIRTS							
US SIZE	**14**	**14.5**	**15**	**15.5**	**16**	**16.5**	**17**
EUROPE SIZE	36	37	38	39	40	41	42
MEN'S SHOES							
US SIZE	**7**	**8**	**9**	**10**	**11**	**12**	**13**
EUROPE SIZE	40	41	42	44	45	46	47.5

BOUTIQUES

Particularly for those coming to Italy from overseas, Rome is one of the best places in the world to sate these forbidden desires. Prices in the boutiques here are usually below those in the US and Australia, though fluctuations in the dollar's value can change that. If you are yearning to shop at Rome's most chic boutiques, V. Colla di Rienzo, and V.d. Corso (and its cross streets toward P.d. Popolo) are lined with name-brand stores. More daring – and unique – shops can be found on V.d. Governo Vecchio and the streets around P.d. Rotonda. Slightly less pricey stores can be found along V. Nazionale. Opening hours in July and August are much less reliable, with a number of shops closing on Saturday morning and reopening only on Tuesday. If you happen to spend over €155 at one store, you are eligible for a tax refund. As if you needed another incentive to splurge.

Bruno Magli, V.d. Gambero, 1 (☎06 679 38 02). Open M-Sa 10am-7:30pm.

Dolce & Gabbana, V.d. Condotti, 51-52 (☎06 699 249 99). Open M-Sa 10am-7:30pm.

Emporio Armani, V.d. Babuino, 140 (☎06 360 021 97). Houses the less expensive end of the Armani line. Same hours as Giorgio Armani.

Ermenegildo Zegna, V. Borgognona, 7E-F (☎ 06 678 91 93). M-Sa 10am-7:30pm.

Fendi, V. Borgognona, 36-40 (☎06 679 48 24). Open daily 11am-2pm, 3-7pm.

Gianni Versace, Men: V. Borgognona, 24-25 (☎06 679 50 37). Women: V. Bocca di Leone, 25-27 (☎06 678 05 21). Open M-Sa 10am-7pm.

Giorgio Armani, V.d. Condotti, 75 (☎06 699 14 60). Open M-Sa 10am-7pm.

Gucci, V.d. Condotti, 8 (☎06 678 93 40). Open M 3-7pm, Tu-Sa 10am-7pm, Su 2-7pm.

Krizia, P. di Spagna, 87 (☎06 679 37 72). Open M 3pm-7pm, Tu-Sa 10am-7pm.

Laura Biagiotti, V. Borgognona, 43-44 (☎06 679 12 05). Open M 3:30-7:30pm, Tu-Sa 10am-1:30pm and 3:30-7:30pm.

Lacoste, V.d. Corso, 61 (☎06 360 018 57). Open M-Sa 10am-7:30pm.

Louis Vuitton, V.d. Condotti, 15 (☎06 699 400 00). Open M-Sa 9:30am-7:30pm, Su 11am-7:30pm.

Max Mara, V.d. Condotti, 17-19 (☎06 678 11 44). Open M-Sa 10am-7:30pm, Su 11am-7pm.

Missoni, P. di Spagna, 77-78 (☎06 679 25 55). Open M 3-7:30pm, Tu-Sa 10am-7:30pm.

Moschino, V. Borgognona, 32a (☎06 699 221 04). Open M noon-8pm, Tu-Sa 9:30am-8pm, Su 10:30am-8pm.

Prada, V.d. Condotti, 88-95 (☎06 679 08 97). Open M 3-7pm, Tu-Sa 10am-7pm, Su 1:30-7:30pm.

RoccoBarocco, V. Bocca di Leone, 65-66 (☎06 679 79 14). Open M 3:30-7:30pm, Tu-Sa 10am-7:30pm.

Salvatore Ferragamo, Men: V.d. Condotti, 64-66 (☎06 678 11 30). Women: V.d. Condotti, 72-74 (☎06 679 15 65). Open M 3-7pm, Tu-Sa 10am-7pm.

Valentino, V.d. Condotti, 13 (☎06 394 20). Open M 3-7pm, Tu-Sa 10am-7pm.

YvesSaintLaurent, P. di Spagna, 77 (☎06 679 77 50). Open M-Sa 10am-7pm, Su 1:30pm-7pm.

CHEAP & CHIC

Designer emporiums such as **Davide Cenci,** V. Campo Marzio, 1-7 (☎06 699 06 81; open M 4-8pm, Tu-F 9:30am-1:30pm and 4-8pm, Sa 10am-8pm), **Antonelo & Fabrizio,** C.V. Emanuele, 242-243, near Chiesa Nuova, (☎06 688 027 49; open daily 9:30am-1:30pm and 4-8pm; in winter 3:30-7:30pm), and **Discount dell'alta Moda,** V. Agostino Depretis, 87 (☎06 478 256 72; open M 2:30-7:30pm, Tu-Sa 9:30am-7:30pm) stock many lines of designer clothes and shoes at sometimes half the original price. Workers won't be as ready to prostrate themselves before you for the contents of your wallet, and you have to buy directly off the rack. These are an especially good deal during the sale months of January and July; look for the *Saldi* or *Disconto* signs in the window. Unless otherwise stated, all accept AmEx/MC/V.

Mariotti Boutique, V.d. Frezza 20 (☎06 322 71 26). This elegant boutique sells clothes for the modern, sophisticated woman. Prices are steep; watch for the significant sales. Open M-F 10am-7:30pm, Saturday 10am-2pm.

David Mayer, V.d. Corso, 168 (☎06 692 020 97), V. Cola di Rienzo, 185 (☎06 324 33 03; www.davidmayer.com). For the inner *fasionista* in all men, David Mayer offers good-looking attire that doesn't require a trust fund. Short-sleeved button-down shirt €45, sweaters €90, their popular shoes run €120. Open daily 10am-8pm.

Diesel, V.d. Corso, 186 (☎06 678 39 33). Off V.d. Condotti. Also at V.d. Babuino, 95. *The* label in retro fashion is surprisingly high-octane. Prices are cheaper than in the US, so it's worth the visit. Open M-Sa 10:30am-8pm, Su 3:30-8pm.

Ethic, V.d. Corso, 85 (☎06 360 021 91), V.d. Pantheon, 46 (☎06 683 010 63), and V.d. Carozze, 20. The hip yet less adventurous can find a balance between the avant garde and tasteful. Prices won't break the bank. Open daily 10am-7:30pm.

Invicta, V.d. Babuino, 28 (☎06 360 017 37) or V.d. Corso, 82-3 (☎06 361 37 42). Chartreuse never looked so good on a backpack. Neither did hot pink or neon blue. Open Tu-S 9:45am-3:30pm and 5:30-11pm.

Max&Co, V.d. Condotti, 46-46a (☎06 678 79 46); also at V. Nazionale, 56. The less expensive line of Max Mara, M.&Co. has more youthful, colorful clothes. Open M-Sa 10am-7:30pm.

Simona, V.d. Corso, 82-3 (☎06 361 37 42 or 06 360 018 36). This lingerie store has an amusing array of name-brand lingerie, as well as colorful bathing suits during the summer. Open M-Sa 10am-7:30pm.

Stefanel, V.d. Corso, 123 (☎06 695 783); also at V. Cola di Rienzo, 223 (☎06 321 14 03), and several other locations in Rome (not all have the same merchandise). The upscale version of Benetton, with higher prices to match. Skirts €45; basic dresses €80; tops €35. For men: jeans €65 and button-down shirts €65. Open daily 10am-8pm.

Xandrine, V.d. Croce, 88 (☎06 678 62 01). Indulge your inner princess in this temple to sequins and chiffon. A couture shop that specializes in evening wear. Many ready-to-wear dresses hang along the walls, but if you'd rather have your ball gown in chartreuse taffeta, get your measurements taken and come back in 3 days. Open M-Sa 10am-7:30pm.

Solo, V.d. Corso, 41 (☎06 360 014 40). A small boutique with cute clothes at great prices. Sundresses start at €50. Open daily 10am-8pm.

DEPARTMENT STORES

While the Romans lap up American entertainment and munch on fries from McDonald's, one American idea can't seem to get off the ground—the department store. Unlike New York or Paris, Rome's department stores tend to cater to the dowdy and conservative, rather than the young and beautiful. The prices are right, however, and these stores are excellent places to buy necessities like socks and underwear, should the need ever arise.

COIN, V. Cola di Rienzo, 173 (☎06 360 042 98), near Castel San Angelo. Also P. Appio, 7 (☎06 708 00 20), M: A-San Giovanni, and V. Mantova, 1 (☎06 841 58 84), near Porta Pia. By far the most useful of Rome's department stores, COIN carries attractive, functional merchandise at reasonable prices. Good deals, especially on cosmetics. The Cola di Rienzo location has a supermarket and cafe; the San Giovanni location has a cafe. All open daily 9:30am-8pm. AmEx/MC/V.

La Rinascente, V.d. Corso, 189 (☎06 679 76 91; www.rinascenteshopping.com). Also at V. Aniene, 1, near P. Fiume. La Rinascente carries sensible, conservative clothing for men, women, and children. Caters toward middle-aged crowd; larger sizes available; wide selection of lingerie in basement. Also a decent stock of perfume, makeup, sunglasses, and other accessories. Open M-Sa 9:30am-10pm, Su 10:30am-8pm. AmEx/MC/V.

UPIM, V. Tritone, 173 (☎06 678 33 36 or 800 824 040), between V. d. Corso and Barberini. Also at V.C. Alberto, 54, near P.S. Maria Maggiore. UPIM is the bargain basement of department stores in Rome, and their goods tend to run toward the uninspiring. But if you need a pair of socks, Upim's a cheap, solid option. Also sells toiletries. M-Sa 9am-8:30pm, Su 10:30am-8:30pm. AmEx/MC/V.

SHOES

It's said that a building's only as good as its foundation. In Italy, you're only as good as your shoes. In a city where Birkenstocks are only sold at religious outfitters (Jesus wore sandals), being well-shod is not a luxury, but a way of life. Rome may have more shoe stores per square kilometer than any other city in the world, and offers everything from €10 sandals at outdoor markets to jewel-encrusted silk numbers whose prices are "available upon request." Luckily, there are many stylish, moderately priced stores—trade your flip-flops for leather sandals, preferably with heels. For the pragmatists, Via Nazionale is home to a number of larger shoe stores that boast a wide selection, quality products, and reasonable prices.

Trancanelli, P. Cola di Rienzo, 84 (☎06 323 45 03). This is where the young and the restless of Rome buy their shoes. A must for anyone looking to return home well-shod, but with their bank account more or less intact (shoes from €65). Open M 3-7:45pm, Tu-Sa 9:30am-7:45pm. AmEx/MC/V.

Bata, V. Nazionale, 88a (☎06 679 15 70), V.d. Due Macelli, 45 (☎06 482 45 29). With 250 shops in Italy and 6000 shops world-wide stocked floor to ceiling with functional, affordable shoes that look great. Bonus points for their ability to turn out shoes that look remarkably like Prada's, but can be yours for a fraction of the price. Open M-Sa 9:30am-8pm, Su 4-8pm. AmEx/MC/V.

Mada, V.d. Croce, 57 (☎06 679 86 60). A very popular women's shoe store, Mada carries conservative, classic, comfortable shoes. Located in a fashionable shopping district, its (relatively) cheap prices make it a favorite among Roman women. Shoes around €100. Open Tu-F 9:30am-7:30pm, Sa 9:30am-1:30pm. AmEx/MC/V.

Elisheva, V.d. Baullari, 19 (☎06 687 17 47), off Campo dei Fiori. Also at P. Irnerio, 41 (☎06 660 160 77), near V. Aurelia southwest of the Vatican. What's going out in Italy without the right shoes? This small boutique solves your shoe problems with their array of sexy sandals, plus a number of daytime flats (from €40). Also a small selection of women's clothing. Open Su-F 10am-8pm. AmEx/MC/V.

Loco, V.d. Baullari, 22 (☎06 688 08 216), near Campo dei Fiori. Sells fun shoes for a younger crowd. Quirky sandals, flats, boots, and sneakers, but fashion comes at a price (starting at €100). Open M 3:30-8pm, Tu-Sa 10:30am-8pm. AmEx/MC/V.

Petrocchi, V. d. Orso, 25 (☎06 687 82 89; www.calzoleriapetrocchi.it), north of P. Navona. Since 1946, Bruno Ridolfi has produced the sort of classy men's and women's shoes that never go out of fashion. All shoes hand-made, but they don't come cheap. €350 pret-a-porter; €750 customized. Open M 4-8pm, Tu-Sa 10am-1pm and 4-8pm. AmEx/MC/V.

Eventi, V. d. Fontanella, 8 (☎06 360 025 33), off V. d. Corso toward P. d. Popolo. Funky men's and women's shoes, with a selection of clothing to match. Heels and flats around €100, but keep an eye out for generous sales. Also at V. d. Serpenti, 134. Open M 3:30-8pm, Tu-Sa 10am-1pm and 3:30-8pm. AmEx/MC/V.

NON-PRODUCE MARKETS

Rome's markets lay the best and the worst of Rome bare. They often have the best deals in town on produce, clothing, and household items, but times and prices vary, pickpockets abound, and successful bargaining is hard work. Arrive at markets early for the best selection, and buy late for the best deals. Expect to bargain, especially on clothing. Often, prices aren't marked in order to allow the vendor to size you up. (So don't come to Porta Portese looking like a clueless tourist who just left the Four Seasons.) The best strategy is to check the prices of other vendors to get a base line cost, and then to bargain in the best Italian you can muster, a little will go a long way. Be prepared to counter the seller's first offer and don't be surprised if a vendor feigns offense—it's all part of the game. Don't be afraid to bust out the *"No, grazie"* and walk away. Also, always, *always* check labels carefully before you buy anything—especially leather jackets. For markets that sell primarily food, see p. 209 (some also sell other goods). Hours are never set in stone—markets begin when everyone gets there and end when they all get bored.

Porta Portese, in Trastevere at Porta Portese. Tram #8 from Torre Argentina. A surreal experience, with booths selling clothing, shoes, jewelry, bags, toilets, and anything else that you can imagine extending beyond the horizon. Keep your money close, as this is a notorious spot for pickpockets. Open Su 5am-1pm.

Rigattieri per Hobby, P. della Marina, 32, Borghetto Flaminio (☎06 588 05 17; www.creativitalia.com), near the Olympic Stadium. Not unlike a giant garage sale, Rigattieri is primarily dedicated to hobbies of all sorts; if you want it, chances are you can probably find it. €1.60 entrance fee. Open Su 10am-7pm.

Via Sannio, near M: San Giovanni, next to the COIN. Here you will find a massive market that lines V. Sannio and sprawls towards the basilica of S. Giovanni in Laterano. Cheap shoes and clothes, plus semi-legal CDs, books, luggage, and more. Open M-Sa 8:30am-1:30pm.

Libri in Campo, P. Santa Maria in Trastevere. An outdoor book sale catering to the dinner and drinks crowd. Most books are in Italian, but the selection is eclectic. Also hosts a variety of events, from poetry readings to panel discussions. Runs late June to late July. Open daily 6pm-midnight.

Piazza Navona

Baskets in Centro Storico

Shopping in P.d. Spagna

MISCELLANEOUS

JEWELRY

Rome boasts a large array of jewelers, many of which carry work that is quite original and creative. **Bulgari's** windows (V. Condotti 11) are the best in Rome, and celebrities are often spotted at **Massoni,** at the corner of V. Condotti and Largo Goldoni.

Alcozer, V.d. Carozze, 48 (☎06 679 13 88). Near P. di Spagna. Gorgeous Old World jewelry at decent prices. Earrings from €20. If you're in the market for a ruby encrusted crucifix, it'll set you back €320. Open M 2-7:30pm, Tu-Sa 10am-7:30pm. AmEx/MC/V.

Furla, V.d. Condotti, 56 (☎06 679 19 73). Also at P. di Spagna, 21 and V.d. Corso, 481. For those who can't afford Bulgari but still like to sparkle, Furla's your place. An Italian staple, Furla sells silver jewelry (necklaces €100; watches from €70). Want shoes and a bag to match? They've got that too. Open M-Sa 10am-8pm. AmEx/MC/V.

Pianegonda, V.d. Croce, 42 (☎06 678 64 02; www.pianegondaitalia.com). Selling provocative jewelry to an upscale clientele, Pianegonda has cornered the market on industrial chic. Open M 3:30-7:30pm, Tu-Sa 10am-7:30pm. AmEx/MC/V.

Luisella Mariotti, V. di Gesu e Maria, 20a (☎06 320 13 20; luisella_mariotti@yahoo.it), between the Spanish Steps and P. Popolo. This tiny boutique carries funky, original costume jewelry. Stylish merchandise, made on-site, but prices are reasonable; €40 will get you a sizeable bracelet. Open M 2:30-7:30pm, Tu-Sa 10:30am-7:30pm; in July M 10am-7:30pm, Sa 10:30am-1:30pm. AmEx/MC/V.

Kelokura, V. d. Minerva, 6 (☎06 699 17 21), near the Pantheon. Also at V. d. Crociferi, 35, off V. d. Corso. If your budget for jewelry tops out at €10, you'll find plenty of funky designs here at the right price. A wide selection of rings, necklaces, and earrings. Open daily 10am-8pm. AmEx/MC/V.

Gioie d'arte, V. d. Gigli d'Oro, 10 (☎06 687 75 24), just north of P. Navona. For the last 15 years, this little workshop has produced original works in gold, silver, and copper–every piece is unique. And with these gorgeous items starting at €50-70, you can afford to stand out a little. AmEx/MC/V.

Cotton Club, V.S. Caterina da Siena, 56 (☎06 679 78 70), right of P.d. Minerva. A small shop with a great array of affordable silver jewelry. Rings go for €20 and up; necklaces and earrings €10 and up. Open M-Su 9:30am-7:30pm. AmEx/MC/V.

Clio, V.d. Croce, 53B (☎06 679 08 86). Handmade costume jewelry featuring unique designs with all different kinds of stones, beads, and shells. Prices vary depending on the size of the piece (rings from €5, elaborate necklaces from €200). Open M-Sa 9am-7:30pm. AmEx/MC/V.

Siragusa, V.d. Carrozze, 64 (☎06 679 70 85). Only in Rome could you find an archaeological jeweler, but Siragusa is just that, and a darn good one. Ancient coins, some dating as far back as the 4th century BC, are set in new gold settings for rings, cuff links, and more. If you happen to have an artifact of your own, they'll set that too. Prices match extremely high quality. Open M-F 10am-1:30pm and 3:30-7:30pm. AmEx/MC/V.

PROFUMERIAS

What's the point of dressing well if you don't smell nice, too? If you don't yet understand the importance that Romans place on their *profumerie*, a quick ride on bus #64 will educate you.

Materozzoli, P.S. Lorenzo in Lucina, 5, off V.d. Corso (☎06 688 926 86). This old-world *profumeria* carries everything from the exclusive Aqua di Parma line to shaving brushes. Specializes in rare perfumes and colognes, including Creed and Lornezo Villoresi. Open M 3:30-7:30pm, Tu-Sa 10am-1:30pm and 3:30-7:30pm. Closed Aug. 10-28. AmEx/MC/V.

Casamaria, V. d. Scrofa 71/72 (☎06 683 30 74), between the Pantheon and P. Navona. Also at Via O. d. Gubbio, 55b. This enormous *profumeria*, which spans two locations in the city center, claims to have the greatest assortment of merchandise in Rome. They might be right. Also famous for their make-up expertise--signed photos of their famous and satisfied customers line the walls. Open M 3:30-7:30pm, Tu-F 9:30am-7:30pm. Closed 2 weeks in Aug. AmEx/MC/V.

Estivi, V.E. Orlando 92-3, (☎06 488 17 31), M: A-Repubblica. Also at P. Bologna, 29, M: B-Bologna. This all-purpose *profumeria* carries everything from designer sunglasses to floral-printed bathing caps, plus a comprehensive selection of designer perfumes. The V.E. Orlando branch also boasts an indoor waterfall. Open M-Sa 9am-8pm. AmEx/MC/V.

Lekythos, V. Ripetta 16 (☎06 320 20 12), near P. d. Popolo. Several other locations around the city, including V.d. Quattro Fontane, near V. Nazionale, V.d. Croce, 23, and V.d. Convertite, 13. A Greek chain that carries a wide variety of international scents and make-up. Open M-Sa 9:30am-10pm. AmEx/MC/V.

Rance, P. Navona, 53 (☎06 688 097 05; fax 06 688 097 05; mail@rance.it). This centuries-old *profumeria* made its name in the early 1600s, when it sold scented gloves to the French aristocracy. Like Napoleon, its most famous customer, the line has since invaded Italy--albeit with a bit less bloodshed. Now, you can find Rance's historic line of perfumes, colognes, and soaps in the equally-historic Piazza Navona. Open M 1:30-7:30pm, Tu-Sa 10:30am-7:30pm. AmEx/MC/V.

STATIONERY STORES

For basic stationery needs, visit one of the many *cartolerie* that you can find on almost any street in the city. In a pinch, you can find pens and pencils at a *tabacchi* or *standa*, but you may be disappointed. The establishments listed below tend to provide greater selection and higher quality at somewhat higher prices.

Campo Marzio Penne, V. Campo Marzio, 41 (☎06 688 078 77; www.campomarziodesign.it). Gorgeous fountain pens (from €12) and leather goods, in addition to brightly colored journals and photo albums. The small address books (€7) make great presents, or check out the antique writing kits (€10). Open M-Sa 10am-1pm and 2-7pm. AmEx/MC/V.

Vertecchi, V. Croce, 70 (☎06 679 01 55; www.vertecchi.com). This should be your first stop for all stationery needs. A wide supply of paper and pens, plus party supplies, notebooks, candles, paintbrushes, and the kitchen sink. Open M 3:30-7:30pm, Tu-Sa 9:30am-7:30pm. AmEx/MC/V.

Leather Goods

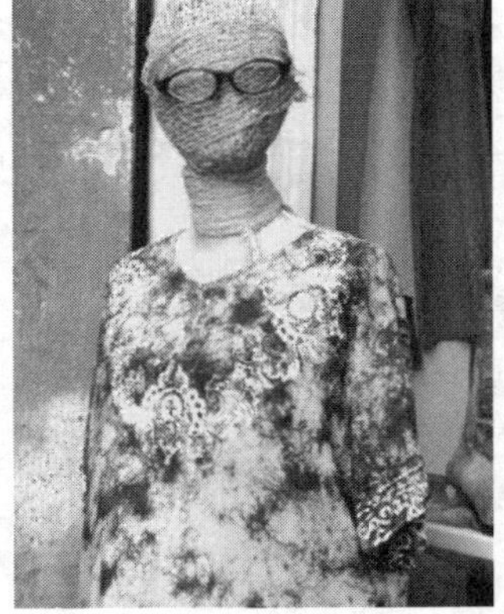
Creative Window Dressing

Shoes

Il Papiro, V.d. Pantheon, 50 (☎06 679 55 97; www.ilpapirofirenze.it), near the Pantheon. Also at V.d. Crociferi, 17, and Salita de'Crescenzi, 28. This stationery store has acquired world fame and countless followers. It features plenty of typical designs, but the customized stationery is the real draw. Open M-Sa 10am-8pm, Su 11am-8pm. AmEx/MC/V.

TOYS

Don Chisciotte, V.A. Brunetti, 21a (☎06 322 45 15; www.gallerisdonchisciotte.com.), near P.d. Popolo. A bit like walking into Alice's Wonderland, Don Chisciotte sells marionettes, puppet theaters, and a wide selection of lead soldiers, many of which are antique. For that special child, or the one that's never grown up. Marionettes and soldiers start at €15. Open daily 10am-1pm and 4:30-7:30pm. Sometimes closed Su; call to confirm. Closed Aug. Cash only.

Al Sogno, P. Navona, 53 (☎06 686 41 98; www.alsogno.com). Step out of the jungle of tourists in P. Navona and into a rainforest filled with gnomes and trees. Children raised on Pokemon might not recognize this enchanting collection of stuffed animals, dolls, and collectible figurines as a toy store—but their parents probably will. Open daily 10am-8pm. AmEx/MC/V.

Berte, P. Navona, 107-111 (☎06 687 50 11). A fantastic collection of old-fashioned, but not antique, toys and games. Dolls, marionettes, rocking horses, puzzles, and more. Also sells Playmobil and LEGO kits. Many items hand-made, and all carefully selected by the owner. Open in summer M-Sa 9:30am-1pm and 4-8pm; in winter 3:30-7:30pm; occasionally open Su. AmEx/MC/V.

HOME FURNISHINGS

B.B.K., V.d. Frezza, 60 (☎06 324 42 59; bbkroma@libero.it). Chic houseware with an earthy feel. Smaller items, like glassware and vases, plus more substantial pieces, like bureaus and tables. Not cheap, but helpful in making your hovel home. Open M 3:30-7:30pm, Tu-Sa 10am-7:30pm. AmEx/MC/V.

C.U.C.I.N.A., V. Mario de' Fiori , 65 (☎06 679 12 75; www.cucinastore.com), near the Spanish Steps. Also at V. Flaminia Vecchia, 679 (☎06 333 22 02), off Corso d. Francia; and P. Euclide, 40 (☎06 807 89 06), north of V. Borghese. Lots of spiffy kitchen gadgets, particularly of the ultra-shiny chrome variety. Open M 3:30-7:30pm, Tu-F 10am-7:30pm, Sa 10:30am-7:30pm. AmEx/MC/V.

House & Kitchen, V. del Plebiscito, 103 (☎06 679 42 08) and C.V. Emanuele II, 20 (☎06 699 255 92). A huge selection of practical and functional housewares. Prices are very reasonable. Open M-Sa 9:30am-8pm, Su 10:30am-2:30pm and 3:30-7:30pm. Closed Su in July and Aug. AmEx/MC/V.

Modigliani, V.d. Condotti, 24 (☎06 678 56 53; Modigliani USA 888-259-7988; www.modigliani.it). A large selection of smaller (and quite elegant) housewares. Some of the glassware and ceramic pieces are simply gorgeous, and are usually priced accordingly. Open M 3-7:30pm, Tu-Sa 10am-2pm and 3-7:30pm. AmEx/MC/V.

Archidomus, V. Leonardo da Vinci, 256 (☎06 547 945), M: B-Basilica S. Paolo. Beds, couches, tables, and other such large objects at discounted prices. Open M 4-8pm, Tu-F 10am-1pm and 4-8pm, Sa 10am-1pm. AmEx/MC/V.

Linn Sui, V.d. Boschetto, 79 (☎06 482 07 61; www.linn-sui.com). If a bed isn't your thing, lay your head on one of their stylish futons (around €300). Also carries glassware, vases, teapots, and various other items. Open M-F 10am-12:45pm and 4-7pm. MC/V.

LUGGAGE

Tedeschi Roma, V. Nazionale 106 (☎06 679 55 75; tedeschi.roma@libero.it). Good selection of luggage and other bags, convenient to Termini. Large backpacks around €100. Open M-F 10am-7:30pm, Sa 10:30am-2pm. AmEx/MC/V.

MUSIC

Those who are in the market for cheap music and are willing to take a walk on the wild side may want to take a gamble with the pirated CDs and PlayStation games sold by street vendors in highly-trafficked areas or in outdoor markets. CDs sell for around €5, but you can often bargain; 3 for €10 is a good offer. A word of warning before you drool over low-cost rip-offs—there is no guarantee of quality and the content may not match what is advertised. For a more savory and legal shopping experience, try the following stores.

Disfunzioni Musicali, V. degli Etruschi, 4 (☎06 446 19 84; mail order 06 444 14 61; disfunzioni.musicali@tiscali.it), in San Lorenzo. CDs, cassettes, and LPs available, including excellent selections of rock, avant-garde classical, jazz, and ethnic. Helpful staff. Bulletin board, with ads for musicians and roommates/apartments. Open M 3-8pm, Tu-Sa 10:30am-8pm. Closed major holidays and Ferragosto. MC/V.

Messaggerie Musicali, V.d. Corso, 472 (☎06 684 401). Standard and dependable, with a large selection at moderate prices (most CDs around €10.50). Bookstore on the second floor. Open M-Sa 10am-11pm, Su 10am-8:30pm; F closes at midnight. AmEx/MC/V.

RicordiMedia, V.d. Corso, 506 (☎06 361 23 70). Also at V.G. Cesare, 88 (☎06 373 515 89), in Prati; Termini Galleria (☎06 874 061 13); V.V.E. Orlando, 73 (☎06 474 62 54), near Repubblica; and V.C. Battisti, 120 (☎06 679 80 22), just off P. Venezia. A chain with an average selection of music and decent prices (CDs €10-15). Comprehensive stock of Italian music, plus a classical wing that also sells sheet music. Open M-Sa 9:30am-8pm, Su 10am-1pm and 3-8pm. AmEx/MC/V.

La Discoteca al Pantheon, V. d. Minerva, 9-10 (☎06 679 86 50). This small store carries a great selection of music, ranging from opera to indie rock to Italian pop. Classical music is the specialty here and they sell a wide range of both Italian and foreign labels. Open Tu-Sa 9:30am-1pm and 3:30-9:30pm. AmEx/MC/V.

BOOKSTORES

Although you already own the only book you'll need during your trip to Rome, sometimes it's nice to read something that's not *so* damn witty and irreverent. **V. di Terme di Diocleziano,** connecting Termini with P. della Repubblica, is lined with booksellers full of dirt-cheap used English paperbacks. **V. di Conciliazione,** the broad avenue leading to St. Peter's, has several bookstores selling English-language histories and guidebooks, as well as devotional materials, but beware of high prices. If you're in Rome for a while, introducing yourself to the staff at these bookstores is a good way to get involved in the expat community.

Libreria Feltrinelli International, V. V. E. Orlando, 84-86 (☎06 482 78 78; www.lafeltrinelli.it), near P. della Repubblica. A Roman fixture, Feltrinelli has an excellent selection of books in several languages, plus dictionaries and a wide range of travel guides. Cheaper than most English-language bookstores, this should be your first stop for basics. Sells early copies of *Wanted in Rome*. Open M-Sa 9am-8pm, Su 10am-1:30pm and 4-7:30pm. AmEx/MC/V.

Anglo-American Bookshop, V.d. Vite, 102 (☎06 679 52 22; www.aab.it). To the right of the Spanish Steps. Fiction, history, and poetry abound in this well-stocked English-language bookshop—*The Joy of Cooking* cohabitates with Henry Kissinger's latest. The bilingual staff really knows its stuff and is always willing to help. The bulletin board in back lists apartments for rent. *Wanted in Rome* sold here. Open in summer M-F 10am-7:30pm and Sa 10am-2pm; winter M 3:30-7:30pm and Tu-Sa 10am-7:30pm, AmEx/MC/V.

The Lion Bookshop, V.d. Greci, 33-36 (☎06 326 540 07; thelionbookshop@hotmail.com), near P. d. Popolo. For the Anglophile, this shop boasts the largest selection of British fiction in Rome. Well-stocked with poetry, fiction, new releases, and children's books. Coffee/tea bar, reading room, and a local bulletin board. Open M 3:30-7:30pm, Tu-Su 10am-7:30pm; in summer closed Su. AmEx/MC/V.

The (Almost) Corner Bookshop, V. del Moro, 45 (☎06 583 69 42), in Trastevere. The Corner Bookshop recently acquired the word "almost" in its title after moving a few doors down but still maintains the hole-in-the-wall charm that keeps its customers returning. They have books in English on just about every topic and can special order anything. Large children's section. Sells early copies of *Wanted in Rome.* Open M-Sa 10am-1:30pm and 3:30-8pm, Su 11am-1:30pm and 3:30-8pm. In Aug., closed Su. AmEx/MC/V.

Economy Book and Video Center, Via Torino, 136 (06 474 68 77; www.booksitaly.com), in Termini. M: A-Repubblica. From P.d. Repubblica, take V. Nazionale 1 block, then turn left on V. Torino. Rome's oldest English bookstore. Specializes in buying, trading, and selling used paperbacks. Also boasts 2500 DVD titles, many in English. Check the message board for posted job and volunteer opportunities. Open M-F 9am-8pm and Sa 9am-2pm. AmEx/MC/V.

ENGLISH LIBRARIES

Centro Studi Americani, V. M. Caetani, 32, 2nd fl. (☎06 688 016 13; www.centrostudiamericani.org). Off P. Mattei, near Largo Torre Argentina, in a pretty *palazzo.* Every section of the Dewey Decimal System represented. You can enter the library for €5/day and with photo ID, but a membership (one-year €150; €50 for students) is required to check out materials. Look at bulletin boards for concerts and cultural events. Open M-Th 10am-6pm, F 10am-2pm. Closed last three weeks of Aug.

Santa Susanna Lending Library, V. XX Settembre, 15, 2nd fl. (☎06 482 75 10; www.santasusanna.org/library), in the Church of Santa Susanna. About 9000 English volumes, including the British Council's Fiction Collection. 3mo. membership €15; 6mo. €20; yearly €30. Prices listed do not include refundable deposit. Occasionally hosts used-book sales; call for information. Open Tu and Th 10am-1pm, W 3-6pm, F 1-4pm, Sa-Su 10am-12:30pm; July and first 2 weeks of Sept. Tu, W, Su; Aug. Su only.

SHOP 'TIL YOU DROP GLOSSARY

ENGLISH	ITALIAN	PRONUNCIATION
On sale	*In offerta*	een of-FAIR-tah
Sales	*Saldi*	SAHL-dee
cheap	*economica*	eh-coh-noh-mee-ka
expensive	*caro*	CA-roh
I'll give you a discount / I would like a discount	*Ti do un sconto/ Vorrei un sconto*	Tee DOH oon skON-toh / vohr-RAY oon skON-toh
I love it!	*Lo adoro!*	loh ah-DOH-roh
I don't like it	*Non mi piace*	nohn mee pee-YAH-chay
design/ style	*il modello*	eel moh-DEL-lo
size	*la misura/ la taglia*	lah mee-SOO-ra/ la tah-GLEE-ah
cloth	*il tessuto/ la stoffa*	eel tes-SOO-toh/ lah STOH-fah
clothing	*abbigliamento*	ab-bee-GLEE-ah-men-toh
color	*il colore*	coh-loh-re
leather	*il cuoio/ la pelle*	eel coo-oy-yoh/ lah pel-lay
silk	*la seta*	lah SEH-ta
cotton	*il cottone*	eel cot-TOH–nay
wool	*il lana*	eel LAH-nah
linen	*il lino*	eel LEE-noh
lace	*il pizzo*	eel PEEZ-zoh
suede	*la pelle scamosciata*	lah pel-LAY ska-mo-SHEE-a-tah
cashmere	*il cachemire*	eel ca-KEH-mee-ray
skirt	*la gonna*	lah GOHN-nah
pants	*il pantelone*	eel pan-teh-loh-nay
hat	*il cappello*	eel kap-PEL-loh
blouse	*la camisa*	lah ka-MEE-sah
dress	*la vestita*	lah veh-STEE-tah
shoes	*le scarpe*	lay SCAR-peh
boots	*i stivali*	ee stee-VAL-ee
tie	*la cravata*	lah cra-VAH-tah
jacket	*la giacca*	lah gee-AH-kah
cash register	*la cassa*	lah CAS-sah
salesperson	*la commessa/ il commesso*	lah com-MES-sah/eel com-MES-so

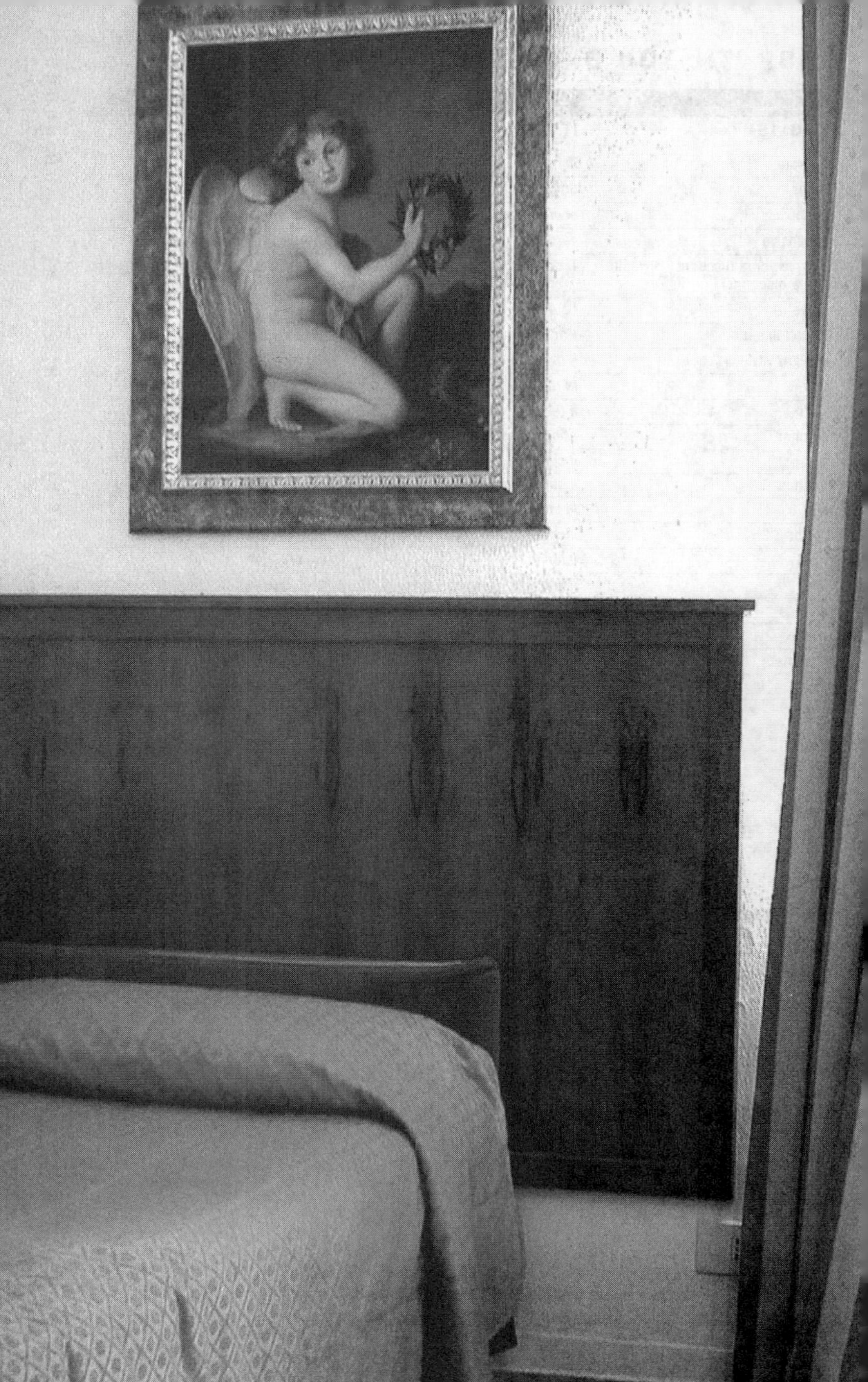

INSIDE

accommodations by price **244**

accommodations by neighborhood **245**

centro storico **245** trastevere **246**

near piazza di spagna **246** borgo & prati (near vatican) **247**

termini & san lorenzo **248** alternative accommodations **254**

long-term accommodations **256**

Accommodations

"Everyone sooner or later comes round by Rome," wrote poet Robert Browning, and chances are they're coming at the same time you are and have the reservations you wanted. Many hotels now let you **book rooms** directly over the Internet, which is significantly cheaper than calling or sending a fax from abroad. English may not be spoken at some smaller places, but this shouldn't dissuade a non-Italian speaker from calling. Useful phrases for making a room reservation in Italian are included in **Let's Speak Italian,** p. 31. When you check in, the proprietor will ask for your passport to register you with the police, as required by Italian law. They should only need it to write down the number—be sure to retrieve it. If the hotel asks for a deposit, send a bank draft (unless a credit card is required). Prices vary widely according to season. You'll pay the most during high season, June and July.

If you arrive in Rome **without reservations,** it is usually possible to find a place to stay, although you may not like it very much and may have to pay more than you ought to for it. Termini is full of officials ready to direct you to a hotel. Some of them are the real thing and have photo IDs issued by the tourist office. Some, however, are sneaky impostors who issue themselves fake badges and cards, and they may well direct you to a sketchy location charging a ridiculous rate, particularly if you arrive late at night. Private tourist agencies like **Enjoy Rome** (see p. 25) are also a good resource.

ACCOMMODATIONS BY PRICE

The accommodations listed below are grouped according to prices as they are posted in the high season (June and July in the Eternal City). Low season prices tend to be anywhere from €5 cheaper than the high season price to half the high season price. The price listed below is for the cheapest single room, dorm room, or equivalent space available (accurate as of August 2003), without any extra amenities such as A/C or bath. The following key to the neighborhoods of Rome (equivalent to the neighborhood breakdown of the rest of the book) will help you to decipher the neighborhood codes listed directly across from the accommodation name.

€25 AND UNDER ❶

Colors (247)	BPV
Pensione Fawlty Towers (248)	TSL
Hotel Papa Germano (248)	TSL
Freedom Traveller (250)	TSL
Pensione Sandy (254)	WT
Hotel Il Castello (253)	ESQ
Pensione di Rienzo (253)	ESQ
Associazione Cattolica Int'l (256)	ESQ
Seven Hills Village (Camping)	

€25-35 ❷

Hotel Bolognese (250)	TSL
Hotel Cervia (250)	TSL
Pensione Tizi (251)	TSL
Pensione Katty (250)	TSL
Hotel Giu' Giu' (254)	ESQ
Hotel Orlanda (253)	ESQ
Hotel San Paolo (254)	WT

€35-45 ❸

Pensione Panda (246)	PS
Hotel Boccaccio (247)	PS
Albergo della Lunetta (245)	CS
Pensione Monaco (251)	TSL
Hotels Castelfidardo & Lazzari (251)	TSL
Hotel Scott House (253)	ESQ
Hotel Sweet Home (253)	ESQ
Pensione Cortorillo (253)	ESQ
YWCA Foyer di Roma (256)	BPV

€45-65 ❹

Albergo Pomezia (245)	CS
Hotel "Rosetta" (245)	CS
Pensione Jonella (247)	PS
Hotel Carmel (246)	TV
Hotel Des Artistes (249)	TSL
Hotel Galli (249)	TSL
Hotel Dolomiti and Hotel Lachea (249)	TSL
Hotel Pensione Cathrine (250)	TSL
Hotel Fenicia (250)	TSL
Hotel Gabriella (250)	TSL
Hotel Aphrodite (250)	TSL
Hotel Baltic (251)	TSL
Hotel Teti (253)	ESQ
Hotel Selene (254)	ESQ
Bed & Breakfast Assoc. of Rome (254)	
Bed & Go (254)	
Santa Maria alle Fornaci (255)	BPV
La Fraterna Domus di Roma (255)	CS

€65 AND OVER ❺

Albergo Abruzzi (245)	CS
Albergo del Sole (245)	CS
Hotel Mimosa (245)	CS
Hotel Navona (245)	CS
Hotel Trastevere (246)	TV
Hotel Pensione Suisse S.A.S. (246)	PS
Hotel Pensione Joli (248)	BPV
Hotel Florida (247)	BPV
Hotel Isa (247)	BPV
Hotel Lady (247)	BPV
Pensione Piave (251)	TSL
Hotel Kennedy (253)	ESQ
Domus Nova Bethlehem (254)	ESQ

BPV Borgo, Prati & near Vatican City **CS** Centro Storico **ESQ** Esquilno **PS** Near Piazza di Spagna **TSL** Termini & San Lorenzo **TV** Trastevere **WT** West of Termini

A Hosteler's Bill of Rights. There are certain standard features that we do not include in our hostel listings. Unless we state otherwise, you can expect that every hostel has no lockout, no curfew, a kitchen, free hot showers, some system of secure luggage storage, and no key deposit.

ACCOMMODATIONS BY NEIGHBORHOOD

Unless explicitly stated (AmEx/D/MC/V), the following accommodations do not accept credit cards. Remember that **price increases** are inevitable at most establishments. When prices are listed as a range, lower prices are for the low season.

CENTRO STORICO

The Centro Storico is the ideal, if increasingly expensive, base for living as the Romans do. Most sights are within walking distance and the market at nearby Campo dei Fiori yields cheap, fresh nourishment. You can expect to pay a 10-15% premium for the classical Roman charm lacking in Termini-area accommodations.

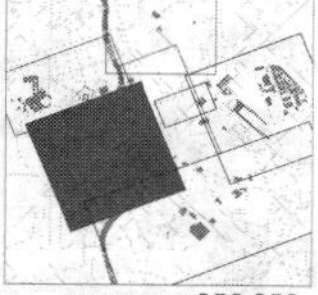

see map p. 358-359

Albergo del Sole, V.d. Biscione, 76 (☎06 688 068 73; fax 06 689 37 87). Off Campo dei Fiori. Allegedly the oldest *pensione* in Rome. 61 comfortable modern rooms with phone, fan, TV, and fantastic antique furniture. Some rooms look out on the rowdy street, while others overlook a pleasant courtyard garden. Some rooms have A/C. English spoken. Checkout 11am. Parking garage €15-18. Singles €65, with bath €83; doubles €95 or €110-140. ❺

Albergo della Lunetta, P. del Paradiso, 68 (☎06 686 10 80; fax 06 689 20 28). The 1st right off V. Chiavari from C.V. Emanuele II behind Sant'Andrea della Valle. Clean, well-lit rooms with phones and a roof garden; some around a small, fern-filled courtyard. Reservations recommended (with credit card or check). Singles €55, with bath €65; doubles €85 or €110; triples €115 or €145). MC/V. ❸

Hotel "Rosetta," V. Cavour, 295 (☎/fax. 06 478 23 069). Located just 2 blocks from the Roman Forum, this family-owned hotel offers spacious rooms at unbeatable prices. While the place is not fancy, each room is equipped with a TV, telephone, fan, and bathroom. Checkout 10:30pm. Singles €60; doubles €80; triples €90; quads €100. AmEx/MC/V. ❹

Albergo Pomezia, V.d. Chiavari, 13 (☎/fax 06 6861371; www.hotelpomezia.it). Off C.V. Emanuele II, behind Sant'Andrea della Valle. The rooms on all 3 floors have recently been renovated and are equipped with new bathrooms. Clean, quiet rooms with phones, fans, and heat in the winter. Breakfast in the pleasant dining room served 8-10:30am. A special handicapped accessible room on the ground floor. Singles €60-105; doubles €80-125; triples €100-160. AmEx/MC/V. ❹

Albergo Abruzzi, P. della Rotonda, 69 (☎06 978 41 351). A mere 200 ft. from the Pantheon, these are indeed rooms with a view. Half of the hotel's rooms were just renovated. Each has a private bath, TV, phone, A/C, fridge, safe, and much higher price. The rest are old-fashioned but clean. Only hall bathrooms here, but every room comes equipped with a sink. Singles €75 or €150; doubles €115 or €195; triples €170 or €240. ❺

Hotel Navona, V.d. Sediari, 8, 1st fl. (☎06 686 42 03; www.hotelnavona.com). Take V.d. Canestrari from P. Navona, cross C. del Rinascimento, and go straight. This recently refurbished 16th-century building has been used as a *pensione* for over 150 years, counting among its guests Keats, Shelley, and the University of Alabama chapter of the ΑΠΘ fraternity. Brand-new bathrooms equipped with the added luxury of heated towel racks (you don't know what you've been missing). Checkout 10:30am. Breakfast included. Reservations with credit card and first night deposit. Singles €90; doubles €120; triples €165. A/C €10. ❺

Hotel Mimosa, V.S. Chiara, 61, 2nd fl. (☎06 688 017 53; www.hotelmimosa.net). Off P. della Minerva behind the Pantheon. This 12-room hotel is located in a quiet and convenient part of the Centro Storico. No elevator, phones, or A/C, but rooms are spacious. Singles €46 or €77, with bath €67 or €88; doubles €60 or €93, with bath €75 or €108. Cash only. ❺

Accommodations

TRASTEVERE

Trastevere is a beautiful old Roman neighborhood famous for its separatism, medieval streets, and pretty-far-from-the-tourist-crowd charm. Hotels here are scattered, most of them flung well beyond the budget traveller's budget, but nice to stay in, if you'd like to be near great restaurants as well as a happening nightlife.

Hotel Carmel, V.G. Mameli, 11 (☎06 580 99 21; www.hotelcarmel.it). Take a right on V.E. Morosini (V.G. Mameli) off V.d. Trastevere. Though a short walk from the heart of Trastevere, this simple hotel offers 9 no-frills, smallish rooms for reasonable prices. A comfortable atrium-like sitting room leads to a beautiful garden terrace with seating for breakfast. All with bath. Breakfast included. Singles €80; doubles €100; triples €120; quads €150. MC/V. ❹

Hotel des Artistes

Hotel Trastevere, V. Luciano Manara, 25 (☎06 581 47 13, fax 06 588 10 16). Take a right off V.d. Trastevere onto V.d. Fratte di Trastevere, which becomes V. Luciano Manara. This homey establishment overlooks P.S. Cosimato. Neighborhood murals give way to 9 simple and airy rooms with bath, TV, and phone. English spoken. Breakfast included. Singles €77; doubles €98-103; triples €129; quads €154. Short-term apartments for 2-6 persons with neat little kitchens and loft beds available. AmEx/D/MC/V. ❺

NEAR PIAZZA DI SPAGNA

see map p. 363

Accommodations in this area might run you a few more euros per day, but can you really put a price tag on living a few steps from Prada? John Keats couldn't.

Pensione Panda, V.d. Croce, 35 (☎06 678 01 79; www.webeco.it/hotelpanda), between P. di Spagna and V.d. Corso. Renovated to add fire proofing and new fixtures, the Panda sports lovely, immaculate rooms and arched ceilings (some with frescoes). Centrally located but shielded from street noise. Always an English speaker on staff. Check-out 11am. Reservations recommended. Mar.-Dec. singles €48, with bath €68; doubles €68, with bath €98; triples with bath €130; quads with bath €170. Off season (Jan.-Feb.) €5 less. Let's Go discount 5% on cash payments during the low season. AmEx/MC/V. ❸

Living in Rome

Hotel Pensione Suisse S.A.S., V. Gregoriana, 54 (☎06 678 36 49; www.hotelsuisserome.com). Turn right at the top of the Spanish Steps. Close to the Steps, but away from the hubbub; at night you'll think you're in another city. Impeccable service, sleek, old-fashioned furniture, comfortable beds, phone and fan in every room; Internet, TV available. Continental breakfast included. All rooms with bath (bathtubs available). Singles €90; doubles €140; triples €194; quads €215. 10-15% discount given on extended stays from Nov.-Feb. MC/V. ❺

Hotel Boccaccio, V.d. Boccaccio, 25 (☎/fax 06 488 59 62; www.hotelboccaccio.com). M: A-Barberini. Off V.d. Tritone. This quiet, well-situated hotel offers 8 elegantly furnished rooms. Reception 9am-11pm, late night access via key, no deposit. Singles €42; doubles €62, with bath €83; triples €84, with bath €112. Reservations with credit card. Discount for extended stays. AmEx/D/MC/V. ❸

Pensione Jonella, V.d. Croce, 41 (☎06 679 79 66; www.lodgingitaly.com), between P. di Spagna and V.d. Corso. Four beautiful rooms. Quiet, roomy, and cool in summer. No reception: you must call to arrange for someone to meet you when you arrive. 4th floor location; no elevator. One bathroom. Singles Mar.-June €62, July-Aug. €52, otherwise generally €45 or less. Doubles Mar.-June €72-25, July-Aug. €62-68, otherwise generally €45-55. Triples Mar.-June €92, July-Aug. €78, otherwise generally €65-75. Quads Mar.-June €110, July-Aug. €92, otherwise generally €85. Cash only. Discount for extended stays. ❹

BORGO & PRATI (NEAR VATICAN CITY)

The *pensioni* on the other side of the Tiber aren't the cheapest in Rome, but they tend to be comfortable, spotless, and fairly quiet (which might appeal to families looking to get plenty of rest). It's convenient to the Vatican but a hike from many central sights. Nearby Metro (A) stops are Lepanto and Ottaviano.

see map p. 364

Colors, V. Boezio, 31 (☎06 687 40 30; www.colorshotel.com). M: A-Ottaviano, or take a bus to P. Risorgimento. Take V. Cola di Rienzo to V. Terenzio. Located in the elegant and quiet Prati area, Colors is patronized by friendly people from all around the English-speaking world and offers 18 beds in rooms painted with a bravado that would put Raphael to shame. Kitchen, hair dryers, Internet €3 per hr. Beautiful terrace and kitchen open 7:30am-11pm. Coed dorm beds €20; doubles €73, with private shower only (shared toilet) €83, with private bathroom €89; triples €83, with private shower only €89, with private bathroom €104. Credit card for private room reservations (dorm beds: call 9pm night before). Cash only. ❶

Hotel Lady, V. Germanico, 198, 4th fl. (☎06 324 21 12; www.hotellady.supereva.it), between V. Fabbio Massimo and V. Paolo Emilio. A non-English-speaking Roman couple has been running this small, peaceful *pensione* for 40 years. The 8 rooms, some with beautiful loft-style open wood-work ceilings and tile floors lack A/C but are miraculously cool in the middle of summer. Spacious common room. All rooms with sinks and desks. Singles without bath €75; doubles without bath €90, with bath €100; with shower €120; triples without bath €120. Prices quoted include a Let's Go discount, so mention it when you reserve. AmEx/MC/V. ❸

Hotel Florida, V. Cola di Rienzo, 243 (☎06 324 18 72 or 06 324 16 08; www.hotelfloridaroma.it), on the 1st-3rd floors, reception on 2nd. Sad that you missed Rome's world-class May flower show? You might like Hotel Florida, a quiet hotel decorated with a distinctly floral decor: floral carpets, floral bedspreads, floral wall paper. A/C (€10/night), TV, phone, and hair dryers in each of the 18 rooms. English-speaking reception. Singles with bath €65-82; doubles with bath €90-113; triples with bath €110-135; quads with bath €130-150. Call ahead to reserve and ask about discounts. 5% discount if you pay in cash. AmEx/MC/V. ❸

Hotel Isa, V. Cicerone, 39 (☎06 321 26 10; www.hotelisa.com). 1 block north of P. Cavour. This 3-star hotel offers all the amenities of a big chain, but with a little more style. Private terraces, telephone, cable TV, and minibar (can of beer €2). American breakfast buffet included, 7-10:30am. 24hr. English-speaking reception. May-Sept. singles €180; doubles €250; Oct.-Apr. singles €130, doubles €180. AmEx/MC/V. ❺

from the road

Queue up

My first day in Rome was not exactly a warm welcome. At the airport, struggling fruitlessly with my bulging, non-Italian suitcases, I accepted a gracious offer to take my luggage to an air-conditioned "taxi." Half-conscious, I slumped into the back seat of a Mercedes that transported me at roughly the speed of light to the city proper. $150 later, I found myself at my hotel. My taxi driver informed me that I had to pay for him to return to the airport. My debating skills were of no use here. Later, I learned that Italians often shouted at each other during the course of normal conversation, and he probably assumed I was thanking him heartily for the ride.

I learned all of my lessons the hard way in Rome, after hours of dragging myself through the Forum, thinking it was downtown and wondering why everything was so dirty and falling down. Profit from my mistakes and follow this advice about surviving La Citta Eterna unscathed.

1. Venturing out of your *albergo* or *ostello* requires fortification in the form of a good, strong coffee drink. After you've taken care of that, find an intersection. This is the first test of your ability.

(continued on next page)

Hotel Pensione Joli, V. Cola di Rienzo, 243, 6th fl. (☎06 324 18 54; www.hoteljoliroma.com), at V. Tibullo, scala A. Winding blue-striped walls and low ceilings make you feel a little like Alice in Wonderland, if Wonderland were a *pensione* with nice beds, ceiling fans, and views of the Vatican. Located on a busy shopping street, Hotel Pensione Joli also offers rooms that face an interior courtyard, for a quieter night. All 18 rooms save a few singles have private baths and telephones. TV available with advance notice.Breakfast 7am-9am. Singles €53, with bath €67; doubles €90 queen, €100 king; triples €135; quads €165; quints €190. AmEx/MC/V. ❹

TERMINI & SAN LORENZO

NORTH OF TERMINI

Although the area right next to the train station has its fair share of tourist traps, there are many comfortable, reasonably priced *pensioni* and hotels. This area has experienced a revival and influx of reasonably-priced lodgings, making it a haven for budget travelers, though it can be a long trek into the city center. But, not only is the area generally cheaper than the historic center, but it is also safer than the sometimes seedy Esquilino area. For a quieter stay, ask for rooms on internal courtyards. Finally, beware of "flexible prices" as some hotels will dramatically increase their rates during peak tourist season.

Pensione Fawlty Towers, V. Magenta, 39 (☎/fax 06 454 359 42; www.fawltytowers.org). From the middle concourse of Termini, exit right (nearest to platform 1), cross V. Marsala onto V. Marghera, and turn right onto V. Magenta; it's on the 5th floor. An extremely popular 15-room hotel/hostel that remains a great value. The flower-filled terrace (open 7am-midnight) provides a peaceful respite from the bustle of Termini. Common room with satellite TV, library, refrigerator, microwave, and free Internet access. Check-out 9am for dorms, 10am for private rooms. Often full, but they will help find a room elsewhere. Reservations possible by fax/email. English speaking staff. No curfew. Dorm quad, €18-20, with bath €23-25; singles €44, with bath €51; doubles €62, with bath €77; triples €82, with bath €90. No credit cards. ❶

Hotel Papa Germano, V. Calatafimi, 14a (☎06 486 919; www.hotelpapagermano.com). From the middle concourse of Termini, exit right, and turn left onto V. Marsala, which shortly becomes V. Volturno; V. Calatafimi is the 4th cross-street on your right. Clean, affordable rooms (all with TV and telephone) and outstanding service from friendly owners Gino and Pina Germano. Still, the real draw here is the four spacious 4-bed dorms at a superb value. English, French, and Spanish spoken. Internet access €2.60 per hr. Check-out 11am. Dorms €18-25, singles €23-40; doubles €45-70, with bath €52-93; triples €54-78, with bath €72-105. Prices vary depending on season and demand; Nov.-Mar. 10% discount. AmEx/MC/V. ❶

Hotel Galli, V. Milazzo, 20 (☎06 445 68 59; www.albergogalli.com). From the middle concourse of Termini, exit right. Take a right on V. Marsala and your first left on V. Milazzo. 12 clean and modern rooms with tile floors and wrought-iron beds. Kind and helpful family owners. All rooms have bath, telephones, TV, fridge, and safe. Breakfast, A/C included. Singles €50; doubles €80; triples €90; quads €110. Winter 10% discount. AmEx/MC/V. ❸

Hotel Des Artistes, V. Villafranca, 20 (☎06 445 43 65; www.hoteldesartistes.com). From the middle concourse of Termini, exit right, turn left onto V. Marsala, right onto V. Vicenza, and then left onto the 5th cross-street. 3-star, 40-room hotel with clean, elegant rooms, some with safes, refrigerators, and TVs. Amenities include a rooftop terrace (open until 1am) and lounge with satellite TV. Free Internet access. You may get a lot for your money, but that doesn't change the fact that you're paying a lot. Breakfast included with bathroom price, otherwise a steep €12. Reception 24 hr. Cancel reservations 5 days before. Check-out 11am. Singles €52-62, with bath €99-149; doubles €59-84 or €109-159; triples €75-112 or €139-179; quads €96-126 or €149-199. Winter 20-30% discount. €15 discount with cash payment. AmEx/MC/V. ❹

Hotel Dolomiti and **Hotel Lachea,** V.S. Martino della Battaglia, 11 (☎06 495 72 56 or 06 491 058; www.hotel-dolomiti.it). From the middle concourse of Termini, exit right, turn left onto V. Marsala and right onto V. Solferino (V.S. Martino della Battaglia). This aging 19th-century *palazzo* houses sparkling new three-star hotels, with the same reception (on 2nd floor) and management, offering a bar, breakfast room, and Internet access (30min. €2.60). Rooms with bathrooms are well-furnished with satellite TV, telephones, minibars, safes, hair-dryers, and A/C. Some rooms with a balcony. Breakfast €6. A/C €13 per night (ouch). Check-out 11am. Check-in 1pm. Singles €37-42, with bath €55-67; doubles €55-68 or €75; triples €60-73 or €88; quads €115-135; quints €145-155. ❸

If you wait until a car stops to let you by, you will be there for the entire day. Do like the real Romans: when there is a small break in traffic, edge your way out into the street and stare the driver directly in the eye, as if daring him to hit you. He may speed up for a perilous few seconds, but he will stop.

2. Lines, queues, whatever you call them, are not Italian. You've finally made your way across the street to McDonald's, a quaint trattoria, or a pizzeria. You encounter a bunch of people standing in what you, simpleton, think is a line. As locals pass you on both sides without regard to the fact that you are patiently waiting in "line," you will become confused and angry...until you wise up and start doing the same thing to beleaguered tourists.

3. On the off chance that you manage to find one of Rome's rare sidewalks, you will undoubtedly be alarmed to find that it is moonlighting as a parking lot, leaving enough space for a small terrier to pass, perhaps, but certainly not enough for you to squeeze your tortellini-swollen body past. Don't be alarmed if a local pulls in front of you while you're walking along, minding your own business.

Caitlin Hurley was a Researcher-Writer for Let's Go: USA 1994. She currently teaches at the Marymount International School in Rome.

Hotel Cathrine, V. Volturno, 27 (☎06 483 634). From the middle concourse of Termini, exit right, and turn left onto V. Marsala (V. Volturno). You get exactly what you pay for: two common bathrooms serve the 8 no frills or thrills singles and doubles that have only a sink. More rooms (and better value) at the modern **Affitacamere Aries** at V. XX Settembre, 58a (☎06 420 271 61; www.afficamereaires.com). Breakfast €2. *Let's Go* discount available, depending on season. Singles €35-45; doubles €47-62, with bath €52-72; €15 per extra bed. ❸

Hotel Gabriella, V. Palestro, 88 (☎06 445 02 52). From the middle concourse of Termini, exit right, cross V. Marsala onto V. Marghera and take the 4th right onto V. Palestro. A friendly family-run hotel with 23 rooms and definite pretensions of grandeur. The newly refurbished doubles, with beautifully tiled bathrooms, are an excellent value. All rooms have private bathroom, A/C (included in high season price) and television. Shared salon with Internet access. 10am checkout. Breakfast included (7-9:30am). Singles €50-100; €80-135; triple €100-182; quads €120-210. AmEx/MC/V. ❹

Hotel Bolognese, V. Palestro, 15 (☎/fax 06 490 045). From the middle concourse of Termini, exit right. Walk down V. Marghera and take your 4th left on V. Palestro. In a land of run-of-the-mill *pensioni,* this place is spruced up by the artist-owner, whose impressive paintings decorate all the rooms. Some rooms have balconies. Probably the only hotel near Termini to have won an award from the Knights of Malta for hospitality. Check-out 10:30am. Singles €31, with bath €43; doubles €47 or €55; triples €55 or €70. Cash only. ❷

Hotel Fenicia, V. Milazzo, 20 (☎/fax 06 490 342 or 338 211 75 41; www.hotelfenicia.it). Same building as Hotel Galli. 15 sparkling, modern rooms with hard-wood floors. Every room with bath, fridge, safe, TV, and A/C. Newly refurbished and especially spacious room upstairs. Singles €45; doubles €70-85. Extra beds €30. ❹

Hotel Cervia, V. Palestro, 55 (☎06 491 057; www.hotelcerviaroma.com). From Termini, exit onto V. Marsala, head down V. Marghera and take the fourth road on the left. The TV room, breakfast room with bar, and clean rooms and bathrooms are nice, but guests stay on for the friendly atmosphere. Rooms with bath include breakfast; otherwise, it's €5. Reception 24 hr. Check-out 11am. Singles €35, with bath €45; doubles €60 or €95; triples €75 or €95. In summer, quad dorm beds available €20. Ask about the Let's Go discount. AmEx/MC/V. ❷

Hotel Aphrodite, V. Marsala, 90 (☎06 491 096; www.accommodationinrome.com). Aphrodite's modern, bright decor, rooftop terrace, and soundproof windows make you forget that you are 10m from Termini. Each room comes with private bath, TV, telephone, A/C, mini-bar, and safe. Breakfast included. Check-out 11am. Singles €60-120; doubles €80-150; triples €105-160; quads €150-200. 10% discount with cash payment. AmEx/MC/V. ❹

Pensione Katty, V. Palestro, 35 (☎06 444 12 16). The 23 rooms are plain but large. Ask for one with an elegant painted ceiling. The second floor has the nicest rooms (with fridges and the option of A/C at €5), but all have high ceilings and sinks. Check-out 11am. Singles €25-40, with bath €35-45; doubles €40-50 or €45-70; triples €45-70 or €55-93; quads €70-80 or €75-100. Big discounts Nov.-Mar. Traveler's checks accepted. MC/V. ❶

Freedom Traveller, V. Gaeta, 25 (☎06 478 238 62; www.freedom-traveller.it). From Termini, exit onto V. Marsala. Walk west down V. Marsala becomes V. Volturno, and make a right onto V. Gaeta. Though lacking in luxuries, the slightly run-down hostel has unbeatable prices. The fun group of guys who run it also organize pub crawls on M and Th nights (€15). No private baths. Dorm bed €17-20; doubles €48-60; triples €66-84; quads €80-100. Cash only. ❶

VIA XX SEPTEMBRE & ENVIRONS

Dominated by government ministries and private apartments, this area is less noisy and touristy than the nearby Termini.

Pensione Monaco, V. Flavia, 84 (☎/fax 06 420 141 80). Go north up V. XX Settembre, turn left onto V. Quintino Sella, and then right onto V. Flavia. Friendly Italian woman and her English-speaking kids keep these 11 sunlit rooms, all with bathroom, remarkably clean. Comfortable mattresses, bright courtyard. Check-out 9am. *Let's Go* discount prices: singles €37; doubles €60; triples and quads €25 per person. Winter 10% discount. ❸

Hotel Castelfidardo and **Hotel Lazzari,** V. Castelfidardo, 31 (☎06 446 46 38; www.castelfidardo.com). Two blocks off V. XX Settmebre. Both run by the same friendly family. Renovated rooms with spanking clean floors and soothing pastel walls. Three floors of modern, shiny comfort. Check-out 10:30am. English spoken. Singles €44, with bath €55; doubles €64/€74; triples €83/€96; quads with bath €110. AmEx/MC/V. ❸

Pensione Tizi, V. Collina, 48 (☎06 482 01 28; fax 06 474 32 66). A 10min. walk from the station. Go north up V. XX Septembre, and turn left onto V. Servio Tullio, then right onto V. Flavia, and left on V. Collina. Or take bus #360 or #217 from Termini. The people at Tizi have served student travelers for years. Marble floors and inlaid ceilings adorn spacious and recently renovated rooms. Check-out 11am. Singles €45; doubles €55, with bath €65; triples €80/€90; quads €100/€110. Cash only. ❸

Hotel Baltic, V. XX Settembre, 89 (☎06 481 47 75); Walk north up V. XX Settembre; go just past the intersection with V. Castelfidardo. Quiet rooms with high ceilings are well maintained and more like those in a business hotel than a typical pensione. All rooms have telephone, TV, mini-bar, and safe. A friendly manager and marble lobby sweeten the deal. Breakfast €5. Check-out 11am. Some rooms with A/C for €10. Singles €48-53; doubles €65-70; triples €83-88; quads €110. AmEx/MC/V. ❹

Pensione Piave, V. Piave, 14 (☎06 474 34 47; www.albergopiave.it). Going north up V. XX Settembre, turn left onto V. Piave. Recently renovated Piave features key cards, sparkling floors and modern decor. All rooms with bathroom, A/C, TV, and phone. Check-in 11:30am. Reservations recommended. Singles €60-90; doubles €75-105. MC/V. ❺

SOUTH OF TERMINI (ESQUILINO)

While it's not the most posh part of town, it has decent rooms at good prices and is still close to many of the major sights.

Pensione di Rienzo, V. Principe Amedeo, 79a (☎06 446 71 31; fax 06 446 69 80). A tranquil, family-run retreat with spacious, recently renovated rooms. Large windows overlook a courtyard. Extremely friendly, helpful, English-speaking staff. It's plain and it's cheap. 20 rooms, with balconies, TVs, and baths. Breakfast €7. Check-out 10am. Singles without bath €20-50; doubles €23-60, with bath €25-70. Prices depend on season. MC/V. ❶

Pensione Cortorillo, V. Principe Amedeo, 79a, 5th fl. (☎06 446 69 34; www.hotelcortorillo.it). This small *pensione* has TVs and A/C in all 14 rooms, and a cheap lobby phone. English, French and Spanish spoken. Breakfast included. Check-out 10am. Singles €30-70, with bath €40-100; doubles €40-80, with bath €50-120; rooms can be made into triples and quads for an additional €10 per person. Prices depend on season. AmEx/D/MC/V. ❸

Hotel Kennedy, V. Filippo Turati, 62-64 (☎06 446 53 73; www.hotelkennedy.net). Classical music in the bar, leather couches, and a large color TV in the lounge. Private bath, satellite TV, phone, and A/C. Some rooms offer a view of Roman ruins. Hearty all-you-can-eat breakfast in three pleasant breakfast rooms included. English, French, Spanish, and Portugese spoken. Check-out 11am. Reservations by fax/email only. Singles €60-80; doubles €85-129; triples €100-149. 10% *Let's Go* discount. AmEx/D/MC/V. ❺

Hotel Scott House, V. Gioberti, 30 (☎06 446 53 79; www.scotthouse.com). Each one of the 34 clean and comfortable rooms features a private bath, A/C, telephone, safe box, satellite TV, and brightly painted walls. After a day of sightseeing, spread out on the large French bed in your single. Breakfast included. Check-out 11am. Singles €35-68, doubles €63-98, triples €75-114, quads, €88-129, quints €100-140. Prices vary by season. AmEx/MC/V. ❸

Hotel Orlanda, V. Principe Amedeo, 76, 3rd fl. (☎06 488 01 24; fax 06 488 01 83; www.hotelorlanda.com). At V. Gioberti. Take the stairs in the vestibule. Frequented by Italian businesspeople. Rooms have TV, phone, and sink, but no bathroom. A/C €15.50. Breakfast included. Reception 24 hr. Check-in noon. Check-out 10am. Singles €30-65, with bath €45-70; doubles €52-75, with bath €60-100; triples €62-90, with bath €80-130; quads €82-110, with bath € 100-160. AmEx/D/MC/V. ❷

Hotel Sweet Home, V. Principe Amedeo, 47 (☎/fax 06 488 09 54; www.hotelsweethome.it). The newly renovated rooms are tidy (with candy on the pillows, no less) and quite spacious, and the proprietors are very welcoming. Breakfast included. Check-out 11am. Singles €35-45, with bath €45-65; doubles €45-65, with bath €55-85. AmEx/D/MC/V. ❸

Hotel Teti, V. Principe Amedeo, 76 (☎/fax 06 489 040 88; hotelteti@iol.it). Take the stairs at the end of the courtyard. Large rooms with satellite TV, bathroom, and telephone. English spoken. A/C included in high season, €10 extra otherwise. Breakfast €5. Check-out 11am. Reservation can be made via email. Singles €45-80; doubles €90-130; triples €120-160; quads €130-170. 10-15% discount for students with ID. AmEx/D/MC/V. ❹

Hotel Il Castello, V. Vittorio Amedeo II, 9 (☎06 772 040 36; www.ilcastello.com). M: A-Manzoni. Far beyond Termini, but well within the backpacker's budget. Walk down V. San Quintino and take the first left. Spartan rooms, but an eager staff (mostly native English speakers). Continental breakfast €3. Check-out 10:30am. Dorms €20; singles (none with bath) €6-37; doubles €45-62, with shower (no toilet) €55-73, with bath €72-82; triples €55-73, with shower (no toilet) €65-83, with bath €75-92. MC/V. ❶

WEST OF TERMINI

Just steps west from all the hustle and bustle of beloved Termini, the neighborhood becomes less decrepit and offers more sights and stores. Streets here are busier than those north of Termini and not nearly as grid-like.

Pensione Sandy, V. Cavour, 136 (☎06 488 45 85; www.sandyhostel.com). Just past the intersection of V.S. Maria Maggiore. Next door to the Hotel Vallet, on the 4th fl. Same ownership as Pensione Ottaviano, but not quite as nice. 25 beds. Free Internet access, bed linens, and individual lockers (bring your own lock) in each room. No curfew, no lock-out. Simple, hostel-style rooms, usually for 3-5 people, in a central location. €12-18. Cash only. ❶

Hotel Giu' Giu', V.d. Viminale, 8 (☎/fax 06 482 77 34; www.hotelgiugiu.com). Though only a few minutes from Termini, the air-conditioned rooms of this elegant but fading *palazzo* will make you forget the hustle and bustle of Rome. Pleasant breakfast area, 12 quiet rooms. English spoken. Breakfast €7. Check-out 10am. Singles (none with bath) €30-40; doubles €50-70, with bath €60-70; triples with bath €90-105; quads with bath €120-140. ❷

Hotel Selene, V.d. Viminale, 8 (☎06 482 44 60; www.hotelseleneroma.it). Above Hotel Giu' Giu'. The newly renovated upper floor offers the amenities of a three-star hotel including A/C, mini-bar, safe box, satellite TV, and telephone in every room. Breakfast included. Check-out 11am. Singles €55-80; doubles €65-170; triples €80-200; quads €96-240. MC/V. ❹

Hotel San Paolo, V. Panisperna, 95 (☎06 474 52 13; 8; www.hotelsanpaoloroma.com). Exit the front of the train station, turn left onto V. Cavour. Pass Santa Maria Maggiore (on the left), then bear right onto V.d. Santa Maria Maggiore (V. Panisperna). 10min. from Termini, San Paolo's 23 rooms are housed in a bright *palazzo* with tranquil, whimsically decorated rooms. English spoken. Breakfast €5. Check-out 11am. Singles €40; doubles €60, with bath €80; triples €80, with bath €110. Large 6-10 person suite €30 per person. AmEx/MC/V. ❸

ALTERNATIVE ACCOMMODATIONS

BED & BREAKFASTS

While Italians may have appropriated the American terminology, the reality of "Bed and Breakfast" services in Rome differs from the New World concept of a quaint countryside inn. Guest rooms are arranged in private homes throughout the city and the owner is generally obliged to provide breakfast every morning, or at least a kitchen so you can make your own. The rooms and apartments vary in quality and size. Be sure to pinpoint just how "centrally located" your place is—generally speaking, the cheaper the place, the longer the metro ride from the city center. Many hotel proprietors also run bed and breakfasts on the side that are often much cheaper. Be wary that bed and breakfasts don't require an extensive licensure process like hotels do (you may find yourself slightly cramped). Owners merely register with tourist offices by promising to offer a maximum of six beds in no more than three rooms. However, Rome's accommodation problems have led many proprietors to illegally pack their rooms with more beds. (One of the principal virtues of the B&B listing agencies listed below is their claim to extensively check every property they list for compliance with basic standards). Don't necessarily rule out the B&B option categorically, as many bed and breakfasts are efficiently run and provide a home-away-from-home experience that hotels can't rival.

Bed & Breakfast Association of Rome, V. A. Pacinotti. 73 (☎06 553 022 48; www.b-b.rm.it), is a reservation service with a superb English website that gives very explicit information and pictures of the rooms and apartments offered (over 100 listings). Prices range from €46 per night for a single room to €268 per night for a 3-bedroom apartment that sleeps 8. Minimum stay usually 2 nights. Call office M-F 9am-1pm to make an appointment.

Bed and Go, V.S. Tommaso d'Aquino, 47 (☎06 397 509 07 or 06 397 464 84; www.bedandgo.com), offers rooms and apartments of all types, with prices in the city center ranging from €165 (+15% during high season and an additional €10 per bed) per night for a 6-bedroom apartment to €59 for a single bedroom. Website includes photos of rooms. Send an email for further information. Open M-F 9:30am-1pm and 2-6pm. ❹

Daphne B&B, V.d. Avignonesi, 20, (☎/fax 06 478 235 29; www.daphne-rome.com) and V. d. San Basilio, 55, just off the Piazza Barberini. English-speaking owners, full amenities, and a prime location, but still a little pricey. A/C, daily maid service, cell phone rental. Check-in 2pm. Check-out 10am. Reservations strongly recommended. Singles €60-95, with bath €75-

120; doubles €70-110, with bath €80-160; triples €90-135, with bath €105-210; quads €120-160, with bath €160-240. MC/V. ❹

RELIGIOUS HOUSING

Even if religiosity isn't on the rise, religious housing in Rome is. Certain convents and monasteries host guests for approximately €30 per night. But don't automatically think cheap; nuns need new habits too, you know. Some of the most popular religious accommodations, catering to wealthy American tourists in search of the quaint and mystical, run up to €155 for a single. Only a few still require letters of introduction from local dioceses; contact your home parish for details. Most are open to people of all religious backgrounds. Religious accommodations often have early curfews; a few involve single-sex housing, services, and light chores.

Domus Nova Bethlehem, V. Cavour, 85/A (☎06 478 244 1 or 06 478 825 11; www.suorebambinogesu.it). Walk down V. Cavour from Termini, past P.d. Esquilino on the right. A clean, modern and centrally located hotel that happens to carry a religious name, decorations, and a 1am curfew along with it. All rooms come with A/C, private bath, safe, TV and phone; some look onto the Domus' beautiful and accessible gardens. Breakfast included. Singles €70; doubles €49.25 per person; triples €43 per person; quads €37 per person. AmEx/MC/V. ❺

Santa Maria Alle Fornaci, P.S. Maria alle Fornaci, 27 (☎06 393 676 32; cifornaci@tin.it). Facing St. Peter's Basilica, take a left (through a gate in the basilica walls) onto V.d. Fornace. Take your third right onto V.d. Gasperi, which leads to P.S. Maria alle Fornaci. Just south of the Vatican, this *casa per ferie,* in the Trinitarian tradition of hospitality, has 54 rooms, each with a private bath and phone. Simple, small, and clean. No curfew. Breakfast included. Singles €50; doubles €80; triples €110. AmEx/MC/V. ❹

La Fraterna Domus di Roma, V. Monte Brianzo, 62 (☎06 688 027 27; domusrm@tin.it). Entrance at V. Cancello, 6. From Ponte Umberto bear left onto V. Monte Brianzo. Take a right on V. Cancello. A safe haven from the noise and commotion of the Centro Storico. Simple rooms with their own bathrooms, and friendly nuns to relieve you of your reasonable room rate. Breakfast included. Optional lunch and dinner €12. Curfew 11pm. Singles €48; doubles €78; triples €98. ❹

CAMPING

In August, when most Italians go on vacation, call ahead or arrive early (well before 11am) to secure a spot. Rates average €7 per person and

in recent news

Foyer faux pas? It's madness!

Is your housing simply not up to snuff? Add a temple! Legend had it that Caligula, Roman Emperor AD 37-41 and interior decorator extraordinaire, converted a temple into his front porch.

In August 2003, after two months of digging near the Forum, at the foot of the Palatine hill, archaeologists discovered Caligula's palace walls to be integrated into to the Temple of Castor and Pollux. Fitting for an emperor who believed himself to be Zeus.

But Dr. Andrew Wilson of Oxford University explained to the *Telegraph*, a British newspaper, that such an architectural move was "just not done" in the ancient world. "It would be like extending your back garden into St. Paul's cathedral."

Evidently this imperial faux pas just confirms Caligula's lunacy under the strain of epilepsy, megalomania and possibly schizophrenia. Before being murdered in AD 41, he supposedly committed incest with all three of his sisters and converted his palace into a brothel. He also proclaimied victory against the sea and appointed Incitatus, his beloved horse, to the coveted position of consul. Catherine the Great would approve!

another €4.50 per tent. Rent a bungalow or apartment for approximately €22-55. The **Touring Club Italiano** (www.touringclub.it) publishes an annual directory of all camping sites in Italy, *Campeggi in Italia,* available in bookstores throughout Italy (€11.30). You can also find a list of camp sites in the Bed and Breakfast book of any tourist office. Camping on beaches, roads, and inconspicuous plots is illegal and dangerous. Respect for property rights is extremely important in Italy: be sure always to ask permission before bedding down. **Seven Hills Village** ❶, a popular campground, is close enough to Rome to be convenient, but far enough to be an escape. Enjoy a lazy pool side afternoon (€4 per day) and then dance the night away at the disco. Seven Hills does not accept cash; guests put money on a camp-issued debit card. To reach Seven Hills, take bus #907 from the Cipro-Musei Vaticani Metro (A), or bus #201 from P. Mancini. Daily shuttles to Rome will take you back and forth between the campgrounds and Ple. Flaminio (8, 9am; return 1, 6pm; €3.50). Reception is open from 7am to 8pm and you may check-in at anytime during the day, but check-out is at noon. (☎06 303 108 26 or 06 303 627 51; www.camping.it/lazio/seven_hills. Open early-Mar. to mid-Nov. €7.90 per person, €4.80 per tent, €3.90 per car; campers €6.50. Bungalows sleep up to 4 and start from €50. AmEx/MC/V.) he converted a temple into a front vestibule for his palace

WOMEN'S HOUSING

Besides the YWCA, your best bet is probably religious housing, which is often single-sex. Beware of the strict curfews and guest policies.

YWCA Foyer di Roma, V.C. Balbo, 4 (☎06 4880 460). From Termini, take V. Cavour turning right onto V. Torino and then the first left onto V. C. Balbo. The YWCA (pronounced EEV-kah and known as the Casa per Studentesse) is a pretty, clean, and secure hostel. Breakfast included, M-Sa 8am-9am. Tell reception by 10am the same day if you want lunch (1-2pm; €11). Reception 7am-midnight. Curfew midnight. Check-out 10am. Singles €37, with bath €47; doubles €31 per person, with bath €37 per person; triples and quads €26 per person; extra bed €26. Cash only. ❸

Associazione Cattolica Internazionale al Servizio della Giovane, V. Urbana, 158 (☎06 4890 45 23; www.acisjf.it). From P. Esquilino (in front of Santa Maria Maggiore), walk down V.d. Pretis and turn left. Church-run establishment that arranges housing for women ages 18-25 of any religion. The gals-only garden is fantastic, the 10pm curfew (midnight on Sa and Su—those rebels) less so. Open M-Sa 6:30am-10pm, Su 7am-10pm. 5- or 8-bed dorms €16; doubles and triples €19 per person. Cash only. ❶

LONG-TERM ACCOMMODATIONS

Finding a long-term rental in Rome can be downright painful. Many potential landlords are wary of renting out properties because Italian law can make the process of evicting a tenant take up to 20 years. Not wanting to have a squatter on their hands, many apartment owners prefer to either keep their properties empty, rent them out to short-term tenants, or lend them to family. Renting short-term is comparatively easier: the months with the most vacancies are July, August, and December. During summer, student apartments become available and homeowners are generally willing to lease out their places. During the rest of the year, the real estate market is extremely tight. In the last decade, prices for even the most simple pad have skyrocketed; expect to pay no less than €900 per month for a one-bedroom in the Centro Storico. The longer you stay, the better your chances of finding cheap rent. In general, the cheaper areas include the Nomentana neighborhood, the area around Piazza Bologna, and San Lorenzo. Utilities are inordinately expensive in Rome; they can push up your rent by 25%. Finding long-term accommodation can be particularly difficult for those who don't speak Italian. **Real estate agencies** can help, but many charge fees—definitely avoid agencies that charge a non-refundable fee. Tourist offices might also be willing to offer a helping hand (see **Service Directory**, p. 343), as may the **Centro Turistico Studentesco,** V. Genova, 16 (☎06 44 11 11). Otherwise, check the English-language ones in bookstores (see p. 232), the Pasquino movie theter (see p. 216), or the All Saints Anglican Church on V. d. Babuino, 153/b (just off P. del Popolo). Finally, consider foreign university programs too: they often rent out vacant dorm rooms in the summer.

HOUSING AGENCIES

The following real estate agents specialize in finding apartments for foreigners. They may be out of your price range, but they're often willing to give advice. Calling well ahead of time will greatly increase your chances of securing a place on time.

Romeguide (www.romeguide.it). A great web site to use while searching for an apartment.

Rome Property Network, V.d. Gesù è Maria, 25 (☎06 321 23 41). Near P. del Popolo. Arranges short- and long-term apartment and villa rentals in various price ranges; specializes in Centro Storico and Trastevere. English spoken. Open M-F 9:30am-6pm, Sa 10am-2pm.

Welcome Home Relocation Services, V. Barbarano Romano, 15 (☎06 303 669 36; fax 06 303 617 06; welcome.home@slashnet.it). Housing placement services plus assistance in documentation (permits, visas, licenses). English spoken. Open M-F 9am-1pm and 4-7pm.

Homes International, V. L. Bissolati, 20 (☎06 488 18 00; fax 06 488 18 08; homeint@tin.it). Arranges short and long-term rentals for apartments and villas; can also locate cheaper places in the outskirts of Rome and in every major city in the western world. English spoken. Open M-F 9am-1pm, 2-7pm, Sa 9am-1pm.

Flat in Rome (www.flatinrome.com). Great no-fee apartment search website.

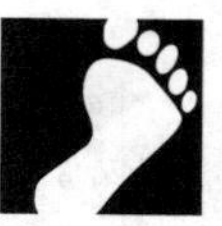

INSIDE

lazio **260**

ostia antica **263** tivoli **267** castelli romani **270**
pontine islands **274** etruia **277**

campania **280**

naples (napoli) **280** bay of naples **285** the amalfi coast **289**
pompeii **292** herculaneum (ercolano) **295** paestrum **296**

Daytripping

Fierce Mediterranean sunshine, sparkling clear waters, and a national predilection for dark tans make Italian beaches an understandably popular summer destination. While most beaches are crowded on weekends, the swarms of scantily clad sunbathers do not become unbearable until August. The farther from the city you go, the better your prospects for sunning and swimming in relative peace. Many of Rome's most popular discos close during the summer months and reappear at the beaches of **Ostia** and **Fregene** (see **Nightlife,** p. 263), although you may need a car to get back late at night. *Rome C'è* lists up-to-date details of the beach scene.

Great stretches of the **Lazio** beaches lie under the thumb of nefarious *stabilimenti balneari*—private companies that fence off the choicest bits of beach and charge admission (usually €5.16-7.75), which includes the use of a changing cabin. Beach chair and umbrella rentals, as well as hot showers, are extra. A little polite inquiry, however, will usually get you to a *spiaggia libera* (public beach).

But beaches aren't the only reason to leave Rome for its surrounding areas. Quaint medieval towns, the world's best pizza, ancient ruins, and clear lakes and rolling hills beckon from the Lazio and Campania regions. Whether you take a picnic to nearby Ostia or spend a weekend in Naples, these daytrips offer an entirely different side of Italy when you are in need of a respite from Rome's insanity.

LAZIO

When the speeding *motorini* and the tourist-choked morass of Rome start to get you down, seek sanctuary nearby in rural **Lazio.** The cradle of ancient Roman civilization, Lazio stretches from the Tyrrhenian coastline through volcanic mountains to the foothills of the Abruzzese Apennines. The territory attracted the Etruscan Empire's attention as early as the 9th century BC, when it colonized Tarquinia and Cerveteri. While Rome was still in its early embryonic stages, just a few mud huts straddling the Palantine Hill, Estruscan and Latin towns throughout Lazio enjoyed relative sophistication. Even as the massive Roman Empire expanded across Europe and the Mediterranean, the imperial city still relied upon Lazio as an important natural resource. Travertine marble quarried from its hills was used to build the Colosseum and St. Peter's Basilica, and fertile volcanic soil fed both farms and vineyards.

SPERLONGA

Take the Naples train from Termini to the Fondi-Sperlonga stop. Takes 1¼hr., leaves every hr. 5:15am-11:32pm, last return 9:57pm. €5.40. From here catch a 10min. CO.TRA.L bus to Sperlonga. Every hr. M-Sa 6:30am-7pm, Su 7am-7pm, last return 8:15pm. €1. From Anzio, head back

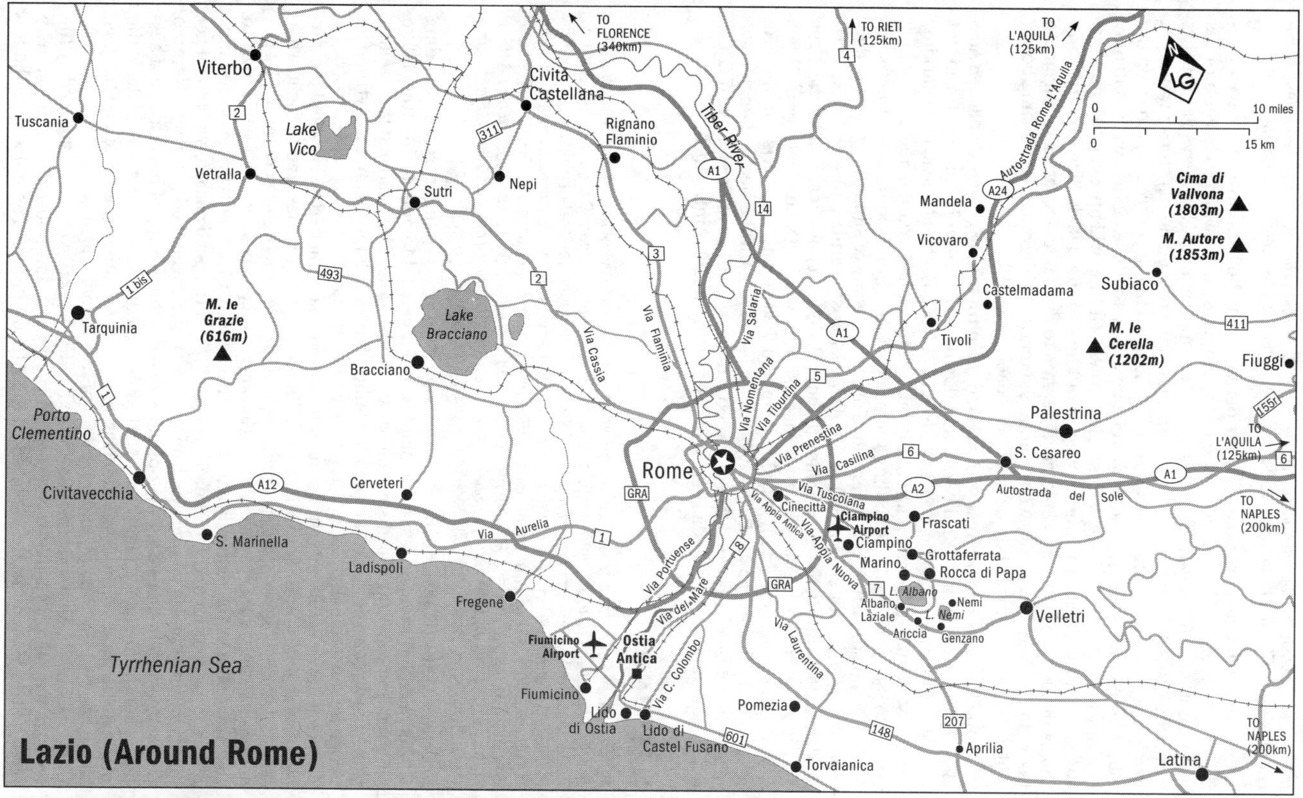

Lazio (Around Rome)

to Rome and transfer at Campoleone for Naples. €5.60. ***Tourist office*** *on C. San Leone just off the piazza, ☎0771 557 00, has maps and hotel listings. Open daily 8am-noon and 3-9pm.*

A tiny coastal hamlet, Sperlonga's name derives from the Latin word for caves, *speluncae.* Emperor Tiberius used one of Sperlonga's caves as an extension of his waterfront villa in the early decades of the first millennium. Nowadays vacationers forgo the caves for luxury rental condos and vine-covered hotels steps away from lovely stretches of beach. Buses arrive at P. Europa in the *centro storico* upon the hill, where chaotically-placed stairwells give way to stores laden with matronly clothing and artsy-craftsy souvenirs. A left on V.d. III Ripa will take you to staircases cascading past cacti growing between boulders to the beach. The hulking **Torre Truglia** divides the beach into **Spiaggia di Levante** to the left and **Spiaggia di Ponente** to the right. Levante has a tiny, well-maintained marina with sailing and fishing boats, while Ponente offers slightly more public beach space.

On the Ponente side of town you will find the ultra-trendy beachside **Albergo Amyclae ❸,** V.C. Colombo, 77. Take V. Roma down the hill from P. Europa, turn right onto V.C. Colombo along the beachfront. (☎0771 548 051. Private beach and parking. Breakfast included. During particularly busy periods, half-board is required, which costs €65-95 per person, including the price of the room. Doubles cost between €100-140 (no singles). If you're famished after a long day of sunbathing, try the delicious *fettuccine alla cozze* (€7) or the *Astice Arrosto* (grilled lobster; €4.50/100g) at **Ristorante La Siesta ❸,** V. Orticello, 15, near P. della Repubblica. Follow the signs for the restaurant from the *piazza* through several winding sidestreets. (☎0771 548 617. €2.50 cover. Open daily 12:30-2:15pm and 7:30-10pm). Otherwise, in the evenings, head for the **Tropical Bar,** V. Colombo, 17-19, just off the beach: inexpensive drinks flow freely and wood-fire-oven-cooked pizzas start at under €4. (☎0771 549 621; www.tropical.it. Open daily 12-3pm and 7pm-midnight; AmEx/MC/V.)

NETTUNO

Take the regional train from Termini to Nettuno, about 1hr.; every hr. 6:10am-9:10pm, additional trains at 2:32pm, 9:50pm, 10:55pm, and 4:58am, return 4:55am-9:52pm; €2.90. Nettuno is the last stop, about 5min. from Anzio. CO.TRA.L buses depart for Anzio every 15-30min. from Piazzale IX Settembre, in front of the train station. Get tickets at the Tabacchi *inside the station, 6:10am-9:30pm, €0.77.* ***Pro Loco tourist office*** *in the right corner of marina. ☎06 980 33 35; www.proloconettuno.it. Open M-F 10am-12:30pm and 5-7:30pm, Sa 10am-12:30pm and 6-8pm. Fortezza Sangallo and Museo dello Sbarco Alleato open Tu-Su 9am-1pm and 2-6pm. Free. Cemetery Information Office open daily 9am-5pm, closed Christmas and New Year's.*

Following the collapse of the Empire, Roman refugees in flight from marauding Goths installed themselves in the shadows of a coastal temple to Neptune 60km south of Rome. World War II saw the partial destruction of Nettuno and the decimation of nearby Anzio, when amphibious Allied forces emerged from the Tyrrhenian Sea to initiate their advance upon Nazi-occupied Rome.

A walk down V. Colombo from the train station takes you to the shore and the perpendicular V. Matteoti. Turn left onto V. Matteoti in order to descend to the marina, teeming with yachts. As in Anzio, many of Nettuno's beaches are controlled by private establishments or *stabilimenti.* Entrance to these beaches is "free," provided that you rent a beach umbrella and a chair for an easy €15. However, if you continue left past the marina and the church, you will reach the **public beach,** which can get quite crowded in the summer as Romans go on their weekend getaways. Nettuno fortunately offers more than over-priced skin-scorching. Sites of historical and aesthetic interest include a highly touristed walled, medieval quarter: to the right of the marina, the walls of the **Borgo Medioevale** preserve a congregation of vaulted passageways, narrow *piazze,* and a handful of less archaic nightspots. A right from V. Colombo onto V. Matteoti will take you to P.S. Francesco, which is dominated by the **Fortezza Sangallo,** a turn-of-the-16th-century fortress that houses the rather musty **Museo dello Sbarco Alleato,** devoted to the Allied landing. The museum is handicapped accessible and contains a piece-meal collection of photographs from the Allied invasion of Italy, various pieces of military paraphernalia, and enlarged American newspaper descriptions of the landing.

Another plaintive reminder of Lazio's unfortunate positioning in the path of the World War II juggernaut is the **Sicily-Rome American Cemetery,** stretching over 77 acres of Italian cypress trees, trickling fountains, and expansive verdant lawns. To reach the cemetery, turn right coming out of the train station and then right again onto V.S. Maria. Arching rows of solemn white crosses extend across the gradually sloping green grass. A walk among the seemingly endless graves of 7861 Americans (as well as a memorial to the 3095 missing) is a disquieting way to spend a day of vacation, but plenty of tourists make the trek. The majority of these soldiers died during the 1943-44 Italian campaign, which began with the invasion of Sicily and ended with the liberation of Rome. The memorial at the top of the park contains a chapel, as well as extensive map murals depicting the Allied drive up the peninsula. Americans run the information office to the right of the entrance, and will provide information and help locate graves.

ANZIO

Take the same regional train from Termini to Nettuno to the next stop. The CO.TRA.L blue bus arrives from and departs for Nettuno in P. Cesare Battisti (6:40am-10pm; €0.77). From the main station, walk down V. Palombi to P.C. Battisti; 3 blocks down and to the left in P. Pia is the ***IAT tourist office,*** *with maps, hotel, and ferry information. ☎06 698 451 47. Open M and W 9am-1pm; Tu and Th-Sa 9am-1pm and 4-7pm. Parco Archeologico della Villa Imperiale di Nerone is a 5 min. walk down V. Fanciulla d'Anzio. Turn right from Riviera Mallozzi onto V. Furio Anziate, and then another right onto V. Fanciulla d'Anzio. Open daily 10:30am-12:30pm and 5-7pm. Guided visits, Sa and Su 5-6pm. Free.*

Majestic palm trees line V. Paolini, the boulevard that runs from the train station to the center of Anzio, past villas that recall Anzio's long-held prominence as the vacation spot of choice for emperors, popes, and pirates. The *vacanza* was interrupted on January 22, 1944 when Allied forces launched an attack from the water upon Anzio and Nettuno, 3km to the south. Within six months, American and British troops would be marching upon the capital. While Rome fared the war reasonably well, the town was decimated during the surprise attack. Anzio is active in the fishing and shipbuilding industries, and the area around the port boasts a shopping center. Anzio is a point of departure for the **Pontine Islands** (see p. 274). As at Nettuno, much of the prime sand is controlled by *stabilimenti,* but if you turn right when you get to the shore, and walk along Riviera Mallozzi, you will find a very appealing swath of public coastline—made easily recognizable by its colorful beach umbrellas. Aside from cost, this public beach has one striking advantage over its privately-controlled neighbors: the ruins of Nero's Imperial Villa descend onto the beach from the overlooking cliffs. After a day at the beach, you can make your way to the **Parco Archeologico della Villa Imperiale di Nerone,** for a closer look at the remains of the emperor's characteristically immodest seaside resort.

OSTIA ANTICA

M: B-Piramide. Exit the platform and follow the signs for the Lido trains to the left of the station. Get off at the Ostia Antica stop. Use same ticket as on Metro. Cross overpass, take road straight until it dead-ends into the parking lot for Ostia Antica. Go left through the parking lot and follow the signs to the entrance. ☎06 563 502 15. Open Tu-Su 8:30am-7pm; in winter Tu-Su 8:30am-4pm; last entrance 1hr. before closing; €4, EU citizens 18-24 €2, EU citizens under 18 and over 65 free. Informative and entertaining audio guide €4.13. Guided tours by reservation only Su mornings, except in Aug., €4. You can pick up a map at the biglietteria for €2.

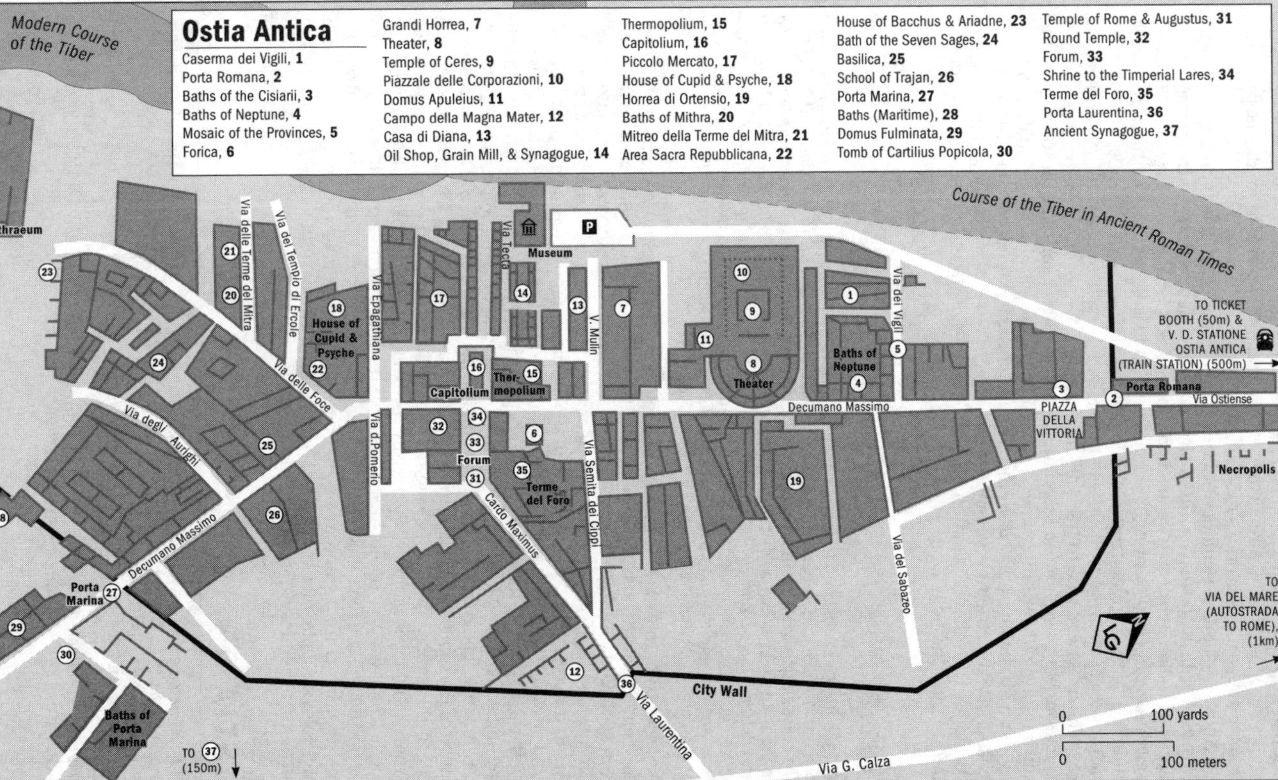
Ostia Antica
Caserma dei Vigili, 1
Porta Romana, 2
Baths of the Cisiarii, 3
Baths of Neptune, 4
Mosaic of the Provinces, 5
Forica, 6
Grandi Horrea, 7
Theater, 8
Temple of Ceres, 9
Piazzale delle Corporazioni, 10
Domus Apuleius, 11
Campo della Magna Mater, 12
Casa di Diana, 13
Oil Shop, Grain Mill, & Synagogue, 14
Thermopolium, 15
Capitolium, 16
Piccolo Mercato, 17
House of Cupid & Psyche, 18
Horrea di Ortensio, 19
Baths of Mithra, 20
Mitreo della Terme del Mitra, 21
Area Sacra Repubblicana, 22
House of Bacchus & Ariadne, 23
Bath of the Seven Sages, 24
Basilica, 25
School of Trajan, 26
Porta Marina, 27
Baths (Maritime), 28
Domus Fulminata, 29
Tomb of Cartilius Popicola, 30
Temple of Rome & Augustus, 31
Round Temple, 32
Forum, 33
Shrine to the Timperial Lares, 34
Terme del Foro, 35
Porta Laurentina, 36
Ancient Synagogue, 37
Modern Course of the Tiber
Course of the Tiber in Ancient Roman Times
Mithraeum
Via delle Terme del Mitra
Via del Tempio di Ercole
House of Cupid & Psyche
Via Epagathiana
Via Tecta
Museum
P
V. Mulin
Via dei Vigil
Baths of Neptune
Theater
Capitolium
Thermopolium
Via delle Foce
Via degli Aurighi
Decumano Massimo
Via d.Pomerio
Forum
Terme del Foro
Via Semita dei Cippi
Cardo Maximus
Via del Sabazeo
PIAZZA DELLA VITTORIA
Porta Romana
Via Ostiense
Necropolis
TO TICKET BOOTH (50m) & V. D. STATIONE OSTIA ANTICA (TRAIN STATION) (500m)
TO VIA DEL MARE (AUTOSTRADA TO ROME), (1km)
Porta Marina
City Wall
Via Laurentina
Via G. Calza
Baths of Porta Marina
TO 37 (150m)
0 100 yards
0 100 meters

The ruins of the Roman port of Ostia are convenient to Rome, and provide the unique experience of exploring a well-preserved abandoned Roman city without having to make the long trip to the more famous ruins at Pompeii and Herculaneum. The extensive site also shows the more practical side of ancient Rome absent in the temples and monuments of the Roman Forum—bakeries, bars, and even public toilets. The excavations are quite large and require the better part of a day to explore well—bring a picnic if you don't want to eat at the cafeteria.

The city, named for the *ostium* (mouth) of the Tiber, was founded around 335 BC as the first Roman colony. Ostia grew alongside its mother city from a mere fortified camp established to guard the salt fields of the Tiber delta into a port and naval base during the 3rd and 2nd centuries BC. After Rome won control of the seas in the Punic Wars, almost all imports to Rome passed through Ostia.

The late Republican and early Imperial periods saw the construction of the most grandiose (and the most well-preserved) structures in the port. By AD 45, the wharves lining the river had reached their maximum capacity, and sand deposits started to block the port, prompting Claudius to dredge an artificial harbor to the northwest (fragments of which have been found near Fiumicino airport). Nonetheless, Ostia remained an important Roman city and continued to expand throughout the Imperial period.

From the entrance gate, **Via Ostiense** (the same highway that now leads out of Rome), leads to a **necropolis** of brick and marble tombs. The road passes through the low remains of the **Porta Romana**—one of the city's three gates, it's framed by Sulla's 1st-century BC walls—and becomes the city's main street, the **Decumanus Maximus.** To the immediate left are a square and the remains of a fountain where *cisiarii* (cart drivers) who ran between Rome and Ostia parked their vehicles.

The following listings are a description of the major ruins and sights in Ostia Antica. The map will help you navigate the city. Visit the **museum** to see a collection of ancient artifacts and obtain additional information about the town's history. (Museum lies on the northern side of Ostia Antica, near the Tiber; see map. Open Tu-Sa 9am-1:30pm and 2:15-6:30pm, Su 9am-1:30pm. Free with park ticket.)

BATHS OF THE CISIARII

After entering the gate, turn right at the large plaza to reach the Baths of the Cisiarii, the mule drivers who transported goods between Rome and Ostia (the Roman equivalent of the Teamsters). Loathe to leave their mules even when bathing, they decorated the floor of their baths with mosaics of long-eared mules at work.

BATHS OF NEPTUNE AND WINE SHOP

The large baths lie on the right a few hundred yards down the road from the entrance gate. Next to the baths is a colonnaded courtyard—the *palestra* where bathers would exercise. A break behind the right wall of the palestra shows how the *calidarium* (hot baths) were heated—they were set on platforms under which hot air circulated. Just beyond the baths is a wine shop in which the mosaic floor depicts a large cup and an advertisement for the shop, "Fortunatus says: if you're thirsty have a cup of wine." In the road in front of the baths is a medieval well—look in the grating next to it to see the piping that distributed water throughout Ostia. Near the well is a small alley alongside the baths, with a mosaic representing the four winds (men with wings on their heads) and the Roman provinces that traded with Ostia (women wearing agricultural products in the hair, and the 3-legged wheel of Sicily).

FULLONICA AND MITHRAEUM

Off the Decumanus to the left of the baths, the **V.d. Fontana,** a well-preserved street lined with stores and apartment houses, leads back to a **Fullonica,** or ancient cleaning shop. Its deep pits were filled with clothing and fresh urine, which contains bleaching agents; slaves had to jump in and splash around to agitate the wash, a means of washing clothes which backpackers probably shouldn't try in their hostel bathrooms. Between V.d. Fullonica and V.d. Palestra are the **Firemen's Barracks** (Caserma dei Vigili), dating from the 2nd century, and built around an arcade courtyard.

THEATER

For events info, check Roma C'è *or call the Teatro Roman Scavi Archeologici di Ostia Antica at* ☎ *333 200 34 29 for advanced ticket sales. Tickets €15-24.*

Built in 12 BC, the Ostian theater is almost completely intact thanks to a restoration effort that has left it in usable condition. The building once housed several small stores in its bottom levels. A vaulted passage leads to the semicircular *cavea.* The stage itself was backed by a wall several stories high, decorated with columns, arches, and statues; only the low wall of its foundation survives. Seating for around 3000. In summer, the theater hosts plays and concerts, including the **International Festival of Ostia Antica.**

PIAZZALE DELLE CORPORAZIONI

Just north of the theater are the remains of this expansive and beautiful plaza for the offices of shipping companies. Lining the walkway are mosaics that advertised the different agencies. Many show ships and their cargos, the lighthouse of Ostia, and describe the original location from which the goods were shipped. At the center of the plaza are the remains of a small temple to Ceres, the goddess of the grain—the prime commodity that poured through Ostia on the way to Rome.

CASA DI DIANA

East of the Theater off V. dei Molini lies the Casa di Diana (named for the terra-cotta relief of Diana in the main courtyard), the best preserved Roman house at Ostia. At the time of its construction, the edifice reached a height of almost 18m, encompassing three or four floors. Buildings like this, known as *insulae,* once filled most Imperial Roman cities. Unlike the large, single-family villas at Pompeii (see p. 292), *insulae* housed several dozen people who shared the courtyard and kitchen facilities. The ground floor housed *tabernae* (shops), which opened onto the street. The grooves in the thresholds show where sliding wooden screens served as doors.

OIL SHOP, GRAIN MILL & SYNAGOGUE

Down the stairs from the museum are the remains of an oil shop. The huge amphorae buried in the ground were used to store oil. Next door are the remains of a small synagogue, decorated with menorahs on top of the pillars. One street over toward the theatre is Via Molini, enter the building with a large dark stone outside to see the remains of a grain mill. Donkeys were used to crank the dark stone contraptions in order to grind grain.

THERMOPOLIUM

Ancestor to the modern coffee/snack bars that adorn the streets of modern Italy, the *Thermopolium* was a great place to get a drink or a quick bite to eat. Many Ostians, lacking kitchens in their own small apartments, ordered entire meals at these establishments. A still life in the central room depicts likely fare of the time.

FORUM

Occupying a wide rectangular space bisected by the Decumano Massimo (to the west of the *thermopolium*), is the Forum of Ostia, anchored by the imposing **Temple to Jupiter, Juno, and Minerva** (called the **Capitolium**). During the 1700s, the temple was used as a sheepfold and dubbed "the red house" by shepherds. At the other end of the forum is the **Temple of Augustus and Rome.** A marble statue representing Rome marks the location of the old shrine. The statue's foot rests on top of a large globe, symbolizing Rome's dominance of the ancient world. Between the two temples is a small well, a monument to the *lares* (household gods) of the imperial family. The largest baths in Ostia, the **Terme del Foro** are just southeast of the Forum. Note the remains of a complex heating system in the subterranean passage and the veined marble columns rising from the *frigidarium*. Near the baths (to the north) is a well-preserved, 20-seat public rest room, the **Forica.**

HOUSE OF CUPID & PSYCHE

From the fork in Decumanus Massimo, V.d. Foce leads to this elaborate, marble-paneled dwelling, where the statue of the two lovers (now in the museum) was found. Several white columns in the courtyard support the last few remaining brick arches, and the base of an old fountain stands in the middle of a side room with a patterned color marble floor. Nearby, on V. di Terme del Mitra, a staircase descends to a shadowy mithraeum and the maze of sewers and cisterns that sprawls beneath the city.

SCHOOL OF TRAJAN

A marbled *exedra* greets the visitor to the Schola of Trajan, believed to be owned by a corporation of shipbuilders. The first-century BC *domus* contains beautiful and rare mosaics; the interior court and fountain are striking.

BATHS OF THE SEVEN SAGES

Considerably less scholarly than the name implies, this bath has a public toilet decorated with famous philosophers providing tips on how to use the bathroom. Those who are already potty-trained should move on to the huge floor mosaic.

DOMUS OF THE NYMPHAEUM & CAUPONA DI ALEXANDER

As you make your way down Decumano Massimo toward Porta Marina, keep an eye out for a rather tall, box-like structure to your right. If you walk around it, you will see the two remaining columns, as well as some very nice, geometrical, mosaics. On the right side of the Decumanus, stop to take a look at the mosaics on the floor of the Caupona di Alexander, which portray two fighters who enjoyed contemporary popularity: Aurelianus Helix and Alexander Alexandrinus.

BATHS OF THE MARINE GATE & TOMB OF L. CARTILIUS POPLICOLA

Like the rest of the large baths, these are decorated with mosaics, showing athletes, philosophers, and a woman resembling the Statue of Liberty. Closer to the gate is a marble wall marking the tomb of a prominent citizen, L. Cartilius Popicola, decorated with the *fasces* of authority. An esteemed politician and magistrate, his tomb was constructed during Augustus' reign. The frieze along the top of the wall initially extended around three sides of the tomb, depicting two military scenes: a naval battle, and the marshalling of infantry on the coast.

ANCIENT SYNAGOGUE

South of the city through the **Porta Marina,** is a large synagogue. The entrance is marked by two steps that lead into a vestibule. On the right lies the *mikvah*, or ritual bath. The tabernacle contains two columns that once held corbels resembling seven-branched candelabra.

TIVOLI

M: B-Rebibbia, 15min. from Termini; exit the station and follow signs for Tivoli through an underpass to reach the other side of V. Tiburtina. Find the marker for the blue CO.TRA.L bus to Tivoli. 40min.; €1.60. Get off just past P. Garibaldi at P. delle Nazioni Unite, the bus back to Rome leaves from the P. Garibaldi ***tourist office****. On the street leading from P. Garibaldi, the tourist stand with a big "i" in front has general information, maps, and bus schedules. ☎0774 311 249. Open M and W 9am-1pm; Tu and Th-Sa 9am-3pm and 4-7pm.*

Only an hour and a half from Termini, this cool hilltop town, perched 120m above the Aniene River, has been the suburban retreat for some of Rome's fin-

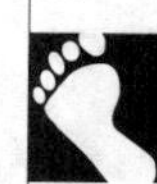

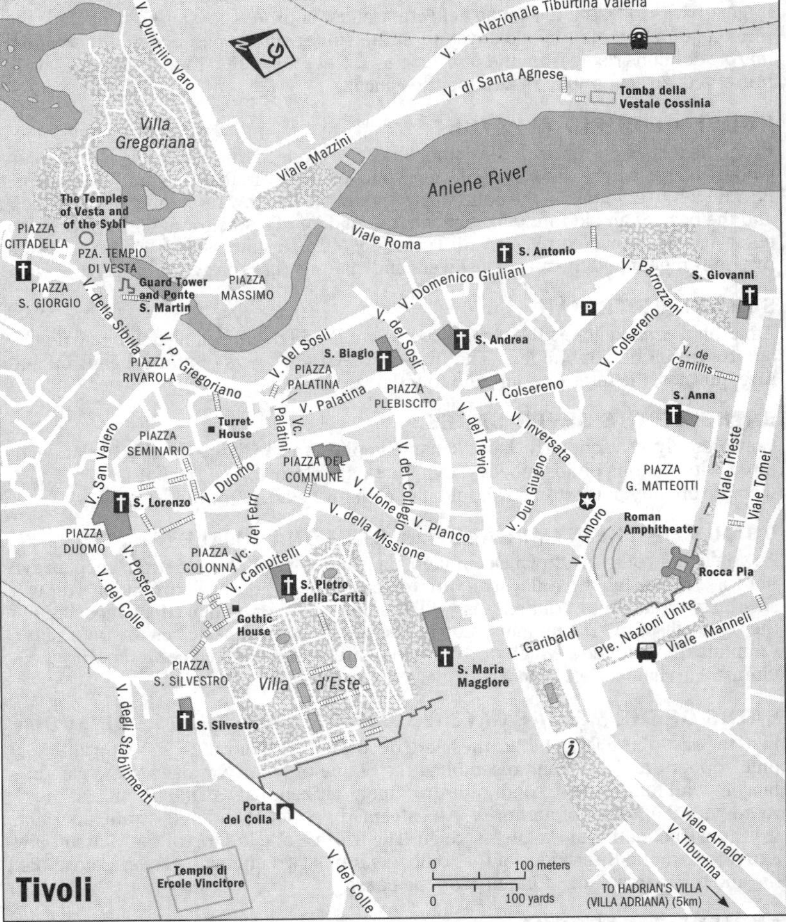

est—Horace, Catullus, and Propertius once vacationed nearby—for centuries. The main attraction in this town of 50,000 is the abundant water, which once filled the baths of emperor Hadrian's magnificent Villa Adriana, and still flows fancifully in the many fountains of the Villa D'Este. Tivoli also boasts a number of 12th-century churches, a 5th-century Cathedral (of S. Lawrence), a 15th-century castle (Rocca Pia), and even a Roman amphitheater.

Though not expressly permitted, the best lunch option in Tivoli is a picnic in the gardens of the Villa D'Este; pick up some water and a panini from any of the bars in P. Garibaldi. If you'd rather not chance getting chased out of a garden by well-meaning guards, head to V. Nicolo Arnaldi, and have a bite to eat under the canopy of one of the restaurants situated there. Tivoli is best visited as a daytrip from Rome, where cheaper accommodations are available.

HADRIAN'S VILLA (VILLA ADRIANA)

Take orange bus #4 or 4x (to V. Adriana) 5km from P. Garibaldi. €0.77. Tickets at the news kiosk. After the bus drops you off, follow signs down a long path to the Villa. The return bus stop is halfway down the street to the right, approximately 75m from the path leading to the villa. ☎0774 382 733. Open daily 9am to 1hr. before sunset. €6.50; €3.25 for EU citizens 18-24; EU citizens under 18 and over 65 free. Audioguide €4. Parking €2. Stop in bookshop for a map and a large bottle of water.

In the valley below Tivoli, Emperor Hadrian, a major patron of art and architecture, built this enormous villa. Hadrian's pad, now scattered in fields of olive trees and purple thistles, is among the best-preserved imperial architecture near Rome. Yet, the enormous complex visible today is only one fifth of the original Villa, which took 16 years to construct. Each section of the estate was built in the style of a monument Hadrian had seen during his travels in Greece and Egypt.

From the entrance, two paved roads in front of you lead to the **Pecile,** a once-colonnaded court built to recall the famous Painted Porch *(Poikile)* in Athens, where the Greek Stoic philosophers met to debate. The large pool of the Pecile is now home to ducks and very hostile swans. To the left of the Pecile, the Philosopher's Hall (which probably held the seven Greek sages' works) leads to the circular **Maritime Theater.** This was the emperor's private bath and exercise room, cloistered inside a courtyard and protected by a green moat.

To the right of the Pecile is the **Stadio,** where Hadrian enjoyed athletic amusements. Taking a left after the Stadio, you'll approach the Piccole and Grande **thermae** (baths) crumbling beneath the remnants of a large dome similar to that of the Pantheon. After the baths is the **Canopus,** a green expanse of water surrounded by plasters of original Egyptian sculptures and broken columns, replicates a famous canal near Alexandria. At the end of the Canopus is the **Serapeum,** a semicircular dining hall modeled after the Alexandria's Temple of Serapis, anchoring the far end of the canal. Here the emperor and his guests dined on a platform completely surrounded by water cascading down from the fountains at rear.

To the left of the Maritime Theater is the so-called **Court of the Libraries,** now believed to have been some form of assembly hall. Beneath the Court of the Libraries lies a shadowy **cryptoporticus,** one of several in the villa which hid the emperor's army of slaves from view as they ran the enormous complex. Other buildings of the palace—the *Hospitali* (guest house), the *Tre Esedere*, and the *Peristilio di Palazzo*—lie nearby in labeled enclaves.

VILLA D'ESTE

From P. Garibaldi, weave your way through busy P. Trento down the path to the villa. ☎0774 332 949. Open May-Aug. Tu-Su 8:30am-7:45pm; Sept.-Apr. 9am-sunset. €6.50; last entrance 1hr. before closing. EU citizens 18-24 €3.25; EU citizens under 18 and over 65 free.

The Villa d'Este was laid out by Cardinal Ercole d'Este (son of Lucrezia Borgia) and his architect, Pirro Ligorio, in 1550 to combine the feel of ancient Roman pleasure palaces with that modern feel of the cutloose 1550s. The palace is decorated with amusing grotesque frescoes, shell-studded grottoes, and large picture windows. The gardens are built along the slope of the hill; cleverly constructed terraces above them offer views of the greenery and the distant countryside. The fountains (the real attractions) and the park are ideal settings for a picnic or some casual frolicking.

Immediately below the villa's main terrace is the **Fontana del Bicchierone,** a shell-shaped goblet of Bernini's design. To the left (with your back toward the villa), a path leads to the **Grotto of Diana,** which contains mythological scenes within its shiny mosaic nooks. To the right, another path leads to the **Rometta** (Little Rome). The stately lady in the center of this fountain is Roma herself, surrounded by emblems of the Eternal City. From the Rometta, along the 130m long **Viale delle Cento Fontane** plumes of water spring from grimacing masks between Este eagles. At the other end,

the BIG $plurge

Hotel Chiaia di Luna (☎0771 801 13; fax 0771 809 821). Above the beach bearing the same name. The views and service here are worth the extra cost; many rooms overlook the awe-inspiring Chiaia di Luna. All quarters with private bath, TV, phone, and elegant hardwood furniture; some have balconies. Also enjoy the large swimming pool and terrace below. Breakfast included. Van service to and from the port at arrival/departure and every morning. Rooms €45.50-90 per person per night, depending on the season; single rooms pay 50% surcharge.

Ristorante Acqua Pazza, P. Carlo Pisacane, 10 (☎0771 80643). Pass a truly unforgettable evening under the awnings of Acqua Pazza. Savor the excellent seafood on beautiful blue and yellow place settings overlooking the harbor. Quite possibly one of the best restaurants on the island, and the bill reflects this fact. Booked solid almost every night in high season; reserve in advance. *Primi* €7.75-17.25 (including great *linguini ai scampi e gamberi;* €11.60), *secondi* are bought by the *etto:* €3.62-4.13 for most whole fish; €10.30 per fillets; expect whole fish to cost €17.60-20.60. Pane €1.55; 10% service charge. Open daily 8pm-"until we finish." AmEx/MC/V.

the **Fontana dell'Ovato or di Tivoli,** designed by Pirro Ligorio, shows a central goddess flanked by nymphs, and Venus trying to emerge from her half-shell in the pool.

Down the semi-circular steps from the center of the Viale delle Cento Fontane is the **Fontana dei Draghi,** a round pool where reclining four dragons are having a spitting contest. To the right of the dragons stand the **Fontana di Proserpina** and the **Fontana della Civetta e degli Uccelli,** which is said to emit bird chirps. Sorry to ruin it, but there are actually unseen pipes inside the fountain creating the peeps. With your back to the villa, the ornate marble and stucco **Fontana dell'Organo Idraulico** is on your right, which once used water pressure to power a hydraulic organ. To the left of the tree in the back of the garden, the **Fountain of the Ephesian Goddess** spouts curved streams of water from each of the goddess' 18 breasts.

VILLA GREGORIANA

Follow the signs to the northern end of the city along the bend in river, then cross the bridge. Open daily 9am-1hr. before sunset. €1.88; under 12 €0.52. The Villa has been ***closed indefinitely*** *for restorations. Check with* ***tourist office*** *☎0774 311 249 for status.*

The **Villa Gregoriana** is a park designed around man-made waterfalls commissioned by Pope Gregory XVI in 1835. The star of the show is the **Great Cascade**, a thundering 160m waterfall. For the best view, bear right at the entrance. If you want more, follow the signs to **Grotta delle Sirene** and the **Grotta della Sibilla,** two natural grottoes carved by the falls. The west exit leads you past the 2nd-century BC **Temple of Vesta** and the **Temple of Tiburnus.**

CASTELLI ROMANI

M:A and take blue CO.TRA.L buses from Rome's Anagnina Station to Rocca Prioria, and get off at Frascati. Run every 30 min. M-Sa 6am-10:50pm, last return 9:30pm; every 1.5 hr. Su 7am-10:30pm, last return 9:30pm. €1. Or to Latina, get off at Albano. Every 30min. M-Sa 5:15-10:25am, last return 11pm, Su 5:20am-11:40pm, last return 11pm. €1. Trains from Termini connect Rome to Frascati and Albano, but are slower. Hourly, 6am-10pm to Frascati, 6am-9pm to Albano. €1.60. For bus travel between the Castelli Romani, ask at the ***tourist office.*** *The best way to see these towns is to rent a motorino or a car, and travel at your own pace.*

Volcanoes are notoriously unfriendly creatures (remember Pompeii?), but the volcanoes that surround Rome have tried to make up for their more inflammatory southern counterparts by providing famed vineyards, crystal clear lakes, and succulent strawberries for world-weary Romans. Nestled between the hills and lakes south of Rome, the thirteen towns that make up the Castelli Romani began as feudal estates for some of Italy's wealthiest families. Today, some of the towns are over-touristed, but the following listings provide a beautiful and relaxing excursion nonetheless.

FRASCATI

Frascati is a 15min. bus ride from Anagnina Station; the bus driver will let you off at the bus depot in P. Marconi. The ***I.A.T. tourist office,*** *P. Marconi, 1, is across the street, next to the town hall ☎ 06 942 03 31. Open M and W 9am-1pm; Tu, Th-F, Sa 9am-1pm and 4-7pm; winter M-F 8am-2pm and 3-6pm. Gardens open M-F 9am-1pm and 3-6pm; winter M-F 9am-1pm and 3-5pm. Get free pass at tourist office. Ethiopian Museum, V. Cardinale G. Massaia, 26. ☎ 06 942 866 01. Open daily 9am-noon and 4-6pm. Free.*

From its commanding position atop an ancient volcanic ridge, Frascati has attracted fugitives from the stifling Roman heat for centuries. Frascati's patrician villas and renowned fruity, dry white wines remain two of the town's finest attractions. Those lucky enough to be in Frascati in October or November can immerse themselves in the fevered dipsomania of the annual **vendemmia,** the celebration of the grape harvest. The **Villa Aldobrandini** dominates the hill above P. Marconi. Up V. Catone from the left side of P. Marconi as you face the villa, hang a right onto V.C.G. Massaia, which leads to the Renaissance villa. Financed by Clement VIII and designed by Giacomo della Porta, the villa was built as a quiet retreat for Clement's favorite nephew, Pietro Aldobrandini. Visit the sculpture-filled gardens, Bernini fountains and the Ninfeo—a "theater of water" featuring Pan, Atlas and a Satyr—and get a true sense for the meaning of the word grandiose.

About 1km uphill from the *villa* on G. Massaia is the tiny 16th-century **Chiesa dei Cappuccini.** A sign on the door announces that you need reservations for marriages, but the unique **Ethiopian Museum,** just next door, is open daily and requires no such foresight. The **Museum,** was built in honor of Cardinal Massaia, who spent 35 years as a missionary in Ethiopia, and houses a collection of weapons, handmade crafts, and the cardinal's personal paraphernalia, including his death mask.

The entrance to **Villa Tuscolana,** the highest of Frascati's villas, is a few meters left of the church's exit. Built on the foundations of the ruins of Cicero's villa, the building has now been turned into an up-scale hotel and restaurant, but provides views of Monteporzio, a neighboring hill town.

While the foundations of Cicero's house are no longer visible, the ruins of nearby Tusculum—an ancient resort for the who's who of Roman society, including Cato and Cicero—can still be seen. From the entrance of the Villa Aldobrandini, turn right onto V. Tusculo, which climbs 5km over winding country roads to reach the ruins of Tusculum. The town was destroyed in 1191 during a feud between its residents and the Romans, but the small Roman theater, scattered ruins and stunning view of Lazio make the ghost town worth the climb.The citadel of Tusculum, marked by an iron cross at the hill's summit, affords a 360° view of southern Lazio, with Rome to the right, the Tyrrhenian Sea in front, and the extinct volcano Monte Cavo to the left. Check at the tourist office in Frascati to see if tours are running; if not, ask for a map.

Frascati's 17th-century cathedral, Basilica Cattedrale Tuscolana San Pietro Apostolo, reconstructed after damage in WWII, rises above P.S. Pietro with a recently restored Baroque facade. Down the street is the **Chiesa del Gesù,** designed by Pietro da Cortona, with interior frescoes by Andrea Pozzi.

Tribal spears and churches notwithstanding, the main attraction here is still wine. Pick up a bottle and other picnic supplies at the **market** in P. del Mercato, off P. S. Pietro, behind Chiesa del Gesù (open M-Sa 8am-1pm), or stop by **Bar Baioni ❶,** V.C. Battisti, 22, to the right of the cathedral, where locals flock for homemade pastries (€0.60-1.40), *panini* (€1.80) and cappuccino. If you are feeling hungry, Bar Baioni also offers pastas (€2.60), mixed vegetables, and meats. (☎06 942 22 05. Open daily 6:30am-midnight.) Another place to soak up the local culture (and wine) is at the **Cantina Il Pergolato ❷,** V. del Castello, 20, off P. del Mercato. It serves homemade wine, pizza, and other fare in a cave-like dining room. (☎06 942 04 64. €11 for *antipasti* and *primi*. Open daily 12:30-2:30pm and 3:30-10:30pm. MC/V.)

Father off the beaten path, **San Martino Al Vicolo,** V.S. Martino, 6, serves affordable food in a charming, intimate location. From P.S. Pietro, take Corso Italia up the hill to the right of the Basilica and turn right on V.S. Martino. *Primi*, including *riso con scampi e zucchine* (rice with shrimp and zucchini; €7) and *secondi*, such as *pesce spada alla griglia* (grilled swordfish; €9) are excellent. (☎06 941 61 02. Open daily 10am-2pm and 6:30pm-midnight. Summer closed Su. Cash only.)

LAKE ALBANO & LAKE NEMI

From Frascati, take bus marked "Albano" from P. Marconi. 1 per hr., 5:50am-9pm. €1. Should let you off in P. Mazzini, the center of Albano. You can buy tickets from the lotto shop near the IAT. Free map at ***tourist office,*** *V. Risorgimento, 1. ☎06 932 40 82 or 06 932 40 81; fax 06 932 00 40. From the piazza, take a right onto Corso Matteotti; after about 7 blocks take a left on V.S. Martino and a right onto V. Cavour, which becomes V. Risorgimento. The tourist office is on the left after the intersection with V. Virgilio. Open M-Sa 9am-1pm, Tu and Th-Sa 4-7pm. Museo Civico, ☎06 932 34 90 or 06 932 57 59. Open Su-F 9am-1pm, additional hours W-Th 4-7pm, Sa 8am-2pm. €2.50; under 6, over 60 €2.*

A few kilometers across the hills from Frascati, the other Castelli Romani cling to the sides of an extinct volcanic crater, now filled with the shimmering blue waters of **Lago Albano,** one of Lazio's cleanest and chilliest swimming spots. Crisp wines, clear mountain views, and a taste of Italian country life are the main attractions among these *castelli*. **Albano** lies on the Appian Way, and was once home to the villa of Emperor Domiziano and the less palatial camp of Septimus Severus' soldiers. As you walk through town, you are likely to encounter some of the ruins of this large military encampment. Especially noteworthy is the central archway of the **Porta Principalis Sinistra,** located a few meters down V. Castro Pretorio (from V. Cavour, turn onto V.S. Francesco, and then right onto V.C. Pretorio). Among the ancient ruins still preserved in Albano is the curious **Tomb of the Horatii and Curiatii,** a Republican-age funeral monument believed to mark the graves of the famous triplets that secured Rome's supremacy over Alba Longa. To get to the tomb, walk down C. Matteotti (will change to Borgo Garibaldi), and make a right onto V.d. Stella; the tomb will be a few meters to your left. Today, emperors and soldiers are harder to find, but Albano remains the largest and most commercial town of the Castelli Romani. Artifacts and pictorial reconstructions of the Paleolithic through Renaissance ages, gathered in Albano and surrounding areas, are housed in the **Museo Civico,** V. Risorgimento, 3, next to the tourist office. You will also need to inquire at the museum in order to get a close-up view of the massive **Roman Cisterns,** the only functioning Roman cisterns in the world today. The cisterns, carved into the side of the mountain with a maximum capacity of 10,000 cubic meters, still supplies the town of Albano with water. At the end of June, look for gladiators (in skimpy costumes wielding daggers, tridents and various blunt objects) duking it out in the town's *Spettacolo Gladiatorio*.

On Thursday mornings, an outdoor market in P. Luigi Sabatini, located up the steps from P. Mazzini, sells the region's fruits, vegetables, and gigantic fish. If you've worked up an appetite walking around town, try **Osteria de San Paolo,** V. Aurelio Saffi, 67. No menu; a variety of pasta dishes will be served. (☎0338 813 38 18. Open daily noon-3:30pm and 7pm-midnight. Closed Su lunch, M and Tu dinner.)

CASTEL GANDOLFO

Buses go to the beach every hour from Castel Gandolfo and Albano. €0.77.

North of Albano, tiny **Castel Gandolfo** owes its fame to the Pope, who occupies its volcanic ridge in the summer. When the Vatican gets too stifling, he comes to enjoy his famed gardens, which spread down the outer rim of the crater toward the sea. The palace, declared an inalienable dominion of the Holy See in 1608, was enlarged according to a plan by Maderno and is topped by a modern dome, the center of the old Vatican Observatory. (Just in case the Pope wants to see if the Big Guy's still up there.) The Pope is in residence in Castel Gandolfo from July to September, and audiences are held Wednesdays at 11am. On Sundays at noon, the Pope says mass.

The town's public street and one tiny *piazza*, dominated by Maderno's early Baroque papal palace, offer glimpses of the lake and mountain scenery which have drawn pontiffs here for centuries. The *piazza* also houses the **Church of San Tommaso di Villanova,** an early work by Bernini. A lake road opens out to several belvederes, from which you can catch better views of Lake Albano. A winding road leads down to a public beach (about 2km), where you can rent sailboats.

ARICCIA

Ariccia, 1km east of Albano along the Appian Way, isn't noted for much other than the soaring viaduct that brings you into town; unless you have a craving for *porchetta* in one of the *piazza*'s many *porchetterias*, it's best to keep driving. Ariccia's *piazza* is graced by the remains of a Republican temple, the medieval **Palazzo Chigi** (spruced up by Bernini in the 17th century), and—for the obsessive Bernini fan—another minor Bernini original, the round **Santa Maria dell'Assunzione.** The spacious **Villa Comunale Menotti Garibaldi,** a free public park on the way into town, is open daily from 8am-8pm.

GENZANO

Catch a CO.TRA.L bus to Nemi; every hr. from P.T. Frasconi. €0.77.

Kings and rock stars get red velvet carpets, Dorothy gets a yellow brick road, and the lucky souls who visit Genzano the Sunday after Corpus Christus get an avenue of flowers. Since 1778, the *Infiorata* has covered Via Livia with elaborate floral designs, often representing famous works of art. (The theme for 2001 was Michelangelo's Sistine Ceiling.) Look for posters in Rome, or consult an ecclesiastical calendar for the exact date.

NEMI

Nemi Museum of Ancient Ships. ☎06 939 80 40. Open in summer daily 9am-7:30pm; in winter daily 9am-2pm; in spring and fall, 9am-1hr before sunset. Closed Su afternoons. €4.

From Ariccia, the road continues southeast to Lake Nemi, another flooded crater where life is a little more tranquil than in other, more touristed *castelli*. Ancient Romans, marveling at Nemi's placid blue waters, called the lake "the Mirror of Diana" and graced its sloping shores with a **temple** to the goddess. Surrounded by a sacred grove, the temple was presided over by a eunuch priest who got his job by killing his predecessor and plucking a golden bough off one of the grove's trees. The village boasts more staircases than streets, but miniature strawberries (*fragoline di Nemi*), grown along the lake's shores, are its real glory. A bowl filled with the tiny fruits, soaked in lemon juice, and topped with a dollop of fresh *panna* (cream) is a specialty at bars lining the belvedere overlooking the lake. **Locanda Specchio di Diana,** Corso V.Emanuele, 13, serves strawberries (€5) with *panna* (€6), with *limone* (€5.20) and, with *gelato* (€6.50). (☎06 936 88 05. Open daily 7:20am-after midnight.) The first Sunday of June, the town hosts a strawberry festival.

The **Nemi Museum of Ships,** 15min. down the road from Nemi, was built to house two of Caligula's Roman barges. Although L. Battista Alberti tried to refloat the Emperor's party boats in 1487, all efforts failed until the ships were dredged from the lake in the late 1920s. During WWII, the ships were torched by the Nazis as they retreated from Italy, so the museum displays two scale models and the few bits of lead and bronze that weren't melted in the blaze.

Cult of San Silverio

Prominently displayed near the cash registers and by the corners and crossroads of much of Ponza is San Silverio, aged graybeard and martyr of choice in the Pontine archipelago. Who is this saintly man, you ask?

Ah. Silverio was a minor deacon when a web of intrigue propelled by the Ostrogothic king Theodehald had him elected pope in 536 to maintain the Goths' influence over Rome. Incensed by her lack of influence over the new pope, Roman Empress Theodora, Justinian's wife, sent her husband's top general to convince Silverio to stand down. When Silverio refused, forged letters of a deal between the pope and the Goths were suddenly brought to light.

Poor Silverio was summarily degraded to the rank of monk, deposed in a hasty trial, forced, by his successor, to sign an abdication, and sent into exile on the island of Pomarola, which is just off the coast of Ponza. He soon died of starvation and the tough island life, but his grave became a center of miracles and cures for the faithful *"Pontinesi."*

In the 11th century, Silverio was elevated to sainthood thanks—in part—to the ardor of his followers, who actively lobbied the Vatican. Still, family connections undoubtedly helped: his father was the equally obscure St. Hormidas. Silverio's image is still enthusiastically plastered about the islands and his somewhat dubious memory is celebrated on June 20th and February 2nd.

ROCCA DI PAPA AND MARINO

Marino is a good place to make CO.TRA.L bus connections back to Rome every 30min. M-Sa 5:20am-10:30pm, Su 6:20am-9pm. €1.

The lake road continues north to the summit of Monte Cavo, where **Rocca di Papa,** the highest Castelli Romani, glowers over Lake Albano. The town, dating from the 3rd century BC, doesn't offer much in the way of architecture anymore, but the views of the lake are worth the hike. On the other side of Monte Cavo, **Marino** closes the circle of *castelli* to the north. If you're in town on the first Sunday in October, you'll see the town's fountains flowing with wine during the annual Sagra dell'Uva.

PONTINE ISLANDS

Several companies run aliscafi *(hydrofoils) and slower, cheaper* traghetti *(larger car ferries). Take the 1hr. train ride from Termini to Anzio. Every hr. 6:10am-11:10pm. €2.90. Then the Linee Vetor hydrofoil from Anzio to Ponza takes 1hr. and 15min. June 13-Sept. 15, 3-5 per day 8:10am-5:15pm, return 9:50am-7pm; from Sept. 15-30 only 1 per day; M-F €20, Sa-Su and Aug, €23. €1.50 per 0-10kg bag, €4.50 per 10-20kg bag. Or, take the slower Caremar ferry from Anzio to Ponza. June 16-Sept. 15 M-F 9:25am, Sa 8:30am, Su and holidays 8:30am and 3pm; return M-F 5pm, Sa 5:15pm, Su and holidays 11am and 5:15pm; €19. Caremar ticket office in Anzio at V. Porto Innocenziano 53, ☎06 986 000 83 or ☎0771 805 65 in Ponza; www.caremar.it. Office in the white booth on the quay. Linee Vetor ticket office in Anzio, ☎06 984 50 83 or ☎0771 805 49 in Ponza; www.vetor.it, is on the quay. From Formia, Caremar runs 2 3hr. boat rides per day. 9am and 5:30pm; return 5:30am and 2:30pm. €10.70. Vetor runs M 1:20pm, Tu and Th 8:30am and 1:20pm; F-Su 8:30am, 1:20, and 4:50pm; return M 6:30pm, Tu and Th 10am and 6:30pm, F-Su 10am, 3, and 6:30pm. €20.*

The Pontine Islands were once believed to be home to the sorceress **Circe,** who captured the Greek hero Odysseus. Homer's *Odyssey* wasn't the last encounter the Pontine Islands would have with history. Nero was expatriated to the *isole*, and Mussolini cast enemies of the state upon the 30 million-year-old volcanic residuum, only to be imprisoned here himself. For nearly two centuries, anarchists and the like were jailed in a Neapolitan king's prison. The **prison** has been out of commission since the 60s, but law-abiding citizens have found it in the meantime.

Not a bad place to be locked up, the Isole Pontine, including Ponza, Palmarola, Zannone, and Ventotene, are awash with beaches connected by rugged Mediterranean coastline knifing into the clean, turquoise-blue water of the Tyrrhenian. The blues are reflected in painted shutters hung on cloud-white cement houses, the domes overrun with fuchsia blossoms. Coves, inlets, and grottoes cut from the volcanic stone lie in all their natural beauty around each turn of the winding roads.

Miles from Rome, the cars slow down, and so do the people. Shoppers don bikinis, tourist-driven *motorini* take the hair-pin turns carefully, and motorboats idle in coves while the occupants enjoy the surrounding beauty. Cocktail "hour" drags on until the sun sets and vacationers begin to swagger towards the restaurants.

A 95km ferry ride is a long way to go, and the €20 fare a lot to pay—but entirely worth it for two, three, or four days (you'll inevitably stay chained to the beach longer than you planned). Join the ranks of Greek heroes, suicidal emperors, and violent hippy revolutionaries; become an exile.

PONZA

To navigate Ponza, Autolinee Isola di Ponza buses leave from V. Dante, every 15-20min. until 1am. Buy tickets from driver. €1. Follow C. Pisacane past the tunnel until it becomes V. Dante; stop is to your left. Buses stop by request; flag them down at stops. Look for private taxis near the main bus stand or call from the tourist office. Water taxis leave near the docks. From €3 round-trip; arrange pick-up time with driver unless going to popular spots. ***Pro Loco tourist office****, V. Molo Musco, at the far right of the port, next to lighthouse, in the long red building. Offers "alternative" tours of the island's many Roman and Bourbon-era archaeological sites. ☎0771 800 31; prolocoponza@libero.it. Open summer M-Sa 9am-1pm and 4-8:30pm, Su 9am-1pm. Emergency: ☎113. Post Office: P. Pisacane. ☎0771 806 72. Open M-F 8am-2pm, Sa 8am-1pm.*

Ponza, the largest of the Pontine Islands, was the favorite victim of Mediterranean pirates until the arrival of the fierce and wealthy Bourbon monarchs in 1734. The crime rate all but disappeared in the same moment that the boats of tourists—the occasional celebrity among them—began arriving from the mainland. Marauding pirates, belligerent royalty, and Gucci-wearing glitterati aside, *dunque, tutti siamo in vacanza*—we're all equal in the eyes of the sun gods.

In Ponza, the laid-back island lifestyle has resulted in a happy disregard for street signs, addresses, or maps. There are only a handful of streets and addresses you'll ever need to know: **Via Banchina Nuova,** which runs along the docks and changes to **Via Dante** on the other side of the **Sant'Antonio tunnel; Corso Pisacane,** which runs along the port above the docks; **Via Molo Musco,** jutting out along the pier to your right as you face the water; and **Piazza Carlo Pisacane,** where V. Molo Musco meets C. Pisacane. Everything you could want is on the docks or nearby, and the locals are friendly and more than helpful in showing you the way, even if they don't know English (which, be forewarned, most Ponzese do not). Pick up *Isole Pontine*, a comprehensive guide to the islands, at newsstands (€6.20).

ACCOMMODATIONS & FOOD

Although Ponza is home to over 15 hotels and pensiones, rooms still hover in the €100 zone. *Let's Go* recommends forgoing hotels entirely and checking out one of many *immobiliare vacanze* (vacation property) offices instead. The tourist office has a list of over 20 helpful agencies that can assist in finding a room or apartment. The folks at **Isotur ❷,** C. Pisacane, 18, are friendly and, more importantly, can set you up with a double room with a bath, kitchen, terrace, and beautiful views by the port or in nearby Santa Maria. (☎0771 803 39; www.isotur.com. Open Mar.-Nov. daily 9:30am-12:30pm and 4-8:30pm. €25-30 per night per person; double €290-650 per wk depending on season and location. MC/D/V.) If you're not up for a trip from the port, **Hotel Mari,** C. Pisacane, 19 has classy decor and comfortable air-conditioned rooms with bathrooms, telephone, and TV. (☎0771 801 01; www.hotelmari.com. Breakfast included. Internet €3/30min. Sept. 1-June 30 singles €42; doubles €62, with ocean view €82; July 1-Aug. 31 singles €64; doubles €94, with ocean view €124. AmEx/D/MC/V.) Another option is the family-owned and operated **Pensione Arcobaleno,** on a hilltop 10min. from the port. The view alone is worth the hike. (V. Scotti di Basso, 6; ☎0771 803 15; arcobalenoponza@libero.it. High season €40 per person, with breakfast and dinner included €60; low season €10 less. Discount for extended stays. MC/V.)

The islands are known for their lentil soup, fish, and spiny lobster. Restaurants and bars line the port and grocery stores, *pizzerie*, and *creperie* crowd the streets running along the docks. The restaurants are a little on the expensive side, with plates of pasta in the €8-12 range, but **Ristorante da Antonio ❹,** on the water at V. Dante, offers good food in a prime location. *Primi* €5-8; *secondi* €10-20; fixed-price menus from €21-30, including wine. (☎0771 809 832. Open Mar.-Dec., daily 6am-midnight. AmEx/MC/V.) If you're up for a little hike from the port, burn off your dinner before you eat it and climb the stairs past C. Pisacane to **Ristorante Arcobaleno ❷,** V. Scotti di Basso 6. (☎0771 803 15. Open daily 9-10:30am, 12:30-1:30pm, and 8:30-10:30pm.) The view is incredible, but go early enough to catch the sunset from the terrace. Menu changes nightly. Don't miss **Ristorante Silvia ❷,** V. Marina S. Maria; walk along Corso Pisacane, through all the tunnels. About 30 yards after you emerge from the last, long tunnel, take a right down a path, and follow the signs for Ristorante Silvia. Indulge in delicious seafood dishes such as *spaghetti alla pescatora* (€8) or the house specialty, swordfish (€13). Better yet, gaze across the harbor at the silly fools who chose to stay at the Port for dinner while you ate like a king for €20-30. (☎0771 800 75. Open daily 8:30-11:15pm. MC/V.)

SIGHTS

Excellent beaches are everywhere on Ponza. **Cala dello Schiavone** and **Cala Cecata** (on the bus line) are excellent spots. **Chiaia di Luna,** an expansive, rocky beach set at the base of a stunning 200m cliffside, accessible only by water (although you can see it from above), provides perhaps the most spectacular view on the island. A 10min. walk from the port will take you to a sightseeing platform. Go down C. Pisacane and turn left before reaching the tunnel. Walk up the hill until the first hair-pin curve in the road at the Hotel Chiaia di Luna. Just don't lean over the edge; most steep drops in Ponza are missing the guard rails that are ubiquitous on the mainland. The most essential points of sunbathing interest are the **Piscine Naturali,** a quick ride through Ponza's lovely hillside. (Take the bus to Le Foma and ask to be let off at the Piscine. Cross the street and make your way down the long, steep path.) Some locals go cliff diving 15m into the pools, although this is ill-advised, especially given the spiny sea urchins lining the rocks.

Water taxis (from €3 roundtrip) run from the port to the beach of Frontone on the east side of the island north of Ponza, **Punta della Madonna** (where you can still see rock-carved pools in which the ancient Romans farmed fish), as well as such unspoiled beaches farther away from Ponza as Core, Spaccapolpi, Cala Fonte, and Cala Feola. Rent kayaks, paddle-boats, motor boats, *motorini*, and scuba gear along the port. **Settemari,** V. Banchina, 25 (☎0771 806 53 or 335 328 69 99 in winter) rents boats with especially helpful guides who will show you around for €7.75 per person per hour. Tours range from €5-25 per excursion or €180 for a personal tour. The tourist office also offers tours of the sites on the island. The **Ponza Diving Center,** V. Banchina (☎0771 809 788; www.ponzadiving.com) charges €31 for 2hr. guided submersions. Open water diver courses start at €310. (Open Mar.-Nov. daily 8am-1pm and 2:30-7:30pm. AmEx/MC/V.)

PALMAROLA

Palmarola is only accessible by boat. Either rent one for €35+ or sign up for a guided boat tour at the many offices at the port advertising una gita a Palmarola. Cooperativa Barcaioli Ponzesi, C. Piscacane at the S. Antonio tunnel, provides excursions to Palmarola, 10:30am, return 6pm. €20. ☎0771 809 929; www.ponza.com/barcaioli.

Palmarola is an uninhabited islet perched off the northeast coast of Ponza. The clear, turquoise water, irregular volcanic rock formations, and steep white cliffs (tinted red by iron deposits and yellow by sulphur) are incredible. As you approach Palmarola, you will see **Cala Brigantina,** a natural lime amphitheater. Most excursions visit the **Pilatus Caves** at Ponza, a breeding ground for fish.

If you're looking for a midday meal, you can try one of the two restaurants on the fairly vacant islet. Both serve excellent island seafood, but you'll pay for the location. Another option is to take a picnic; tour boats often have an icebox where you can stash perishables.

ZANNONE

Zannone is only accessible by boat. Trips, with guided trekking, offered by Cooperativa Barcaioli Ponzesi, C. Pisacane at the S. Antonio tunnel, 10:30am, return 7pm. €16-20. ☎0771 809 929; www.ponza.com/barcaioli.

Zannone is a nature and wildlife preserve whose lands are encompassed by the **National Park of Circeo.** Zannone offers the nature-lover a refreshing break from the beach and the opportunity to see various forms of Mediterranean wildlife. Tours will take you around the coast, allowing time for walks on the *mufloni*-strewn island, through the *lecci* forrests, and to the large medieval monastery of S. Spirito.

VENTOTENE

Motorboat rentals from the port €32. Aliscafi ALILAURO hydrofoils go from Ponza to Ventotene July 1-Sept. 1. 45min., 5:30pm, no return to Ponza. ☎0771 700 710. €15. Aliscafi SNAV makes the same trip Oct.-June. ☎081 428 55 55. 40min.; 11:15am and 6:15pm, return 10:05am and 5pm, €8. Sa-Su. €12. ***Pro Loco tourist office****, V. Roma, 2, can help arrange tours of the island. ☎0771 85 257. Open summer daily 9am-1pm. Archaeological Museum ☎0771 853 45. €3. Tours: Villa Giulia, €4. Cisterna Romana, €7. Carcere of Santo Stefano, €11.50 includes round-trip boat fare.*

Ventotene is far less accessible than Ponza (and free from summer vacationing hordes). The island lifestyle is untainted even by the roar of engines—cars and *motorini* are forbidden; the only homage to internal combustion is the outboard motor. The **Archaeological Museum** of Ventotene covers everything from Roman ruins and underwater archaeology to the prison Mussolini built here for "enemies of the state." The tourist office also arranges Italian-language tours of archaeological sites, including **Villa Giulia,** a well-preserved villa where Augustus exiled his daughter, Giulia, for crimes of indecency; the prehistoric **Necropoli;** and the **Carcere of Santo Stefano,** the citadel where Mussolini enjoyed locking up anti-Fascists.

ETRURIA

The rolling hills north of Rome were once home to the Etruscans, who ruled much of the Mediterranean prior to the rise of the Roman Empire. Though little is known about life under their rule, the Etruscans had a strong influence on early Roman art and culture. Outside what is now Cerveteri, wealthy Etruscans built thousands of large tombs, while a necropolis with well-preserved wall paintings lies outside the medieval walls of Tarquinia. Many of the objects and statues originally found in the tombs are now in the **Villa Giulia** and the Vatican Museums. Bracciano, near Cerveteri, has no Etruscan sites but does boast a medieval castle and a large lake for swimming and boating.

CERVETERI

M: A-Lepanto or bus #70, then take the blue CO.TRA.L bus to Cerveteri from Lepanto. Every 30min.-1hr., 6:25am-9:10pm, €2.80. Last bus to Rome 8pm. Less frequent on Su. The bus will drop you off outside Ruspoli Castle. From the castle, it's about 2km to the necropolis along what becomes a country road; follow the signs downhill and then to the right onto V.d. Necropoli. Whenever you see a fork in the road without a sign to guide you, bear right, but don't follow detours indi-

cated by restaurant signs. ***Tourist office****, V.d. Necropoli, 2, will answer queries. ☎06 995 23 04. Open Tu-Su 9:30am-1pm; in winter, additional hours 5-7pm. Tomba dei Rilievi ☎06 994 00 01. Open Tu-Sa 8:30am until one hour before sunset. €4. Museo Nazionale di Caerite ☎06 994 13 54. Open Tu-Su 8:30am-7:30pm. Free.*

Cerveteri's main attraction is its extensive Etruscan necropolis, a remnant of the port of Kysry, which conducted a lively trade economy throughout the Mediterranean from the 7th to 5th century BC. The town was actually much larger than is visible from the excavated area; archaeologists estimate that Kysry was about 20 times larger than modern Cerveteri.

The **Banditaccia Necropolis** is made up of dozens of Etruscan tombs up to 30 ft. high, designed to look like the round-roofed houses the Etruscans once lived in and laid out in semi-orderly streets. The grass growing on top makes them resemble huge haystacks, but while the scene is reminiscent of Monet's painting, exploring the necropolis is an experience straight out of Indiana Jones. Only a few tombs are lighted, yet almost all are accessible, so you can wander freely around the tombs and underground chambers. The earliest tombs in the necropolis date to the seventh century, and the evolution of Etruscan architecture is evident in the increasingly complex floor plans and ornamentation.

Archaeologists have removed the objects of daily life (chariots, weapons, cooking implements) with which the dead were equipped, but the carved *tufa* columns and couches remain. Small rooms off each tomb's antechamber were the resting places of slaves and lesser household members, the central room held the bodies of the rest of the family, and the small chambers off the back were reserved for the most prominent men and women. Triangular headboards on a couch mark women's graves, while a circular headboard indicates that the deceased was male. Only some 50 of an estimated 5000 tombs have been excavated, mostly in a cluster of narrow streets at the heart of this city of the dead. Don't miss the **Tomb of the Shields and the Chairs,** the smaller **Tomb of the Alcove** (with a carved-out matrimonial bed), and the **row houses** where less well-to-do Etruscans rested in peace. Look for the colored stucco reliefs in the **Tomba dei Rilievi**—the only ones visible in the necropolis.

Also worthwhile is the **Museo Nazionale di Caerite,** on the P.S. Maria Maggiore, in the 2200-year-old **Ruspoli Castle,** whose crenellations and ancient walls now guard Etruscan artifacts, such as the painted vases and funerary statues excavated from the necropolis in the last 10 years. Exploring the side streets of the village will yield many cheap places to grab a snack, but for a garden terrace and castle views, **La Rupe ❷,** V.d. Lavatore, 12, is your best bet, offering hearty pastas as well as fish and meats *alla brace*. *Primi* €6.80; *secondi* €12. (Walk right facing the steps to the museum and follow signs. ☎06 994 28 96. Open 12:30-3pm and 7:30-11:30pm; MC/V).

TARQUINIA

Trains, sometimes with a bus connection at Civitavecchia, leave Termini 1hr., 11 per day, last train leaves Tarquinia at 10:38pm, €5.60. Buses run from the train station to the beach €0.60 and to the city center €0.80 every 25-45min. Last bus 9:10pm. Buses link the town with Viterbo 1hr., €3.50. For bus schedules and info on Etruria, try the ***tourist office*** *in P. Cavour, near the medieval walls. ☎0766 856 384. Open daily 9am-7pm. Museo Nazionale ☎0766 850 080. Open Mar.-Nov. Tu-Su 8:30am-7:30pm; Dec.-Feb. Tu-Su 2-7:30pm. Necropolis ☎0766 840 000; www.arteo.it. Open 8:30am until one hour before sunset, usually 7:30pm in summer. Call ahead for details. Museum and necropolis €6.50 combined; €4 each.*

When Rome was little more than a mud hut shanty town clinging to the Palatine Hill, Tarquin kings held the fledgling metropolis under their sway. Their vibrantly decorated tombs make their hedonistic lives seem vivid despite the intervening centuries. The city of Tarquinia is an attraction in itself, with a large and excellent Etruscan museum, stunning countryside vistas, and medieval churches.

Buses stop just outside the medieval ramparts. Just inside P. Cavour is the magnificent **Museo Nazionale,** one of the most comprehensive collections of Etruscan art outside of Rome. It houses a superb collection of sarcophagi (some with bright paintings still visible), frescoes removed from tombs in the nearby necropolis, votive statues, and an enormous range of Etruscan and (occasionally explicit) Greek vases. Look for the famous 4th-century BC terra cotta **Winged Horses** upstairs.

The **necropolis** is a 15min. walk from the **museum.** Head up C.V. Emanuele from P. Cavour past the main square with its fountain and turn right on V. Porta Tarquinia (V. Tombe Etruschi); walk through the city gate, then continue left. The tombs are decorated with paintings of their occupants feasting, dancing, and hunting, depicted quite realistically in warm red, yellow, and green paints and surrounded with beautiful abstract patterns. D. H. Lawrence's section on Tarquinia in *Etruscan Places* will give you a picture of the tombs as they were before they were made into museums.

Tarquinia's medieval churches are also worth exploring. Don't miss **San Pancrazio,** with its distinctive spiky tower, or **San Martino,** with its simple interior and Romanesque arches. The most interesting church, the crumbling **Santa Maria del Castello,** must be reached by the old city bastions overgrown with climbing honeysuckle—from P. Cavour follow V. Mazzini until the medieval gates. The asymmetrical facade results from the fact that the 12th-century church was built over the foundations of an earlier edifice. The white marble flooring, inscribed with cabalistic pictures, can still be seen at the edges of the later multi-colored mosaic. Ask the custodian to unlock the church doors—she lives to the left of the church. The brick towers dotting the city were once private fortresses during those crazy Middle Ages. For local cuisine, try **Le Due Orfanelle ❷,** V. Breve, 4, near the Church of San Francesco. (☎0766 856 307. Open M and W-Su noon-2:30pm and 7:30-11pm). **Lo Scacciapensieri ❷,** V. M. Garibaldi, 12 (☎0766 857 826) is a good choice for whole fish and roast lamb. Open Th-M noon-3pm and 7-10pm. MC/V.

There are several B&Bs within the medieval walls as well as a few cheaper accommodations toward the outskirts. **San Marco Hotel ❷,** Piazza Cavour, 18, just inside the city wall, offers comfortable rooms at reasonable prices (☎0766 842 234; www.sanmarco.com). English-speaking reception 7am-midnight; TV, telephone, all rooms with bath. Breakfast included in the price. Singles €50; doubles €65; triples €80; quads €95. AmEx/MC/V.

LAKE BRACCIANO

*M: A-Lepanto, then take the CO.TRA.L buses every hr. 7:40am-8:35pm, last bus from Bracciano at 5:20pm, €2. Anguillara and Bracciano are more accessible by train on the Rome-Viterbo line every hr. from Rome's San Pietro station 4:44am-9:47pm, last train to Rome 10:43pm; from Termini €2.50, from San Pietro €2.10. Orsini-Odescalchi Castle ☎06 998 043 48; www.odescalchi.it. Open via mandatory tour Tu-Sa 10am-noon and 3-6pm; Su 9am-12:30pm and 3-6:30pm tours every 30min.-1hr. €6, military and children under 12 €5. Tours in English at 3:30, 4:30, and 5:30pm; no English tours on Su. For more information on Bracciano, try the **tourist office**, P. Venti Novembre, 5, ☎06 998 400 62. Open Tu-Sa 9am-1pm and 3-5pm; Su 10am-noon and 3-5pm.*

Lake Bracciano lies in the hills an hour north of Rome, surrounded by small beaches and wooded farms on the nearby slopes. Bracciano's large and imposing medieval castle towers over the quiet town below and local restaurants serve up platters of savory fish or eel from the lake.

To get to Bracciano's main attraction, the **Orsini-Odescalchi Castle,** take V.A. Fausti from P. Roma to V. Umberto and turn right. The castle was built in the late 15th century for the Orsini, an ancient, independent-minded Roman family who managed to provoke (and more impressively, to withstand) the jealous rages of a succession of autocratic Renaissance popes. Even Cesare Borgia, Alexander VI's Machiavellian son and commander-in-chief, never breached the castle's towers. The castle only succumbed in the 1670s, when the Odescalchi family tried a weapon more powerful than any pillaging army or battering ram—cold, hard, beautiful cash. Inside, a series of salons and chambers wraps around two medieval courtyards, their walls and ceilings frescoed with the bears and roses of the Orsini arms and a few stellar cycles by Antoniazzo Romano (a pupil of Pinturicchio), Taddeo, and Federico Zuccari. The rooms house more arms and armor than you can shake a halberd at and a **furry collection** of stuffed wild boars. Don't miss the sala di Isabella with its wooden door covering a pit lined with blades, used by Isabella di Medici to ensure that her one-night stands would not give her a bad reputation, or the more pleasant views of the lake from the castle.

To get to the lake from the castle (about 2km), head down V. Umberto and turn right, following the signs along V.d. Lago (follow porticciolo signs if no sign says "lake" at an intersection, until the sign for "lago & batello"). The narrow strip of rough sand stretches in both directions, and stands rent paddle boats and **canoes** (€6-8 per hr.) and umbrellas and chairs (€3 per day), while large swaths of the beach are free. During the week, the beaches are sparsely populated, though on weekends many day-trippers pour in from Rome.

If all that swimming makes you hungry, you have plenty of options. Cafes and *ristoranti* line the lakefront, and the historic center has several *alimentari* if you want a cheap, self-catered snack. For local seafood and big plates of pasta, try **Trattoria del Castello ❷,** in Piazza Mazzini, in the shadow of the castle (☎06 998 043 39). *Gelaterie* abound, and for the meat lover, *porchetta* (meat from an entire roast baby pig; €10-20/kg depending on cut). *Primi* €7-10. Hours vary. Open 12:15pm for lunch and 8pm for dinner.

CAMPANIA

The fertile crescent of Campania, in the shadow of Mt. Vesuvius, cradles the Bay of Naples and the larger Gulf of Salerno. The fiery fields of Hades to the west and the ruins of Pompeii hiding beneath the crater captivate visitors year after year. The region remains justly proud of its open-hearted populace, strong traditions, classical ruins, and relatively untouristed beaches.

NAPLES (NAPOLI)

Italy's third-largest city is also its most chaotic: shouting merchants flood markets and summer traffic jams clog the broiling city. The city's color and vitality, evident in the street markets and family-run pizzerias, have gradually overcome its rough-edged image. In recent years, aggressive restoration has opened monuments for the first time, revealing exquisite architectural works of art.

TRANSPORTATION

Flights: Aeroporto Capodichino, V. Umberto Maddalena ☎789 67 42, northwest of the city, has flights to all major Italian and European cities. A CLP **shuttle bus** ☎531 17 06 leaves from P. Municipio; 20min., 6am-10:30pm, €1.55.

Trains: Ferrovie dello Stato trains go from **Stazione Centrale** to **Milan** (8hr., 13 per day, €50) and **Rome** (2hr., 34 per day, €9.60). **Circumvesuviana** (☎772 24 44) heads for Herculaneum €1.55; and Pompeii €1.90. **FS** goes to Salerno €2.74.

Ferries: depart from **Molo Angioino** and **Molo Beverello,** at the base of P. Municipio. From P. Garibaldi take the R2 bus to P. Municipio. **Caremar,** Molo Beverello (☎551 38 82), goes frequently to Capri and Ischia (both 1½hr., €5). **Tirrenia Lines,** on Molo Angioino, goes to Cagliari, Sardinia and Palermo, Sicily; ☎720 11 11. Schedules and prices change frequently, so check Qui Napoli.

Public Transportation: Giranapoli public transport tickets (1½hr. €0.77, full-day €2.32, month €23.24) are valid on **buses, metro, trams,** and **funiculars.** Everything stops running around midnight, except for the unreliable notturno (nighttime) buses.

Taxis: Napoli, ☎556 44 44. Take metered taxis.

Car Rentals: Avis, C. A. Lucci, 203 (☎554 30 20), rents cars from €165.20 for 2 days; €355.82 per wk. Another office is in the airport (☎780 57 90). Additional 12% tax applies.

Open daily 7am-midnight. AmEx/MC/V. **Maggiore Budget** (☎081 28 78 58) in Stazione Centrale rents from €78 per day and €312 per week. Open M-F 8am-1pm and 3-7pm, Sa 8:30am-1:30pm. AmEx/MC/V.

ORIENTATION AND PRACTICAL INFORMATION

Think of Naples as divided into five areas: **train station, waterfront, hilltop, downtown,** and **historic center.** The main train and bus terminals are in the immense **Piazza Garibaldi** on the east side of Naples. From P. Garibaldi, broad **Corso Umberto I** leads southwest to P. Bovi, from which V. Depretis leads left to **Piazza Municipio,** the city center, and **Piazza Trieste e Trento** and **Piazza Plebiscito.** Below P. Municipio lie the **Stazione Marittima** ferry ports. From P. Trieste e Trento, **Via Toledo** (also known as **Via Roma**) leads through the Spanish quarter to **Piazza Dante.** Make a right into the historic **Spaccanapoli** neighborhood, which follows **Via dei Tribunali** through the middle of town. If you plan to be in town for a few days, the tourist office, hostels, museums, and the like eagerly hand out detailed maps. Be sure to pick up the free *Napoli by Bus* brochure to assist you in using the bus system. Finally, though violence is rare in Naples, theft is relatively common so watch your belongings.

Tourist Office: EPT tourist office, at Stazione Centrale, helps with hotels and ferries and has copies of *Qui Napoli*, a monthly tourist publication full of schedules and listings. **Branch:** P. dei Martiri 58 and Stazione Mergellina (☎081 26 87 79). Open M-Sa 9am-7pm.

Consulates: Canada, at V. Carducci 29 (☎081 40 13 38); **South Africa,** at Corso Umberto 1 (☎551 75 19); **UK,** at V. dei Mille 40 (☎081 423 89 11); and **US,** P. della Repubblica, at the west end of Villa Comunale (☎081 583 81 11, emergency ☎081 03 37 94 50 83).

Currency Exchange: Thomas Cook, at the airport (☎081 551 83 99). Open M-F 9:30am-1pm and 3-6:30pm.

Emergency: ☎113. **Police** ☎113 or 794 11 11. **Ambulance** ☎081 752 06 96.

Hospital: Cardarelli ☎081 747 28 59, on the R4 bus line.

Internet Access: Internetbar, P. Bellini 74; €2.50 per hr. Open M-Sa 9am-2am, Su 8am-2am; or **Internet Multimedia,** V. Sapienza 43;

the insider's CITY

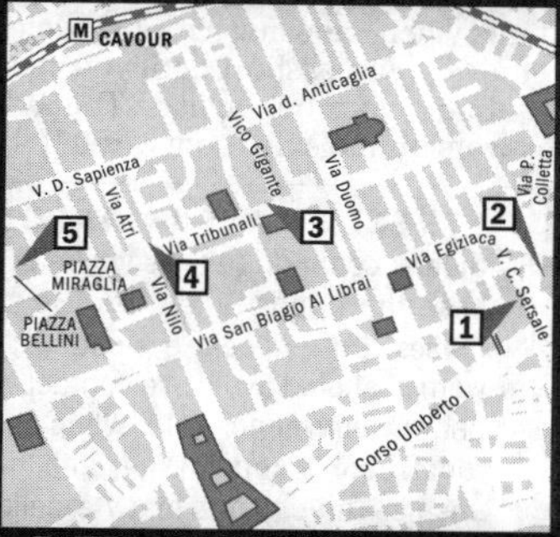

PIZZA PARADISO

A tour of the pizza capital of the world is best for two—it would take prodigious gastronomic capabilities to single-handedly devour an entire pizza at each of the four best Neapolitan *pizzerie.* Consider fasting for a couple days, or just take a friend.

1 Start with the basics at Antica Pizzeria da Michele—only *margherita* and *marinara* pizzas grace their purist menu. (☎553 92 04).

2 Cross the street to Pizzeria Trianon da Ciro, and try a sizzling pie by da Michele's rival. (☎553 94 26).

3 Re-ignite your appetite with a short walk to the lively Pizzeria di Matteo, where Bill Clinton once ate. (☎45 52 62).

4 Polish off another version of the pie from the inventors of the *calzone* at Gino Sorbillo (☎44 66 43).

5 Retreat to the open-air bars of Piazza Bellini, to bask in the sun and brag about your monstrous feat over a cold drink.

€1.55 per hr. Scanning and printing available. Open daily 9:30am-9:30pm.

Post Office: P. Matteotti, at V. Diaz on the R2 line. Address mail to be held: First name, SURNAME, In Ferme Posta, P. Matteotti, Naples **80100**, ITALIA. ☎081 552 42 33. Open M-F 8:15am-6pm, Sa 8:15am-noon.

Phone Code: ☎081.

ACCOMMODATIONS

Although Naples has some fantastic bargains, especially near **Piazza Garibaldi,** be cautious when choosing a room. Avoid hotels that solicit customers at the station, never give your passport until you've seen the room, and consider the security of yourself and your belongings. The **ACISJF/Centro D'Ascolto,** at Stazione Centrale, helps women find safe rooms. (☎081 28 19 93. Open M, Tu, and Th 3:30-6:30pm.)

STREET SMART IN NAPOLI. Though violent crime is rare in Naples, theft is common (unless you're in the *Camorra,* the Neapolitan mafia, in which case the opposite is true). Be smart. Don't carry your money in wallets or purses. Do not wear eye-catching jewelry or flaunt expensive cameras. Young women should avoid eye contact with strangers and should travel in mixed company whenever possible. When choosing accommodations, *always* ask to see a room before committing, and never stay anywhere that feels even a little unsafe. The city has many excellent hotels, hostels, and pensions, and many lousy ones too; no matter the duration, the quality of your stay can rest heavily on your choice of accommodation.

Casanova Hotel, 2 entrances; C. Garibaldi, 333 and V. Venezia 2. (☎081 26 82 87; www.hotelcasanova.com). From P. Garibaldi, head down C. Garibaldi; turn right before V. Casanova. Tucked into a vine-covered corner, it features 18 airy rooms and breezy rooftop bar. All rooms with A/C, some with TV, fridge, and phone. Breakfast €4. Luggage deposit. Check-out noon. Reserve ahead. Singles €23-26, with bath €26-30; doubles €38-42/€47-52; triples €55-68; quads €69-78. 10% *Let's Go* discount. AmEx/MC/V. ❷

Hostel and Pensione Soggiorno Imperia, P. Miraglia, 386, 6th fl. (☎/fax 081 45 93 47). From train station, take R2, exit at University, take V. Mezzocannone through P. S. Domenico Maggiore. Buzz at 1st green doors to left on P. Miraglia. Refurbished 16th-century *palazzo* houses 9 bright and clean rooms. Kitchen facilities available. Reservation recommended. Dorm €18; singles €35; doubles €50, with bath €70; triples €75/€90; quad €90/€100. 10% *Let's Go* discount. Cash only. ❷

Hostel Pensione Mancini, V. Mancini, 33 (☎081 553 6731; www.hostelpensionemancini.com), off far end of P. Garibaldi from station. The only real option for backpackers, and a top-notch value. Multilingual, tourist-friendly owners share their encyclopedic knowledge of Naples. Simple, spacious, and newly renovated; guests feel safe and at home. Breakfast included. Check-in and check-out at noon. Reservations suggested 1 week in advance. Dorms €18. Singles €35; doubles €45, with bath €55; triples €80; quads €90. Cash only. ❷

6 Small Rooms, V. Diodato Lioy, 18 (☎081 790 1378; www.at6smallrooms.com). From P. Monteoliveto, turn right on V. Diodato Lioy, and go up half a block. There is no sign; look for the name on the call button. A bit out of the way, but worth the trek. Key (€5 deposit) available for after midnight curfew. Big rooms and *cornetti* and coffee every morning. Dorms €16, €15 for longer stays; singles €20.66. ❷

Pensione Margherita, V. Cimarosa, 29, 5th fl. (☎081 578 2852; fax 556 7044), in the same building as the Centrale funicular station. Go outside and around the corner to the right and buzz to enter. 19 big rooms. Endearing management, excellent views of Vesuvius and Capri, and the lowest prices available in this posh, peaceful residential area. Check-out 11am. Curfew 1am. Closed Aug. 1-15. Singles €32; doubles €58; triples €82. MC/V. ❸

FOOD

If you ever doubted that Neapolitans invented **pizza,** Naples's *pizzerie* will take that doubt, beat it into a ball, throw it in the air, spin it on their collective finger, toss it down, cover it with sauce and mozzarella, and serve it *alla margherita* (see the **Insider's City** sidebar on p. 281 for the full tour of Naples's top *pizzerie*). While certainly the best meal ever concocted, pizza can get a little old, so don't shy away from exploring Naples's other establishments.

RESTAURANTS AND TRATTORIE

La Cantina di Albi Cocca, V. Ascensione, 6 (☎081 41 16 58). Take V. Vittoria Colonna from P. Amedeo, take the 1st right down a flight of stairs, turn right, then left onto V. Ascensione. This hard-to-find place has traditional Neapolitan fare in a small, romantic setting. *Primi* €6-8, *secondi* €8-10. Cover €1. Open M-Sa 1-3pm and 8pm-midnight. MC/V. ❷

Umberto, V. Alabardieri, 30/31 (☎081 41 85 55; www.umberto.it). V. Alabardieri leads out of P. dei Martiri; restaurant on the left. Replete in tealights and bamboo, this waterfront locale serves local fare with flare. House specials are *tubettoni d' 'o treddata* (tube pasta stuffed with seafood, €9.30) and *polpettine di nonna Ermelinda* (meatballs in tomato sauce, €4.65). Closed 2 weeks in Aug. Reservations recommended. Open Tu-Su noon-3pm and 7:30pm-midnight. AmEx/MC/V. ❸

Antica Trattoria Campagnola, Piazzetta Nilo, 22 (☎081 339 207 3149). Heaping portions of regional cuisine at this outstanding trattoria, including excellent *fritto di aliei.* Simple outdoor seating is a calm, quiet alternative to bustling *pizzerie* nearby. Efficient service and wide selection of wines. *Secondi* around €12. Open daily 10am-11pm. AmEx/MC/V. ❷

GELATERIE

Gay Odin, V. V. Colonna, 15b (☎081 41 82 82; www.gay-odin.it), off P. Amedeo; V. Toledo, 214 (☎40 00 63); and V. Luca Giordano, 21 (☎081 57 83 80). No Norse gods, just delicious chocolate treats that have been poured in *fabbriche* (factories) on V. Vetriera since 1824. Try the *foresta*, a sweet and crumbly chocolate stalk (from €2.20 for a small twig, to €8.40 for a branch best devoured with friends). Open M-Sa 9:30am-1:30pm and 4:30-8pm, Su 10am-2pm. AmEx/MC/V. ❶

Pintauro, V. Toledo, 275 (☎081 41 73 39), near the Centrale funicular station. This tiny bakery invented *sfogliatella* in 1785. Try one piping hot for €1.30. Open M-Sa 9:15am-8:15pm. ❶

Fantasia Gelati, V. Toledo, 381 (☎081 551 1212) comes close to gelato perfection. The shop's fruit flavors, including heavenly *arancia* (orange) and tangy papaya, are made with real juices, yielding tart, refreshing results. Very generous scoops. Cones €1.30-€2. Open daily 7am-11pm. ❶

SIGHTS

A **Campania ArteCard** (☎800 60 0601; www.artecard.it; €13, ages 18-25 €8) is a good investment for those planning to spend some time in Naples's museums and sights. The card grants free admission to two of 48 museums and sites in and around Naples (including Pompeii), and half-price admission to the rest, as well as free public transportation, special ArteCard transportation on weekends, and discounts on audio guides. Those with a flare for archaeology should consider the **Biglietto comprensivo** (€8.50), which includes admission to the Museo Nazionale, the Museo Archeologico dei Campi Flegrei and the archaeological sites of Pozzuoli, Baia, and Cuma.

MUSEO ARCHEOLOGICO NAZIONALE. This world-class collection houses exquisite treasures from Pompeii and Herculaneum. Highlights include the massive Farnese Hercules, showing the exhausted hero after his last labor. Also check out the Farnese Bull, the largest extant ancient sculpture. The bull was carved out of a single piece of marble, then touched up by Michelangelo. The mezzanine contains a room filled with exquisite mosaics taken from Pompeii, ranging from pictures of food to the Alexander Mosaic, which shows a young and fearless Alexander the Great routing a Persian army. The Secret Collection showcases another side of antiquity, with its display of erotic paintings and objects from Pompeii. Call ahead to gain entrance to the room. Also of note are the Jewels, a collection of ancient ornaments that includes the sparkling Farnese Cup. *(M: P. Cavour, turn right and walk 2 blocks. ☎081 44 01 66; www.marketplace.it/museo.nazionale. Open M and W-Su 9am-7:30pm. €6.50.)*

SPACCANAPOLI. This neighborhood overflows with gorgeous architecture, meriting at least a 30min. meander. From P. Dante, walk through Porta Alba and P. Bellini before turning on V. dei Tribunali, where the churches of **San Lorenzo Maggiore** and **San Paolo Maggiore** lie. Turn right on V. Duomo and right again on V. S. Biago to pass the **University of Naples** and the **Chiesa di San Domenico Maggiore.** *(In P. S. Domenico Maggiore. Open daily 7:15am-12:15pm and 4:15-7:15pm. Free.)*

CHIESA DI SAN DOMENICO MAGGIORE. This 13th-century church, founded when Naples was a center of learning in Europe, has been restructured several times over the years, finally settling on a 19th-century, spiked Gothic interior. To the right of the altar in the Chapel of the Crucifix hangs the 13th-century painting that allegedly spoke to St. Thomas Aquinas, when he lived in the adjoining monastery. Fine Renaissance sculptures decorate the side chapels. *(P. S. Domenico Maggiore. ☎081 45 91 88. Open M-F 8:30am-noon and 5-8pm, Sa-Su 9:30am-1pm and 5-7pm.)*

DUOMO. The main attraction of this 14th-century *duomo* is the Cappella del Tesoro di San Gennaro. A beautiful 17th-century bronze grille protects the high altar, which holds a gruesome display of relics like the saint's head and two vials of his coagulated blood. Supposedly, disaster will strike if the blood does not liquefy on the celebration of his *festa;* miraculously, it always does. *(3 blocks up V. Duomo from Corso Umberto I or take the #42 bus from P. Garibaldi. Open M-F 8am-12:30pm and 4:30-7pm, Sa-Su 9am-noon. Free.)*

PIO MONTE D. MISERICORDIE. This small chapel was built by a group of nobles who dedicated themselves to helping the needy and sick, housing pilgrims, and ransoming Christian slaves held prisoner by infidels. The church houses seven arches, each with its own altar and painting, and the main archway boasts Caravaggio's *Our Lady of Mercy*, the central attraction. In an archway to the left is the creepy *Resurrection of Tabatha;* teeming with vivid characters, it merits more than a passing glance. In the *piazza* outside, a spire reaches to the sky; its dedicated to S. Gennaro for having saved the city from the 1656 plague. *(1 block down V. Tribunali after V. Duomo, in a small piazza. ☎081 44 69 44. Call in the morning to book a tour.)*

NAPOLI E LA CITTA SOTTERANEA/NAPOLI SOTTERRANEA. These tours of the subterranean alleys beneath the city are fascinating, but not for the claustrophobic: they have people crawling through narrow underground passageways, grottoes, and catacombs, spotting Mussolini-era graffiti, and exploring Roman aqueducts. *Napoli e la Città* explores the area underneath Castel Nuovo and downtown, and *Napoli Sotterranea* drags the intrepid underneath the historic center. *(**Napoli e La Città' Sotteranea,** office at Vco. S. Anna di Palazzo. ☎081 40 02 56. Tours Th 9pm; Sa 10am and 6pm; Su 10am, 11am, and 6pm. €5. Tours leave from Bar Gambiunes in P. Trieste e Trento, but call first. **Napoli Sotterranea,** P. S. Gaetano, 68. Take V. Tribunali and turn left right before San Paolo Maggiore. ☎081 29 69 44; www.napolisotterranea.com. Tours every 2hr. M-F noon-4pm, Sa, Su, and holidays 10am-6pm. €5.)*

CASTEL NUOVO. It's impossible to miss this huge, five-turreted landmark, towering mightily over the Bay of Naples. Known also as the **Maschio Angioino,** the fortress was built in 1286 by Charles II of Anjou to be his royal residence in Naples. Its most stunning feature is the triumphal entrance, with reliefs commemorating the arrival of Alphonse I of Aragon in 1443, is the *castel*'s most stunning feature. The magnificent cubical **Hall of the Barons,** where King Ferdinand once trapped rebellious barons and where Naples's city council holds spirited meetings today, is also inside. The splendid **Capella Palatina,** also called the Chapel of St. Barbara, is a cool and beautiful retreat from the castel's open churchyard. *(P. Municipio. Take the R2 bus from P. Garibaldi or walk from anywhere in the historical center. Open M-Sa 9am-7pm. Admission €5.)*

MUSEO AND GALLERIE DI CAPODIMONTE. This museum, in a royal *palazzo*, is surrounded by a pastoral park and sprawling lawns. In addition to its plush royal apartments and their furnishings, the palace houses the National Picture Gallery. The **Farnese Collection** on the first floor is full of artistic masterpieces, many of them removed from Neapolitan churches for safety's sake, including Bellini's *Transfiguration*, Masaccio's *Crucifixion*, and Titian's *Danae.* The 2nd floor traces the development of the Neapolitan realistic style and its dramatic use of light. *(Take bus #110 from P. Garibaldi to Parco Capodimonte, and then enter by Portas Piccola or Grande. Open Tu-F and Su 8:30am-7:30pm. €7.50, after 2pm €6.50.)*

PALAZZO REALE AND CASTEL NUOVO. The 17th-century **Palazzo Reale** contains opulent royal apartments, the **Museo di Palazzo Reale,** and a fantastic view from the terrace of the **Royal Chapel.** The **Biblioteca Nazionale** stores 1.5 million volumes, including the scrolls from the **Villa dei Papiri** in Herculaneum. The **Teatro San Carlo** is reputed to top the acoustics in Milan's La Scala. From P. Trieste e Trento, walk up V. Vittorio Emanuele III to P. Municipio for the five-turreted **Castel Nuovo,** built in 1286 by Charles II of Anjou. The double-arched entrance commemorates the arrival of Alphonse I of Aragon in Naples. Inside, admire the **Museo Civico.** *(Take the R2 bus from P. Garibaldi to P. Trieste e Trento and go around to the P. Plebiscito entrance. Palazzo open M-Tu and Th-F 9am-8pm. €4.15. Castel open M-Sa 9am-7pm. €5.20.)*

CHIESA DI SANTA CHIARA. One of the best Angevin monuments in Naples, the **Chiesa di Santa Chiara** was originally built in the 1300s by the rulers of the house of Anjou and has been renovated several times, most recently after a World War II bombing in 1943. The church is littered with sarcophagi and tombs from the Middle Ages, and the 14th-century tomb of Robert of Anjou can be seen behind the main altar. Spend some time in the adjoining garden and monastery, adorned with Gothic frescoes and brightly colored majolica tiles. *(From P. Dante, head down V. Toledo and turn left on V. B. Croce. The church sits on P. Gesù Nuovo. ☎081 552 62 09. Open M-F 9:30am-1pm and 3:30-5:30pm, weekends and holidays 9:30am-1pm. €4, students €2.50.)*

MUSEO NAZIONALE DI SAN MARTINO. Once a monastery, the massive Certosa di S. Martino is now home to an excellent museum of Neapolitan history and culture. In addition to extensive galleries, the monastery includes a chapel lavishly decorated in Baroque marbles and statuary, featuring one of Ribera's finest works, *The Deposition of Christ*, and an excellent *Nativity* by Guido Reni. Numerous balconies and a multilevel garden provide superb views. The massive **Castel Sant'Elmo** next door was built to deter rebellion and hold political prisoners. Ignore the oppressive past; there are great panoramic views from the battlements. *(From V. Toledo, take the funicular to Vomero, and make a right on V. Cimarosa. A left on V. Morghen and a right onto V.P.L. Architetto lands you in Piazzale S. Martino. ☎081 578 1769. Open Tu-F 8:30am-7:30pm, Sa 9am-7:30pm. €6, EU students €3, EU citizens under 18 or over 65 free. Castel: ☎081 578 4030. Open Tu-Su 9am-2pm. €1.)*

NIGHTLIFE

Piazza Vanvitelli in Vomero is where the cool kids go to relax and socialize. Take the funicular from V. Toledo or the C28 bus from P. Vittoria. Outdoor bars and cafes are popular in **Piazza Bellini,** near P. Dante. **Itaca,** P. Bellini 71, mixes eerie trance music with dark decor. (Cocktails from €6. Open daily 10am-3am.) **Camelot,** V. S. Pietro A Majella 8, just off P. Bellini in the historic district, plays mostly pop and house. (Open Sept.-June Tu-Su 10:30pm-5am.) **ARCI-Gay/Lesbica** has information on gay and lesbian club nights. (☎081 551 82 93.)

BAY OF NAPLES

Off the shores of the Bay of Naples, the pleasure islands **Capri** and **Ischia** beckon weary travelers with promises of breathtaking natural sights, comfortable accommodations, and gorgeous beaches. The islands can be reached by ferries *(traghetti)* or the faster, more expensive hydrofoils *(aliscafi)*. For trips to Capri, Sorrento is the closest starting point. The busiest route to Capri and Ischia is through Naples's Mergellina and Molo Beverello ports. To reach **Molo Beverello** from Naples's Stazione Centrale (trains from Rome: 2hr., every 15min.-1hr. 6:10am-10:30am, €9.61), take tram #1 from P. Garibaldi to P. Municipio on the waterfront. Ferries and hydrofoils also run between the islands.

CAPRI & ANACAPRI

Caremar ferries run from Naples to Marina Grande; 1¼hr., 7 per day, 5:50am-8:05pm; €8.44; and Sorrento 50 min.; 4 per day, 7:05am-6:15pm; €6.53. ☎837 07 00. LineaJet runs hydrofoils from Naples 40min.; 10 per day, 8:30am-6:25pm; €11.50; and Sorrento 20min., €8.51. Ferries and hydrofoils to Ischia and Amalfi run with much less frequency and regularity; check with the lines at Marina Grande for details. ☎837 08 19. The ***Capri tourist office*** *sits at the end of Marina Grande dock. ☎837 06 34. The* ***Anacapri tourist office*** *is at V. Orlandi 59, to the right of the P. Vittoria bus stop; ☎837 15 24. Both open June-Sept. M-Sa 8:30am-8:30pm; Oct.-May M-Sa 9am-1:30pm and 3:30-6:45pm. Take the funicular from Marina Grande to Capri proper; every 10min.; 6:30-12:30am in summer; €1.50. To reach Anacapri, catch the bus at V. Roma in Capri, every 15min until 1:40am.*

Augustus fell in love with Capri's fantastic beauty in 29 BC but traded it in for the fertility of Ischia. His successor Tiberius passed his last decade on Capri, leaving a dozen scattered villas. Visitors today pay exorbitant rates to tour the renowned **Blue Grotto,** a sea cave where the water shimmers bright blue, and to gawk at the rich and famous. Away from the throngs flitting between Capri's expensive boutiques, Anacapri is home to budget hotels, spectacular vistas, and empty mountain paths. In the summer months crowds and prices increase, so the best times to visit are in the late spring and early fall.

For quick access to the beach and center of Capri, stay at the **Bed and Breakfast Tirrenia Roberts ❸,** V. Mulo 27. Walk away from P. Umberto on V. Roma and take the stairs on your right just before the fork. (☎837 61 19; bbtirreniaroberts@iol.it. Reserve well in advance. 3 doubles €80-105.) Another good option is **Pensione 4 Stagioni ❸,** V. Marina Piccola 1. From P. Umberto, walk five minutes down V. Roma, turn left at the triple fork, and look for the green gate on the left. (☎837 00 41; www.hotel4stagionicapri.com. Breakfast included. Singles €40-70; doubles €70-130. Open April to November AmEx/MC/V.) Bear right at the fork to reach **Dimeglio supermarket.** (Open M-Sa 8:30am-1:30pm and 5-9pm.) At night, dressed-to-kill Italians come out for Capri's *passegiatta;* bars around **Piazza Umberto** keep the music pumping late, but Anacapri is cheaper and more fun.

Should you tire of Capri's crowds and prices, Anacapri offers a much more reasonable alternative. Reserve ahead of time for the great value and super-friendly hosts at **Alla Bussola di Hermes ❶,** V. Traversa La Vigna, 14. (☎838

20 10; bus.hermes@libero.it. Dorms €20-24; doubles €50-65 with bath and breakfast. AmEx/MC/V.) Tired of buses? **Il Girasole ❶**, V. Linciano, 47, will pick you up at Marina Grande and take you to their serene and picturesque locale. (☎837 23 51; www.ilgirasole.com. With *Let's Go* discount, singles €20-32; doubles €70-95; triples €100-120. Groups of 8 or more €15 per person. AmEx/MC/V). Once settled, make your way over to **Ristorante Il Cucciolo ❷**, V. Fabbrica, 52, and enjoy wonderful food served on a seaside terrace at a great price (thanks to your *Let's Go* discount). The *bruschette pomodori* antipasto (€3.50) is unsurpassed. (☎837 19 17. Open daily Mar.-June and Sept.-May noon-2:30pm and 7:30-11pm; July-Aug. 7:30-11pm. AmEx/MC/V.)

CAPRI'S COAST

To reach Bagni di Tiberio, take a bus or a 10min. walk down the path on left fork where V. Roma splits in three leads to the gorgeous southern stretch of Marina Piccola. Buy tickets and get info for all boat tours at the Grotta Azzurra Travel Office, V. Roma, 53, across the street from the bus stop. ☎837 07 02; g.azzurra@capri.it. Open M-Sa 9am-1pm and 3-8pm, Su 9am-12:30pm.

Every day, **boat tours** reveal Capri's coast from Marina Grande for €11.50, and leave at 9:30, 10:30, and 11:30am. Many rock and pebble **beaches** surround the island. Take a boat from the port (€5) or descend between vineyards from P. Umberto to **Bagni di Tiberio,** a bathing area amid the ruins of an imperial villa. Cavort in the clear water among lava rocks or rent a **motor boat** (€80 for two hours) from **Banana Sport.** (☎081 837 5188. Main office on the dock at Marina Grande. Open daily 9am-6pm.)

CAPRI'S CLIFFS

To get to the Villa Jovis, head out of P. Umberto on V. Longano, and don't miss the left onto V. Tiberio. Open daily 9am-6pm.

For those who prefer land to sea, Capri's hiking trails lead to some stunning panoramas; less known than Capri's legendary shopping, the island's natural beauty can be a needed break from the crowded *piazze.* Take a short but very uphill hike to check out the Roman Emperor Tiberius's ruined but magnificent **Villa Jovis,** the largest of his 12 Capri villas. Always the gracious host, Tiberius tossed those who displeased him over the precipice. The view from the **Cappella di Santa Maria del Soccorso,** built onto the villa, is unrivaled. A path winds along the cliffs, connecting the **Arco Naturale,** a majestic stone arch on the eastern cliffs, and the **Faraglioni,** three massive rocks seen on countless postcards. The walk between the two takes about an hour, and offers a vista around every bend. V. Tragara goes from Capri Centro to the Faraglioni, while the path to the Arco Naturale connects to the route to Villa Jovis through V. Matermania. The tourist office map details several walking tours of the less-populated parts of the island.

THE BLUE GROTTO

Take the bus marked Grotta Azzurra from the intersection of V. De Tomaso and V. Catena.

La Grotta Azzurra is a water-filled cave where light shining through the water creates the illusion of brilliantly blue walls. Some who visit are amazed by the bright blue color of the water; others think it's pretty, but certainly nowhere near pretty enough to justify the €8.50 fee for a six-minute boat ride. Despite the sign warning that it is "strictly forbidden," and the danger of the narrow cave opening, many choose to go for a swim in the Grotto after the boats stop at 5pm.

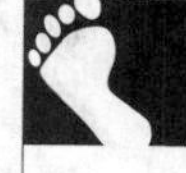

VILLA SAN MICHELE

Upstairs from P. Vittoria and to the left, past Capri's Beauty Farm. Open daily 9:30am-6pm. €5.

American author Henry James once declared this Anacapri villa a clustering of "the most fantastic beauty, poetry, and inutility." Built in the early 20th century by Swedish author and physician Axel Munthe on the site of a Tiberian villa, it houses 17th-century furniture and ancient Roman sculpture. The gardens boast a remarkable view and are a site for concerts on Friday nights. (Concerts June-Aug.)

OTHER SIGHTS

From P. Vittoria in Anacapri, a 12min. climb in a chairlift takes you to the summit of Monte Salerno. Open Mar.-Oct. daily 9:30am-4:45pm. Round-trip €5.50.

From the top of **Monte Solaro** on a clear day, you can see the Apennines to the east and the mountains of Calabria to the south. You can also take a difficult hike up the mountain, starting from the base near the Villa San Michelle. A bus from P. Vittoria leads to the **Faro,** Italy's second-tallest lighthouse. Countless Italians tan, snorkel, and dive off its rocks.

ISCHIA

Caremar ferries arrive from Naples, 1½hr., 14 per day, 6:40am-8:10pm; €5.06. ☎98 48 18. Alilauro runs hydrofoils from Sorrento 6 per day, 8:35am-5:20pm. ☎99 18 88; www.alilauro.it. Orange SEPSA buses #1, CD, and CS depart from the ferry landing and follow the coast in a circular route, stopping at: Ischia Porto, a port formed by the crater of an extinct volcano; Casamicciola Terme, with a crowded beach and legendary thermal waters; Lacco Ameno, the oldest Greek settlement in the western Mediterranean; and popular Forio, home to lively bars. Every 20 min.; €1.20, half-day pass €2.63, full-day pass €4.84.

Upon first setting foot on Ischia (EES-kee-yah), you may think you have left Italy entirely, not just because the island is an Edenic vision with luscious beaches, natural hot springs, ruins, vineyards, lemon groves, and a once-active volcano, but also because the signs, newspapers, and conversations are all in German. The island is immensely popular with German tourists, who take over for much of the summer. In August, however, Italians on holiday swarm to Ischia and reclaim it, leading to sky-high prices and boisterous crowds. Bargains and breathing room become hard to find, but with good reason: Ischia's beaches possess the perfection of Hollywood's digitally enhanced notion of a beach. Its hot springs have drawn tourists since ancient times, meriting mention in the *Iliad* and the *Aeneid*.

Stay in Ischia Porto only if you want to be close to the ferries and nightlife—most pensioni are in Forio. **Pensione Di Lustro ❷,** V. Filippo di Lustro 9, is near the beach. (☎99 71 63. Breakfast included. Singles €34; doubles €50-65.) The **Ostello "Il Gabbiano" (HI) ❷,** Strada Statale Forio-Panza, 182, is accessible by buses #1, CS, or CD, and near the beach. (☎90 94 22. Breakfast included. Lockout 9:30am-1pm. Curfew 2am. Open Apr.-Sept. Dorms €16.) In Ischia Porto, **Albergo Macri ❷,** V. Lasolino, 96, is a quiet, family-run hotel away from the noise and bustle of V. Porto. Though somewhat plain, the 22 rooms have comfortable beds and spotless baths. (☎99 26 03. With *Let's Go* discount singles €22-27; doubles €51-64; triples €70-83. AmEx/MC/V.)

CASTELLO ARAGONESE

Bus #7 runs to Ischia Ponte from Porto Ischia. Castle ☎99 28 34. Open daily 9am-7:30pm. €8.

Providing some brooding time away from fun and surf, this castle resides on a small island of its own, Ischia Ponte, connected to the rest of civilization by a 15th-century footbridge. The stronghold, built in 1441, contains both the holy and the macabre. The **cathedral** in the castle, mostly destroyed by World War II bombing, displays a mix of Roman and Baroque styles. Below, the **crypt** houses colorful 14th-century frescoes crafted by those in the school of Giotto. The **nuns' cemetery** has a ghastly history; when a nun died, the order would prop the decomposing body on a stone as a (fragrant) reminder to the other nuns of their mortality. For more family fun, visit the castle's **Museum of Arms and Instruments of Torture,** 200m past the main ticket booth.

BEACHES, HOT SPRINGS & HIKING

To reach Maronti, take #5 bus from Ischia Porto to the Maronti stop. The #1 and #3 buses head to Citara directly from Ischia Porto. Reach the beach at Sorgeto from Panza by a 20min. hike or from Sant'Angelo by boat taxi. €5 per person, with possible group discounts and arranged pick-ups.

Ischia's best and most popular beach is at **Maronti,** on the island's south coast. Another popular choice is the beach at **Citara,** 1km down the coast from Forio. For steamier adventures, the hot springs at **Sorgeto** (on the far side of the island) range from tepid to boiling. The beach is the perfect spot to lounge and soak aching feet. Locals say that the cleansing lather formed by rubbing the light-green porous rocks together is fantastic for the skin. **Lacco Ameno** and **Casamicciola Terme** are densely packed with the thermal baths that originally attracted visitors to Ischia. Hikers should take the CS or CD bus to **Fontana,** which rests above most towns, making it a good departure point. Head for **Mt. Epomeo** (788m); on a clear day the summit has an incredible view extending from Capri to Terracina.

SORRENTO

*Caremar ferries go to Capri; 20min., €5.70. ☎081 807 3077. The **tourist office**, L. de Maio 35, is off P. Tasso. ☎081 807 4033. Open Apr.-Sept. M-Sa 8:45am-7:45pm; Oct.-Mar. M-Sa 8:30am-2pm and 4-6:15pm.*

The most heavily touristed town on the peninsula, lively Sorrento makes a convenient base for daytrips around the Bay of Naples and Amalfi Coast. With 20,000 residents, it is the largest town in the area, and with 13,000 hotel beds, the most touristed. Despite its popularity among tourists, Sorrento is not home to many traditional Italian attractions: the *duomo-torre-palazzo* combination. Still, Sorrento has its charms—the streets of the old city and the **Marina Grande.** Frequent ferry connections provide links to the rest of the bay. The pretty Marina Grande provides a beautiful setting for a late afternoon stroll, far from the crowded Piazza Tasso, and the walk goes through the equally charming streets of the **old city.** The walk to Punta del Capo is picturesque as well, with the ruins of the **Villa di Pollio** around a beautiful cove fit for exploring at the tip of the cape. Take bus A (€0.93) from P. Tasso to the end of the route and take the footpath from the right of the stop. Bring your suit and a towel for a memorable swim among the ruins.

Halfway to the free **beach** at **Punta del Capo** (bus A), **Hotel Elios ❷**, V. Capo 33, has comfy rooms. (☎878 18 12. Singles €25-30; doubles €40-50.) For extensive amenities, stay at **Hotel City ❸,** C. Italia 221. Turn left on C. Italia from the station. (☎877 22 10. Singles €37-46; doubles €40-50.) It's easy to find good, affordable food in Sorrento. **Davide ❶**, V. Giuliani 39, off Corso Italia, two blocks from P. Tasso, has divine *gelato*. (60 flavors. 2 scoops for €2. Open daily 10am-midnight.)

The old city and the area around P. Tasso heat up after dark, as locals and tourists stroll the streets, gaze over the bay, and cavort about town on mopeds. Hands down the most stylish bar in Sorrento, **Gatto Nero,** V. Correale, 21, has a garden and creative interior—each wall is painted in the style of a modernist painter, among them Picasso and Matisse. Jazz and blues animate the crowd that gathers by 11pm in the summer. (☎877 36 86. Open Tu-Su noon-3pm and 7pm-midnight.) In the rooftop lemon grove above **The English Inn,** C. Italia, 56, a fun-loving crowd gathers after 10:30pm on summer evenings to dance to 80s music. Shout to be heard over the blaring speakers. (☎081 807 4357. Open daily 9am-1am, much later on weekends.)

Pompeii

Inside Pompeii

Pottery

THE AMALFI COAST

Trains run directly to Salerno from Naples; 45min., 29 per day, €5-10; and Rome 2.5-3hr., 19 per day, €20-30. The coast is accessible by ferry and blue SITA buses from Naples, Sorrento, Salerno, and the Bay of Naples islands of Capri and Ischia. From Salerno, Travelmar runs ferries to Amalfi; 35min., 6 per day, €3.50. ☎ 089 87 31 90. From Sorrento, Linee Maritime Partenopee ferries run to Capri; 40min., 5 ferries per day 8:30am-4:50pm, €6.50; 20min., 17 hydrofoils per day 7:20am-5:40pm, €8.50. ☎ 807 18 12. Area code: 089.

The beauty of the Amalfi Coast is one of contrasts and extremes. Immense rugged cliffs plunge downward to crashing waves, and the sides of narrow ravines are dotted with tightly nestled coastal towns offering delicious food and throbbing nightlife. The natural splendor and unique character of these towns attracts many tourists. Although some coastal areas may cost you an arm and two (or three) legs, budget gems exist as well. The coast is easily accessible from Naples, Sorrento, Salerno, and the islands by ferry or SITA buses. The harrowing bus ride along the Amalfi Coast is unforgettable—just remember to sit on the right side of the bus heading south (from Sorrento to Amalfi) and on the left heading back. Those with weaker stomachs should opt for sea service.

AMALFI & ATRANI

*Buses arrive at and depart from Amalfi at P.F. Gioia, on the waterfront. Buy tickets at bars and tabacchi on the piazza. Blue SITA buses connect Amalfi to: Positano, 50min., 14 per day, 6:30am-8pm, €1.30; Salerno, 1.25hr., 20 per day 6am-10pm, €1.65; and Sorrento, 1.25hr., 13 per day, 6:30am-8pm, €1.86. ☎ 089 87 10 16. Ticket booths and departures for ferries and hydrofoils are at the dock off P.F. Gioia. Travelmar runs hydrofoils to: Minori, 5min.; 3 per day, 12:35-7pm; €1.50; Positano, 25min.; 7 per day, 8:45am-4:20pm; €4; Salerno, 35min.; 6 per day, 10:35am-7pm; €3.50; Sorrento, 80min.; 2 per day, 9:15am and 3pm; €7. ☎ 089 87 29 50. All times and prices subject to change; check with tourist office or ferry line. Taxis: ☎ 089 87 22 39. The **AAST tourist office**, C. delle Repubbliche Marinare, 27, is through a gate on the left as you head up the road towards Atrani. ☎ 87 11 07. Open May-Oct. daily 8am-2pm and 3-8pm; Nov.-Apr. M-Sa 8am-2pm.*

Breathtaking natural beauty surrounds the narrow streets and historic monuments of **Amalfi.** Visitors crowd the P. del Duomo to admire the elegant 9th-century **Duomo di Sant'Andrea** and the nearby **Fontana di Sant'Andrea,** a marble nude with water spouting from her breasts. The cathedral features a facade of varied geometric designs typical of the Arab-Norman style.

The **Chiostro del Paradiso** (Cloister of Paradise), a 13th-century cemetery, has become a graveyard for miscellaneous columns, statues, and sarcophagus fragments. The elegant interlaced arches, like the *campanile* in the square, show the Middle Eastern influence. Its museum houses mosaics, sculptures, and the church's treasury. Underneath is the crypt containing the body of the church's namesake, Saint Andrew the Apostle. (Open June-Sept. daily 9am-6:45pm. Free multilingual guides available. Cloister, museum, and crypt €1.50.)

The 9th-century Arsenal on the waterfront, by the entrance to the city center, contains relics of Amalfi's former maritime glory. As you walk up V. D'Amalfi, the road changes its name to **Valle dei Mulini** (Valley of the Mills). Find here the **Paper Museum** with collections of, surprisingly enough, sundry paper items and the water-powered medieval machines that made Amalfi a paper-producing powerhouse. (☎089 830 45 61; www.museodellacarta.it. Open Tu-Su 10am-6pm. €1.50.)

A'Scalinatella ❶, P. Umberto 12, has hostel beds and regular rooms all over Amalfi and Atrani. (☎089 87 19 30. Camping €5; dorms €10-21; doubles €26-50. Cash only.) If you plan to stay in town, **Hotel Lidomare ❸,** V. Piccolomini, 9, through the alley across from the *duomo*, left up the stairs, then across the *piazzetta*, provides spacious rooms with terraces. The common areas are decked with local antiques. The 15 rooms feature bath, TV, phone, fridge, and A/C. (☎089 87 13 32; www.lidomare.it. Breakfast included. Singles €34-43; doubles €70-120. AmEx/MC/V.)

Food in Amalfi is good, but expensive. Seafood is probably your best bet, topped off with a healthy swig of the omnipresent *limoncello*. **Da Maria ❷** should be your one and only stop for quality Neapolitan cuisine. In this family-run restaurant, owners instruct the adventurous on the daily specials and the house favorites like the Amalfitan Pasta, *scialatelli* and seafood for €4.50. (☎089 87 18 80. *Primi* from €10.33, pizza from €2.58. Reservations recommended. Open Tu-Su 11am-3pm and 7pm-midnight. AmEx/MC/V.)

Nearby **Atrani,** which is a 15-20min. bus ride around the bend from Amalfi, is a much better (and free) beach option. The village of Atrani used to be home to the Amalfi Republic's leaders; with about 1000 inhabitants today, it's a quiet place to escape Amalfi's crowds by day and enjoy lively bars and music at night. Try **Casbah'r,** P. Umberto, 1, with super-friendly bartenders and a fun-filled atmosphere. (☎089 87 10 87. Open daily, 7am-1pm.) Those who can find the beach and travel up Atrani's cobbled V. dei Dogi to P. Umberto will arrive at the **Chiesa di San Salvatore de Bireto.** The 11th-century bronze doors come from Constantinople. **Path of the Gods,** a spectacular 3hr. hike, runs the coast from Bomerano to Positano.

POSITANO

*The **tourist office**, V. del Saraceno 4 (☎089 87 50 67), is below the duomo.*

When John Steinbeck visited Positano in the 1950s, the town was a posh haven for artists and literati. Jack Kerouac and Tennessee Williams sought solitude in this bohemian retreat, where the fashion avant-garde invented the bikini and creativity ran wild like the bounganvilla. But this classy reputation soon drew ordinary millionaires in addition to the writers, painters, actors, and filmmakers who made it famous. Today, its beachfront teems with teenage backpackers, honeymooners, and older, more moneyed types. Steinbeck had estimated that Positano's cliffs could stack no more than 500 visitors at a time. He clearly underestimated local ingenuity. The *Positanesi* managed to squeeze in over 2000 hotel beds, and crowds now overrun the tiny footpaths and narrow stairways. As Steinbeck observed, "Positano bites deep." Indeed, though merchants squeeze tourist wallets like lemons and crowds pile onto the legendary beaches, Positano is the most fashionable of the Amalfitan coastal towns—for better or worse.

For some, Positano's gray beaches are its main attractions. Each has public (free) and private sections. The biggest, busiest, and priciest is **Spiaggia Grande**, in the main part of town. At the private **Lido L'incanto**, spend the day with the other people who shelled out €10 for a beach chair *(lettino)*, umbrella, shower, and changing room. (☎089 81 11 77.) Outside the entrance, **Noleggio Barche Lucibello**, rents motorboats from €30 per hour and rowboats from €10.50 per hour. (☎089 87 50 32 or 87 53 26.) To reach the quieter, smaller **Spiaggia del Fornillo**, take V. Positanese d'America, a footpath that starts above the port and winds past Torre Trasita. While parts of the Fornillo are public, you can get your own spot at one of three private beaches. **Marinella beach** (€5) features a little sand underneath a time-worn boardwalk; **Fratelli Grassi beach** (€12) offers boat excursions; and **Puppetto beach** (€5-7) gives guests from Hostel Brikette a 10-15% discount. The three **Isole dei Galli**, off Positano's coast, were home to Homer's mythical sirens, who lured unsuspecting victims with their spellbinding songs. In 1925, perhaps to honor this tradition, the quartet of Stravinsky, Picasso, Hindemith, and Massine bought one of the isole. While swimming around these beautiful islands is permitted, setting foot on land is not.

Positano offers tremendous hikes for those with quads of steel. **Montepertuso**, a high mountain pierced by a large *pertusione* (hole), is one of three perforated mountains in the world (the other two are in India). To get there, hike the 45-minute trail up the hillside, or take the bus from P. dei Mulini, near the port or from any other bus stop. For those who want to lighten their pocketbooks by several pounds, Positano offers endless possibilities. The tragically chic spend afternoons in the exorbitantly priced city boutiques. Others take boat excursions to tour the coast and neighboring islands. The adventurous (or really hungry) take squid-fishing expeditions at night. Frequent cruises embark to the **Emerald and Blue Grottoes**, beautiful water-filled caves in the area. As numerous boating companies compete for these excursions, the prices can sometimes be reasonable for shorter trips; check the tourist office and booths lining the port area.

Ostello Brikette 2, V.G. Marconi 358, 100m up the main coastal road to Sorrento from Viale Pasitea, has incredible views from two large terraces. (☎089 87 58 57. Breakfast and sheets included. Dorms €20; doubles €65.) **Casa Guadagno** 3, V. Fornillo 22, has 15 spotless rooms. (☎089 87 50 42; fax 81 14 07. Breakfast included. Reserve ahead. With Let's Go: doubles €85; triples €95. MC/V.) Prices in the town's restaurants reflect the high quality of the food. For a sit-down dinner, thrifty travelers head toward the beach at **Fornillo**.

POMPEII (POMPEI)

The easiest way to get to Pompeii is to take one of many Rome-based bus tours. Enjoy Rome's self-guided tour (p. 25) is a deal at €33 per person. On your own from Termini, take the train to Naples, every 15min.-1hr., 6:10am-10:30pm, €9.77-20.30. From there, take the Circumvesuviana train and get off at "Pompeii Scavi/Villa dei Misteri;" ignore "Pompeii Santuario." ☎081 772 21 11. Eurailpasses are not valid. Stop by the ***tourist office,*** *V. Sacra, 1, for a free map. ☎081 850 72 55. Open M-F 8am-3:30pm, Sa 8am-2pm. Store your pack for free at the entrance to the ruins. There is a police station at the entrance to the ancient site, but the main station is at P. Schettini, 1, in the modern town, on the corner of P. B. Longo, at the end of V. Roma. ☎081 850 61 64. Food at the ruins cafeteria is expensive, so bring a lunch. Of the few restaurants and fruit stands that cluster outside the excavation entrances, the best is La Vinicola, V. Roma, 29. ☎081 863 12 44. Cover €0.77. Open daily 9am-midnight. Guidebooks from €4.13. Useful audio guide recommended. While the city map lists eateries and accommodations, Pompeii is best seen as a one-day trip from Naples, Sorrento, or another nearby city. Area code: 081*

On the morning of August 24th, AD 79, a deadly flow of lava from Mt. Vesuvius overtook the Roman city of Pompeii, engulfing the city in suffocating black clouds and

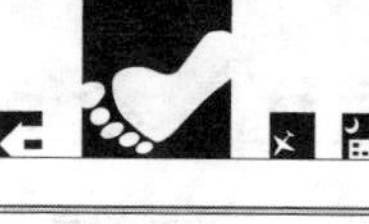

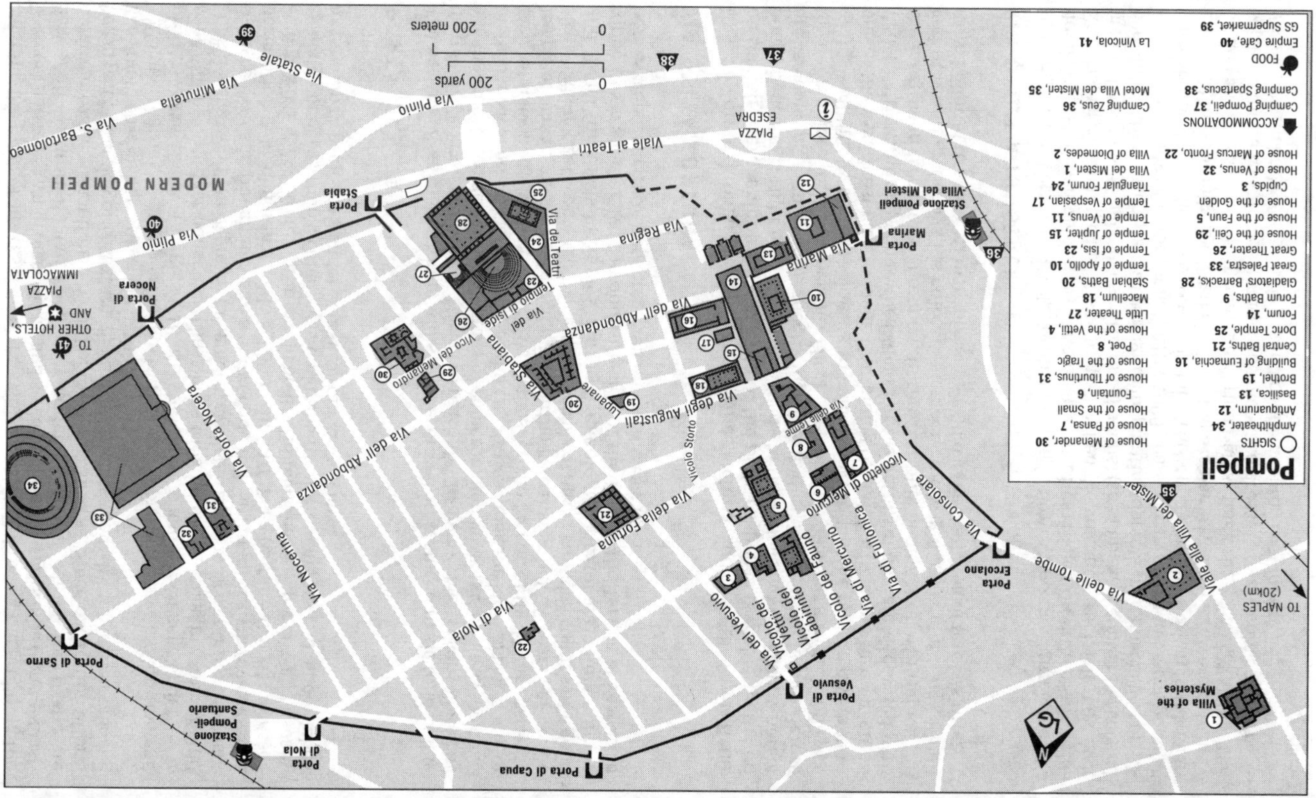
Pompeii
SIGHTS
Amphitheater, 34
Antiquarium, 12
Basilica, 13
Brothel, 19
Building of Eumachia, 16
Central Baths, 21
Doric Temple, 25
Forum, 14
Forum Baths, 9
Gladiators' Barracks, 28
Great Palestra, 33
Great Theater, 26
House of the Ceii, 29
House of the Faun, 5
House of the Golden Cupids, 3
House of Venus, 32
House of Marcus Fronto, 22
House of Menander, 30
House of Pansa, 7
House of the Small Fountain, 6
House of Tiburtinus, 31
House of the Tragic Poet, 8
House of the Vettii, 4
Little Theater, 27
Macellum, 18
Stabian Baths, 20
Temple of Apollo, 10
Temple of Isis, 23
Temple of Jupiter, 15
Temple of Venus, 11
Temple of Vespasian, 17
Triangular Forum, 24
Villa dei Misteri, 1
Villa of Diomedes, 2
ACCOMMODATIONS
Camping Pompeii, 37
Camping Spartacus, 38
Camping Zeus, 36
Motel Villa dei Misteri, 35
FOOD
Empire Cafe, 40
GS Supermarket, 39
La Vinicola, 41
Villa of the Mysteries
TO NAPLES (20km)
Viale alla Villa dei Misteri
Via delle Tombe
Porta Ercolano
Via Consolare
Porta di Vesuvio
Porta di Capua
Porta di Nola
Stazione Pompei-Santuario
Porta di Sarno
Via del Vesuvio
Vicolo dei Vettii
Vicolo del Labirinto
Vicolo del Fauno
Via di Mercurio
Via di Fullonica
Vicoletto di Mercurio
Via delle Terme
Via della Fortuna
Vicolo Storto
Via degli Augustali
Lupanare
Via di Nola
Via Nocerina
Via dell' Abbondanza
Via Porta Nocera
Via Stabiana
Vico del Menandro
Via del Tempio di Iside
Via dei Teatri
Via Regina
Via Marina
Porta Marina
Stazione Pompeii Villa dei Misteri
Porta Stabia
Porta di Nocera
TO OTHER HOTELS, AND
PIAZZA IMMACOLATA
MODERN POMPEII
Via Plinio
Via S. Bartolomeo
Via Minutella
Via Statale
Viale ai Teatri
PIAZZA ESEDRA
200 yards
200 meters

catching the prosperous residents largely by surprise. Following the eruption, the lava reached the town in mere hours and sealed buildings, works of art, and—ghastliest of all—contorted human bodies in hardened casts of ash. Visitors to the site today can witness an intimate record of the town's demise. Since excavation efforts began in 1748, archaeologists turn up new discoveries every decade in their ongoing mission to shed light on daily life in the Roman era.

Pompeii entrances are open 8:30am to 7:30pm. A comprehensive exploration will probably take all day. (Tickets €10, EU students €5, and EU citizens under 18 or over 65 free). Budget-conscious Classicists looking for an engaging tour should consider the excellent digital audio guides, available at the park's entrance. Consult the free map and punch in a site's audio code to hear an informative, accessible description. (€6, children's guide €4.50.) Call **GATA Tours** (☎081 861 5661) or **Assotouring** (☎081 862 2560) for information on **Guided Tours,** more expensive and usually available only to groups. Otherwise, endure hefty admission fees and a poor labeling system to get a peek under 2000-year-old molten lava.

PORTA MARINA

The **basilica** (Roman law court) walls are decorated with stucco made to look like marble. Walk farther down V.d. Marina to reach the **Forum,** which is surrounded by a colonnade. Once dotted with statues of emperors and gods, this site was the commercial, civic, and religious center of the city. Cases along the side display some of the gruesome body-casts of Vesuvius's victims. To the far end of the Forum rises the **Temple of Jupiter,** mostly destroyed by an earthquake that struck 17 years before the city's bad luck got worse. To the left, the **Temple of Apollo** contains statues of Apollo and Diana (originals in Naples' Museo Archeologico Nazionale) and a column topped by a sundial. On the opposite side of the forum, the **Temple of Vespasian** houses a delicate frieze depicting preparation for a sacrifice.

VIA DELLA FORTUNA

Exit the Forum through the upper end, by the cafeteria, and enter the **Forum Baths** on the left. Here, chipping away parts of the body casts has revealed teeth and bones beneath. A right on V.d. Fortuna leads to the **House of the Faun,** where a bronze dancing faun and the spectacular Alexander Mosaic were found. Before the door, a floor mosaic proclaims *Have* (welcome). The sheer size and opulence of this building lead archaeologists to believe that it was the private dwelling of one of the wealthiest men in town. Continuing on V.d. Fortuna and turning left on V. dei Vettii will bring you to the **House of the Vettii,** on the left, decorated with the most vivid frescoes in Pompeii. In the vestibule, a depiction of Priapus, the god of fertility, displays his colossal member. And while in ancient times, phalli were believed to scare off evil spirits; these days they only make tourists titter.

VIA DEGLI AUGUSTALI

Back down V.d. Vetti, cross V.d. Fortuna over to V. Storto, and then turn left on V. degli Augustali, which displays the deep ruts of carriages on either side. The Romans who were repaving this worn path when the volcano struck left their task incomplete. A quick right leads to the small **brothel** (the Lupenar) containing several bed stalls. Above each stall, a pornographic painting depicts with unabashed precision the specialty of its occupant. After 2000 years, this remains the most popular place in town; you may have to wait in line. The street continues down to the main avenue, V.d. Abbondanza. To the left lie the **Stabian Baths,** which were privately owned and therefore fancier than the Forum Baths (think ritzy spa vs. YMCA). The separate men's and women's sides each include a dressing room, cold baths *(frigidaria)*, warm baths *(tepidaria)*, and hot steam baths *(caldaria)*.

VIA DEI TEATRI

V.d. Teatri, across the street, leads to a huge complex consisting of the **Great Theater,** constructed in the first half of the 2nd century BC, and the **Little Theater,** built later for music and dance concerts. North of the theaters stands the **Temple of Isis,** Pompeii's monument to the Egyptian fertility goddess. Through the exit on the right, the road passes two fine houses, the **House of Secundus** and the **House of Menander.** At the end of the street, a left turn will return you to the main road. The Romans believed that crossroads were particularly vulnerable to evil spirits, so they built altars (like the one here) designed to ward them off.

VIA DELL'ABBONDANZA

On V.d. Abbondanza, red writing glares from the walls, expressing everything from political slogans to love declarations. Popular favorites include "Albanus is a bugger," "Restitutus has deceived many girls many times," and the lyrical "Lovers, like bees, lead a honey-sweet life"—apparently graffiti hasn't changed much in 2000 years. At the end of the street rest the **House of Tiburtinus** and the **House of Venus,** huge complexes with gardens replanted according to modern knowledge of ancient horticulture. The nearby **amphitheater** (80 BC), the oldest standing in the world, held 12,000 spectators. When battles occurred, crowds decided whether a defeated gladiator would live or die with a casual thumbs up or thumbs down.

To reach the **Villa of the Mysteries,** go to the far west end of V.d. Fortuna, turn right on V. Consolare, and walk all the way up Porta Ercolano. The best preserved of Pompeii's villas, it includes the Dionysiac Frieze, perhaps the largest painting from the ancient world, depicting the initiation of a bride into the cult of Dionysus. Head through the door in the Porta for a great view of the entire city.

HERCULANEUM (ERCOLANO)

Take a Circumvesuviana train from Naples's Stazione Centrale to the "Ercolano" stop. Walk 500m downhill to the ticket office. The ***Municipal Tourist Office,*** *V. IV Novembre, 84 is on the way. Open M-Sa 9am-3pm. ☎081 788 1243. The archaeological site is open daily 8:30am-7:30pm. €10, EU students €5, EU citizens under 18 or over 65 free. Inquire at the tourist office for guided tours. Grab an illustrated guidebook at any of the shops flanking the entrance €4-6, or get the free* Brief Guide to Herculaneum *and map at the entrance.*

Neatly excavated and impressively intact, the remains of the prosperous Roman town of Herculaneum (modern Ercolano) hardly deserve the term "ruins." Indeed, exploring the 2000-year-old houses, complete with frescoes, furniture, mosaics, small sculptures, and even wooden doors, feels like an invasion of privacy.

Though archaeologists long held the opinion that most of Herculaneum's residents escaped the eruption that destroyed Pompeii, recent discoveries of tangled remains suggest that much of the fleeing population was buried in avalanches of volcanic mud. Only a small part of the southeastern quarter, about 45% of the city, has been excavated, and between 15 and 20 houses are open to the public. One of the more alluring is the **House of Deer,** named for the delightful courtyard statues of deer being mauled by packs of ghoulish creatures. Here, archaeologists also found the statues *Satyr with a Wineskin* and *Drunken Hercules,* trying desperately to relieve himself. The **palestra,** a gym and exercise complex, still holds wooden shelves once laden with massage oils and the *strigiles* used to scrape the skin clean after a rubdown. The large vaulted swimming pool, *caldarium* (hot steam bath), and *frigiadarium* (cold bath) in the **baths** are still largely intact. Towering columns in the atrium and bits of delicate stone carving attest to ancient opulence. The **House of the Mosaic of Neptune and Anfitrite** is famous for its breathtaking namesake **mosaic.** Two textured, shimmering figures stand beneath a vivid fan of blues and greens, and to the left, bizarre masks cast indelible expressions over some exquisite hanging flower garlands. In front of the house is a remarkably well-preserved **wine shop.** A mock colonnade of stucco distinguishes the **Samnise House.** Down the street, the **House of the Wooden Partition** still has a door in its elegant courtyard, and an ancient clothes press is around the corner. Outside the site, 250m to the left on the main road, lies the theater, perfectly preserved underground. (☎081 739 09 63. Occasionally open for visits; call to check.) The **Villa dei Papiri,** 500m west of the site, recently caused a stir when a trove of ancient scrolls in the library appeared to include works by Cicero, Virgil, and Horace. (Rarely open to the public; Campania ArteCard holders can view the site by special arrangement. Contact the municipal tourist office.)

MT. VESUVIUS

Trasporti Vesuviani buses run from the Ercolano Circumvesuviana station to the crater of Vesuvius. Schedule available at tourist office; buy tickets on the bus €3.10. Otherwise €4.65.

Peer into the only active volcano on mainland Europe. It's a 20 to 30min. walk from the bus stop to the top of Mt. Vesuvius, so bring plenty of water and wear sturdy shoes. Scientists say volcanoes should erupt about every 30 years—Vesuvius hasn't erupted since March 31, 1944. Nevertheless, experts say the trip is safe.

PAESTUM

*From Termini, take the train to Naples (see p. 280), then take the train to Paestum via Salerno, 40min.; 16 per day, 5:52am-9:52pm; €3.11. CTSP buses from Salerno stop at Via Magna Graecia, the main modern road. 1hr.; hourly 7am-7pm; €2.79. The **tourist office** in Salerno provides a helpful list of all return buses from Paestum. The AAST Information Office, V. Magna Graecia, 155, is next to the museum. ☎082 811 016. Open June-Sept. 15 M-Sa 9am-1pm and 2-7pm, Sept. 16-June 9am-1pm, 2-5pm Temples open daily 9am-7:30pm in summer; 9am-4pm in winter. Closed 1st and 3rd M of each month. Ruins and museum €6.50, EU students half-price, EU citizens under 18 and over 60 free.*

Not far from the Roman ruins of Pompeii and Herculaneum, the three Doric Greek temples of Paestum are among the best preserved in the world, even rivaling those of Sicily and Athens. They rank among the best preserved in the world. Originally built without any mortar or cement (they were simply covered by roofs of terra-cotta tiles supported by wooden beams) the temples remained standing even after the great earthquake of AD 69 reduced Pompeii's streets to a pile of rubble. When excavators first uncovered the three temples, they misidentified (and thus misnamed) them, and the names have stuck. Misnomers have been Paestum's M.O. from the beginning. Greek colonists from Sybaris founded Paestum as Poseidonia in the 7th century BC, and it became a flourishing commercial and trade center. After a period of native Italian control in the 5th and 4th centuries BC, Poseidonia fell to the Romans in 273 BC, was renamed Paestum, and remained a Roman town until the deforestation of nearby hills turned the town into a swampy mush. Plagued by malaria and syphilitic pirates, Paestum's ruins lay relatively untouched until they were rediscovered in the 18th century. Because Paestum is not urbanized, you may think that you missed your stop as you step off the train or bus. Fear not the dearth of modern urban squalor; the ruins alone are a must-see, especially when the *Sovrintendenza Archeologica* lets visitors walk around on the temples (sometimes they are fenced off). If visiting the temples puts you in the mood for worship, bow to the sun-god on the golden **beach,** 2km to the west. Unfortunately, much of it is owned by resorts that charge for beach access and chair rental. For a free dip in the Mediterranean, head to a *spiaggia pubblica*—ask for directions.

The pleasant beachside **Ostello "La Lanterna" (HI),** V. Lanterna, 8, in **Agropoli,** is the nearest budget accommodation. ☎/fax 0974 838364. 56 beds. Sheets and shower included. To get to Agropoli, take the CTSP buses from Paestum, (10min.; hourly, 7:30am-9:15pm; €1.10; or from Salerno, 1hr.; 23 per day, 6:30am-8:15pm; €2.53.) Agropoli is also connected by train to Paestum, (10min.; 9 per day, 6:10am-10:22pm; €1.15.)

TEMPLE OF CERES & ENVIRONS

There are three entrances to Paestum's ruins. The northernmost entrance leads to the Temple of Ceres. Built circa 500 BC, this temple became a church in the early Middle Ages but was abandoned in the 9th century. The ancient Greeks built Paestum on a north-south axis, marked by the paved V. Sacra. Farther south on V. Sacra is the Roman **forum,** which is even larger than the one at Pompeii (p. 292). The Romans leveled most of the older structures in the city's center to build this proto-*piazza*, the commercial and political arena of Paestum. To the left, a pit marks the pool of an ancient **gymnasium.** To the east gymnasium lies the Roman **amphitheater.**

TEMPLE OF POSEIDON

Museum open daily 9am-6:30pm. Ticket office open daily 9am-5:30pm; closed 1st and 3rd Monday of each month. €4, EU citizens over 60 and under 18 free.

South of the forum lies the 5th-century BC Temple of Poseidon (actually dedicated to Hera), which incorporates many of the optical refinements that characterize the Parthenon in Athens. Small lions' heads serve as gargoyles on the temple roof. The southernmost temple, known as the **basilica,** is the oldest, dating to the 6th century BC. Its unusual plan, with a main interior section split by a row of columns down the middle, has inspired the theory that the temple was dedicated to two gods, Zeus and Hera, rather than one. A **museum** on the other side of V. Magna Graecia houses an extraordinary collection of pottery, paintings, and artifacts taken primarily from Paestum's tombs, with outstanding bilingual descriptions and essays on site. It also includes samples of 2500-year-old honey and paintings from the famous **Tomb of the Diver,** dating to 475 BC.

INSIDE

when to go **299**
embassies and consulates **300**
documents & formalities **300**
passports **300** visas & work permits **301** identification **303** tourist offices **304**
health **304** insurance **305** packing **306** customs **306**
money **307**
currency & exchange **307** traveler's checks **307** credit, debit & atm cards **308**
costs **309** safety & security **309**
getting to rome **311**
by plane **311** by train **314** by bus **315** by car **315**
specific concerns **316**
other resources **320**

Planning Your Trip

WHEN TO GO

*For information about **National Holidays** and **Festivals**, see **Discover**, p. 2.*

Few would dare call a Roman **spring** anything less than heaven. The weather is pleasantly balmy (hovering around 50 to 70°F), but the tourists haven't caught on. By June, the rains have ceased and hotels are booming. A Roman **summer** is sweltering (65-85°F) and congested, but you can catch major exhibitions, exciting festivals, and concerts under the stars. When the city gets too thick, cool off in the Mediterranean or in cold volcanic lakes. In August, the Romans leave town; you may not find as many hole-in-the-wall *trattorie* open, but the crowds will subside a bit. The trend continues into the **fall,** when the temperatures drop (45-60°F) and the prices do, too. **Winter** brings cold (expect temperatures between 40°F and 55°F), rain, and some of the lowest prices of the year, but it also brings the holidays, which are a major to-do in the city of St. Peter.

EMBASSIES & CONSULATES

*For foreign **consular services** in Rome, check the **Service Directory**, p. 338.*

ITALIAN CONSULAR SERVICES ABROAD

Address questions concerning visas and passports to consulates, not embassies.

Australia: Embassy: 12 Grey St., Deakin, **Canberra** ACT 2600 (☎02 6273 3333; www.ambitalia.org.au). Open M-F 8:30-4pm; consular services hours 9am-noon. **Consulates:** Level 14 AMP Place, 10 Eagle St., **Brisbane** QLD 4000 (☎00617 3229 8944; itconqldnt@ecn.net.au). Open M-F 9am-1pm, Th 9am-3pm); 509 St. Kilda Rd., **Melbourne** VIC 3004 (☎613 867 5744; itconmel@netlink.com.au). Level 45, "The Gateway," 1 Macquarie Pl., **Sydney** NSW 2000 (☎612 9392 7939; italcons@wantree.com.au). All consulate information is available through the embassy website.

Canada: Embassy: 275 Slater St., 21st fl., **Ottawa,** ON K1P 5H9 (☎613-232-2401; www.italyincanada.com). **Consulate:** 3489 Drummond St., **Montréal,** QC H3G 1X6 (☎514-849-8351; www.italconsul.montreal.qc.ca).

Ireland: Embassy: 63 Northumberland Rd., **Dublin** (☎3531 660 1744; www.italianembassy.ie/eng). Consular section open M-F 10am-12:30pm.

New Zealand: Embassy: 34-38 Grant Rd., **Wellington** (☎006 4473 5339; www.italyembassy.org.nz).

South Africa: Embassy: 796 George Ave., Arcadia 0083, **Pretoria** (☎012 4305541; www.ambital.org.za). **Consulates:** 2 Grey's Pass, Gardens 8001, **Cape Town** (☎021 424 1256; italcons@mweb.co.za); Corner 2nd Ave., Houghton 2196, **Johannesburg** (☎011 430 5541).

UK: Embassy: 14, Three Kings Yard, **London** W1K 4EH (☎020 7312 2200; www.embitaly.org.uk). **Consulates:** 38 Eaton Pl., **London** SW1X 8AN (☎440 20 7235 9371); Rodwell Tower, 111 Piccadilly, **Manchester** M1 2HY (☎161 236 9024); 32 Melville St., **Edinburgh** EH3 7HA (☎131 330 3695).

US: Embassy: 3000 Whitehaven St., **Washington, D.C.** 20008 (☎202-612-4400; www.italyemb.org). **Consulates:** 100 Boylston St., #900, **Boston,** MA 02116 (☎617-542-0483; www.italconsboston.org); 500 N. Michigan Ave., #1850, **Chicago,** IL 60611 (☎312-467-1550; www.italconschicago.org); 12400 Wilshire Blvd., #300, **Los Angeles,** CA 90025 (☎310-820-0622; www.conlang.com); 690 Park Ave. (visa office 54 E. 69th St.), **New York,** NY 10021 (☎212-737-9100; www.italconsulnyc.org).

DOCUMENTS & FORMALITIES

All applications should be filed several weeks or months before departure. Keep in mind that demand for passports is highest between January and August.

PASSPORTS

REQUIREMENTS

Citizens of Australia, Canada, the EU, Ireland, New Zealand, South Africa, the UK, and the US need valid passports to enter Italy and to re-enter their home countries. At most hotels and hostels in Italy, you will be required to show your passport.

PHOTOCOPIES

Be sure to photocopy the page of your passport with your photo, passport number, and other identifying information, as well as any visas, travel insurance policies, plane tickets, or traveler's check serial numbers. Carry one set of copies in a safe

ONE EUROPE. The idea of European unity has come a long way since 1958, when the European Economic Community (EEC) was created in order to promote solidarity and cooperation. Since then, the EEC has become the European Union (EU), with political, legal, and economic institutions spanning 15 member states: Austria, Belgium, Denmark, Finland, France, Germany, Greece, Ireland, Italy, Luxembourg, the Netherlands, Portugal, Spain, Sweden, and the UK.

What does this have to do with the average non-EU tourist? In 1999, the EU established **freedom of movement** across 14 European countries—the entire EU minus Denmark, Ireland, and the UK, but plus Iceland and Norway. This means that border controls between participating countries have been abolished, and visa policies harmonized. While you're still required to carry a passport (or government-issued ID card for EU citizens) when crossing an internal border, once you've been admitted into one country, you're free to travel to all participating states. Britain and Ireland have also formed a **common travel area,** abolishing passport controls between the UK and the Republic of Ireland. This means that the only times you'll see a border guard within the EU are traveling between the British Isles and the Continent and in and out of Denmark.

For more important consequences of the EU for travelers, see **The Euro** (p. 301) and **European Customs** and **EU customs regulations** (p. 300).

place, apart from the originals, and leave another set at home. Consulates also recommend that you carry an expired passport or an official copy of your birth certificate in a part of your baggage separate from other documents.

LOST PASSPORTS

If you lose your passport, immediately notify the local police and the nearest embassy or consulate of your home government. To expedite its replacement, you will need to know all information previously recorded and show ID and proof of citizenship. In some cases, a replacement may take weeks to process, and may only be valid for a limited time. Any visas stamped in your old passport will be irretrievably lost. In an emergency, ask for immediate temporary traveling papers that will permit you to re-enter your home country. Your passport is a public document, which technically belongs to your nation's government. You may have to surrender it to a foreign government official, but if you don't get it back in a reasonable amount of time, inform the nearest consulate of your home country.

NEW PASSPORTS

Citizens of Australia, Canada, Ireland, New Zealand, the United Kingdom, and the United States can apply for a passport at the nearest post office, passport office, or court of law. Citizens of South Africa can apply for a passport at the nearest office of Foreign Affairs. Any new passport or renewal applications must be filed well in advance of the departure date, although most passport offices offer rush services for a very steep fee. Citizens living abroad who need a passport or renewal services should contact the nearest consular service of their home country.

VISAS & WORK PERMITS

British, Irish, and **EU** citizens need only carry a valid passport to enter Italy, and they may stay in the country for as long as they like. Citizens of **Australia, Canada, New Zealand,** and the **US** do not need visas for tourism or business stays of up to three months. Citizens of South Africa need a visa—a stamp, sticker, or insert in your passport specifying the purpose of your travel and the permitted duration of your stay—in addition to a valid passport for entrance to Italy. Any

VISA INFORMATION

Italy will throw load of confusing paperwork at you before you can take part in that utopia that is European living. Private companies such as the **Center for International Business and Travel,** 25 W. 23rd St., #1420, New York, NY 10036 (☎ 800-925-2428), can obtain documentation for a fee.

Long term visa: Non-EU citizens are required to obtain a visa for any stay longer than 3 months. Contact the Italian embassy or consulate in your country.

Permit to Stay: All non-EU citizens are also required to obtain a permesso di soggiorno (permit to stay) within 8 days of arriving in Italy. If you are staying in a hotel or hostel, this requirement is generally waived, but if you are living on your own, you must apply at a police station or the foreigner's office at the main police station (Questura Centrale), V. Genoa, 2. (☎06 46861. Open M-F 9am-12:30pm.) EU citizens must apply for a permit to stay within 3 months.

Residency: Once you find a place, bring your permit to stay (it must have at least one year's validity) to a records office (circoscrizione; for the nearest location, look up Come di Rome: Circoscrizione in the phone book). This certificate, which confirms your registered address, will expedite such procedures as clearing goods from abroad through customs and making large purchases.

visa granted by Italy will be respected by the following countries: which make up the Schengen area: Austria, Belgium, France, Germany, Greece, Luxembourg, Portugal, Spain, and The Netherlands. All applications should be filed several weeks or months before departure.

IDENTIFICATION

When traveling, always carry two or more forms of identification on your person, including at least one photo ID; a passport combined with a driver's license or birth certificate is usually adequate. Many establishments, especially banks, may require several IDs in order to cash traveler's checks. Never carry all your forms of ID together; keep copies and split them up in case of theft or loss.

TEACHER, STUDENT & YOUTH IDENTIFICATION. The **International Student Identity Card (ISIC),** the most widely accepted form of student ID, provides discounts on sights, accommodations, food, and transport; access to 24hr. emergency helpline (in North America call ☎877-370-ISIC; elsewhere call US collect ☎1 715-345-0505); and insurance benefits for US cardholders (see **Insurance,** p. 305). The ISIC is more likely to be recognized and honored abroad than institution-specific cards (such as a university ID). Applicants must be degree-seeking students of a secondary or post-secondary school and must be of at least 12 years of age. Because of the proliferation of fake ISICs, some services (particularly airlines) require additional proof of student identity, such as a school ID or a letter attesting to your student status, signed by your registrar and stamped with your school seal. The **International Teacher Identity Card (ITIC)** offers teachers the same insurance coverage as well as similar but limited discounts. For travelers who are 25 years old or under but are not students, the **International Youth Travel Card** (**IYTC;** formerly the **GO 25** Card) also offers many of the same benefits as the ISIC.

Each identity card costs US$22 or equivalent. ISIC and ITIC cards are valid for roughly one and a half academic years; IYTC cards are valid for one year. Many student travel agencies (see p. 311) issue the cards, including STA Travel in Australia and New Zealand; Travel CUTS in Canada; USIT in the Republic of Ireland and Northern Ireland; SASTS in South Africa; STA Travel in the UK; and STA Travel in the US. For a listing of issuing agencies, or for more information, contact the International Student Travel Confederation (ISTC), Herengracht 479, 1017 BS Amsterdam, Netherlands (☎31 20 421 28 00; www.istc.org).

TOURIST OFFICES

The privately owned **Enjoy Rome** (p. 25) and the official **APT** (p. 26) and **PIT** (p. 26) are the best places to turn when you have questions about Rome.

Italian Government Tourist Board (ENIT), 630 5th Ave., #1565, **New York,** NY 10111 (☎212-245-5618; www.italiantourism.com). Write or call ☎212-245-4822 for a free copy of *Italia: General Information for Travelers to Italy.* Branch offices: 12400 Wilshire Blvd., #550, **Los Angeles,** CA 90025 (☎310-820-1898; fax 820-6357; enitla@earthlink.net); 175 E. Bloor St., #907 South Tower, **Toronto,** ON M4W 3R8 (☎416-925-4882; enit.canada@on.aibn.com); 1 Princess St., **London** W1R 2AY (☎020-7355 1557 or 7355 1439; www.italiantouristboard.co.uk). Italian Chamber of Commerce and Industry in Australia, Level 26, 44 Market St., **Sydney** NSW 2000 Australia (☎02 9262 1666; enitour@ihug.com.au).

Italian Cultural Institute, 686 Park Ave., **New York,** NY 10021 (☎212-879-4242; www.italcultny.org). Often more prompt than ENIT. Has useful links about Italian culture and sites.

HEALTH

Common sense is the simplest prescription for good health while you travel. Drink lots of fluids to prevent dehydration and constipation, and wear sturdy, broken-in shoes and clean socks.

BEFORE YOU GO

In your **passport,** write the names of any people you wish to be contacted in case of a medical emergency, and list any allergies or medical conditions. Matching a prescription to a foreign equivalent is not always easy, safe, or possible, so carry up-to-date, legible prescriptions or a statement from your doctor stating the medication's trade name, manufacturer, chemical name, and dosage. For tips on packing a basic **first-aid kit** and other health essentials, see p. 306. For a searchable online database of all medications, try www.rxlist.com.

IMMUNIZATIONS. Travelers over two years old should be up to date on the following vaccines: MMR (for measles, mumps, and rubella); DTaP or Td (for diptheria, tetanus, and pertussis); OPV (for polio); HbCV (for haemophilus influenza B), and HBV (for hepatitus B). For recommendations on immunizations and prophylaxis, consult the CDC (see below) in the US, the IAMAT (see below), or the equivalent in your home country, and check with a doctor for guidance. Meningitis shots are usually advisable, especially among college-age backpackers who plan to stay in hostels.

USEFUL ORGANIZATIONS AND PUBLICATIONS. The US **Centers for Disease Control and Prevention** (**CDC;** ☎877-FYI-TRIP; www.cdc.gov/travel) maintains an international travelers' hotline and an informative website. The CDC's comprehensive booklet *Health Information for International Travel,* an annual rundown of dis-

STAI MALATO? Feeling sick? Here are some Italian translations of common maladies you might encounter on the road:
allergies: delle allergie.
appendicitis: appendicite.
asthma: asma.
birth control: controllo di nascita.
blood pressure: pressione sanguigna.
fever: una febbre.
infection: infezione
heart disease: malattia di cuore.
sore throat: mal di gola.
stomach ache: mal de stomaco.

ease, immunization, and general health advice, is free online or US$25 via the **Public Health Foundation** (☎877-252-1200; www.hhs.gov). For information on health and travel warnings, contact the **Overseas Citizens Services,** Bureau of Consular Affairs, #4811, US Department of State, Washington, D.C. 20520 (☎888-407- 4747; between 8pm and 8am ☎202-647-4000; http://travel.state.gov/overseas_citizens), or ask a passport agency, embassy or consulate abroad. For information on medical evacuation services and travel insurance firms, see http://travel.state.gov/medical.html or the **British Foreign and Commonwealth Office** website at (www.fco.gov.uk).

MEDICAL ASSISTANCE ON THE ROAD. The quality of health care in Italy varies throughout the country and is generally better in the north and in private medical institutions. In most large cities doctors speak English or can find a translator. If you are concerned about obtaining medical assistance while traveling, you may wish to employ special support services. The *MedPass* from **GlobalCare, Inc.,** 2001 Westside Pkwy., #120, Alpharetta, GA 30004, USA (☎800-860-1111; www.globalems.com), provides 24hr. international telephone triage, assessment, referral, medical evacuation, and claims administration. The **International Association for Medical Assistance to Travelers** (**IAMAT;** US ☎716-754-4883, Canada ☎416-652-0137, New Zealand ☎03 352 20 53; www.sentex.net/iamat) has free membership, lists English-speaking doctors worldwide, and offers detailed information on immunization requirements, sanitation and climactic conditions. If your regular **insurance** policy does not cover travel abroad, you may wish to purchase additional coverage.

Those with medical conditions (such as diabetes, allergies to antibiotics, epilepsy, heart conditions) may want to obtain a **Medic Alert** membership (first year US$35, annually thereafter US$20), which includes a stainless steel ID tag, among othr benefits, like a 24hr. collect-call number. Contact the Medic Alert Foundation, 2323 Colorado Ave, Turlock, CA 95382, USA (☎888-633-4298; outside US ☎209-668-3333; www.medicalert.org).

WOMEN'S HEALTH

Emergency contraception, or the morning after pill, is available in Italy by prescription. Abortion is legal and may be performed in a public hospital or authorized private facility at the woman's discretion for the first 90 days. Except in urgent cases, a weeklong reflection period is required. Women under 18 must have permission. Actual availability may be limited in some areas of Italy, particularly the south, due to Vatican resistance and a "conscience clause" that allows physicians to opt out of performing the procedure.

INSURANCE

Travel insurance covers four basic areas: medical/health problems, property loss, trip cancellation/interruption, and emergency evacuation. Though your regular insurance policies may well extend to travel-related accidents, you may consider purchasing travel insurance if the cost of potential trip cancellation/interruption is greater than you can absorb. Prices for travel insurance purchased separately generally run US$50 per week for full coverage, while trip cancellation/interruption may be purchased separately at a rate of about US$5.50 per US$100 of coverage.

Medical insurance (especially university policies) often covers costs incurred abroad; check with your provider. **US Medicare** does not cover foreign travel. **Canadians** are protected by their home province's health insurance plan for up to 90 days after leaving the country; check with the provincial Ministry of Health or Health Plan Headquarters. **Australians** traveling in Italy are entitled to many of the services that they would receive at home as part of the Reciprocal Health Care Agreement. **Homeowners' insurance** (or your family's coverage) often covers theft during travel and loss of travel documents (passport, plane ticket, railpass, etc.) up to US$500.

ISIC and **ITIC** (see p. 306) provide basic insurance benefits, including US$100 per day of in-hospital sickness for up to 60 days, US$3000 of accident-related medical reimbursement, and US$25,000 for emergency medical transport. Cardholders have access to a toll-free 24hr. helpline for medical, legal, and financial emergencies overseas (US and Canada ☎800-626-2427, elsewhere call US collect ☎1 713-267-2525). **American Express** (US ☎800-528-4800) grants most cardholders automatic car rental insurance (collision and theft, but not liability) and ground travel accident coverage of US$100,000 on flight purchases made with the card.

Council and **STA** (see p. 311) offer a range of plans that can supplement your basic coverage. Other private insurance providers in the US and Canada include: Access America (☎800-284-8300); Berkely Group/Carefree Travel Insurance (☎800-323-3149; www.berkely.com); Globalcare Travel Insurance (☎800-821-2488; www.globalcare-cocco.com); and Travel Assistance International (☎800-821-2828; www.worldwide-assistance.com). Providers in the UK include Campus Travel (☎01865 25 80 00) and Columbus Travel Insurance (☎020 7375 0011). In Australia, try CIC Insurance (☎9202 8000).

PACKING

IMPORTANT DOCUMENTS. Don't forget your passport, traveler's checks, ATM and/or credit cards, and ID (see p. 306). Check that you have any of the following that might apply to you: a hosteling membership card, driver's license, travel insurance forms, and rail or bus pass.

CLOTHING. Bring along a **warm jacket** or wool sweater, a **rain jacket** (Gore-Tex® is waterproof and breathable), sturdy shoes or **hiking boots,** and **thick socks. Flip-flops** or waterproof sandals are crucial for hostel showers. If you want to go clubbing, bring at least one pair of slacks, a nice shirt, and a nice pair of shoes. If you plan to visit churches, bring an outfit that covers your torso, upper arms and knees.

CONVERTERS AND ADAPTERS. In Italy, electricity is 220V AC, enough to fry any 110V North American appliance. 220/240V electrical appliances don't like 110V current, either. Americans and Canadians should buy an adapter (which changes the shape of the plug) and a converter (which changes the voltage; US$20). Don't use only an adapter (unless appliance instructions explicitly state otherwise). New Zealanders and South Africans (who both use 220V at home) as well as Australians (who use 240/250V) won't need a converter, but will need a set of adapters.

OTHER USEFUL ITEMS. Bring a **money belt** and small **padlock.** Basic **outdoors equipment** (plastic water bottle, compass, waterproof matches, pocketknife, sunglasses, sunscreen, insect repellent, hat) may also prove useful. **Quick clothing repairs** can be done on the road with a needle and thread; also consider bringing electrical tape for patching tears. Doing your **laundry** by hand (where allowed) is both cheaper and more convenient than doing it at a laundromat—bring detergent, a small rubber ball to stop up the sink, and string for a makeshift clothes line.

CUSTOMS

Upon entering Italy, you must declare certain items from abroad and pay a duty on the value of those articles that exceeds the allowance established by the Italian customs service. Note that goods and gifts purchased at **duty-free** shops abroad are not exempt from duty or sales tax and thus must be declared upon entering Italy as well; "duty-free" merely means that you need not pay a tax in the country of purchase. Duty-free allowances were abolished for travel between EU member states on July 1, 1999, but they still exist for those arriving from outside the EU.

Upon returning home, you must declare all articles acquired abroad and pay a duty on the value in excess of your home country's allowance. Keep receipts for all goods acquired abroad. Upon departure from the EU, non-EU citizens can claim a refund for the value added tax (VAT or IVA) paid on major purchases.

CUSTOMS IN THE EU. As well as freedom of movement of people within the EU (see p. 301), travelers in the countries that are members of the EU (Austria, Belgium, Denmark, Finland, France, Germany, Greece, Ireland, Italy, Luxembourg, the Netherlands, Portugal, Spain, Sweden, and the UK) can also take advantage of the freedom of movement of goods. This means that there are no customs controls at internal EU borders (i.e., you can take the blue customs channel at the airport), and travelers are free to transport whatever legal substances they like as long as it is for personal use—up to 800 cigarettes, 10L of spirits, 90L of wine, and 110L of beer. Duty-free was abolished on June 30, 1999 for travel between EU member states; however, travelers between the EU and the rest of the world still get a duty-free allowance when passing through customs.

MONEY

CURRENCY & EXCHANGE

The former Italian currency unit was the lira (plural: lire). Italy, as a member of the EU, has converted to the Euro; you are likely to see nary a lira in circulation these days, even in the most remote parts of Italy. The chart below is based on August 2002 exchange rates between European Union Euros (EUR€) and US dollars (US$), Canadian dollars (CDN$), Australian dollars (AUS$), New Zealand dollars (NZ$), Irish pounds (IR£), South African Rand (ZAR), Czech crowns (Kč), British pounds (UK£). Check the currency converter on financial websites such as www.bloomberg.com and www.xe.com, or a large newspaper for the latest exchange rates.

EUROS (EUR€)	
AUS$1 = EUR€0.58	EUR€1 = AUS$1.73
CDN$1 = EUR€0.64	EUR€1 = CDN$1.57
NZ$1 = EUR€0.52	EUR€1 = NZ$1.93
ZAR1 = EUR€0.12	EUR€1 = ZAR8.36
UK£1 = EUR€1.41	EUR€1 = UK£0.71
US$1 = EUR€0.89	EUR€1 = US$1.16

As a general rule, it's cheaper to convert money in Italy or Europe at large than at home. While currency exchange will probably be available in your arrival airport, it's wise to bring enough foreign currency to last for the first 24 to 72 hours of a trip.

When changing money abroad, try to go only to banks or cambii that have at most a 5% margin between their buy and sell prices. Since you lose money with every transaction, **convert large sums** (unless the currency is depreciating rapidly), **but no more than you'll need.**

TRAVELER'S CHECKS

Traveler's checks are one of the safest means of carrying funds. American Express and Visa are the most widely recognized brands. Many banks and agencies sell them for a small commission. Check issuers provide refunds if the checks are lost or stolen, and many provide additional services, such as toll-free refund hotlines abroad, emergency message services, and stolen credit card assistance. **American Express:** Checks available with commission at select banks and all AmEx offices. US residents can also purchase checks by phone (☎888-269-6669) or online (www.aexp.com). AAA (see p. 21) offers commission-free checks to its members. Checks available in US, Australian, British, Canadian, Japanese, and Euro curren-

THE EURO. The official currency of 12 members of the European Union—Austria, Belgium, Finland, France, Germany, Greece, Ireland, Italy, Luxembourg, the Netherlands, Portugal, and Spain—is now the euro.

The currency has some important—and positive—consequences for travelers hitting more than one euro-zone country. For one thing, money-changers across the euro-zone are obliged to exchange money at the official, fixed rate (see below), and at no commission (though they may still charge a small service fee). Second, euro-denominated travelers cheques allow you to pay for goods and services across the euro-zone, again at the official rate and commission-free.

At the time of printing, 1€=US$1.12=1.58CAD=0.70£. For more info, check a currency converter (such as www.xe.com) or www.europa.eu.int.

cies. *Cheques for Two* can be signed by either of 2 people traveling together. For purchase locations or more information contact AmEx's service centers: In the US and Canada ☎800-221-7282; in the UK ☎0800 521 313; in Australia ☎800 25 19 02; in New Zealand 0800 441 068; in Rome 06 7228 03 08; elsewhere US collect ☎+1 801-964-6665. **Visa:** Checks available (generally with commission) at banks worldwide. For the location of the nearest office, call Visa's service centers: In the US ☎800-227-6811; in the UK ☎0800 89 50 78; elsewhere UK collect ☎+44 020 7937 8091. Checks available in US, British, Canadian, Japanese, and Euro currencies. **Travelex/Thomas Cook:** In the US and Canada call ☎800-287-7362; in the UK call ☎0800 62 21 01; elsewhere call UK collect ☎+44 1733 31 89 50.

CREDIT, DEBIT & ATM CARDS

Where they are accepted, credit cards often offer superior exchange rates—up to 5% better than the retail rate used by banks and other currency exchange establishments. They are sometimes required to reserve hotel rooms or rental cars, and may also offer services such as insurance or emergency help. MasterCard (a.k.a. EuroCard or Access in Europe) and Visa (a.k.a. Carte Bleue or Barclaycard) are the most welcomed; American Express cards work at some ATMs and at AmEx offices and major airports.

Depending on the system that your home bank uses, you can most likely access your personal bank account from an ATM in Italy. ATMs get the same wholesale exchange rate as credit cards, but there is often a limit on the amount of money you can withdraw per day (around US$500). There is typically also a surcharge of US$2-5 per withdrawal.

Debit cards are a relatively new form of purchasing power that are as convenient as credit cards but have an immediate impact on your funds. A debit card can be used wherever its associated credit card company (usually Mastercard or Visa) is

PINS & ATMS. To use a cash or credit card to withdraw money from a cash machine (ATM) in Europe, you must have a four-digit **Personal Identification Number (PIN).** If your PIN is longer than four digits, ask your bank whether you can just use the first four, or whether you'll need a new one. **Credit cards** don't usually come with PINs, so if you intend to hit up ATMs in Europe with a credit card to get cash advances, call your credit card company to request one.

People with alphabetic, rather than numerical, PINs may also be thrown off by the lack of letters on European cash machines. The following handy chart gives the corresponding numbers to use: 1=QZ; 2=ABC; 3=DEF; 4=GHI; 5=JKL; 6=MNO; 7=PRS; 8=TUV; and 9=WXY. Note that if you mistakenly punch the wrong code into the machine three times, it will swallow your card for good.

accepted, yet the money is withdrawn directly from the holder's checking account. Debit cards often also function as ATM cards and can be used to withdraw cash from associated banks and ATMs throughout Italy.

The two major international money networks are **Cirrus** (to locate ATMs US ☎800-424-7787, Italy ☎800-870-866 or www.mastercard.com) and **Visa/PLUS** (to locate ATMs US ☎800-843-7587, Italy ☎800-874-155 or www.visa.com). Most ATMs charge a transaction fee that is paid to the bank that owns the ATM.

COSTS

STAYING ON A BUDGET

To give you a general idea, a bare-bones day in Rome (sleeping in hostels/, buying food at supermarkets) would cost about US$45 and for a luxurious day, the sky's the limit. Also, don't forget to factor in emergency reserve funds of at least US$200 when planning how much money you'll need.

TIPS FOR SAVING MONEY

Considering that saving just a few dollars a day over the course of your trip might pay for days or weeks of additional travel, the art of penny-pinching is well worth learning. Learn to take advantage of freebies: for example, **museums** in Rome are typically free once a month, and Rome hosts free open-air **concerts** and **cultural events** (especially in summer). Bring a **sleepsack** to save on sheet charges in hostels, and do your own laundry in the sink (unless you're explicitly prohibited from doing so). You can split **accommodations** costs (in hotels and some hostels) with trustworthy fellow travelers; multi-bed rooms almost always work out cheaper per person than singles. The same principle will also work for cutting down on the cost of restaurant meals. You can also buy food in **supermarkets** like STANDA instead of eating out.

TAXES

The **Value-Added Tax** (**VAT,** *imposto sul valore aggiunta*, or IVA) is a sales tax levied in the EU. VAT (ranging from 15-25%) is usually part of the price paid for goods and services. If you live outside the EU, you may be able to claim some VAT back through the **Retail Export Scheme.** This only applies to articles that are being exported out of the EU; meals and lodging do not qualify. Only larger stores in heavily-touristed areas normally participate in the scheme, and there is a €155 minimum purchase. If the store participates, you will need to request a VAT refund form from the shopkeeper. On leaving the country, take this form and the goods to the "Tax-Free Refund" desk at the airport, where officers will ensure the items are being exported and stamp your forms (this process can take up to an hour). After going through passport control, mail the form back to the shop, which will then eventually send you a refund (less an administrative fee) by check or credit it to your credit card. "Tax-Free Shopping for Tourists" at some stores enables you to get a refund in cash at the airport or a border crossing.

SAFETY & SECURITY

Travel in Italy is generally safe, and incidents of physical violence against tourists are quite rare. While your person may be safe, however, your pocket-book is likely to be somewhat less secure. If you find yourself victim to a robbery or other assault, try to find an English-speaking Italian and have him or her report the incident--the carabinieri generally speak limited English. The vast chasm that separates the north from the south in terms of tourism infrastructure also applies to safety issues. In general, Naples and farther south is more dangerous than the north. Travelers of color may not feel wholly safe south of Naples.

PROTECTING YOUR VALUABLES

There are a few steps you can take to minimize the financial risk associated with traveling. First, bring as little with you as possible. Second, buy a few combination padlocks to secure your belongings either in your pack or in a hostel or train station locker. Third, carry as little cash as possible. Keep your traveler's checks and ATM/credit cards in a money belt—not a "fanny pack"—along with your passport and ID cards. Fourth, keep a small cash reserve separate from your primary stash. This should be about US$50 sewn into or stored in the depths of your pack, along with your traveler's check numbers and important photocopies.

CON ARTISTS & PICKPOCKETS

Vespa bandits cruise the city atop their mopeds in search of people carrying purses or cameras that they can snatch as they drive by. Keep valuables out of the reach of these mobile thugs.

GETTING TO ROME

BY PLANE

When it comes to airfare, a little effort can save you a bundle. If your plans are flexible enough to deal with the restrictions, courier fares are the cheapest. Tickets bought from consolidators and standby seating are also good deals, but last-minute specials, airfare wars, and charter flights often beat these fares. The key is to hunt around, to be flexible, and to ask persistently about discounts. Students, seniors, and those under 26 should never pay full price for a ticket.

AIRFARES

Airfares to Rome peak between mid-June and early September; holidays are also expensive. Midweek (M-Th morning) round-trip flights run US$40-50 cheaper than weekend flights, but they are generally more crowded and less likely to permit frequent-flier upgrades. Traveling with an "open return" ticket can be pricier than fixing a return date when buying the ticket. Round-trip flights are by far the cheapest; arriving in and departing from different cities tends to be pricier. Patching one-way flights together is the most expensive way to travel. **Fares** for roundtrip flights to Rome from the US or Canadian east coast cost around US$600 or US$400 off season; from the US or Canadian west coast US$900/US$500; from the UK $200/$175; from Australia $1100/$900; from New Zealand $950/$1100.

BUDGET & STUDENT TRAVEL AGENCIES

While travel agencies can make your life easy, they may not find you the lowest possible fare—they get paid on commission. Travelers holding **ISIC and IYTC cards** (see p. 306) qualify for big discounts from student travel agencies. Most flights from budget agencies are on major airlines, but in peak season some are on chartered aircraft.

STA Travel, 7890 S. Hardy Dr., Ste. 110, Tempe AZ 85284, USA (24hr. reservations and info ☎800-781-4040; www.sta-travel.com). A student and youth travel organization with hundreds of offices worldwide, including US offices in Boston, Chicago, L.A., New York, San Francisco, Seattle, and Washington, D.C. Recently acquired Council Travel and operates hundreds of offices under that name. Ticket booking, travel insurance, railpasses, and more. In the UK, walk-in office 11 Goodge St., **London** W1T 2PF or call 0207-436-7779. In New Zealand, Shop 2B, 182 Queen St., **Auckland** (☎09 309 0458). In Australia, 366 Lygon St., **Carlton** Vic 3053 (☎03 9349 4344).

CTS Travel, 44 Goodge St., **London** W1T 2AD, UK(☎0207 636 0031; ctsinfo@ctstravel.co.uk).

Travel CUTS (Canadian Universities Travel Services Limited), 187 College St., **Toronto,** ON M5T 1P7 (☎416-979-2406; www.travelcuts.com). 60 offices across Canada. Also in the UK, 295-A Regent St., **London** W1R 7YA (☎0207-255-1944).

FLIGHT PLANNING ON THE INTERNET. Many airline sites offer special last-minute deals on the Web. Alitalia (www.alitalia.com) offers the best last minute budget tickets. These sites will do the legwork for you: www.bestfares.com, www.flights.com, www.hotdeals.com, www.lowestfare.com, www.onetravel.com, and www.travelzoo.com.

StudentUniverse (www.studentuniverse.com), **STA** (www.sta-travel.com), **Council** (www.counciltravel.com), and **Orbitz.com** provide quotes on student tickets, while **Expedia** (www.expedia.com) and **Travelocity** (www.travelocity.com) offer full travel services. **Priceline** (www.priceline.com) allows you to specify a price, and obligates you to buy any ticket that meets or beats it; be prepared for antisocial hours and odd routes. **Skyauction** (www.skyauction.com) allows you to bid on both last-minute and advance-purchase tickets.

An indispensable resource on the Internet is the *Air Traveler's Handbook* (www.cs.cmu.edu/afs/cs/user/mkant/Public/Travel/airfare.html), a comprehensive listing of links to everything you need to know before you board a plane.

Wasteels, Skoubogade 6, 1158 Copenhagen K. (☎3314-4633; www.wasteels.dk/uk). A huge chain with 165 locations across Europe. Sells Wasteels BIJ tickets discounted 30-45% off regular fare, 2nd-class international point-to-point train tickets with unlimited stopovers for those under 26 (sold only in Europe).

COMMERCIAL AIRLINES

The commercial airlines' lowest regular offer is the Advance Purchase Excursion (APEX) fare, which provides confirmed reservations and allows "open-jaw" tickets. Generally, reservations must be made seven to 21 days ahead of departure, with seven- to 14-day minimum-stay and up to 90-day maximum-stay restrictions. These fares carry hefty cancellation and change penalties (fees rise in summer). Book peak-season APEX fares early; by May you will have a hard time getting your desired departure date. Low-season fares should be appreciably cheaper than the high-season (mid-June to Aug.) ones listed here.

TRAVELING FROM NORTH AMERICA

Basic round-trip fares to Western Europe range from roughly US$200-750. Standard commercial carriers like American (☎800-433-7300; www.aa.com) and United (☎800-241-6522; www.ual.com) offer the most convenient flights, but they may not be the cheapest, unless you manage to grab a special promotion or airfare war ticket. Flying one of the following airlines may be a better deal, if any of their limited departure points is convenient for you.

Icelandair, (☎800-223-5500; www.icelandair.com). Stopovers in Iceland for no extra cost on most transatlantic flights. For last-minute offers, subscribe to their email list.

Finnair, (☎800-950-5000; www.us.finnair.com). Cheap round-trips from San Francisco, New York, and Toronto to Helsinki; connections throughout Europe.

Martinair, ☎800-627-8462; www.martinair.com.

TRAVELING FROM THE UK & IRELAND

Because of the many carriers flying from the British Isles to the continent, we only include discount airlines or those with cheap specials here. The **Air Travel Advisory Bureau** in London (☎020 7636 5000; www.atab.co.uk) provides referrals to travel agencies and consolidators that offer discounted airfares out of the UK.

Aer Lingus, Ireland (☎0818 365 000; www.aerlingus.ie).

British Midland Airways, UK (☎0870 607 05 55; www.flybmi.com). Departures from throughout the UK.

easyJet, UK (☎0870 600 00 00; www.easyjet.com). Online tickets.

Go-Fly Limited, UK (☎09063 020 150, elsewhere call UK 44 1279 66 63 88; www.go-fly.com). A subsidiary of British Airways.

KLM, UK (☎0870 507 40 74; www.klmuk.com). Cheap return tickets.

TRAVELING FROM AUSTRALIA & NEW ZEALAND

Air New Zealand, New Zealand (☎0800 73 70 00; www.airnz.co.nz).

Qantas Air, Australia (☎13 13 13), New Zealand (☎0800 808 767; www.qantas.com.au).

Singapore Air, Australia (☎13 10 11), New Zealand (☎0800 808 909; www.singaporeair.com).

Thai Airways, Australia (☎1300 65 19 60), New Zealand (☎09 377 02 68; www.thaiair.com).

TRAVELING FROM SOUTH AFRICA

Air France: ☎011 770 16 01; www.airfrance.com/za.

British Airways: ☎0860 011 747; www.british-airways.com/regional/sa. Cape Town and Johannesburg to the UK and the rest of Europe from SAR3400.

Lufthansa: ☎0861 842 538; www.lufthansa.co.za.

AIR COURIER FLIGHTS

Those who travel light should consider courier flights. Couriers help transport cargo on international flights by using their checked luggage space for freight. Generally, couriers must travel with carry-ons only and must deal with complex flight restrictions. Most flights are round-trip only, with short fixed-length stays, which are usually one week, and a limit of a one ticket per issue. Most of these flights also operate only out of major gateway cities, mostly in North America. Round-trip courier fares from the US to Rome run about US$200. Most flights leave from New York, Los Angeles, San Francisco, or Miami in the US; and from Montreal, Toronto, or Vancouver in Canada. Generally, you must be over 21 (in some cases 18). In summer, the most popular destinations usually require an advance reservation of about two weeks (you can usually book up to two months ahead). Super-discounted fares are common for "last-minute" flights (three to 14 days ahead).

FROM NORTH AMERICA

Round-trip courier fares from the US to Western Europe run about US$200-500. Most flights leave from New York, Los Angeles, San Francisco, or Miami in the US; and from Montreal, Toronto, or Vancouver in Canada. The organizations below provide members with lists of opportunities and courier brokers for an annual fee. Prices quoted below are round-trip.

Air Courier Association, 350 Indiana St. #300, Golden, CO 80401 (☎800-282-1202; www.aircourier.org). Ten departure cities throughout the US and Canada to Rome and other western European cities (high-season US$150-360). One-year membership US$49.

International Association of Air Travel Couriers (IAATC), PO Box 980, Keystone Heights, FL 32656 (☎352-475-1584; www.courier.org). From 9 North American cities to Western European cities, including Rome. One-year membership US$45.

Global Courier Travel, PO Box 3051, Nederland, CO 80466 (www.globalcouriertravel.com). Searchable online database. Six departure points in the US and Canada to Rome and other western European cities. Lifetime membership US$40, 2 people US$55.

NOW Voyager, 315 W 49th St., New York, NY 10019 (☎212-459-1616; fax 262-7407). To Rome (US$499-699). Usually one-week max. stay. One-year membership US$50. Non-courier discount fares also available.

FROM THE UK, IRELAND, AUSTRALIA & NEW ZEALAND

The minimum age for couriers from the **UK** is usually 18. **Brave New World Enterprises,** P.O. Box 22212, London SE5 8WB (www.courierflights.com) publishes a directory of all the companies offering courier flights in the UK (UK£10, in electronic form UK£8). **Global Courier Travel** (see above) also offers flights from London and Dublin to continental Europe. **British Airways Travel Shop** (☎0870 240 0747; www.batravelshops.com) arranges some flights from London to destinations in continental Europe (specials may be as low as UK£60; no registration fee). From **Australia** and **New Zealand, Global Courier Travel** (see above) often has listings from Sydney and Auckland to London and occasionally Frankfurt.

STANDBY FLIGHTS

Traveling standby requires considerable flexibility in arrival and departure dates. Companies dealing in standby flights sell vouchers rather than tickets, along with the promise to get to your destination (or near your destination) within a certain window of time (typically 1-5 days). Carefully read agreements with any company offering standby flights as tricky fine print can leave you in a lurch. To check on a company's service record in the US, call the Better Business Bureau (☎212-533-6200). It is difficult to receive refunds, and clients' vouchers will not be honored when an airline fails to receive payment in time.

TICKET CONSOLIDATORS

Ticket consolidators, or **"bucket shops,"** buy unsold tickets in bulk from commercial airlines and sell them at discounted rates. Look in the Sunday travel section of any major newspaper, where many bucket shops place tiny ads. Not all are reliable, so insist on a receipt that gives full details of restrictions, refunds, and tickets, and pay by credit card (2-5% fee) so you can stop payment if you never receive tickets. Check out www.travel-library.com/air-travel/consolidators.html.

Travel Avenue (☎800-333-3335; www.travelavenue.com) searches for best available published fares and then uses several consolidators to attempt to beat that fare. **NOW Voyager,** 74 Varick St., Ste. 307, New York, NY 10013 (☎212-431-1616; fax 219-1793; www.nowvoyagertravel.com) arranges discounted flights, mostly from New York, to Barcelona, London, Madrid, Milan, Paris, and Rome. Other consolidators worth trying are **Interworld** (☎305-443-4929; fax 443-0351); **Pennsylvania Travel** (☎800-331-0947); **Rebel** (☎800-227-3235; travel@rebeltours.com; www.rebeltours.com); **Cheap Tickets** (☎800-377-1000; www.cheaptickets.com). Yet more consolidators on the web include the **Internet Travel Network** (www.itn.com); **Flights.com** (www.flights.com); **TravelHUB** (www.travelhub.com); and **The Travel Site** (www.thetravelsite.com). Keep in mind that these are just suggestions to get you started in your research; *Let's Go* does not endorse any of these agencies.

CHARTER FLIGHTS

Charters are flights a tour operator contracts with an airline to fly extra loads of passengers during peak season. Charter flights fly less frequently than major airlines, make refunds particularly difficult, and are usually fully booked. Schedules and itineraries may also change or be cancelled at the last moment (as late as 48 hours before the trip, and without a full refund), and check-in, boarding, and baggage claim are often much slower. However, they can also be cheaper.

Discount clubs and **fare brokers** offer members savings on last-minute charter and tour deals. **Travelers Advantage,** Trumbull, CT, USA (☎203-365-2000; www.travelersadvantage.com; US$60 annual fee includes discounts and cheap flight directories) specializes in European travel and tour packages.

BY TRAIN

Most major Italian cities and European hubs lie on a direct line to Rome or can reach it with a single change. **Tickets** can be bought and **reservations** made in any train station and at many travel agencies (see **Tourist Offices,** p. 25). Reservations are mandatory for **Eurostar** (☎440 20 7298 5163; www.eurostar.com,) trains and some express trains (usually less than €5.16). Machines opposite the ticket counter at Termini station provide instructions in English and handle most transactions, accepting cash, ATM, Diner's Club, Mastercard, and Visa. While economical, efficient, and romantic, riding the train exposes you to a greater risk of robbery. Sleep wearing your money belt or neck pouch, and if you are traveling with a companion, try to sleep in shifts (see **Personal Safety,** p. 316). **Termini,** the transportation hub of Rome, is the focal point of most train lines and Rome's subway. Services including hotel reservations (across from track #20), ATMs, luggage storage (at track #1), and police (at track #13, or call 112) are in the station. Not to be missed are **Termini's bathrooms,** a black lit wonderland off track #1 (€0.51). Be warned, they become a way of life.

The various other stations on the fringe of town—Tiburtina, Trastevere, Ostiense, San Lorenzo, Roma Nord, Prenestina—are connected by bus and/or subway to Termini. Trains that arrive in Rome after midnight and before 5am or so usually arrive at Tiburtina or Ostiense, which are connected to Termini during these hours by the 40N and 20N-21N buses respectively. **Be particularly wary of pickpockets and con artists in and around the stations.**

For information on **train service within Italy,** contact **Ferrovie dello Stato (FS),** the Italian state railway (☎06 4730 6599; www.fs-on-line.com). FS offers **Cartaverde** for people under 26; the card (€23.24) is valid for one year, and entitles you to a 20% and 30% discount on first- and second-class seats, respectively. If you qualify and plan to travel extensively, it should be your *first* purchase upon arrival. Families of four or more and groups of up to 10 adults traveling together also qualify for discounts on Italian railways. Persons over 60 receive a 20% discount on train tickets with purchase of a **Carta d'argento** (€23.24 per year).

For more information on service from outside Italy, contact Rail Europe (US ☎877 456-RAIL; www.raileurope.com); for extended travel, a variety of passes are available. The following are rates and times for second-class seats, one-way to Rome from: **Florence** (1-2hr., €35.50); **Venice** (5hr., €53.25); **Milan** (4½hr., €55.62); **Naples** (2hr., €28.41); **Vienna** (13hr., US$50); **Paris** (14½hr., US$295).

BY BUS

An often cheaper alternative to rail passes for travelers visiting many cities is an **international bus pass,** which allows unlimited travel between major cities. Buses are most popular among non-American backpackers.

Busabout, 258 Vauxhall Bridge Rd., London SW1V 1BS (☎207 950 1661; www.busabout.com). Offers 5 interconnecting bus circuits covering 70 cities and towns in Europe; rolls into Rome twice daily. Consecutive Day Passes and FlexiPasses both available. Connections to Rome available from **Florence** (4hr.); **Sorrento** (5hr.); and **Venice** (9hr.). Consecutive Day Standard/student passes allow unlimited travel to all destinations, and are valid 2 weeks (US$249/219), 3 weeks (US$359/329), 1 month (US$479/429), 2 months (US$739/659), 3 months (US$909/829), or season (US$1089/979). Flexicards also available, which allow travelers to allow themselves more time in locations.

Eurolines, 52 Grosvenor Gardens, London SWIW OAG (☎1582 404 511; www.eurolines.com). Unlimited 15-day (UK£109; under 26 and over 60 UK£90), 30-day (UK£222, under 26 and over 60 UK£179) or 60-day (UK£259/195) travel in 30 major European cities.

BY CAR

For specific information on traveling by car in Italy, check out **When in Rome,** p. 21.

INTERNATIONAL DRIVING PERMIT (IDP)

If you plan to drive a car while in Italy, you must have an International Driving Permit (IDP). Your IDP, valid for one year, must be issued in your own country before you depart, and is generally available at the local automobile club, for a fee of US$10. An application for an IDP usually needs to include one or two photos, a current local license, an additional form of identification.

CAR INSURANCE

Most credit cards cover standard insurance. If you rent, lease, or borrow a car, you will need a **green card,** or **International Insurance Certificate,** to certify that you have liability insurance and that it applies abroad. Green cards can be obtained at car rental agencies, car dealers (for those leasing cars), some travel agents, and some border crossings. Rental agencies may require you to purchase theft insurance in countries that they consider to have a high risk of auto theft.

SPECIFIC CONCERNS

WOMEN TRAVELERS

Italy can be a difficult destination for female travelers, largely due to the amount of unsought attention they routinely, constantly, and universally receive from Italian men. In general, that attention does not go beyond honking, whistling, obnoxious hissing noises, and raucous "compliments." To minimize harassment, adopt the attitude of Roman women: walk like you know where you are going, avoid eye contact—**sunglasses** are indispensable—and meet all advances with dignity, silence, and an impassive gaze. Try not to show too much skin if you aren't comfortable attracting attention; avoiding "touristy" attire (college shirts, sneakers, Tevas, or Birkenstocks) can also prevent unwanted attention.

The Italian conception of **personal space** might be different from that to which you are accustomed. The guy crowded next to you on the bus or the woman gesticulating madly in your face is not necessarily threatening you or being rude; it is fairly normal in Italian culture to stand close to the person you're addressing and to gesture wildly. However, if you are physically harassed on the bus or in some public place, it is better to find another Italian (especially middle-aged or older women) than to talk to the person directly (this can encourage him). Most Italians are embarrassed by the treatment that foreign women receive in Italy and will be supportive and helpful. Try to avoid traveling alone at night. Memorize Italy's **emergency numbers** (☎113 and 112). Always carry a phone card and enough extra money for a bus or taxi, and consider carrying a whistle.Some travelers recommend wearing a fake (or real) wedding or engagement ring and even carrying pictures of their "children," who are back at the "hotel" with their "husband."

Hitchhiking is never safe for lone women, or even for two women traveling together. When choosing a train compartment, look for other women, couples, or, better yet, nuns. Nuns, both on and off trains, rival the police, guard dogs, and the most state-of-the-art personal protection devices in effectiveness. **Never sit in an empty train compartment.** If you are touched by someone, a loud *"non mi toccare"* ("don't touch me") will alert other riders that you're being bothered.

TRAVELING ALONE

There are many benefits to traveling alone, including independence and greater interaction with locals. However, lone travelers need to be well organized and look confident at all times. Try not to stand out as a tourist. **If questioned, never admit that you are traveling alone.** Maintain regular contact with someone at home who knows your itinerary. For more tips, pick up *Traveling Solo* by Eleanor Berman (Globe Pequot Press, US$17) or subscribe to **Connecting: Solo Travel Network,** 689 Park Road, Unit 6, Gibsons, BC V0N 1V7 (☎604-886-9099; www.cstn.org; membership US$28). Alternatively, several services link solo travelers who desire companions with travelers that have similar travel habits and interests; contact the **Travel Companion Exchange,** P.O. Box 833, Amityville, NY 11701 (☎631-454-0880; www.whytravelalone.com; US$48).

OLDER TRAVELERS

Older travelers in Italy are generally treated with considerable respect, and senior travelers are often entitled to travel-related discounts. Always ask about them, and be prepared to show proof of age (you probably look younger than you are). Agencies for senior group travel are growing in enrollment and popularity.

For more info, check out: *No Problem! Worldwise Tips for Mature Adventurers*, by Janice Kenyon (Orca Book Publishers, US$16); *A Senior's Guide to Healthy Travel*, by Donald L. Sullivan (Career Press, US$15); *Unbelievably Good Deals and Great Adventures That You Absolutely Can't Get Unless You're Over 50*, by Joan Rattner Heilman (Contemporary Books, US$13). For more information, contact one of the following organizations:

Elderhostel, 11 Ave. de Lafayette, Boston, MA 02111 (☎877-426-8056; www.elderhostel.org). Organizes 1- to 4-week "educational adventures" in Rome for those 55+.

The Mature Traveler, P.O. Box 15791, Sacramento, CA 95852 (☎800-460-6676; www.thematuretraveler.com). Deals, discounts, and travel packages for the 50+ traveler. Subscription$30.

BGLTQ TRAVELERS

While Rome does not have a thriving queer community like those in many northern Italian cities, the queer scene is slowly but surely expanding. Italian society is, unfortunately, not the most queer-friendly. Straight Roman men and women are open in showing affection for members of the same sex; embracing, holding hands or walking arm-in-arm is common, but this "homosocial" ease hasn't translated into tolerance of same-sex couples. Still, however concealed public queer life may be, the scene is on the rise. In 2000, Rome hosted World Pride 2000, drawing thousands of men and women from around the world. Sexual acts between members of the same sex has been legal for those above the age of consent (16) since 1889—more than most Anglo-Saxon countries can say.

The national organization for gay men, **Arci-Gay,** has its headquarters in V.D. Minzoni, 18 (☎051 649 3055; www.arcigay.it). Arci-gay Ora, has an office in Rome at V. Goito 35/b (☎339 618 1131 or 340 347 5710; www.gruppoora.org) It might be a good idea to buy an Arci-Gay membership card (€10 annually), which gives admission to many gay clubs all over Italy.

Rome's Arci-Gay office publishes the monthly newsletter *Pegaso*. In addition, the monthly *Babilonia* (published by Babilonia Edizioni, V. Ebro, 11, 20141 Milan; ☎02 569 64 68) and the annual *Guida Gay Italia* (available at most newsstands) address gay issues and list community events. Finally, the **Italian Gay and Lesbian Yellow Pages** (www.gay.it/guida/italia/info.htm) includes listings of gay bars, hotels, and shops. Other useful websites include www.women.it and www.gay.it.

In Rome, the **Circolo Mario Mieli di Cultura Omosessuale,** V. Corinto, 5, provides info about gay life in Rome. Take M: B-San Paolo, walk one block to largo Beato Placido Riccardi, hang a left, and walk 1½ blocks to V. Corinto to find gay-related brochures, pamphlets, and a bulletin board with announcements and special events. The staff offers group discussions and social events every Friday at 7pm, and info sessions on topics such as gay health concerns. (☎06 5413985; fax 06 5413971; www.mariomieli.org. Open M-F 9am-1pm and 2-6pm; closed Aug.)

Unfortunately, there isn't much organized lesbian activity for the traveler in Rome. The best source of info is the **Coordinamento Lesbico Italiano,** V.S. Francesco di Sales, 1a (☎06 6864201), off V.d. Lungara in Trastevere. Rome's one and only gay bookstore, **Libreria Babele,** V.d. Banchi Vecchi, is across the bridge from Castel Sant'Angelo. (☎06 6876628. Open Tu-Sa 10am-2pm and 4-7:30pm. M 4-7:30pm.) It is also one of the only places that sells the *Gay and Lesbian Map of Rome* (€1).

Gay and lesbian Romans crowd the **gay beach** *Il Buco* at Lido di Ostia, which accommodates a relaxed, younger crowd. Take the train from Piramide or Magliana (M: A-Lido di Ostia), then bus #7 to the *capolinea;* from there, walk 2km south along the beach.

FURTHER READING: BISEXUAL, GAY, & LESBIAN

Spartacus Internation Gay Guide 2001-2002. Bruno Gmunder Verlag (US$33).

Damron Men's Guide, Damron's Accommodations, and *The Women's Traveller.* Damron Travel Guides (US$14-19). For more info, call ☎800-462-6654 or visit www.damron.com.

The Gay Vacation Guide: The Best Trips and How to Plan Them, Mark Chesnut. Citadel Pres (US$15).

Listed below are contact organizations, mail-order bookstores, and publishers that offer materials addressing some specific concerns. **Out and About** (www.planetout.com) offers a bi-weekly newsletter addressing travel concerns and a comprehensive site addressing gay travel concerns.

Gay's the Word, 66 Marchmont St., London WC1N 1AB, UK (☎+44 20 7278 7654; www.gaystheword.co.uk). The largest gay and lesbian bookshop in the UK, with both fiction and non-fiction titles. Mail-order service available.

Giovanni's Room, 1145 Pine St., Philadelphia, PA 19107, USA (☎215-923-2960; www.queerbooks.com). An international lesbian/feminist and gay bookstore with mail-order service (carries many of the publications listed below).

International Lesbian and Gay Association (ILGA), 81 rue Marché-au-Charbon, B-1000 Brussels, Belgium (☎+32 2 502 2471; www.ilga.org). Provides political information, such as homosexuality laws of individual countries.

TRAVELERS WITH DISABILITIES

Romans are making an increased effort to meet the needs of people with disabilities. Still, many of the sights (like the Ancient City) can be difficult to navigate in a wheelchair, and in general, establishments are not wheelchair accessible unless stated otherwise. The **Italian Government Travel Office (ENIT)** will let you know which hotels and buildings are wheelchair accessible. Many of the larger **Ferrovie dello Stato (FS)** trains are marked wheelchair accessible; they suggest that you call ahead to reserve a space (☎ 800 888088). For more info, call the **Italian State Railway Representative** in New York (☎ 212 730-2121). If you plan to bring a **seeing-eye dog** to Italy, contact your vet and the nearest Italian consulate. You'll need import documents and records certifying your dog's health. For additional info, try **Global Access** (www.geocities.com/Paris/1502/disabilitylinks.html), which has several great links for disabled travelers in Italy.

Those with disabilities should inform airlines and hotels of their disabilities when making reservations; some time may be needed to prepare special accommodations. **Guide dog owners** should inquire as to the quarantine policies of each destination country. At the very least, they will need to provide a certificate of immunization against rabies. **Rail** is probably the most convenient form of travel for disabled travelers in Europe: many stations have ramps, and some trains have wheelchair lifts, special seating areas, and specially equipped toilets. All Eurostar, some InterCity (IC) and some EuroCity (EC) trains are wheelchair-accessible and CityNightLine trains and Conrail trains feature special compartments. In general, Italy has one of the most **wheelchair-accessible rail networks** in Europe; all Pendolino and many EC and IC trains are accessible. Some major **car rental** agencies (Hertz, Avis, and National) offer hand-controlled vehicles.

USEFUL ORGANIZATIONS

Mobility International USA (MIUSA), P.O. Box 10767, Eugene, OR 97440 (☎541-343-1284; www.miusa.org). Sells *A World of Options: A Guide to International Educational Exchange, Community Service, and Travel for Persons with Disabilities* (US$35).

Society for Accessible Travel & Hospitality (SATH), 347 Fifth Ave., #610, New York, NY 10016 (☎212-447-7284; www.sath.org). An advocacy group that publishes free online travel information and the travel magazine *OPEN WORLD* (US$18, free for members). Annual membership US$45, students and seniors US$30.

Directions Unlimited, 123 Green Ln., Bedford Hills, NY 10507 (☎800-533-5343). Books individual and group vacations for the physically disabled; not an info service.

MINORITY TRAVELERS

Until recently, the Roman population was relatively homogeneous. Immigration in the latter half of the 20th century from Eastern Europe, North Africa, the Philippines, and former Italian colonies like Somalia and Ethiopia has changed the make-up of the city. Many Romans have not quite gotten used to these newcomers and blame them for—among other things—the rise in crime and social unrest. Although immigrants of color do experience discrimination, tourists of color from the West, who are easily distinguishable by Western clothes and language, are not the usual targets of racism. Women of Asian heritage may be referred to as *giapponese*. Women from India may be called *Indiana*. African-American women may find that Italian men can't get past *bellissima*.

Let's Go does not list known discriminatory establishments. If, in your travels, you encounter discriminatory treatment, let us know so that we can check the establishment and warn travelers.

TRAVELERS WITH CHILDREN

Long bus rides and longer walks are usually required to see just about anything in Rome, making traveling with children quite challenging. But Rome boasts a bountiful supply of *gelaterias*, candy stores, and free water fountains, which are surprisingly helpful in keeping a kid's morale up. Don't forget to schedule an afternoon nap for *everyone*, which will correspond with the siesta planned right into Roman business hours anyway.

If you're going beyond Rome, note that while car rental is convenient, train travel might be more fun for the kids, and certainly cheaper. **Discount Eurailpasses** are available for groups, families, and children.

Caffè della Palma (near the Pantheon) and **Jolly Pop candy stores** (in P. Navona and in the entrance of Termini Station) are always good for a rest stop or a bribe. The **Villa Borghese** park is a cool respite from ancient monuments and churches, and you can rent bicycles or a rowboat to paddle in the small lake. There are **horse-drawn carriage rides** around the city, originating from P. di Spagna. Sailing along the Tiber River can be entertaining for both parents and children. Commentated tours leave from Ponte S. Angelo and cost €10. (For more information on these boat tours, visit www.battellidiroma.it, call 06 67 89 361, or stop by V.d. Tribuna Tor de'Specchi, 15.) Children also love the **caricatures** and portraits done in P. Navona—either watching or posing. There are puppet shows in English on Saturday and Sunday at **Teatro dei Satiri,** V.d. Grotta Pinta, 19, off Campo dei Fiori. (☎06 68806244.) Check out the genuine Sicilian puppet shows at the **Teatro Crisogno,** V.S. Gallicano, 8, off viale di Trastevere. **LUNEUR** park (see p. 146) is an old-fashioned amusement park, with a hokey wax museum, roller coaster, and carnival attractions.

FURTHER READING: TRAVELING WITH CHILDREN

Gutsy Mamas: Travel Tips and Wisdom for Mothers on the Road, Marybeth Bond Travelers' Tales, Inc. (US$8).

Have Kid, Will Travel: 101 Survival Strategies for Vacationing With Babies and Young Children, Claire and Lucille Tristram. Andrews McMeel Publishing (US$9).

Young Children, Claire and Lucille Tristram. Andrews McMeel Publishing (US$9).

How to take Great Trips with Your Kids, Sanford and Jane Portnoy. Harvard Com mon Press (US $10).

Trouble Free Travel with Children, Vicki Lansky. Book Peddlers (US$9).

DIETARY CONCERNS

*Also see **Food and Wine,** p. 192.*

EATING VEGETARIAN, VEGAN, OR KOSHER

Vegetarians should have no problems in Italian restaurants, since the majority of first courses (*primi,* the pasta course) are meatless and most restaurants will supply a mixed plate of their vegetable side dishes upon request—ask for *verdure miste* (mixed vegetables). *Let's Go: Rome* includes restaurants that offer vegetarian and vegan options, and you can always ask for a dish *senza carne* (without meat). If you aren't sure of the contents of a particular dish, ask *"c'è carne?"* Be wary, since Italians don't believe that fish is meat and many seemingly veggie treats may hide meat ingredients. Soups are never vegetarian unless the menu specifies otherwise; they're usually made with a meat base, even if no meat is added.

One useful resource for vegetarians is the North American Vegetarian Society, P.O. Box 72, Dolgeville, NY 13329 (☎518-568-7970; www.navs-online.org), which publishes information about vegetarian travel, including *Transformative Adventures, a Guide to Vacations and Retreats* (US$15), and the *Vegetarian Journal's Guide to Natural Food Restaurants* in the US and Canada (US$12). For more information, visit your local bookstore, health food store, or library, and consult *The Vegetarian Traveler: Where to Stay if You're Vegetarian,* by Jed and Susan Civic (Larson Publications; US$12.95) and *Europe on 10 Salads a Day,* by Greg and Mary Jane Edwards (Mustang Publishing; US$10).

Many Italian dishes count pork as their principal ingredient, and those that don't still often combine meat and cheese, making it hard to keep kosher in Rome. If going vegetarian is an option, you should have no trouble getting by, but a good place to get more information is the Synagogue of Rome in the Jewish Ghetto (☎06 687 50 51). Our **Food & Wine** chapter also offers a few options (p. 192). Your own synagogue or college Hillel should have access to lists of Jewish institutions across the nation. If you are strict in your observance, you may have to prepare your own food. A good resource is the *Jewish Travel Guide,* by Michael Zaidner (Vallentine Mitchell; US$17).

OTHER RESOURCES

TRAVEL PUBLISHERS & BOOKSTORES

Hippocrene Books, Inc., 171 Madison Ave., New York, NY 10016 (☎212-685-4371; www.netcom.com/~hippocre). Free catalog. Publishes foreign language dictionaries and language learning guides.

Hunter Publishing, 130 Campus Dr., Edison, NJ 08818, USA (☎800-255-0343; www.hunterpublishing.com). Extensive catalog of travel guides and diving and adventure travel books.

Rand McNally, 150 S. Wacker Dr., Chicago, IL 60606, USA (☎800-234-0679 or 312-332-2009; www.randmcnally.com), publishes road atlases (each US$10).

Adventurous Traveler Bookstore, P.O. Box 2221, Williston, VT 05495, USA (☎800-282-3963; www.adventuroustraveler.com).

Bon Voyage!, 2069 W. Bullard Ave., Fresno, CA 93711, USA (☎800-995-9716, from abroad 559-447-8441; www.bon-voyage-travel.com). They specialize in Europe but have titles pertaining to other regions as well. Free newsletter.

Travel Books & Language Center, Inc., 4437 Wisconsin Ave. NW, Washington, D.C. 20016, USA (☎800-220-2665; www.bookweb.org/bookstore/travelbks/). Over 60,000 titles from around the world.

THE ART OF BUDGET TRAVEL

How to See the World, (www.artoftravel.com). A compendium of great travel tips, from cheap flights to self defense to interacting with local culture.

Travel Library, (www.travel-library.com). A fantastic set of links for general information and personal travelogues.

Lycos, (cityguide.lycos.com). General introductions to Rome, accompanied by links to applicable histories, news, and local tourism sites.

Backpacker's Ultimate Guide, (www.bugeurope.com). Tips on packing, transportation, and where to go. Also tons of country-specific travel information.

WWW.LETSGO.COM Our website, www.letsgo.com, now includes introductory chapters from all our guides and a wealth of information on a monthly featured destination. As always, our website also has info about our books, a travel forum buzzing with stories and tips, and additional links that will help you make the most of a trip to Rome.

INFORMATION ON ROME

Foreign Language for Travelers, (www.travlang.com). Provides free online translating dictionaries and lists of phrases in Italian.

MyTravelGuide, (www.mytravelguide.com). Country overviews, with everything from history to transportation to live web cam coverage of Rome.

Geographia, (www.geographia.com). Highlights, culture, and people of Italy.

Atevo Travel, (http://www.atevo.com/guides/destinations). Detailed introductions, travel tips, and suggested itineraries.

World Travel Guide, (www.travel-guides.com/navigate/world.asp). Helpful practical info.

TravelPage, (www.travelpage.com). Links to official tourist office sites in Italy.

PlanetRider, (www.planetrider.com). A subjective list of links to the "best" websites covering the culture and tourist attractions of Italy.

A.S. Roma and **S.S. Lazio,** (www.asromacalcio.it and www.sslazio.it). Rome's two soccer teams. Figure out who you like before talking to the locals.

Comune di Roma, (www.comune.roma.it). An intimidating Roman site with up-to-the-minute events information and metric tons more.

Romeguide, (www.romeguide.it). An amazingly complete site; particularly strong in the area of accommodations, transportation, and cultural events.

INSIDE

volunteering 326
for the environment 326 social issues 327
the arts 328 utilizing ongs (ngos) 328
studying abroad 327
universities 329 language schools 330
options less ordinary 331
working 331
long term work 332 short term work 334

Alternatives to Tourism

When we started out in 1961, about 1.7 million people in the world were traveling internationally each year; in 2002, nearly 700 million trips were made, and that number is projected to be up to a billion by 2010. The dramatic rise in tourism has created an interdependence between the economy, environment, and culture of many destinations and the tourists they host. As a popular tourist destination, Italy receives a whopping 30 million visitors each year. In recent decades tourism has become an increasingly important sector of the economy, employing 6-7% of the Italian workforce. The industry provides jobs for foreigners as well, serving the expanding need for skilled and unskilled seasonal work and speakers of different languages.

In the spirit of sustainable tourism, this year's *Let's Go* aims to offer travelers a chance to give back to the communities they visit. In this chapter we describe social and economic issues facing Rome, along with listings of volunteer organizations dedicated to these concerns. As the capital of Italy and home to the Vatican, Rome feels the sway of the State and Pope John Paul II's edicts more than any other city in Italy. Yet perhaps because of its large university population and urban diversity in Rome, Lazio remains one of the nation's most liberal provinces. Environmentalist groups are active in Rome, addressing recent concerns for its shrinking, darkly polluted, and often putrid Tiber river. Currently, environmentalists estimate that two-thirds of the fish passing though the city die on the river banks, leading many to suspect that the river suffers from illegal toxic waste and sewage dumping. Cleaning the city itself has been an important item on the agenda for new center-left mayor Walter Veltroni. In the style of the London's Thames, the Tiber is destined to be refurbished from an eyesore into a site worthy of a €10 cruise ride.

However, pollution is not the only issue concerning the Roman mind. Due to continuing economic downturn since 2001, those at the margins of Roman society, including gypsies (also known as the "Roma minority") and the ever-increasing immigrant population, feel the brunt of high unemployment and relatively scattered social services for the homeless. Immigrants seeking economic opportunity and/or a milder climate continue to arrive in Rome from Ukraine, Albania, North Africa, Sri Lanka, Pakistan and Kurdish communities. Ever wary of *i stranieri* (foreigners) placing a drain on social services, some Italians respond to poor immigrants with fear and condescension. Charitable organizations such as the Salvation Army, Sant'Egidio, and Caritas, the Catholic aid agency, offer aid to the poor. However, these organizations rely on regional church and state funding to subsist.

FIND THE PATH. To read more on specific organizations that are working to better their communities, look for our **Giving Back** features. For a first-hand interview, see p. 143.

Those looking to **volunteer** have many options. Depending on your interests, volunteering can become either a weekend endeavor or the main component of your trip. Later in this section, we recommend organizations that can help you find the opportunities that best suit your interests, whether you're looking to pitch in at a soup kitchen or in art restoration; whether you're moving-in or just staying for two weeks.

Other than volunteering, there are any number of other ways that you can participate in the communities you visit. **Studying** at a college or language program is one option. Bella Roma also offers unique opportunities in archaeological study and perfecting your Italian. Many travelers also structure their trips by the **work** that they can do along the way—either odd jobs as they go, or full-time stints in cities where they plan to stay for some time.

For those who seek more active involvement, **Earthwatch International, Operation Crossroads Africa,** and **Habitat for Humanity** offer fulfilling volunteer opportunities all over the world. For more on volunteering, studying, and working in Rome and beyond, consult Let's Go's alternatives to tourism site, www.beyondtourism.com.

Before handing your money over to any volunteer or study abroad program, make sure you know exactly what you're getting into. It's a good idea to get the names of **previous participants** and ask them about their experience, as some programs sound much better on paper than in reality. The **questions** below are a good place to start:

-Will you be the only person in the program? If not, what are the other participants like? How old are they? How much will you be expected to interact with them?

-Is room and board included? If so, what is the arrangement? Will you be expected to share a room? A bathroom? What are the meals like? Do they accommodate dietary restrictions?

-Is transportation included? Are there any additional expenses?

-How much free time will you have? Will you be able to travel around?

-What kind of safety precautions will be taken? Will you still be covered by your home insurance? Does the program have an emergency plan?

A NEW PHILOSOPHY OF TRAVEL

We at *Let's Go* have watched the growth of the 'ignorant tourist' stereotype with dismay, knowing that the majority of travelers care passionately about the state of the communities and environments they explore—but also knowing that even conscientious tourists can inadvertently damage natural wonders, rich cultures, and impoverished communities. We believe the philosophy of **sustainable travel** is among the most important travel tips we could impart to our readers, to help guide fellow backpackers and on-the-road philanthropists. By staying aware of the needs and troubles of local communities, today's travelers can be a powerful force in preserving and restoring this fragile world.

Working against the negative consequences of irresponsible tourism is much simpler than it might seem; it is often self-awareness, rather than self-sacrifice, that makes the biggest difference. Simply by trying to spend responsibly and conserve local resources, all travelers can positively impact the places they visit. Let's Go has partnered with **BEST** (**Business Enterprises for Sustainable Travel,** an affiliate of the Conference Board; see www.sustainabletravel.org), which recognizes businesses that operate based on the principles of sustainable travel. Below, they provide advice on how ordinary visitors can practice this philosophy in their daily travels, no matter where they are.

TIPS FOR CIVIC TRAVEL: HOW TO MAKE A DIFFERENCE

Travel by train when feasible. Rail travel requires only half the energy per passenger mile that planes do. On average, each of the 40,000 daily domestic air flights releases more than 1700 pounds of greenhouse gas emissions.

Use public mass transportation whenever possible; outside of cities, take advantage of group taxis or vans. Bicycles are an attractive way of seeing a community first-hand. And enjoy walking–purchase good maps of your destination and ask about on-foot touring opportunities.

When renting a car, ask whether fuel-efficient vehicles are available. Honda and Toyota produce cars that use hybrid engines powered by electricity and gasoline, thus reducing emissions of carbon dioxide. Ford Motor Company plans to introduce a hybrid fuel model by the end of 2004.

Reduce, reuse, recycle–use electronic tickets, recycle papers and bottles wherever possible, and avoid using containers made of styrofoam. Refillable water bottles and rechargable batteries both efficiently conserve expendable resources.

Be thoughtful in your purchases. Take care not to buy souvenir objects made from trees in old-growth or endangered forests, such as teak, or items made from endangered species, like ivory or tortoise jewelry. Ask whether products are made from renewable resources.

Buy from local enterprises, such as casual street vendors. In developing countries and low-income neighborhoods, many people depend on the "informal economy" to make a living.

Be on-the-road-philanthropists. If you are inspired by the natural environment of a destination or enriched by its culture, join in preserving their integrity by making a charitable contribution to a local organization.

Spread the word. Upon your return home, tell friends and colleagues about places to visit that will benefit greatly from their tourist dollars, and reward sustainable enterprises by recommending their services. Travelers can not only introduce friends to particular vendors but also to local causes and charities that they might choose to support when they travel.

VOLUNTEERING

Volunteering can be one of the most fulfilling experiences you have in life, especially if you combine it with the thrill of traveling in a new place. Most people who volunteer in Rome do so on a short-term basis, at organizations that make use of drop-in or once-a-week volunteers.

For better or worse, volunteer work (like any kind of work in Rome) can be difficult to come by unless you have contacts. Some of the more popular sites for tourists might be looking for part-time docents to give tours in English or other foreign languages. You'll get better results if you go through the site offices directly, instead of through a placement agency. A good resource to begin your search is **www.adventuretravelabroad.com.** More intensive volunteer services may charge you a fee to participate. These costs can be surprisingly hefty (although they frequently cover airfare and most, if not all, living expenses). Most people choose to go through a parent organization that takes care of logistical details and frequently provides a group environment and support system. There are two main types of organizations—religious and non-sectarian—although there are rarely restrictions on participation for either. If you're flexible about your location, the agencies listed below are much more likely to place you somewhere in southern Italy.

FOR THE ENVIRONMENT

Recently, both environmental organizations and the municipal government have made stemming pollution in Rome a hot topic. In August 2003, Rome inaugurated a water taxi service along the Tiber River—after a hiatus of over 100 years—in an attempt to alleviate the notoriously frustrating traffic congestion and smog in Rome's streets. The taxi service was possible only after dredging 38 tons of trash from the river. To be sure, environmentalism in Rome extends beyond its city walls. It is home to most national organizations that are dedicated to preserving wildlife and natural resources ranging from the mountains of Piedmont to the woods of Calabria.

Earthwatch, 3 Clocktower Pl. Suite 100, Box 75, Maynard, MA 01754 (☎800-776-0188 or 978-461-0081; www.earthwatch.org). Arranges programs in Italy to promote conservation of natural resources. 1-3 wks. Fees vary based on program location and duration; costs average $1700 plus airfare.

Greenpeace Italia, national office: V. Manlio Gelsomini, 28, 00153 Roma (☎06 572 99 91; www.greenpeace.it). From protesting genetically modified foods to preserving the forests, Greenpeace Italia is active in a wide range of regional campaigns (check Lazio for Rome). To get involved locally at the Castelli Romani, email: castelli.romani@greenpeace.it. Duration of projects varies. Free.

Lega Italiana Protezione Uccelli, Lazio Regional Office, Via Aldrovandi, 2, 00197 Roma, (☎/fax: 06 321 107 52; www.lipuostia.it, in English and Italian). Works to preserve the natural habitat of birds and teach environmental awareness. Organizes bird-watching excursions and courses. Website includes a link to volunteer opportunities throughout Italy. Regional office is also the location of the **Wildlife Rescue Center:** Centro Recupero Fauna Selvatica (☎06 320 19 12). Open daily 9:30am-5:30pm.

Torre Argentina Cat Shelter, V. Marco Papio, 15, 00175 Roma (☎06 687 21 33; torreargentina@tiscali.it). Roman city ordinances dictate that no cat can be evicted from the place it was born. Thankfully Torre Argentina cares for these stray kitties. Manned 24hr. a day by volunteers and supported by donations. For more information contact Silvia Vivarini.

World Wide Foundation Italia, Rome office: Via G. Allegri, 1 CAP, 00198, Rome (☎06 844 972 06; fax 06 844 972 07; www.wwf.it/lazio). Based in Milan, the WWF sponsors a host of conservation and environmental activism campaigns and publishes an annual list work camps (In Italian). For information specifically related to volunteering, email volontariato@wwf.lazio.it.

SOCIAL ISSUES

Poverty in Rome is expected to worsen in the coming year, as the intense drought of the summer of 2003 imposed a severe energy drain on the city and has decreased agricultural production in grapes, olives, peaches, and apricots by almost 50%. Unskilled laborers in agriculture are now flocking to the city for work, only to encounter stiff competition from immigrants and resentment from the locals. Refugees continue to pour in from North Africa despite Italy's tightened immigration laws of 2002. The following listings feature organizations dedicated to helping those in Rome who are most in need. Their goals range from providing health care and alleviating poverty to granting various groups political asylum and expanding the country's scholarship on an array of social issues.

AFSAI, Associazione per la Formazione gli Scambi e le Attivita Interculturali (Association for Inter-cultural Exchanges and Activities), National office: Viale dei Colli Portuensi, 345 B2, 00151, Roma (☎06 537 03 32; www.afsai.it) Founded independently in 1958, AFSAI collaborates with the European Voluntary Service (EVS) and Youth for Europe (a work exchange program) to arrange cultural exchange and volunteer programs with home stays for Italians and non-Italians aged 16-30. Note that while an allowance is provided, volunteers may not select the location of their service.

Amnesty International Italia, Via Giovan Battista De Rossi 10, 00161 Roma (☎06 449 01). Dedicated to peace and asylum for refugees worldwide.

Centro Nazionale per il Volontariato, Via A. Catalani, 158, C.P. 202, 55100 Lucca, (☎05 834 195 00; cnv.cpr.it) Founded in 1984 as a center for research, publishing and networking for volunteers. Based in Lucca.

Child Family Health International, 953 Mission St., Suite 220, San Francisco, CA 94103, USA (☎415-957-9000; www.cfhi.org). Sends pre-med undergraduate and medical students to work with physicians in Italy, although the focus is more on working with the community and learning about health care rather than actually providing medical assistance. Program fees are around US$1500, excluding airfare.

Croce Rossa Italiana (Italian Red Cross), Via Toscana, 12, 00187, Roma (☎ 06 475 93 36; www.cri.it) An ever ready and helpful branch of the international Red Cross, volunteers in this nationwide organization provide free emergency medical treatment and organize blood donations. The Italian branch also organizes special chapters for women's health needs and "*I Pioneri*" or youth groups.

Elderhostel, Inc., 11 Avenue de Lafayette, Boston, MA 92111-1746, USA (☎877-426-8056; www.elderhostel.org). Sends volunteers (age 55 and over) worldwide to work in construction, research, teaching, and other projects. Costs average $100 per day plus airfare.

F.O.C.S.I.V. (Federazione Organismi Cristiani di Servizio Internazionale Volontario), Via S. Francesco di Sales, 18, 00165 Roma (☎06 687 77 96; www.focsiv.it).

Global Volunteers, 375 E. Little Canada Rd., St. Paul, MN 5517 USA (☎800-487-1074). Operates a year-round volunteer program to teach English in the Puglia region of southern Italy. $2395-2995 for 1-2 wks.

Habitat for Humanity International, 121 Habitat St., Americus, GA 31709, USA (☎229-924-6935 ext. 2551; www.habitat.org). Volunteers build houses in over 83 countries for anywhere from 2 weeks to 3 years. Short-term program costs range from US$1200-4000.

Italian Foundation for Voluntary Service, Via Nazionale, 39, 00184 Roma (☎06 474 81; www.fivol.it). National organization dedicated to providing financial and counseling support to volunteer organizations, regardless of social and economic affiliation.

Service Civil International Voluntary Service (SCI-IVS), SCI USA, 3213 W. Wheeler St., Seattle, WA 98199, USA (☎/fax 206-350-6585; www.sci-ivs.org). Arranges placement in work camps in Italy for those 18+. Registration fee US$65-125. You can also contact the regional office in Rome (Via de Laterani 28, 00134).

Salvation Army, Italia, Via degli Apuli, 39, 00185 Roma (☎ 06 446 26 14 or 06 494 10 89; www.esercitodellasalvezza.org) A Christian organization dedicated to providing emergency and social services, including youth and school programs and family tracing.

THE ARTS

As a city full of art and archaeological resources, opportunities abound for working in the arts. Contact **Museums** directly (p. 150) for volunteer docent openings. Local colleges and universities in your home country are an excellent source of information on archaeological digs and other projects. Check with the departments of the classics, archaeology, anthropology, fine arts, and/or other relevant area studies; many excavations send information and applications directly to individual professors or departments rather than to the general public.

The Archaeological Institute of America, 656 Beacon St., Boston, MA 02215-2010 (☎ 617-353-9361; www.archaeological.org), puts out the *Archaeological Fieldwork Opportunities Bulletin* (US$16 for non-members), which lists over 250 field sites throughout the world. The bulletin can also be purchased from Kendall/Hunt Publishing, 4050 Westmark Dr., Dubuque, Iowa 52002 (☎800-228-0810).

Centro Comune di Studi Preistorici, 25044 Capo di Ponte, Brescia (☎036 442 091; globalnet.it/ccsp/ccsp.htm), a research center involved with the management of cultural property and the organization of congresses, research projects, and exhibitions. They publish *BCSP*, the world journal of prehistoric and tribal art, and offer volunteer work, grants, and research assistant positions for prehistoric art. Write to the above address for info on anthropology, archaeological digs, and art history in Italy.

Gruppi Archeologici d'Italia, Via degli Scipioni 30a, 00192 Roma (☎/fax 06 3973 3637; www.gruppiarcheologici.org). Provides updated listings on upcoming and ongoing volunteer archaeological digs throughout Italy. The Gruppo Archeologicio Romano organizes digs or "camps" located in 2003 at the Villa Farnese Rofalco. Average cost €198-302 per wk.

Capitoline Museums, Piazza del Campidoglio 1, 00186 Roma (☎06 671 024 75). Interested volunteers should send a resume and letter of introduction to the address above.

Volunteers for Peace, 1034 Tiffany Rd., Belmont, VT 05730, USA (☎802-259-2759; www.vfp.org). Arranges 2- to 3-week placements in work camps worldwide, 183 of which are in Italy. Tasks and location vary from year to year and range from Environmental Studies and homestays to archaeology and art conservation. Membership required for registration. Programs average US$200-500.

UTILIZING ONGS (NGOS)

Italian ONGs (Italian Non-governmental organizations), also known as the *terza settore* (Third Sector) also provide volunteer and internship opportunities. Many registered ONGs, which are designed to assist a range of clientele from the disabled to prisoners to the blind, are based in Rome. For listings organized by region contact the **Dipartimento Generale per la Cooperazione allo Sviluppo,** Ufficio 11, Ministero degli Affari Esteri at Viale delle XVII Olimpiadi, 8, Roma (☎ 06 324 02 01). For more information check out **No Profit Italia** (www.noprofit.org), which offers a plethora of articles on ONGs, co-ops, changing Italian laws and immigration.

STUDYING ABROAD

Study abroad programs in Rome range from basic language and culture courses to college-level classes that count for credit at most American institutions. In order to choose a program that best fits your needs, you should research as much as possible before making your decision—determine costs and duration, as well as what kind of student participates in the program and the status of room and board. A good website to begin your search is **www.internationalstudent.com.**

STUDENT VISAS. EU citizens do not need a visa to study in Italy, but everyone else must obtain a *permesso di studio* (permit to study) prior to departure from the nearest embassy or consulate. You will need to provide proof of enrollment from your home institution or the school in Italy. US citizens must also present a notarized statement that the student has adequate financial means, and that the student will purchase an Italian health insurance policy in Italy as a supplement to American health insurance. The visa fee for US citizens is $32.34 (payable in money order only) and for Australian citizens is AUS$51. Upon arrival in Italy, students must register with the Foreigners' Bureau (*Ufficio degli Stranieri*) of the local questura in order to receive their permit of stay. For more information on visas see p. 301.

In programs that have large groups of students who speak the same language, you face a trade-off between feeling comfortable and practicing a foreign language and befriending other international students. For accommodations, dorm life provides a better opportunity to mingle with fellow students, but there is less of a chance to experience the local scene. If you live with a family, there is a potential to build lifelong friendships with natives and to experience day-to-day life in more depth, but conditions can vary greatly from family to family.

UNIVERSITIES

Some American schools still require students to pay them for credits obtained elsewhere. Most university-level study-abroad programs are meant as language and culture enrichment opportunities, and therefore are conducted in Italian. Still, many programs do offer classes in English and beginner and intermediate Italian. Those relatively fluent in Italian, on the other hand, may find it cheaper to enroll directly in a university abroad, although getting college credit may be more difficult. A good resource for finding programs that cater to your particular interests is **www.studyabroad.com,** which has links to various semester abroad programs based on a variety of critera, including desired location and focus of study. The following is a list of organizations that can help place students in university programs abroad, or have their own branch in Italy.

AMERICAN PROGRAMS

American Institute for Foreign Study, College Division, River Plaza, 9 West Broad St., Stamford, CT 06902, USA (☎800-727-2437 ext. 5163; www.aifsabroad.com). Organizes programs for high school and college study in universities in Italy.

Arcadia University for Education Abroad, 450 S. Easton Rd., Glenside, PA 19038, USA (☎866-927-2234; www.arcadia.edu/cea). Operates programs in Italy. Costs range from $2200 (summer) to $29,000 (full-year).

Council on International Educational Exchange (CIEE), 633 3rd Ave., 20th floor, New York, NY 10017-6706 (☎800-407-8839; www.ciee.org/study) sponsors work, volunteer, academic, and internship programs in Rome.

Institute for the International Education of Students (IES), 33 N. LaSalle St., 15th fl., Chicago, IL 60602, USA (☎800-995-2300; www.IESabroad.org). Offers year-long, semester, and summer programs for college study in Rome. US$50 application fee. Scholarships available.

School for International Training, College Semester Abroad, Admissions, Kipling Rd., P.O. Box 676, Brattleboro, VT 05302, USA (☎800-336-1616 or 802-257-7751; www.sit.edu). Semester and year-long programs in Italy. Cost US$10,600-13,700. Also runs the **Experiment in International Living** (☎800-345-2929; www.usexperiment.org), 3- to 5-week summer programs that offer high-school students cross-cultural homestays, community service, ecological adventure, and language training in Rome and cost US$1900-5000.

State University of New York, New Paltz, 75 South Manheim Boulevard, Suite 9, New Paltz, NY 12561, USA (☎845-257-3125; www.newpaltz.edu/studyabroad) Art History Department and the Center for International Programs offers an on-site summer course on a specific geographical area and limited chronological span (Summer 2003 was the mosaics of Venice, Rome and Ravenna). All lectures take place at the actual monuments. Tuition $2100.

Temple University, International Programs, 200 Tuttleman Learning Center, 1809 N. 13th St., Philadelphia, PA 19122, USA (☎215-204-0720; www.temple.edu/studyabroad) Rome branch offers both semester and summer programs in topics ranging from Art History to Business Administration and Management. Tuition plus housing (term time): $4123-$7300.

PROGRAMS IN ITALY

Universities in Rome are generally very crowded, but if you apply early, your chances of finding an open class or two are significantly increased. **The Ufficio Centrale Studenti Esteri in Italy (UCSEI),** Lungovetere dei Vallati 14, 00186 Rome (☎06 8804 062; fax 06 8804 063), a national organization for foreign students who have already started their course of study in Italy, can also provide assistance.

La Sapienza, one of the main universities in Rome. M:B-Policlinico. From the Metro station, walk up V. Regina Margherita/Elena past the hospital and Blockbuster to V. Università. For application info, write to the nearest Italian consulate (see p. 300). In Rome, contact the **Segretaria Stranieri,** Città Universitaria, P. Aldo Moro 5, 00185 Roma (switchboard ☎06 499 11; direct ☎06 499 127 07; www.uniroma1.it. Open M, W, and F 8:30am-1pm). Though the university does not offer any week- or month-long classes, the range of activities on campus is as good as any major university; theatrical, musical, and dance productions, debates, and sports—all in Italian, of course.

John Cabot University, V.d. Lungara, 233, 00165 Roma (☎06 681 91 21; fax 06 6832088). US office at 339 South Main St., Sebastopol, CA 95472 (☎707-824-9800; www.johncabot.edu; jcu@johncabot.edu.) This American international university in Trastevere offers undergraduate degrees in art history, business, English literature, and international affairs. Foreign students can enroll for summer, semester ($5500), and year-long ($10,600) sessions. Students are aided in finding internships in their fields of study. Like any college named after a confused British navigator who stumbled upon Canada, John Cabot has a number of conferences, lectures, and dramatic productions that are open to the public.

LANGUAGE SCHOOLS

Unlike American universities, language schools are frequently independently run international or local organizations or divisions of foreign universities that rarely offer college credit. Language schools are a good alternative to university study if you desire a deeper focus on the language or a slightly less-rigorous course load. These programs are also good for younger high school students that might not feel comfortable with older students in a university program. Some good programs include:

Italidea, Via dei Due Macelli, 47/I floor, 00187 Roma (☎06 699 413 14; www.italiaidea.com). Offers every level of Italian study from an intensive short-term course to more advanced, semester-long courses meeting once or twice per week. Intensive groups meet 3hr. per day for 4 weeks, at a total price of €465 and a €35 registration fee. The less intensive group meets 3hr. per day twice a week for 4 weeks, at the same price. Private lessons are also available at higher prices. Flexible scheduling. College credit courses offered through some US college and university programs in Italy. Homestays with Italian families are also available.

DILIT-ih, V. Marghera, 22, 00185 Roma (☎06 446 25 92 or 06 446 25 93; www.dilit.it). Near Termini. Resources include a language lab, video and listening center, a computer, and reading room. Intensive courses 15-30 hrs per week (min. 2 weeks), prices range from €455 to €808 (plus a €40 enrollment fee). Individual courses also available. Students of all levels of Italian are accommodated according to a placement exam. Private and home-stay lodgings available. Open summer daily 8:30am-8pm.

Eurocentres, 101 N. Union St. Suite 300, Alexandria, VA 22314, USA (☎703-684-1494; www.eurocentres.com) or in Europe, Head Office, Seestr. 247, CH-8038 Zurich, Switzerland (☎+41 1 485 50 40; fax 481 61 24). Language programs for beginning to advanced students with homestays in Rome.

Istituto Italiano Centro di Lingua e Cultura, V. Macchiavelli 33, 00185 Roma (☎06 704 521 38; www.istitutoitaliano.com). Near the Manzoni Metro stop on Linea A. Courses offered for students who want a slower pace or for those who seek an intensive setting. Bills on a per week schedule, with the average price decreasing with length of stay. Intensive programs are 30 lessons per week (€135-165). The less intensive entails 15hr. per week (€100-125). Groups size 3-12. 1 month of accommodations with a family (€96-128) or a student flat with a kitchen (€85-107) are available through the office. Open M-F 8:30am-7pm. AmEx/MC/V.

Language Immersion Institute, 75 South Manheim Blvd., SUNY-New Paltz, New Paltz, NY 12561-2499, USA (☎845-257-3500; www.newpaltz.edu/lii). 2-week summer language courses and some overseas courses in Italian. Program fees are around US$1000.

Torre di Babele, V. Bixio 74, 00185 Roma (☎06 700 84 34; www.torredibabele.com). Small groups of students (max. 12) enjoy personal attention from the instructor in non-intensive or intensive courses for an even number of weeks (min. 2 weeks). 2-week intensive program (4hr. per day) €325; 4-week intensive program (4hr. per day) €588. Additional weeks €147 apiece. Students can find lodging through the school. MC/V.

OPTIONS LESS ORDINARY

Professione Futura Culinary School, Via Aurelia, 1100/21, Roma 00166 (☎ 06 661 837 77; fax 06 669 00 69). This tasty option offers 3-month and 6-month courses on "High Italian Cooking" including the history of food and gastronomy. Also dishes up a yummy 3-month course on Pastry and Ice Creamery. Course tuition ranges from €18700-12920, including accommodations, an Italian language course, and 5 meals a week.

Intercultura, subsidiary of **AFS (American Field Service) Intercultural Programs,** Corso Vittorio Emanuele II 187, 00186 Roma (☎06 687 72 41; www.intercultura.it). Organizes long to short-term homestays and study abroad for high school students, ages 16-18 and community service volunteer programs with homestays for persons age 18 and over.

WORKING

Unfortunately, **unemployment** is high in central and southern Italy (approximately 9.5%) making job searches in Rome difficult and sometimes fruitless. Italian law requires employers to pay substantial sums of money for pensions and benefits even for short-term employees, making new hires very substantial investments.

In such a situation, firms are inclined to prefer naturalized Italian labor to your foreign sweat and blood. Work with Italian companies is almost impossible to find if you are not an EU citizen; your best bet is either a position in a foreign firm from an English-speaking country (preferably your own), or under-the-table jobs in the tourism sector. However, it's not easy in this sector, either. Over the past fifteen years, Italy has experienced a tremendous surge in immigration, chiefly from Northern Africa and Eastern Europe. Thus, competition can be fierce even for menial jobs.

Unofficially, there is the cash-based, untaxable **underground economy** *(economia sommersa* or *economia nera)*. Many permitless agricultural workers go untroubled by local authorities, who recognize the need for seasonal labor. Many foreigners go the agricultural route, though this is a less popular alternative. Rather, many expats find work (cash-based and official) with well-to-do families as nannies or English teachers. Again, your best resource for these jobs is community bulletin boards and magazines such as *Wanted in Rome*, or placement organizations such as those listed below.

The **ability to speak Italian** can be immensely useful both in being hired and developing networks of contacts. If you have the time and resources before heading off to Rome, acquiring at least a basic knowledge of conversational Italian could give you a distinct advantage. However, lack of Italian will not necessarily bar you from obtaining English speciality work (such as ESL and work in the tourist industry). For **US college students, recent graduates, and young adults,** the simplest way to get legal permission to work abroad is through **Council Exchanges Work Abroad Programs.** Council Exchanges can help you obtain a three- to six-month work permit/visa and also provides assistance finding jobs and housing. Fees US$300-425.

LONG-TERM WORK

So you yearn to tread in the footsteps of Goethe, Keats, Shelley, and Hemingway (not to mention scads of former *Let's Go* researchers). The good news is that Rome offers some of the best walks in the history of Western civilization. The bad news is that you need money, desperately. Not to fear, gentle, penniless reader. A little planning before you jump on that plane can save you months of wandering around Rome looking for gainful (or somewhat less than gainful) employment.

If you're planning on spending a substantial amount of time (more than three months) working in Rome, search for a job well in advance. Newcomers to Italy may be disgruntled to learn how important contacts are in finding a job. Even in Rome, who you know, from the friendly bar tender to a sympathetic pensione owner, could be the ticket to a part-time job via connections. Aside from who you know, Americans in particular should not be scandalized by the nonchalance of employers in inquiring about age, appearance, and nationality. Especially in sales, expect to see want-ads requesting an "attractive young woman, age 18-27, smartly dressed, with a warm personality." Employment laws change for job-seekers over 30, making it more difficult to find jobs at entry-level positions.

International placement agencies are often the easiest way to find employment abroad, especially for teaching English. **Internships,** usually for college students, are a good way to segue into working abroad, although they are often unpaid or poorly paid. Be wary of advertisements or companies that claim the ability to get you a job abroad for a fee—often times the same listings are available online or in newspapers, or even out of date. It's best, if going through an organization, to use one that's somewhat reputable. Some good ones include:

Wanted in Rome, V.d. Delfini, 17 00186 (☎06 679 01 90; www.wantedinrome.com). This bi-weekly magazine (€0.75) offers cultural information and a wealth of classified advertisements, all delivered in a very British tone. Annual subscription (21 issues) €30-40 overseas, €15-30 within Italy. Available at most newsstands, English-language bookstores, and from their main office. For the best selection, you might want to get an early copy at **The (Almost) Corner Bookshop** (V.d. Moro, 45, p. 240), or **Libreria Feltrinelli** (L. di Torre Argentina, 7).

Vacation Work Publications, 9 Park End St., Oxford OX1 1HJ, UK (☎01865 24 19 78; www.vacationwork.co.uk). Publishes variety of directories with job listings and info for the working traveler. Opportunities for summer or full-time work in numerous countries.

WORK VISAS. Officially, everyone except EU citizens must have a visa to work in Italy. Non-EU citizens seeking work must apply for an Italian **work permit** (Autorizzazione al lavoro in Italia) before entering the country. The employer must receive a work permit from the Provincial Employment Office where the foreigner will be working. The Employment Office, upon determining that there are no Italian workers willing or able to fill the position, may issue a permit (or they may not–this is, after all, Italy). The employer proceeds with the permit to the appropriate questura for the necessary approval. Finally, the employer must send the work permit to the prospective employee in his home country, where he presents the document along with a valid passport to the nearest embassy or consulate in order to obtain a work visa. Whew. For more information, see **Visas,** p. 301.

USEFUL JOB SEARCH ENGINES FOR ROME

CESOP Recruitment and Career Opportunities (www.cesop.it, in conjunction with www.recruititaly.it) In English and Italian, the site is divided into living, working and studying in Italy, with information on embassies, career fairs and workshops taking place in Rome.

Kata Web Lavoro (www.kwlavoro.kataweb.it). In Italian. A well organized site which allows you to search for employment by criteria including skills, sector, and geographic area. Also offers news, advice on interviews and an index which calculates the value of stipends.

Job Italy (www.jobitaly.it). In Italian. Registered members can post their CVs, search job listings, and read short articles on the job market.

Lavoro Oggi (www.lavorooggi.it) In Italian. Provides links on living in Italy and advice for foreigners on everything from health to auto insurance. See also (www.straneiritalia.com).

TEACHING ENGLISH

If tilling the soil in rural Lazio as a member of the *economia sommersa* begins to lose its charm, consider teaching English to foreigners. While it won't make you a millionaire, it will at least pay your *telefonino* bill. No more than minimal Italian is necessary to teach conversation, though many language institutes require a bachelor's degree and/or some sort of **Teaching English as a Foreign Language (TEFL)** certificate. Though a TEFL certificate is not always necessary (and does not guarantee employment), job seekers will find it increasingly difficult to get interviews without one. One place where you may want to consider obtaining your certificate is at the **International House Academia Britanica,** V. Manzoni, 22, one block from the Manzoni (A) Metro stop (☎06 704 768 94; www.ihromamz.it; Open M-F 9am-1pm and 3-7:30pm). Courses for a Cambridge/RSA CELTA certificate (equivalent to a TEFL) run from €767 to €1414. This helpful House also has a good bulletin board and advertises teaching jobs throughout Italy. On a related note, if your Italian skills are worth bragging about, the IH office on Via Marghera 22, Roma 00185, offers diplomas on **teaching Italian as a foriegn language**, (☎ 06 446 25 92), €995 per course. **Interlingue,** Via Ennio Quirino Visconti, 20 (☎06 321 5740; tefl.rome@interlingue-it.com) also offers TEFL certificate courses. An intensive course of over 120 hours per week for 4 weeks costs €950.

Currently private schools tend to offer the most openings, and are frequently the most profitable option. Native English speakers working in private schools are most often hired for English-immersion classrooms where no Italian is spoken. Those volunteering or teaching in public, poorer schools, are more likely to be working in both English and Italian. Placement agencies or university fellowship programs are the best resources for finding teaching jobs in Italy. The alternative is to make contacts directly with schools or just to try your luck once you get there. Listings in **Wanted in Rome,** the **Porta Portense** (www.porta-portese.it), or in Rome's daily newspaper, **Il Messagero,** will usually indicate which qualifications are necessary for each position. Some schools will simply post signs in stores, hair salons, or cafes. Most people poster around universities and on community bulletin boards. In almost all cases, you must have at least a bachelor's degree to be a full-fledged teacher, although college undergraduates can often get summer positions teaching or tutoring. The best time of the year to look for a job is several weeks before the start of the school year. Often, a good strategy is to call schools listed in the yellow pages under *Scuole di Lingua* and ask if they have any openings. Also try:

International Schools Services (ISS), 15 Roszel Rd., Box 5910, Princeton, NJ 08543-5910, USA (☎609-452-0990; www.iss.edu). Hires teachers for more than 200 overseas schools, including 2 in Rome; candidates should have experience teaching or with international affairs, 2-year commitment expected.

International Schools Services, Educational Staffing Program, P.O. Box 5910, Princeton, NJ 08543 (☎609-452-0990; www.iss.edu). Recruits teachers and administrators for American and English schools in Italy. All instruction in English. Applicants must have a bachelor's degree and two years of relevant experience. Nonrefundable US$100 application fee. Publishes *The ISS Directory of Overseas Schools* (US$35).

PROFESSIONAL TEACHING

You may be able to secure a teaching position with an American school in Italy through the **Office of Overseas Schools,** Room H328, SA-1, Dept. of State, Washington, DC 20522. (☎202-261-8200; www.state.gov.) **International Schools Services,** Educational Staffing Program, 15 Roszel Rd., P.O. Box 5910, Princeton, NJ 08543, can also assist in finding a teaching job. (☎609-452-0990; www.iss.edu.) Another short-term option, albeit horrifying, is to be a substitute teacher at one of the American or British schools; generally, you need a college degree, nerves of steel, and a *Codice Fiscale* (tax code).

AU PAIR WORK

Au pairs are typically women, aged 18-27, who work as live-in nannies, caring for children and doing light housework in foreign countries in exchange for room, board, and a small spending allowance or stipend. Most former au pairs speak favorably of their experience, and of how it allowed them to really get to know the country without the high expenses of traveling. Drawbacks, however, often include long hours of constantly being on-duty and the somewhat mediocre pay (generally €60-80 per week in Italy). Much of the au pair experience really does depend on the family you're placed with. If you go directly to an Italian agency, beware that you may be asked to pay a substantial registration fee. The agencies below are a good starting point for looking for employment as an au pair.

Accord Cultural Exchange, 750 La Playa, San Francisco, CA 94121, USA (☎415-386-6203; www.cognitext.com/accord).

Au Pair Homestay, World Learning, Inc., 1015 15th St. NW, Suite 750, Washington, DC 20005, USA (☎800-287-2477; fax 202-408-5397). Offers postings throughout Western Europe.

Au Pair in Italy, V. Demetrio Martinelli, 11d, 41033 Bologna (☎051 383 466; www.aupairitaly.com). No fee program places foreigners directly with Italian families.

Au Pair in Europe, P.O. Box 68056, Blakely Postal Outlet, Hamilton, Ontario, Canada L8M 3M7 (☎905-545-6305; www.princeent.com). Offers postings throughout Italy.

Childcare International, Ltd., Trafalgar House, Grenville Pl., London NW7 3SA (☎44 020 8906 3116; www.childint.co.uk).

Mix Culture Au Pair Agency, Via Baccina, 32/a, I-00184 Roma, (☎ 06 678 38 87; web.tiscalinet.it/mixculturroma) in English and Italian.

Rome Au Pair, V. Vicenzo Bellini, 10, 00198 Roma (☎06 853 545 49; www.romaaupair.com).

SHORT-TERM WORK

Traveling for long periods of time can get expensive; therefore, many travelers try their hand at odd jobs for a few weeks at a time to make some extra cash to carry them through another month or two of touring around. Although you will have to secure these jobs through unofficial channels, the questura rarely see fit to spend their time enforcing the laws regarding employment in Italy. Those looking into part-time work in the **food and beverage sector** may find that even the most "laid-back" employers will insist upon you having a **Tessere Santiaria** (hygiene certificate) even if workers are not handling food. The Tessere Sanitaria can be obtained at the Unitaria Sanitaria Locale. **The Roman tourism industry** is primarily targeted at the English-speaker, and with some persistence, you may be able to find a position there, albeit with little financial security. Many tourist offices look for tour guides over the summer. These jobs are usually not salaried; you work for a commission by convincing people to come to expensive tours given by the agency. Often, this entails giving free "teaser" tours all day in the hot sun at Roman ruins, working for tips, and begging your fellow countrymen to come to paid events and say that you sent them there. It's not for the faint of heart nor quiet of mouth, but it just might be enough to pay the bills. One possible agency to try would be **Walks of Rome,** Via Urbana 38 (☎06 484 853). Walks of Rome describes their guides as young, native English speakers, usually art or history students, "who know how to make the monuments come alive."

Another popular option is to work several hours a day at a **hostel** in exchange for free or discounted room and/or board. Most often, these short-term jobs are found by word of mouth, or simply by talking to the owner of a hostel or restaurant. Many places, especially due to the high turnover in the tourism industry, are always eager for help, even if only temporary.

Italy's three largest **temp job** search engines are **Adecco Lavoro Temporaneo** (www.adecco.it), **Ali Temporaneo** (www.alispa.it), and **Manpower.it** (www.manpower.it). For those who have advanced technical skills, which are in high demand, these temp jobs are likely to lead to permanent employment. Technical employers are also more likely to help with work permit paperwork than are employers in the service sector. All of these search engines are in Italian, and it is likely that a prospective employer will expect you to be fluent before you depart. Also keep your eyes open for jobs posted on **Notice boards.** Likely spots include the numerous offices of the **Centro Turistico Studentesco (CTS)** (www.cts.it) at Via Genova (☎ 06 462 0431). Open M-F 9:30am-1pm and 2:30-6:30pm, Sa 9:30am-1pm.

Working in **agriculture** may be a no-go operation even for most EU citizens. With the large influx of African and Central European immigrants there is no shortage of eager laborers willing to work for low wages. Jobs picking for grape and olive harvests, while plentiful, are often controlled among locals and unemployed Italians. However, outside Rome it is possible to be involved with the **Willing Workers on Organic Farms (WWOOF)** based in Liguria. Located at Via Casavecchia 109, Castagneto Carducci, 57022, LI, (☎05 6576 5742; www.wwoof.it) WWOOF facilitates placement on organic farms, beginning with a €25 membership fee.

FOR FURTHER READING ON ALTERNATIVES TO TOURISM

How to Get a Job in Europe, by Sanborn and Matherly. Surrey Books, 1999 ($US11).

How to Live Your Dream of Volunteering Overseas, by Collins, DeZerega, and Heckscher. Penguin Books, 2002 (US$17).

International Directory of Voluntary Work, by Whetter and Pybus. Peterson's Guides and Vacation Work, 2000 (US$16).

International Jobs, by Kocher and Segal. Perseus Books, 1999 (US$18).

Living, Studying, and Working in Italy: Everything You Need to Know to Live La Dolce Vita by Monica Larner and Travis Neighbor Ward. Owl Books; 2nd edition, 2003 (US$12).

Work Abroad: The Complete Guide to Finding a Job Overseas, by Hubbs, Griffith, and Nolting. Transitions Abroad Publishing, 2000 ($US16).

Work Your Way Around the World, by Susan Griffith. Worldview Publishing Services, 2001 (US$18).

TAXI

Service Directory

ACCOMMODATION AGENCIES

See also ***Tourist Services,*** p. 343.

Welcome Home Relocation Services, V. Barbarano Romano, 15 (☎06 303 669 36; welcome.home@flashnet.it). English spoken. Open M-F 9am-1pm and 4-7pm.

Property Center, V.d. Gesù è Maria, 25 (☎06 321 23 41; www.romeproperty.com). English spoken. Open M-F 9:30am-6pm. Call for an appointment.

At Home International, V. L. Bissolati, 20 (☎06 488 18 00; homeint@tin.it). English spoken. Open M-F 9am-7pm, Sa 9am-1pm. Call for an appointment.

Italian Youth Hostels Association (HI-IYHF), V. Cavour, 44 (☎06 487 11 52). English spoken. Open M-Th 8am-5pm, F 8am-3pm, Sa 8am-noon.

Associazione Cattolica Internazionale al Servizio della Giovane, V. Urbana, 158 (☎06 488 00 56). For youth ages 15-27. Open M-Sa 6:30am-10pm, Su 7am-10pm.

Bed and Go, V. S. Tommaso d'Aquino, 45 (☎06 397 509 07; www.bedandgo.com). Open M-F 9am-1pm and 2-6pm.

Bed & Breakfast Association of Rome, P. del Teatro Pompeo, 2 (www.b-b.rm.it).

AIRPORTS

Aeroporti di Roma, (flight info: ☎06 659 536 40 or 06 659 540 01; www.adr.it).

Ciampino Airport, (central and flight info: ☎06 794 941).

Fiumicino Airport, (central: ☎06 659 51); also known as Leonardo da Vinci International.

BANKS

Banca Popolare di Milano, Pl. Flaminio, 1 (☎06 322 902); V. Vittorio Veneto, 1 (☎06 481 43 48); P. Popolo (☎06 320 854).

Banca Nazionale del Lavoro, P. Venezia, 6 (☎06 678 09 78); V. Veneto, 119a (☎06 427 455 23); P. Risorgimento, 27 (☎06 397 381 60); V. Ostiense, 107 (☎06 574 16 98). Cirrus/PLUS.

Banca di Roma, V. Ravenna, 31 (☎06 442 529 90); P. Vitorrio Emanuele II, 136 (☎06 443 409 73). Also at V. Tiburtina, P. Barberini, V.d. Monti Tiburtini, V.d. Corso. Cirrus/PLUS.

Banca Credito Italiano, P. di Spagna, 20 (☎06 679 13 13); P. Navona, 46 (☎06 683 074 13); V. Cola di Rienzo, 168 (☎06 687 42 31).

Banca Commerciale Italiana, V. Corso, 226 (☎06 679 08 23); V. Veneto, 78 (☎06 420 135 95); V. Nazionale, 181 (☎06 488 20 40); P. di Spagna, 18 (☎06 679 11 41).

BIKE & MOPED RENTAL

AutoCity, in Rome, V. Colina, 22 and V. Bomarzo, 32; in Ostia, V. d. Baleari, 201. (☎06 332 219 08 or 06 420 202 07; www.auto-city.it). V. Colina branch open daily (always closed Su in winter), 9am-1pm and 3-7pm; other locations closed Su. Scooters €35-55 per day plus €0.25 for each km over 100km and taxes; discounts for longer rentals. AmEx/MC/V.

Happy Rent, V. Farini, 3 (☎06 481 81 85). Take a bus to V. Cavour. Scooters and motorcycles €50-120 per day. Open daily 9am-7pm. AmEx/MC/V.

Romarent, V.d. Bovari, 7a (☎06 689 65 55). Bikes €12 per day, €36 per week; motorbikes €65-75 per day. Open daily 9am-7pm. AmEx/MC.

Scooters for Rent, V.d. Purificazione, 84 (☎06 488 54 85), off P. Barberini. Bicycles €10 per day, €50 per week; mopeds €30/155 per week. Open daily 9am-7pm. AmEx/MC/V.

Collalti, V.d. Pellegrino, 82 (☎06 688 010 84). Bikes €7.80 for 12 hrs, €10.45 for 24 hrs. Tu-Sa 9am-1pm and 3:30pm-7:30pm, Su 9am-7pm. AmEx/MC/V.

BUSES

See ***Transportation,*** *p. 331.*

CAR RENTAL (AUTONOLEGGIO)

Avis, toll free: ☎199 100 133, at Fiumcino Airport ☎06 650 115 31; www.avis.com.

Maggiore, toll free car reservations ☎848 867 067; for vans 848 848 844, at Fiumicino 06 650 106 78; www.maggiore.it.

Hertz, toll free ☎199 112 211, at Fiumicino 06 650 115 53; www.hertz.com or www.hertz.it.

Europcar, toll free ☎800 418 418, at Fiumicino ☎06 650 108 79; www.europcar.it.

CLINICS

See also ***Hospitals*** *(p. 340) and* ***Emergency Services*** *(p. 339).*

Ospedale San Camillo in Monteverde, Circonvallazione Gianicolense, 87 (☎06 587 01), in Gianicolo. Pregnancy tests, STD tests, gynecological exams, and pap smears. Open for daily 8am-7pm; call for appointment.

Unione Sanitaria Internazionale, V. Machiavelli, 22 (☎06 704 535 44), M: A-Vittorio Emanuele. Open for info daily 7am-7pm; tests daily 7-11am.

Analisi Cliniche Luisa, V. Padova, 96a (☎06 442 914 06). M: B-P. Bologna. Pregnancy, STD, HIV tests (€10-50). Open M-F 7:30am-10:30pm, Sa 8am-10:30pm.

Studio Polispecialistico Nomentano, V. Nomentana, 550/552 (☎06 868 956 11). HIV tests €45. Open M-F 7am-7:30pm, Sa 7am-1pm.

Circolo di Cultura Omosessuale Mario Mieli. See p. 338.

COMMUNITY RESOURCES

See also ***Gay & Lesbian Resources,*** *p. 339.*

Welcome Home (☎06 303 669 36). Events and support groups for English speakers. Open M-F 9am-1pm and 4-7pm.

CONSULATES & EMBASSIES

Australia, V. Alessandria, 215 (☎06 852 721, emergency 800 877 790). Consular and passport services at C. Trieste, 25. Open M-F 8:30am-12:30pm and 1:30-5:30pm.

Canada, Consulate, V. Zara, 30 (☎06 445 981; fax 06 445 989 12, www.canada.it.). Office open M-F 8:30am-4:30pm. Consular and passport services open M-F 10am-noon and 2-4pm. **Embassy,** V.G.B. De Rossi, 27 (☎06 445 981).

Ireland, Consulate, P. Campitelli, 3 (☎06 697 91 21). Passport services open M-F 10am-12:30pm and 3-4:30pm.

New Zealand, V. Zara, 28 (☎06 441 71 71, emergency 335 203 760). Consular and passport services open M-F 9:30am-noon. Open M-F 8:30am-12:45pm and 1:45-5pm.

South Africa, V. Tanaro, 14 (☎06 852 541, emergencies: 333 989 68 87; www.sudafrica.it). Bus #86 from Termini to P. Buenos Aires. Open M-F 8:30am-4:30pm.

U.K., V. XX Settembre, 80/A (☎06 482 54 41; consulate 06 422 026 00, www.grbr.it), near the corner of V. Palestro. Consular and passport services open M-F 9:15am-1:30pm.

United States, V. Veneto, 119/A (☎06 46741). Passport and consular services open M-F 8:30-noon and 1:30-3:30pm. Visas M-F 8:30-10:30am; IRS M-F 9am-noon in person, 1:30-3:30pm by phone. Closed US and Italian holidays.

CRISIS LINES

Centro Anti-Violenza, V.d. Torrespaccata, 157 (☎06 232 690 49 or 06 232 690 53). For victims of sexual violence. Branch offices for legal and psychological consultation throughout the city. Available 24hr.

Telefono Rosa, V. Tor di Nona, 43 (☎06 637 518 261/62/82). For victims of sexual abuse or harassment. Open M-F 10am-1pm and 4-7pm.

Samaritans, V. San Giovanni in Laterano, 250 (☎06 704 544 44). English speakers. Anonymous or face-to-face counseling. Open for calls and visits (call ahead) daily 1-10pm.

Alcoholics Anonymous, V. XX Settembre, 7 (c/o St. Andrew's Church) or V. Napoli, 58 (c/o St. Paul's Within the Walls) (☎06 474 29 13).

Narcotics Anonymous, ☎06 860 47 88.

Arche-HIV+ Children and their Families, ☎06 688 053 77.

Overeaters Anonymous, ☎06 884 51 05.

Ryder Italia, ☎06 329 43 23. Support for cancer patients and their families.

CURRENCY SERVICES

*See also **Banks,** p. 338.*

American Express, P. di Spagna, 38 (☎06 676 41; lost or stolen cards/checks ☎06 722 82). Open Sept.-July M-F 9am-7:30pm, Sa 9am-3pm; Aug. M-F 9am-6pm, Sa 9am-12:30pm.

Thomas Cook, (toll free: ☎800 004 48. Barberini, 21a (☎ 06 420 201 50). Open M-Sa 9am-8pm, Su 9:30am-5pm. Also at V.d. Conciliazione, 23/25 (☎06 683 004 35/6; open M-Sa 8:30am-6pm, Su 9am-5pm); V.d. Corso, 23 (☎06 320 02 24 open M-Sa 9am-8pm, Su 9am-1:30pm).

Western Union, V.d. Babuino, 51 (toll free ☎800 220 055, 06 367 131; fax 06 320 81 52). Open M-F 8:30am-11pm, Sa-Su 8:30am-10:30pm.

EMBASSIES

*See **Consulates & Embassies,** p. 300.*

EMERGENCY SERVICES

*See also **Police** (p. 341) and **Hospitals** (p. 340).*

Carabinieri: ☎112.

Police/Fire/Ambulance: ☎113.

Medical Emergencies: ☎118.

Fire Service: ☎115.

Policlinico Umberto I, V.le di Policlinico, 155 (emergency ☎06 491 911, non emergency 06 499 71). M: B-Policlinico or #9 bus. Free first aid *(pronto soccorso).* Open 24hr.

Nuovo Regina Margherita, V. Trastevere, 72 (☎06 584 41). Walk-in first aid. Open 24hr.

ENTERTAINMENT

*See **Tickets,** p. 343.*

GAY & LESBIAN RESOURCES

Check out the end of *Roma C'e* for the latest gay and lesbian hot spots or pick up a free copy of AUT magazine at any gay/lesbian establishment.

Circolo Mario Mieli di Cultura Omosessuale, V. Corinto, 5 (☎06 541 39 85; www.mariomieli.it). M: B-San Paolo. Open M-F 9am-1pm and 2-6pm; closed Aug.

Libreria Babele (☎06 687 66 28), V.d. Banchi Vecchi, across the bridge from Castel Sant'Angelo. Rome's only gay and lesbian bookstore. *Gay and Lesbian Map of Rome* €6.20. Open M-Sa 10am-2pm and 3-7:30pm.

Libreria Queer, V.d. Boschetto, 25 (06 474 06 91; libreriaqueer@hotmail.com). Offers a wide selection of gay/lesbian/bisexual/transsexual videos and books, many in English.

Italian Gay and Lesbian Yellow Pages, (www.gay.it/guida/italia/info.htm).

Coordinamento Lesbico Italiano, V. S. Francesco di Sales, 1a (☎06 686 42 01).

GROCERS

*See **Supermarkets,** p. 342.*

HEALTH CLUBS

Big Gym, Stadio dei Marmi at the Foro Italico (☎06 320 86 66; www.biggym.it).€5, fitness classes €8, €1.55 discount with stamped bus ticket. Open Jun. 1-Aug. 5 daily 5pm-12:30am.

Roman Sport Center, V.d. Galoppatoio, 33 (☎06 320 16 67). M: A-Spagna. 1-day membership €25, yearly membership €1,137. Open M-Sa 9am-10pm and Su 9am-3pm.

Associazione Sportiva Augustea (A.S.A.), V. Luciani, 57 (☎06 232 351 12). M: A-Cinecittà. Open daily 9am-5:30pm.

Navona Health Center, V.d. Banchi Nuovi, 39 (☎06 689 61 04). €10 per day, €67 per month, €60 for students per month. Open M-Sa 9:30am-9:30pm; closed Aug.

HOSPITALS

*See also **Emergency Services** (p. 339) and **Clinics,** (p. 338).*

International Medical Center, V.G. Amendola, 7 (☎06 488 23 71; nights and Su 06 488 40 51). Call first. Prescriptions filled, paramedic crew on call, referral service to English-speaking doctors. General visit €68. Open M-Sa 8:30am-8pm. On-call 24hr.

Rome-American Hospital, V. E. Longoni, 69 (☎06 225 51 for 24hr. service or 06 225 52 90 for appointments; www.rah.it). Private emergency and laboratory services, HIV tests, and pregnancy tests. No emergency room. On-call 24hr.

Salvator Mundi International Hospital Vle. delle Mura Gianicolensi, 67 (☎06 588 961, www.smih.pcn.net).

Fatebenefratelli, P. Fatebenfratelli, 2, Isola Tiberina (☎06 683 72 99 or 06 683 73 24). Has emergency services.

HOTLINES

*See **Crisis Lines,** p. 339.*

INTERNET ACCESS

Trevi Tourist Service: Trevi Internet, V.d. Lucchesi, 31-32 (☎/fax 06 692 007 99). €2.50 per hr., €4 for 2hr. Open daily 9:30am-10pm.

Splashnet, V. Varese, 33 (☎06 493 820 73), 3 blocks north of Termini. Offers a match made in heaven: a laundromat with Internet access. Clothes get clean (€3 per load), you get 15 min. of Internet time free. Internet access €1 for 30min., or €1.50 for 1hr., ask about Let's Go discount. Open daily 9am-1am; in winter daily 9am-11pm.

Internet Café, V.d. Marrucini, 12 (☎/fax 06 4454953; www.Internetcafe.it). €4 per hour, €2.50 per half hr.; students €2.50 per hr. Open M-F 9am-2am, Sa-Su 5pm-2am.

Bolle Blu (p. 340). Laundromat with Internet access (€2 per hr.).

Freedom Traveller, V. Gaeta, 25 (☎06 478 238 62; www.freedom-traveller.it). North of P. del Cinquecento. Run by a youth hostel, Internet cafe with full bar and couchful common room. €2.60 per hr. with card; otherwise €4.13. Open daily 9am-midnight.

Internet Café, V. Cavour, 213 (☎06 478 230 51). €3.20 per hr. Open daily 9am-1am.

The Netgate Internet Point, P. Firenze, 25 (☎06 689 34 45). W and Sa free 8pm-8:30pm; otherwise per hr.

Metropolis, Borgo Vittorio, 75 (☎06 682 106 76; metropolis@romaguide.it). €3 per hr, €2 per hr with purchase of 10 hr. student card.

X-plore, V.d. Gracchi, 83-85 (☎06 507 974 74; www.xplore.it). €5.16 per hr. Open M-Th 10-1am, F-Sa 10-3am.

Internet Café, V. Cavour, 213 (☎06 478 236 82). Just south of the Cavour metro stop. There's nothing particularly exciting about this place, but it gets the job done and has video games if you're bored. €3 per hour. Or, time card ranges from €8 for 200min to €50 for 2000min. Open daily 9am-1am.

LAUNDROMATS

OndaBlu, V. La Mora, 7 (info ☎800 861 346). Other locations throughout Rome. Wash €3.20 per 6½kg load; dry €3.20 per 6½kg load; soap €0.75. Open daily 8am-10pm.

Bolle Blu, V. Palestro, 59/61 (☎06 446 58 04), and V. Milazzo, 20b. Wash and dry €6.20

for 6.5kg load. 15mins of free Internet while you do laundry. Open daily 8am-midnight.

Acqua & Sapone Lavanderia, V. Montebello, 66 (☎06 5488 32 09). Wash €3.20 per 6-8kg; dry €3.20 per 6-8kg. Open daily 8:30am-10pm.

LIBRARIES

Biblioteca Universitaria Alessandrina, P. Aldo Moro, 5 (☎06 447 40 21). La Sapienza's hard-to-use but open-to-all library. Open M-F 8:30am-7:45pm, Sa 8:30am-1:30pm.

Biblioteca Nazionale, V. Castro Pretorio, 105 (☎06 498 91 or 06 498 92 49). M-F 8:30am-7pm, Sa 8:30am-12:30pm. Closed mid-Aug.

Centro Studi Americani, V. M. Caetani, 32, 2nd fl. (☎06 688 016 13). Open M-Th 10am-7pm, F 10am-2pm. Closed part of Aug.

Santa Susanna Lending Library, V. XX Settembre, 15, 2nd fl. (☎06 482 75 10; www.santasusanna.org). Open Tu and Th 10am-1pm, W 3-6pm, F 1-4pm, Sa-Su 10am-12:30pm.

LOST PROPERTY

*See also **Police**, p. 341.*

Oggetti Smarriti, V. Nicolo Bettoni, 1 (☎06 581 60 40; items lost on trains 06 473 066 82). Open Tu and F 8:30am-1pm, M and W 8:30am-1pm and 2:30-6pm, Th 8:30am-6pm.

Termini, in the glass booth in the main entrance. Open daily 7am-11pm.

MARKETS

*See **Supermarkets**, p. 342. For outdoor markets, see (p. 235) or (p. 209).*

MOPED RENTAL

*See **Bike & Moped Rental**, p. 338.*

PHARMACIES

*Most **Hospitals** (p. 340) have pharmacies.*

Farmacia Internazionale, P. Barberini, 49 (☎06 482 54 56). Open 24hr. MC/V.

Farmacia Piram, V. Nazionale, 228 (☎06 488 07 54). Open 24hr. MC/V.

Farmacia Arenula, V. Arenula, 73 (☎06 688 032 78). Open M-F 24hr., weekends vary.

Farmacia Grieco, P. della Repubblica, 67 (☎06 488 04 10). Open 24hr.

Farmacia Di Stazione Notturna, P. del Cinquecento, 51 (☎06 488 00 19). Open 24hr.

Farmacia Cola di Rienzo, V. Cola di Rienzo, 23/25 (☎06 324 31 30). Open 24hr.

PHONE SERVICES

*See **Telehone Services**, p. 341.*

POLICE

Police: Foreigner's Office (Ufficio Stranieri), V. Genova, 2 (☎06 468 637 11 or 06 468 631 63). Open 24hr. daily.

Police Headquarters (Questura Centrale), V.d. San Vitale, 15 (☎06 468 61). Open 24hr.

Railway Police (☎06 473 069 59), track #1 and facing track #2 in Termini. Open 24hr.

POSTAL SERVICES

Information about all Italian postal services and post offices is available by phone: ☎160.

Main Post Office (Posta Centrale), P. San Silvestro, 19 (☎06 679 50 44 or 06 678 07 88; fax 06 678 66 18). Open M-F 9am-6:30pm, Sa 9am-2pm. Another main office is located at V.d. Terme di Diocleziano, 30 (☎06 481 82 98; fax 06 474 35 36), near Termini. Same hours as San Silvestro branch.

Vatican Post Office (☎06 698 834 06), 2 locations in P. San Pietro. No *Fermo Posta*. Open M-F 8:30am-7pm, Sa 1-6pm. Branch office 2nd fl. of Vatican Museum. Open museum hours.

FedEx, V. Barberini, 115-119 (☎800 123 800; www.fedex.com). Open M-F 8am-7pm. AmEx/MC/V.

UPS, V. della Magliana, 329. (☎800 877 877; www.ups.com). Open M-F 9am-1pm, 3-7:30pm. AmEx/MC/V.

RADIO TAXIS

*See **Taxis & Radio Taxis**, p. 342.*

RELIGIOUS SERVICES

All Saints Church (Anglican), V.d. Babuino, 153/b (☎06 360 018 81). All services in English. Communion M, W, F noon; Su 8:30am and 10:30am.

St. Andrew's Church (Presbyterian), V. XX Settembre, 7 (☎06 482 76 27). Services in English Su 11am. Another congregation holds Korean services in the same building daily 6am and Su 7am, 2 and 4pm.

Comunita Ebraica di Roma, Tempio Maggiore (Jewish), Lungotevere Cenci (☎06 684 00 61). Hebrew services M-F 7:30am and sunset, Sa 8:30am.

Confessionals (Catholic) are in St. Peter's (p. 115), Santa Maria Maggiore (p. 130), San Giovanni in Laterano (p. 136), San Paolo Fuori le Mura (p. 144), Il Gesù (p. 91), and Santa Maria sopra Minerva (p. 95). Languages spoken by priest noted on door.

La Moschea di Roma (Muslim), V.d. Moschea (☎06 808 22 58). Prayers in Arabic daily 3:22am, noon, 1:15, 5:13, 8:50, and 10:20pm. Services W and Su 9-11:30am.

Ponte Sant'Angelo Church (Methodist), P. Ponte Sant'Angelo (☎06 686 83 14). Su service 10:30am. Communion 1st Su each month.

Rome Baptist Church, P. di San Lorenzo in Lucrina, 35 (☎06 687 66 52). Su service 10am; Bible study 11am. Confession M-W 10am-1pm, F 6-8pm.

San Silvestro (Roman Catholic), P. San Silvestro, 1 (☎06 679 77 75). Mass in English Su 10am and 5:30pm.

Santa Susanna (Catholic), V. XX Settembre, 15 (☎06 420 145 54). Mass in English M-Sa 6pm, Su 9 and 10:30am.

San Paolo Fuori le Mura (Episcopalian), V. Napoli, 58 (☎06 488 33 39). English services Su 8:30 and 10:30am.

The Rome Buddhist Vihara, V. Mandas, 2 (☎06 224 600 91).

SPORTS FACILITIES

*See also **Health Clubs,** p. 340.*

Bowling Brunswick, Lungotevere dell'Acqua Acetosa, 10 (☎06 808 61 47). Cosmic bowling! €3.90 per game per person, shoes included, after 9pm €5.20. Open Su-Th 10am-2am, F-Sa 10am-4am.

Bowling Roma, V.R. Margherita, 181 (☎06 855 11 84). Shoes included. Open 9am-3pm €1; 3pm-9pm €2; 9pm-2am €3.50.

Centro Sportivo Italiano, Lungotevere Flaminio, 59 (☎06 323 47 32). Swimming pool. One-time membership fee €5; full day €8; Su and holidays €11; half-day €5. Open June-Sept. daily 10:45am-10:30pm.

Circolo della Stampa, P. Mancini (☎06 323 245 2). Tennis. €9.30 per court per hr. Lights €2.10. Open M-F 8am-11pm, Sa-Su 8am-8pm.

Federazione Italiana Yoga, V. Belisario, 7 (☎06 428 701 91).

Palaghiacco di Marino, V. Appia Nuova (☎06 930 94 80). Ice skating. 1½hr. skating sessions. Rentals of skates and pads €5, on weekends €6.50. Rentals M-F 5, 9, and 11pm; Sa-Su 3, 5, 7, 9, and 11pm; Su also 11am. Open late-Aug. to June.

Piscina delle Rose, V. America, 20 (☎06 592 67 17). Full-day swim in the outdoor pool €10, half-day €8. Open June-Sept. daily 9am-7pm.

SC Ostiense, V.d. Mare, 128 (☎06 591 55 40). Tennis. €8.50 per singles match per hr., €12.50 per doubles match per hr. Open daily 9am-6:30pm; closed Aug.

SUPERMARKETS

STANDA (☎800 358 758). V. Cola di Rienzo, 173 (in Prati, near the Vatican, in the basement of COIN), V.d. Trastevere, 60 (in the basement of Oviesse ☎06 581 14 67), V. Caffaro, 57 (☎06 512 65 18).

Despar, V. Giustiniani, 18b (☎06 683 331 66). Off the P. della Rotonda, between the Pantheon and P. Navona. A real bargain, especially given its location. Open daily 9am-10pm.

SMA (☎800 824 038) P. dei Re di Roma, 15-18 (☎06 772 078 01), P. Pio XI, 20 (☎06 393 665 73), P. Bologna, 60 (☎ 06 442 913 89) and other locations. All open 8am-8pm.

Alimentari Coreani (Korean Grocery Store), V. Cavour, 84. Near P. di Santa Maria Maggiore. Open M-Sa 9am-1pm and 4-8pm.

Billo, V. S. Ambrogio, 7, off V. Portico, in the Jewish Ghetto. Kosher.

Castroni, V. Cola di Rienzo, 196-198 (☎06 687 43 83). Coffee bar and phenomenal foreign foods market. Other locations include V. Ottaviano, 55 (☎06 397 232 79), and V.d. Quattro Fontane, 38 (☎06 448 24 35).

TAXIS & RADIO TAXIS

Radiotaxi: ☎06 3570.

Radiotevere: ☎06 4157.

Prontotaxi: ☎06 6645.

La Capitale Radio Taxi: ☎06 4994.

Taxi 8822: ☎06 885 216 73 (for advance booking).

TELEPHONE SERVICES

See **When in Rome,** p. 27.

TICKETS

Teatro Argentina Box Office, Largo di Torre Argentina, 52 (☎06 688 046 01 or 06 687 54 45). Tickets for all goings-on in Rome. Open M-F 10am-2pm and 3-7pm, Sa 10am-2pm.

Interclub, P. Ippolito Nievo, 3 (☎06 588 05 64), in Trastevere. Covers just about everything.

Orbis, P. Esquilino, 37 (☎06 482 74 03). Rock/pop and sporting events. Open M-Sa 9:30am-1pm and 4-7:30pm.

RicordiMedia, Box Office (☎06 320 37 90). Open 10am-1:30pm and 2:30-7pm. 2 store locations: V.d. Corso, 506 (☎06 361 23 70), and V.G. Cesare, 88 (☎06 373 515 89). Rock/Pop concerts. Both open daily 9:30am-8pm.

Auditorio Pio Box Office, V.d. Conciliazione, 4 (☎06 320 27 90). Classical music. Open Th-Tu 11am-7pm and until showtime on concert days.

Villa Giulia/Santa Cecilia ticket office, P. della Villa Giulia, 9 (☎06 361 10 64, credit card reservations ☎06 688 010 44). Summer classical music. Open M-F 10am-5pm and until showtime on performance days Closed Aug. 10-20.

TOURIST SERVICES

*For a list of tourist offices in Rome, see **When in Rome,** p. 25.*

Call Center Comune di Roma (☎06 06 06). Open 24hr. in Italian; available in English, French, Spanish, German, Chinese and Arabic, M-Sa 4-7pm. All manner of city information.

Italian Youth Hostels Association (HI-IYHF), p. 337.

TOURS

Enjoy Rome: Walking Tours of Rome, V. Marghera 8A (☎06 445 18 43; www.enjoyrome.com). Five three-hour English tours (maximum 25 people; all tours, except the Catacombs tour, €20; Catacombs and Appian Way tour €35. ISIC card discount €6 off. 6 fantastic tours including a nighttime tour of Ancient Rome and **bike tour** from Villa Borghese to the Circus Maximus (€25, with ISIC card €20, bike and helmets provided). Day-long Pompeii bus trips, Apr.-Oct. €55, under 26 €45. Other bus tours offered. Tickets sold at Enjoy Rome (p. 25), Pensione Fawlty Towers (p. 248), Colors (p. 247), and Pensione Sandy (p. 254).

Appian Line, P. dell'Esquilino, 6 (☎06 487 866 01; fax 06 474 22 14; www.appianline.it). To the left facing Santa Maria Maggiore. 11 different bus tours of the city including Papal Blessing (Su, €30.50) and various daytrips (€47-100). Free pick-up from hotel. English, French, Spanish, and German spoken. Open daily 6:30am-8pm. AmEx/MC/V.

American Express, P. di Spagna, 38 (☎06 676 424 13; fax 06 679 49 53). All expenses paid 4hr. bus and walking tours of Vatican City, Ancient City, and Tivoli daily except Su and winter holidays 9:30am and 2:30pm (€47-60, 20% discount for under 8). Daytrips to Florence, Pompeii, Capri, Assisi, and Sorrento (€70-120). English spoken. Open M-F 9am-5:30pm, Sa 9am-2:30pm. AmEx.

Associazione Culturale dell'Italia, V. Trionfale, 148 (☎06 397 281 86). Guided tours of the city in English, French, Spanish, and German. €6.20 per person, 15-20 people €77.50 for 2hr. of whatever sights you want to see. Closed Aug.

ATAC 110 City Tour, (☎06 469 522 56). City transit authority. 2hr. bus tour along bus #110 line, leaving from Termini (€7.75). Sightseeing Tour (2½hr.; daily departure 10:30am, 2, 3, 5, 6pm) and Basilicas Tour (3hr.; daily departure 10am and 2:30pm). Buy tickets at info booth inside train station. English spoken. Reservations possible.

TRANSPORTATION

*See also **Airports** (p. 337), **Bike & Moped Rental** (p. 338), **Car Rental** (p. 338), **Taxis & Radio Taxis** (p. 342).*

Aziende Tramvie Autobus Communali (ATAC), ☎800 555 666. Open daily 8am-8pm.

CO.TRA.L: ☎06 591 55 51.

Ferrovie dello Stato (FS), ☎1 478 880 88; www.fs-on-line.com.

VESPA RENTAL

See Bike & Moped Rental, p. 338

INDEX

SYMBOLS

'Gusto 206

NUMERICS

360° 216
6 Nations Cup 229

A

A'Scalinatella 291
Abbazia delle Tre Fontane 145
Abbey Theatre 213
Academia Nazionale di Santa Cecilia 224
Accademia di Francia 107
accommodation agencies 337
Accommodations 243–257
adapters
  see converters.
Aeneas 176
Africa 197
Al 39 197
airplane travel
  courier 313
  fares 311
  standby 314
airports
  Ciampino 16
  Fiumicino 15
  luggage storage 16
Al Presidente 193
Alaric 45
Albergo della Lunetta 245
Alberic the Younger 46
Albero del Pane 208
Alcazar 224
Alcoholics Anonymous 339
Alexander Mosaic 294
Alexanderplatz Jazz Club 227
Alien 218
alimentari 208
Amalfi 290
The Amalfi Coast 289
Amato, Giuliano 51
American Express 308
  tours 343
  traveler's checks 307
Amnesty International 327
Anacapri 286
Ancient City 4
  food 188
  sights 69
Antica Caciara Trasteverina 208
Antico Caffè Greco 202
Antilia 215
Antiquarium Forense 76
Antiquarium, Palatine 81
apartments 25, 256
Apicius 207
Appian Way 138
APT (Rome Tourist Authority) 15, 26
Aquarela 219
aqueducts
  Acqua Vergine 108
Ara Pacis 113
Arancia Blu 197
Arancio d'Oro 192
arch
  of the Argentarii 87
  of Augustus 74
  of Banchi 99
  of Constantine 77
  of Janus 87
  of Septimius Severus 71
  of Titus 76, 56
archaeology
  studies 328
  volunteering 328
Archeobus 139
architecture glossary 146
Arco Naturale 287
Teatro Argentina 222
Ariccia 273
Armani 232
art and architecture
  glossary 146
  history 55
art exhibitions 181, 219
Art Glossary 182
Teatro dell'Arte Studio 223
Artu Cafe' 214
Associazione Cattolica Internazionale al Servizio della Giovane 256, 337
ATAC 18
ATM cards 308
Atrani 290
Attila the Hun 45
au pair work 334
Augusto 196
Augustus 44, 69, 113
Aurelian 45
Australia consulates and embassies 300
Australian consulates 300
Australian embassies
  Italy 300
Aventine Hill 137

B

Babington's Tea Rooms 201
Babylonian Captivity 47
banks
  Banca di Roma 16
  directory 338
Bar Da Benito 206
Bar della Pace 217
Bar Guilia 201
Bar San Calisto 201
Barberini
  bees 174
  Cardinal Antonio 109
  palazzo 110, 174
  piazza 109
  Pope Urban VIII 93
Bar del Fico 217
Baroque 58
bars 211–218
Bartaruga 213
basilicas 57
  Aemilia 70
  Santi Apostoli 91
  Argentaria 83
  Santa Cecilia in Trastevere 125
  Julia 74
  San Lorenzo Fuori le Mura 133
  Santa Maria Maggiore 130
  of Maxentius and Constantine 75
  San Paulo Fuori le Mura 144
  St. Peter's 115
  San Marco 91
  di San Sebastiano 140
  Ulpia 84
bathroom, best in Rome 213
baths

of Caracalla 85
of Diocletian 128
of Flavian 81
Bay of Naples 285
beaches
Atrani 291
Citara 288
gay 317
Maronti 288
Paestum 296
bees, Barberini 174
Ben Hur 82
Berlusconi, Silvio 51
Bernini, Gian Lorenzo 58, 106, 112
Apollo and Daphne 166
Baldacchino 118
Beata Lodovica Albertoni 124
Bee Fountain 109
bust of St. Peter 140
Fontana dei Quattro Fiumi 97
Fontana delle Tartarughe 105
Palazzo Montecitorio 92
Pulcin della Minerva 95
Palazzo del Quirinale 126
Rape of Proserpina 166
Santa Maria dell'Azzunzione 273
Santa Maria della Vittoria 127
Santa Maria di Montesanto 112
tomb 131
bicycles 25
Big Mama 227
Big Splurge 217, 270
bikes 25
rental 338
Black Out 218
Blackshirts 50
The Blue Grotto 287
boat rentals 277, 279
Bocca della Verità 87
bookstores 240
gay/lesbian 317
Borghese, Paolina
statue of 166
Borghese, Villa
secret gardens 114
Borgia Apartments 157
Borgo, Prati, & Vatican City 5
food 194
museums 150
sights 115
Borromini, Francesco 59
Church of San Carlino 127
clock tower 99
Botanical Gardens 126
Bramante, Donato 47, 111
cloisters 98
Tempietto 125
bridges
Cestio 124
Fabricio 124
Four Heads 124
Michelangelo's 103
Palatino 124
Rotto 124
Il Brillo Parlante 193
I Buoni Amici 188
buses 18
ATAC 18
CO.TRA.L 20
night routes 19
routes 19

C

Cacio e Pepe 194
Caelian Hill 134
Caesar, Julius 44, 69, 100
Cafe Peru 201
caffè 201
calcio 228
Caligula 44
calling cards 28
camping 256
Campo dei Fiori 99
food 190
market 209
Mercato di Campo dei Fiori 209
Campo Verano 133
Canada consulates and embassies 300
Canaletto 168
Cantina Il Pergolato (Frascati) 271
Il Capellaio Matto 198
Capitoline Hill 84–85
Capitoline Museums 168
Capri 286
Capri's Cliffs 287
Capri's Coast 286
Capuchin crypt 110
car rentals 25
at airport 16
directory 338
carabinieri. See police.
Caracalla 45, 85
Caravaggio 174
The Calling of St. Matthew 95
Conversion of St. Paul 111
Crucifixion of St. Matthew 95
Crucifixion of St. Peter 111
Deposition from the Cross 165
Madonna of the Pilgrims 96
Rest during the Flight in Egypt 177
Self Portrait as Bacchus 167
St. Jerome 167
St. John the Baptist 170
St. Matthew and the Angel 95
cars 21
Ristorante a Casa di Alfredo 196
Casa di Dante 124
Casa Valadier 114
Casamicciola Terme 289
Casbah'r 291
Case Romane 135
Castelli Romani 270
castles
Aragonese 288
Castelli Romani 270
Gandolfo 272
Orsini-Odescalchi 279
Castor and Pollux 84
Castroni 208
cat shelter 103
catacombs
along Appian Way 139
San Callisto 140
Santa Domitilla 141
Naples 284
Santa Priscilla 114
Sant'Agnese Fuori le Mura 129
San Sebastiano 140
use of by Christians 54
Cato the Censor 42
Cave Canem 196
CDs, see shopping, music
cemeteries
Campo Verano 133
Jewish 133
Protestant 143
Sicily-Rome American 263
Centers for Disease Control (CDC) 304
Centro Macrobiotico Italiano-Naturist Club 194
Centro Storico 4, 89–105
clubs 218
food 190
pubs 212
sights 89
Cerveteri 277
La Cestia 198
chapels
Abbazia delle Tre Fontane 145

Bufalini 85
Santa Caterina 134
Cerasi 111
Chigi 98, 111
Cornaro 127
Della Rovere 111
of Urban VIII 157
Saint Zeno 132
Charlemagne 46
Charles V 85
Charro Cafe 219
Chic and Kitsch 219
Chiesa Nuova 99
children and travel 319
Chirico, Giorgio di 60
Christian Democratic Party 50
Christina, Queen of Sweden 152, 168, 175
churches 65
Sant'Agnese in Agone 97
Sant'Andrea delle Fratte 106
Sant'Andrea al Quirinale 127
Sant'Andrea della Valle 103
Sant'Angelo in Pescheria 104
Santi Apostoli 91
San Bartolomeo 124
Santa Bibiana 132
Santa Brigida 101
San Carlino 127
San Carlo alle Quattro Fontane 59, 127
Santa Cecilia in Trastevere 125
Chiesa Nuova 99
San Clemente 134
of Consolation 87
Santi Cosma e Damiano 83, 75
Counter Reformation style 91
San Crisogno 124
Santa Croce in Gerusalemme 131
Santa Francesca Romana 76
of San Francesco a Ripa 124
Il Gesù 91
Chiesa del Gesù 271
San Giorgio in Velabro 87
San Giovanni in Laterano 2, 136
Santi Giovanni e Paolo 135
San Giovanni dei Fiorentini 103
San Giuseppe dei Falegnami 70
Sant'Ivo 95
L'Immacolata Conezione 109
San Lorenzo in Damaso 100
San Lorenzo in Miranda 75
Santi Luca e Martina 70
San Luigi dei Francesi 95
San Marcello al Corso 92
Santa Maria degli Angeli 128
Santa Maria dell'Anima 98
Santa Maria in Aracoeli 85
Santa Maria in Cosmedin 87
Santa Maria Maggiore 130
Santa Maria Sopra Minerva 95
Santa Maria della Pace 98
Santa Maria della Vittori 127
Santa Maria Antiqua 74
Santa Maria in Campitelli 104
of Santa Maria dei Miracoli 112
Santa Maria di Montesanto 112
Santa Maria in Palmis 141
Santa Maria del Popolo 111
Santa Maria in Trastevere 125
San Nicola in Carcere 88
San Pantaleo 101
Pantheon (Santa Maria ad Martyres) 93
San Paulo Fuori le Mura 144
St. Peter's 115
San Pietro in Carcere 85
San Pietro in Vincoli 133
San Pietro in Montorio 125
of Santa Pudenziana 132
Santil Quattro Coronati 135
Santa Sabina 138
Chiesa di San Salvatore de Bireto 291
Sant'Agostino 96
Sant'Andrea al Quirinale 59
Sant'Ignazio di Loyola 92
Santa Maria ad Martyres 93
San Stefano Rotondo 136
Santa Susanna 128
San Tommaso di Villanova 272
Santa Trinita' dei Monti 106
Santi Vincenzo and Anastasio 109
See also basilicas
churchs
San Sebastiano 140
Ciampino. See airports.
Cicero 69
cinema 223
Circus Maximus 82
Cirrus 309
citadel of Tusculum 271
Citara 288
Civic Center 70
Classico Village 219
Claudius 44
climate 2, 299
clinics 338
Cloaca Maxima 74
clothing 231
clothing size conversions 232
clubs 218–219
CO.TRA.L 20
coffee. See *caffè*
collect calls 28
Collegio di Propaganda Fide 106
Colors 247
Teatro Colosseo 222
The Colosseum 76
columns
of the Immaculata 106
Ionic (ruins) 88
of Marcus Aurelius 92
of Phocas 71
of Trajan 84
Coming Out Pub 219
Commodus 45
Comunità Israelitica di Roma 341
Concordat of Worms 47
Constantine 45
Constantinople 56
consulates
see Australia consulates and embassies
see Canada consulates and embassies
see Irish consulates
see New Zealand consulates and embassies
see South African consulates
see UK consulates and embassies
see US consulates and embassies
converters and adapters 306
Cooperative Latte Cisternino 209
La Cordonata 85
Cornetto Free Music Festival Roma Live 227
counterculture 219
courier flights 313
Coyote 219
Creation of Adam 161
crêche museum 181
credit cards 308
crib of Jesus 131
Crisca Nimagiu 212
Crusade, first 54
Cul de Sac 206
culinary schools 331
Curia di Bacco 207
currency 307

D

Da Benito e Gilberto 195
Da Quinto 199
Dagnino 200
Dalhu' Pub 217
dance 228
dance clubs 218
Dar Poeta 196
David
  Bernini's 59
David, Jacques-Louis 59
Daytripping 259–297
department stores 234
Deposition from the Cross 107
desserts 198
Diesel 233
dietary concerns 320
Diocletian 45
  baths 128
disabled travelers 318
discos 218
Discover Rome 1–90
Dolce & Gabbana 232
La Dolce Vita (Fellini) 109
Domine quo vadis? 141
Domitian
  Imperial Complex 80
domus
  Augustana 80
  Aurea 81
  Flavia 80
Domus Aurea 86
driving 21
driving permits 21, 315
Drogheria Innocenzi 209
Drome 217
Druid's Rock 215
The Drunken Ship 212
Le Due Orfanelle 279

E

Edict of Milan 45
Elefantino 95
email 30
embassies
  see Australia consulates and embassies
  see Canada consulates and embassies
  see Irish consulates and embassies
  see New Zealand consulates and embassies
  see South Africa consulates and embassies
  see UK consulates and embassies
  see US consulates and embassies
emergency medical services 305
Emperors
  Justinian 45
emperors
  Hadrian 93
ENIT 304
Enjoy Rome 25
  tours 343
Enoteca Buccone 207
Enoteca Cavour 313 206
Enoteca Reggio 207
Enoteca Trastevere 214
Enotecantica 207
enoteche (wine shops) 206
Entertainment 221–229
Esquiline Hill 129
Estate Romana 225
Etruria 277
Etruscan museum 170
Etruscans 42, 277
EUR 145
  sights 145
exchange rates
  Italy 307
exhibitions 181

F

Fabius Maximus 42
families
  Barberini 174
  Caetni 142
  Cosmati 136
  Farnese 101
  Frangipane 76
  Odescalchi 279
  Orsini 279
Faro 287
Fatebenefratelli Hospital 123
female travelers 316
Ferrazza 216
festivals. See holidays and festivals
Fiesta 228
Film, about Rome 7
films
  recommended viewing 8
Fiumicino 15
FM radio 27
Fonclea 227
Fontana 289
Fontana, Domenico 126
Fontana, Lavinia
  Cleopatra 175
Food and Wine
  caffè 201
  dessert 198
  menu reader 187
  restaurant types 186
  restaurants by location 188
  restaurants by price 189
  the Italian meal 186
  wine 202
  wine bars & enoteche 206
footprints of Christ 140, 141
Il Fornaio 200
forums
  of Augustus 83
  Foro Boario 87
  of Caesar 83
  Foro Italico 60
  Fori Imperiali 82
  of Nerva 83
  of Peace 75
  Roman 69
  of Trajan 84
  Transitorium 83
  of Vespasian 83
fountains
  Acqua Felice 127
  delle Api (of the Bees) 109
  della Baraccia 106
  of the Four Rivers 97
  del Mascherone 103
  del Moro 97
  Moses 113
  Neptune 97
  di Sant'Andrea 290
  Tortoise 105
  Trevi 107
  Triton 109
Four XXXX Pub 218
Franchi 194, 208
Franco e Cristina Pizzeria 192
Frascati 270
Fratelli Fabbi 208
Freddo Giovanni Fassi 200
fresco 55
Friend's 215
frozen yogurt 200
furnishings 238
furniture 238

G

Galleria Nazionale d'Arte Moderna 170
gardens
  Garden for the Blind 126
  Botanical Gardens 126
  Degli Aranci 137
  Roseto Comunale 137
Garibaldi, Giuseppe 49
gay and lesbian travelers

gay beach 317
gay beach 317
gay travelers 317
Gay Village nel Testaccion Village 227
gelaterie 198
gelato flavors 198
Il Gesù 91
Teatro Ghione 223, 225
Giadini Degli Aranci 137
Gianicolo 125
Il Giardini di Adone 218
Giolitti 199
Giulio Cesare 224
Gladiator 8, 76
glossaries
architecture 146
art 182
menu 187
GO25 card 303
Goethe, Heinrich von 179
Golden Gala 229
GRA
death wish 20
Grande Raccordo Anulare (GRA) 21
granita 199
Great Western Schism 47
Greenwich 224
Groove 218
Il Guernico 176
Guido 195
Guiscard, Robert 47
gynecology 338

H

Hadrian 44
temples
of Hadrian 92
Hannibal 42
heads of Saints Peter and Paul 136
health 304
women 305
help lines 339
Herculaneum 295
heresy, a field guide 48
hills
Aventine 137
Caelian 134
Capitoline 84–85
Esquiline 129
Janiculum 125
Oppian 133
Quirinal 126
Hippodrome 80
history 41–52
art and architecture 55–60
of Roman cuisine 43
hitchhiking 25
holidays and festivals
antique fair 3
art festival on V. Margutta 3
Capodanno 3
Carnevale 3
Christmas 3
complete chart 3
Festival d' Autunno 222
Estate Romana 225
Festa dell'Immacolata Connezione 3
Good Friday 2
Festa della Madonna della Neve 2
medieval crafts fair 3
more music festivals 227
New Opera Festival di Roma 226
Noantri 2, 123
La Festa di Primavera 2
Festival Roma-Europe 222
Rome's birthday 2
rose show 2
Festa di Sant'Antonio 3
Festa dei Santi Pietro e Paolo 2
Spoleto Festival 226
Vinitaly 202
Holy Roman Emperor
Charlemagne 46
Charles V 85
Otto I 46
home furnishings 238
horse show 229
hospitals 340
Hostaria da Bruno 197
Hostaria da Nerone 189
hot springs
Casamicciola 289
Lacco Ameno 288
Sorgeto 288
Hotel Carmel 246
Hotel Il Castello 253
Hotel Cervia 250
Hotel Des Artistes 249
Hotel Dolomiti 249
Hotel Florida 247
Hotel Galli 249
Hotel Giu' Giu' 254
Hotel Kennedy 253
Hotel Lachea 249
Hotel Lady 247
Hotel Lazzari 251
Hotel Lindomare 291
Hotel Orlanda 254
Hotel Pensione Joli 248
Hotel Pensione Suisse 246
Hotel San Paolo 254
Hotel Selene 254
Hotel Sweet Home 253
Hotel Trastevere 246
hotels
Borgo, Prati, Vatican City 247
Centro Storico 245
near Piazza di Spagna 246
north of Termini 248
south of Termini (Esquilino) 253
Trastevere 246
west of Termini 253

I

identification 303
IDP 21
Il Giardino Romano 191
immunizations 304
innoculations 304
Inquisition 48
L'Insalata Ricca 191
Insider's City, The
Naples, Un Paradiso di Pizza 281
insurance 305
International Driving Permit (IDP) 315
International Student Identity Card (ISIC) 303
International Teacher Identity Card (ITIC) 303
International Youth Discount Travel Card 303
Internet cafes 30, 340
Irish consulates and embassies 300
Ischia 288
ISIC card 303
Isola Tiberina 123
Italian Cultural Institute 304
Italian Government Tourist Board (ENIT) 304
Italian Open Tennis Championship 229
ITIC card 303
itineraries 9

J

jazz 226
Jesuits 91
Jesus' crib 131
jewelry 238
Jewish Cemetery 133
Jewish Ghetto
food 191
sights 104

jobs 331
John Cabot University 330
Jonathan's Angels 213
Julius Caesar 69, 100, 215
Jungle 219

K

Keats, John 143, 178
Keats-Shelley Memorial House 178
Ketumbar 217
Korean grocery store 342

L

L'Alibi 219
L'Oasi della Pizza 191
La Reppublica 26
Lacco Ameno 288
Lacus Juturnae 74
Laghetto Artificiale 146
Lake Bracciano 279
lakes
 Albano 272
 Artificiale 146
 Bracciano 279
 Nemi 272, 273
Lancelot 216
language schools 330
Laocoön 153
Lapis Niger 71
Largo Argentina 103
Last Judgement 158, 161
Last Judgment 58
Lateran Treaty 115
laundromats 340
Lawrence, D.H. 279
learning Italian 31
Legend Pub 216
lesbian travelers 317
libraries
 directory 341
 English 240
Life & Times 41–60
Literature
 about Rome 6
Lo Spuntino 195
Loggia di Pische 173
lost passports 301
lost property 341
Lucretia 42
Ludovisi Throne 173
luggage storage 16
Luigi, Trattoria da 191
Luna Piena 198
LunEUR 146
Luther, Martin 47
Luzzi 189

M

Maderno, Carlo 126, 128
mail
 papal mail 30
 See also post office 29
Mamertine Prison 70, 85
maps
 Let's Go map guide 17
marble steps 136
March on Rome 50
Marcus Aurelius 44
Il Margutta 193
markets 235
 Campo dei Fiori 100
 indoor 208
 Mercati Generali(Ostiense) 144
 non-produce 235
 outdoor 132, 209
 produce 209
 of Trajan 83
Maronti 288
MasterCard 308
Mausoleo delle Fosse Ardeatine 141
mausoleum
 of Cecilia Metella 142
 Constanza 129
 of Augustus 112
 Ossario Garibaldino 126
 delle Fosse Ardeatine 141
Mazzini, Carlo 49
media
 brochures and pamphlets 26
 magazines 26
 newspapers 26
 radio 27
 television 27
Medic Alert 305
medical assistance 305
menu reader 187
Il Messaggero 26
Metropolitana 20
Michelangelo 58
 Christ the Redeemer 95
 Creation of Adam 161
 footbridge
 La Cordonata 85
 Last Judgement 158, 161
 Santa Maria degli Angeli 128
 Moses 133
 Palazzo Farnese 101
 St. Peter's Basilica 116
 Pietà 117
 Porta Pia 129
 Sistine Chapel 163
minority travelers 319
Mithraism 53
monastery
 Trappist 145
money 307
Monte Solaro 287
Monte Testaccio 143
mopeds 25, 338
Moro, Aldo 50
Morrison's 214
mosaics 55
mosque 342
Mount Epomeo 289
Mount Gay Music Bar 218
Mt. Vesuvius 296
movies 223
Muro Torto 114
Museums 149–182
museums
 tessere (passes) 150
 dell'Alto Medioevo 176
 archaeological museum (Ventotene) 277
 Arms and Instruments of Torture 288
 Barracco 101
 Canonica 114
 Capitoline 168
 della Casina della Civette 129
 della Casina delle Civette 179
 del Casino dei Principi 129
 Centrale del Vittoriano 182
 Centrale Termoelettrica Montemartin 177
 delle Cere 178
 Civico (Albano) 272
 della Civilità Romana 176
 Comunale Birreria Peroni 179
 del Corso 182
 Ethiopian Museum (Frascati) 271
 EUR Museums 176
 Galleria Colonna 177
 Galleria Comunale d'Arte Moderna e Contemporanea di Roma 179
 Galleria Nazionale d'Arte Moderna 170
 Goethe 179
 Internazionale del Cinema e dello Spettacolo 179
 Jewish Community Museum 179
 Mario Praz 178
 delle Mura 141
 Mura Porta San Sebastiano 181
 Nazionale d'Arte Antica 174
 Nazionale delle Arti e

Tradizioni Popolari 176
Nazionale di Caerite (Cerveteri) 278
Nazionale d'Arte Orientale 177
Nazionale delle Arti e Tradizioni Popolari 176
Nazionale di Palazzo Venezia 91, 182
Nazionale Etrusco di Villa Giulia 170
Nazionale delle Paste Alimentari 181
Nazionale(Tarquinia) 278
Nazionali Romani 174
Piccolo Museo delle Anime del Purgatorio 181
Preistorico ed Etnografico Luigi Pigorini 177
di Risorgimento 179
Sacrario delle Bandiere 179
Sala del Bramante 182
dello Sbarco Alleato (Nettuno) 262
of Ships (Nemi) 273
Spada 175
Teatrale del Burcardo 179
Tipologio Nazionale del Presepio 181
Vatican 150–165
della Via Ostiense 143
Villa Farnesina 173
of Zoology 179
music 239
classical and opera 224
jazz 226
live 224
rock and pop 227
summer events 225
Musicain 225
Mussolini
Alessandra 50
Benito 49, 182

N

The Nag's Head 214
Naples 280–285
Napoleon 48
Teatro Nazionale 223
necropolis
Forum 75
Ventotene 277
neighborhoods 4
Nemi 273
Neoclassicism 59
Nero 44, 81, 86
Netgate 340
Nettuno 262
New Zealand consulates and embassies 300
NGOs 328
Nicene Creed 54
Night and Day 213
Nightlife 211–219
Nuovo Regina Margherita 339
Nuovo Sacher 223

L'Oasi della Pizza 191
obelisks
Egyptian at P.d. Rotonda 93
of Pharaoh Ramses II 112
in Piazza della Minerva 95
at Santa Trinità dei Monti 107
Octavian 44
Odoacer the Goth 45
Of Bread and Circuses 43
Oggetti Rinvenuti 341
Old Bridge, The 199
older travelers 317
Teatro Olimpico 225
Ombre Rosse Caffè 214
opera 60, 224
Teatro dell'Opera di Roma 225
Oppian Hill 133
Oratorio dei Filippini 99
Orbis Agency 229
Orti Farnesiani 79
Orto Botanico 126
Osteria dei Belli 196
Ostiense
sights 144
Our Lady of Mercy 284
Ouszeri 196

P

Caffè della Pace 201
Paestum 296
Palatine 77–81
palazzi
dei Conservatori 169
di Banco di Santo Spirito 99
Barberini 110, 174
della Borsa 92
Cenci 104
Chigi 92
Civilization of Labor 145
dei Congresso 145
dei Conservatori 85, 168
della Consulta 127
Corsini 175
del Freddo Giovanni Fassi 200
della Cancelleria 100
Doria Pamphilj 91
Farnese 101
Massimo 171
Massimo "Alle Colonne" 101
Montecitorio 92
Nuovo 85, 168
Piccola Farnesina 101
Poli 107
del Quirinale 126
Ruspoli 182
dei Senatori 85
Spada 102, 175
dello Sport 145
Venezia 89, 182
Wedekind 92
dei Senatori 71
Palladium 74
Palmarola 276
panificio 208
La Pantera Rosa 198
Pantheon 93
papal mail 30
Parco della Musica 225
parks
Parco Adriano 146
Campo Verano 146
Jewish Cemetery 133
LunEUR 146
Pincio 113
Villa Borghese 113
Villa Torlonia 129
Il Pasquino 223
passports 300
pasta museum 181
pasta, types of 192
Pasticceria Ebraica Boccione 200
Pavarotti, Luciano 61
Pax Romana 44
pay phones 28
Pensione Cortorillo 253
Pensione Fawlty Towers 248
Pensione Jonella 247
Pensione Katty 250
Pensione Panda 246
Pensione Papa Germano 248
Pensione Piave 251
Pensione di Rienzo 253
Pensione Tizi 251
La Pergola (Cavalieri Hilton) 194
phalli
Priapus's member 294
phones 27
calling cards 28
collect calls 28
pay phones 28
piazza
Piazza Vittorio Emanuele II

132
- Piazza di Spagna & the Corso 4, 105–109
  - food 192
  - sights 105
- Mercato di Piazza Mazzini 209
- Mercato di Piazza San Cosimato 209
- Mercato di Piazza Vittorio Emanuele II 209
- *piazze*
  - Augusto Imperatore 112
  - Barberini 109
  - del Campidoglio 84
  - di Campitelli 104
  - Campo dei Fiori 99
  - dei Cavalieri di Malta 138
  - Colonna 92
  - *del Collegio Romano* 91
  - Dell'Orologio 99
  - *della Minerva* 95
  - Giuseppe Garibaldi 126
  - Sant'Ignazio 91
  - *San Luigi dei Francesi* 95
  - Marconi 145
  - Mattei 105
  - di Montecitorio 92
  - Pasquino 99
  - San Pietro in Montrorio 125
  - Popolo 111
  - *Quirinale* 126
  - della Rotonda 93
  - Sant'Agostino 96
  - Sidney Sonnino 124
  - Spagna 105
  - Venezia 89
  - San Bernardo 127
  - di Pietra 92
- *piazzi*
  - Farnese 101
- Al Piccolo Arancio 193
- Il Piccolo 207
- pickpockets 311
- *Pietà* 117
- Pigmalione 217
- Pincio 113
- Pinturicchio 85, 111
  - *Adoration* 111
  - *Coronation of the Virgin* 111
- Piper 218
- PIT 26
- Pizza e Festa 192
- Pizza Rè 193
- Pizzeria Baffetto 190
- Pizzeria Corallo 190
- Pizzeria La Maschere 198
- Pizzeria San Calisto 195
- plague 47
- **Planning Your Trip** 299–321
- PLUS 309
- Plutei of Trajan 70
- police 341
- Policlinico Umberto I 339
- La Pollarola 191
- Pompeii 292
- Pompey the Great 44
- *ponte*, see bridges
- Pontifex Maximus 74, 170
- Pontine Islands 274–277
- Ponza 275
- Pope
  - hearts and lungs 109
  - love for executions 111
  - Alexander VI 95, 101, 157, 279
  - Alexander VII 112, 121
  - Benedict XIV 59
  - Boniface IV 93
  - Boniface VIII 47
  - Caius 128
  - Calixtus 125
  - Clement 134
  - Clement III 47
  - Clement VII 48
  - Formosus 46
  - Gregory IV 91
  - Gregory the Great 45
  - Gregory XI 47
  - Hildebrand 46
  - Innocent III 47
  - Innocent X 97, 102, 177
  - Joan 46
  - John XII 46
  - Julius II 47, 58, 102, 121, 152, 213
  - Julius III 170
  - Leo I 45, 156
  - Leo III 46
  - Leo IV 157
  - Leo X 48, 103, 111, 157, 174
  - Liberius 130
  - Mark 91
  - Martin V 47
  - Pascal I 125
  - Pascal II 111
  - Paul III 48, 85, 101, 121
  - Paul IV 104
  - Paul V 131
  - Paul VI 158
  - Pius I 132
  - Pius IV 128
  - Pius IX 49, 106, 155
  - Pius V 155, 162
  - Pius VI 48
  - Pius VII 76
  - Sixtus IV 168
  - Sixtus V 92, 127
  - Stephen II 45
  - Stephen VI 46
  - Urban I 125
  - Urban IV 156
  - Urban VIII 97, 110, 118, 174
- *Porta*
  - Magica 132
  - San Paolo 143
  - Pia 129
  - Sancta 117
  - San Sebastiano 141
- *Porta Portense*(publication) 333
- Il Portico 191
- Portico d'Ottavia 89
- post office
  - at airport 16
  - main branch 29
  - Vatican City 341
  - Vatican Museum 30
- poverty in Rome 327
- Prada 233
- Praz, Mario 178
- pregnancy testing 338
- Premio Roma 137
- prisons
  - Mamertine 70, 85
  - Santo Stefano 277
- Protestant Cemetery 143
- Protestant Reformation 47, 55
- Protestants 47
- The Proud Lion Pub 214
- Pub Hallo'Ween 216
- public transportation. See transportation.
- Borgo, Prati, & Vatican City 214
- pubs 211–218
- *Pulcin della Minerva* 95
- Il Pulcino Ballerino 197
- Punic Wars 42
- Pyramid of Gaius Cesius 142

- Questura 341
- Quirinal Hill 126

- Radio Londra Caffè 219
- radio taxis 20
- rape 341
- Raphael 58, 174
  - Chigi Chapel 111
  - *Coronation of the Virgin* 164
  - home 102
  - *Madonna of Foligno* 164
  - *Prophet Isaiah* 96, 96
  - School of Athens 156
  - *Stanza della Segnatura*

156
The Sybils 98
Transfiguration 164
Triumph of Galatea 173
real estate agencies 256
recommended viewing 8
Regia 74
religion 52
Catholicism 53
Mithraism 53
see also gods 52
religious services 341
rental bikes 25
rental cars 25
reporting crime 341
Republic, modern Roman 49
restaurants
Ancient City 188
Borgo 194
Centro Storico 190
cover charges 186
Jewish Ghetto 191
Piazza di Spagna 192
Piazza Navona 190
Prati 194
Termini & San Lorenzo 196
Testaccio 198
Trastevere 195
Vatican City 194
vegetarian 193, 198
Retail Export Scheme 309
revolving exhibitions 181
di Rienzo, Cola 85
Mercato Rionfale 209
Mercato Rionfale di Monte 209
Risorgimento 49
Ristorante Acqua Pazza 270
Ristorante Arnaldo ai Satiri 191
Ristorante de Costanza 101
Ristorante al Fontanone 196
Ristorante San Pancrazio 101
Rivegauche2 217
robbery 311
Rocca di Papa 273
Rock Castle Café 213
Roma C'è 26
Roma Incontra il Mondo 228
Roman gods 52
a field guide 53
Roman Holiday 87
Rome-American Hospital 340
Romulus and Remus 41
Romulus Augustulus 45
rose show 2
Roseto Comunale 137
Rostra 69, 70
rowboat rentals 114
Rubens, Peter Paul 99, 175
ruins
Paestum 296
Pompeii 294

S

Sack of Rome 48
Sacrario delle Bandiere 179
Sacred Trees of Rome 71
safety 309
Saint
Agnes 97, 129
Augustine 54
Bernard 145
Cecilia 125
Cyril 135
heads of Peter and Paul 136
Ignatius Loyola 91
Jerome 54
Paul 54, 144, 145
Peter 54
Sebastian 140
Teresa of Avila 127
St. Peter's Basilica 115
Sala del Bramante 182
Sala delle Prospettive 173
Sala of Galatea 173
salumeria 208
Salvi, Nicola 59, 107
Samaritans 339
San Crispino 199
San Giovanni 136
San Lorenzo. See Termini & San Lorenzo 5
San Marco 195
San Silverio 274
Il Caffè Sant'Eustachio 201
La Sapienza University 330
Saracens 46
La Scala 215
Scala Santa 136
Scalforo, Oscar Luigi 51
Scalinata di Spagna 105
scams 311
School of Athens 156
seasonal events 2
security 309
Seneca 86
Septimius Severus 87
Service Directory 337–343
sewers 74
sexual abuse 341
Shanti (pub) 217
shoes 231
Shopping 231–240
shopping 231
clothing and shoes 231
glossary 241
home furnishings 238
jewelry 238
markets 235
music 239
Sicily-Rome American Cemetery 263
Sights 65–146
sights
Ancient City 69–89
Centro Storico 89–105
Southern Rome 134–146
Termini and San Lorenzo 126–129
Trastevere 122–126
Vatican City 115–122
Il Simposio 215
Il Simposio di Piero Costantini 207
Teatro Sistina 223
Sistine Chapel 58, 158
contested legacy 163
restoration efforts 163
Sloppy Sam's 212
soccer 228
Social Wars 42
Il Sodoma 174
solo travelers 316
Sorgeto 288
Sorrento 289
South Africa consulates and embassies 300
South African embassies
Italy 300
Southern Rome 5
food 198
Spanish Steps 105
Spartacus 42
speaking Italian 31
special concerns
dietary concerns 320
specific concerns
bisexual, gay, and lesbian travelers 317
children and travel 319
disabled travelers 318
minority travelers 319
solo travel 316
women travelers 316
Sperlonga 260
sports 228
Italian International Tennis Tournament 2
STA Travel 311
Stadio Olimpico 228
STANDA 208
standby flights 314
Stardust 227
statistics 2
statue
di Rienzo, Cola 85
statues
Apollo and Daphne 166
Apollo Belvedere 153

Belvedere Torso 153
of Castor and Pollux 84, 126
Colossus of Constantine 169
Laocoön 153
Marcus Aurelius 85, 168
Pietà 117
of St. Peter 117
Santa Cecilia 125
subway 20
suggested itineraries 9
Sulla 42
superlatives
oldest ampitheater, Pompeii 295
supermarkets 208
synagogues
Ashkenazita 104
Comunita Israelitica di Roma 341
Ostia Antica 267

T

Tabularium 71
Tacitus 6, 53, 81
Tangentopoli 51
Tarquinia 278
Tarquinius Superbus (Tarquin) 42, 74
tartufo 199
Taverna Angelica 195
Taverna dei Quaranta 188
Taverna del Campo 212
La Taverna del Ghetto "Kosher" 192
Taverna Lucifero 190
taxes 309
taxis 20, 342
Tazza d'Oro 201
teaching English 333
Teatro dell'Opera 228
telephones 27
services 343
temperature 2, 299
Tempietto of Bramante 125
temples
Aesculapius 114
of Antoninus and Faustina 75
of Apollo (Pompeii) 294
of Apollo Sosianus 89
of Castor and Pollux 74
Circular (Hercules Victor) 87
of Concord 71
of Deified Julius 74
of Jupiter (Pompeii) 294
of Mars Ultor 83
Portunus (Fortuna Virilis) 87
of Romulus 75
of Saturn 71
of Venus and Rome 81
of Venus Genetrix 83
of Vespasian (Pompeii) 294
of Vespatian 71
of Vesta (Foro Boario) 87
Vesta (Roman Forum) 74
Termini
police 341
Termini & San Lorenzo 5
clubs 218
food 196
pubs 215
sights 126
terrorist bombs 136
tesserae 56
Testaccio
clubs 219
sights 142
Mercato Testaccio 209
theater & cinema 221
Theater of Marcellus 88
Theater of Pompey 100
theft 311, 341
Theodora 46, 57, 132, 274
Thirty Years' War 48
Thomas Cook 308
currency exchange 339

throwing corpses in the Tiber 123
Tiberius 44
Time Out 26
time zones 28
Titus 44
Tivoli 267–270
tombs
Bernini 131
King Vittorio Emanuele II 93
Pope Adrian VI 98
pope's failed 58
Raphael 93
Romulus 142
Saint Ignatius Loyola 91
Unknown Soldier 89
Torre degli Anguillara 124
Touring Club Italiano 256
tourist offices 25, 343
trains
Fiumicino to Rome 16
Trajan 44, 83
trams
routes 19
transportation 343
buses 18
metro 20
planes 311
taxis 20
trains 314
Trastevere 5
food 195
pubs 214
sights 122–126
Trattoria "da Dante" 195
Trattoria da Bucatino 198
Trattoria da Giggetto 191
Trattoria dal Cav. Gino 190
Trattoria Gino e Pietro 190
Trattoria Da Luigi 191
Trattoria da Sergio 190
travel agencies 311
traveler's checks 307
Tre Scalini 199
Trevi Fountain 107
Trimani 208
Trimani Wine Bar 206
Trinity College 213
Mercato Trionfale 209
trompe l'oeil 55
Trovaroma 26
true cross 131
Il Tulipano Nero 196
Il Tunnel 197
Tusculum 271
Twelve Tables 70

U

Ufficio Centrale Beni Culturali 150
Ufficio Stranieri (Foreigner's Office) 341
UK consulates and embassies 300
UKIYO Japanese Restaurant 193
Umbilicus Urbis 69
Unam Sanctam 47
underground economy 30
universities
branches in Italy 329
Italian 330
student housing 255
US consulates and embassies 300
US embassies
Italy 300
US State Department 31

V

vaccinations 304
Teatro Valle 223
valuables, protecting 311
Vatican City 115–122
baldacchino 118
Museums 150–165
post offices 341
St. Peter's Basilica 115

Sistine Chapel 158
St. Peter's dome 118
Treasury of St. Peter's 119
Vatican II 55
Vatican Museums 150–165
Apollo Belvedere 153
Belvedere Courtyard 152
Borgia Apartments 157
Chiramonti 152
Egyptian 152
Etruscan 154
Gallery of Statues 153
Laocoön 153
minor museums 165
Pietà 117
Pinacoteca 164
Pio-Clementine 152
Raphael Rooms 155
Room of the Immaculate Conception 155
School of Athens 156
Sistine Chapel 158
Stanza della Segnatura 156
vegan monks 107
vegetarian 198
vegetarian restaurants
Centro Macrobiotico Italiano-Naturist Club 194
Il Margutta 193
vegetarians 320
Velabrum 86
Velando 195
Veltroni, Walter 52
Ventotene 277
Versace 232
Vespa bandits 311
Vespas 25
Vestal Virgins 69
house of the 74
Vesuvius 296
Via
Appia Antica 138
Giulia 102
del Governo Vecchio 98
Nomentana 129
Vittorio Veneto 110
XX Settembre 127
Mercato di Via del Lavatore 209
Mercato di Via Milazzo 209
Victoria House 213
Villa Borghese 4, 113–114
Villa Jovis 287
Villa San Michele 287
villas
Ada 113
Aldobrandini (Frascati) 271
Borghese 113
Celimontana 135
d'Este (Tivoli) 269
Farnesina 173, 174
Giulia 114
Giulia (Ventotene) 277
Hadrian's (Tivoli) 268
L. Licinius Lucullus 114
Ludovisi 110
of Maxentius 142
Medici 107
Torlonia 129
Tuscolana 271
La Vineria 207
Vini e Buffet 192
Vinitaly 202
violence 341
Visa 308
visas 301
Visigoths 45
Vitruvius 56
Vittorio Emanuele II
the man 49
the monument 89
Volpetti Piu 198
volunteering 326
vomitorium 185

W

Wanted in Rome 26
Warner Village Moderno 223
water taxis 275
wax museum 178
weather 2, 299
Western Union 31
When in Rome 15–39
wildlife preserve 277
wine 202
wine shops, see *enoteche*
wine tasting 203
wiring money 31
women travelers 305, 316
minority women 319
wong. See robbie.
work 331
work permits 306
WWII monuments 263, 141

X-plore 340

Yogufruit 200
YWCA 256

Z

Zampano' 190
Zannone 277
zoo
Museum of Zoology 179
Villa Borghese 113, 114

Maps

inside

rome: map overview 356
centro storico & trastevere 358
termini & san lorenzo 360
spanish steps & the corso 363
vatican city 364
villa borghese 365
southern rome 366
piazza barberini 367
the appian way 368

MAP LEGEND

ABBREVIATIONS

Abbreviation	Meaning
C.	Corso
L.	Lungotevere
Pta.	Porta
Pte.	Ponte
Pza.	Piazza
Pzle.	Piazzale
V.	Via
Vic.	Vicolo
Vle.	Viale

SYMBOLS

Embassy
Hospital
Police
Post Office
Tourist Office
Service
Site or Point of Interest
Airport
Bus Station
Metro Station
Parking
Train Station
Church
Synagogue
Museum
Hotel/Hostel
Camping
Food & Drink
Entertainment
Nightlife
Shopping
Theater
Library
Gate or Entrance
Mountain
Railroad Tracks
Stairs

The Let's Go compass always points NORTH

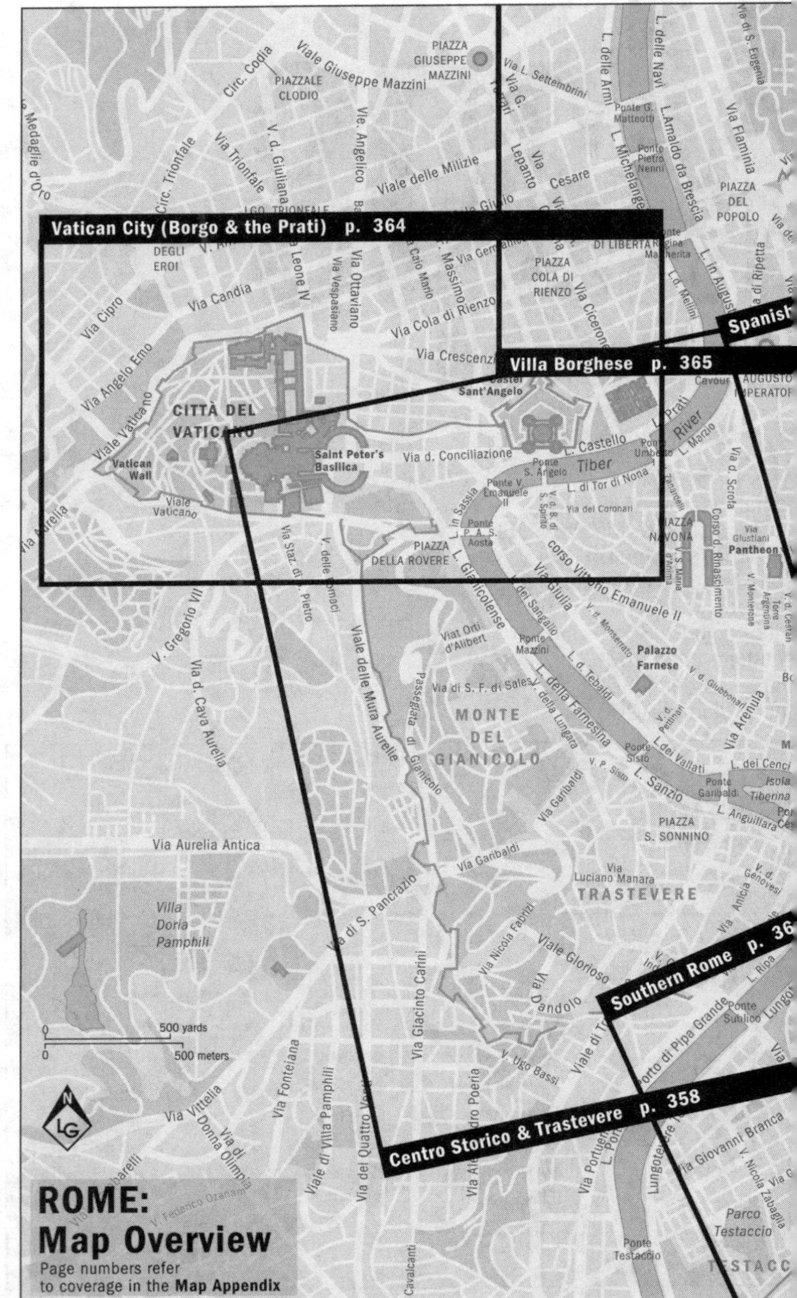

ROME:
Map Overview
Page numbers refer to coverage in the Map Appendix
Vatican City (Borgo & the Prati) p. 364
Villa Borghese p. 365
Centro Storico & Trastevere p. 358
Southern Rome p. 36
Spanish
CITTÀ DEL VATICANO
Saint Peter's Basilica
Castel Sant'Angelo
Tiber River
MONTE DEL GIANICOLO
TRASTEVERE
Villa Doria Pamphili
PIAZZA GIUSEPPE MAZZINI
PIAZZALE CLODIO
PIAZZA DEL POPOLO
PIAZZA COLA DI RIENZO
PIAZZA NAVONA
PIAZZA DELLA ROVERE
PIAZZA S. SONNINO
Palazzo Farnese
Pantheon
Parco Testaccio
Isola Tiberina
Vatican Wall
500 yards
500 meters

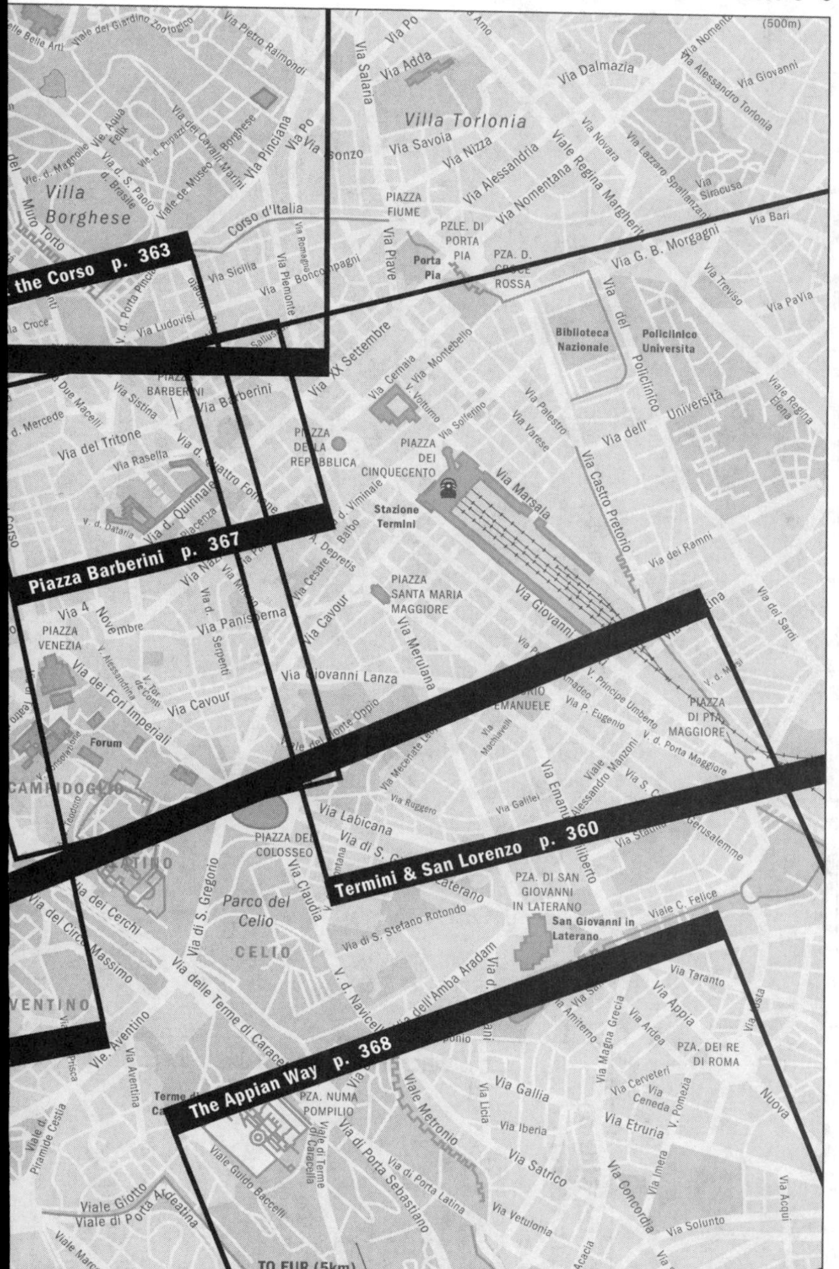

the Corso p. 363
Piazza Barberini p. 367
Termini & San Lorenzo p. 360
The Appian Way p. 368
Villa Borghese
Villa Torlonia
Stazione Termini
Biblioteca Nazionale
Policlinico Università
PIAZZA DELLA REPUBBLICA
PIAZZA DEI CINQUECENTO
PIAZZA SANTA MARIA MAGGIORE
PIAZZA VENEZIA
Forum
PIAZZA DEL COLOSSEO
Parco del Celio
CELIO
PZA. DI SAN GIOVANNI IN LATERANO
San Giovanni in Laterano
PIAZZA DI PTA. MAGGIORE
PZA. NUMA POMPILIO
PZA. DEI RE DI ROMA
PIAZZA FIUME
PZLE. DI PORTA PIA
Porta Pia
PZA. D. CROCE ROSSA
TO EUR (5km)
(500m)
Via Salaria
Via Po
Via Dalmazia
Via Nomentana
Corso d'Italia
Via XX Settembre
Via Nazionale
Via Cavour
Via Merulana
Via Giovanni Lanza
Via dei Fori Imperiali
Via del Tritone
Via Marsala
Via Castro Pretorio
Via Labicana
Via Appia Nuova
Viale Metronio
Via di Porta Sebastiano
Via delle Terme di Caracalla
Viale Aventino

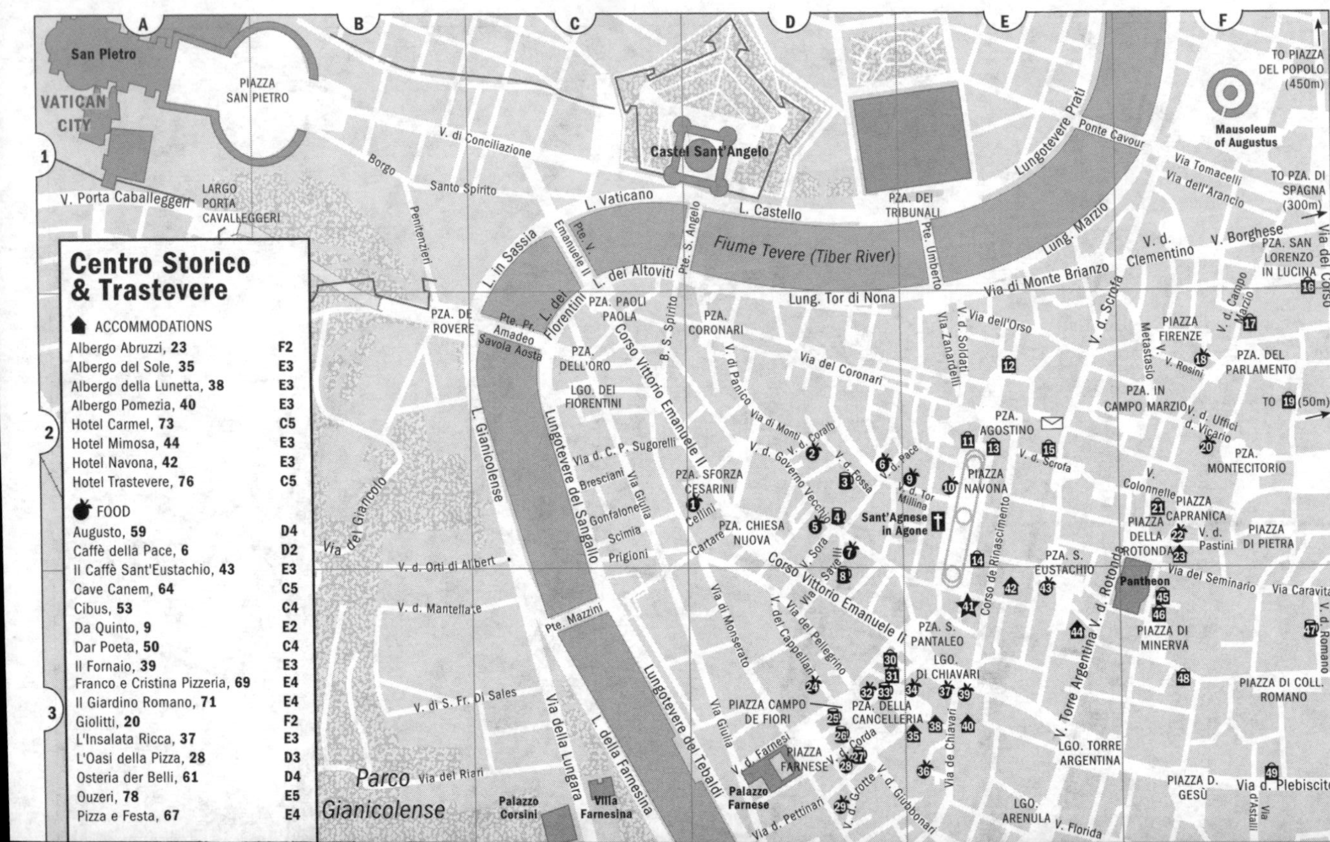
Centro Storico & Trastevere
ACCOMMODATIONS
Albergo Abruzzi, 23 F2
Albergo del Sole, 35 E3
Albergo della Lunetta, 38 E3
Albergo Pomezia, 40 E3
Hotel Carmel, 73 C5
Hotel Mimosa, 44 E3
Hotel Navona, 42 E3
Hotel Trastevere, 76 C5
FOOD
Augusto, 59 D4
Caffè della Pace, 6 D2
Il Caffè Sant'Eustachio, 43 E3
Cave Canem, 64 C5
Cibus, 53 C4
Da Quinto, 9 E2
Dar Poeta, 50 C4
Il Fornaio, 39 E3
Franco e Cristina Pizzeria, 69 E4
Il Giardino Romano, 71 E4
Giolitti, 20 F2
L'Insalata Ricca, 37 E3
L'Oasi della Pizza, 28 D3
Osteria der Belli, 61 D4
Ouzeri, 78 E5
Pizza e Festa, 67 E4
San Pietro
VATICAN CITY
PIAZZA SAN PIETRO
Castel Sant'Angelo
Fiume Tevere (Tiber River)
Mausoleum of Augustus
TO PIAZZA DEL POPOLO (450m)
TO PZA. DI SPAGNA (300m)
Pantheon
PIAZZA NAVONA
Sant'Agnese in Agone
PIAZZA CAMPO DE FIORI
PIAZZA FARNESE
Palazzo Farnese
Villa Farnesina
Palazzo Corsini
Parco Gianicolense

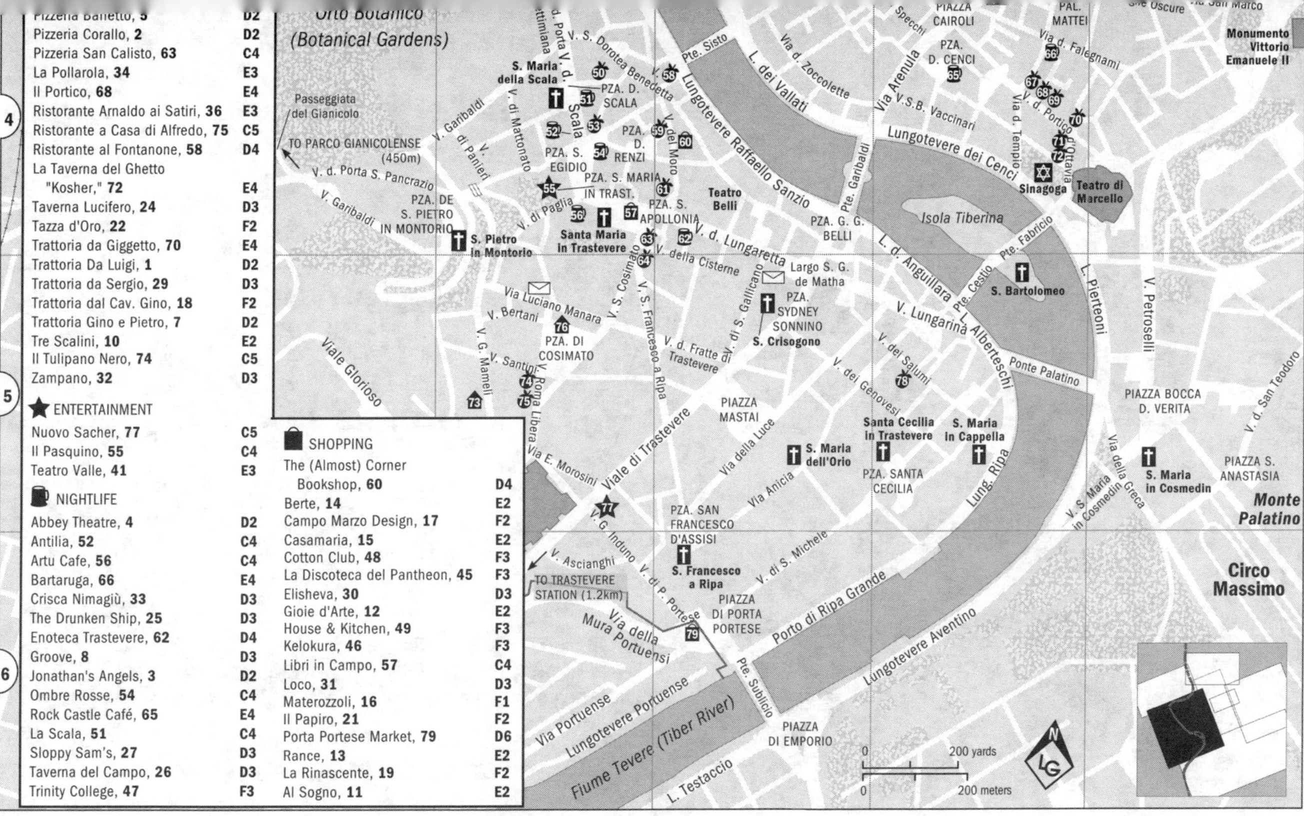

Pizzeria Corallo, 2 D2
Pizzeria San Calisto, 63 C4
La Pollarola, 34 E3
Il Portico, 68 E4
Ristorante Arnaldo ai Satiri, 36 E3
Ristorante a Casa di Alfredo, 75 C5
Ristorante al Fontanone, 58 D4
La Taverna del Ghetto "Kosher," 72 E4
Taverna Lucifero, 24 D3
Tazza d'Oro, 22 F2
Trattoria da Giggetto, 70 E4
Trattoria Da Luigi, 1 D2
Trattoria da Sergio, 29 D3
Trattoria dal Cav. Gino, 18 F2
Trattoria Gino e Pietro, 7 D2
Tre Scalini, 10 E2
Il Tulipano Nero, 74 C5
Zampano, 32 D3
ENTERTAINMENT
Nuovo Sacher, 77 C5
Il Pasquino, 55 C4
Teatro Valle, 41 E3
NIGHTLIFE
Abbey Theatre, 4 D2
Antilia, 52 C4
Artu Cafe, 56 C4
Bartaruga, 66 E4
Crisca Nimagiù, 33 D3
The Drunken Ship, 25 D3
Enoteca Trastevere, 62 D4
Groove, 8 D3
Jonathan's Angels, 3 D2
Ombre Rosse, 54 C4
Rock Castle Café, 65 E4
La Scala, 51 C4
Sloppy Sam's, 27 D3
Taverna del Campo, 26 D3
Trinity College, 47 F3
SHOPPING
The (Almost) Corner Bookshop, 60 D4
Berte, 14 E2
Campo Marzo Design, 17 F2
Casamaria, 15 E2
Cotton Club, 48 F3
La Discoteca del Pantheon, 45 F3
Elisheva, 30 D3
Gioie d'Arte, 12 E2
House & Kitchen, 49 F3
Kelokura, 46 F3
Libri in Campo, 57 C4
Loco, 31 D3
Materozzoli, 16 F1
Il Papiro, 21 F2
Porta Portese Market, 79 D6
Rance, 13 E2
La Rinascente, 19 F2
Al Sogno, 11 E2
4
5
6
(Botanical Gardens)
Passeggiata del Gianicolo
TO PARCO GIANICOLENSE (450m)
V. d. Porta S. Pancrazio
V. Garibaldi
PZA. DE S. PIETRO IN MONTORIO
S. Pietro in Montorio
S. Maria della Scala
PZA. D. SCALA
Scala
PZA. S. EGIDIO
PZA. D. RENZI
PZA. S. MARIA IN TRAST.
Santa Maria in Trastevere
PZA. S. APOLLONIA
Teatro Belli
V. d. Lungaretta
V. della Cisterne
Via Luciano Manara
PZA. DI COSIMATO
V. G. Mameli
Viale Glorioso
Viale di Trastevere
Via E. Morosini
V. Ascianghi
TO TRASTEVERE STATION (1.2km)
Via della Mura Portuensi
Via Portuense
Lungotevere Portuense
Fiume Tevere (Tiber River)
Pte. Sublicio
PIAZZA DI EMPORIO
PIAZZA DI PORTA PORTESE
S. Francesco a Ripa
PZA. SAN FRANCESCO D'ASSISI
PIAZZA MASTAI
Via della Luce
Via Anicia
V. di S. Michele
Porto di Ripa Grande
Lungotevere Aventino
L. Testaccio
S. Maria dell'Orio
Santa Cecilia in Trastevere
PZA. SANTA CECILIA
S. Maria in Cappella
Lung. Ripa
V. dei Genovesi
V. dei Salumi
PZA. SYDNEY SONNINO
S. Crisogono
Largo S. G. de Matha
PZA. G. G. BELLI
Pte. Garibaldi
Lungotevere Raffaello Sanzio
L. dei Vallati
Pte. Sisto
Via d. Zoccolette
Via Arenula
V.S.B. Vaccinari
Lungotevere dei Cenci
Isola Tiberina
S. Bartolomeo
Pte. Fabricio
Pte. Cestio
L. d. Anguillara
V. Lungarina
L. Alberteschi
Ponte Palatino
L. Pierteoni
V. Petroselli
Sinagoga
Teatro di Marcello
PZA. D. CENCI
PIAZZA CAIROLI
PAL. MATTEI
Via d. Falegnami
V. d. Portico d'Ottavia
Via d. Tempio
Monumento Vittorio Emanuele II
PIAZZA BOCCA D. VERITA
S. Maria in Cosmedin
Via della Greca
V. S. Maria in Cosmedin
PIAZZA S. ANASTASIA
V. d. San Teodoro
Monte Palatino
Circo Massimo
0 200 yards
0 200 meters

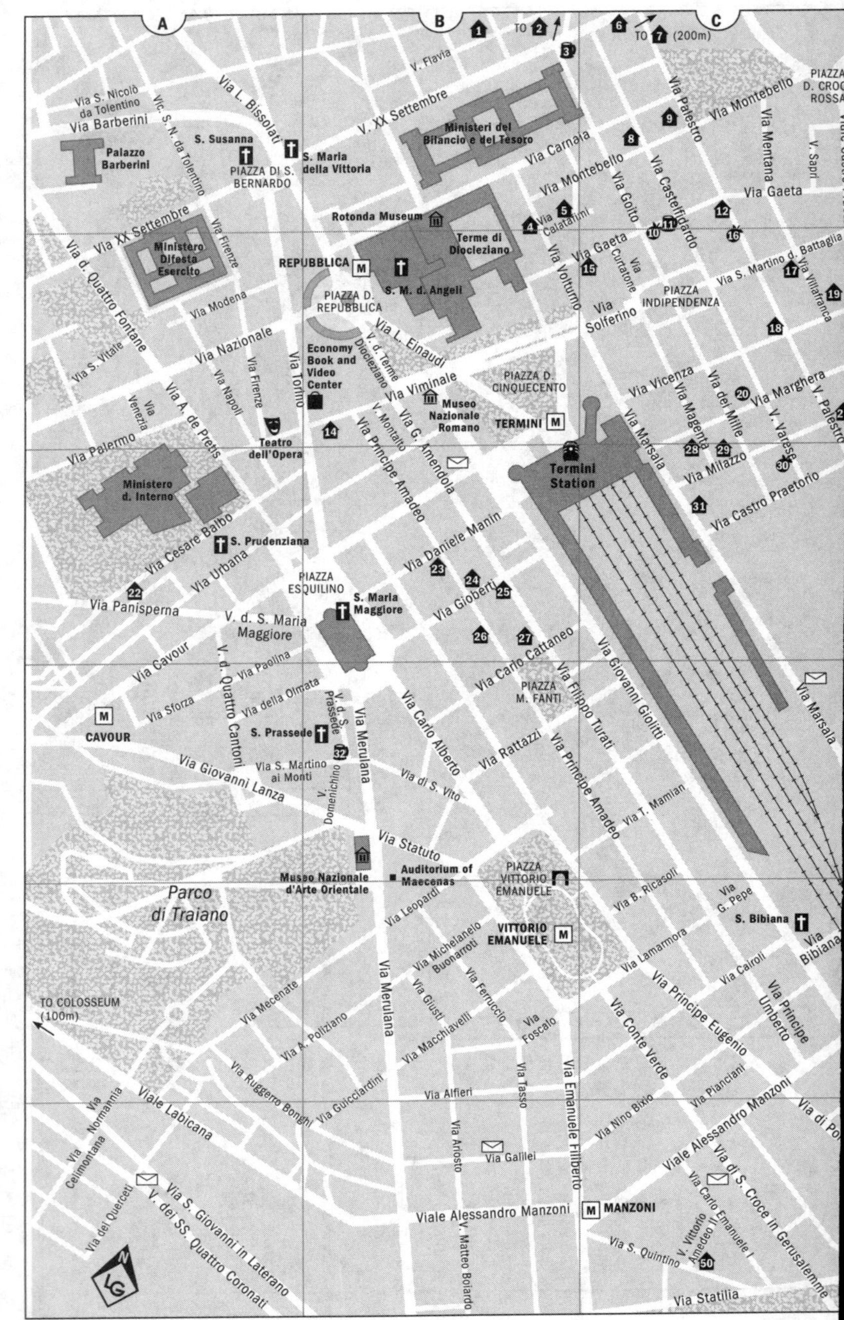

A
B
C
TO 2
TO 7 (200m)
Via S. Nicolò da Tolentino
Via Barberini
Palazzo Barberini
Vic. S. N. da Tolentino
Via L. Bissolati
V. Flavia
V. XX Settembre
S. Susanna
PIAZZA DI S. BERNARDO
S. Maria della Vittoria
Ministeri del Bilancio e del Tesoro
Via Carnaia
Via Montebello
Via Palestro
Via Mentana
V. Sapri
Via Gaeta
PIAZZA D. CROCE ROSSA
Via Castelfidardo
Via Goito
Via Calatafimi
Rotonda Museum
Terme di Diocleziano
Via XX Settembre
Ministero Difesa Esercito
Via Firenze
Via d. Quattro Fontane
REPUBBLICA
S. M. d. Angeli
PIAZZA D. REPUBBLICA
Via Modena
Via Volturno
Via Gaeta
Via Curatone
Via Solferino
PIAZZA INDIPENDENZA
Via S. Martino d. Battaglia
Via Villafranca
Via Nazionale
Via S. Vitale
Via Napoli
Via Firenze
Via Torino
Economy Book and Video Center
V. d. Terme Diocleziano
Via L. Einaudi
Via Viminale
PIAZZA D. CINQUECENTO
Via Vicenza
Via Magenta
Via dei Mille
Via Marghera
V. Palestro
Via Venezia
Via A. de Pretis
Teatro dell'Opera
V. Montalto
Via G. Amendola
Museo Nazionale Romano
TERMINI
Via Principe Amadeo
Via Marsala
Termini Station
Via Milazzo
V. Varese
Via Castro Praetorio
Via Palermo
Ministero d. Interno
Via Cesare Balbo
S. Prudenziana
Via Urbana
Via Daniele Manin
PIAZZA ESQUILINO
S. Maria Maggiore
Via Gioberti
Via Panisperna
V. d. S. Maria Maggiore
Via Cavour
V. d. Quattro Cantoni
Via Paolina
Via Carlo Cattaneo
PIAZZA M. FANTI
Via Filippo Turati
Via Giovanni Giolitti
Via Marsala
Via Sforza
Via della Olmata
V. d. S. Prassede
Via Merulana
Via Carlo Alberto
CAVOUR
S. Prassede
Via Rattazzi
Via Principe Amadeo
Via Giovanni Lanza
Via S. Martino ai Monti
V. Domenichino
Via di S. Vito
Via T. Mamiani
Via Statuto
Museo Nazionale d'Arte Orientale
Auditorium of Maecenas
PIAZZA VITTORIO EMANUELE
Via B. Ricasoli
Via G. Pepe
Parco di Traiano
Via Leopardi
S. Bibiana
Via Bibiana
VITTORIO EMANUELE
Via Michelangelo Buonarroti
Via Lamarmora
Via Cairoli
Via Merulana
Via Giusti
Via Ferruccio
Via Principe Eugenio
Via Principe Umberto
TO COLOSSEUM (100m)
Via Mecenate
Via A. Poliziano
Via Macchiavelli
Via Foscolo
Via Conte Verde
Via Ruggero Bonghi
Via Guicciardini
Via Alfieri
Via Tasso
Via Emanuele Filiberto
Via Pianciani
Via Nino Bixio
Viale Alessandro Manzoni
Via di Po
Via Normannia
Viale Labicana
Via Celimontana
Via Ariosto
Via Galilei
Via di S. Croce in Gerusalemme
Via Carlo Emanuele I
Via dei Querceti
V. dei SS. Quattro Coronati
Via S. Giovanni in Laterano
Viale Alessandro Manzoni
V. Matteo Boiardo
MANZONI
Via S. Quintino
V. Vittorio Amedeo II
Via Statilia
LG

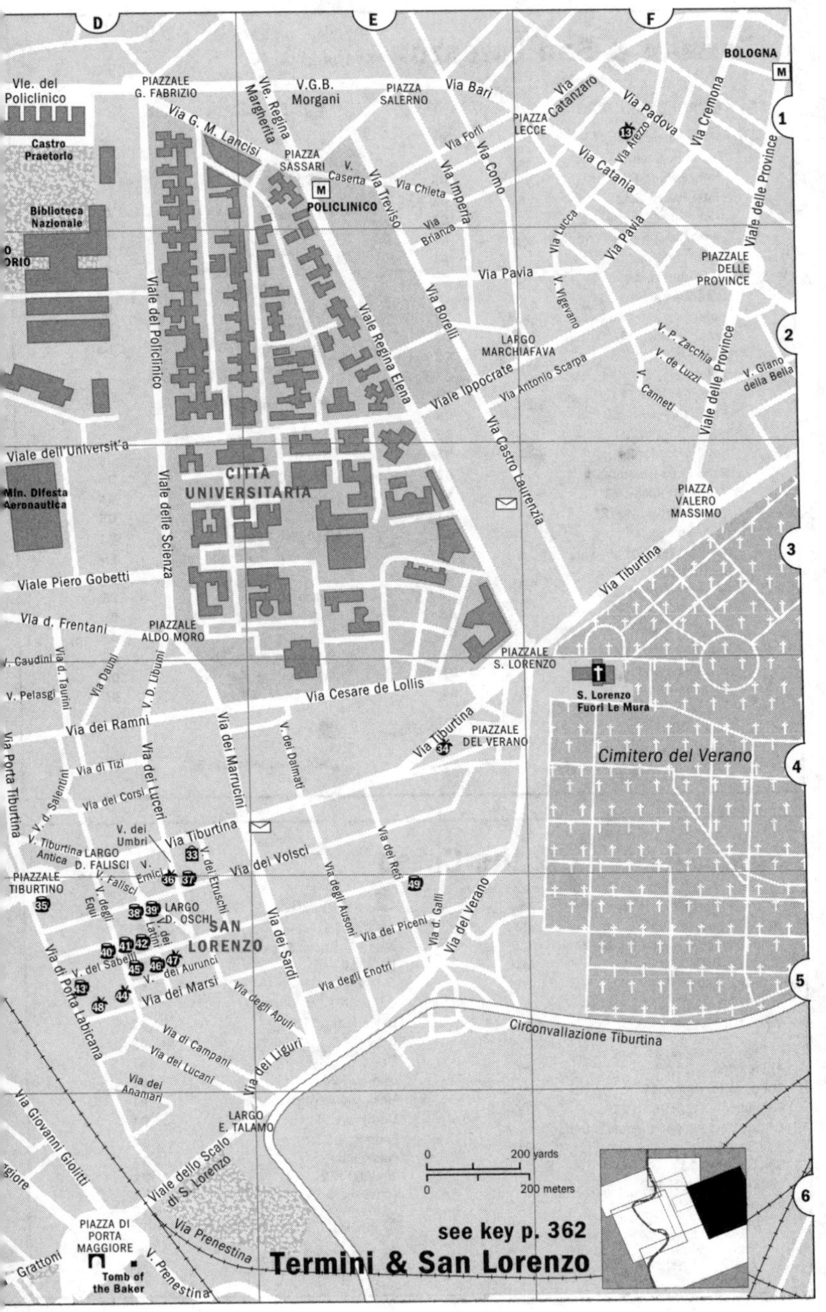

see key p. 362

Termini & San Lorenzo

Termini & San Lorenzo see map p. 360

ACCOMMODATIONS

Affitacamere Aries, **7**	**C1**
Freedom Traveler, **15**	**C2**
Hotel Aphrodite, **31**	**C3**
Hotel Baltic, **6**	**C1**
Hotel Bolognese, **9**	**C1**
Hotel Castelfidardo and Hotel Lazzari, **8**	**C1**
Hotel Cathrine, **2**	**B1**
Hotel Cervia, **18**	**C2**
Hotel Des Artistes, **19**	**C2**
Hotel Dolomiti and Hotel Lachea, **17**	**C2**
Hotel Fenicia, **29**	**C2**
Hotel Gabriella, **21**	**C2**
Hotel Galli, **29**	**C3**
Hotel Giu' Giu', **14**	**B2**
Hotel Il Castello, **50**	**C6**
Hotel Kennedy, **27**	**B3**
Hotel Orlanda, **24**	**B3**
Hotel Papa Germano, **5**	**B1**
Hotel San Paolo, **22**	**A3**
Hotel Scott House, **25**	**B3**
Hotel Selene, **14**	**B2**
Hotel Sweet Home, **23**	**B3**
Hotel Teti, **24**	**B3**
Pensione Cortorillo, **26**	**B3**
Pensione di Rienzo, **26**	**B3**
Pensione Fawlty Towers, **28**	**C3**
Pensione Katty, **12**	**C1**
Pensione Monaco, **1**	**B1**
Pensione Piave, **2**	**B1**

SERVICES

Enjoy Rome, **20**	**C2**

FOOD

Africa, **10**	**C2**
AL 39, **16**	**C2**
Arancia Blu, **47**	**D5**
Il Capellaio Matto, **48**	**D5**
Il Pulcino Ballerino, **44**	**D5**
Il Tunnel, **13**	**F1**
La Pantera Rosa, **34**	**E4**
Pizzeria La Maschere, **36**	**D5**
Hostaria da Bruno, **30**	**C3**

NIGHTLIFE

360°, **45**	**D5**
Dalhu' Pub, **40**	**D5**
Drome, **39**	**D5**
Druid's Rock, **32**	**B4**
Ferrazza, **38**	**D5**
Friend's, **3**	**B1**
Il Giardini di Adone, **49**	**E5**
Julius Caesar, **11**	**C1**
Lancelot, **37**	**D5**
Legend Pub, **42**	**D5**
Pigmalione, **43**	**D5**
Pub Hallo'Ween, **35**	**D5**
Rivegauche2, **41**	**D5**
Il Simposio, **46**	**D5**

SHOPPING

Disfunzioni Musicali, **33**	**D4**

Spanish Steps & the Corso

ACCOMMODATIONS

Hotel Boccaccio, **26**	**C3**
Hotel Pensione Suisse S.A.S., **21**	**C2**
Pensione Jonella, **3**	**B1**
Pensione Panda, **6**	**B1**

FOOD

Al Piccolo Arancio, **25**	**C3**
Al Presidente, **24**	**C3**
Antico Caffè Greco, **13**	**B1**
Babington's Tea Rooms, **11**	**B1**
Centro Macrobiotico Italiano-Naturist Club, **16**	**A2**
San Crispino, **23**	**C3**
UKIYO (Japanese), **14**	**A2**
Vini e Buffet, **15**	**A2**

SHOPPING

Alcozer, **10**	**B1**
Anglo-American Bookshop, **19**	**B2**
Bata, **20**	**C2**
Clio, **2**	**B1**
C.U.C.I.N.A., **9**	**B1**
David Mayer, **17**	**A2**
Diesel, **18**	**A2**
Furla, **7**	**B1**
Linn Sui, **28**	**D5**
Messaggerie Musicali, **1**	**A1**
Modigliani, **8**	**B1**
Petrocchi, **22**	**A3**
Pianeginda, **4**	**B1**
Siragusa, **12**	**B1**
Vertecchi, **5**	**B1**

NIGHTLIFE

The Nag's Head, **28**	**B5**
Trinity College, **27**	**A4**

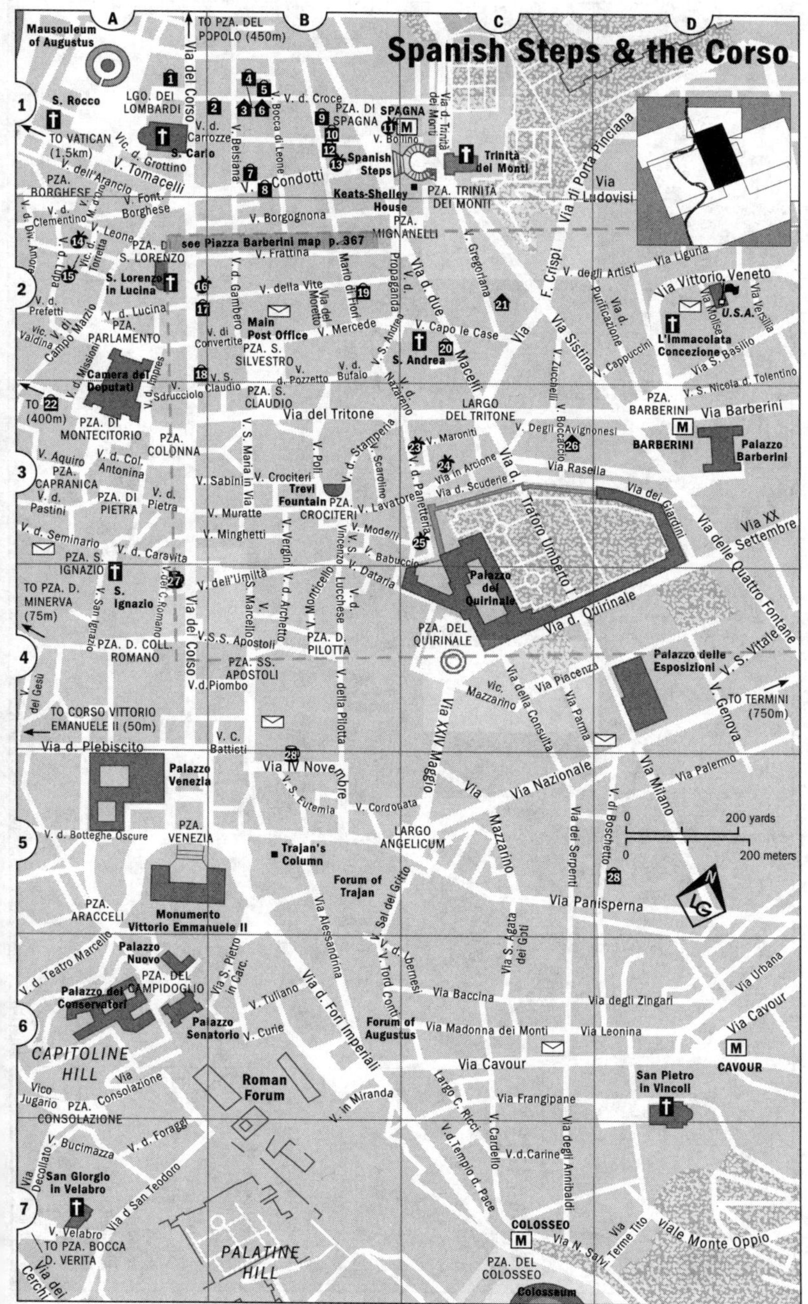

Spanish Steps & the Corso
Mausouleum of Augustus
TO PZA. DEL POPOLO (450m)
S. Rocco
LGO. DEI LOMBARDI
TO VATICAN (1.5km)
S. Carlo
PZA. DI SPAGNA
SPAGNA
Spanish Steps
Trinità dei Monti
PZA. TRINITÀ DEI MONTI
Keats-Shelley House
PZA. MIGNANELLI
see Piazza Barberini map p. 367
Via Ludovisi
Via di Porta Pinciana
Via Vittorio Veneto
U.S.A.
L'Immacolata Concezione
S. Lorenzo in Lucina
PZA. D. S. LORENZO
Main Post Office
PZA. S. SILVESTRO
S. Andrea
PZA. PARLAMENTO
Camera dei Deputati
TO 22 (400m)
PZA. S. CLAUDIO
Via del Tritone
LARGO DEL TRITONE
PZA. BARBERINI
Via Barberini
BARBERINI
Palazzo Barberini
PZA. DI MONTECITORIO
PZA. COLONNA
PZA. CAPRANICA
PZA. DI PIETRA
Trevi Fountain
PZA. CROCITERI
Via Rasella
Via XX Settembre
Via delle Quattro Fontane
Palazzo del Quirinale
Via d. Quirinale
PZA. DEL QUIRINALE
Traforo Umberto I
PZA. S. IGNAZIO
S. Ignazio
TO PZA. D. MINERVA (75m)
PZA. D. COLL. ROMANO
PZA. SS. APOSTOLI
PZA. D. PILOTTA
Palazzo delle Esposizioni
TO TERMINI (750m)
TO CORSO VITTORIO EMANUELE II (50m)
Via d. Plebiscito
Via del Corso
Palazzo Venezia
Via IV Novembre
Via XXIV Maggio
Via Nazionale
Via Milano
PZA. VENEZIA
Trajan's Column
LARGO ANGELICUM
Forum of Trajan
Via Mazzarino
Via dei Serpenti
Via Panisperna
200 yards
200 meters
PZA. ARACCELI
Monumento Vittorio Emmanuele II
Palazzo Nuovo
PZA. DEL CAMPIDOGLIO
Palazzo dei Conservatori
Palazzo Senatorio
CAPITOLINE HILL
Via d. Fori Imperiali
Forum of Augustus
Via Cavour
CAVOUR
Roman Forum
Via Frangipane
San Pietro in Vincoli
PZA. CONSOLAZIONE
San Giorgio in Velabro
TO PZA. BOCCA D. VERITA
PALATINE HILL
COLOSSEO
PZA. DEL COLOSSEO
Colosseum
Viale Monte Oppio

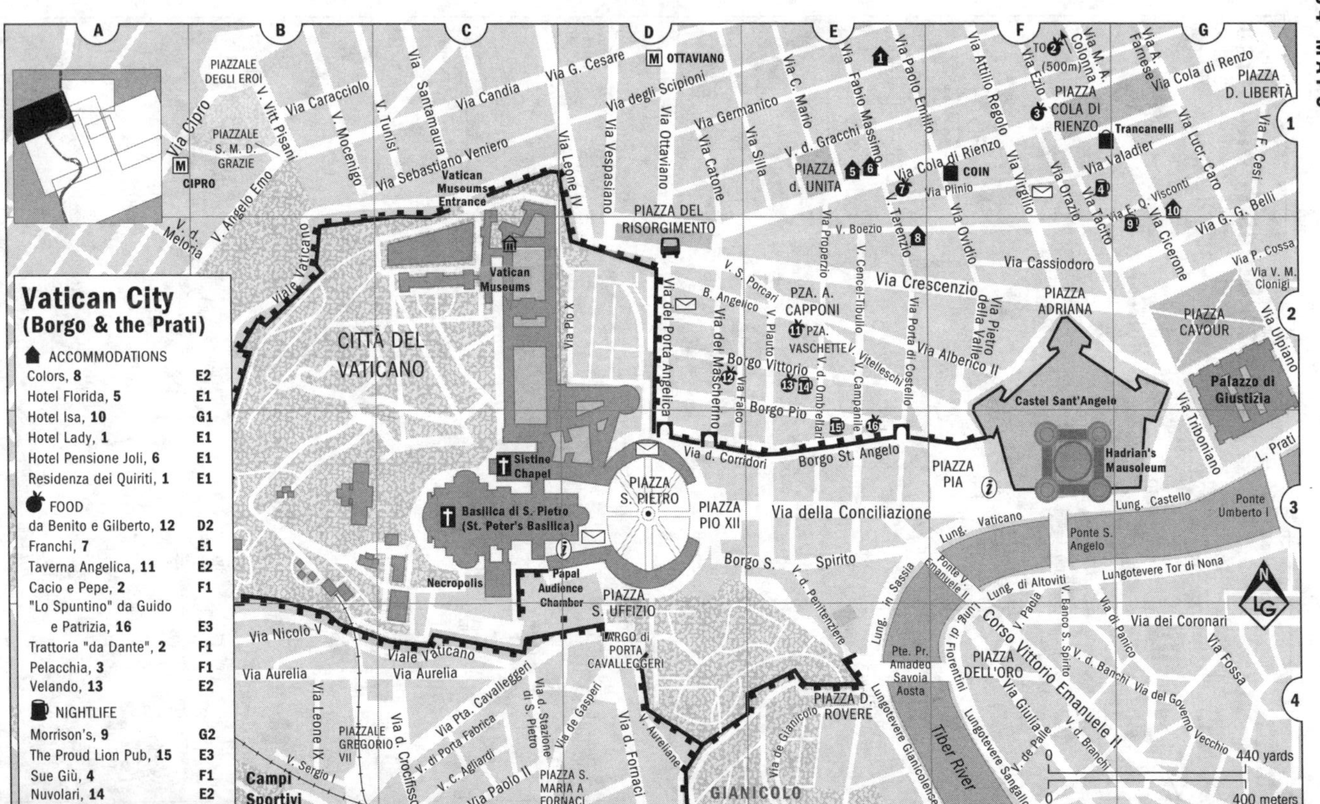
Vatican City
(Borgo & the Prati)
ACCOMMODATIONS
Colors, 8 E2
Hotel Florida, 5 E1
Hotel Isa, 10 G1
Hotel Lady, 1 E1
Hotel Pensione Joli, 6 E1
Residenza dei Quiriti, 1 E1
FOOD
da Benito e Gilberto, 12 D2
Franchi, 7 E1
Taverna Angelica, 11 E2
Cacio e Pepe, 2 F1
"Lo Spuntino" da Guido e Patrizia, 16 E3
Trattoria "da Dante", 2 F1
Pelacchia, 3 F1
Velando, 13 E2
NIGHTLIFE
Morrison's, 9 G2
The Proud Lion Pub, 15 E3
Sue Giù, 4 F1
Nuvolari, 14 E2
A
B
C
D
E
F
G
1
2
3
4
PIAZZALE DEGLI EROI
PIAZZALE S. M. D. GRAZIE
CIPRO
Via Cipro
V. Vitt Pisani
Via Caracciolo
V. Mocenigo
V. Tunisi
Via Santamaura
Via Sebastiano Veniero
Via Candia
Via G. Cesare
OTTAVIANO
Via degli Scipioni
Via Leone IV
Via Vespasiano
Via Ottaviano
Via Germanico
Via Catone
Via Silla
Via C. Mario
V. d. Gracchi
PIAZZA d. UNITA
Via Fabio Massimo
Via Paolo Emilio
Via Cola di Rienzo
Via Plinio
COIN
Via Attilio Regolo
Via Ezio
PIAZZA COLA DI RIENZO
TO (500m)
Via M. A. Colonna
Via A. Farnese
Trancanelli
Via Valadier
Via Lucr. Caro
Via F. Cesi
PIAZZA D. LIBERTÀ
Via Virgilio
Via Orazio
Via Tacito
Via E. Q. Visconti
Via Cicerone
Via G. G. Belli
Via P. Cossa
Via V. M. Clonigi
Via Ulpiano
V. d. Meloria
V. Angelo Emo
Viale Vaticano
Vatican Museums Entrance
Vatican Museums
PIAZZA DEL RISORGIMENTO
V. Terenzio
V. Boezio
Via Ovidio
Via Cassiodoro
Via Crescenzio
PIAZZA ADRIANA
PIAZZA CAVOUR
Palazzo di Giustizia
CITTÀ DEL VATICANO
Via Pio X
Via del Porta Angelica
B. Angelico
V. S. Porcari
Via del Mascherino
V. Plauto
PZA. A. CAPPONI
PZA. VASCHETTE
Via Properzio
V. Cencel-Tibullo
V. Vitelleschi
Via Porta di Costello
Via Pietro della Valle
Via Alberico II
Borgo Vittorio
V. d. Ombrellari
V. Campanile
Via Falco
Borgo Pio
Castel Sant'Angelo
Hadrian's Mausoleum
Via Triboniano
L. Prati
Sistine Chapel
Basilica di S. Pietro (St. Peter's Basilica)
Via d. Corridori
Borgo St. Angelo
PIAZZA PIA
PIAZZA S. PIETRO
PIAZZA PIO XII
Via della Conciliazione
Lung. Castello
Ponte Umberto I
Lung. Vaticano
Ponte S. Angelo
Borgo S. Spirito
Necropolis
Papal Audience Chamber
PIAZZA S. UFFIZIO
V. d. Penitenziere
Lung. in Sassia
Ponte V. Emanuele II
Lung. di Altoviti
Lungotevere Tor di Nona
V. Banco S. Spirito
Via di Panico
Via dei Coronari
Via Fossa
Via Nicolò V
Viale Vaticano
LARGO di PORTA CAVALLEGGERI
Via Aurelia
Via Leone IX
PIAZZALE GREGORIO VII
Via d. Crocifisso
V. di Porta Fabrica
Via Pta. Cavalleggeri
V. C. Agliardi
Via d. Stazione di S. Pietro
Via de Gasperi
Via Paolo II
PIAZZA S. MARIA A FORNACI
Via d. Fornaci
V. Aureliane
GIANICOLO
Via de Gianicolo
PIAZZA D. ROVERE
Lungotevere Gianicolense
Pte. Pr. Amadeo Savoia Aosta
Tiber River
Lung. di Fiorentini
V. Paola
Corso Vittorio Emanuele II
PIAZZA DELL'ORO
Via Giulia
V. de Palle
V. d. Banchi
V. d. Branchi
Via del Governo Vecchio
Lungotevere Sangallo
Campi Sportivi
V. Sergio I
0
440 yards
0
400 meters

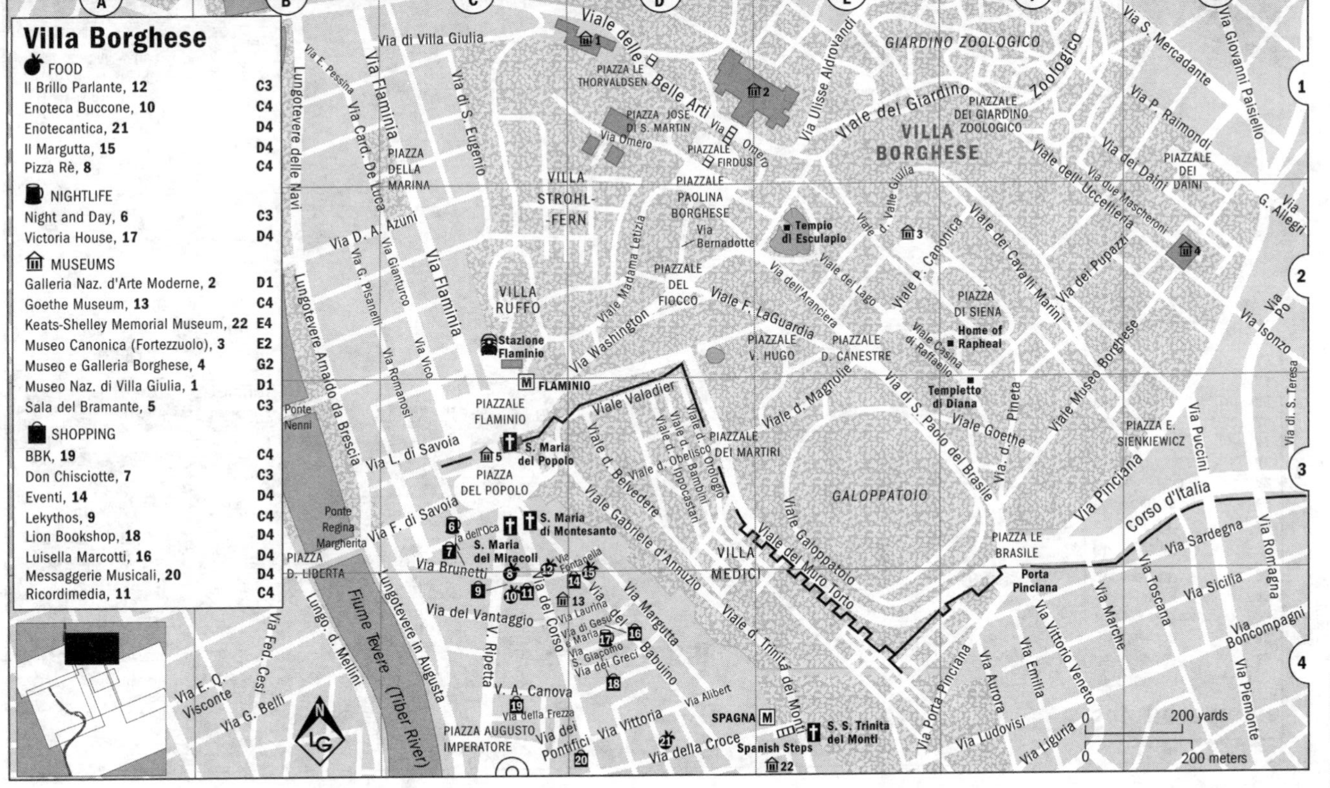
Villa Borghese
FOOD
Il Brillo Parlante, 12 C3
Enoteca Buccone, 10 C4
Enotecantica, 21 D4
Il Margutta, 15 D4
Pizza Rè, 8 C4
NIGHTLIFE
Night and Day, 6 C3
Victoria House, 17 D4
MUSEUMS
Galleria Naz. d'Arte Moderne, 2 D1
Goethe Museum, 13 C4
Keats-Shelley Memorial Museum, 22 E4
Museo Canonica (Fortezzuolo), 3 E2
Museo e Galleria Borghese, 4 G2
Museo Naz. di Villa Giulia, 1 D1
Sala del Bramante, 5 C3
SHOPPING
BBK, 19 C4
Don Chisciotte, 7 C3
Eventi, 14 D4
Lekythos, 9 C4
Lion Bookshop, 18 D4
Luisella Marcotti, 16 D4
Messaggerie Musicali, 20 D4
Ricordimedia, 11 C4
GIARDINO ZOOLOGICO
VILLA BORGHESE
VILLA STROHL-FERN
VILLA RUFFO
VILLA MEDICI
GALOPPATOIO
Tempio di Esculapio
Home of Rapheal
Tempietto di Diana
Stazione Flaminio
FLAMINIO
SPAGNA
S. Maria del Popolo
S. Maria di Montesanto
S. Maria del Miracoli
S. S. Trinita del Monti
Spanish Steps
Porta Pinciana
PIAZZALE FLAMINIO
PIAZZA DEL POPOLO
PIAZZA AUGUSTO IMPERATORE
PIAZZA D. LIBERTA
Fiume Tevere (Tiber River)
Via Flaminia
Via del Corso
Via Veneto
Corso d'Italia
Via Pinciana
Via di Porta Pinciana
Via Vittorio Veneto
Via del Babuino
Via Margutta
Via della Croce
Viale del Muro Torto
Via di Villa Giulia
Viale delle Belle Arti
Viale del Giardino Zoologico
200 yards
200 meters

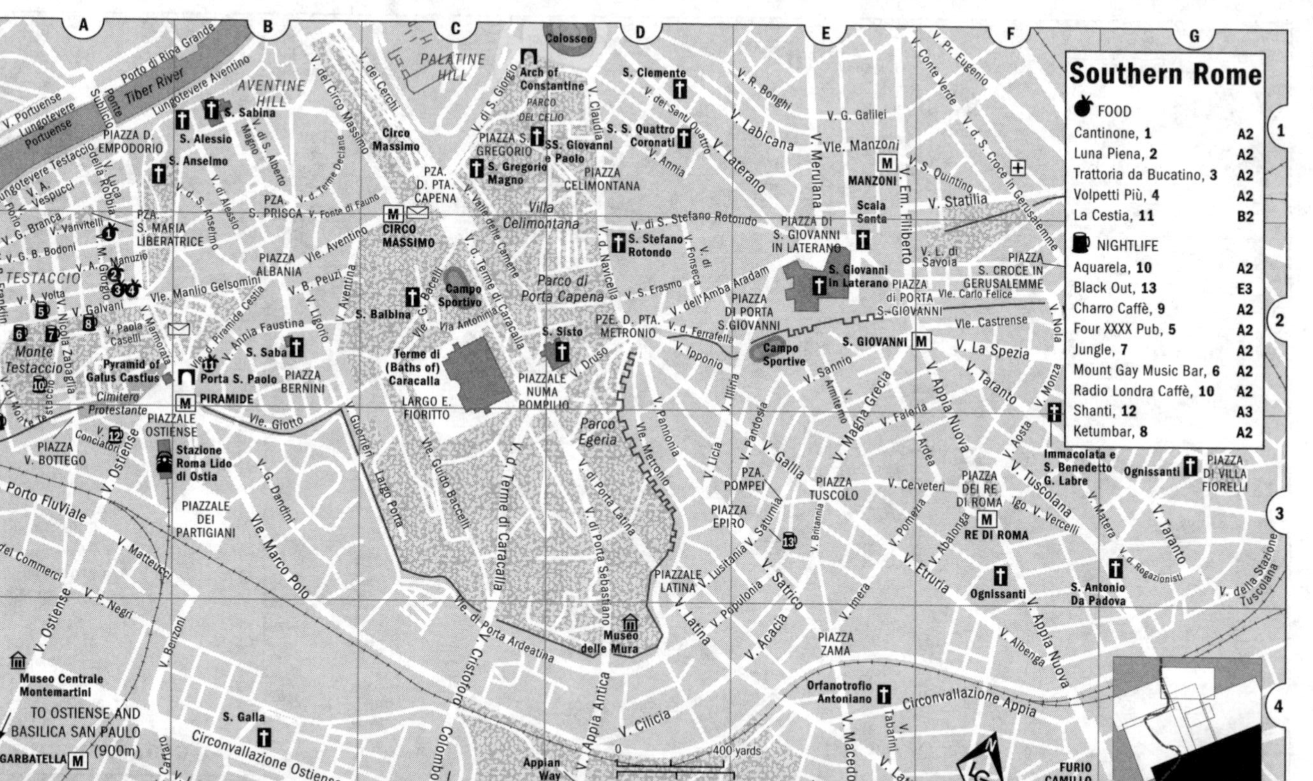
Southern Rome
FOOD
Cantinone, 1 A2
Luna Piena, 2 A2
Trattoria da Bucatino, 3 A2
Volpetti Più, 4 A2
La Cestia, 11 B2
NIGHTLIFE
Aquarela, 10 A2
Black Out, 13 E3
Charro Caffè, 9 A2
Four XXXX Pub, 5 A2
Jungle, 7 A2
Mount Gay Music Bar, 6 A2
Radio Londra Caffè, 10 A2
Shanti, 12 A3
Ketumbar, 8 A2
Colosseo
Arch of Constantine
PALATINE HILL
AVENTINE HILL
Tiber River
TESTACCIO
Circo Massimo
CIRCO MASSIMO
Villa Celimontana
Parco di Porta Capena
Terme di (Baths of) Caracalla
S. Giovanni in Laterano
S. GIOVANNI
MANZONI
PIRAMIDE
RE DI ROMA
Pyramid of Galus Castius
Porta S. Paolo
Stazione Roma Lido di Ostia
Museo delle Mura
Museo Centrale Montemartini
Parco Egeria
Appian Way
TO OSTIENSE AND BASILICA SAN PAULO (900m)
GARBATELLA
FURIO CAMILLO
400 yards

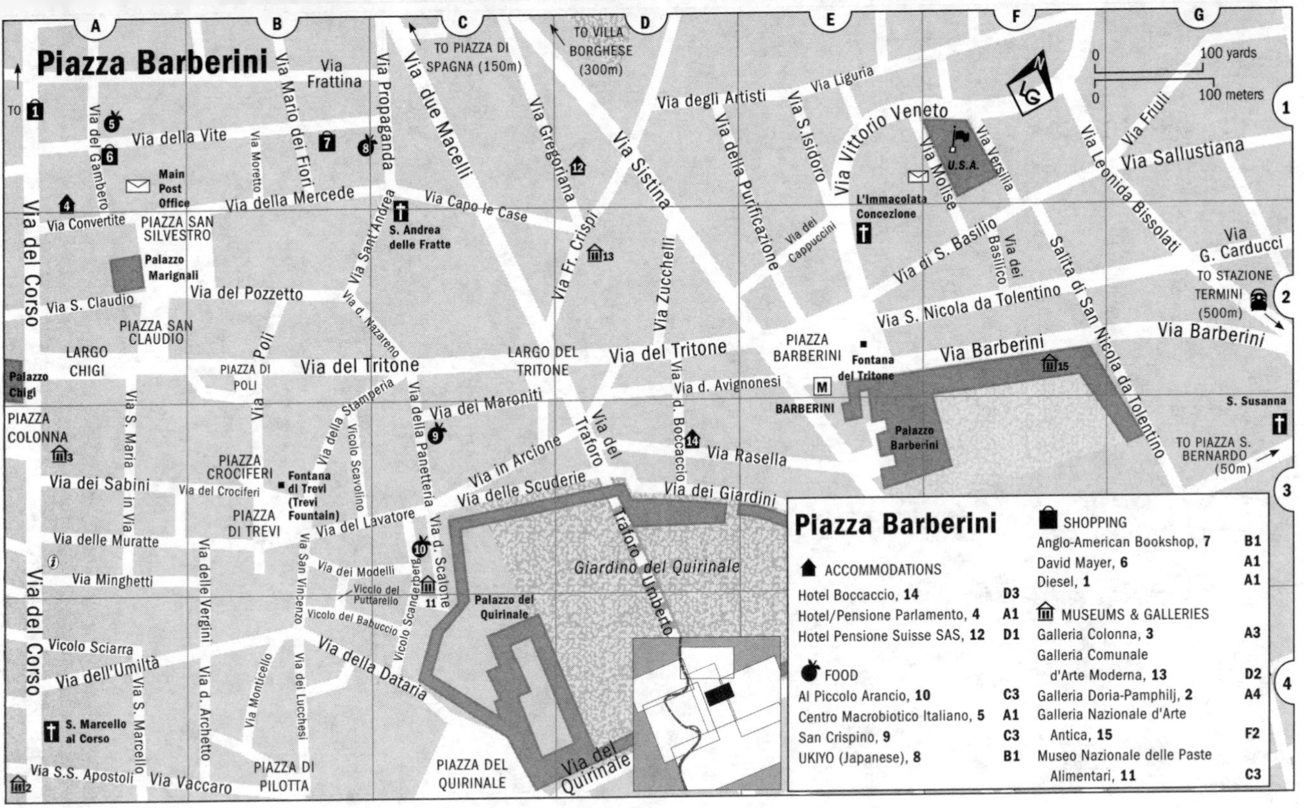

Piazza Barberini

ACCOMMODATIONS

Hotel Boccaccio, **14**	D3
Hotel/Pensione Parlamento, **4**	A1
Hotel Pensione Suisse SAS, **12**	D1

FOOD

Al Piccolo Arancio, **10**	C3
Centro Macrobiotico Italiano, **5**	A1
San Crispino, **9**	C3
UKIYO (Japanese), **8**	B1

SHOPPING

Anglo-American Bookshop, **7**	B1
David Mayer, **6**	A1
Diesel, **1**	A1

MUSEUMS & GALLERIES

Galleria Colonna, **3**	A3
Galleria Comunale d'Arte Moderna, **13**	D2
Galleria Doria-Pamphilj, **2**	A4
Galleria Nazionale d'Arte Antica, **15**	F2
Museo Nazionale delle Paste Alimentari, **11**	C3

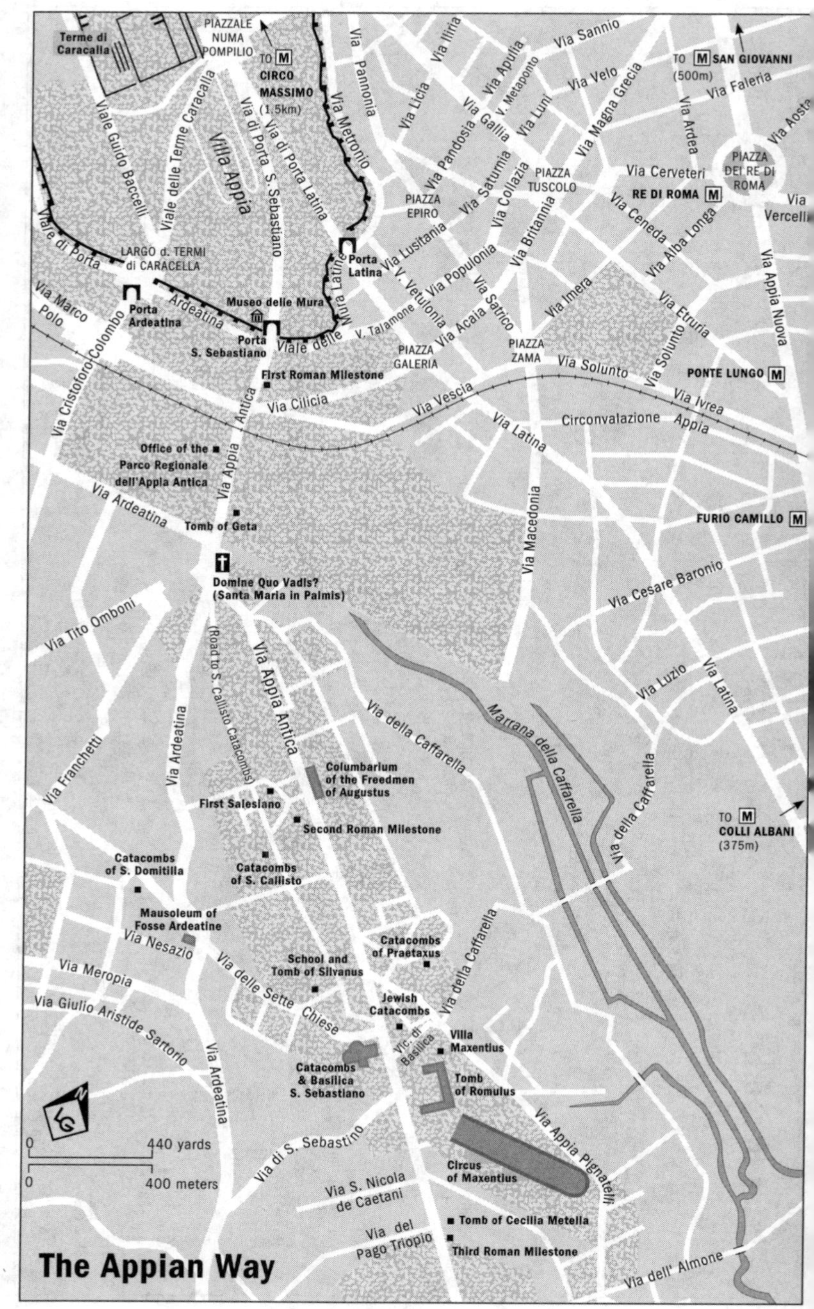
The Appian Way
Terme di Caracalla
PIAZZALE NUMA POMPILIO
TO M CIRCO MASSIMO (1.5km)
TO M SAN GIOVANNI (500m)
Via Sannio
Via Ilirla
Via Pannonia
Via Metronio
Via Licia
Via Apulia
V. Metaponto
Via Velo
Via Magna Grecia
Via Faleria
Via Aosta
Via Ardea
PIAZZA DEI RE DI ROMA
Via Cerveteri
RE DI ROMA M
Via Vercelli
Via Gallia
Via Luni
Via Pandosia
PIAZZA TUSCOLO
PIAZZA EPIRO
Via Saturnia
Via Collazia
Via Britannia
Via Ceneda
Via Alba Longa
Via Appia Nuova
Viale Guido Baccelli
Viale delle Terme Caracalla
Villa Appia
Via di Porta S. Sebastiano
Via di Porta Latina
Viale di Porta Ardeatina
LARGO d. TERMI di CARACELLA
Porta Latina
Via Lusitania
V. Vetulonia
Via Populonia
Via Satrico
Via Imera
Via Etruria
Via Marco Polo
Porta Ardeatina
Museo delle Mura
Via Mura Latine
Porta S. Sebastiano
Viale delle Mura Latine
V. Talamone
Via Acaia
PIAZZA GALERIA
PIAZZA ZAMA
Via Solunto
PONTE LUNGO M
Via Cristoforo Colombo
First Roman Milestone
Via Cilicia
Via Vescia
Via Ivrea
Circonvalazione Appia
Via Latina
Office of the Parco Regionale dell'Appia Antica
Via Appia Antica
Via Ardeatina
Tomb of Geta
Via Macedonia
FURIO CAMILLO M
Domine Quo Vadis? (Santa Maria in Palmis)
Via Cesare Baronio
Via Tito Omboni
(Road to S. Callisto Catacombs)
Via Luzio
Via della Caffarella
Marrana della Caffarella
Via Franchetti
Columbarium of the Freedmen of Augustus
First Salesiano
Second Roman Milestone
TO M COLLI ALBANI (375m)
Catacombs of S. Domitilla
Catacombs of S. Callisto
Mausoleum of Fosse Ardeatine
Via Nesazio
Catacombs of Praetaxus
School and Tomb of Silvanus
Via Meropia
Via delle Sette Chiese
Jewish Catacombs
Via Giulio Aristide Sartorio
Vic. di Basilica
Villa Maxentius
Catacombs & Basilica S. Sebastiano
Tomb of Romulus
Via Appia Pignatelli
0 440 yards
0 400 meters
Via di S. Sebastino
Circus of Maxentius
Via S. Nicola de Caetani
Tomb of Cecilia Metella
Via del Pago Triopio
Third Roman Milestone
Via dell' Almone

Rome Mass Transit

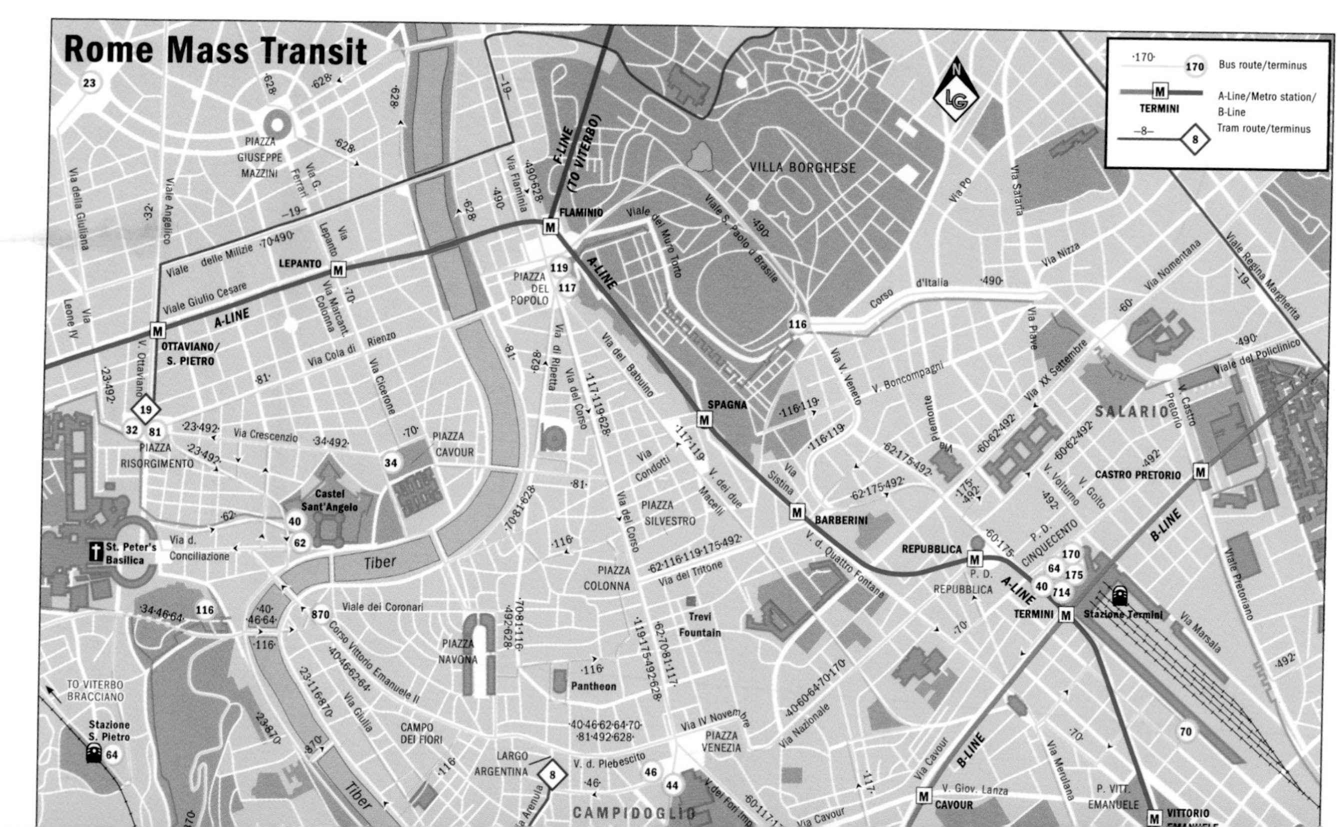

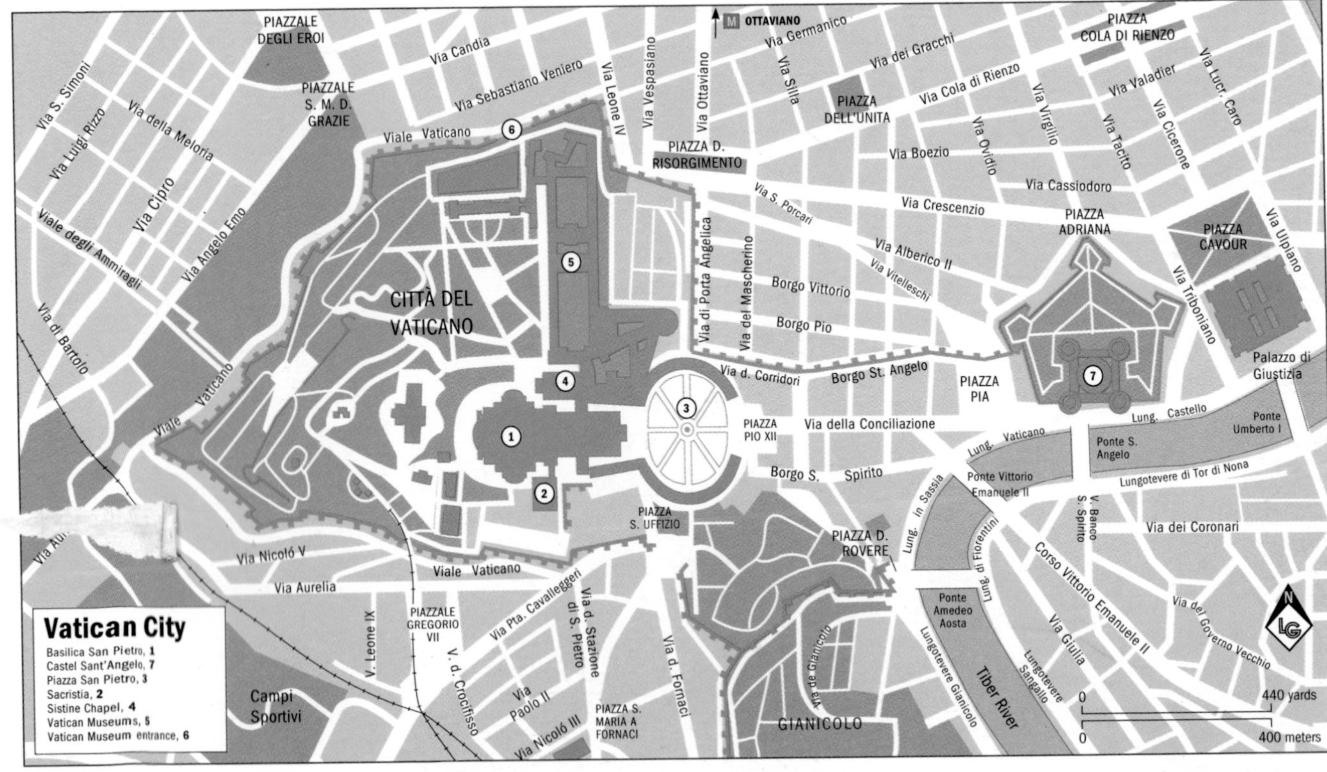

Vatican City
Basilica San Pietro, 1
Castel Sant'Angelo, 7
Piazza San Pietro, 3
Sacristia, 2
Sistine Chapel, 4
Vatican Museums, 5
Vatican Museum entrance, 6
PIAZZALE DEGLI EROI
PIAZZALE S. M. D. GRAZIE
OTTAVIANO
PIAZZA COLA DI RIENZO
Via S. Simoni
Via Luigi Rizzo
Via della Meloria
Via Cipro
Viale degli Ammiragli
Via Angelo Emo
Via di Bartolo
Via Candia
Via Sebastiano Veniero
Viale Vaticano
Via Leone IV
Via Vespasiano
Via Ottaviano
Via Germanico
Via Silla
Via dei Gracchi
PIAZZA DELL'UNITA
Via Cola di Rienzo
Via Valadier
Via Lucr. Caro
Via Virgilio
Via Ovidio
Via Tacito
Via Cicerone
Via Boezio
PIAZZA D. RISORGIMENTO
Via S. Porcari
Via Cassiodoro
Via Crescenzio
PIAZZA ADRIANA
PIAZZA CAVOUR
Via Ulpiano
Via Alberico II
Via Vitelleschi
Via Tribonano
CITTÀ DEL VATICANO
Via di Porta Angelica
Via del Mascherino
Borgo Vittorio
Borgo Pio
Via d. Corridori
Borgo St. Angelo
PIAZZA PIA
Palazzo di Giustizia
PIAZZA PIO XII
Via della Conciliazione
Lung. Castello
Ponte Umberto I
Lung. Vaticano
Ponte S. Angelo
Borgo S. Spirito
Ponte Vittorio Emanuele II
Lungotevere di Tor di Nona
Lung. in Sassia
V. Banco S. Spirito
Via dei Coronari
PIAZZA S. UFFIZIO
PIAZZA D. ROVERE
Lung. di Fiorentini
Corso Vittorio Emanuele II
Via Nicoló V
Viale Vaticano
Via Aurelia
Ponte Amedeo Aosta
Via del Governo Vecchio
V. Leone IX
PIAZZALE GREGORIO VII
Via Pta. Cavalleggeri
Via d. Stazione di S. Pietro
Via d. Fornaci
Via Giulia
V. d. Crocifisso
Via Paolo II
Via de Gianicolo
Lungotevere Gianicolo
Tiber River
Lungotevere Sangallo
Campi Sportivi
Via Nicoló III
PIAZZA S. MARIA A FORNACI
GIANICOLO
0
440 yards
0
400 meters

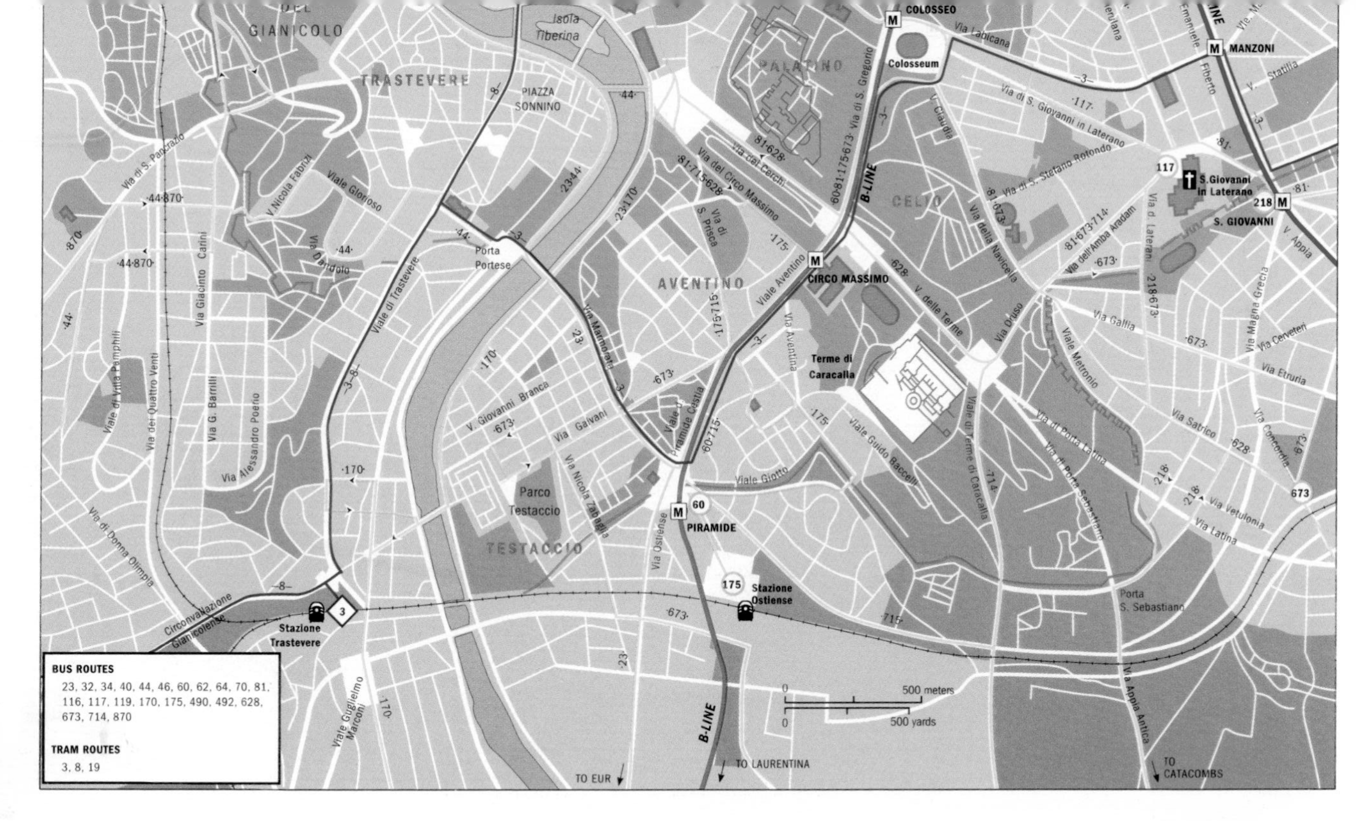
GIANICOLO
TRASTEVERE
Isola Tiberina
PIAZZA SONNINO
PALATINO
COLOSSEO
Colosseum
MANZONI
CELIO
AVENTINO
TESTACCIO
CIRCO MASSIMO
Terme di Caracalla
S.Giovanni in Laterano
S. GIOVANNI
PIRAMIDE
Parco Testaccio
Porta Portese
Porta S. Sebastiano
Stazione Trastevere
Stazione Ostiense
B-LINE
Via Labicana
Via di S. Giovanni in Laterano
Via di S. Stefano Rotondo
V. Claudia
Via della Navicella
Via dell'Amba Aradam
Via d. Laterani
Via di S. Gregorio
Via dei Cerchi
Via del Circo Massimo
Via di S. Prisca
Viale Aventino
Via Aventina
V. delle Terme
Via Druso
Via Gallia
Viale Metronio
Via Magna Grecia
Via Cerveteri
Via Etruria
Via Satrico
Via Concordia
Via di Porta Latina
Via di Porta Sebastiano
Via Vetulonia
Via Latina
Viale di Terme di Caracalla
Viale Guido Baccelli
Viale Giotto
Viale d. Piramide Cestia
Via Marmorata
V. Giovanni Branca
Via Galvani
Via Nicola Zabaglia
Via Ostiense
Via Appia Antica
V. Appia
Via di S. Pancrazio
V. Nicola Fabrizi
Viale Glorioso
Via Dandolo
Viale di Trastevere
Via Giacinto Carini
Via G. Barrilli
Via Alessandro Poerio
Via dei Quattro Venti
Viale di Villa Pamphili
Via di Donna Olimpia
Circonvallazione Gianicolense
Viale Guglielmo Marconi
0
500 meters
500 yards
TO EUR
TO LAURENTINA
TO CATACOMBS
BUS ROUTES
23, 32, 34, 40, 44, 46, 60, 62, 64, 70, 81, 116, 117, 119, 170, 175, 490, 492, 628, 673, 714, 870
TRAM ROUTES
3, 8, 19

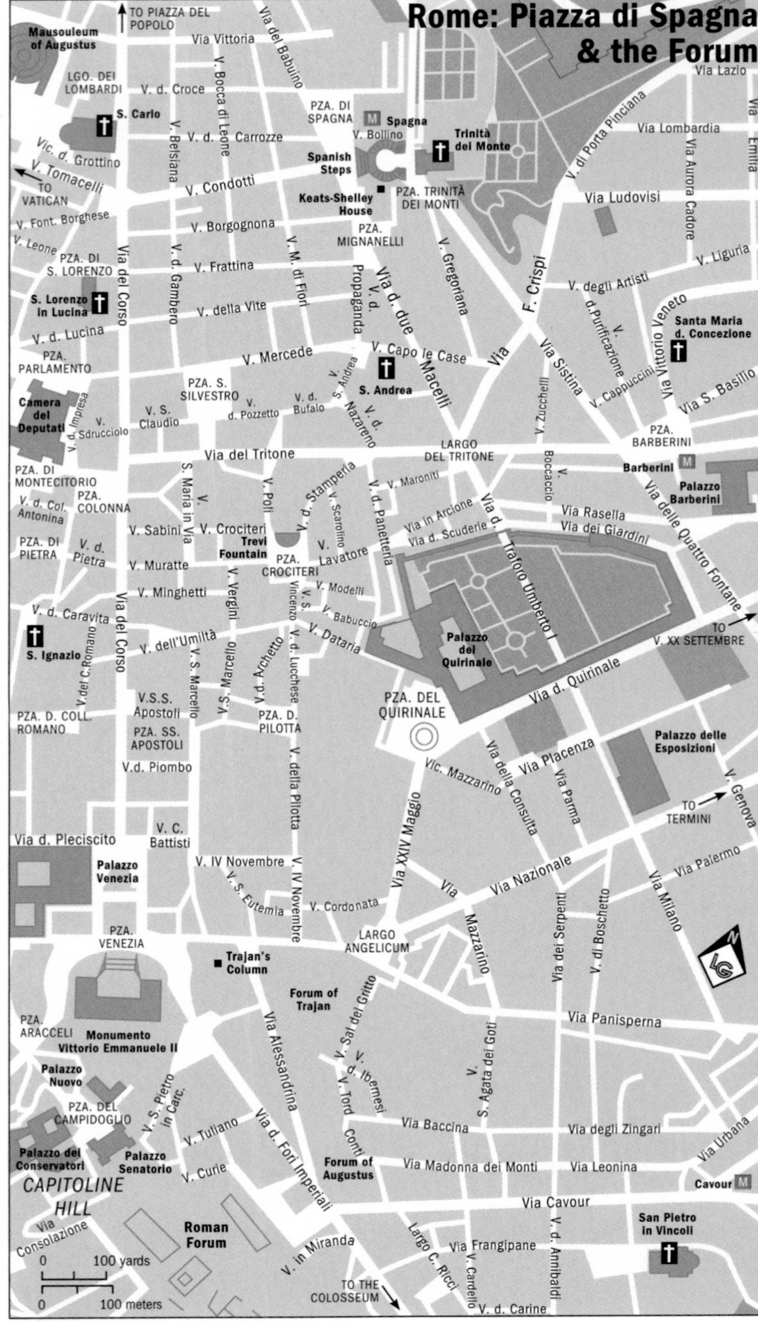
Rome: Piazza di Spagna & the Forum
TO PIAZZA DEL POPOLO
Mausouleum of Augustus
Via Vittoria
Via del Babuino
LGO. DEI LOMBARDI
V. d. Croce
V. Bocca di Leone
PZA. DI SPAGNA
Spagna
S. Carlo
V. Belsiana
V. d. Carrozze
V. Bollino
Trinità dei Monte
Spanish Steps
Vic. d. Grottino
V. Tomacelli
TO VATICAN
V. Condotti
Keats-Shelley House
PZA. TRINITÀ DEI MONTI
V. Font. Borghese
V. Borgognona
PZA. MIGNANELLI
V. Leone
PZA. DI S. LORENZO
V. Frattina
V. d. Gambero
V. M. di Fiori
V. d. Propaganda
Via d. due Macelli
V. Gregoriana
S. Lorenzo in Lucina
Via del Corso
V. della Vite
V. d. Lucina
PZA. PARLAMENTO
V. Mercede
V. Capo le Case
S. Andrea
PZA. S. SILVESTRO
Camera dei Deputati
V. d. Impresa
V. Sdrucciolo
V. S. Claudio
V. d. Pozzetto
V. d. Bufalo
V. S. Andrea
V. d. Nazareno
Via del Tritone
LARGO DEL TRITONE
PZA. DI MONTECITORIO
V. S. Maria in Via
V. Poli
V. d. Stamperia
V. Scarolino
V. d. Panetteria
V. Maroniti
V. d. Col. Antonina
PZA. COLONNA
V. Sabini
V. Crociteri
Trevi Fountain
V. Lavatore
Via in Arcione
Via d. Scuderie
PZA. DI PIETRA
V. d. Pietra
V. Muratte
PZA. CROCITERI
V. Minghetti
V. Vergini
V. Vincenzo
V. Modelli
V. S.
V. Babuccio
V. d. Caravita
V. Dataria
V. dell'Umiltà
V. S. Marcello
V. d'Archetto
V. d. Lucchese
S. Ignazio
V. del C. Romano
V.S.S. Apostoli
PZA. D. PILOTTA
PZA. D. COLL. ROMANO
PZA. SS. APOSTOLI
V. della Pilotta
V.d. Piombo
V. C. Battisti
Via d. Pleciscito
Palazzo Venezia
V. IV Novembre
V. S. Eutemia
V. Cordonata
PZA. VENEZIA
Trajan's Column
Forum of Trajan
PZA. ARACCELI
Monumento Vittorio Emmanuele II
Palazzo Nuovo
PZA. DEL CAMPIDOGLIO
V. S. Pietro in Carc.
V. Tuliano
Palazzo dei Conservatori
Palazzo Senatorio
V. Curie
CAPITOLINE HILL
Via Consolazione
Roman Forum
0
100 yards
100 meters
Via Alessandrina
Via d. Fori Imperiali
V. in Miranda
TO THE COLOSSEUM
V. Sal del Gritto
V. d. Ibernesi
V. Tord Conti
Forum of Augustus
Via Baccina
Via Madonna dei Monti
Largo C. Ricci
Via Frangipane
V. Cardello
V. d. Carine
Via Cavour
V. d. Annibaldi
San Pietro in Vincoli
Cavour
Via Leonina
Via degli Zingari
Via Urbana
V. S. Agata dei Goti
Via Panisperna
Via Mazzarino
Via dei Serpenti
V. di Boschetto
Via Milano
LARGO ANGELICUM
Via XXIV Maggio
Via Nazionale
Via Palermo
TO TERMINI
V. Genova
Vic. Mazzarino
Via della Consulta
Via Placenza
Via Parma
Palazzo delle Esposizioni
PZA. DEL QUIRINALE
Palazzo del Quirinale
Via d. Quirinale
V. XX SETTEMBRE
TO
Via d. Traforo Umberto I
Via Rasella
Via dei Giardini
Via delle Quattro Fontane
Palazzo Barberini
Barberini
PZA. BARBERINI
V. Boccaccio
V. Zucchelli
Via Sistina
Via F. Crispi
V. Cappuccini
Via Vittorio Veneto
Santa Maria d. Concezione
Via S. Basilio
V. d.Purificazione
V. degli Artisti
V. Liguria
Via Ludovisi
Via Aurora Cadore
Via Lombardia
V. di Porta Pinciana
Via Lazio
Via Emilia

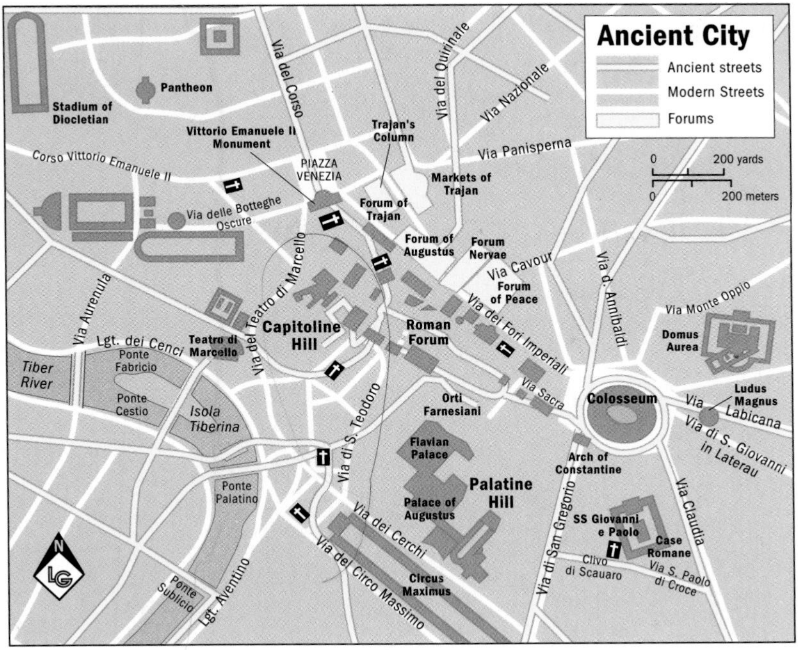

Ancient City

Ancient streets
Modern Streets
Forums

0 200 yards
0 200 meters

Pantheon
Stadium of Diocletian
Vittorio Emanuele II Monument
Via del Corso
Via del Quirinale
Via Nazionale
Trajan's Column
Via Panisperna
Corso Vittorio Emanuele II
PIAZZA VENEZIA
Markets of Trajan
Via delle Botteghe Oscure
Forum of Trajan
Forum of Augustus
Forum Nervae
Via Cavour
Forum of Peace
Via del Teatro di Marcello
Via Aurenula
Capitoline Hill
Roman Forum
Via dei Fori Imperiali
Via d. Annibaldi
Via Monte Oppio
Domus Aurea
Lgt. dei Cenci
Teatro di Marcello
Ponte Fabricio
Tiber River
Ponte Cestio
Isola Tiberina
Via di S. Teodoro
Orti Farnesiani
Via Sacra
Colosseum
Ludus Magnus
Via Labicana
Via di S. Giovanni in Laterau
Flavian Palace
Arch of Constantine
Palatine Hill
Ponte Palatino
Palace of Augustus
Via dei Cerchi
Via di San Gregorio
SS Giovanni e Paolo
Via Claudia
Case Romane
Clivo di Scauaro
Via S. Paolo di Croce
Via del Circo Massimo
Circus Maximus
Ponte Sublicio
Lgt. Aventino
N
LG

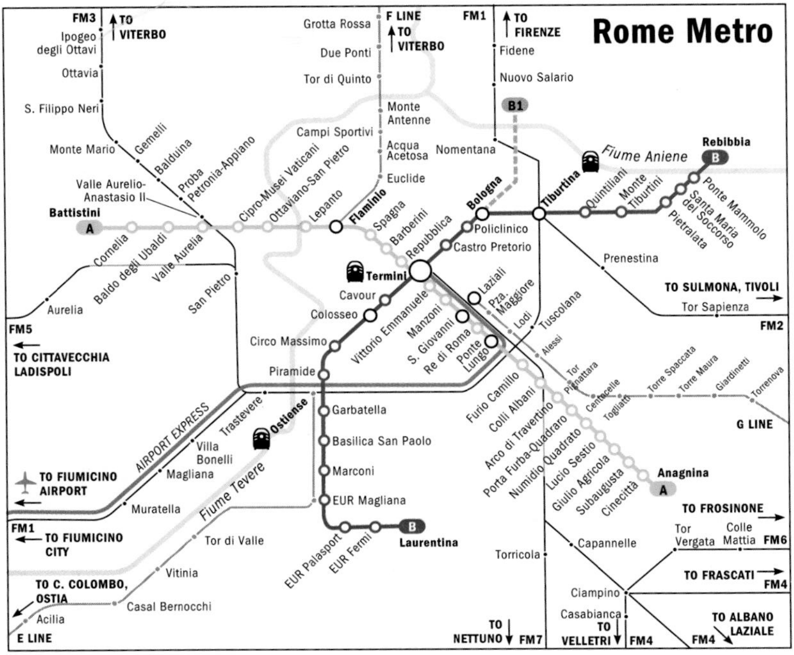

Rome Metro

FM3 TO VITERBO
Ipogeo degli Ottavi
Ottavia
S. Filippo Neri
Monte Mario
Gemelli
Balduina
Proba Petronia-Appiano
Valle Aurelio-Anastasio II
Battistini
A
Cornelia
Baldo degli Ubaldi
Valle Aurelia
Cipro-Musei Vaticani
Ottaviano-San Pietro
Lepanto
San Pietro
Aurelia
FM5 TO CITTAVECCHIA LADISPOLI
F LINE TO VITERBO
Grotta Rossa
Due Ponti
Tor di Quinto
Monte Antenne
Campi Sportivi
Acqua Acetosa
Euclide
Flaminio
Spagna
Barberini
Repubblica
Termini
Cavour
Colosseo
Circo Massimo
Piramide
Vittorio Emanuele
Manzoni
S. Giovanni
Re di Roma
Ponte Lungo
Garbatella
Basilica San Paolo
Marconi
EUR Magliana
EUR Palasport
EUR Fermi
B
Laurentina
Ostiense
Trastevere
AIRPORT EXPRESS
Villa Bonelli
Magliana
Muratella
TO FIUMICINO AIRPORT
Fiume Tevere
FM1 TO FIUMICINO CITY
Tor di Valle
Vitinia
TO C. COLOMBO, OSTIA
Casal Bernocchi
Acilia
E LINE
FM1 TO FIRENZE
Fidene
Nuovo Salario
B1
Nomentana
Bologna
Policlinico
Castro Pretorio
Tiburtina
Fiume Aniene
Quintiliani
Monte Tiburtini
Pietralata
Santa Maria del Soccorso
Ponte Mammolo
Rebibbia
Prenestina
TO SULMONA, TIVOLI
Tor Sapienza
FM2
Laziali
Pza. Maggiore
Lodi
Tuscolana
Alessi
Tor Pignattara
Centocelle
Togliatti
Torre Spaccata
Torre Maura
Giardinetti
Torrenova
G LINE
Furio Camillo
Colli Albani
Arco di Travertino
Porta Furba-Quadraro
Numidio Quadrato
Lucio Sestio
Giulio Agricola
Subaugusta
Cinecittà
Anagnina
TO FROSINONE
Capannelle
Tor Vergata
Colle Mattia
FM6
TO FRASCATI FM4
Torricola
Ciampino
Casabianca
TO ALBANO LAZIALE FM4
TO NETTUNO FM7
TO VELLETRI FM4

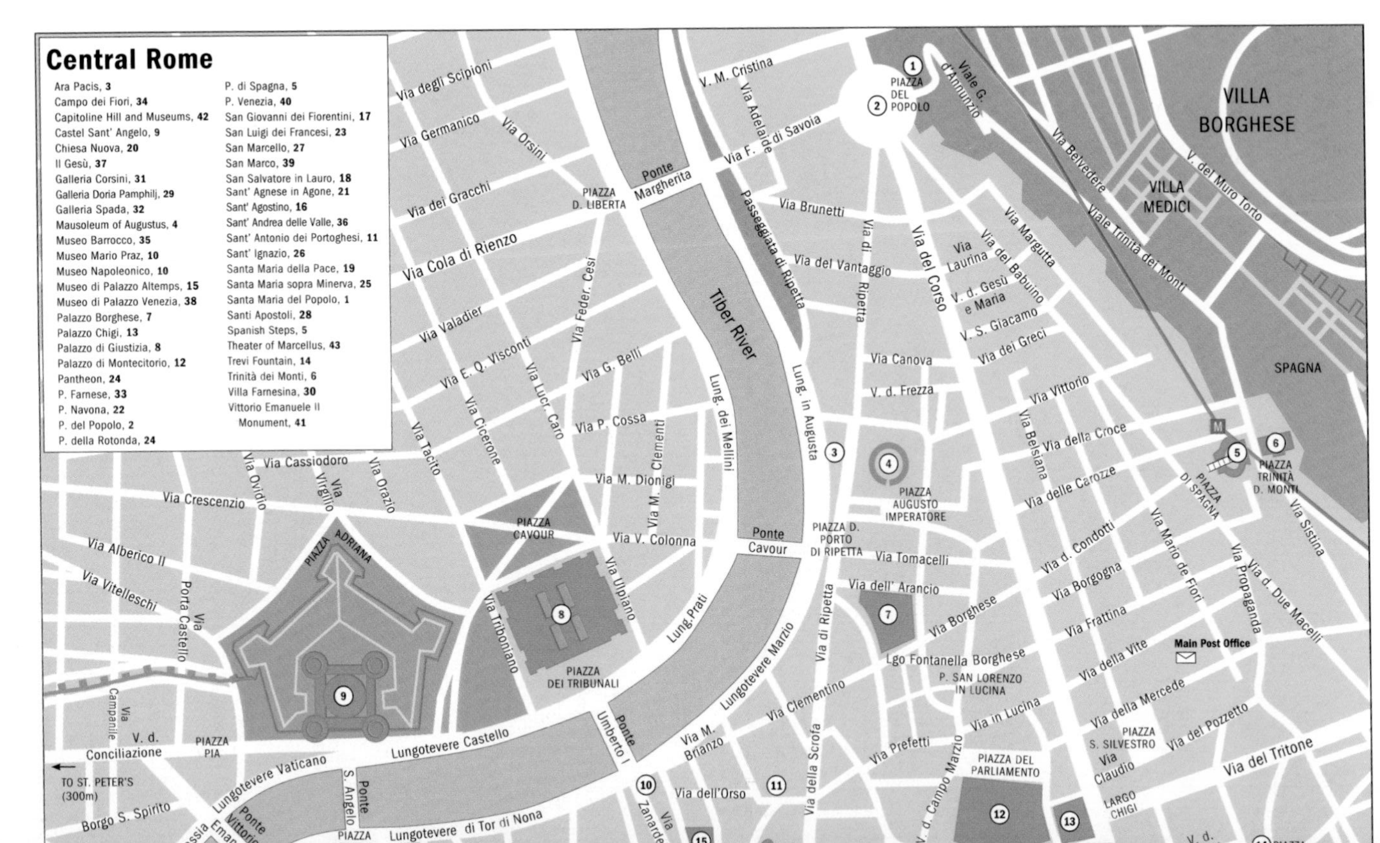

Central Rome
Ara Pacis, 3
Campo dei Fiori, 34
Capitoline Hill and Museums, 42
Castel Sant' Angelo, 9
Chiesa Nuova, 20
Il Gesù, 37
Galleria Corsini, 31
Galleria Doria Pamphilj, 29
Galleria Spada, 32
Mausoleum of Augustus, 4
Museo Barrocco, 35
Museo Mario Praz, 10
Museo Napoleonico, 10
Museo di Palazzo Altemps, 15
Museo di Palazzo Venezia, 38
Palazzo Borghese, 7
Palazzo Chigi, 13
Palazzo di Giustizia, 8
Palazzo di Montecitorio, 12
Pantheon, 24
P. Farnese, 33
P. Navona, 22
P. del Popolo, 2
P. della Rotonda, 24
P. di Spagna, 5
P. Venezia, 40
San Giovanni dei Fiorentini, 17
San Luigi dei Francesi, 23
San Marcello, 27
San Marco, 39
San Salvatore in Lauro, 18
Sant' Agnese in Agone, 21
Sant' Agostino, 16
Sant' Andrea delle Valle, 36
Sant' Antonio dei Portoghesi, 11
Sant' Ignazio, 26
Santa Maria della Pace, 19
Santa Maria sopra Minerva, 25
Santa Maria del Popolo, 1
Santi Apostoli, 28
Spanish Steps, 5
Theater of Marcellus, 43
Trevi Fountain, 14
Trinità dei Monti, 6
Villa Farnesina, 30
Vittorio Emanuele II Monument, 41
VILLA BORGHESE
VILLA MEDICI
SPAGNA
PIAZZA DEL POPOLO
PIAZZA D. LIBERTA
PIAZZA CAVOUR
PIAZZA ADRIANA
PIAZZA DEI TRIBUNALI
PIAZZA AUGUSTO IMPERATORE
PIAZZA D. PORTO DI RIPETTA
PIAZZA DI SPAGNA
PIAZZA TRINITÀ D. MONTI
P. SAN LORENZO IN LUCINA
PIAZZA DEL PARLIAMENTO
PIAZZA S. SILVESTRO
LARGO CHIGI
PIAZZA PIA
Main Post Office
Tiber River
Ponte Margherita
Ponte Cavour
Ponte Umberto I
Ponte S. Angelo
Ponte Vittorio
TO ST. PETER'S (300m)
Via degli Scipioni
Via Germanico
Via Orsini
Via dei Gracchi
Via Cola di Rienzo
Via Valadier
Via E. Q. Visconti
Via Cicerone
Via Tacito
Via Lucr. Caro
Via Feder. Cesi
Via G. Belli
Via P. Cossa
Via M. Clementi
Via M. Dionigi
Via V. Colonna
Via Ulpiano
Via Triboniano
Via Cassiodoro
Via Ovidio
Via Virgilio
Via Orazio
Via Crescenzio
Via Alberico II
Via Vitelleschi
Via Porta Castello
Via Campanile
V. d. Conciliazione
Borgo S. Spirito
Lungotevere Vaticano
Lungotevere Castello
Lungotevere di Tor di Nona
Lung. dei Mellini
Lung. Prati
Lungotevere Marzio
Lung. in Augusta
Passeggiata di Ripetta
V. M. Cristina
Via Adelaide
Via F. di Savoia
Via Brunetti
Via del Vantaggio
Via di Ripetta
Via del Corso
Via Laurina
V. d. Gesù e Maria
V. S. Giacamo
Via dei Greci
Via del Babuino
Via Margutta
Via Canova
V. d. Frezza
Via Vittorio
Via Belsiana
Via della Croce
Via delle Carozze
Via d. Condotti
Via Borgogna
Via Frattina
Via della Vite
Via della Mercede
Via del Pozzetto
Via del Tritone
Via Mario de Fiori
Via Propaganda
Via d. Due Macelli
Via Sistina
Via Tomacelli
Via dell' Arancio
Via Borghese
Lgo Fontanella Borghese
Via Clementino
Via in Lucina
Via Prefetti
V. d. Campo Marzio
Via della Scrofa
Via M. Brianzo
Via dell'Orso
Via Zanardelli
Via Claudio
Viale G. d'Annunzio
Via Belvedere
Viale Trinità dei Monti
V. del Muro Torto

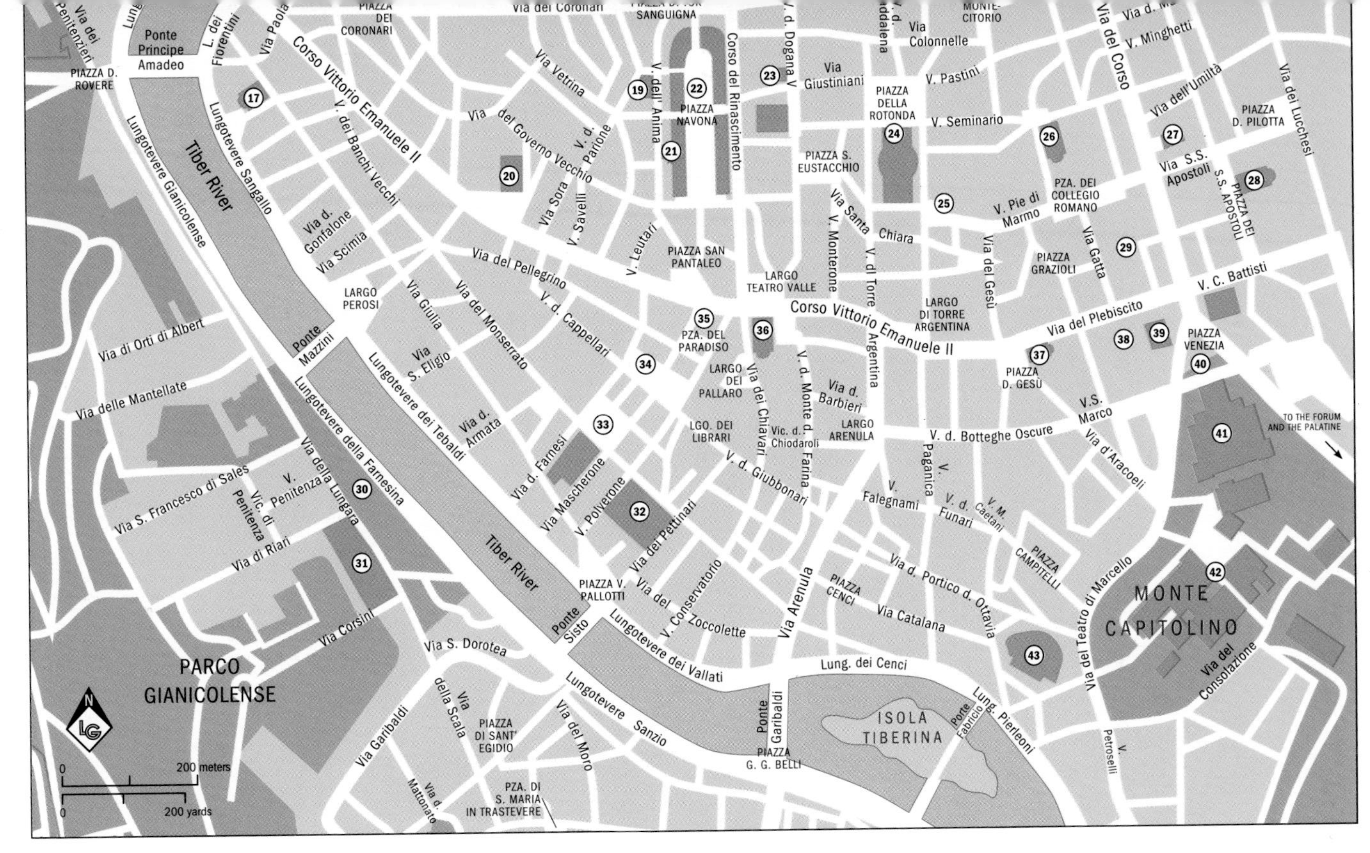

MONTE CAPITOLINO
PARCO GIANICOLENSE
ISOLA TIBERINA
Tiber River
Tiber River
TO THE FORUM AND THE PALATINE
Via del Corso
Corso Vittorio Emanuele II
Corso Vittorio Emanuele II
Corso del Rinascimento
Via del Plebiscito
V. C. Battisti
Via dei Lucchesi
Via dell'Umiltà
V. Minghetti
Via S.S. Apostoli
PIAZZA D. PILOTTA
PIAZZA DEI S.S. APOSTOLI
PIAZZA VENEZIA
PZA. DEI COLLEGIO ROMANO
PIAZZA GRAZIOLI
Via Gatta
V. Pie di Marmo
Via del Gesù
PIAZZA D. GESÙ
V.S. Marco
Via d'Aracoeli
V. d. Botteghe Oscure
LARGO DI TORRE ARGENTINA
V. dl Torre Argentina
V. Seminario
V. Pastini
Via Colonnelle
Via Giustiniani
PIAZZA DELLA ROTONDA
PIAZZA S. EUSTACCHIO
Via Santa Chiara
V. Monterone
LARGO TEATRO VALLE
PIAZZA SAN PANTALEO
PIAZZA NAVONA
V. dell' Anima
V. d. Dogana V
Via Vetrina
Via del Governo Vecchio
V. d. Parione
Via Sora
V. Savelli
V. Leutari
Via del Pellegrino
V. d. Cappellari
PZA. DEL PARADISO
LARGO DEI PALLARO
LGO. DEI LIBRARI
Via dei Chiavari
V. d. Monte d. Farina
Via d. Barbieri
Vic. d. Chiodaroli
LARGO ARENULA
V. d. Giubbonari
V. Paganica
V. Falegnami
V. d. Funari
V. M. Caetani
PIAZZA CAMPITELLI
Via del Teatro di Marcello
Via del Consolazione
V. Petroselli
Via d. Portico d. Ottavia
Via Catalana
PIAZZA CENCI
Via Arenula
Lung. dei Cenci
Lung. Pierleoni
Ponte Fabricio
Ponte Garibaldi
PIAZZA G. G. BELLI
Lungotevere dei Vallati
Via del Zoccolette
V. Conservatorio
Via dei Pettinari
PIAZZA V. PALLOTTI
Ponte Sisto
Via Mascherone
V. Polverone
Via d. Farnesi
Via d. Armata
Via del Monserrato
Via Giulia
Via S. Eligio
Lungotevere dei Tebaldi
LARGO PEROSI
Ponte Mazzini
V. dei Banchi Vecchi
Via d. Gonfalone
Via Scimia
Via Paola
L. dei Fiorentini
Lungotevere Sangallo
Ponte Principe Amadeo
PIAZZA D. ROVERE
Via dei Penitenzieri
Lungotevere Gianicolense
Lungotevere della Farnesina
Via della Lungara
V. Penitenza
Vic. di Penitenza
Via di Riari
Via Corsini
Via S. Francesco di Sales
Via delle Mantellate
Via di Orti di Albert
Via S. Dorotea
Lungotevere Sanzio
Via del Moro
Via della Scala
PIAZZA DI SANT' EGIDIO
PZA. DI S. MARIA IN TRASTEVERE
Via d. Mattonato
Via Garibaldi
Via dei Coronari
PIAZZA DEI CORONARI
SANGUIGNA
MONTE-CITORIO
V. d. Maddalena
0
200 meters
0
200 yards
N
LG
17
19
20
21
22
23
24
25
26
27
28
29
30
31
32
33
34
35
36
37
38
39
40
41
42
43

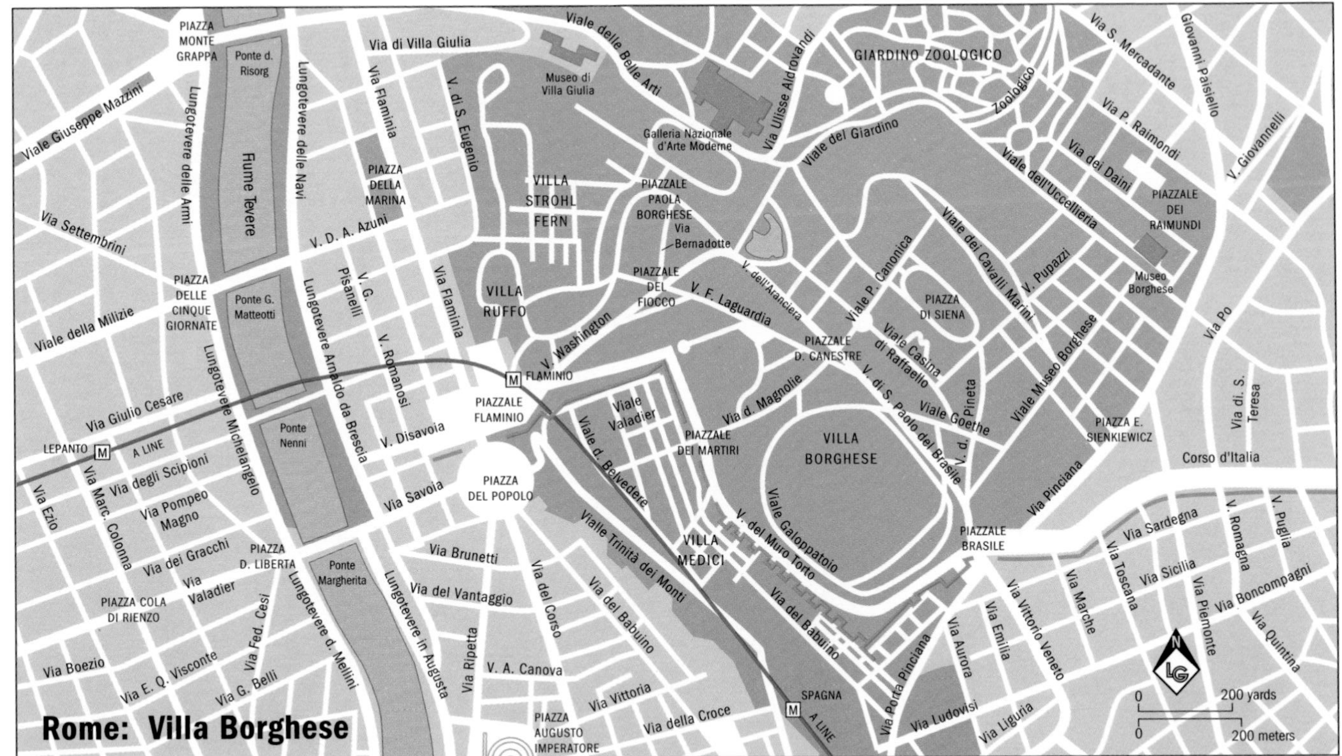
Rome: Villa Borghese
PIAZZA MONTE GRAPPA
Ponte d. Risorg
Viale Giuseppe Mazzini
Lungotevere delle Armi
Fiume Tevere
Lungotevere delle Navi
Via di Villa Giulia
Via Flaminia
V. di S. Eugenio
Museo di Villa Giulia
Viale delle Belle Arti
Via Ulisse Aldrovandi
GIARDINO ZOOLOGICO
Zoologico
Via S. Mercadante
Giovanni Paisiello
V. Giovannelli
Via P. Raimondi
Via dei Daini
PIAZZALE DEI RAIMUNDI
Museo Borghese
Viale dell'Uccellieria
Viale del Giardino
Galleria Nazionale d'Arte Moderne
PIAZZA DELLA MARINA
VILLA STROHL FERN
PIAZZALE PAOLA BORGHESE
Via Bernadotte
Via Settembrini
V. D. A. Azuni
V. G. Pisanelli
PIAZZA DELLE CINQUE GIORNATE
Ponte G. Matteotti
Lungotevere Arnaldo da Brescia
V. Romanosi
VILLA RUFFO
PIAZZALE DEL FIOCCO
V. F. Laguardia
V. dell'Aranciera
Viale P. Canonica
Viale dei Cavalli Marini
V. Pupazzi
PIAZZA DI SIENA
Viale Casina di Raffaello
Viale Museo Borghese
Via Po
Viale della Milizie
V. Washington
FLAMINIO
PIAZZALE D. CANESTRE
Via Giulio Cesare
Lungotevere Michelangelo
PIAZZALE FLAMINIO
Viale Valadier
Via d. Magnolie
V. di S. Paolo del Brasile
Viale Goethe
V. d. Pineta
Via di S. Teresa
LEPANTO
A LINE
Ponte Nenni
V. Disavoia
PIAZZALE DEI MARTIRI
VILLA BORGHESE
PIAZZA E. SIENKIEWICZ
Corso d'Italia
Via Ezio
Via Marc. Colonna
Via degli Scipioni
Via Pompeo Magno
Via Savoia
PIAZZA DEL POPOLO
Viale d. Belvedere
Via Pinciana
Viale Galoppatoio
Vialle Trinità dei Monti
VILLA MEDICI
V. del Muro Torto
PIAZZALE BRASILE
Via Sardegna
V. Romagna
V. Puglia
Via dei Gracchi
PIAZZA D. LIBERTA
Ponte Margherita
Via Brunetti
Via del Corso
Via Toscana
Via Sicilia
Via Valadier
PIAZZA COLA DI RIENZO
Lungotevere d. Mellini
Via del Vantaggio
Via del Babuino
Via Marche
Via Piemonte
Via Boncompagni
Via Fed. Cesi
Lungotevere in Augusta
Via Vittorio Veneto
Via Emilia
Via Aurora
Via Quintina
Via Boezio
Via E. Q. Visconte
Via G. Belli
Via Ripetta
V. A. Canova
Via Vittoria
Via della Croce
SPAGNA
Via Porta Pinciana
Via Ludovisi
Via Liguria
PIAZZA AUGUSTO IMPERATORE
N
LG
0
200 yards
200 meters